American Education

American Education
A History

Fourth Edition

Wayne J. Urban
University of Alabama

Jennings L. Wagoner, Jr.
University of Virginia

Routledge
Taylor & Francis Group

NEW YORK AND LONDON

First edition published by McGraw-Hill 1996
Second edition published by McGraw-Hill 2000
Third edition published by McGraw-Hill 2004
This edition first published 2009
by Routledge
270 Madison Ave, New York, NY 10016

Simultaneously published in the UK
by Routledge
2 Park Square, Milton Park, Abingdon, Oxon OX14 4RN

Routledge is an imprint of the Taylor & Francis Group, an informa business

© 1996, 2000, 2004 McGraw-Hill
© 2009 Taylor & Francis

Typeset in Minion by
RefineCatch Limited, Bungay, Suffolk
Printed and bound in the United States of America on acid-free paper by
Sheridan Books, Inc.

Library of Congress Cataloging in Publication Data
Urban, Wayne J.
American education : a history / Wayne J. Urban, Jennings L. Wagoner, Jr.—4th ed.
p. cm.
Includes bibliographical references and index.
1. Education—United States—History.
I. Wagoner, Jennings L. II. Title.
LA205.U73 2008
370.973—dc22
2008007152

ISBN10: 0–415–96529–2 (pbk)

ISBN13: 978–0–415–96529–3 (pbk)

For Judy and Shirley
who shared the journey with us

Contents

Chapter 6

Chapter 7

Chapter 8

Chapter 9

**The Effects of Depression and War on American Education:
1930–1946**   293

Chapter 10

Education during and after the Crucial Decade: 1945–1960   325

Chapter 11

The Pursuit of Equality: 1960–1980   355

Preface

In a very real sense, this book had its beginning in the late 1960s. As fellow graduate students at Ohio State University, we were part of a group of passionate, if not always enlightened, graduate students caught up in the turmoil of that era. Questions forced on us by scholarly debate and social and political events of the day challenged us to question long-held values and beliefs while trying to make sense of a world caught up in ideological and generational whirlwinds. Personal and professional contact through the years enabled us to pursue that dialogue as the tide of change has continued to ebb and flow.

This book is a continuation of that dialogue. In it, we invite you, our readers, to join in the conversation. Running throughout our conversation is a question: what is the point of studying the history of American education (or any other history)? Does it really make any difference if we understand what has happened in the past? For that matter, can we with our post-modern consciousness really know what happened in the past and why things happened as they did?

Some people are prone to agree with Voltaire that "history is a pack of lies we play on the dead," or with Henry Ford that "history is more or less bunk." Still others find merit in Harry Truman's observation that "the only thing new in the world is the history you don't know" or resonate to George Santayana's aphorism that "those who cannot remember the past are condemned to repeat it."

It occurs to us, however, that history's most ardent detractors and defenders are both wrong. The critics appear to expect too little from history and the proponents too much. As historians, we must confess to occasional ambivalence and to finding ourselves sometimes caught in tangled webs of disagreement regarding matters of interpretation. Making sense of the past is difficult. In our continuing dialogue, we try to confront each other and our sources in as direct a manner as possible in an effort to wrestle with the demands of historical explanation.

One concern that we share after having taught history of education courses for four decades is that educators, like most people, tend to "use" history to prove their own particular point of view. Some history of education authors do this by pronouncing at the outset that their purpose essentially is to show either how wonderful or how terrible American schools and school people are and have been down through the years. Some choose to see only successes and triumphs; others focus on the failures and mistakes.

We find such orientations to be reductionist and worrisome. They bring to mind H. L. Mencken's observation that "for every complex problem there is an answer that is clear, simple, and wrong." We tend to have little sympathy for those who cling to neatly packaged answers in their history and close their minds to alternative explanations of the past. For us, the fabric and design of history, like the threads of experience in our own lives, are woven in intricate and complex patterns. Moreover, we regard history as an ongoing process. Not only does the past influence the present, but the concerns and issues of the present prompt historians to reform and rephrase questions about the past and to think in new ways about old problems. History is thus fluid, dynamic, and shifting. The past, properly understood, is far from being a simple story of linear events that led us to some inevitable present or that has determined in some fixed sense a single direction in which we must now go. All of us are very much in the stream of history and, like those who lived in earlier times, face decisions and make choices that define our present and shape the history that others will someday seek to understand. All history, therefore, is to some degree socially constructed.

In this book, we have tried to set forth as honestly as we can our examination of the tremendously important and diverse phenomena of our nation's educational experiences. While striving to be conscientious in our research and adhering to the accepted conventions of scholarship, we recognize that our interpretation at times differs in detail and tone with some other histories of American education. As already noted, we hold that there is no single interpretation of facts, no single story to which all need give assent. Every history represents an attempt to "make sense" of the past from the perspective of the present. And for every historian, the way one experiences the present affects to some degree the way one comprehends the past. Facts need not be in dispute in order for the story to vary in important particulars or in general viewpoint. The way the facts are sorted and arranged to form the structure of a story produces a mosaic that varies from historian to historian, and from reader to reader. Every reader, like every historian, has an individual past and a particular present that color perception.

Each of us sees the world through a different set of lenses—and with varying degrees of clarity. It is natural, when at times our vision seems fuzzy and out of focus, to strain to rid ourselves of the blur. However complex are life and history, each of us has a need to see clearly, to understand, to make sense of it all.

We share the conviction that clear vision and making sense are vitally important. We believe too that it matters greatly how each of us makes sense of ideas and events, past or present. One's own understanding in itself becomes part of history, part of the story. Each person's view of the past heavily influences his or her view of the present and the future; it shapes one's conception of what is desirable or undesirable, possible or impossible.

How people conceive of the reality of the past or see their own times thus takes on a dimension of validity. What people think, feel, and believe, determines both their values and behavior patterns. Quantitative data of various kinds may demonstrate what is "real" in a measurable sense—and thus are important in helping us to make sense of past and present—but belief patterns and myths are also a measure of reality. If we are told often enough that our system of education is the best in the world—or among the worst—or that, whatever our national problems, schools can—or cannot—help solve them, then our actions will tend to reinforce that conventional "wisdom." It may matter little or not at all that evidence to the contrary can be readily found.

Our own approach has been to try to avoid one-sided judgments and to look at evidence that supports multiple views of particular events and individuals. Thus, we stress the narrative, the story of American educational history, as well as the interpretive, in our treatment.

Furthermore, we try to examine the interplay between social reality and perceptions of that reality as defined and described by participants. The lives lived in earlier times, like our own, reflect perceptions of reality that influenced choices, defined options, and both limited and expanded horizons. It is this more complicated, complex, and unsettled sense of reality that we have attempted to reconstruct and to interpret.

The history in the pages that follow adheres for the most part to a chronological ordering, but the reader will quickly discover that it is clearly not a rendering of straightforward linear development, a simple story of progress (or decline) from then to now. Rather, we have undertaken to present a narrative history of men and women who tried to understand and order and improve their lives and their world as best they could, given their perception of the facts and fears and hopes that characterized their world. We should be prepared to extend a bit of compassion and sympathy to those who in an earlier time made decisions whose outcomes even now can be understood only partially. We might hope for the same understanding from those who follow us.

This Fourth Edition

When we began work on this book in the early 1990s, we had no idea that it would go into multiple editions. As we complete work on this fourth edition, we want to thank our publisher for the first three editions, McGraw-Hill, and offer our gratitude to our new publisher, Routledge. More specifically, in working with Routledge we are especially pleased to be reunited with the editor who worked with us initially in developing this volume, Lane Akers. Lane has been a good friend to both of us over the years and we are delighted to have the opportunity to work with him again.

In addition to a new Epilogue, this fourth edition contains new material in almost every chapter. End Notes and supplementary bibliographical sections throughout the book have been updated with more recent references. New illustrations and photographs have been added throughout the text. Additional material has been added to our discussion of the social and economic currents of the Jacksonian era that formed the background for the emergence of the common school. In several chapters, attention given to the relationship between elementary and secondary with higher education has been expanded.

In Chapter 6 the impact on changing patterns of college-going associated with the Land Grant College Acts, the rise of the research university, and the emergence of the junior/community college are given expanded attention. New material on urbanization, immigrant life, and Catholic dissatisfaction with the common school movement has been added to this edition. We have also inserted new material on the character building efforts of youth organizations such as the YMCA, the Boy Scouts and associations for girls. Increased attention has been given as well to the upheaval and displacement of hundreds of thousands of individuals and families who left their homes in the Midwest and Southwest "Dust Bowl" during the Great Depression.

We would like to address a suggestion that has been made to us before publication of this edition that we have not embraced. The suggestion and our resistance to it merit an explanation. Almost from the beginning, some readers of our book have sought the addition of a chapter or long section of a chapter that deals exclusively with competing educational philosophies or theories. We have considered this suggestion seriously, but have chosen not to extract and rarify various philosophies of education out of their historical context. Philosophies such as traditionalism or essentialism, perennialism, and social reconstructionism were given definition and substance in reaction to the progressive education movement and were grounded in specific social, economic, and political settings. Each theory deserves attention, critical analysis, and debate. However, we contend that progressive education and the various reactions to it need to be addressed as historical phenomena. We believe that progressive education is the reigning ideology in professional educational circles today, and further that reactions to progressivism constitute one of the more potent critiques of professional education. Our treatment of progressive educational theory begins in Chapter 3 with our discussion of the Enlightenment. In the last several chapters of the book our focus moves to progressive education in both theory and in practice. We attempt to account for variations among advocates of progressive education as well as critical reactions from opponents who have advocated alternative approaches to education. We have elaborated on the growth and appeal of progressivism in most of these chapters in the hope that readers will more clearly understand the concept and its development in schools (and in the family and the larger society), appreciate its significance both conceptually and in practice, and conclude that we have treated progressive education *and* opposing philosophies fairly, neither automatically embracing nor denigrating them condescendingly. Inasmuch as the fundamentals separating different philosophies of education are still quite alive and meaningful, *current* debates within the *current* context are most appropriate. The historian's task is to explain how those fundamentals emerged and developed over time.

In this edition, a point from the Preface to the previous edition is worth repeating. There we noted that the interpretive aspect of our work invites serious consideration. We continue to be attentive to the challenge of interpretation. As we stated before, we choose not to use our text to wage war with other historians or social scientists or philosophers on interpretative questions. We certainly have our own points of view, and they are not always identical between the two of us. More importantly, however, we are interested in presenting the evidence behind interpretations, both our own and the judgments reached by others. In the final analysis, we hope our readers will gain information and insights on which to draw their own conclusions.

Over the years we have been heartened by the positive reception of our book by colleagues and students across the country. We sincerely hope that this new edition, with its additional material and updating, will merit the same reception that was given to earlier editions. It is the teachers of the history of American education and allied subjects and their students who animate our effort at improving this work. We salute both groups and look forward to continuing positive interaction with them.

Wayne J. Urban
University of Alabama

Jennings L. Wagoner, Jr.
University of Virginia

About the Authors

WAYNE J. URBAN, since January 2006, has served as Associate Director of the Education Policy Center and Professor of Education at the University of Alabama. Prior to going to Alabama, he taught for over three decades in the Department of Educational Policy Studies and the Department of History at Georgia State University. His other books are *Accountability in American Education: A Critique.* (Princeton, NJ: Princeton Publishing. 1976.); *Why Teachers Organized.* (Detroit: Wayne State University Press, 1982.); *Black Scholar: Horace Mann Bond, 1904–1972.* (Athens, GA: University of Georgia Press, 1992.); *More than the Facts: The Research Division of the National Education Association, 1922–1977.* (Lanham, MD: University Press of America, 1997.); *Gender, Race, and the National Education Association: Professionalism and Its Limitations.* (New York: Routledge Falmer, 2000.); and an edited volume, *Essays in Twentieth Century Southern Education: Exceptionalism and Its Limits.* (New York: Garland Publishing, 1999.) He has served as president of the History of Education Society and of the American Educational Studies Association, and as vice president of Division "F" (History and Historiography) of the American Educational Research Association. He is also the immediate past president of the International Standing Conference for the History of Education.

JENNINGS L. WAGONER, JR. is Professor Emeritus of the History of Education at the University of Virginia. He is author of numerous articles on educational history and has a special interest in the educational views of Thomas Jefferson. Previous books include *Thomas Jefferson and the Education of a New Nation.* (Bloomington, IN: Phi Delta Kappa, 1976.); *The Changing Politics of Education.* (Berkeley, CA: McCutcheon Publishing Co., 1978.); and *Jefferson and Education.* (Monticello Monograph Series, Chapel Hill NC: University of North Carolina Press, 2004.) He taught at the University of Virginia from 1968 through 2005 where he also served as Director of the Center for Higher Education for ten years and as Chair of the Department of Leadership, Foundations and Policy for twelve years. He is a past president of the History of Education Society and has served as a member of the Editorial Board of the History of Education Quarterly and Educational Studies. He has served as vice president of Division "F" (History and Historiography) of the American Educational Research Association. In 1987 he received the Outstanding Professor Award from Virginia's Curry School of Education, and in 1996 he was honored by the University of Virginia Alumni Association with its Distinguished Professor Award.

1
Education in Precolonial America
Native American Cultural Traditions

Overview: The Indigenous Foundations of American Education

As soon as the first groups of Europeans began establishing outposts in the new world, they became learners as well as teachers. They and the Native Americans with whom they came in contact engaged in a process of cultural exchange that was educative in the broadest meaning of that term. Two "old worlds" had met and the inhabitants of neither would be the same again.

The cultural roots from which old world and new world people had drawn their nourishment were, of course, markedly different. Although humans everywhere have the same fundamental needs and share many of the same basic hopes and fears, what was believed and valued by those who lived on opposite sides of the Atlantic Ocean was by no means the same during the Age of Discovery. In the process of encounter, the beliefs and values of those separate worlds were shared and altered, but not in equal measure. European cultural traditions and values rather quickly became dominant, as confrontation and conquest soon followed initial contact.

With this understanding in mind, perhaps we can disabuse ourselves of the notion that education and knowledge were brought to the new world by the small bands of Englishmen who dropped anchor along the coast of North America in the early seventeenth century. Neither should we argue that earlier Italian, Spanish, Portuguese, Dutch, or French explorers, missionaries, or traders should be credited with introducing learning, culture, and religion as they penetrated the vast American continent. Well-established societies and rich cultural legacies existed long before anyone "discovered" anyone else, as is dramatically exemplified by the great civilizations of the Aztecs, Incas, and Mayas.

Cultural Diversity in Pre-Columbian America

Until recent years, archeological scholarship has held that the first inhabitants of the North American continent crossed over the Bering Land Bridge around 13,000 B.C. Today that notion is contested. The most current research findings suggest that Native Americans were here far longer and in greater numbers than previously thought. Archeological digs in Chile over the past few years have yielded evidence of artifacts dating back more than 30,000 years. In 2003, archeologists discovered ancient seeds from cultivated squashes in coastal Ecuador that may be older than any other agricultural remains thus far identified. It now appears that the Euroasians who traversed across the 55-mile-wide Bering corridor some 13,000 years ago may have constituted the most recent of *three* such migrations. However far back in time "Native" American origins may be, before their encounter with Europeans some 500 years ago, these people shared the land only with the animals that were native to the Western Hemisphere or that, like their own ancestors, had migrated from the steppes of Asia and Siberia before the last glacial melt turned the Bering Land Bridge into the Bering Strait.[1]

As the original Americans spread across the continent and southward into Central and South America, they developed a variety of indigenous societies. Although some societies remained rather simple hunting-and-gathering communities, others evolved into large and complex agrarian settlements. During the period when English barons were securing limited rights under the terms of the Magna Carta (1215), the Cahokia federation was supporting a "city" with a population of some 30,000 inhabitants at the confluence of the Illinois, Mississippi, and Missouri rivers. Today, within sight of the Gateway Arch and skyscrapers of downtown St. Louis, Missouri, one can still walk to the top of Monk's Mound, a terraced 100-foot high ceremonial site that was the centerpiece of this Cahokian city that flourished five centuries before Columbus found his way to the new world. Other tribal groups left their mark with earthworks by the thousands spread from southern Canada and the Great Plains to the Atlantic coast and the Gulf of Mexico. While most of these mounds took the form of rounded pyramids, some were sculpted into the shapes of gigantic birds, lizards, bears, and alligators with long tails. In southern Ohio the remains of a 1,330 foot earthen serpent are still visible.[2]

Other impressive reminders of the communal achievements of some pre-Columbian inhabitants of North America attest to their survival skills and social sophistication. By the first half of the eleventh century, a people the Navajo called the Anasazi ("the ancient ones") were building five-story stone houses with 500 rooms each into the walls of Chaco Canyon in what is now New Mexico. Thirteen major housing complexes and several hundred smaller ones were constructed, linked by a remarkable system of roads and irrigation canals. Granaries were erected to store surplus corn, and pottery and basket remains indicate artistic as well as utilitarian skillfulness. Two centuries later and 80 miles to the north, at Mesa Verde, Colorado, the Anasazi created another extensive network of stone dwellings—these built into a huge cave on a high cliff. Hand and toeholds dug into the cliff face provided the only means of entering and leaving the community dwelling area to farm or hunt on the Mesa above or in the valley below.

Climatic changes that resulted in long periods of drought brought an end to these elaborate farming cultures of the Southwest just two or three centuries before the arrival of the first Spanish explorers. The Anasazi moved on in search of more arable land. Indigenous peoples in the Southwest became hunter-gatherers, adopting a nomadic lifestyle much like their distant kinsmen along the eastern seaboard. When European colonists began arriving in North America, they had no comprehension of what the Native Americans had achieved in the interior. As one historian put it: "They saw not the great cities that once had been, but tribal societies with a subsistence economy, [people] living in wigwams and mud huts, and deserving, it seemed to them, the designation of savages."[3]

Native Americans in both the Northern and Southern Hemispheres had long endeavored to "make sense" of their world and to prepare themselves and their children for survival in that world and happiness in the next. In this respect they were no different from Europeans, Africans, Asians, and other peoples in distant parts of a largely uncharted world. The essentials of sense-making produced a variety of social and cultural arrangements as the widely scattered groups of Native Americans adapted to the varied requirements of life in the American wildernesses, deserts, and plains. Although they were indiscriminately called "Indians" (*los Indios, les Indiens, die Indianer*) by the European invaders, the separate native societies revered their own special identities and cultures, identifying only members of their own group as "the original people" or "the humans." All others, even other native groups, were considered outsiders or nonentities.[4]

Hundreds of Native American tribes and scores of nations developed ways of living that in many respects were as distinctive as those that characterized various European ethnic and national groups similarly separated by barriers of terrain, language, and traditions. Among the native inhabitants of North America alone, for example, more than 160 language families, with 1,200 or more dialects are known to have been spoken. Warfare and trade among native groups provided opportunities for the exchange of material goods as well as some aspects of non-material culture, but basically, each group lived in a separate and insular world. Within this special world everyone spoke a common language and shared a common spiritual outlook, a common past, and a common set of customs. The young were taught what they needed to know in order to belong, that is, to be "human."[5]

Education among the Native Americans

Although education among the Native Americans differed from tribe to tribe, the basic elements were similar. Boys and girls had to master certain skills and gain specific understandings before they could be accepted as mature members of the tribal society. Survival skills were, of course, essential. For many boys, survival depended on their abilities as hunters and warriors. A Jesuit priest in the eighteenth century observed that Abenaki boys began practicing with bows and arrows as soon as they began to walk, and by the age of 10 or 12, "they do not fail to kill the bird at which they shoot."[5]

Hunting skills alone, however, were hardly sufficient for survival. Adaptations dictated by place of dwelling—coastal, inland forest, plains, or desert—as well as seasonal and ecological changes meant that, in some groups, skill in agriculture, fishing, gathering edibles from fields, forests, and waterways, and making implements for all of these activities became essential knowledge. Moreover, food, regardless of how it was obtained, had to be preserved and prepared; shelter and clothing had to be provided. In all indigenous societies, subsistence alone required that the young be well instructed in the ways of their elders.[6]

Spiritual lessons were no less critical to survival than manual and physical skills. Native youth had to learn of the spirits that governed the world and of the accustomed ways of living in harmony and balance with all living things. Among some groups, such as the Cherokee, daily personal prayers and rituals were an essential part of life. Festivals and rites closely linked to the agricultural seasons, hunts, and special events of life and death were integral aspects of existence and education among all Native Americans.

Acknowledging a "creative force" in all things, native cultural groups typically did not separate the spiritual from the material, the natural from the supernatural, or the human from the animal. Illustrative of the closeness of the spiritual world to the world of physical existence was the practice among the Iroquois, Otos, and Omaha, among others, of cutting a hole in the moccasins of infants on the cradleboard lest they be enticed back to the spirit world by an unseen spirit following the mother on the forest path. The hole would inform the messenger from the spirit world that the child could not accompany him because his moccasins were worn out.[7]

Native American children learned of the essentials of life by being exposed from infancy to the shared wisdom and heritage of their group. Down through the generations, children were surrounded by concentric circles of people who served as teachers. The immediate family was most important, but members of the extended family and the entire tribe also played significant roles in perpetuating traditions and directing the footsteps of youths along the proper path. Education was not something special and separate from life; it was integral to life itself.

Instruction in cultural and spiritual matters often took the form of storytelling. The elders held in memory all that was retained of their people's past. Through repeated tellings, this store of knowledge was passed from one generation to the next. Cultural ideals and moral attitudes were formed by means of the oral tradition. Youth who exhibited, among other talents, a keen memory and storytelling abilities were selected to become the anointed "culture bearers" among the people: the ceremonial leaders among the Hopi, the medicine men among the Navajo, or the ritual leaders among the Seneca.

The onset of puberty symbolized a sharp dividing line between childhood and adulthood. Significant coming-of-age rituals occurred at this time. Among some tribes, youth were initiated into secret societies responsible for some aspect of the group's ceremonial life. The duration of the initiation rites varied from a few days among the Pueblos of the Rio Grande area to more than a year among the Taos Pueblos. Other tribes tested and isolated their young men and women for a period of time during which the youths fasted and went in quest of a guardian spirit. The quest involved overcoming physical hardships and discomfort until, in a vision or dream, a "spiritual guide"—an animal or some other living thing—would appear that would aid and guide the youth for the remainder of his or her life. At this time, the maturing youth would also often be given a new name, symbolic of his or her new status or guardian spirit.

Despite the rigorous demands of many aspects of life, in matters of discipline most Native Americans tended to be lenient, at least in terms of avoiding corporal punishment. Because most native cultures idealized the ability to withstand pain, suffering without flinching was seen as a sign of maturity. Among some south eastern tribes for example, boys would deliberately anger yellow jackets to see who could withstand the most stings. Instead of physical punishment, which might have been counterproductive, ridicule, praise, and appeals to supernatural forces were employed as means of behavioral control.[8]

Patterns of ridicule or shame varied, but among the Blackfeet a particularly embarrassing means of exposing a youth's misdeeds was sometimes employed. The Blackfeet made a person who had committed an especially offensive act the subject of community verbal abuse. At night one person would loudly announce the act of wrongdoing. The story would then be shouted from tepee to tepee until it had circulated throughout the tribe. The disgraced youth often tried to remain hidden until he or she could complete some feat that might help erase the memory of his or her mistake.

This type of public humiliation was extreme. Derisive laughter, taunts, mild ridicule, or admonition from friends, relatives, or elders were usually sufficient to bring one into conformity. The supernatural also was used as a means of controlling the behavior of children. For many tribes, different varieties of owls were omens of danger. Children were warned that if they misbehaved, the large birds would swoop down and snatch them away. Other animals and evil spirits, including "masked beings" such as "Solid Face" among the Delaware or the hideous "Spotted Face" of the Flatheads, became part of the legends and ritual dances that frightened children into obedience.

Praise and rewards for good deeds were also used effectively as means of character development. The Yakima acknowledged a boy's first deer with a feast in his honor. Among the Blood, people of the northern plains, a young man who had proved himself in battle no longer had to carry wood and water or tend the fire; these were the chores of boys who were as yet untested as warriors. Szasz notes that "in many groups, marriage was prohibited until the youth had met certain tests—the killing of the first seal, proven proficiency as a hunter, or the preparation of skins."[9]

Native peoples then, despite varying customs and conventions, developed specific traditions through which they inculcated essential skills, understandings, and attitudes among their children. The rearing of children was everyone's concern, for they understood that the life of the tribe—the life of "the people"—could be preserved and extended only for as long as the rising generations followed the ways of the old. However, native life, instead of enduring for "as long as the rivers may run and the wind may blow," began to be altered forever once European explorers found their way to the Atlantic coastline and began to penetrate into the vast wilderness beyond.

Conquest, Colonization and the "New" Americans

At Christmastime in 1492, Christopher Columbus addressed a journal entry to the Spanish sovereigns under whose flag he had sailed. The Italian navigator penned a description of the inhabitants of the new world and his intentions toward them:

> I assure Your Highnesses that I believe that in all the world there is no better people nor better country. They love their neighbors as themselves, and have the sweetest talk in the world, and gentle, and always with a smile. They go naked, men and women, as their mothers bore them. But . . . they have very good manners. . . . Your Highnesses should feel great joy, because presently they will be Christians, and instructed in the good manners of your realms.[10]

However benign Columbus's designs may have been, his arrival on the eve of the sixteenth century profoundly affected native life in ways he could not have anticipated. His crews and the European explorers who followed not only introduced strange cultural patterns and alien ways of thinking, but also brought new diseases and weapons of war. As Euro-Americans established villages in areas once inhabited only by natives, they began to insist that native children be civilized and Christianized. This meant undergoing a new and different kind of education, adopting new customs and manners, and embracing new spiritual doctrines and practices. Those native inhabitants who were not killed by guns or disease or who were not immediately driven from their lands were henceforth to be educated for life and death on new terms. It mattered little that many natives objected and resisted. The invading European explorers, missionaries, traders, and settlers considered themselves superior people. Their duty to God and their king, if not to the financial backers who subsidized their undertakings, was to impose their cultural and religious views on everyone who came into their sphere of influence and survived—especially the "savages," who in their eyes were backward, superstitious, and lacking in the skills and sensibilities of "civilized" people.[11]

European Outposts along the American Frontier: The Sixteenth Century

Spanish and English Settlements

Three-quarters of a century separated Columbus's initial voyage to America in 1492 from the establishment of the first permanent European settlement in the territory that eventually became the United States of America. St. Augustine, Florida, was founded in 1565 under the leadership of Pedro Menéndez de Avilés, a veteran of earlier treasure-seeking expeditions to Mexico. Spain's Philip II financed Menéndez's colonization effort in hopes of dislodging the French, who a year before had established a small outpost on the Florida coast near present-day Jacksonville.

Unlike previous Spanish forays into Mexico, this Florida colonization venture was to be more than a "land and loot" undertaking. Five ships loaded with 600 men, twenty-six of whom brought their families with them, left Spain in June and arrived in Florida in August 1565. Two hundred and fifty soldiers were in the party, at least half of whom were *labradores*, experienced farmers who could immediately begin the process of planting crops and providing food for the colonists. Others who made the voyage with Menéndez also possessed useful skills: stonecutters, blacksmiths, carpenters, smelters, weavers, tanners, weapons makers, coopers, bakers, brewers, and barbers who doubled as surgeons. This ready-made urban population came prepared to reproduce down to the last detail a Spanish municipality, complete with priests, church bells, and even a notary supplied with twenty-four reams of paper and a pot of ink.[12]

Within a month after the settlement of St. Augustine, the Spanish Catholics had rid the territory of the French Huguenots 40 miles to the north. Franciscan friars began establishing missions along the coast and into the interior. Each mission became a school of instruction for the natives in the cultural and religious doctrines of the colonizers. A classical school for the children of Spanish settlers was in existence in St. Augustine at least as early as 1606.[13]

Farther west, the village of San Gabriel in northern New Mexico, which was approached overland from Mexico rather than by sea, was settled by Spaniards in 1598. A decade later, Philip III declared New Mexico a royal colony and designated the newly founded town of Santa Fe as its capital. Gradually, missions spread into what later became the territories of Texas and Arizona. By the beginning of the eighteenth century, Jesuits as well as Franciscans were planting missions along the California coast. These mission communities laid the foundation for the extension of Spanish religious and cultural influence throughout the western region of the country.[14]

The first English attempt to gain a foothold in North America occurred in the mid-1580s and came to an abrupt if temporary halt with the disappearance of the "Lost Colony." A small band of settlers sent to the new world in 1585 by Sir Walter Raleigh survived for almost a year on Roanoke Island off the coast of North Carolina before returning to England. A second group recruited by Raleigh reestablished the colony in 1587. Virginia Dare, the first child of English parents born in America, made her appearance within a month after the colonists arrived on the island. Running low on supplies, the governor of the colony, John White, then departed for England with a small crew, expecting to return with ample provisions by the spring. However, war with Spain delayed White's departure from England for three years. When he did return in

August 1590, he found the settlement abandoned. No trace of the colonists could be found; only the word CROATOAN carved on a tree offered an undecipherable clue as to what may have happened to the Lost Colony. Whether they were killed by neighboring Indians or by Spaniards from St. Augustine, or whether they died in an attempt to sail back to England or moved inland and mingled with the Croatans (the present-day Lumbee Indians of Robeson County), or met some other fate will never be known with certainty. What can be said is that the failure of Raleigh's venture stymied English colonization attempts until the Jamestown settlement in Virginia almost two decades later.[15]

French, Italian, and Dutch Exploration

French and Italian explorers also passed along the Atlantic shoreline during the sixteenth century. As early as 1524, Giovanni da Verrazano, an Italian navigator sailing under a commission from the King of France, made landfall on the coast of North Carolina and then sailed northward to Newfoundland. During the 1530s, the French explorer Jacques Cartier laid claim to portions of Canada, but no lasting settlements were made. As the seventeenth century dawned, however, Samuel de Champlain began a series of voyages between France and Canada in the service of the Company of New France.

Champlain crossed the Atlantic twenty-nine times between 1603 and 1635—averaging almost a crossing a year over a span of thirty-two years. A series of government-sponsored French trading camps appeared in Acadia (now Nova Scotia), but only in 1608 did the first enduring French settlement get underway on Canadian soil. In that year, Champlain directed the construction of a fortified log village on the St. Lawrence River. He braved the winter there with twenty-eight men. Eight lived to see spring come to this bare-bones settlement they had named Quebec.

Henry Hudson, an English navigator, was hired by the Dutch East India Company to give the people of the Netherlands a chance to explore and exploit the new world. In 1609 Hudson entered New York Bay and sailed 350 miles up the river that was to bear his name. He reached the point at which Albany now exists without discovering a passage to the Northwest. Finding instead a water level of only seven feet, he turned his ship around and headed back down the river.

However, Hudson's explorations proved valuable to the Dutch. In 1625, Peter Minuit, representative of a second Dutch joint-stock company, the West India Company, bought an island at the mouth of the Hudson River from the local Native Americans and began a settlement. The island was named Manhattan; the settlement, New Amsterdam; the colony surrounding the area, New Netherland.

New Netherland might be said to be the first truly multicultural society in North America. In addition to the Dutch, who by 1643 made up less than half of the population of 1,600, Germans, French, and Scandinavians also settled in the area. The population included Protestants, Catholics, Jews, and Muslims;

eighteen European and African languages were spoken. The people drawn to the New Netherland colony were clearly motivated by the lure of profits in the fur trade rather than religious freedom. In 1642, the colony had seventeen taverns but not a single house of worship.[16]

The search for riches continued to spur French adventurers to explore and chart the rivers and bays of the Northeast in search of a passage to the Orient. French frontiersmen failed in that endeavor, but they eventually found their way to the Mississippi River and from there to New Orleans. Unfortunately for the French, their reliance on river routes did not motivate them to establish permanent settlements as the English were doing along the Atlantic coast and into the interior. By the time these two powers finally collided in the eighteenth century, the English had established a dense settlement with a population of 2 million. The French, by contrast, numbered less than 100,000 and controlled only Quebec on the St. Lawrence and New Orleans on the Mississippi. Only a handful of forts linked these two settlements that were separated by 2,000 miles of wilderness.

It should be stressed that the settlements established by the English, French, and other nations before the seventeenth century—except for the ill-fated "Lost Colony" of North Carolina—were intended to be temporary commercial outposts, not permanent communities. Churches, schools, and other institutions of fixed societies were not considered necessary in trading camps and frontier outposts.

As the sixteenth century drew to a close, Spain was the only European power with established *colonies* within the territory that would become the United States. Contrary to conventional Anglocentric versions of American history, the first white men to establish permanent settlements in the United States were not the Protestant religious dissidents of Plymouth or the agents of English mercantile companies in Jamestown. The first settlements were put down by the loyal and orthodox emissaries of the Catholic empire of Spain. Contrary also to the oft-told stories of the first American schools as New England institutions, Catholic mission schools in Florida and in the "New Spain" of the West were established well before the Pilgrims came ashore near Plymouth Rock.[17]

In a somewhat different fashion, French missionaries had begun living among the Hurons of Georgian Bay as early as 1615. French missionaries tended to become immersed in tribal society, learning a great deal about Native American languages, culture, and skills even as they were trying to teach and convert their hosts. Indeed, had it not been for Native American efforts, however inconsistent, to share their survival skills as well as food with early Spanish, French, English, and other migrating groups, the European conquest of the continent would have been delayed considerably.

The Consequences of Cultural Exchange

Contact with Europeans, even when on friendly terms, proved increasingly to be disruptive and finally disastrous to large segments of the Native American population. The ever-precarious balance of nature became even more strained as the fur trade encouraged Native Americans as well as colonists to overhunt and overkill. In exchange for guns, knives, and trinkets, some tribal groups abandoned their religious rituals and hunting taboos. For example, to satisfy the demand of French fur traders and their own newly acquired tastes and desires, some Iroquois tribes began breaking into beaver dams, releasing water and tons of stored-up topsoil as they searched for more and more animals. As ponds were drained and beaver and other animal populations were decimated, the ecology began to shift, and with it ways of life that had endured for centuries. Moreover, fierce competition over shrinking hunting grounds superimposed on traditional rivalries provoked intense intertribal warfare. After a half-century of conflict known as the "Wars of the Iroquois," the powerful (and flintlock-supplied) Iroquois had annihilated the Illinois, nearly wiped out the Hurons, and pushed tribes of the Great Lakes and Ohio Valley farther west.[18]

Diseases of epidemic proportions added to the destruction of Native American life as families and entire villages succumbed to diphtheria, measles, typhus, and numerous other alien illnesses. Smallpox, the deadliest malady to strike the Native Americans, reduced some tribes by as much as 90 percent in a single outbreak. Even whooping cough, mumps, and chicken pox, childhood diseases now considered relatively benign, turned deadly among the native peoples lacking prior exposure and natural immunization. According to some estimates, by the midpoint of the eighteenth century, the Native American population in the New England area had been reduced by disease by at least 80 percent. Alcohol brought additional devastation to North American Indians in terms of the disease and the violent actions it sometimes triggered—the latter outcome being aggravated all the more as European firearms became staples of trade and bounty of warfare.

New lessons were thus being taught and learned all along the American frontier. Some lessons were helpful, some not; some were offered in friendship, others in hatred. The exchange worked both ways. As Indians and the new Euro-Americans increased contact with each other, they not only made biological and material exchanges but cultural adaptations as well. Members of each group redefined themselves in reaction to what they were learning of the other. At the time, of course, no one could anticipate fully the outcome.

Conclusion

Long before the beginnings of recorded history, the inhabitants of the American continent developed cultural traditions and social organizations that formed the core of education for successive generations. Gradual adjustments and alterations occurred over time as environmental conditions, spiritual insights, and cultural change seemed to warrant. By and large, however, the education of children proceeded down through the centuries along the same lines and involved the same learnings as had long been the pattern. Education served to unite the generations and to define one's place among "the people."

One need not romanticize the hardships and limitations of life faced by the Native Americans in order to appreciate the disruptive changes that occurred as a consequence of the European invasion of the Western Hemisphere. Although the Europeans overpowered Native Americans in scientific, techno-logical, and literary sophistication and formality of religious doctrine, the latter tried to preserve cultural and spiritual traditions based on customs that had proved effective as far back as their collective memories could recall. In the process of encounter, however, both Native Americans and Euro-Americans experienced change. If some elements of education continued to tie new gener-ations to those of the past, other lessons were being pressed to the fore as new challenges forced both old and new inhabitants to adjust to the demands of two worlds undergoing the process of cultural transfer and transformation. Although they were themselves willing teachers, Native Americans typically found themselves cast in the role of unwilling learners. Although the European colonizers had much to learn, from the outset they assumed the role of master.

Over the course of the next century, patterns of life changed markedly in North America. English Protestants, dissenters and Anglican conformists alike, brought to the eastern shores of the continent linguistic, political, social, and religious traditions and beliefs that eventually enabled them to establish cultural hegemony in thirteen diverse and far-flung colonies. Other European colonists (in growing numbers), as well as Indians (in declining numbers), con-tinued to share the land with the English settlers, but increasingly on terms laid down by the British Crown and its colonials.

Further Reading

Axtell, James. *The European and the Indian: Essays in the Ethnohistory of Colonial North America.* New York: Oxford University Press, 1981. A cultural and historical interpretation of early encounters that draws on a wide variety of sources, including archaeological findings, linguistics, accounts of colonists, art, and published scholarship.

Axtell, James. *Natives and Newcomers: The Cultural Origins of North America.* New York: Oxford University Press, 2001. An ethnohistory of the cultural consequences resulting from the encounters that marked Indian and European interactions in the colonial era.

Crosby, Alfred W., Jr. *The Columbian Exchange: Biological and Cultural Consequences of 1642.* Westwood, CT: Greenwood Press, 1972. A "biohistorian's" analysis of the important inter-play between biological and cultural forces that followed in the wake of European-Indian contact.

Grumet, Robert S., ed. *Northeastern Indian Lives, 1632–1816.* Amherst, MA: University of Massachusetts Press, 1996. The history and culture of northeastern Indian tribes from the time of their initial encounter with white settlers to the early nineteenth century, with an introduction by the anthropologist Anthony F. Wallace.

Jennings, Francis. *The Invasion of America: Indians, Colonialism, and the Cant of Conquest.* Chapel Hill: University of North Carolina Press, 1975. A pro-Indian/anti-European assessment of colonial "imperialist" policies toward the Indians.

Krech, Shepard III. *The Ecological Indian: Myth and History,* New York: W. W. Norton Co., 2000. A carefully researched and reasoned probe by an anthropologist into the myth that Indians lived in complete harmony with nature and did no ecological harm.

Kupperman, Karen Ordahl. *Indians and the English: Facing Off in Early America.* Ithaca, NY: Cornell University Press, 2000. A vivid reconstruction of the impressions English migrants (based on their writings) and Algonquin natives (based on their oral traditions) formed of each other as they interacted and tried to make their way into an uncertain future.

Mann, Charles C. *1491: New Relevations of the Americas Before Columbus.* New York: Vintage, 2006.

An engaging and provocative disclosure of new facts and interpretations about human origins and life in the New World before the arrival of Europeans.

Morgan, Ted. *Wilderness at Dawn: The Settling of the North American Continent.* New York: Simon and Schuster, 1993. An engaging account of the ordinary people—Indians and Europeans—who from prehistoric times to the formation of the new nation confronted the challenges of the American wilderness.

Reyhner, Jon and Jeanne Eder. *American Indian Education: A History.* Norman, OK: University of Oklahoma Press, 2004. The authors briefly examine pre-Columbian native life and then focus the rest of the book on nineteenth and twentieth century boarding schools and government policies.

Richter, Daniel K. *Facing East from Indian Country: A Native History of Early America.* Cambridge, MA: Harvard University Press, 2002. A recasting of early American history from the Native American point of view, which provides an alternative view of early American history. Takes its cue from historian Carl Becker's famous assertion that history is an "imaginative creation."

Sale, Kirkpatrick. *The Conquest of Paradise: Christopher Columbus and the Columbian Legacy.* New York: Alfred A. Knopf, [1990], 2006. A revised view of the myths surrounding the journey of Christopher Columbus, with new translations of historical documents that reveal the European motivations for exploration.

Szasz, Margaret Connell. *Indian Education and the American Colonies, 1607–1783.* Albuquerque, NM: University of New Mexico Press, 1988. The varieties of Indian cultural traditions and values prior to and following contact with European settlers.

Wilson, James. *The Earth Shall Weep: A History of Native America.* New York: Macmillan Co., 1998. A reassessment of the Native Americans' struggle for survival against the tide of invading peoples and cultures that reduced their numbers from an estimated seven to ten million to only 250,000 today.

Notes

1. Charles C. Mann, *1491: New Revelations of the Americas before Columbus.* New York: Vintage, 2006, pp. 18–19, passim.
2. Mann, pp. 284–290; Ted Morgan, *Wilderness at Dawn: The Settling of the North American Continent.* New York: Simon & Shuster, 1993, pp. 18–30, 30–40, *passim.*
3. Morgan, pp. 44–46.
4. We use the terms *Native American* and *Indian* interchangeably throughout this text. It should be kept in mind that both terms are "imposed" in that neither is derived from an indigenous tribal language.
5. An excellent general account on which much of the following discussion is based is Margaret Connell Szasz, *Indian Education in the American Colonies, 1607–1783.* Albuquerque: University of New Mexico Press, 1988, pp. 1–24.
6. European invaders, insensitive to the ethnocentrism inherent in their views, often criticized Native American men for engaging in "pleasurable" pursuits such as hunting and fishing while "their wives set their corn and do all their other work." See James Axtell, *The European and the Indian: Essays in the Ethnohistory of Colonial North America,* New York: Oxford University Press, 1981, pp. 52–54.
7. Among the Omaha, the hole in the moccasins was also a form of "prayer" (i.e., an appeal to the spirit world to allow the child to live long and travel far). See Szasz, pp. 7–8, 266; William N. Fenton, "Northern Iroquoian Culture Patterns," in William C. Sturtevant (gen. ed.), Bruce G. Trigger (ed.), *Handbook of North American Indians, Northeast,* vol. 15. Washington, D.C.: Smithsonian Institution, 1978, p. 314.
8. Charles M. Hudson, *The Southeastern Indians.* Knoxville: University of Tennessee Press, 1976, p. 324. Cf. Szasz, pp. 18–21.
9. Szasz, pp. 20–22.
10. Christopher Columbus, *Journal,* December 24 and 25, 1492, in Samuel Eliot Morrison (ed.), *Journals and Other Documents on the Life and Voyages of Christopher Columbus.* New York: Heritage Press, 1963, pp. 133, 136.
11. Of course, native groups also sought to impose their cultural patterns and values on those who came, voluntarily or otherwise, into their midst. For a dramatic account of a Puritan minister's daughter who chose to stay with her Mohawk captors, see John Demos, *The Unredeemed Captive: A Family Story from Early America.* New York: Alfred A. Knopf, 1994.
12. Morgan, p. 79.

13. On southeastern missions, see Mary Ross, "The Restoration of the Spanish Missions in Georgia, 1598–1606," *The Georgia Historical Quarterly*, vol. 10, 1926, pp. 171–199.

14. James A. Burns, *The Principles, Origin and Establishment of the Catholic School System in the United States*. New York: Arno Press, [1908], 1969, pp. 39–65.

15. See Karen Ordahl Kupperman, *Roanoke: The Abandoned Colony*. Totowa, NJ: Rowman & Allanheld, NJ, 1984; Hugh Talmage Lefler and Albert Ray Newsome, *North Carolina: The History of a Southern State*. Chapel Hill: University of North Carolina Press, 1954, pp. 3–12.

16. In 1638, New Sweden was established in the lower Delaware Valley and was annexed by New Netherland in 1655. In turn, New Netherland was taken over by the British in 1664 and renamed New York. Paul S. Boyer, Clifford E. Clark, Jr., Joseph F. Kett, Thomas L. Purvis, Howard Sitkoff, and Nancy Woloch, *The Enduring Vision: A History of the American People*. Lexington, MA: D. C. Heath, 1990, p. 35.

17. Morgan, pp. 88, 100, passim; Burns, pp. 39ff.

18. See Axtell, *The European and the Indian*, pp. 245–315, for an illuminating analysis of both the English colonial impact on the Indians and the Indian impact on the English colonials. Axtell's text and references provide useful guides to sources drawn upon in the commentary that follows. See also Alfred W. Crosby, Jr., *The Columbian Exchange: Biological and Cultural Consequences of 1492*. Westport, CT: Greenwood Press, 1972; Francis Jennings, *The Invasion of America: Indians, Colonialism, and the Cant of Conquest*. Chapel Hill: University of North Carolina Press, 1975; and Kirkpatrick Sale, *The Conquest of Paradise: Christopher Columbus and the Columbian Legacy*. New York: Alfred A. Knopf, 1990.

2

Colonization and Cultural Transplantation
1607–1776

Overview

Over the course of the first six decades of the seventeenth century, a massive number of people migrated from England, Scotland, and Wales and sailed west and south across the Atlantic. Beginning slowly, perhaps 25,000 to 30,000 people ventured toward Ireland, the islands in the Caribbean, and the North American continent during the first thirty years of the exodus. Over the next thirty years, however, from 1630 to 1660, the "great migration" occurred. Probably no fewer than 240,000 and possibly as many as 295,000 people left Britain between the century's dawn and the year 1660.

The first contingent of adventurers to create a permanent English settlement in North America arrived in Jamestown, Virginia, in 1607. Virginia, along with its neighboring Chesapeake colony, Maryland, founded in 1634, became the destination of approximately 50,000 settlers by 1660. Farther up the Atlantic coast, a small band of Pilgrims migrated to Plymouth in 1620, thus initiating the settlement of the New England seaboard. Between 1629 and the early 1640s, an additional 20,000 to 25,000 English people, many dissatisfied with social and economic as well as religious conditions in their native land, poured into Massachusetts Bay and began to spill over into the new colonies of Connecticut, Rhode Island, and New Haven.[1]

In Search of American Beginnings

The dominant interpretation of American history, including its educational history, has long maintained that our most important and enduring cultural and ideological legacies are of New England origin. Perry Miller's pronouncement that, in order to understand America, one must begin with the Puritans and Puritanism, contains a great deal of truth. So ingrained is this notion that generations of historians have told the story of America largely from a New England perspective. The prevailing assumption has been that the main line of political and cultural development extended from Plymouth and Massachusetts Bay southward and westward. The histories of other regions of the country, particularly the South and Midwest, have fostered the view that development in those regions was merely a rude copy of New England's established social, religious, and educational institutions adjusting to frontier conditions. As far as the South was concerned, its institutions and mores were set aside as being deviations that had to be overcome before America could finally realize its true self and live up to its New England legacy.[2]

A process of revisionism in educational history initiated by Bernard Bailyn and Lawrence Cremin in the 1960s only partially called this dominant interpretation into question. They, and others, condemned historians of earlier generations, and especially the pioneer educational historian, Ellwood P. Cubberley, for a host of scholarly sins. Cubberley was criticized for locating in the "Puritan mind" and the New England experience the intentional foundations of American public education—and much else that is accepted as "typically American." He was chastised also for being too narrow and parochial in his focus on schools and formal education and for ignoring other educative forces such as the family, church, or community. His acceptance of the "providentiality" of public schooling was considered anachronistic, moralistic, and too "celebratory."[3]

The revisionist history proposed by Bailyn, Cremin, and others called for a broader view of education. "The history of education," said Bailyn, "should consider not only schools and 'formal pedagogy,' but the entire process by which a culture transmits itself across the generations." Cremin likewise emphasized the need to understand all the agencies and institutions that educate—all the elements that comprise the "configurations of education" present in society at particular points in time.[4]

In all of the clamor for reconceptualization, however, the "New England origins" concept has not been fundamentally challenged. Neither the "liberal" or "cultural revisionists" who followed the lead of Bailyn and Cremin, nor the more "radical revisionists" who joined the fray a few years later, questioned seriously the "Massachusetts myopia" syndrome that has long dominated discussions of American life and education. Recent historical research and interpretation, however, are suggesting that reassessment may be long overdue.

Reassessing Our Origins

In the examination that follows, we side with those who suggest that the New England experience of the seventeenth century ought to be viewed as atypical rather than prototypical of American development. Much of New England history—and this certainly includes its educational traditions—can be best appreciated as a series of reactionary efforts aimed at fostering and preserving a rigidly homogeneous or "tribal" way of life. By contrast, the Chesapeake region and the Middle Atlantic colonies, marked from the outset by dissent, diversity, individualism, and economic competition, reflected the upheaval and change that were coming to characterize "old England" and other parts of Europe as well as other regions of Atlantic settlement. Seen in this light, it is New England, with its attempts to create static, intimate, and rigidly cohesive enclaves, and not the other colonies, that appears to have been at odds with the dominant patterns of development in both the changing "old world" as well as the new.

Historian Jack Greene has argued that the most important element in the emerging British-American culture was not a vision of a closed and homogeneous religious society on the New England model. Rather, it was the conception of the country as a place in which free people could pursue their own individual happiness in safety and with a fair prospect of success. The American colonies eventually forged a new nation by moving away from, rather than toward, the New England model of social and religious conformity. As New Englanders gradually relinquished their grand vision of creating a new holy commonwealth, they worked their way back into the mainstream of British-American social and cultural development.[5]

To say that New England's influence in terms of America's "origins" has been exaggerated is by no means to suggest that it lacked significance. Far from it. Nor are we about to suggest that the southern or the middle colonies, or the western empire of "New Spain," or any other section of the country holds "the key" to defining the American experience. What we do suggest is that those who seek to understand our educational past must try to comprehend the people who lived in earlier times and places on their terms, not ours. We also stress the need to keep in mind that most, if not all, people who came to this country in the seventeenth century intended in one degree or another to re-create societies here that were recognizably European. There were indeed differences among colonists and colonies, and dissimilar geographic and climatic conditions forced still more adjustments that had telling consequences. However, the new arrivals to America expected to build societies that in most respects were like those from which they had come.

To understand both the continuity and the change that marked their efforts, including educational transplantations and transformations, we must first attend briefly to the patterns of settlement that were attempted. It is to the Chesapeake region and the experience of the settlers of that section that we now turn in our efforts to comprehend the predominantly English underpinnings of the American social and educational experience.

Jamestown and the Chesapeake Experience

The Formative Stage: Struggle for Survival

The English settlers who established Jamestown in 1607 had no intention of creating a new society, religious or otherwise. Their motive for coming to the new world was much less grandiose. They were, first and foremost, Englishmen who were restless, hungry for adventure, and in search of economic opportunities they lacked at home. They set sail for the Virginia shores in hopes of obtaining riches for themselves and turning a profit for their financial backers, the stockholders of the London Company. The London Company operated the colony as a private venture for the first seventeen years of its existence. In 1624, Virginia became a royal colony and control was transferred to a Crown-appointed governor.

The Englishmen who had obtained a charter creating the London Company in 1606 were speculators willing to put their capital at risk in the hope that a passage to the Orient might yet be discovered or, failing that, at least realizing some profit from their investment in a colony in the new world. Their dream that a quick passage to the East might still be found was reflected in the company's instructions to the adventurers they recruited. They were told to establish their base on the river "which bendeth most toward the Northwest, for that way you shall soonest find the other sea."[6]

Three ships carrying just over a hundred male adventurers and thirty-nine crewmen sailed into Chesapeake Bay in late April 1607, and, as instructed, entered one of several broad rivers that curved toward the northwest. After several weeks of searching for a suitable site to establish a fort, they began erecting a settlement on the north shore of the river that had been named for King James I. English adventurers were once again attempting to plant a colony in the new world. Their survival this time was no more assured than it had been for Raleigh's fateful adventurers on Roanoke Island two decades earlier.

As Christians, the Jamestown colonists and investors believed that without God's favor the enterprise was hopeless. Moreover, religious justifications for English expansion were expressed from the outset of the venture. In the original charter granted in 1606, James I had instructed the leaders of the expedition to carry the Christian religion to the "Infidels and Savages" who "as yet live in Darkness and miserable Ignorance of the true Knowledge and Worship of God." Numerous sermons preached on behalf of the backers of the colonization scheme emphasized the need for settlers whose concerns were Godly rather than worldly. In 1609, for example, the Reverend William Crashaw sermonized to a group about to make passage to Jamestown: "if you should aime at nothing but your private ends, and neglect religion and God's service, looke for no blessing, nay looke for a curse."[7]

Curses were certainly abundant during the first several years of the colony's life. The site picked for the settlement was surrounded by marshlands and brackish water, a suitable breeding ground for mosquitoes but not for humans. Typhoid, malaria, dysentery, and other illnesses took a heavy toll, as did periodic attacks by the native Powhatans with whom relations alternated abruptly between periods of civility and outbreaks of hostility. The situation deteriorated to the point at which (noted George Percy in his journal in September 1607), they were "in miserable distress." Day and night for week upon week, there was "groaning in every corner of the fort, most pitiful to hear . . . some departing out of the world, many times three or four in a night." At daybreak, those who could walk pulled the bodies of the dead out of their cabins "like dogs to be buried." When replacements arrived in January 1608, they found

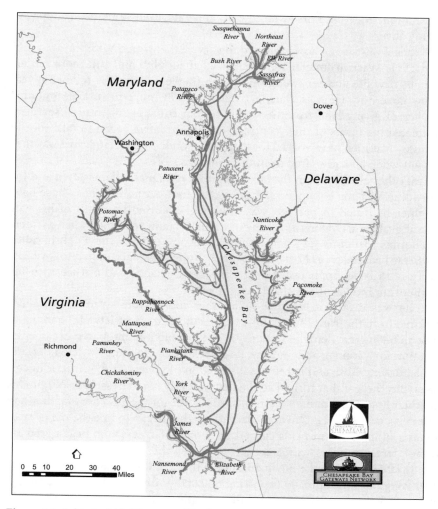

Figure 2.1 John Smith's Voyages of Exploration: June 2–21, 1608.

Credit: Map courtesy of the National Park Service.

thirty-eight settlers alive of the original 104. Percy closed his account of this tragic episode by commenting that, "had it not been for aid given them by sympathetic Indians—'our mortal enemies'—all would have perished."[8]

Successive waves of new recruits replenished the colony, at least temporarily. By the fall of 1608, the colony numbered about 200, including the first two women and a few German and Polish glassmakers. A year later there were close to 500 settlers in Jamestown. The winter of 1609 to 1610, however, became known as "the starving time." As famine and disease inside the fort and hostile natives outside reduced their numbers, some colonists turned in desperation to eating horses, dogs, cats, and rats, even humans, in hopes of staying alive.[9]

Sixty colonists somehow managed to survive the winter. With the arrival of Lord De la Warr in June 1610, much-needed supplies and still more settlers brought new life and renewed hope to the fragile colony. The following year a new governor, Thomas Dale, arrived with 300 more men. Dale initiated a policy of giving land to settlers who, having come as indentured servants, completed the terms of their contract. Private initiative began to take root in Jamestown as men now worked for themselves on their own lands in a way they had not when all had shared from the common stores.

Two other events within the next couple of years placed Jamestown and the expanding Virginia colony on a more secure footing. John Rolfe, whose baby daughter had died in passage, was doubly grieved by the death of his wife soon after their arrival in the colony in 1610. When in 1613 the Indian maiden, Pocahontas, daughter of Chief Wahunsonacock (whom the English called Powhatan) was taken as hostage, the lonely Rolfe soon succumbed to love. His marriage to Pocahontas resulted in a hostage exchange and a truce with the neighboring Indians that lasted for eight years.[10]

Rolfe was also instrumental in another momentous event. With seeds acquired from the West Indies, Rolfe began cultivating a variety of tobacco that came to be in great demand in Europe. The production of tobacco became the salvation for Virginia, and, in time, its curse as well. Tobacco depleted the soil, was labor-intensive, and led to the installation of slavery in the American colonies. But the leaf that turned gold when properly cured became to Virginians and their English investors a welcomed substitute for the gold ore that they had little success in finding. On large plantations that began to line the major river routes and in scattered fields cleared by yeomen farmers who began arriving in ever larger numbers, tobacco spread across the coastal plain of Virginia and into Maryland to the north and down into the Carolinas to the south. By 1630, Virginia was annually exporting 500,000 pounds of the "joviall weed." Historian Ted Morgan has asserted that shipping the first barrels of tobacco to England "was the most momentous fact in the history of Virginia, and one of the most momentous for all America."[11]

As tobacco became the staple crop of the Virginia colony, all aspects of life began to reflect its dominion. In 1619 a Dutch ship unloaded the first Africans to come to North America. These indentured servants were followed by others whose eventual enslavement became inexorably tied to the emerging plantation economy. In the same year, ninety "mail-order brides" arrived in Jamestown, each of whom was claimed by payment of 120 pounds of tobacco leaf. Families, both free and slave, were henceforth to become indispensable components of Virginia's destiny.

Representative government also made its appearance in the expanding colony in 1619. Under terms of a new charter, delegates were elected from each of the major settlements in the Virginia colony to join with the governor and his six counselors in order to regulate the affairs of the colony. The Virginia House of Burgesses thus became the first elected legislative body in the English colonies.

The Burgesses drafted legislation fixing the price of tobacco and instructed the settlers to plant grapes, hemp, and mulberry trees, the latter necessary for silkworm cultivation. Of more immediate importance than diversifying the economy however, was the need to rescue the growing colony from barbarism. The assembly enacted a statute requiring everyone to attend worship services twice on Sunday. Laws against idleness, gambling, drunkenness, and other breaches of Christian decorum were restored or established. That such laws were needed might be surmised from the descriptions made of some who came—or were sent—to the Virginia shores. Captain John Smith wrote in 1608 that among the early settlers were "many unruly gallants packed thither by their friends to escape their destinies," and that "all the trash they could get in London was sent to us in Virginia." Even less flattering was George Sandy's appraisal some years later of a half-dozen Italian glassmakers recruited to the colony: "A more damned crew hell never vomited," he recorded caustically in 1623.[12]

Even as laws were being passed to ensure civility, a hundred destitute boys and girls, most of whom were orphans and waifs, were rounded up in London and shipped to the colony to become apprentices. They, and a contingent of convicts that King James also directed to be deported to Virginia, were among over 1,200 new arrivals who in 1619 came to the Chesapeake region to confront life on new terms.

Early Attempts to Establish Schools in Virginia

That the leaders of the Virginia colony were serious about planting a permanent outpost of English civilization on the American frontier was underscored by their attempts to improve relations with the natives surrounding them. One early directive required each town, city, borough, and plantation to educate Indian children in their vicinity "in true religion" and the principles of civilized life. The Virginia Company of London directed that Indian boys of promise "should be fitted for the College intended for them." This college, which had been in the planning stage for at least two years, was to be built at Henrico City, just south of present-day Richmond. Ten thousand acres of land were set aside for the purpose, and over the next few years, additional gifts of money, books, and materials, including ornaments for a communion table in the college chapel, were donated or pledged in support of the institution.

The Henrico College venture, as well as plans for the East India School, a free school in Charles City intended for the education of white children, disintegrated on Good Friday morning, March 22, 1622. Whatever the colonists' intentions about improved relations might have been, the Indians, after years of peace, apparently grew tired of intrusion into their lands. With amazing coordination and ferocity, Indians suddenly attacked settlements stretched

140 miles along both sides of the James River. More than 350 settlers—men, women, and children—were killed. At Henrico City, twenty-two settlers were killed and the foundations of the college were put to the torch. The first attempts to establish schools in English North America thus met a dismal fate.[13]

Southern Diversity: Piedmont and Backcountry Settlements

Indian uprisings and repeated epidemics of disease delayed but did not long deter the expansion of settlements around and to the south of the Chesapeake Bay. By 1634, under terms of a royal grant given to the family of George Calvert (Lord Baltimore), the colony of Maryland was established as a "for-profit" venture and as a peaceful haven for Catholic immigrants. Protestants settled in the colony in greater numbers than did Catholics, however, and the Calverts themselves eventually reconverted to Protestantism.

The Carolinas originated in a grant bestowed by Charles II on eight friends who anticipated wealth as proprietors of the colony. As the region developed, the section that became North Carolina was characterized by fewer large plantations and a more diverse population than Virginia. German and Scottish-Irish as well as English immigrants settled in the colony's piedmont and mountain areas. The South Carolina coastal region developed an extensive plantation economy based on rice and indigo and came to resemble Virginia's social and economic structure more than its northern sister state. Charleston in time became the commercial center of the region, the largest and wealthiest town in the colonial South. North Carolina and South Carolina became separate royal colonies in the 1720s.

Georgia, the least populated and last settled of the southern colonies, resulted from proposals of some British philanthropists to provide a new start in life for formerly imprisoned debtors. That the colony would serve to buffer the Carolinas from the Spanish in Florida was also a consideration. Settlement began at Savannah in 1733. By 1753, Georgia went the way of the other southern colonies and fell under direct royal control. Its eighteenth-century social and economic situation more closely resembled the Carolina and Virginia backcountry than that of the Chesapeake or South Carolina tidewater, however.

The backcountry sections of the South were settled largely after the 1730s. Successive waves of immigrants made their way from Pennsylvania southward by way of "the Great Wagon Road" that followed Indian trails down the Shenandoah Valley and through mountain gaps into the Carolina piedmont. By the mid-eighteenth century, connections had been extended to Charleston and Augusta. Tens of thousands of humble families traveled this narrow, rutted intercolonial thoroughfare in hopes of finding a better life than they had known before.

Inhabitants of the interior tended to settle in tight ethnic enclaves, isolated from the more cosmopolitan influences that shaped life along the coast. In keeping with long-established patterns in the borderlands of North Britain and

Ireland, from which many of these people came, clan ties connected one nuclear family to another and joined one generation to the next. Their world view was defined by and largely restricted to the folkways of those who shared the same surname and ancestors. In the shadows socially, economically, and politically, as well as geographically, these backcountry settlers clung stubbornly to their native languages, dialects, and customs. The rigidity with which some held to their opinions is exemplified by the prayer of one stiff-necked Scottish-Irish Presbyterian who was heard to say: "Lord, grant that I may always be right, for Thou knowest that I am hard to turn."

The Quakers, Moravians, German Reformed, and Presbyterian Calvinists who settled in the piedmont region held strong religious views and attended seriously to their spiritual as well as their physical needs. Some other migrants to the region, however, especially among those who made their way into the remote mountain backcountry, boasted of being staunch "nothingarians" and complained bitterly of being "eaten up by teachers and preachers" who intruded into their closed world spreading conflicting and unwelcomed versions of Christianity. In exasperation, one Anglican missionary described backcountry inhabitants who rejected his sermonizing as "the lowest vilest Scum of Mankind," a people plainly beyond the reach of the Gospel. In disgust he concluded: "They delight in their present low, lazy, sluttish, heathenish, hellish life, and seem not desirous of changing it." For many in the rugged and isolated Appalachian backcountry, the poverty of their spiritual life mirrored the poverty of their physical circumstances.[14]

Class and Caste in the Colonial South

With the backcountry dwellers excepted, southern colonists tended to maintain rather close ties with Britain until the eve of the Revolution. This affinity with the mother country and the feeling that they remained English subjects explain in large measure that region's tendency to emulate many aspects of English social life and institutions. An agrarian social order based on the dictates of class and caste gradually took hold, increasingly shaping life in the Chesapeake and coastal Carolina colonies.

The large majority of Virginia's earliest arrivals were humble people of low rank, but beginning in the 1640s, emigrants who were descended from families of substance and culture in England began arriving in Virginia. These younger sons of eminent English families were Royalists or "Cavaliers," many of whom had served in the English Civil War as military officers. Those with university backgrounds had ties to Oxford colleges—especially Christ Church, Merton, and Queens—all associated with the royal family. With but few exceptions, these migrating Cavaliers tended to be solid members of the Church of England, loyal Anglicans who intended to fashion their lives in Virginia as much as possible along the accustomed lines of their ancestors. In customs, dress, habits, and values, these founders of the plantation gentry class reflected the lifestyles of English rural squires. Descendants of the original Carters,

Lees, Randolphs, Byrds, and other "first families of Virginia" intermarried frequently and came to dominate the public life of the colony for some two centuries.[15]

Upwardly mobile families in Virginia and neighboring colonies tended to follow the lead of the cultural and economic elite of the tidewater. Throughout the colonial period, about half of the white immigrants to the South came to the new world as indentured servants. Some eventually found a measure of success as farmers, craftsmen, and merchants in the coastal and piedmont areas. Others moved toward the backcountry in search of good land, hoping that through effort and divine blessing they too might someday prosper.

While class lines could be somewhat fluid, the caste barrier was fixed. Although African "indentured servants" had been a part of the workforce since 1619, in 1661 the Virginia General Assembly made legal the slave system that by then existed in practice. Massachusetts in 1641 and Connecticut in 1650 had already recognized the legality of the slave trade in supporting ship captains who found captive Africans to be a profitable cargo. The African American slave population grew rapidly as the forests and their original inhabitants yielded to the spread of tobacco and other extractive crops. Slavery also became an accepted part of urban life as seaport and river towns grew in importance.

Education in the Chesapeake and Southern Colonies

Education in the southern colonies was influenced by the social and economic developments that defined life in the coastal, piedmont, and backcountry regions. The dispersed agrarian pattern of settlement worked against close communal ties and activities, thus deterring the development of anything resembling a "system of schools" in the southern colonies. Moreover, the Church of England, although by 1758 legally established to varying degrees throughout the South, failed to emerge as a powerful force in the region. The absence of a resident bishop and widely scattered clergymen of sometimes dubious qualifications and character thwarted attempts at effective hierarchical control. As a result, the vestries of most southern parishes conducted their churches on an independent and often informal basis. Except in areas with a fair population density, Anglican churches did not become centers of sustained spiritual or intellectual activity. A Virginia clergyman noted in 1662 that the scattered and sparse population "has resulted [in] their almost general want of Schooles for the education of their Children," a sad situation "most of all bewailed of Parents there."[16]

Educational policies and practices in the Chesapeake and coastal Carolina colonies were also shaped by deliberate attempts to transplant familiar English customs and institutions to the new world. Most southern colonists tended to accept without question the prevailing European precept that education was essentially a private matter, a family concern. Virginia's governor, Sir William Berkeley, clearly expressed the attitude of many in his colony when he reported in 1671 that as far as education was concerned, Virginians were following "the same course that is taken in England out of towns; every man according to his own ability in instructing his children."[17]

Tutors, Parents, and Home Schooling

"Every man according to his own ability" meant, of course, that the economically secure could provide much better for their children than could colonists of more humble circumstances. Beginning in the seventeenth and continuing through most of the eighteenth century, some planters and wealthy merchants sent their children "back home," as they referred to England, for a proper education. Others brought the tradition of the English schools and classical education to the colonies by employing English- and Scottish-trained tutors and governesses. As the number of American colleges slowly increased during the eighteenth century, students or graduates of some of those institutions served for a time as "live-in" tutors.

The best-known tutor of the late colonial period was Philip Fithian, a Princeton-bred theological student who taught the children of Robert Carter of Nomini Hall from October 1773 to October 1774. Fithian's diary and letters to relatives and friends during his year in Virginia provide a detailed and illuminating account of his duties as a tutor and offer insight into the daily routines of plantation life. His entry of November 1, 1773, for example, is suggestive of the range of studies he supervised. He recorded that the oldest son, 17 years of age, was studying Latin grammar and reading Sallust. The second son, age 14, and a cousin of the same age, were studying English grammar and "cyphering in subtraction." The oldest of five daughters, a 15-year-old, was improving her command of English with writing exercises and by reading *The Spectator*. She was also "beginning to cypher." The younger daughters were working in spelling books at various levels, except for the youngest, a 4-year-old who was just "beginning her letters." Music teachers came in once a week to give the children lessons on the pianoforte, harpsichord, and guitar, as well as in dancing.

It is clear from Fithian's *Journal* that tutors were given responsibility for discipline as well as for teaching. His methods ranged from mild admonishment to corporal punishment. Some situations that demanded his attention clearly perplexed him. He noted on 8 February 1774:

> Before Breakfast Nancy & Fanny had a Fight about a Shoe Brush which they both wanted—Fanny pull'd off her Shoe & threw [it] at Nancy, which missed her and broke a pane of glass of our School Room. [T]hey then enter'd upon close scratching &c. which methods seem instinctive in Women. . . . I made peace, but with many threats—.[18]

Obviously, few parents could afford live-in tutors. "Home schooling" by a parent was sometimes an option, but Patrick Henry's experience of having a college-educated father as a tutor was clearly exceptional. More commonly, some well-meaning parents who were capable made efforts to teach their children to read and possibly write. Many children of the less cultured members of society, however, had little chance of receiving even the basic rudiments of literary training. With the notable exception of some religious groups such as the Moravians, who settled in piedmont North Carolina in the eighteenth century, the farther into the backcountry people lived, the less likely they were to have access to books or literate neighbors. Consequently, many lives were passed in ignorance of any learning that could not be transmitted orally or by way of demonstration.

Church and School in the Southern Context

The role of the church in educational matters in the Chesapeake and southern colonies varied by denomination and circumstance. Among adherents of the Church of England (Anglicans), it was expected that ministers would provide basic instruction in religious matters. As noted earlier, among the first acts of the Virginia General Assembly in 1619 was legislation requiring colonists to attend church services twice on Sunday. In 1631 the legislature reminded Anglican ministers of their legal duty to preach at least one sermon every Sunday. Another legislative enactment in the same year required ministers to "examine, catechize, and instruct the youth and ignorant persons" in the Ten Commandments, The Lord's Prayer, and The Articles of Faith for a half-hour before evening prayer on Sundays. The law placed responsibility on "all fathers, mothers, masters, and mistresses" in the parish to bring their children, servants, or apprentices to church at the appointed time, under threat of censure by the local court. Children who refused to learn were also threatened with punishment.[19]

In England, local parishes were units of civil government and provided literary as well as religious training. This arrangement was repeated in parts of Maryland, Virginia, and the Carolinas, although to a lesser degree. Among Anglicans in the Chesapeake region, the most common and direct "church-school" connection occurred when ministers, to supplement their income, conducted "parson's schools." In these schools, the quality of instruction mattered less than the fact that a minister served as the teacher. In some instances ministers opened up their homes to fee-paying students and provided room and board as well as instruction. The Reverend James Maury of Fredericksburg Parish in Virginia, for example, began conducting a parson's boarding school in 1740. In boarding schools such as Maury's, students whose parents could afford the tuition fees could prepare for college as well as equip themselves for life among the established gentry. Among the young men who lived and studied with Maury over time were George Washington, James Madison, James Monroe, and Thomas Jefferson.

Ministers who did not take in students as boarders sometimes taught in the local church or in a specific building set aside as a school. Still others, usually unmarried ministers, functioned as tutors and, in exchange for their room and board and perhaps a small fee, taught the children of their host family.

It did not become the custom in Virginia, as it was in England, for parishes to provide schoolhouses as an inducement for masters to conduct schools. If a special building were constructed as a school, then it was typically the work of interested parents and neighbors or perhaps the parson himself. Anglican colonists also departed from the English custom of using parish funds to pay for the tuition of poor children in private schools. A careful examination of vestry books in Virginia by Guy Wells turned up only five instances in which this occurred. Thus, while the Anglican church was certainly involved in secular (as well as religious) education through the work of its ministers, it was not parish policy to support education directly by either building and maintaining schools or by providing tuition assistance to children of the poor.[20]

Missionary societies representing various denominations stepped in to fill the educational breach. In northern, middle, and southern colonies alike, missionary groups established "charity schools," in which instruction was provided to poor and indigent children without charge. The Anglican-sponsored Society for the Propagation of the Gospel in Foreign Parts (SPG), chartered in 1701, was perhaps the most active and influential of these societies. The SPG was quite explicit in stating the need for its adherents to support the efforts of missionaries to combat atheism, infidelity, and the "popish superstition and idolatry" that threatened the colonists abroad. By the time of the Revolution, the society had established approximately 170 missionary stations, extending from New Hampshire to Georgia and into backcountry counties of Pennsylvania and New York. More than eighty schoolmasters and eighteen catechists devoted themselves for periods ranging from a few weeks to a quarter-century to teaching charity-school children the principles of Anglicanism and to "read, write, and cast accounts." Their duties also included leading prayers in the absence of clergymen and distributing Bibles, prayer books, sermons, and textbooks printed not only in English, but also in French, German, Dutch, and various Indian dialects.[21]

The SPG was the largest but by no means the only missionary society working in the colonies. Missionary work was carried on by a number of societies representing different Christian denominations. Some dissenting sects operated "denominational schools" that offered literary as well as religious instruction to the unchurched as well as to children of their own faith. Dissenting Protestant sects such as the Moravians, Quakers, and Presbyterians actively planted schools in the piedmont sections of Virginia and North Carolina. In Maryland Jesuits began establishing schools for Catholic children in the 1640s. While some schools were engaged in mission work with Native and African Americans, many were founded specifically to preserve and advance the religious and cultural knowledge of the children of adherents of the sponsoring faith.

In Virginia from the mid-seventeenth century forward, ecclesiastical pronouncements and legislative enactments periodically proclaimed that teachers in all schools and at all levels had to be licensed by officials of the church or "state." The extent to which these regulations were ignored obviously increased as more and more groups of dissenters entered the colony during the eighteenth century.[22]

Endowed "Free" Schools

Virginia's Governor Berkeley, who was quite satisfied with the notion of parental responsibility for education, was both incorrect and uncharitable when he informed the Commissioners of Trade and Plantations in 1671 that, "thank God, there are no free schools nor printing [in Virginia]." Berkeley continued: "I hope we shall not have these [for a] hundred years; for learning has brought disobedience and heresy, and sects into the world, and printing has divulged them, and libels against the best government. God keep us from both."

Governor Berkeley notwithstanding, there were benevolent souls in the colonies as in the mother country who were moved to make provision in their wills for "free schools" for the education of children in their vicinity. As early as 1635, a Virginia planter named Benjamin Syms bequeathed 200 acres of land and the produce and increase of eight cows for a free school "to educate and teach the children of the adjoining parishes of Elizabeth City and Poquoson." In 1642 a school in Elizabeth City received a charter under the terms of Syms's will and opened soon thereafter.[23]

A surgeon, Dr. Thomas Eaton, whose brother Nathaniel was Harvard's first head, followed Syms's example and left an even larger bequest in 1659: 500 acres of land; two slaves; twenty hogs; twelve cows; two bulls; and an assortment of pots, pans, and other miscellany. The "Eaton School" that resulted was also situated in Elizabeth City. Apparently both benefactors, whose schools later merged and then in 1805 became Hampton Academy, intended their school to be free to all children in the vicinity regardless of ability to pay. It is too far a stretch to claim, as has one historian, that the Syms school should be considered "the forefather of the American system of free education." However, it is worth noting that Syms and Eaton were at the forefront of a small number of individuals who transplanted to the American colonies the British tradition of endowing schools, thus extending educational opportunity in at least a few communities during the colonial period and beyond. Outside Virginia, endowed free schools were also established before the Revolution in the southern coastal cities of Annapolis, New Bern, Charleston, and Georgetown.[24]

"Old Field Schools"

In some rural areas where population density was sufficient and interest warranted, groups of citizens erected schoolhouses on worn-out parcels of land. Tobacco was a demanding crop, usually exhausting fields in about seven years. Abandoned fields were thus abundant and basically useless—except as sites for schools, and perhaps, churches and graveyards. Unlike endowed free schools, which were open without charge to children of a neighborhood, teachers in "old field schools" were supported by fees paid by parents of children who attended. Schools of this type were also variously referred to as "rate schools," "subscription schools," or "fee schools"—and eventually as "district schools." In some cases itinerant teachers staffed these schools for short periods of time, "boarding round" with various families. Parish priests also served on occasion as schoolmasters in old field schools, but, as noted previously, not as part of their regular ministerial duties. Conversely, some men hired as schoolmasters also served as readers in parish churches, but in a lay capacity. Seldom did these schools in the colonial era offer instruction much beyond the basics, but for many students that was all that was deemed necessary.

Apprenticeship Training

The apprenticeship method of education was predominant in all the colonies, as it had been in England for at least three centuries. Apprenticeship had emerged from the guild system of medieval Europe as a means by which master craftsmen could protect their incomes as well as the quality of workmanship by restricting practice in a craft or trade to men who had been properly trained. By the sixteenth and seventeenth centuries, the apprenticeship system had acquired other important functions as well. It had become a system of community social control and welfare relief, a way of alleviating the burden of the poor on society, a penalty for idleness, and a means by which a person could work one's way out of indebtedness. This latter arrangement made it possible for perhaps one half to one third of all immigrants to the American colonies to pay for their passage by "binding" themselves out as indentured servants for a specified number of years. Of course, not all indentured servants had the good fortune to become apprentices to master craftsmen or tradesmen. Many were bound to the hardest kind of labor: working someone else's land or toiling in public workhouses.[25]

In a law enacted in 1563, the English parliament had legalized the principle of "no work, no money" by decreeing that anyone between the ages of 12 and 60 who lacked visible means of support was to be "bound out" or apprenticed for a period of seven years. The English Poor Law of 1601 further empowered each parish to designate overseers of the poor. These men had the power to levy taxes for the establishment of workhouses to which illegitimate, indigent, or orphaned children or adults could be assigned as apprentices.

Apprenticeship laws derived from these English precedents were enacted in all the American colonies, along with laws that required parents and masters of apprentices to ensure that children under their care were properly catechized in religion. In 1646, the Virginia General Assembly adopted an apprenticeship statute that was clearly derived from existing English law. The legislation empowered local authorities to round up and send to public workhouses boys and girls who, whether by parental neglect or absence, were not being instructed "in some good and lawful calling."

The Virginia statute is significant in several respects. For one thing, it indicates that the problems being faced in the colonies, while aggravated by frontier conditions and the importation of indigent children, were by no means unique. The orphans and waifs being sent to Virginia were, after all, taken from the streets and alleys of London. Sending unwanted children to the colonies may have seemed a promising way to alleviate the problem for Londoners, but it only added to difficulties in the colonies where unruly children and negligent or incapable parents were already a matter of concern.

The 1646 Virginia statute and others of a similar nature also reveal that colonial authorities recognized the need to encourage parents and masters to give proper attention to their charges. These laws empowered justices, vestrymen, or other public officials to intercede in family matters for the welfare of the community as well as on behalf of children. In both the old world and the new, parental sovereignty clearly had its limits, especially if parents or masters were judged incompetent or inattentive to their children's—and the community's—welfare.

While Virginia's initial apprenticeship law is of interest as a reflection of English precedent and as a reaction of colonial officials to economic and social problems, educationally this particular law was limited. In keeping with the English Poor Law of 1601, the Virginia statute made no mention of instruction in reading or writing. As far as dependent or problem children were concerned, the focus of this law was on education for employment, not literacy or even "salvation." Although the Virginia Assembly in 1643 had "enjoyned" guardians of orphans to "educate and instruct them according to their best endeavors in Christian religion and in the rudiments of learning," legislation requiring masters to provide for the literacy training of children placed in their care was not adopted until 1705.[26]

Virginia was the only colony to enact legislation providing for "workhouses" for indigent children, but the public flax houses envisioned in the 1646 law were never built. Just over a century later, however, at least six Virginia parishes were operating workhouses or poorhouses. Only one of these, the Upper Parish of Nansemond County, had made provision for teaching reading and writing to poor children, and that was the direct result of an endowment given for that purpose. Vestry officials were forced to close even this workhouse school within four years since enrollment proved insufficient to warrant its continuance.

Beyond the Basics: Approaches to Secondary Education

Familial interest and social standing, religious affiliation, geographic location, and community support (or lack thereof) all affected the educational opportunity available to children in the Chesapeake and southern colonies. The "schooling" options described above varied considerably from family to family and from region to region. The duration and quality of schooling also differed widely. While some families could afford private tutors and boarding schools for their children, others had neither the means nor the inclination to consider any sort of formal schooling for their children.

Of the dozen or so endowed free schools in southern colonies during the pre-Revolutionary period, only King William's School in Annapolis, the Eaton School in Elizabeth City, Virginia, and the Free School of Charleston appear to have offered instruction above the elementary level. By the mid eighteenth century, some Presbyterian academies in Maryland and North Carolina and Moravian schools in Wachovia (now Winston-Salem) had begun providing advanced instruction for some children within their reach.

In southern colonies as well as in those in the Middle Atlantic and New England regions, schools of another sort began to appear in urban areas and even in outlying districts. These proprietary or "private venture schools" were conducted by individuals who, for a fee, offered to teach a wide range of subjects. Some private schoolmasters, such as the Scottish-born Reverend Maury who taught Washington, Jefferson, Madison, and others of the Virginia gentry, had been educated abroad and were accomplished men of learning. Others had attended one of the fledgling colonial colleges or in some other fashion had acquired something of a classical education. Still others could offer little by way of formal credentials, but rested their claims on practical experience and native intelligence and fashioned curricula that appealed to ambitious young men eager to learn nonagrarian crafts or trades.

For the most part, these entrepreneurial schools were secular in orientation and, especially in towns that were becoming commercial centers, tended to give greater attention to practical skills than to classical studies. Enterprising schoolmasters advertised widely and sometimes immodestly in attempts to attract students to their "schools." Some offered to teach at convenient hours in the evening, while others volunteered to move to a new neighborhood if a sufficiently attractive offer were forthcoming. While their services were beyond the reach of most colonial inhabitants, private teachers of both classical and practical studies filled an important niche in the educational configurations of the southern colonies and even more so in colonies to the north.

The College of William and Mary

As noted earlier, some southern colonials had from the earliest days of settlement sent their offspring back across the ocean for secondary and higher education. A few children were sent abroad at a very tender age, but most boys were over the age of ten when arrangements were made for them to enroll in secondary boarding schools in England. From there, sons of Virginia's colonial elite entered the colleges of Oxford, Cambridge, Edinburgh, and occasionally Aberdeen, or one of the Inns of Court in London. Over time, however, the appeal of education abroad dimmed, as parents began to conclude that education on the western shores of the Atlantic posed less danger in terms of travel, was less expensive, and very likely was more useful as well.

Access to institutions of higher education in the American colonies posed

---

EIGHTEENTH CENTURY PRIVATE SCHOOL ADVERTISEMENTS

JOHN WALKER

Lately arriv'd in Williamsburg from London, and who for ten Years past has been engag'd in the Education of Youth, undertakes to instruct young Gentlemen in Reading, Writing, Arithmetic, the most material Branches of Classical Learning, and ancient and modern Geography and History; but, as the noblest End of Erudition and Human Attainments, he will exert his principal Endeavors to improve their Morals, in Proportion to their Progress in Learning, that no Parent may repent his Choice in trusting him with the Education of his Children.

MRS. WALKER, likewise, teaches young Ladies all Kinds of Needle Work; makes Capuchins, Shades, Hats, and Bonnets; and will endeavour to give Satisfaction to those who shall honour her with their Custom.

The above-mentioned JOHN WALKER, and his Wife, live at MR. COBB's new House, next to MR. COKE's near the Road going down to the Capitol Landing; where there is also to be sold, Mens Shoes and Pumps, Turkey, Coffee, Edging and Lace for Ladies Caps, and some Gold Rings.

The Virginia Gazette, 1752

NOTICE is hereby GIVEN that JOHN SEARSON

Who teaches School at the House of Mrs. Coon opposite to the Post Office, proposes (God Willing) to open an Evening School, on Thursday the 25th of this Instant September; where may be learn'd Writing, Arithmetic Vulgar and Decimal, Merchants Accounts, Mensuration, Geometry, Trigonometry, Surveying, Dialling, and Navigation in a short, plain, and methodical Manner, and at very reasonable Rates. Said Searson having a large and commodious Room, together with his own diligent Attendance, the Scholars will have it in their Power to make a good Progress in a short time.

N.Y. Gazette or Weekly Post Boy, 1755

Figure 2.2 School Advertisements.

Credit: These and other advertisements may be found in Sol Cohen, ed., *Education in the United States: A Documentary History*, vol. 1. New York: Random House, 1974, pp. 438–452.

another set of difficulties, however. They were, quite literally, few and far between, especially south of the Chesapeake. After the abortive attempt to launch a "college" at Henrico City[27] in the 1620s, Virginia officials allowed decades to pass without giving sustained attention to education at any level. In 1661 the Virginia General Assembly passed an act authorizing a "colledge and free school." Although contributions of both money and tobacco were raised on behalf of the project, the undertaking failed. When a group of English merchants raised subscriptions to support a college in 1688–1689, their efforts also came to naught. In the early 1690s, however, over seventy years after the initial undertaking, the Reverend James Blair, Episcopal Commissary for Virginia, secured a charter for a college from skeptical English officials. When he argued that a college in the Anglican outpost of Virginia would prepare ministers who would be able to save souls, the attorney general for the Crown is said to have bellowed: "Souls! Damn your souls! Make tobacco!"

If the Virginians had needed a reminder as to why their colony had been established in the first place, the attorney general's response surely made the point. Even so, in 1693 a college named for the English sovereigns, William and Mary, received a charter. Within a few years a grammar (or secondary) school was in operation, and the institution's first building was completed in 1700. College-level instruction did not begin until about 1712, and not until 1729 did the faculty grow to the full complement of six as specified in the founding charter.[28]

The College of William and Mary, the second college to be founded in the colonies, was an Anglican institution. Like its predecessor, Harvard, which had been founded in the Massachusetts Bay colony in 1636, the Virginia college had the mission of preparing young men for positions of leadership in both church and state. Also like its New England counterpart, William and Mary received support from the government as well as from the church and individual donors. In the case of William and Mary, the king and queen signaled their approval of the enterprise by making a gift of money to the college. The colonial legislature made land grants and gave the college income from taxes on exported skins, furs, and tobacco and on imported liquor. Following English parliamentary practice, the college was also allowed to send a representative to the colonial legislative assembly.

The College of William and Mary was the only institution of higher learning to be successfully established south of the Chesapeake in the colonial period, although similar attempts had been made during the eighteenth century in Maryland, the Carolinas, and Georgia. With only a few exceptions, higher education south of the Chesapeake during the colonial era tended to be a realistic aspiration only for the sons of the most economically privileged. As in England and on the continent, extensive formal schooling at any level, and especially on the collegiate or university level, generally was regarded with suspicion by the majority of seventeenth- and eighteenth-century migrants to the Chesapeake and southern colonies.

A different attitude toward education was displayed by many who settled along the shores and into the backcountry north of Chesapeake Bay. That difference resulted from a number of factors, including dissimilar motives for immigration, distinctive religious and social class backgrounds, variations in the density of settlements, and different climatic and geographic conditions. To understand better the diversity as well as similarities among seventeenth- and eighteenth-century migrants to the North American continent, we turn to a consideration of developments in New England.

Pilgrims, Puritans, and the New England Experience

The Founding of Plymouth Colony

The 102 passengers who sailed out of Plymouth, England, on the *Mayflower* on September 16, 1620, constituted an odd assortment of Englishmen. They were, first of all, not all men. Twenty women and thirty-two children were among those cramped "tween-decks" in the squat ship that measured only 96 feet long and 25 feet wide. Their presence gave witness to the fact that families as well as individuals were among the refugees who hoped to find asylum in the region Captain John Smith had scouted four years earlier and given name to in his pamphlet, *A Description of New England* (1616).[29]

While some of those who made the sixty-seven-day crossing were related by family and religious ties, there were also strangers in their midst. In fact, the Pilgrims themselves were in a minority and considered with suspicion and disdain their fellow passengers who had been haphazardly recruited without regard to their religious convictions. William Bradford, who governed the colony from 1621 until his death in 1657, offered the opinion that the non-Pilgrims among them were an "ill-conditioned people, who will never do good, but corrupt and abuse others." This distrust and fear of rebellion, compounded by the fact that they were over 3000 miles from "home" and had landed beyond the lands specified in their patent from the Virginia Company of London, prompted the adult males aboard the *Mayflower* to forge a civil compact among themselves so that order might be maintained. Signed by all but nine of the adult males on board (some had been hired as seamen for only a year, others were probably too sick to write their names), the Mayflower Compact is seen by some historians to have provided the basis for a secular government in America and is considered to rank with the Declaration of Independence and the Constitution as a seminal American text.[30]

The Pilgrims were a people unhappy with their neighbors and with themselves. Those who established the Plymouth colony in 1620 were a splinter group of Puritans who were dissatisfied with the Church of England in spite of changes that had occurred since the Reformation. In their view, the Anglican church continued to exhibit too many traces of Roman Catholicism. They wanted to see the further "purification" of the church and voiced objections to such practices as the wearing of priestly vestments, the use of elaborate church decorations, and even the exchange of weddings rings in marriage ceremonies. They could find no biblical precedent for making the sign of the cross when uttering Christ's name, thought hymns were a corruption of God's word, and saw no need to kneel when taking communion since there was no evidence that the apostles had done so during the Last Supper. High on the list of reforms the Pilgrims thought necessary was abandonment of the concept of a state church and the tradition of hierarchical governance external to the local congregation.[31]

Dissatisfaction with the established Church of England had caused these

Figure 2.3 "The pilgrims signing the compact, on board the Mayflower, Nov. 11th, 1620 / painted by T.H. Matteson ; engraved by Gauthier" Source: LC-USZ61-206

disgruntled Christians to initiate their pilgrimage more than a decade before they sailed for the new world. Believing that they and their descendants would be corrupted if they remained in England, members of a congregation in the hamlet of Scrooby had "separated" from both church and country and made their way to Amsterdam and then to Leiden, Holland, about the same time the Jamestown founders were establishing their new world outpost. After living in exile in Holland for over a decade, this band of "Separatist Puritans" pronounced themselves "well weaned from the delicate milk of our mother country" and ready to venture into the unknown difficulties of "a strange and hard land." Intending to turn their backs forever on both England and Holland, they entrusted themselves to the care of the Almighty, pledging:

> We are knit together as a body in a most strict and sacred bond and covenant of the Lord, of the violation whereof we make great conscience, and by virtue whereof we do hold ourselves straitly tied to all care of each other's good and of the whole, by every one and so mutually.[32]

Such were the convictions held by those who set out to establish the second permanent English colony in the new world. They expected severe trials and difficulties. In this they were not disappointed. Half of the company, including all but a few of the women, died during the first winter.

Those who somehow survived that first terrible New England winter were soon reinforced by new arrivals. Yet the Plymouth colony grew slowly and could claim no more than 400 people after a decade and only a few thousand by 1660. However, its slow growth gave it more stability than some of the other colonial settlements. In the Chesapeake and southern colonies, for example, the discovery of tobacco heightened the demand for labor and not only led to the institutionalization of African slavery, but encouraged the voluntary emigration of distressed Europeans.

The lower colonies soon became heavily populated by immigrants who came on the guarantee of being given land and freedom in return for a specified period of labor as indentured servants. For the remainder of the century, indentured laborers became the largest single source of European immigration to the Chesapeake, accounting for perhaps 80 to 90 percent of the 130,000 to 150,000 Europeans who migrated to the area before 1700. Few of those who came as indentured servants had much of a stake in English society; they were predominantly young, male, and not highly skilled.

In contrast, immigration to the Plymouth colony occurred at a more moderate pace and consisted mostly of families, although indentured servants settled there as well. But most of the Puritan shoemakers, coopers, joiners, weavers, carpenters, tradesmen, farmers, and ministers and their families had been able to withstand the economic difficulties that afflicted many of their countrymen. Their distress was religious, not economic. Although few were wealthy, far fewer were the sort of beggars and vagabonds that were migrating to the lower colonies.[33]

The high rate of family migration to the Massachusetts colonies is remarkable. In one contingent of 700 who sailed from Great Yarmouth (Norfolk) and Sandwich (Kent), 94 percent consisted of family units. In another group of 680 emigrants, 73 percent came as nuclear families and at least 88 percent traveled with a relative. These proportions are perhaps the highest in the history of American immigration.

From the beginning, Plymouth was characterized by a fair degree of religious pluralism. As a result, the colony continually experienced dissent and threats to community. Dissatisfied groups moved on to form hamlets and villages ever farther from the original center. "Strangers," those outside the communion of the local congregation, placed a heavy strain on attempts by the Separatist Puritan leaders to create and maintain an essentially homogeneous community. Laws requiring church attendance by everyone, including non-members, and stringent attempts to suppress "heretical" views could not stem the tide.[34]

Most Puritans were not as adamant about a complete divorce from the Anglican church as were the Plymouth settlers. "Non-Separatist" Puritans believed they could support the idea of a reformed state church as long as individual congregations were allowed latitude in self-governance. Their hope was to improve the Church of England from within. Some believed this could and should be done by remaining in England; their commitment threw the country into civil war in 1642. Others became convinced that only with a new start in a new Eden could the way be cleared for the complete purification of the church. These non-Separatist Puritans, who still considered themselves spiritual members of the Church of England, formed the backbone of the "great migration" that populated the Massachusetts Bay colony between 1630 and 1660.

"Errand into the Wilderness"

Fear of falling short of God's commands and into the ways of the world was certainly a factor that motivated the Pilgrims to seek refuge in Plymouth in 1620. This same fear was also a driving force that induced 400 other Puritans to make their way to Salem, Massachusetts, at the end of the decade; but those who settled in Salem in 1629 were guided by "vision" as well as by fear. They were the vanguard of those who came to the Massachusetts Bay colony to shame England into repenting. John Winthrop, leader of the "great fleet" of eleven ships and 700 passengers bound for New England the following year, sermonized in mid-voyage about their utopian vision. "We shall be as a city upon a hill," he proclaimed; "the eyes of all people are upon us." Winthrop encouraged his determined soulmates to envision building a society that would be an example for all the world, a society about which "men shall say of succeeding plantations: 'The Lord make it like that of New England.' " Theirs was to be a redemptive community of God's chosen people, a "holy commonwealth."[35]

Winthrop's great fleet sailed into Boston harbor in June 1630, and by fall six towns had been formed within what is now Boston's city limits. Thirteen hundred more settlers arrived the next summer, and hundreds and then thousands followed. Although nominally Anglicans, the New England Puritans preferred a congregational style of governance that ignored the authority of distant bishops. Instead, each congregation fell under the dominion of the male "saints" or "the elect" in their midst. These saints determined who among the flock gave true evidence of being blessed with the gift of salvation and who, therefore, could join the church, take communion, and baptize their children. They directed the congregational examinations required of those who claimed to have reached a state of grace by having had a profound conversion experience.

The "visible saints" not only governed the local congregation, but by extension, the entire colony, even though church and state were formally separate. Saints became the town selectmen and members of the Massachusetts General Court (legislature), which controlled affairs of the colony. These civil authorities required all adults to attend and contribute financially to worship services, whether or not they were confirmed members of the church. Thus, the Puritan or Congregational churches in the Bay colony became officially established or state-sponsored institutions. The intertwined relationship of church and civil government was symbolized by the fact that often a single building—termed a meeting house rather than a church—was used for both religious services and town business.[36]

By 1640, the population in the Massachusetts Bay colony had grown to about 15,000. The Plymouth population had reached the 3,000 mark, with around twice that number in Connecticut and an additional 2,000 farther north. With the near extinction of the Pegouts by the late 1630s, the way was cleared for the steady advance of Euro-Americans.

Pegouts and other natives not downed by colonists' muskets and swords fell victim to "the pox" that had been thinning their numbers since their first contact with European fishing parties several years before the Pilgrims arrived. William Bradford described a scene along the Connecticut River in 1634 in which the Indians were dying "like rotten sheep." Too sick to go for water or gather wood for fire, they were burning their bows and arrows and wooden bowls for fuel when some English traders from a settlement at Windsor happened by. The English, "seeing their woeful and sad condition and hearing their pitiful cries and lamentations," cared for the few survivors and buried the dead. Not one of the colonists became ill, a sure sign to them that God was preparing their way.[37]

Literacy in New England

By and large, those who settled the New England colonies during the period of the great migration were a literate as well as religious people. In England before 1640, only about one-third of the adult male population could be considered literate as measured by the ability to sign one's name. However, half to two-thirds of the adult male emigrants to New England in the seventeenth century could write their names. Others could read but not write.

Although growth in literacy increased rather slowly over the first three generations, after the 1720s New England literacy rates increased significantly. By the eve of the American Revolution, adult male literacy in New England was nearly universal, whereas in old England only half to two-thirds of the male population gave evidence of literacy. In Virginia and Pennsylvania, male literacy prior to the Revolution reached into the 60 to 70 percent range, driven upward by selective in-migration of literate English and German settlers rather than by advances in schooling. In Virginia and Pennsylvania, as in England, there remained a strong correlation between social status and literacy that had all but disappeared in the New England colonies by the end of the colonial era.

Thus, in spite of laws compelling the education of apprentices, missionary and charity school initiatives, endowed and proprietary schools, and itinerant schoolmasters, colonial children outside New England did not make gains in literacy comparable to those of their New England counterparts. These differences in literacy rates among the various colonies and between New England and old England raise a number of important questions. What factors or developments might account for these rather significant differences in patterns of literacy?[38]

Puritan Origins

Certainly one factor helping to explain variations in literacy rates had to do with migrants' origins. While the builders of Massachusetts were drawn from all over England, approximately 60 percent came from nine eastern counties, the most densely settled and highly urbanized parts of England. Among the colony's leaders, East Anglia was disproportionally represented. Well over three-fourths of the 129 university-educated ministers and magistrates who joined the 1630–1660 exodus to New England had been born, married, educated, or employed for long periods of time within an area bounded by seven eastern counties. Nearly half had studied at three Cambridge colleges: Emmanuel, Magdalen, and Trinity. Thus, the nucleus of the New England leadership consisted of a rather highly educated group of Puritans who had interconnected family and friendship ties long before emigration.

East Anglians shared other things in common. Here was the heart of the Protestant Reformation in England. During the brief but bloody reign of Queen Mary (1553–1558), no fewer than 225 (82 percent) of the 273 Protestant men and women burned at the stake resided in East Anglia. The martyrdom of these early dissenters and the determination of their progeny to purify the Church of England, even if it required leaving their homeland, was clear evidence that these people took their religion seriously. The intensity of their Protestant beliefs motivated them to take literacy seriously as well. The Puritans were becoming a "people of the book."[39]

Puritanism and Literacy

The commonly held view that pictures the Puritans as rigid fundamentalists and biblical literalists is misleading. To be sure, they accepted the Bible as the inspired word of God and committed themselves to living in accordance with its teachings. Puritans insisted, however, that God's word be interpreted in the light of reason and scientific knowledge of the day. Within prescribed limits, Puritans could agree to disagree, for they conceived of their religion as a highly complex, subtle, and intellectualized affair.

Puritan ministers were learned men who expected their communicants to be able to follow their enlightened discourses. As a young minister, John Cotton peppered his sermons with Greek quotations and criticized some of the early church fathers for their lack of knowledge of Hebrew and of "the Scripture in the original." While Cotton and other Puritan ministers eventually moved toward a simpler style of preaching, they did not abandon their scholastic inheritance. They struggled in the pulpit as well as in private with difficult passages of scripture and theological enigmas that had perplexed scholars since the rise of the medieval universities.

Puritans placed faith in the concept of the priesthood of the individual believer. They maintained that the individual Christian could approach God in prayer and confession, without the intercession of a priest or minister, if one could read and understand scripture intelligently. John Cotton reflected this Reformation doctrine when he encouraged his parishioners in England to reflect on "whether the things that have been taught were true or no." Puritan hostility toward Catholicism was in part based on the view expressed by Thomas Hooker, clerical leader of the settlement in Connecticut, who asserted that uncritical acceptance of doctrine was an affront to individual judgment that, in effect, demanded that the faithful "put out his own eyes to see by another man's."[40]

The survival of the Puritan spirit depended on learned ministers and on enlightened and literate parishioners. The survival of congregations and communities, however, depended on shared understandings and common commitments. Their "city on a hill" had to grow out of "communities of believers." The Puritan congregations in the Massachusetts Bay area held communion with their God and with each other to be of the utmost importance. The regeneration and sanctification of those whom God had chosen were to be realized within what might be best understood as a "tribal" society.

Puritanism and Tribalism

The ties that bound the Puritans into a tribal society were analogous to those that gave identity to each of the Native American tribes in whose midst the Puritans had settled. Shared ancestry, language, experiences, stories, meanings, values and shared fears and visions set them apart from others whose ways of seeing and knowing were different.

For the Puritans, maintaining these tribal bonds meant that diversity of opinion on the *essentials* of Protestant Christianity could not be permitted. This included the belief that although they were God's chosen people, they, like all humans, were by nature sinful, imperfect creatures who were chained and enslaved by evil until liberated by the undeserved and redeeming grace of Christ. They held that "enthusiasts" and misguided individuals such as Anne Hutchinson, who made pretenses to immediate revelation that contradicted the "known" precepts of the Bible or the wisdom of the saintly tribal leaders, were guilty of blasphemy. Regenerate persons, using the faculty of reason that grace had restored, and following the guidance of an educated clergy, should be able to interpret the revealed word of God properly. All those whose thinking was "rightly done" could come to only one sound conclusion on matters of fundamental importance. It was therefore vital that those recognized as God's elect should live by His commandments, search for His will, and enforce His discipline on the unregenerate. In a word, membership in the tribe demanded conversion, rebirth, and confidence in those anointed by God as leaders of the biblical commonwealth.[41]

The Puritans' shared assumptions and interconnected lives had been threatened in the old world. They soon found that conditions in the new world were hardly more encouraging. The depth of their concern for literacy and schooling comes into sharper focus if one understands that their educational efforts emerged not out of some vague vision of establishing a system of universal education, but rather out of an immediate and alarming sense that their tribal religion and way of life were extremely vulnerable.

Education and Community in the Wilderness

Bernard Bailyn, in his *Education and the Forming of American Society* (1960), maintained that fear was the energizing force behind the education laws and concerns for literacy among the Puritans. They had a deepening fear of the "breakdown of traditional European society in its wilderness setting." Bailyn pointed especially to the strains of frontier life on the family, the primary agency that had traditionally shouldered most of the burden of education. He asserted that even in Virginia, where distance and sparseness of population made formal education difficult, there emerged a "veritable frenzy" of concern that, unless bold measures were taken to provide for education, the present and coming generations would succumb to the savage environment.[42]

In advancing his thesis, Bailyn argued that the Puritans (and other colonists) had good reason to believe that the younger generations were falling away from the faith, that they were, in effect, on the verge of "incipient savagery." Bailyn posited that the lure of open land, a spirit of independence and religious indifference on the part of children, and dissent and disrespect within the fragile Puritan household were unraveling the ties that had long held extended families together. Moreover, as strangers moved into what were initially rather homogeneous communities, it became increasingly difficult to prevent new and offending ideas from entering the minds of children and susceptible adults. Fearful that their families, communities, and their holy mission were disintegrating, New England Puritans, contended Bailyn, made determined attempts to push back the surrounding wilderness. In desperation they searched for ways to reinforce and strengthen the threatened agencies of education: the family, community, and the church. Alarmed by the less respectful and less reverential attitudes of the younger generation, Puritan leaders enacted laws requiring stricter parental and community control over children and public support of schools. The fate of Western civilization, and particularly the Puritan version of Protestant Calvinism, demanded no less. Of much greater significance than the survival of Western culture and the Puritan commonwealth, however, was Puritan concern over the fate of their souls and the souls of their children for all eternity. They perceived themselves engaged in an all-important battle with the forces of darkness.

More recent studies have suggested that Bailyn's use of "wilderness" conditions to explain family and community changes in seventeenth-century America tended to ignore similar changes occurring in England and Europe at about the same time. According to Helena Wall, "one of the many ironies of early American society is that the European colonists sought to reproduce, even to freeze in time, patterns of family and community life that were already beginning to erode in Europe." Kenneth Lockridge, who stresses the importance of "population concentration" and the driving force of "intense Protestantism" in explaining the spread of schools and literacy, similarly contends that "there is no evidence that the wilderness shattered the essentially nuclear families which arrived in America." Lockridge agrees with Wall, Philip Greven, and others in maintaining that, if anything, the new environment actually strengthened family bonds for several generations as communities became more impersonal and less intrusive.[43]

Child Rearing in Seventeenth Century New England

Whatever the verdict of historians may be, to seventeenth-century Puritans it surely must have seemed as if the wilderness was the devil's special weapon that would be their undoing. Child rearing was difficult enough in settled communities with the support of extended families, but frontier conditions appeared to add special strains to parent–child relationships.

The duty of children to honor and obey their parents was, of course, a mainstay of Christian sermons. An extensive body of literature, composed in both old and New England, emphasized that the Fifth Commandment must be properly obeyed. Children (and their parents) were advised that "obedience is the best lesson" that a parent can teach a child. Children were instructed to respect their parents and "all Superiors in age or Office." Accompanying such admonishments were reminders that, as one Pilgrim minister phrased it:

> [There] is in all children, though not alike, a stubbornness, and stoutness of mind arising from natural pride, which must, in the first place, be broken and beaten down; that so the foundation of their education being laid in humility and tractablenes, other virtues may, in their time, be built thereon.[44]

Sermons, proverbs, the admonitions of elders, appeals to filial love, reasoning, parental example, and the corrective rod were all called into service in attempts to direct children in the ways of God. Despite all such efforts, however, it seemed to many Puritans that not all children were growing in favor with God and mankind. In the eyes of some, children were growing away from rather than closer to God. Perhaps the gravity of the situation is revealed most vividly in the tone of some laws that were adopted by Puritan legislatures in Massachusetts and Connecticut in the mid seventeenth century. In 1646 the Massachusetts General Court decreed that:

> If any child[ren] above sixteen years old and of sufficient understanding shall curse or smite their natural father or mother, they shall be put to death, unless it can be sufficiently testified that the parents have been very unchristianly negligent in the education of such children, or so

provoked them by extreme and cruel correction that they have been forced thereunto to preserve themselves from death or maiming.

Connecticut passed an identical law in 1650.[45]

While there is no evidence that colonial magistrates ever pronounced the maximum sentence under these laws, a couple of lads had close calls. For "stricking and abusing his parents," Edward Bumpas of Plymouth was publicly whipped and, had he not been thought to be "crasey brained," would have been put to death in 1679. John Porter of Essex County, Massachusetts, was jailed for "his prophane, unnatural and abusive carriages to his natural parents" on more than one occasion. Since John gave no sign of repentance, he was sentenced in 1664 "to stand upon the ladder at the gallowes, with a roape about his neck, for one hower, & afterwards to be severely whipt," then fined and jailed. Only his mother's intervention and tearful pleas before the court saved John Porter from becoming New England's sole casualty of the capital laws against disobedient and rebellious children.[46]

A less dramatic piece of legislation adopted by the Massachusetts General Court in 1642 in some respects has greater significance. Although often (and inaccurately) referred to as the first "school" law in the colonies, the law in question was in fact an apprenticeship law. The 1642 Massachusetts law compelled heads of households to provide occupational training and ensure that their children learned "to read and understand the principles of religion and the capital laws of this country." Parents or masters who were judged by town officials to be derelict in their duty could be fined and have their children removed from the household and "put forth as apprentices" under the care of more diligent guardians.[47]

This Massachusetts law was in keeping with tradition and contained several features worthy of comment. The statute affirmed the value of literacy skills (unlike the 1646 Virginia law) as well as skills valuable for productive employment. Civic as well as religious instruction was held to be important. Moreover, the law underscored the supportive—even intrusive—role of the community in education. While parents or masters were still vested with primary responsibility for the education and welfare of their children, civil authorities empowered themselves to intervene in family matters when it seemed in the best interests of the colony and, supposedly, the child. If the family proved incapable or unwilling to fulfill its functions, outside authorities were prepared to take up the slack. In addition to Connecticut's adoption of this same law in 1650, similar laws were passed in New Haven in 1655, New York in 1665, Plymouth in 1671, and Pennsylvania in 1683.[48]

Transplantation and Transformation of English Educational Traditions

To varying degrees, emigrants to all sections of colonial America made attempts to transplant into their communities laws and institutions that were familiar to them. The Puritans were no exception. The apprenticeship laws and subsequent legislation pertaining to the educational obligations of families and communities made clear their valiant efforts to overcome religious and cultural degeneracy. Perry Miller stressed that, in contrast to all other pioneers, the Puritans "made no concessions to the forest, but in the midst of frontier conditions, in the very throes of clearing the land and erecting shelters, they maintained schools and a college, a standard of scholarship and of competent writing, [and] a class of men devoted entirely to the life of the mind and of the soul."[49]

In light of Miller's assertion, it is revealing to note that the Plymouth colony, for all the fervor and commitment of the founding congregation, failed to establish a single school during its first forty years of existence. In part this might be taken as a natural consequence of the demands of frontier existence, Miller's assessment of Puritan zeal notwithstanding. Further, one could argue that the lack of attention given to formal schooling reflected the Plymouth settlers' conviction that the family, particularly the father, should direct children's education. However, a more compelling explanation for the lack of formal schools in Plymouth can be traced to the continuing dispersal of the population into the surrounding countryside. Sparsely populated communities had great difficulty in maintaining schools.

In his study of literacy patterns in pre-Revolutionary America, Kenneth Lockridge concluded that "social concentration," along with an intense commitment to Protestantism, were the two most significant variables that account for differences in the development of schools and the subsequent spread of literacy within and among the various colonies. Before schools could be established and maintained over time, villages and towns had to grow to a size sufficient to make their existence both feasible and worthwhile.[50]

The Massachusetts Bay colony's experience provides support for the conclusions reached by both Miller and Lockridge. Unlike Plymouth, which grew slowly, the Bay colony rapidly expanded in population and moved quickly to establish formal modes of education. In April 1635, Boston town officials agreed to hire a schoolmaster "for the teaching and nurturing of children with us." The Boston Latin Grammar School opened the next year. The town of Ipswich may have begun a short-lived grammar school that same year, as did Charleston. In 1638, Cambridge set off three acres of land to be used "for a public school or college." In 1639, Dorchester, Salem, and Newbury took steps to establish schools for the children of their communities. Within the first decade of settlement, seven of the twenty-two towns in Massachusetts had taken some public action on behalf of schooling.

Towns in neighboring colonies also moved toward providing support and encouragement for formal schools. In 1642 the general court of New Haven ordered that a free school be established and that it be supported by funds drawn from the "common stock of the town." In the same year, Hartford officials voted to direct £30 a year toward the support of a school in their town.[51]

While community initiative was certainly in evidence in these and some other New England towns, the impetus to found schools appears to have waned somewhat in the 1640s. As noted, the Massachusetts General Court in 1642 considered it necessary to remind parents and masters of their duties, even though the Apprenticeship Act passed in that year did not make provision for schools or require school attendance. Within five years, however, the Massachusetts court enacted a stronger and more important law that influenced the educational history of New England for the remainder of the colonial period. The basic pattern for the development of "town schools" was set with the passage of the "Old Deluder Satan Act" in 1647.

The "Old Deluder" law asserted that Satan, master of deception, was keeping people from true knowledge of the scriptures. Acknowledging dissent and a fear that the learning of the church and civic elders might not survive into future generations, the law required that towns with fifty or more families must make provision for instruction in reading and writing. The law indicated that the teacher's wages could be paid by the students' parents or shared by all in the community. The law further specified that as towns grew to a hundred households, they were to establish grammar schools that would prepare boys for Harvard College. Noncompliance could result in a fine levied against the town.

While there was nothing novel about the establishment of basic reading and writing schools or secondary-level grammar schools, it is instructive to note that throughout all of colonial New England (except Rhode Island), responsibility for providing education gradually became an obligation undertaken by the community. Parents were still fined for not adhering to the strictures of the 1642 law and similar statutes, but now *towns* also faced the prospect of fines if schools, however financed, were not provided.

Passing education laws was one matter, enforcing them another. While some towns established schools as required by the 1647 law, others had fines levied against them. During the first decade after passage of the Old Deluder law, all eight of the Massachusetts towns with a hundred families established grammar schools, but only a third of the towns with fifty or so families complied with the reading-and-writing school requirement. As the century progressed, efforts at both compliance and enforcement varied considerably.

The Path to Literacy

Throughout the colonial period and beyond, household education remained important, even as schools became more and more of a community concern. In New England as in old England, children of the "middling classes" typically gained their first steps toward literacy under the tutelage of their parents, siblings, or other members of the family. Children in households without a literate adult could sometimes attend a nearby "dame school" if they lived in a village or town. Dame schools were very basic reading sessions conducted by a neighboring housewife who, for a modest fee, gave instruction to other children along with her own.

By memorizing the alphabet and passages of Scripture and connecting these verbal lessons with the printed word, children gained rudimentary reading skill. Hornbooks, primers, psalters, catechisms, the Bible, and textbooks such as Edmund Coote's *The English Schoole-Maister* were used to teach reading. Coote's text, an instructional manual and spelling book, was first published in London in 1596 and was reprinted fifty-four times by 1737. Thomas Dilworth's *A New Guide to the English Tongue*, reprinted in Philadelphia in 1747 by Benjamin Franklin, was another of scores of books written in England that were used in the colonies up to the time of the American Revolution.[52]

Hornbooks, another imported teaching aid, presented the alphabet, a few syllables combining vowels and consonants (the "syllabarium"), and the the Lord's Prayer, the Apostles' Creed, or some other biblical lesson. The single page of parchment containing this material was affixed to a wooden paddle that in turn was covered by a thin sheet of transparent horn. The layer of horn protected the parchment from the wear and tear and smudges of little hands.

Figure 2.4 Colonial child ("Miss Campion") with hornbook, 1661.

Source: http://en.wikipedia.org/wiki/Image:Campion-Hornbook.jpg

Reading instruction involved much more than gaining skill in decoding printed symbols. For Protestants, skill in reading meant access to the Scriptures. To advance both literacy skills and biblical understanding, catechisms and devotional writings became important adjuncts to the Bible itself. After 1641, when the Massachusetts General Court encouraged Puritan elders to "make a catechism for the instruction of youth in the grounds of religion," a steady flow of native catechisms began to appear, rivaling the Westminster Catechism and others acquired from England. In 1646, John Cotton, minister of Boston's First Church, set forth his admonitions for children in *Spiritual Milk for American Babes, Drawn Out of the Breasts of Both Testaments for Their Souls' Nourishment.* Cotton's catechism was but one of hundreds that set forth questions and answers that the faithful were to master in print and memory.

One of the most powerful "devotional lessons" for children and adults alike was the Reverend Michael Wigglesworth's *The Day of Doom.* Published in 1662, Wigglesworth's poem, 224 stanzas in length, described in vivid detail God's final judgment and the horrible punishment that awaited the wicked. Readers were told of how the damned would be cast into the lake "where Fire and Brimstone flameth" and where, "day and night, without respite, they wail, and cry, and howl/ For tort'ring pain, which they sustain in Body and in Soul." Lines such as these were read and reread, often aloud and in groups, and much of it memorized and repeated so often that it passed into the oral tradition.[53]

Along with the Bible, catechisms, and devotional texts of various types, psalters (collections of Psalms) and primers were used in reading instruction. Primers, initially manuals used in conjunction with worship, eventually combined the alphabet drills of ABC books with catechisms to become the essential texts for teaching reading and religion. The most famous of the colonial primers, *The New England Primer,* continued in use until well into the nineteenth century. Although no copy of the first edition of *The New England Primer* exists and the exact date of its first printing cannot be stated with certainty, a Boston printer, Benjamin Harris, produced the initial American version sometime between 1687 and 1690. It quickly became so popular that virtually every New England book shop and general store regularly stocked the little book (or facsimiles) along with the Bible itself.[54]

The New England Primer, and others modeled upon it, began with the letters of the alphabet in capital and lowercase forms, followed by the standard syllabarium (presented as a list of "Easy Syllables for Children" such as "ab, eb, ib, ob, ub," followed by "ac, ec, ic, oc, uc," and so forth through the alphabet). Words of one syllable were followed by those of two and three syllables, until by degrees six-syllable vocabularies were displayed for pronunciation and spelling drills.

"An Alphabet of Lessons for Youth," consisting of a series of instructive lessons drawn from the Bible, became a common feature of the primers. Here children not only perfected their reading (and memorization) skills, but reinforced moral precepts as well:

A Wise Son makes a glad Father, but a foolish son is the heaviness of his mother.

Better is a little with the fear of the Lord, than great treasure and trouble therewith.

Come unto CHRIST all ye that labor and are heavy laden, and He will give you rest.

On through the alphabet ran the verses, pounding biblical truths into the souls of young readers whose minds were straining to decipher the symbols on the printed page. These alphabetized exhortations were usually followed by the Lord's Prayer, the Apostles' Creed, and the Ten Commandments.

The most famous feature of *The New England Primer* was the twenty-four woodcut illustrations of alphabetical rhymes, beginning with "In Adam's Fall/ We sinned all." Of all the twenty-four stanzas, only this first one relating to original sin remained unchanged through all the known editions of *The New England Primer*. Some of the changes were slight, while others reflected interesting shifts in doctrinal and political opinion. The rhymes that accompanied the letter K, for example, clearly signaled changes over time in American colonists' attitudes toward the British monarchy. Using the word and woodcut impression of a king, the earliest known version read "King Charles the Good/ No Man of Blood." As American hostility toward England and the Crown increased near the end of the eighteenth century, the verse underwent a change: "Kings should be good/ Not men of Blood." Then, rejecting the very concept of monarchy, a 1797 version proclaimed: "The British King/Lost States thirteen." A later edition further extended the democratic orientation of the new nation: "Queens and Kings/Are gaudy things."

To all the above were added catechisms, names of the books of the Bible, instructions on the "Duty of Children toward Their Parents," numbers in Arabic and Roman style, and John Rogers' "Exhortation to His Children," a poem written by the Protestant minister a few days before he was burned at the stake during the reign of Queen Mary, as his wife and nine children looked on. However unenlightened or awkward the methods of developing literacy may have been in colonial times, from the opening reminder that "In Adam's Fall/We sinned all" to the concluding poem of the martyred Rogers, there was certainly no thought of allowing "process" to overshadow "content."

Depending on the ability of the teacher and the availability of texts, lessons in writing, arithmetic, singing, and civility or manners might also be offered in reading or "petty" schools. Reading literacy, however, was the basic objective, and the process of instruction sometimes began quite early in life. Some children as young as three or four were set to reading at home or in dame schools. At age six, John Barnard was teaching children both older and younger to read and claimed to have "read My Bible through thrice" by that age. Jane Coleman at age four "could say the greatest part of the [Westminster] Assembly's Catechism, many of the Psalms, some hundred lines of the best poetry, read

A — In ADAM's Fall, We finned all.

B — Heaven to find, The BIBLE mind.

C — CHRIST crucify'd, For Sinners dy'd.

D — The Deluge drown'd The Earth around.

E — ELIJAH hid, By Ravens fed.

F — The Judgment made Felix afraid.

G — As runs the Glafs, Our Life doth pafs.

H — My Book and Heart Muft never part.

J — Job feels the Rod, Yet bleffes GOD.

K — Proud Korah's Troop Was fwallow'd up.

L — Lot fled to Zoar, Saw fiery Shower On Sodom pour.

M — Mofes was he Who Ifrael's Hoft Led thro' the Sea.

N — Noah did view The old world & new.

O — Young Obadias, David, Jofias, All were pious.

P — Peter deny'd His Lord and cry'd.

Q — Queen Efther fues, And faves the Jews.

R — Young pious Ruth, Left all for Truth.

S — Young Samuel dear, The Lord did fear.

T — Young Timothy Learnt Sin to fly.

V — Vafhti for Pride, Was fet afide.

W — Whales in the Sea, GOD's Voice obey.

X — Xerxes did die, And fo muft I.

Y — While youth do chear Death may be near.

Z — Zaccheus he Did climb the Tree, Our Lord to fee.

Figure 2.5 *New England Primer*, Boston: 1762.

distinctly, and make pertinent remarks of many things she read." While these children were clearly exceptional in ability, their experience of becoming literate by memorizing passages from religious texts was clearly the norm.[55]

Writing Schools

Although some children were taught the basics of writing as well as reading in petty schools, serious instruction in the skill of penmanship had a domain of its own. Penmanship was considered a craft and was largely a male concern. Certainly there were exceptions, but in the customary New England way, women taught reading and men taught writing. Writing was taught as a specialized skill, one requiring years of practice before mastery could be attained. Whereas primers and other books helpful in learning to read were cheap and in abundant supply, writing manuals or copybooks were scarce and expensive. Writing masters carefully guarded their copybooks and the techniques of the craft, not wanting to lose the income that some parents were willing to pay in order for their sons to acquire a skill of importance to future ministers, lawyers, clerks, and men of business affairs.

In a growing shipping and commercial center such as Boston, both "private" and "public" writing masters coexisted. Boston town leaders first employed a "public" writing master, who was to serve as an assistant to the teacher in the original town Latin Grammar school, in 1666. In 1682 Boston officials decided to maintain a "free" school devoted solely to "the teachinge of Children to write & Cypher." That writing school opened in 1684 and was followed by a second in 1700 and a third in 1720. Hundreds of boys passed through these town writing schools each year. Many others studied with one of the twenty or so private writing teachers who offered instruction in penmanship, book-keeping, and arithmetic in Boston between 1616 and 1776. While some older boys attended a classical grammar school as well as a writing school, many found that the town writing schools provided all the instruction they needed for useful careers in business.[56]

"Classical Literacy": Secondary and Higher Education

For boys whose talents (or parents) pointed them toward collegiate education and the professions, the grammar school was a necessity. Although these schools usually offered intensive study in Greek as well as Latin (and often Hebrew as well), they were commonly referred to as "Latin" grammar schools. Students in New England Latin schools, like their southern counterparts who had tutors or attended boarding schools, drilled in the grammars of Latin, Greek, and Hebrew as they plowed their way through a series of successively demanding texts. Geography, history, and the fundamentals of mathematics were incorporated as the instructor's knowledge and the availability of texts permitted. Typically, mornings were devoted to grammar drill, afternoons to reading in the classic texts, Fridays to review and testing, Saturdays to writing themes, and Sundays to catechizing and religious exercises. This regimen, which was surely taxing even to the most dedicated sons of the Puritan elite, began when boys reached the age of seven or eight, or as soon after as they had acquired the basics of reading English. Those who completed the entire curriculum spent about seven years in the process.

The Boston Latin School

The school "for the teaching and nurturing of children with us" called for by the Boston officials in the spring of 1635 was a grammar school of the type just described. The Boston Latin Grammar School opened in 1636 and is recognized as the first formal "public" secondary school in the original British colonies. The Boston Latin School, adhering to an institutional form transplanted from England, was public in the sense that it was under civic or public control, partially supported by public funds, and accessible to children in the local community. Together with the Old Deluder law of 1647, it reflected early and decisive commitment on the part of civic leaders to provide public support for educational undertakings in the American colonies.[57]

The terms "public" and "free," when used in the colonial and early national periods of American history, can be confusing if interpreted in their modern sense. In historical context, both terms generally implied that a school (or teacher) received some "public" financial support (often in addition to student fees), whether through land grants, endowment, taxes, gifts, or other means. Schooling that was absolutely free (that is, no fee or payment "in kind") was sometimes made available to orphans or the children of paupers, but rarely to all the children in a community.

Harvard College

Close on the heels of the Boston Latin School was the beginning of Harvard College. In the fall of 1636, the Massachusetts General Court agreed to set aside £400 "toward a schoale or colledge." The court appointed a board of overseers to govern the "colledge at Newetowne," and by the end of 1637, the overseers announced that Nathaniel Eaton, a graduate of Emmanuel College, Cambridge, had been engaged as "master." Arriving on the same ship with Eaton was another Master of Arts from Emmanuel College, John Harvard. Soon after Master Eaton began holding recitations with the first students late in the summer of 1638, John Harvard fell ill. Before his death in September 1638, the 31-year-old Harvard dictated in an oral will that his entire library of some 400 books and half of his property should go to the college. The remainder of his property went to his childless widow. Soon thereafter the "colledge" was named in his honor, and "Newetowne" was renamed Cambridge. In 1642, nine young men became the first graduates of Harvard College.[58]

The fact that the president of the General Court was an alumnus of Magdalen Hall, Oxford, and that a number of the other members of the court were alumni or relatives of alumni of other Oxford or Cambridge colleges, helps explain in part their interest in establishing a college. They were, after all, educated Englishmen who were a long way from the colleges and the cultural way of life that to them were so important. But there is more to the founding of Harvard than a desire to keep alive the intellectual and cultural traditions of an educated elite. As historian Frederick Rudolph put it, "the really important fact about Harvard College is that it was absolutely necessary." Rudolph stressed that the Puritan sense of mission compelled the leaders of the Massachusetts Bay colony to begin a college. Their Protestant commonwealth needed competent rulers, the church required a learned clergy, and the perpetuation of civilized society depended on the knowledge, standards of taste, and values of cultured men. Harvard came into being to educate ministers, schoolmasters, and magistrates—the men who could make all the difference between civilization and barbarism as well as between heaven and hell.[59]

The Halfway Covenant

Before the generation that founded Harvard had passed from the scene, the very continuance of the covenanted community was thrown into question by internal and external challenges. By the middle of the seventeenth century, Puritan elders had to face the disturbing fact that their second generation admitted itself to be deficient in grace. The children of the elect were not giving evidence of election in sufficient numbers and zeal to maintain the supply of saints. In a desperate effort to reverse this situation, the "Halfway Covenant" was adopted in 1662. This adjustment in church policy enabled the children of the saints, after making a profession of obedience, to join the church, baptize their children, and pray that in due course they too might have a conversion experience.

The Halfway Covenant, like the Puritan stress on literacy, community schooling, and the founding of Harvard, represented yet another determined effort to keep alive the covenant faith. Yet the return to tradition had begun. In spite of the sincerity of the young and the old, it gradually became obvious that the religious experiences, piety, and tribal covenant of the first generation were not to become hereditary endowments.[60]

In England it seemed for a moment, during the rule of Oliver Cromwell, that theocracy just might take root there, but the restoration of Charles II put a quick end to that possibility. Thus, in old and New England, utopian visions of a society ruled by God's chosen few fell victim to the demands of toleration and to the separation of church and state brought on by an increasingly pluralistic and secularizing culture.[61]

Revivalism, Sectarianism, and the Collapse of Orthodoxy

However necessary Harvard may have seemed to its founders, the religious and cultural traditions it was created to defend proved over time to be all too vulnerable. The founding of Yale, Princeton, and a half-dozen other colleges during the colonial period occurred as both population growth and doctrinal schisms fed religious pluralism. Yale, for example, was founded in 1701 by disgruntled Congregationalists who felt that Harvard had veered too far toward toleration and liberalism in religious matters. Cotton Mather, while still a member of the Harvard Board of Overseers, made clear his disillusionment with the Cambridge institution when he encouraged Elihu Yale to memorialize himself by endowing in New Haven a new college that would bear his name and hold to the faith of the fathers. Yale College thus set out to become a purer version of what Harvard had promised to be but failed to become—a solid and unwavering defender of a purified and conservative form of Christianity.

Yale's intolerance with the evangelical spiritualism that grew out of the "Great Awakening" of the 1730s and 1740s led to the founding, at least indirectly, of Princeton. Revivalistic preachers such as Jonathan Edwards and George Whitefield reignited the smoldering embers of religious enthusiasm that had been all but extinguished for many. With a fervor that proved embarrassing to conservative Congregationalists, evangelists preached on the uncertainties of life and the certainty of coming death and judgment in graphic terms. Their images of hell and damnation were not new, but the passion with which the evangelists described the wrath of God roused their listeners into outbursts of religious frenzy. During a revival in 1735, for example, Jonathan Edwards sermonized on "Sinners in the Hands of an Angry God." Edwards warned that "The God that holds you over the pit of Hell, much as one holds a spider or other loathsome insect over the fire, abhors you. His wrath toward you burns like fire; He looks upon you as worthy of nothing else but to be cast into the fire." The prospect of such a horrible fate moved thousands to declare their repentance and in tears to reject their worldly ways.

When the charismatic English minister George Whitefield began a preaching tour of Connecticut in 1740, there were 630 church members. A year later church membership had jumped to 3,217. By mid-decade, every fifth man and woman in the colony under the age of 45 claimed to have been "born again." As the Great Awakening spread, church membership soared in all the colonies, swelling the ranks of Presbyterians, Baptists, and Methodists while Anglican and Congregational influence waned.

Rather than bringing harmony and unity to American Protestants, the Great Awakening created new divisions. Churches split into "Old Light" (conservative and rationalistic) and "New Light" (revivalist and enthusiastic) factions. Gilbert Tennent, a New Light preacher, gave evidence of the heat generated by the schism when he denounced Boston's established clergymen as "dead Drones." Charles Chauncy, speaking for the Congregational clergy, blasted back. He ridiculed enthusiasts who had "a certain wildness" in their eyes, "quakings and tremblings" of their limbs, and foaming at the mouth as being struck by "a sort of madness."[62]

It is in the context of this schism that Princeton's founding takes on special meaning. The chartering of Princeton in 1746 (initially known as the College of New Jersey) was a vivid expression of the unhappiness of some Presbyterians with the rigidness of Yale and their desire to have a college that would be friendlier to their "awakened" religious ways. In establishing Princeton, New Light Presbyterians, convinced that soul-shaking religious conversions counted for more than biblical learning and quiet decorum, aimed to prepare learned ministers who also understood and encouraged the workings of the Holy Spirit.

Princeton was followed by colleges founded by other sectarian groups. In New Hampshire a group of Congregationalists stirred by the enthusiasm of the Great Awakening founded Dartmouth in 1763. Dartmouth was an outgrowth of a school that had been founded for Indians in Lebanon, New Hampshire, by the Reverend Eleazar Wheelock. Its name changed and its mission broadened when the institution relocated to Hanover, New Hampshire. Over in Rhode Island, Baptists began a college in Providence in 1765. This institution became Brown University. The next year, Dutch Reformed Protestants started a second college in New Jersey. The college they named Queen's eventually became Rutgers.

While sectarian rivalry accounts for the founding of most of the colleges established before the American Revolution, there were instances of cooperation in the founding and administration of colonial colleges, most notably at two colleges founded in the mid-1750s: the College of Philadelphia (now the University of Pennsylvania) and King's College (now Columbia). In these two "urban" colleges, efforts were made to appease various congregations by judicious appointments to college posts and by reserving some seats on the boards of trustees for members of various faiths. Thus, at Philadelphia the chief executive officer was Anglican, but the second in rank was Presbyterian. At King's College, although it was officially an Anglican institution, the college charter reserved four seats on the board for ministers from rival denominations. In these institutions, as at others in more subtle ways, the religious atmosphere had moderated considerably since the days when the Massachusetts Puritans had given birth to their little college on the banks of the Charles River.

Although colleges broadened their purposes and eased their religious expectations over time, one should not lose sight of the fact that their fundamental mission at the time of their founding was to preserve and pass down the learning, religious and secular, most valued by their sponsors. Schools and colleges in colonial America were purposefully conservative institutions. While competing sects and groups differed over what aspects of their religious and cultural beliefs were most worth preserving, they established their schools and colleges in order to hold onto and advance those beliefs. Colonial educational institutions were not established to push children to new frontiers, but to enable them to hold back the frontiers of change that to their parents and the older generations represented decline and regression. That schools and colleges in time came to serve liberating as well as conserving ends underscores the power of the written word and the multiple uses of literacy as well as the impact of increasing population growth and cross-cultural contact.

Diversity in the Middle Colonies

Attempts to employ education in the service of conserving particularistic values and traditions were certainly in evidence among the mixture of people who colonized the Middle Atlantic region. Here localized settlements of Dutch, Germans, English, Scots, Swedes, French, Norwegians, Irish, and other immigrants tended to isolate themselves from other groups and to establish church-related schools to preserve their linguistic, religious, and cultural distinctiveness. However, rapid economic expansion and population growth in the eighteenth century worked against these isolationist tendencies. Cultural distinctives long remained, but cultural barriers began to fall as interaction among the diverse groups led to increasing consolidation and coherence.

From New Netherlands to New York and New Jersey

The thirty Dutch families that landed on Manhattan Island in 1624 were the vanguard of a short-lived attempt by Holland to establish a commercial base in the new world. Much more intent on the profits to be made in the fur trade than in converting souls or extending empire, the Dutch built only a few settlements and the colony grew slowly.

Within forty years of its founding, New Netherlands came under English dominion when four British men-of-war arrived at Staten Island on August 26, 1664. Without a shot being fired, New Amsterdam became the property of the king of England's brother, James, the Duke of York. Nearly all the Dutch inhabitants, including the deposed governor, Peter Stuyvesant, remained in the colony on generous terms. The colony, renamed New York, then numbered about 10,000. Immigration from New England, Britain, and France pushed the population to around 20,000 by 1700, of whom just 44 percent were descended from the original Dutch colonizers.

New Jersey was also carved out of New Netherlands. Held for a time by absentee British proprietors and then divided into two colonies, East and West Jersey, the territory was inhabited by Quakers, Anglicans, Puritans, Scottish Presbyterians, Dutch Calvinists, Swedish Lutherans, and several thousand Native Americans. These quarreling groups got along poorly with each other and even worse with the proprietors. Finally disillusioned, the proprietors relinquished their political powers to the crown and in 1702 New Jersey was proclaimed a royal province.[63]

Pennsylvania and Delaware

With the restoration of the British monarchy in 1660 and the ascension of Charles II to the throne of England, prominent royalist supporters clamored for rewards for their services. Some favorites of the king were given land grants that led to the establishment of the "Restoration colonies" of Carolina, New York, New Jersey, and Pennsylvania. William Penn, whose father had served the cause of the House of Stuart as an admiral in the Royal Navy, was rewarded for his father's loyalty with dominion over the last unallocated tract of American territory at the king's disposal.

The younger Penn proved to be less concerned with social standing and royal favor than his father had been. In 1667, at the age of 23, William Penn turned his back on his father's military profession, social standing, and religious beliefs by adopting the faith of the Society of Friends. The Society of Friends, or

Quakers, had a strong appeal among men and women at the bottom of the social order, and stood well beyond the fringe of respectability in late seventeenth-century England. The conversion of Admiral Penn's son to Quakerism has been likened by historian Ted Morgan to one of the Joint Chiefs of Staff having a college-age son come home one weekend with his head shaved, wearing a saffron robe, and announcing that he had become a Hare Krishna![64]

As the founding governor of the new colony bearing the family name, William Penn set about creating a "holy experiment" of a sort different than had been attempted earlier by Puritan settlers. Penn's colony was to be a haven for oppressed Quakers and other harassed people. The Quaker migration to Pennsylvania began in 1681. Some 8,000 English Quaker refugees had migrated to the colony by 1687; most came in family groups. Beginning in 1683, German immigrants began arriving, adding more diversity to a population that already included Dutch and Swedish as well as English settlers. Although the heaviest concentrations of early German settlement remained in Pennsylvania, German migrants moved into New York, Maryland, Virginia, and down to the Carolinas. By the time of the Revolution, German settlers had spread their language, culture, and a variety of pietistic religious sects into all the colonies along the Atlantic seaboard and into the backcountry as well.[65]

Although dissenting religious groups from various parts of Europe found refuge in Pennsylvania, the colony was hardly the "peaceable kingdom" its founder had envisioned. The Swedes and Dutch who had acquired good lands along the lower Delaware River resisted Quaker domination and in 1704 separated from the Pennsylvania colony. Schisms within the Society of Friends led to disaffection within that community of faith. By the time Penn's heirs abandoned Quakerism and embraced Anglicanism in 1748, it must have been abundantly clear that religious, linguistic, and ethnic differences were to be enduring characteristics of the Middle colonies.

Even though dissension was marked and little went according to the expectation of founders such as Penn, his colony and others established during the Restoration period can be considered to have been successful ventures. They survived not as homogeneous, closely knit, well-ordered communities on the New England model, but as a collection of pluralistic entities. People of English descent probably never constituted much more than half of the population in any of the Middle colonies at any point in their history. An array of separate ethnic and religious groups maintained self-contained and self-supporting communities and endeavored, with varying degrees of success, to follow their religious and ethnic customs in relative isolation.

Over time, however, as contact among groups did increase, so too did tolerance for diversity and recognition of the need for civility and accommodation. As the port towns of New York and Philadelphia grew into heterogeneous urban centers, it became increasingly necessary, politically and economically, to find ways to transcend differences and settle disputes. Ethnic and religious distinctions, individual competitiveness, and limited concern for achieving social uniformity produced both conflict and at the same time made cooperation a social imperative. During the course of the eighteenth century, the Middle colonies, like the Chesapeake area and unlike New England, moved not from coherence to incoherence but from incoherence to coherence. Through economic, political, and religious disagreements, a consensus was being formed that fostered a spirit of "live and let live" and a pragmatic acceptance of differences.

The Middle colonies, in which conflict was always present, thus demonstrated that colonial America could benefit by encouraging pluralism. Pennsylvania, New Jersey, and Delaware provided an early and telling marker of the growth of toleration by refusing to require residents to pay support for any official church. Another sign of compromise and conciliation has already been noted: the interdenominational cooperation in the sponsorship and governance of Kings College and the College of Philadelphia. As the eighteenth century evolved, there was a coming together, not a falling apart, of Middle colony society. Residents of the region were coming to terms with their extraordinarily heterogeneous society.[66]

Educational Patterns in the Middle Colonies

Patterns of education among the inhabitants of the Middle colonies reflected the diversity of the region. Essentially, each religious group sought to educate its children within the confines of the home, church, and community along the general lines being followed in other sections of the emerging nation. For some groups, structured schooling was deemed important; for others, formal educational arrangements were considered unnecessary and undesirable.

The Dutch West India Company established and initially financed a town school in New Amsterdam in 1638 and encouraged the establishment of similar schools in the outlying villages. In 1659 a classical secondary school was operating in New Amsterdam. Dutch schools existed in eleven of the twelve Dutch communities established before the English conquest in 1664.

Anglicans in New York, Pennsylvania, and other Middle colonies, like their counterparts in the Chesapeake region, tended to regard schooling as a private matter. While the Society for the Propagation of the Gospel in Foreign Parts (SPG) was active in establishing charity schools in the Middle colonies as elsewhere, self-sufficient Anglicans did not expect any type of "free" education for their children. SPG schools were for indigent children and Indians, not for those whose tithes supported the Society. For respectable adherents of the faith, schoolmasters were available for a fee to offer instruction to their children.

Members of other religious groups, such as the Presbyterians, Baptists, Catholics, Dutch Reformed, Jews, and Quakers, also established schools in their communities when population density warranted. Despite their disdain for theologically sophisticated ministers, Quakers advocated literacy and provided for parochial elementary schools in their communities. Quaker schools were controlled and supported financially by the local congregations and were free and open to all, including blacks and Indians, who were typically excluded from other schools. Quaker schools were also coeducational.

One of the most famous schoolmasters in the Middle colonies was Christopher Dock, a German who settled in Pennsylvania around 1714. Dock, a Mennonite, opened a school in Montgomery County soon after his arrival and taught until his death in 1771. He wrote *Schulordnung (School Management)*, which in 1770 became the first book on pedagogy to be printed in America. Dock instructed schoolmasters to be sensitive to individual differences and to base discipline on love and understanding. He described his own methods for individualizing instruction and his use of older students to help younger ones with their lessons.

Perhaps most significant in terms of the sectarian divisions in the Schuylkill Valley of Pennsylvania, Dock managed to deal with children of various religious persuasions without exciting sectarian controversy. In *Schulordnung* he provided what is probably the earliest systematic treatment of a fundamental problem of common schooling in a pluralistic society. Of course, the schools in which Dock taught were religiously diverse only in a limited sense. The students were ethnically homogeneous (although Germans were a minority group), and the religious pluralism was confined within a Christian framework.[67]

As New York and Philadelphia developed into commercial centers, private teachers opened schools as profit-making ventures, as was the case in other emerging towns and cities of size throughout the colonies. As noted earlier, these more secular and utilitarian schools had special appeal to young men with commercial interests and served to highlight the gap that existed between traditional classical education for a leadership elite and the more "useful" training that promised to advance the careers of young men aspiring to "make it" in commercial society.

Benjamin Franklin and Education for Success in Life

Perhaps no individual in early American history so well personifies the "rise to respectability" attributes of the self-made man as does Benjamin Franklin. In Franklin's own estimation, in his ascent "from the poverty and obscurity" into which he was born to "a state of affluence and some degree of reputation in the world," he had fashioned a life worth emulating. With the purpose of instructing his son and others in the merits of Protestant virtues and the value of self-help, Franklin began working on his *Autobiography* in 1771. He made his last entries just a couple of years before his death in 1790, but had chronicled his life's story only to the year 1757. He was thus unable to leave to posterity his accounting of his greatest achievements in statesmanship. What he did leave, however, was a description of his life's journey for the edification of those who wished to follow the paths of self-education to advantage.[68]

Born the tenth son of a Boston candlemaker in 1706, the youngest member of the Franklin family appeared to his father to have a bit more promise than his older brothers, all of whom received training as apprentices in various trades. When Franklin was eight years old and already showing a keen appetite for reading, his father placed him in a Latin grammar school "as the tithe of his sons to the service of the church." Although by his own accounting Franklin performed well in his early schooling, his father, having concluded that he could not afford to educate his son through college, withdrew him from the grammar school and placed him under the tutelage of George Brownell, a teacher of writing and arithmetic. "I failed in the arithmetic," admitted Franklin, and at the age of 10 "was taken home to assist my father in his business."

Two years working with his father was more than enough to convince Franklin that boiling tallow for soap and candles was not to his liking. An apprenticeship with his cousin Samuel, who was a cutler, proved equally unsatisfying. He found the printing trade more rewarding and worked as an apprentice in his brother James's print shop until 1723 when, at the age of 17, he broke his indenture. After an odyssey that carried him to Philadelphia, London, and back to Philadelphia, Franklin and a partner purchased *The Pennsylvania Gazette* in 1728. Two years later, at the age of 24, Franklin became the sole owner and began a series of publishing ventures that brought him both fame and fortune. By 1748 he was able to retire from business and devote his energies for the remainder of his life to public affairs and a succession of projects, experiments, and observations in numerous areas of interest.

Franklin's remarkable life is fascinating in its own right, but his career and writings are of special note in terms of his educational experiences and opinions. As Franklin himself made clear, his ambitions and his accomplishments were the direct result of his determination and ability to learn from experience. With less than two years of formal schooling, Benjamin Franklin became one of the most learned, original, and respected men of the Revolutionary generation.

Franklin and the Doctrine of Self-Education

Franklin's oft-quoted comment that "Most of the learning in use is not of much use" nicely captures his disdain for much of the attention to the "dead languages" and other trappings of the conventional education of his day. However, by no means was Benjamin Franklin anti-intellectual. His quarrel was against the current forms of institutionalized education, not against learning.

In his *Autobiography*, Franklin described in detail the various ways in which he had acquired knowledge without relying on formal schooling. He gave special attention to the Junto, a club for mutual improvement that he and some friends began in 1727. Franklin and his friends agreed to gather every Friday evening to discuss topics of importance and interest. Franklin noted in his *Autobiography*:

> The rules I drew up required that every member in his turn produce one or more queries on any point of morals, politics, or natural philosophy,

to be discussed by the company, and once in three months produce and read an essay of his own writing on any subject he pleased. Our debates were . . . to be conducted in the sincere spirit of inquiry after truth, without fondness for dispute, or desire for victory.[69]

The Junto continued to serve as a local discussion and debating group for forty years, and similar associations began to appear in other colonies. In the 1760s the Philadelphia Junto merged with the American Philosophical Society (APS). The APS had been organized in 1744 in Philadelphia as a kind of inter-colonial junto intended to maintain a constant correspondence among "virtu-osi or ingenious men residing in the several colonies." While Franklin was not the originator of the APS idea, he sponsored the plan in his *Proposal for Promoting Useful Knowledge among the British Plantations in America* (1743). The APS soon became the organizational hub for a network of the colonial intelligentsia.

The colonial commerce in ideas was broadened considerably as the APS began to exchange correspondence, reports, abstracts and transactions of various sorts with the New York Society for the Promotion of Useful Knowledge (founded in 1748), the Virginia Society for the Promotion of Useful Knowledge (founded in Williamsburg in 1773), and other societies including the Royal Society of London and the Dublin Society. In Societies such as these, and hundreds of more ephemeral organizations that came and went, Americans were learning important lessons in the uses of informal education. In his *Autobiography* and in other writings, Benjamin Franklin repeatedly extolled the virtues of these efforts at mutual education.[70]

Franklin also noted the value of individual correspondence as an enterprise in self-education. He engaged in extensive correspondence with knowledgeable men and women on both sides of the Atlantic, tapping into their investigations and opinions on matters relating to science, religion, politics, agriculture, and scores of other topics.

When they were available, of course, books could yield the knowledge of the ages as well as ideas useful in the present; but in colonial America, private library collections were limited to the very wealthy and even then were often small in size. Cotton Mather took great pride in his "well-furnished library" of around 4,000 volumes—probably the largest and best of its time in the colonies. William Byrd II's brick mansion at Westover in Virginia housed over 3,000 books and pamphlets. The library holdings of Harvard, William and Mary, and other colonial colleges approximated but did not exceed these private collections in size. But these treasure troves were indeed the exceptions. Many families had only a Bible. Those who could boast of more books might also lay claim to a catechism, a devotional pamphlet, and perhaps an almanac or two. A family with a dozen or more books could with justification consider itself a literary household.

Franklin and some of his Junto colleagues maintained personal libraries, but came to the realization that, individually, their shelves were rather bare. As related by Franklin in his *Autobiography*, in 1731 he and his associates undertook to develop the first subscription library in the American colonies. Junto members agreed to donate books to a common collection and to form an association of subscribers whose initial contribution of forty shillings and subsequent annual assessment of ten shillings would enable the library to expand its holdings. Franklin was intimately involved in selecting the first publications for the newly founded Library Company of Philadelphia. Included were such varied titles as Homer's *Iliad* and *Odyssey*, Plutarch's *Lives*, Algernon Sidney's *Discourses Concerning Government* (1698), and *The Tatler, The Spectator,* and *The Guardian.* Atlases, histories, and handbooks that would interest enterprising young men formed an important part of the collection. "Significantly," observed Lawrence Cremin, "there was not a theological title in the initial collection."[71]

No title is more closely associated with the name of Benjamin Franklin than *Poor Richard's Almanack.* Writing under the pseudonym Richard Saunders, Franklin issued his first edition in December 1732 and continued its publication for twenty-five years. In the same vein as his discussion group, library company, and conversations and communications with other knowledgeable people, Franklin saw his *Almanack* as an avenue for extending useful education. Writing of his purpose, he said:

> I intended to make it both entertaining and useful . . . I considered it a proper vehicle for conveying instruction among the common people, who bought scarce any other books. I therefore filled all the little spaces that occurred between the remarkable days in the calendar, with proverbial sentences, chiefly such as inculcated industry and frugality, as the means of procuring wealth and thereby securing virtue, it being more difficult for a man in want to act always honestly, as (to use here one of those proverbs) it is hard for an empty sack to stand upright.

Franklin's emphasis on the worldly payoff of good Puritan values—hard work, thriftiness, moderation, honesty, and the like—has been interpreted by some as a "secularization of the Protestant ethic." There can be little argument that Franklin contributed to and even encouraged a more materialistic and pragmatic outlook associated with the emerging capitalistic "middle class" in American society. However, Franklin was reflecting values already being turned to secular purposes. Moreover, learning at every level was becoming more and more valued for its economic utility and its promise of material success. While Franklin certainly understood that material progress and moral progress are not synonymous, he sometimes lost sight of this in both his aphorisms and in his own conduct. Even so, Franklin's admonitions and instructions in the art of self-education and self-responsibility included a genuine concern for civic virtue and moral betterment, as well as useful instructions that pointed the way toward individual success.[72]

Franklin and the Institutionalization of Useful Education

Franklin saw in self-education and mutual endeavors the keys to the successful conduct of life for ambitious men like himself who had neither the time, the money, nor the inclination to attend traditional grammar school and colleges. His self-help suggestions in his *Autobiography* and *Almanack* were not intended, however, as substitutes for educational institutions that, if reformed, could be made more useful and relevant to the needs of the new middle class. Franklin acknowledged that it would be wonderful if students could be taught "everything that is useful and everything that is ornamental," but he also observed that "art is long, and their time is short." This line of reasoning prompted Franklin to propose a new type of school in which students would "learn those things that are likely to be most useful and most ornamental," with special attention given to the occupational interests of the students.

Franklin's plan for an English grammar school was first sketched in 1743 and published in 1749 as *Proposals Relating to the Education of Youth in Pennsylvania*. In essence, Franklin's design for the "Philadelphia Academy" involved grafting a program of practical studies that theretofore had been outside the province of "formal" secondary schooling on to the conventional classical curriculum. The heart of Franklin's new school, however, was clearly to be studies that were useful rather than ornamental. English and *modern* foreign languages were to hold center stage, along with various branches of mathematics and courses in the natural and physical sciences. Penmanship, accounting, drawing, commercial studies, gardening (including field trips to neighboring farms), and physical exercise rounded out the curriculum of the English or practical side of the institution. Franklin envisioned his academy as laying the foundation for healthy habits of mind and body and cultivating a spirit of service which he regarded as "the great aim and end of all learning."[73]

In a companion essay published in 1751, *Idea of the English School*, Franklin elaborated upon his earlier proposals. Beyond refinements in the curriculum, however, Franklin emphasized again that the purpose of his modernized program of studies was not designed to turn out scholars, but rather to produce men of practical affairs. Those destined for the ministry or other learned professions might have need of Latin, Greek, and similar studies, but young American tradesmen and artisans had little use for such studies. In arguing for the primacy of English grammar and literature along with geography, mechanics, and other practical studies, Franklin wrote:

> Thus instructed, youth will come out of this school fitted for learning any business, calling or profession, except such wherein languages are required; and tho' unacquainted with any ancient or foreign tongue, they will be masters of their own, which is of more immediate and general use.[74]

Franklin readily acknowledged that many of his ideas were drawn from the writings of other men more learned than he. He noted in particular his indebtedness to John Milton's *Of Education* (1644), John Locke's *Some Thoughts Concerning Education* (1745), Charles Rollin's *The Method of Teaching and Studying Belles-Lettres* (1726–1728), and George Turnbull's *Observations upon Liberal Education in All Its Branches* (1742). These and other educational treatises influenced Franklin, but the driving impulse behind his design for a new kind of secondary school came from his own experiences in trying to obtain an education that could be put to the service of self and society.

In spite of Franklin's insistence that his generation break from the educational conventions of the past, his success with the Philadelphia Academy was short-lived. The English School paled in the shadow of the Classical Department, not in terms of student popularity, but rather in terms of domination of the academy by the "Latinists." As the academy faded, the more advanced segment of Franklin's scheme, the College of Philadelphia, prospered. In 1789 the institution was renamed the University of Pennsylvania.

Reviewing the minutes of the board of trustees in 1789, a year before his death, Franklin sadly noted that "the original Plan of the English School has been departed from; . . . the subscribers to it have been disappointed and deceived." Franklin lamented that there appears to be in mankind "an unaccountable prejudice in favor of ancient customs and habitudes" which allows practices to continue long "after the circumstances, which formerly made them useful, cease to exist."[75]

Conclusion

It is rather ironic that the ideas of an old man about to leave the world seemed for the moment too novel to gain acceptance by a new nation about to be born. Yet the fact that Franklin's academy did not develop as he had planned must be noted as a commentary on the power of the prevailing educational institutions and arrangements of colonial America. The educational landscape, like the country's topography, revealed a bewildering range of peaks and valleys. For all their newness, the European outposts in the new world long held on to inherited customs, traditions, and assumptions, in education as in other matters. For all its openness, colonial America fostered educational institutions and arrangements that were essentially hierarchical, class bound, and markedly uneven in terms of opportunity. With only a few exceptions, education remained authority oriented in pedagogy and purpose; it was intended to reinforce the religious, ethnic, and political traditions and institutions of those in control.[76]

All that being said, the role of schools in colonial society must be acknowledged as being subordinate to more powerful educational agencies: the family, the community, and, for many, the church of their fathers. Even so, as the eighteenth century progressed, currents of change loosened but did not dislodge the old order. As the flow of people, books, and ideas quickened in the second half of the eighteenth century, the boundaries of clan, community, and church began to soften. Education was making a difference, although schooling remained a haphazard affair.

Further Reading

Berkin, Carol. *First Generations: Women in Colonial America*. New York: Hill & Wang, 1997. A readable and scholarly multicultural account of the lives and contributions of mostly unknown women of varied backgrounds who struggled to find their place in the new world.

Brands, H. W. *The First American: The Life and Times of Benjamin Franklin*. New York: Anchor Books, 2002. A broad-ranging portrayal of the central role played by the Founding "Grandfather" in the creation of the United States of America.

Clinton, Catherine, and Michele Gillespie, eds. *The Devil's Lane: Sex and Race in the Early South*. New York: Oxford University Press, 2002. An important new work highlighting legal and cultural conflicts pertaining to matters of sexuality, race, and gender in the South from the seventeenth into the nineteenth centuries.

Crass, David C., et al., eds. *The Southern Colonial Backcountry: Interdisciplinary Perspectives on Frontier Communities*. Knoxville: University of Tennessee Press, 1998. A multidisciplinary analysis of community formation and maintenance in the backcountry areas of Virginia, North Carolina, South Carolina, and Tennessee.

Cremin, Lawrence A. *American Education: The Colonial Experience, 1607–1783*. New York: Harper & Row, 1970. A comprehensive volume by the "dean" of twentieth century educational historians that details multiple and intersecting paths to knowledge in colonial America.

Daniels, Christine. *Negotiated Empires: Centers and Peripheries in the New World, 1500–1820*. New York: Routledge, 2002. Essays representing recent historiographical analyses of the interactions and experiences of the colonials on the peripheries of European empires.

Earle, Alice Morse. *Child Life in Colonial Days*. Williamstown, MA: Corner House Publishers, [1899], 1989. A broad survey with illustrations of a broad range of children's activities at home, school, church, in recreational activities.

Fischer, David Hackett. *Albion's Seed: Four British Folkways in America*. New York: Oxford University Press, 1989. A fascinating cultural revisionist inquiry into the ways in which the religious and social roots of four British districts helped build four distinctly separate cultures in seventeenth and eighteenth century America.

Hall, David D. *Worlds of Wonder, Days of Judgment: Popular Religious Belief in Early New England*. Cambridge, MA: Harvard University Press, 1990. An innovative study of the ways in which religion was embedded in the fabric of everyday life in colonial New England.

Main, Gloria L. *Peoples of a Specious Land: Families and Cultures in Colonial New England*. Cambridge, MA: Harvard University Press, 2001. An examination of aspects of family life, such as sexuality, courtship, marriage, child rearing, old age, and death in pre-Revolutionary America. Includes comparisons of the lifestyles of Native Americans and European settlers.

Morgan, Edmund S. *Benjamin Franklin*. New Haven: Yale University Press, 2002. An excellent one volume biography by a leading American historian.

Philbrick, Nathaniel. *Mayflower: A Story of Courage, Community, and War*. New York: Viking, 2006. Evokes the drama of the voyage, encounters with Indians, explorations, and the first half-century of life among the Pilgrims and their descendants.

Roundtree, Helen, Wayne Clark, and Kent Mountford. *John Smith's Chesapeake Voyages 1607–1609*. Charlottesville: University of Virginia Press, 2007. The definitive book on the Chesapeake Bay region's natural environment and native cultures at the time of Smith's expeditions.

Sloan, Kim. *A New World: England's First View of America*. Chapel Hill: University of North Carolina Press, 2007. A collection of watercolors by John White, Governor of the Lost Colony, depicting Algonquian Indians and the flora and fauna of coastal North Carolina.

Wood, Gordon S. *The Americanization of Benjamin Franklin*. New York: Penguin Press, 2005. A penetrating study of Franklin the man, the myth, and the roots of American character.

Notes

1. A migration that began in 1612 brought 3,000 to 4,000 people to the island of Bermuda, while perhaps as many as 110,000 to 135,000 left England, Scotland, and Wales to settle in the Caribbean during this period. In addition 70,000 to 100,000 emigrés settled in Ireland. See Jack P. Greene, *Pursuits of Happiness: The Social Development of Early Modern British Colonies and the Formation of American Culture*. Chapel Hill: University of North Carolina

Press, 1988, pp. 7–8. On the turmoil that fueled the seventeenth-century migration, see Carl Bridenbaugh, *Vexed and Troubled Englishmen, 1590–1642.* London: Oxford University Press, 1968.

2. Perry Miller and Thomas H. Johnson, eds., *The Puritans: A Sourcebook of Their Writings,* vol. 1. New York: Harper Torchbooks, 1963, p. 1. A mid-twentieth century assessment of this theme by an outstanding historian of the South is provided by C. Vann Woodward, "The Southern Ethic in a Puritan World," *William and Mary Quarterly,* 3rd series, 25, 1968, pp. 343–370. For a penetrating challenge to the New England hegemony theme, see Greene, *Pursuits of Happiness.*

3. While other historians of an earlier era also were targeted for criticism, the major focus was on Ellwood P. Cubberley, *Public Education in the United States: A Study and Interpretation of American Educational History.* Boston: Houghton Mifflin, 1919.

4. The key works in the early phase of the "revisionist debate" are Bernard Bailyn, *Education in the Forming of American Society.* Chapel Hill: University of North Carolina Press, 1960; and Lawrence A. Cremin, *The Wonderful World of Ellwood P. Cubberley.* New York: Bureau of Publications, Teachers College, 1965. Among many useful reviews of the shifting currents in the field before the "radical" critique (to be discussed later) got underway, see Sol Cohen, "The History of the History of American Education, 1900–1965: The Uses of the Past," *Harvard Educational Review,* vol. 46, August 1976, pp. 298–330.

5. Greene, pp. 5, 165–166, and passim.

6. Ted Morgan, *Wilderness at Dawn: The Settling of the North American Continent.* New York: Simon and Schuster, 1993, p. 110.

7. Sadie Bell, *The Church, the State, and Education in Virginia.* Philadelphia: Science Press Printing Co., 1930, pp. 6–8.

8. Morgan, pp. 110–115. See George Percy, *Observations Gathered out of "A Discourse on the Plantation of the Southern Colony in Virginia by the English, 1606," Written by that Honorable Gentlemen, Master George Percy.* David B. Quinn, ed., Charlottesville: University Press of Virginia, 1967.

9. Two gruesome tales of cannibalism were recorded during that winter. In one instance, some colonists disinterred an Indian they had recently killed and ate him, "boiled and stewed with roots and herbs." The second case was of a man who murdered his pregnant wife, threw the unborn child into the James River, chopped up and salted the mother, and then ate her! The man confessed after being hanged by his thumbs with weights attached to his feet. See George Percy, *A Trewe Relacyon of the Proceedings and Ocurrentes of Momente which Have Happened in Virginia from 1609 until 1612,* reprinted in Ralph Hamor, et al., *Virginia: Four Personal Narratives.* New York: Arno Press, 1972, pp. 259–282, at p. 267. Cf. Morgan, p. 118.

10. Pocahontas was eleven or twelve years old when she supposedly saved the life of Captain John Smith in late December, 1607. While the legend endures as a cherished part of American history, recent scholarship has cast increasing doubt about its accuracy. See Helen C. Roundtree, *Pocahontas, Powhatan, Opechancanough: Three Indian Lives Changed by Jamestown.* Charlottesville: University of Virginia Press, 2005, pp. 36, 77–82, 104–107.

11. Morgan, p. 120.

12. Virginius Dabney, *Virginia: The New Dominion.* Garden City, N.Y.: Doubleday, 1971, pp. 29–33, passim. The quotations, varying in wording and attribution, may be found in Morgan, pp. 116, 117–118, and 125, and Dabney, p. 34. See also Susan Myra Kingsbury, ed., *Records of the Virginia Company of London.* Washington, D.C.: U.S. Government Printing Office, 1906.

13. Dabney, pp. 35–36; Bell, pp. 14–23. Documents pertaining to efforts to establish Henrico College, the East India School, and a 1624 bequest to fund a university to be called *Academia Virginiensis et Oxoniensis* are in Edgar W. Knight, ed., *A Documentary History of Education in the South before 1860,* vol. 1. Chapel Hill: University of North Carolina Press, 1949, pp. 1–31.

14. Carl Bridenbaugh, *Myths and Realities: Societies of the Colonial South.* New York: Atheneum, [1952], 1975, pp. 119–200, quotations at 177, 179, 182, and 183.

15. On the social origins and characteristics of the American colonists, see David Hackett Fischer, *Albion's Seed: Four British Folkways in America.* New York: Oxford University Press, 1989, esp. pp. 212–256.

16. Sheldon S. Cohen, *A History of Colonial Education, 1607–1776.* New York: John Wiley, 1974, pp. 112–119. See also Bell, p. 112.

17. Sir William Berkeley, "Report to the Commissioners of Trade and Plantations, 1671," in William Walter Hening, ed., *Statutes at Large; Being a Collection of All the Laws of Virginia,*

from the First Session of the Legislature, in the Year 1619, vol. 2. Richmond: Samuel Pleasants, Jr.,1809–1823, pp. 511–517.

18. [Philip V. Fithian], *Journal and Letters of Philip Vickers Fithian, 1773–1774: A Plantation Tutor of the Old Dominion*, Hunter Dickinson Farish, ed. Williamsburg: Colonial Williamsburg, Inc., 1943, pp. 25–26, 34, 85, passim.

19. Hening, ed., vol. 1, p. 157.

20. Guy Fred Wells, *Parish Education in Colonial Virginia*. New York: Teachers College, Columbia University, 1923, pp. 17–29, passim.

21. Lawrence A. Cremin, *American Education: The Colonial Experience, 1607–1783*. New York: Harper & Row, 1970, pp. 341–342. See also John Calam, *Parsons and Pedagogues: The S.P.G. Adventure in American Education*. New York: Colombia University Press, 1971.

22. See Bell, pp. 106–111.

23. That Berkeley was aware of the Syms endowment is clear from the fact that he was governor of the colony when the school was incorporated in 1642. See Knight, vol. 1, pp. 666–667. Berkeley's full report is in Hening, ed., vol. 1, pp. 511–517.

24. See Helen Jones Campbell, "The Syms and Eaton Schools and Their Successor," *William and Mary Quarterly*, vol. 20, January 1940, pp. 1–61, at 1. Wells, pp. 30–57, identified nine endowed schools in Virginia during the colonial period. Inasmuch as parish officials (ministers, vestrymen, or church wardens) sometimes served as "trustees" of these endowments, these schools also show up in the literature as "endowed parish schools." See also James A. Burns, *The Principles, Origin and Establishment of the Catholic School System in the United States*. New York: Arno Press, [1908], 1969, pp. 94–101, who points to endowments for Catholic schools in Maryland dating from the 1650s.

25. Joshua Rosenbloom, "Indentured Servitude in the Colonial U.S.," *EH.Net Encyclopedia*, Robert Whaples, ed., January 16, 2006 at http://eh.net/encyclopedia/article/Rosenbloom. Indenture. See also John E. Murray and Ruth Wallis Herndon, "Markets for Children in Early America: A Political Economy of Pauper Apprenticeship," *The Journal of Economic History*, 62 (June 2002), pp. 356-ff.

26. Wells, pp. 66–69, 73–75; Cohen, *Colonial Education*, pp. 124–126; Hening, ed., vol. 1, pp. 336–337.

27. See p. 15.

28. Bridenbaugh, *Myths and Realities*, pp. 35–36; Cohen, *Colonial Education*, pp. 131–137; Herbert Baxter Adams, *The College of William and Mary: A Contribution to the History of Higher Education*. Washington, D.C.: U.S. Government Printing Office, 1887, pp. 11–15; Susan H. Godson, et al., *The College of William and Mary: A History, 1693–1888*. Williamsburg: King and Queen Press, Society of the Alumni, 1993.

29. One male passenger died en route, but a son born at sea to Elizabeth and Stephen Hopkins kept the gender ratio fixed. The child was named, appropriately enough, Oceanus. A complete passenger list is provided in William Bradford, *Of Plymouth Plantation, 1620–1647*, Samuel Eliot Morison, ed., New York: Alfred A. Knopf, 1979, pp. 441–448.

30. Bradford, pp. 75–76, 95; cf. Morgan, pp. 134–139; Nathaniel Philbrick, *Mayflower: A Story of Courage, Community, and War*. New York: Viking, 2006, pp. 41–43. The Pilgrims had been given a patent for lands in the northern reaches of the Virginia colony, near present-day New York City.

31. Philbrick, p. 9. The journalist and humorist H. L. Mencken offered a more cynical assessment of Puritan beliefs by asserting that "Puritanism is the haunting fear that someone, somewhere, may be happy."

32. Bradford, pp. 33, 37. It is interesting to note that the covenant made in Holland was spiritual whereas the Mayflower Compact was a civil document.

33. See Fischer, p. 25; T. H. Breen and Stephen Foster, "Moving to the New World: The Character of Early Massachusetts Immigration," in Breen, *Puritans and Adventures: Change and Persistence in Early America*. New York: Oxford University Press, 1980, p. 51; and Virginia DeJohn Anderson, "Migrants and Motives: Religion and the Settlement of New England, 1630–1640," *New England Quarterly*, vol. 58, 1985, p. 348.

34. Greene, pp. 10, 18–19; John Demos, *A Little Commonwealth: Family Life in Plymouth Colony*. New York: Oxford University Press, 1970, pp. 6–12, passim.

35. John Winthrop, "A Model of Christian Charity" (1630), in Miller and Johnson, vol. 1, pp. 195–199.

36. Boyer et al., pp. 46–48. "Saint" in Puritan terminology did not imply canonization. Rather, it carried the Biblical meaning of being one of God's chosen people. The term "Puritan," like "Quaker," was originally one of reproach, not accepted until the late

seventeenth century by the people to whom it was applied. The Puritans called themselves "God's people."

37. Bradford, pp. 279–271; Morgan, pp. 172–187. Bradford reported that of approximately a thousand Indians in this village, only fifty survived the "great sickness it pleased God to visit [upon them]."

38. "Literacy" is a slippery concept and one that continues to provoke considerable debate among both historians and educators. However defined and measured, throughout the colonial period, literacy rates among women appear to have been about half those of the male population at a given time. In most instances, the literacy rates given here are based on counts of signed wills as presented in Kenneth A. Lockridge, *Literacy in Colonial New England: An Enquiry into the Social Context of Literacy in the Early Modern West.* New York: W. W. Norton, 1974. See also Cremin, *Colonial Experience*, p. 526, passim. Insightful critiques and useful discussions of the relationship between literacy and social development are offered by Harvey J. Graff, *The Labyrinths of Literacy: Reflections on Literacy Past and Present.* London: Falmer Press, 1987, esp. pp. 73–93; and Carl F. Kaestle, Helen Daman-Moore, Lawrence C. Stedman, Katherine Tinsley, and William Vance Trollinger, Jr., *Literacy in the United States: Readers and Reading since 1880.* New Haven: Yale University Press, 1991.

39. Fischer, pp. 31–205, passim.

40. John Cotton, *Christ the Fountaine of Life* (1651), and Thomas Hooker, *The Soules Vocation or Effectual Calling* (1637), as quoted in Andrew Delbanco, *The Puritan Ordeal.* Cambridge, MA: Harvard University Press, 1989, p. 83. Too much can be made of this independent spirit among Protestants, however, and especially with regard to seventeenth-century Puritans. There were indeed dangers in encouraging critical thought and in attempting to blend piety with learning and revelation with community, as is attested to by the difficulties the Puritan elders experienced with Anne Hutchinson and Roger Williams.

41. The concept of "Puritan tribalism" was introduced into Puritan studies by Edmund S. Morgan to emphasize the importance of infant baptism and other acts of "bonding" within the covenant community. Here we use the concept in a more expanded fashion. See Morgan, *The Puritan Family: Religion and Domestic Relations in Seventeenth-Century New England.* New York: Harper & Row, [1944], 1966, chap. 7. See also Alan Simpson, *Puritanism in Old and New England.* Chicago: University of Chicago Press, 1955, p. 24; "Introduction" in Miller and Johnson, pp. 1–79. For justifications of theocracy and intolerance of "erroneous" religious views, see, among other writings, John Winthrop's "Little Speech on Liberty" (1645), and Nathaniel Ward's "The Simple Cobbler of Aggawam" (1645), in Miller and Johnson, pp. 205–207 and 226–236.

42. Bailyn, pp. 14, 28, passim.

43. Helena M. Wall, *Fierce Communion: Family and Community in Early America.* Cambridge, MA: Harvard University Press, 1990, p. 1; Lockridge, p. 104; Philip J. Greven, Jr., *Four Generations: Population, Land and Family in Colonial Andover, Massachusetts.* Ithaca, NY: Cornell University Press, 1970. See also Jay Fliegelman, *Prodigals and Pilgrims: The American Revolution against Patriarchal Authority, 1750–1800.* New York: Alfred A. Knopf, 1977; and Lawrence Stone, *The Family, Sex, and Marriage in England, 1500–1800.* New York: Harper & Row, 1977.

44. John Robinson, "Of Children and Their Education" (1625), in Robert Ashton, ed., *The Works of John Robinson,* London: John Snow, 1851, vol. 1, p. 246. See also Cremin, *Colonial Experience,* p. 132; James Axtell, *The School upon a Hill.* New Haven: Yale University Press, 1974, pp. 147–148.

45. "Instructions for the Punishment of Incorrigible Children in Massachusetts" (1646), in Sol Cohen, ed., *Education in the United States: A Documentary History,* vol. 1. New York: Random House, 1974, pp. 370–371. Although we have found no examples of children being put to death for the "crimes" specified in these laws, some young people were put to death for unnatural and unlawful acts. For example, William Bradford recorded the sordid details of "A Horrible Case of Bestiality" that resulted in the invocation of the death penalty in the case of a teenage boy convicted of "buggery" in 1642. See Bradford, pp. 320–321.

46. Porter's age, 26, did not exempt him from facing the charge of being disobedient to his parents. Axtell, pp. 156–159.

47. "Massachusetts School [sic] Law of 1642," in Cohen, *A Documentary History,* vol. 1, p. 393.

48. The New Haven colony, founded by Puritans in 1638, was absorbed into Connecticut in 1665. A new charter combined Massachusetts Bay, Plymouth, and Maine into the single

royal colony of Massachusetts in 1691. Maine remained tied to Massachusetts until it gained statehood in 1820.

49. Miller and Johnson, vol. 1, p. 12.
50. Demos, p. 143; Lockridge, pp. 43–71.
51. Cremin, *Colonial Education*, pp. 180–181.
52. E. Jennifer Monaghan, "Literacy Instruction and Gender in Colonial New England," in Cathy N. Davidson, ed., *Reading in America: Literature and Social History*. Baltimore: Johns Hopkins University Press, 1989, p. 57.
53. Michael Wigglesworth, *The Day of Doom: or A Poetical Description of the Great and Last Judgement* (1662), in Miller and Johnson, vol. 2, pp. 585–606. On the relationship between literacy and religion among the Puritans, see David D. Hall, *Worlds of Wonder, Days of Judgment: Popular Religious Belief in Early New England*. Cambridge, MA: Harvard University Press, 1990, pp. 21–70, and Cremin, *Colonial Experience*, pp. 128–137.
54. The oldest extant American primer was composed by John Eliot as part of his efforts to convert the Massachuset Indians to Christianity. Written in the Algonquian language and published in 1669, the title (in its English version) stated its purpose clearly: *The Indian Primer; or, in the Way of Training up of Our Indian Youth in the Good Knowledge of God, in the Knowledge of the Scriptures and in an Ability to Read*. Our discussion of primers is indebted to Paul Leicester Ford, ed., *The New England Primer*, Classics in Education no. 13. New York: Teachers College, Columbia University, 1962.
55. Hall, *Worlds of Wonder*, pp. 36–37; Monaghan, "Literacy Instruction and Gender," pp. 53–80; Cremin, *Colonial Experience*, pp. 173–174. Axtell, in *School upon a Hill*, p. 176, provides information of the extreme youthfulness of some pupils by noting that a girl of only two and a half accidentally drowned in a river as she was making her way to school.
56. E. Jennifer Monaghan, "Readers Writing: The Curriculum of the Writing Schools of Eighteenth Century Boston," *Visible Language*, vol. 21, Spring 1987, pp. 167–213; and Monaghan, "Literacy Instruction and Gender," pp. 53–80. Monaghan notes that although the writing schools were essentially male institutions, some masters offered private instruction to girls after hours.
57. See Cremin, *Colonial Experience*, p. 193. The modern American "free public school system" is a creation of the nineteenth century, not the seventeenth, as we explain in Chapter 4.
58. In Latin America, the Spanish already had three universities in operation by this time: at Mexico City, Lima, and Cordoba. The Jesuits had opened a school in Quebec that soon evolved into a university, and, as noted previously, the earlier Henrico College venture in Virginia had been aborted. On Harvard's development, see Samuel Eliot Morison, *Three Centuries of Harvard, 1636–1936*. Cambridge, MA: Harvard University Press, 1936, p. 5, passim and Seymour Martin Lipset and David Riesman, *Education and Politics at Harvard*. New York: McGraw-Hill, 1975.
59. Frederick Rudolph, *The American College and University: A History*. Athens, GA: University of Georgia Press, [1962], 1990, pp. 3–6.
60. For a touching commentary on the dashed hopes of the pioneering generation of Puritans, see Bradford, *Of Plymouth Plantation*, p. 33, n. 6. See also Simpson, *Puritanism in Old and New England*, pp. 33–38.
61. On the English Civil War and Restoration, see Diane Purkiss, *The English Civil War: Papists, Gentlewomen, Soldiers and Witchfinders in the Birth of Modern Britain*. New York: Basic Books, 2006; Tim Harris, *Restoration: Charles II and His Kingdom, 1660–1685*. London: Penguin Books, [2005], 2006.
62. Boyer et al., *The Enduring Vision*, pp. 120–121.
63. Morgan, *Wilderness at Dawn*, pp.152–154; Boyer, et al., pp. 86–87.
64. Morgan, p. 277. When the religion's founder, George Fox, was tried on one occasion for blasphemy, he warned the judge to "tremble at the word of the Lord." Fox was ridiculed as a "quaker," and the name came to be applied to all who followed his teachings.
65. German pietism sprang up in reaction to the formalism and intellectualism of Lutheranism, Calvinism, and Catholicism. Among the bands of German-speaking pietists who placed emphasis on a "religion of the heart" and who sought to preserve their identity as a "special people" were Moravians, Mennonites, Amish, Dunkers, Seventh-Day Adventists, and Rappites.
66. Greene, *Pursuits of Happiness*, pp. 140–141, passim, is most instructive on this transition.
67. Cremin, *The Colonial Experience*, pp. 178, 308–309.
68. See Leonard W. Labaree, Ralph L. Ketcham, Helen C. Boatfield, and Helene H. Fineman, eds., *The Autobiography of Benjamin Franklin*. New Haven: Yale University Press, 1964.

Franklin intended his narrative to be used as a "conduct manual" in the genre of Francis Osborne's *Advise to a Son* (1656) and William Penn's *Fruits of a Father's Love* (1726). Cf. Cremin, The *Colonial Experience*, p. 373, n. 20.

69. Labaree, et al., eds., *Autobiography*, p. 116.
70. In addition to Franklin's *Autobiography*, see Cremin, *The Colonial Experience*, p. 410, passim for an extended discussion of this theme. See also Joseph F. Kett, *The Pursuit of Knowledge under Difficulties*. Palo Alto, CA: Stanford University Press, 1994.
71. Cremin, *The Colonial Experience*, p. 399.
72. See John Hardin Best, ed., *Benjamin Franklin on Education*. New York: Teachers College, Columbia University, 1962, pp. 1–21.
73. Franklin's *Proposals* and other writings can be found in Leonard W. Labaree and Whitfield J. Bell, Jr., *The Papers of Benjamin Franklin*. New Haven: Yale University Press, 1959. The most convenient single-volume collection of Franklin's major educational writings is Best, ed., *Benjamin Franklin on Education*.
74. As quoted in Best, ed., p. 171.
75. Cremin, *The Colonial Experience*, p. 403; S. Alexander Rippa, *An Education in a Free Society: American History*, 6th ed. New York: Longman, 1988, pp. 53–56.
76. See Rush Welter, *Popular Education and Democratic Thought in America*. New York: Columbia University Press, pp. 17–22.

3
Education and the Building of a New Nation
1776–1830

Overview: The Impact of the Enlightenment

During the course of the seventeenth and eighteenth centuries, new currents of thought began circulating among the intelligentsia of Europe and the American colonies. As these new ideas took root, they began to take on a life and power of their own. The constellation of ideas that eventually became known as the Enlightenment provoked momentous changes in nearly every aspect of Western society. Traditional assumptions regarding religion and philosophy—the latter then encompassing the domains of the natural and physical sciences, politics, economics, psychology, educational theory, and more—were altered in dramatic and profound ways by Enlightenment doctrines. In all of Western history, few ideas have proved more forceful, for good or ill, than those unleashed by the Enlightenment.

What were these new ideas? In brief, we might say that they were the foundational ideas that shaped our modern society—ideas that, at least until recent years, we have tended to think of as "progressive." To be enlightened implied freedom from the past. It offered hope, welcomed change, and questioned entrenched authority. The Enlightenment was youthful, if not always in terms of the actual age of those who gave it definition, then certainly in terms of their spirit of optimism and belief in "the future." Indeed, the very notions of reform and progress grew directly out of Enlightenment thought. In a word, the Enlightenment ushered in our contemporary understanding of what it means to be "modern."

The course of Enlightenment thought was uneven and erratic in both Europe and America. In some ways it represented a mood or outlook on life as much as a set of fixed principles. Initially spreading through the ranks of the middle and upper classes in industrializing Europe, Enlightenment ideas did not begin to circulate widely in America until well into the second half of the eighteenth century. Although somewhat later in taking hold, Enlightenment thought in America proved to have a more profound and more enduring ideological influence, at least in the political realm, than in Europe. As one historian put the matter: "The Old World imagined the Enlightenment and the New

World realized it. The Old World invented it, formulated it, and agitated it; America absorbed it, reflected it, and institutionalized it."[1]

While Enlightenment thought initially captured the attention of only the most educated in Europe and America, ideas associated with the movement soon began to be discussed among broader segments of the population. Within the diverse bands of European settlers scattered across a still largely unexplored continent were literate ministers, teachers, merchants, lawyers, gentry, and some self-improving artisans and farmers who lived in the world of print culture. These people could no more escape the new currents of thought than could their literate kinsmen who had stayed behind in Europe. Clearly, the large majority of working-class people on both sides of the Atlantic had little time for or interest in the speculations and scribblings of theorists. Nonetheless, no matter how tradition-bound and insular some individuals and communities tended to be, the trans-Atlantic migration and communication routes kept ideas as well as people and supplies floating back and forth across the sea. Through varied channels—books, newspapers, almanacs, sermons, political tracts, letters, and conversations—popularized bits and pieces of "enlightened thought" seeped into people's consciousness. Sometimes these new ideas were received agreeably; sometimes they were mixed with fear and confusion.[2]

The impact of the Enlightenment in the new world was perhaps doubly powerful precisely because this was a new world. In a very real sense, the American colonies came to represent a clean canvas on which innovative ideas and a new order could be sketched. Enlightenment thinkers of the eighteenth century fleshed out in bold strokes and with sharp hues novel theories and daring convictions that radically altered the drab picture of the old world order. As one world view slipped into decline, a new world view—and indeed, a new world—came into being.

Sources of Enlightenment Thought

The roots of Enlightenment thought reached far back across the centuries. In some respects, the scholastic debates that pitted advocates of logic against defenders of the faith and that stimulated the rise of universities in the twelfth and thirteenth centuries can be viewed as a precursor of the Enlightenment. Renaissance culture, with its emphasis on humanism and almost obsessive admiration of the artistic and intellectual achievements of classical Greece and Rome, also diminished the stagnation that had for centuries enveloped Western Europe. The Protestant Reformation, which challenged Papal authority and splintered the Christian church into quarreling factions, jarred the very foundations of Western political, as well as religious, tradition. Most important, the range of scientific discoveries that stretched from Copernicus to Isaac Newton quickened the pace of change that altered centuries-old assumptions and beliefs on which Western culture had been built.

There is no exaggeration in saying that the Enlightenment moved both heaven and earth. The cumulative effect of the astronomical investigations of Copernicus, Tycho Brahe, Johannes Kepler, Galileo, and Newton was the dismantling of the biblical and Aristotelian belief in a fixed and unchanging universe. In its place these investigators erected a "scientific" conception of a solar system constantly in motion. More than that, their calculations and observations demonstrated that the sun, not the earth, is the center of our solar system. More alarming still to those who sensed the crumbling of their tidy medieval world view, these men of science posited the existence of a great universe outside our planetary system and asserted that the whole was governed by immutable, universal laws which, as they were discovered, could be formulated as precise mathematical principles.

In other realms of science, new discoveries and inventions brought forth still other challenges to the human perspective on nature and our place in the scheme of things. In 1628 William Harvey published his conclusion that the human heart was in essence a mechanical device—a pump that forces the blood to circulate through the body. In a similar fashion, Giovanni Borelli demonstrated that the human arm operates as a lever and that muscles do mechanical "work." Moreover, just as the telescope had made possible the scanning of the heavens, the microscope, invented just before the opening of the seventeenth century, made possible the probing of the vast universe of micro-organic life.

The period leading into the Enlightenment witnessed not only the genius of the likes of Kepler, Galileo, and Newton, but also was stirred by the speculations of such theorists as Francis Bacon, Thomas Hobbes, René Descartes, and John Locke. The seventeenth century also marked the founding of the first great scientific societies, such as the Royal Society (1660) and the French *Académie des Sciences* (1666). Increasingly, thinkers of a scientific and philosophical bent quickened the assault on long-revered authorities and dogmas by widely communicating the discoveries and insights that were resulting from patient, meticulous investigation of the empirical world. Just before the dawn of the eighteenth century, advancing knowledge in the physical sciences had reached a stage that made possible Newton's great synthesis that provided the intellectual structure for the Enlightenment. Newton's majestic achievement was, of course, to conceive of the whole world of nature as an immense and intricate mechanism governed by precise mathematical laws.

Newton's grand mathematical formulation of the relation of the planets and the laws of gravity, mass, and motion seemed to demonstrate to his contemporaries the essential harmony, reasonableness, and predictability of the workings of natural phenomena. In a similar vein, John Locke's inquiries into the nature of human reason and conduct seemed to show how Newton's principles could be applied to the study of human affairs. As Crane Brinton observed, "Together, Newton and Locke set up those great clusters of ideas, Nature and Reason, which were to the Enlightenment what such clusters of ideas as grace, salvation, and predestination were to traditional Christianity."[3]

The Ideology of the Enlightenment

The Primacy of Reason

Central among the concepts that forged the Enlightenment ideology was the belief that Reason—with a capital R—was the only infallible guide to knowledge. It was Reason that would enable humankind to understand Nature—its importance, too, often signified by capitalization. Conceiving of the universe as a machine governed by unalterable laws, Enlightenment thinkers forged an ideology that in significant ways tested the underpinnings of traditional Judeo-Christian cosmology. Knowledge previously grounded in faith, revelation, or tradition was replaced with knowledge—or at least with questions—derived from empirical sense experience and from mathematical and naturalistic reasoning. "Science," the fruit of the union between Reason and Nature, was, from Newton forward, to become the germinator of most new conceptions of humanity and the universe.[4]

Most (although not all) true believers of the Enlightenment interpreted "science" or the natural order as wholly benign. As the concept spread, nature came to be understood as the orderly, untroubled, beautifully simple working of the universe *properly understood*. Once humanity comprehended the true nature of human affairs, ran the logic, all that would be necessary would be to regulate human actions accordingly and there would be no more "unnatural" behavior. The possibilities were limitless. Everything that was unnatural, once exposed as such, would surely be cast aside. No longer would corrupt leaders or inhumane institutions and customs be allowed to rob individuals of their happiness. No longer would any "enlightened" person accept the artificial inequalities and injustices of life as if they were natural occurrences that could not be changed. They could be changed—and would be changed—as the light of reason and understanding of the principles of nature spread among the common people. As one enthusiast proclaimed during the upheaval of the French Revolution, "*le bonheur est une idee neuve en Europe*"—"happiness is a new idea in Europe!"[5]

The Idea of Progress

Happiness was indeed a new idea in Europe—and in the awakening continent far to the west as well. How could one not be happy when, at long last, it seemed more and more certain that the growing force of reason was directing the ascent of humankind ever upward on the road toward unlimited improvement? A fundamental belief that emerged as a cornerstone of Enlightenment ideology was the conviction that progress was inevitable and that, in time, the perfect—or at least, near perfect—society would come into existence.

The importance of this new attitude cannot be overstated. For the first time in Western history, people in growing numbers began to believe that the future would be better than the past and that the Golden Age was not some bygone era, but a time yet to be. The history of humankind was not a record of decline—in spite of a long "middle age" of relative darkness that had separated two great periods of civilization, the "ancient" and the "modern" worlds. On the contrary, the Enlightenment held that history, properly conceived, was the story of continuing, if somewhat uneven, human progress. The present, for all its problems, was better than the past. Far more exciting, and as a direct consequence of the emergence of scientific and enlightened thinking, the future would be far better than the present. Whereas Christian cosmology held forth the prospect of a better life only after death, the Enlightenment ideology promised a state in which all would be happy in this world—and within the near future.

A New View of Human Nature

The belief in progress that captured the imagination and aspirations of Enlightenment thinkers was based on yet another revolutionary aspect of the new cosmology. That new aspect was the abandonment of the traditional biblical teaching of the natural sinfulness of man and the acceptance instead of a modified if not totally opposite view. Just as the eighteenth century was about to dawn, John Locke launched the assault on the doctrine that humans are by nature "evil" when he rejected the concept of "innate ideas" and asserted that the human mind starts as a *tabula rasa* or "blank tablet"—"a white paper void of all characters." We know what we know and become what we become, Locke reasoned, because of our experiences and sensations and our reflections on those experiences and sensations. If we do evil things, it is not because it is in our nature to do so, said Locke, but because of the experiences or environmental influences that have shaped us and to which we have grown accustomed.[6]

In 1762, Jean Jacques Rousseau moved the enlightened view of human nature even farther away from the curse of Adam when he wrote in the opening sentence of *Émile*: "Everything is good as it comes from the hands of the Maker of the world but degenerates once it gets into the hands of man." Similarly, Rousseau began *The Social Contract*, published in the same year, by asserting: "Man is born free; and everywhere he is in chains." With Locke, Rousseau believed that every person is shaped by education or experience, but Rousseau's basic premise was strikingly different: man is not born merely neutral or malleable, but definitely "good" and, ideally, at least, free. It is our artificial, unnatural, and degenerate environment that corrupts and enslaves, proclaimed Rousseau.[7]

The Faith of the Enlightened

Point by point, the ideology of the Enlightenment crashed headlong into long-held beliefs and powerful institutions, not the least of which were many associated with traditional Christianity. For some who eagerly placed their faith in the new ideology, neither Christianity nor any other conventional religion seemed capable of passing the test of reasonableness. At the extreme were some of the newly enlightened who proudly proclaimed themselves atheists. Unlike skeptics or agnostics, atheists had no doubt about God's existence: they were convinced that He did not exist. There was no need for a God. The universe, these materialists maintained, was a system of "matter" in motion, a system that could be understood fully by the use of human reason and scientific investigation. To many atheists, then as now, their assertion became a positive belief, a definite form of faith—in its own strange way, a kind of religion that they embraced devoutly.[8]

If atheism or agnosticism appealed to some whose faith in the traditional Christian religion was shaken, others followed the dictates of reason toward a different set of conclusions. Some of the enlightened in the eighteenth century, including such leading figures as Voltaire and Condorcet in France and Franklin and Jefferson in America, found in deism a comfortable compromise between conventional Christianity and stern rationalism. Deists tended to believe firmly in the existence of God. To the deist, God *had* to exist. His existence was made evident by two very old, and to them, solid arguments: the argument from a First Cause, and the argument from Design. More simply put, God was the Supreme Craftsman, the Great Clockmaker who created the universe and set it in motion according to laws of His design. Unlike the personal and intervening God of the Jews and the Christians, however, God as envisioned by deists had no cause to interfere with His creation after the fact. God had wound up His clock-universe at the moment of creation, and ever since it had been running and would run for all eternity according to the laws Newton and others were now discovering and explaining. As part of God's creation, humans were on their own, save for the power to use their reason to discover and live in accordance with the laws God had designed to govern the universe.

Although some deists, on occasion, claimed to be good Christians, typically they rejected the mysteries and miracles that to the orthodox were essential to the faith. The French philosopher Voltaire illustrates well the religious passion and rejection of "fundamentalism"—a characteristic of some of the enlightened. Early one morning in 1774, the aged philosopher asked a visitor at Ferney to join him to see the sunrise. The two friends made a strenuous climb and then rested on a hill to survey the magnificent panorama about to unfold before them. As the sun appeared in radiant splendor, Voltaire turned toward the heavens and declared: "I believe! I believe in you! Powerful God, I believe!" Then he rose, looked at his friend, and added dryly: "As for monsieur the Son, and madame His Mother, that's a different story."[9] Thomas Paine, the American patriot whose call to reason is well known, was more direct. "The Christian system of religion," he wrote in 1804, "is an outrage on common sense. Why is man afraid to think?"[10]

Certainly there were men and women of the Enlightenment as in our own times who managed to reconcile their religious faith with acceptance of scientific knowledge. If the answers to some questions appeared to be contradictory or shrouded in mystery, eventually the light of reason would provide the illumination necessary for clearer understanding. In the meantime, the faithful followers of the Enlightenment—whatever their particular spiritual beliefs— embraced the idea that life here on earth could be made better. If sin existed, it was the sin of ignorance. The faith of the Enlightenment was a faith that reason could remove ignorance and that human nature, if not inherently good and perfectible, was at least improvable. It was possible, they maintained, to improve human institutions and thus humanity itself. It was possible, through the use of intelligent action, to engage in *reform*.

Basic to the reform agenda that took root in the eighteenth century was a rising faith in the potential of *education* or *enlightenment* as the key weapon in the fight against ignorance and injustice. However, in constant tension with that faith was the uneasy and deep-seated fear that the American experiment in enlightened progress and self-government might yet fail, that ignorance might defeat reason after all.[11]

Enlightenment, Education, and the Republican Experiment

The fifty-six men who, in the summer of 1776, pledged their lives, their fortunes, and their sacred honor in support of a set of ideals did so in the belief that they were starting the world anew. Their Enlightenment faith was eloquently expressed by Thomas Jefferson in the Declaration of Independence:

> We hold these truths to be self evident: that all men are created equal; that they are endowed by their Creator with certain inalienable rights; that among these are life, liberty, and the pursuit of happiness; that to secure these rights, governments are instituted among men, deriving their just powers from the consent of the governed; that whenever any form of government becomes destructive of these ends, it is the right of the people to alter or abolish it, and to institute new government, laying its foundations on such principles, and organizing its powers in such form, as to them shall seem most likely to effect their safety and happiness.[12]

As stirring as were Jefferson's words and as committed as he and his compatriots were, the outcome of the Revolution was not at all certain. Of the 2.5 million "Americans" in 1776, considerably less than half initially sided with Jefferson and the Whigs who advocated Enlightenment ideals and revolutionary change. Perhaps another third or more, including most of the slave and Native American populations, opposed the insurrection, while the remainder of the inhabitants were too concerned with their own personal affairs to care much one way or the other about the outcome.[13]

Descendants of Africans composed about 20 percent of the total population in 1776. All but about 25,000 were slaves, many of whom realized rather quickly that the Revolution was not intended to benefit them. During the war at least 20,000 slaves escaped and signed on as laborers or soldiers in the British

Figure 3.1 Reenactment of the signing of the Declaration of Independence, Independence Hall, Philadelphia, PA.

Credit: Value RF © Comstock/Corbis

Army, although approximately 5,000 African Americans, some slave and some free, did fight for the Continental forces. Native Americans, who also had good reason to resent the white colonists, tended to support the Crown against the Revolutionaries, but here too there were exceptions.

Even though the American Revolution was initially a "minority movement," the leaders of the rebellion began immediately to lay plans for a new nation—or rather, at the outset, a confederation of thirteen independent nations. The Articles of Confederation that were ratified by each of the states in 1781 reserved to each state "its sovereignty, freedom and independence" and established a form of government in which Americans were citizens of their own states first and of the United States second. The new American states' distrust of England was matched by an almost similar distrust of each other.

It was in this context that various American statesmen and men of letters turned their attention to education. There was little or no debate about the necessity of having an educated leadership class. There was considerably less agreement, however, about how much formal education, if any, should be extended to the general population.

There were some, following the lead of Jefferson, who firmly believed that the new states (and eventually, the new nation), could not survive long if the general population remained ignorant of the "true" laws of government and social order that were being discovered by enlightened inquiry. Jefferson informed a friend in 1816 that "If a nation expects to be ignorant and free, in a state of civilization, it expects what never was and never will be." He had expressed similar sentiments thirty years earlier when he wrote to George Washington: "It is an axiom in my mind that our liberty can never be safe but in the hands of the people themselves, and that too of the people with a certain degree of instruction." Jefferson pointedly added: "This it is the business of the state to effect, and on a general plan."[14]

To Jefferson and Washington, as well as to a number of other "Founding Fathers," it was one thing to make stirring declarations about independence and inalienable rights; it was another to cooperate in the prosecution of the war. It would be another matter still, after the war, to maintain the newly proclaimed rights and liberties if ignorance, apathy, or distrust characterized the population. Education, then, emerged as an essential consideration in the minds of those who faced the momentous task of establishing the new nation. As various spokesmen articulated their political goals, some of the most thoughtful also set forth educational "reform" proposals. In so doing, these architects of the American nation clearly and deliberately fused educational theory with political theory.

Education also took on a new importance in terms of its role in the individual pursuit of happiness. Well before the Revolution, Benjamin Franklin had articulated another strain of Enlightenment doctrine when he stressed that education should be useful and should contribute to the self-advancement of young men on the rise in society. As noted in the previous chapter, in the middle of the eighteenth century Franklin had encouraged his fellow citizens in Philadelphia to create a new type of school, an academy, that would offer practical as well as classical studies. Others picked up on Franklin's concern for an education "useful" to Americans. Thus, hand in hand with attempts to design arrangements that would serve *political ends* and the *social good* were attempts to determine the type of education most appropriate for the *individual good* of the enterprising American people. What indeed was to be the character of the new American society and the new American citizen? What kind and how much formal schooling did Americans need? Who should provide it? To what degree should schooling be public in terms of support and access? Such questions concerning the conduct and content, or the means and ends of schooling, were from the very founding of our nation intensely political and sometimes bitterly contested educational issues. No one was more directly involved in proposing answers to these questions than Thomas Jefferson.[15]

Jefferson and Education for Republican Citizenship

Having completed his momentous work as a member of the Continental Congress, Jefferson left Philadelphia in the fall of 1776 and returned to Virginia, eager to take up the business of framing a new government for his commonwealth. He took his seat as a member of the House of Delegates in October, determined to take full advantage of every opportunity to translate human rights into legal forms. Jefferson played the leading role as a member of a special legislative committee appointed to review and revise the laws of Virginia. Within a period of three years, 1776–1779, Jefferson and his fellow committeemen, George Wythe and Edmund Pendleton, drafted 126 bills. More than 50 of those bills were enacted into law by 1786.

Among the proposals that Jefferson advanced were several designed explicitly to "lay the ax to the roots of pseudo-aristocracy." These included measures to end inheritance practices circumscribed by the legal doctrines of "entails" and "primogeniture." In both Europe and the American colonies, these traditions had long served to keep large parcels of land intact. The doctrine of entails enabled wealthy landowners to place binding restrictions on inheritances down through the generations, while primogeniture specified that, unless a will stipulated otherwise, the entire estate would pass directly to the first-born son. By these customs, the power and wealth of a narrow landed aristocracy could be perpetuated indefinitely.[16]

Jefferson certainly did not oppose ownership of property and, in concert with other gentry of his day, believed that the right to vote should be restricted to property owners, those who had a stake or investment in society. Jefferson, however, thought it vital to expand the opportunity for land ownership and thus include new arrivals and poorer people in the social contract. In a draft of a new constitution for Virginia, he proposed that at least 50 acres of land (and thus the franchise) should be provided to every citizen. Jefferson's draft of a constitution for his native state was not adopted by the legislature, and thus

Figure 3.2 Thomas Jefferson.
Life Portrait by Rembrandt Peale, 1800.

Credit: Courtesy, Special Collections, University of Virginia Library.

his notion of providing a grant of land to every citizen—as well as another provision designed to effect the gradual emancipation of slaves—was quietly laid to rest.

Although these and a number of other progressive legislative and constitutional recommendations made by Jefferson failed to gain adoption, a bill that did win approval was his Statute of Virginia for Religious Freedom. This act, which "disestablished" the Anglican Church in Virginia, was later prized by Jefferson as second only to the Declaration of Independence in fostering liberty. The act for religious freedom declared that no one could be compelled to attend any church or be made to support any religion not of his own choosing; that no one could be made to suffer reprisals for belief or non-belief in religion; that, in sum, "all men shall be free to profess, and by argument to maintain, their opinions in matters of religion, and that the same shall in no wise diminish, enlarge, or affect their civil capacities."[17]

The Bill for the More General Diffusion of Knowledge

There was, however, yet another bill that Jefferson considered to be of tremendous importance. He wrote to George Wythe that Bill Number 79, the "Bill for the More General Diffusion of Knowledge," was "by far the most important bill in our whole code." Years later he confided to John Adams that, had this education bill been adopted by the legislature, "our work would have been complete."[18]

Jefferson's education bill, drafted in 1778, came before the legislature in June 1779. His plan called for the division of counties into wards or "hundreds." Jefferson envisioned each ward functioning as a "little republic" in which local citizens would provide for an elementary school to which "all the free children, male and female," would be admitted without charge. Schooling at this level would equip all citizens with the basic literacy and computational skills they would need in order to manage their own affairs. Furthermore, Jefferson recommended that these elementary schools provide for the study of ancient and modern history along with reading, writing, and arithmetic. The study of history, he contended, would improve the citizens' moral and civic virtues and enable them to know and exercise their rights and duties. Essentially then, Jefferson conceived of elementary education as basic education for citizenship; it was to be a public investment in the possibility of self-government and human happiness, at both the individual and the social levels.

For the majority of boys and for all the girls, publicly supported schooling would end after three years. Of course, children whose families could afford to pay for additional years of education could remain in school for as long as their parents or guardians thought proper. Jefferson's scheme of public support of and provision for education was not set up in opposition to private schooling. Rather, his plan was based on the proposition that, in a free society, the "public" had a vital interest in providing for equality of opportunity and responsible citizenship. In fulfilling this obligation, the right of individuals to opt for alternative or additional schooling was not challenged.

With these local elementary schools serving as a base, Jefferson's bill called for a second tier of 20 boarding schools placed at convenient locations throughout the state. These secondary schools, which were to receive public subsidies, were to accept each year, without charge, the most promising boy from each of the lower schools scattered throughout every county. By means of a rather rigorous selection process, the ranks of these publicly supported scholars would be thinned over the next two years until in each secondary school only one student, the most promising in intellect and character (and whose parents were unable to pay the tuition), would remain on a "scholarship" for four additional years of study. By this means, Jefferson later wrote, "twenty of the best geniuses will be raked from the rubbish annually, and be instructed, at the public expense, so far as the grammar schools go." Upon completion of this college preparatory phase, half of these students—in odd numbered years, those living south and west of the James River, and in even numbered years, those living north and east of that line—would then receive public support to attend the College of William and Mary. In a companion bill, Jefferson proposed that William and Mary, his alma mater, be made more modern academically and converted into a state university that would be the capstone of a complete educational pyramid.[19]

Jefferson's commitment to the idea of a system of education based on public support grew directly out of his concept of classical democracy and his vision of America as a virtuous and enlightened republic. He believed that humans were by nature social and were morally equipped for life in a political community. However, he held that only as a result of proper civic education and active participation in community life could individuals refine their sense of republican virtue and thus secure themselves against oppression and tyranny. The extension of a basic degree of education to the citizenry was necessary, wrote Jefferson to John Adams, in order "to raise the mass of the people to the high ground of moral respectability necessary to their own safety, and to orderly government." In a letter to James Madison, Jefferson acknowledged that "I am not a friend to a very energetic government. It is always oppressive." Nonetheless, he stressed to Madison that "the most certain, and the most legitimate engine of government" is providing for the education of the people. "The people," Jefferson stated, "are the only sure reliance for the preservation of our liberty."[20]

Educating the Natural Aristocracy

Jefferson's plan for a general system of education embodied both democratic and meritocratic principles. He believed that his scheme would provide opportunity for virtuous and talented youngsters, members of the "natural aristocracy" who were to be found in every segment of society. If given a chance—equal opportunity—children from undistinguished backgrounds might compete successfully against those of the "artificial aristocracy." This latter group, Jefferson said, often lacked either virtue or talent. Jefferson was well aware that children born into wealth not only had the advantage of a head start in life but, in essence, were guaranteed a spot at the finish line. Jefferson's intention was to open up the race to commoners and, if their talents warranted, to have them take their place in the winner's circle.

Underlying Jefferson's educational and political theory was the conviction that academic competition and the cultivation of the best and the brightest ought not to be used primarily as a pathway to material gain and the private pursuit of happiness. Rather, equal educational opportunity was to allow the identification and proper education of those capable of leadership and worthy of public trust. Jefferson placed himself in opposition to those of his own social background, many of whom constituted the "artificial aristocracy." Content with private education for their own children, they were willing to leave the education of others to random local initiative, church benevolence, or perhaps to the well-meaning charity of a concerned citizen benefactor. To Jefferson, however, the education required for participation and leadership in the new American social order was far too important to be left to chance, parental whim, or restricted to a traditional elite.

Frustrated by the refusal of his native state to move forward with his educational plan, Jefferson nonetheless threw himself into other educational ventures. He continued to refine his ideas regarding a state-wide system of schools and even gave serious thought for a time to the idea of creating a national university. Jefferson founded the United States Military Academy at West Point in 1802, giving life to an institution not only designed to educate military engineers, but that eventually could evolve into a branch of the national university. Jefferson and the Academy's Superintendent, Colonel Jonathan Williams, conspired unsuccessfully in plans to move the Military Academy from West Point to the nation's capital.

It is worth noting as well that throughout his Presidency, 1801–1809, Jefferson also served as President of the Washington, D.C. School Board. In spite of his own increasing indebtedness, he contributed $200 to the campaign undertaken to initiate the building of the first two public elementary schools to open in the District. He also served as President of the American Philosophical Society headquartered in Philadelphia at the same time, thus acting on his advocacy of education from the primary level to the most advanced studies at the university level and beyond.[21]

Jefferson's provisions in his 1779 bill and in a similar proposal in 1817 certainly did not place upon the schools the total burden of maintaining freedom and enlightenment. His education bills were only a part, although an essential part, of a complete system of laws and institutions designed to protect the rights boldly proclaimed in the Declaration of Independence. In addition to formal schooling, Jefferson, like Franklin, valued and encouraged informal approaches to education. He frequently advised friends and relatives on the best methods of educating their children and proposed, along with the 1779 education bill, the establishment in Richmond of a public research library. Years later, expressing concern for the continuing education of the adult population, he recommended the creation of small circulating libraries in every county.

Jefferson was also highly conscious of the educational value of a free press and declared on one occasion: "The basis of our government being the opinion of the people, the very first object should be to keep that right; and were it left to me to decide whether we should have a government without newspapers, or newspapers without a government, I should not hesitate a moment to prefer the latter." Jefferson promptly added, however: "But I should mean that every man should receive those papers and be capable of reading them."[22]

When viewed in the light of later developments, Jefferson's educational ideas and proposals may seem quite modest. After all, his major legislative initiative would have granted only limited education to the white female population and made no provision at all for Native or African Americans, slave or free. Even so, during the Revolutionary era and in later years, his efforts to extend educational opportunity to the citizenry at public expense proved to be much too radical—and much too expensive—to win the favor of the Virginia legislature. In 1819, forty years after Jefferson had begun his "crusade against ignorance," he realized only partial success with his plan when the legislature granted a charter for the creation of the University of Virginia, the institution that in fact became the "capstone" of his proposed educational edifice. As proud as he was of this accomplishment, however, it represented but a part, although surely an important part, of his larger scheme.

Thomas Jefferson did not live long enough to see a system of publicly supported elementary and secondary schools established as the foundation of a complete system of education in Virginia. To have done so, he would have had to live yet another forty years and more—too much to expect, one is tempted to say, even of Thomas Jefferson! Thus, when Jefferson died on July 4, 1826, at the age of 83, educational opportunity in his state was still limited largely to the sons of the artificial aristocracy.[23]

Other Theorists and Educational Plans

Thomas Jefferson was by no means alone in his concern over the educational requirements of the new nation. A number of other prominent Americans, some of whom differed quite sharply with Jefferson (and each other) on certain political, religious, and educational particulars, nonetheless shared his general sense of urgency regarding the necessity of a new form of education for the new nation. And well they might. On both sides of the Atlantic there were predictions that the American experiment in political and cultural independence was destined to fail. Many believed that the American Revolution was less likely to go down in history as an act of national independence than as an act of national suicide.

Fear of failure can be a mighty stimulus to action. David Tyack has insightfully suggested that, just as the Puritans had experienced frustration and feared failure in their errand into the wilderness, "so too many leaders in the early Republic, charged with a deep sense of destiny, masked a dark vein of anxiety by assertive nationalism." Newly self-conscious American nationalists saw internal disorder and the rise of political factions as ominous threats to enlightened self-government and the fragile concept of republican community. In their determination to turn the tide and save the republic, Federalists (Whigs) and Anti-Federalists (Jeffersonian Republicans) alike turned to education for national salvation.[24]

Benjamin Rush and "Republican Machines"

Benjamin Rush, a professor of chemistry and medicine at the University of Pennsylvania, had served as surgeon general of the Continental Army during the Revolution. Rush was among those patriots who believed that the new

American citizen and a new American culture were yet to be created. A decade after Rush had signed his name to the Declaration of Independence, he reminded a correspondent that the war for independence was only "the first act of the great drama. We have changed our forms of government," he wrote, "but it remains yet to effect a revolution in principles, opinions, and manners so as to accommodate them to the forms of government we have adopted."[25]

The revolution in principles, opinions, and manners Rush thought essential for republican citizens was to be effected in large measure through education. To the patriotic Rush, as well as to George Washington, Noah Webster, Thomas Jefferson, and some other notable Americans of the Revolutionary generation, it was a given that their countrymen should be educated at home, not abroad. From 1766 to 1769, while in his early twenties, Rush himself had studied medicine at the University of Edinburgh. That, however, was before the War for Independence and after, he might say, his attachment to his homeland was firmly fixed. As he put the issue in 1786, "The principle of patriotism stands in need of the reinforcement of prejudice, and it is well known that our strongest prejudices in favor of our country are formed in the first one and twenty years of our lives." Jefferson likewise maintained that "the consequences of foreign education are alarming to me as an American" and observed that the men "most beloved by their country and most trusted and promoted by them" are those who have been educated among them. So strongly did the Georgia legislature feel on this matter that it passed a law in 1785 disbarring its residents from civic office for as many years as they had studied abroad.[26]

Writing in 1786, before the Constitution had been adopted and thus while the future direction of the country was still very much in doubt, Rush issued a call for a comprehensive system of education in Pennsylvania that was in many respects similar to Jefferson's plan for Virginia.[27] Rush announced that "the business of education has acquired a new complexion by the independence of our country." The new form of government carried with it new duties and responsibilities, he advised, and thus American ideas on education needed to be altered accordingly. To those who would argue that the tax burden to support these schools would be too great, Rush countered that "These institutions are designed to lessen our taxes." Education would increase our understanding of finance, promote more profitable agriculture and manufacturing, and lead to improvements in transportation. More to the point, Rush argued:

> But, shall the estates of orphans, bachelors, and persons who have no children be taxed to pay for the support of schools from which they can derive no benefit? I answer in the affirmative to the first part of the objection, and I deny the truth of the latter part of it. . . . The bachelor will in time save his tax for this purpose by being able to sleep with fewer bolts and locks on his doors, the estates of orphans will in time be benefitted by being protected from the ravages of unprincipled and idle boys, and

the children of wealthy parents will be less tempted, by bad company, to extravagance. Fewer pillories and whipping posts and smaller jails, with their usual expenses and taxes, will be necessary when our youth are properly educated than at present.

Rush then suggested that the expenses of confining, trying, and executing criminals each year would doubtless exceed the cost of maintaining the schools he proposed. In making this appeal, Rush was advancing an argument in favor of public support of education that would reappear in every generation.[28]

Even though Rush in this particular document proposed a plan of education for Pennsylvania, his proposal by extension applied to the needs of the American people in general. The national reach of his ideas was anticipated in his contention that "Our schools of learning, by producing one general and uniform system of education, will render the mass of the people more homogeneous and thereby fit them more easily for uniform and peaceable government."[29]

The homogeneity desired by Rush frames in bold relief what David Tyack alluded to as "a fundamental tension and paradox in republican educational theory." Tyack pointed out that Rush and others maintained that, in order for freedom to exist, restraints have to be internalized by the citizenry. American liberty was to be ordered or bounded liberty. A degree of shared understandings and even conformity was considered necessary in order for Americans to enjoy freedom without loosening the common bonds that united them in a republican society. Rush could see no irony in proclaiming that it was possible (and desirable) to convert men into "republican machines." Indeed, the Philadelphia physician declared that "this must be done if we expect them to perform their parts properly in the great machine of the government of the state." To avoid the evils of tyranny, Rush contended somewhat paradoxically, the wills or sentiments of the people "must be fitted to each other by means of education before they can be made to produce regularity and unison in government."[30]

Rush was quite explicit in identifying the attributes of a sound republican education and the sentiments and duties that marked the homogeneous republican citizen. He held that republican education and citizenship must be grounded in religion. "Without this," he asserted, "there can be no virtue, and without virtue there can be no liberty, and liberty is the object and life of all republican governments." Rush expressed veneration for every religion that revealed the attributes of the Deity, but left no doubt about his belief that Christianity was best suited to promote the happiness of society and the well-being of civil government. "A Christian cannot fail of being a republican," he stated. Maintaining that the story of the creation of man in the Old Testament "is the best refutation that can be given to the divine right of kings and the strongest argument that can be used in favor of the original and natural equality of all mankind," Rush reasoned further:

A Christian, I say again, cannot fail of being a republican, for every precept of the Gospel inculcates those degrees of humility, self-denial, and brotherly kindness which are directly opposed to the pride of monarchy and pageantry of a court. A Christian cannot fail of being useful to the republic, for his religion teacheth him that no man "liveth to himself." And lastly, a Christian cannot fail of being wholly inoffensive, for his religion teacheth him in all things to do to others what he would wish, in like circumstances, they should do to him.[31]

Rush did not stop with an advocacy of some sort of "general Christianity" in the education process. He thought it "necessary to impose" upon children the doctrines and discipline of a particular denomination, although he refrained from recommending one denomination above all others. That determination was to be left to parental choice.

In essence, Rush was advocating public support for the establishment of religious schools. In contrast to Jefferson, he did not believe that sectarian religion was harmful. Rather, he was convinced that the best way to ensure universal education was to allow each sect to educate children in the faith of their parents. He believed that doctrinal differences were gradually giving way to a common and unified set of values toward which each sect could make its own unique contribution. Not surprisingly in light of his religious views, Rush favored the use of the Bible as a schoolbook, although some devout Christians frowned upon the practice as being too casual toward and disrespectful of religion. Noah Webster, for example, observed that the Bible "is as common as a newspaper and in schools is read with nearly the same degree of respect."[32]

To Rush, nonetheless, love of country was next only to love of God. In his advocacy of unqualified patriotism, he did not shrink from charges of political indoctrination. He insisted that while American children should be taught to love their fellow creatures in every part of the world, it was essential that they be taught to "cherish with a more intense and peculiar affection the citizens of Pennsylvania and of the United States." He admonished further: "Let our pupil be taught that he does not belong to himself, but that he is public property. Let him be taught to love his family, but let him be taught at the same time that he must forsake and even forget them when the welfare of his country requires it." To Rush it was Sparta, not Athens, that offered the best ideal of patriotism.[33]

Rush's educational plans broadened and became more explicitly nationalistic when, in the 29 October 1788 issue of the *Philadelphia Federal Gazette*, he proposed that one of the first acts of the new Congress should be to create a federal university. The year before Rush made his proposal, the Continental Congress had enacted the Northwest Ordinance (Land Ordinance of 1787), which proclaimed that in the western lands surveyed under terms of the Ordinance of 1785, "religion, morality, and knowledge, being necessary to good government and the happiness of mankind, schools and the means of education shall forever be encouraged." The Land Ordinance of 1785 had specified that the sixteenth section of each township laid out in the new territories to the north and west of the Ohio River should be set aside for the funding of public schools. Thus, in terms of federal support for education, it can be argued that there was precedent for Rush's proposal. However, Rush's plan called for more than federal support or encouragement: It specified federal *establishment*.

The institution Rush envisioned was to provide the culminating educational experience for graduates of public and private colleges throughout the states who aspired to positions of responsibility in the new nation. Rush was so convinced that the federal university could furnish exemplary republican leaders that he proposed that within 30 years after the institution opened, Congress should legislate that no person could be "chosen or appointed into power or office who has not taken a degree in the federal university." Rush concluded his proposal by arguing that the United States could not hope to survive without an educated leadership group that shared common principles. He reasoned:

> We shall never restore public credit, regulate our militia, build a navy, or revive our commerce, until we remove the ignorance and prejudices, and change the habits of our citizens, and this can never be done 'till we inspire them with federal principles, which can only be effected by our young men meeting and spending two or three years together in a national University, and afterwards disseminating their knowledge and principles through every county, township and village of the United States. 'Till this be done—Senators and Representatives of the United States, you will undertake to make bricks without straw. Your supposed union in Congress will be a rope of sand.[34]

Others, including some members of the Constitutional Convention, saw merit in the proposal to create a federal university. The idea was debated seriously in committee by the drafters of the Constitution, but in the end a majority of the delegates in the Committee on Detail determined that it would be unwise to burden the Constitution with too many specifics.

Although the Constitution as adopted made no mention of education, it was taken for granted by some that Congress could in fact launch a federal university and undertake other projects to advance the general welfare whenever it decided to do so, with or without specific Constitutional authorization. Even after the adoption of Article X, which clearly circumscribed federal power, each of the first six presidents of the United States at one time or another agreed on the desirability of establishing a national university. George Washington referred to the idea in his first annual message to Congress in 1790, devoted part of his "Farewell Address" to the measure in 1796, and even pledged his personal financial support for the institution. Thomas Jefferson, a self-declared opponent of "energetic government," nonetheless as president encouraged Congress to consider amending the Constitution if necessary in order to promote a version of the plan submitted by Joel Barlow in 1806. James

Madison reiterated familiar themes in 1810 when he argued that a national university would enlighten the opinions, expand the patriotism, and harmonize the principles of those who attended it, thereby strengthening the foundations "of our free and happy system of government."[35]

In spite of presidential support for the national university idea and initiatives such as the ordinances of 1785 and 1787, it remained basically at the local and state, not the federal level, that governments made provision for the public support of education at all levels. Seven of the 14 states that had joined the Union by 1800 had made explicit in their constitutions state responsibility for education. In time all states were to do so. Beginning with Georgia in 1785 and then North Carolina in 1789, legislatures began chartering "state universities." In many sections of the emerging nation, the enterprise of religious denominations and booster spirit of men of standing in local communities figured even more prominently in college and university development than did state initiative. Although Rush developed elaborate plans for governmental involvement in education, he himself testified to the strength of local initiative by playing a prominent role in the founding of Dickinson College.

Noah Webster and the Vocabulary of Republicanism

Noah Webster, whose "blue-backed" *American Spelling Book* and *American Dictionary of the English Language* did much to help define the new nation, also had some very definite ideas about the educational needs of the new American nation. A schoolmaster and later a founder of Amherst College, Webster was in full agreement with Jefferson and Rush regarding the need for an educated citizenry as well as an educated leadership class. Indeed, he considered the role of education so central to the working of a free government that he flatly asserted it to be the most important business in civil society.

Although he was basically in agreement with Jefferson and Rush regarding the need for the general diffusion of knowledge, Webster, as a Federalist, worried that republican government might foster too much freedom and thus fall victim to anarchy. Webster wanted America to be composed of "quiet Christians," citizens educated to be humble, devout, and submissive to legitimate authority. His disagreement with Rush over the value of Bible reading in schools was grounded, not in a greater degree of tolerance, but rather in his fear that "familiarity, contracted by a careless disrespectful reading of the sacred volume," would weaken rather than strengthen its message. "My wish," he said in this regard, "is not to see the Bible excluded from schools but to see it is used as a system of religion and morality." Thus, unlike Jefferson, whose main concern tended to be the extension of liberty, for Webster as for Rush, the greater concern was to promote "order" and to prevent social disruption.[36]

Webster used the pages of his own *American Magazine* as well as his schoolbooks to popularize his views on education. In a series of essays published during 1787 and 1788, Webster argued for a system of education that would "implant in the minds of American youth the principles of virtue and liberty" and at the same time would inculcate "an inviolable attachment to their own country." This required, he said, less attention to dead languages and more attention to our own. In common with Franklin, he held that "what is now called a *liberal education* disqualifies a man for business," and he urged that young people be given more opportunity to acquire knowledge related directly to their occupational callings. He condemned the lax manner in which parents chose instructors for their children, and found it contemptible that "the most important business in civil society" is in many places "committed to the most worthless characters." Webster maintained that "it is better for youth to have *no* education than to have a bad one, for it is more difficult to eradicate habits than to impress new ideas."[37]

Webster was explicit about the "new ideas" he thought should be inculcated in American youth. In addition to the principles of Christian morality, the basics of language and mathematics, and skills useful in commerce, Webster wrote that, as soon as children were capable of receiving instruction, they should be taught American history. As he put it, "As soon as [the child] opens his lips, he should rehearse the history of his own country; he should lisp the praise of liberty and of those illustrious heroes and statesmen who have wrought a revolution in her favor." Elsewhere he admonished: "Begin with the infant in his cradle; let the first word he lisps be 'Washington.'"[38]

Believing that America should become free of European domination in literature and language as well as in politics and social practices, Webster devoted himself to shaping an American language as the basic structure by which to define the American character. In essence calling for an American revolution at the linguistic level, Webster asserted in 1789 that "As an independent nation, our honor requires us to have a system of our own, in language as well as government. Great Britain, whose children we are, and whose language we speak, should no longer be our standard; for the taste of her writers is already corrupted, and her language on the decline." He gave further testimony to the potentially corrupting influence of European linguistic as well as political and social forms when he warned: "For America in her infancy to adopt the maxims of the old world would be to stamp the wrinkles of old age upon the bloom of youth, and to plant the seeds of decay in a vigorous constitution."[39]

Webster's dictionary, speller, and other texts were designed to instill the "correct" rules of spelling, pronunciation, and grammar—and moral precepts—that would bind Americans together. His aim was nationalistic: "to diffuse uniformity and purity" in the language that would remove regional and ethnic variations in dialect and at the same time free Americans from European habits of thought.

In a society marked by regional and ethnic diversity, common pronunciation and proper diction would prove difficult to attain, no matter how carefully marked were the pronunciation symbols. However, in terms of establishing uniformity of spelling and a shared understanding of word meanings, Webster may be said to have succeeded. In 1825, after devoting twenty-five years of intensive labor to the project, Webster completed his American *Dictionary of the English Language*, consisting of 70,000 entries, all written by hand. By the middle of the nineteenth century, the name "Webster" had become synonymous with "dictionary" in American minds. His speller, the first edition of which was published in 1783, sold 1.5 million copies by 1801; 20 million by 1829; and 75 million by 1875. Moreover, Webster's speller became the model followed by other textbook writers throughout the nineteenth century.[40]

Robert Church and Michael Sedlak have advanced the interesting notion that the power of Webster's speller might also be assessed over time in terms of the popularity of spelling bees in American schools. Even though the spelling bee may have served to ingrain rather than obscure regional peculiarities of speech, there was in the event something of the uniformity and shared understanding that Webster had promised. As Church and Sedlak contend:

> The spelling bee dramatized equality: any person of any background could win and children and their parents could prove their ability to "use" language as well as any person of whatever background. That someone in their community could spell a word from the last pages of Webster's speller assured the people that their village was as good as any other place, whether village or urban cultural center. It also proved that the promises of democracy were real; the most sophisticated and cultured "use" of language, the possession of only the upper classes in despotic Europe, was available to all in America.[41]

Whatever the contributions of the spelling bee and Webster's "blue-backed" speller to American ideas of equality, there is little doubt that his texts had a more profound impact on the development of American education than did his theoretical schemes. The same can be said for some other writers of the period. The first U.S. history textbooks for schoolchildren were compiled in the 1780s and 1790s by John M'Culloch, a Philadelphia printer. These first history texts, essentially composed of cut-and-paste items gleaned from other sources, nonetheless presented an ordered account of American history from its initial settlement to the Revolution. Jedidiah Morse published his *Geography Made Easy* in 1784. His geography provided descriptions of each state's climate, topography, inhabitants, institutions, and commercial basis. Noah Webster's reader, the third volume of his *A Grammatical Institute of the English Language*, published in 1785, soon encountered competition from new entries to the field, such as Caleb Bingham's *The American Preceptor* (1795), Lindley Murray's *The English Reader* (1799), and, in time, William Holmes McGuffey's *Eclectic Reader* (1836) series.

While theorists essayed about grand schemes, textbooks in fact provided what little system there was to education in the early National period. Spellers often contained reading lessons and sometimes even elementary arithmetic problems as well as long lists of words to be memorized. Readers included a wide range of stories, poems, expositions, historical narratives, speeches, and excerpts from belles lettres, all arranged in order of complexity and difficulty, and often followed by catechisms and lists of words to be mastered.

As the eighteenth century drew to a close, a notable shift in the content of readers could be noted. Heavily religious content remained, but it was now more frequently leavened with stories about animals and children, especially tales that illustrated moral lessons. Increasingly, too, orations from Revolutionary days, sketches of Revolutionary heroes, and other patriotic material were included in readers. As the nineteenth century unfolded, and especially after the introduction of the McGuffey readers in the 1830s, stories with patriotic and moralistic content had become standard fare in elementary reading books.[42]

Obviously, one cannot assume that the lessons presented in the textbooks were necessarily taught, much less learned. However, given the relative lack of other information sources available and the "read and memorize" teaching techniques then in vogue, textbooks undoubtedly played a much more important part in defining the content of education in the late eighteenth and early nineteenth centuries than is the case today. The histories, geographies, readers, and companion books offered a view of the world that consistently celebrated the assumed superiority of white Anglo-Saxon Protestant Americans, their heroes, and their institutions. As it happened, the unity so eagerly sought by Jefferson, Rush, Webster, and others was embedded more deeply in the moral and patriotic lessons in the readers, histories, and geographies than in the numerous ephemeral "systems of education" that were proposed during the early National period of our history.

The American Philosophical Society and American Education

The peak of "system building" proposals was reached in the closing years of the eighteenth century. Jefferson, Rush, and Webster may have been among the most notable of the self-appointed advisors to the American people on the subject of republican education, but they were certainly not alone. In addition to fugitive essays published here and there, in 1795 the American Philosophical Society (APS) invited focused attention on the question of "the best system of liberal education and literary instruction, adapted to the genius of the United States," by announcing an essay contest. Offering a prize of $100 for the best entry, the APS called for proposals detailing the best scheme of education suitable for the new republic.

Although only eight essays were submitted, the judges deliberated for a year before reaching a decision, and even then they declared a tie. In December 1797, the announcement was made: The two winning essayists were the Reverend Samuel Knox, a Presbyterian minister who had only recently migrated from Ireland to Bladensburg, Maryland; and Samuel Harrison Smith of Philadelphia. The prize money was divided between the men, and their essays were subsequently published.[43]

The prize-winning essays differed in particulars but carried the same general theme that characterized the proposals of Rush and others. Smith proposed that a board of literature and science be established to create and conduct a national system of education reaching from primary schools up to a national university. In Smith's view, this national board of education, each member of which was to be "distinguished by eminent attainments in some department of learning," should have the power "to determine what authors shall be read or studied" in American schools. The board would also be given authority over a national system of libraries, including the right to direct "all original productions of merit to be introduced into them."[44]

Samuel Knox also recommended a "uniform system of national education." Undoubtedly Knox, like Smith and other essayists, was influenced at least in part by similar plans for a national system of education being advanced in France at about the same time. The compelling desire of educational reformers in both countries was to "educate out" old views associated with monarchies, entrenched ruling classes, and established churches and to "educate in" new views that would advance nationalism and loyalty to the new ideals that had stirred revolution in both countries. As Knox saw the matter, it was of the utmost importance that in the United States, "even the poorest and most uninstructed of its citizens" be made aware early in life of the "happy constitution under which they live" and of the awesome responsibility that citizenship entailed. Republican citizens, he advised—in harmony with other theorists—should be instructed in the principles of good government, religion, and morality. To this end, Knox recommended that teachers in the public schools "begin and end the business of the day with a short and suitable prayer and address to the great source of all knowledge and instruction." As a further aid to the inculcation of correct moral and civic values, Knox recommended a catechism that contained lessons on "natural theology or the proofs of the existence of the Deity from his works," the first principles of ethics, and the basic axioms of republicanism.[45]

The Social Foundations of Republican Theory

Republican Paradoxes

From conservative and liberal theorists alike, the dominant message of the Revolutionary and early National periods was the same: America needed a schoolmaster. The principles of republicanism were not innate; they had to be learned. For some, but certainly not for all, this suggested an "energetic government"—assuming, of course, that the government was to be in the hands of those who were "best qualified" to govern.

The educational rhetoric of this period abounds with paradoxes, especially when theory is compared to practice. Rush Welter has pointed to a number of these paradoxes and strains between the real and the ideal in his insightful *Popular Education and Democratic Thought in America*. For example, Welter noted that republican advocates of education championed the idea that the general diffusion of knowledge would maximize happiness and opportunity for individuals as well as be of benefit to society. For the most part, however, republican theory manifested a far greater concern for the community or the state than for the individual. Republican theorists argued that an educational system should be established by the government, at the state or national level, less out of a concern for individual happiness and advancement than out of concern for the social good. In order for individuals to enjoy the right to pursue happiness, they reasoned, it was essential that they be educated into an understanding of their shared responsibilities and loyalties as republican citizens. Clearly, education was championed more as a social necessity than as any sort of individual right.[46]

Seen in this light, republican educational theory becomes thoroughly utilitarian and instrumental. Just as the Puritans and other religious leaders of the Colonial era saw in education a means of heavenly salvation and earthly social harmony, so too did republican theorists envision educational schemes that would serve the ends of national salvation and social control. Education should be diffused, they contended, in order that the larger good, the republican social order, might be preserved.

For all the talk about extending education to the masses, educational plans and practices of the era remained essentially hierarchical. Jefferson may have desired to "rake geniuses from the rubbish of mankind" to form the ranks of the natural aristocracy, but his plan was not so radical as to remove the existence of the rubbish. Jefferson and the other republican theorists did not envision a Utopian social order composed of citizens equal in all respects. There were to be gradations in education as in society, although merit and talent, not accidents of birth or wealth, ideally would determine one's place in the hierarchy. While acknowledging that Jefferson was clearly not a radical democrat, we would certainly agree with Merle Curti's assertion that Jefferson's quest for genius among the poor and his encouragement of equal opportunity were far more democratic than anything else that existed at the time, or for a long time thereafter.[47]

If the major innovation of the Founders in the realm of educational theory was their explicit commitment to broadening the dissemination of knowledge, one might wonder why so little was accomplished in that regard. Certainly one of the major obstacles was the expense, as James Madison informed Jefferson when his plan for Virginia was voted down in 1786. At the time, Jefferson's argument that the expense of school support would be trifling compared to the cost of ignorance fell largely on deaf ears.

Between 1795 and 1825 nearly every state, following the precedent of Connecticut, established a literary fund, but for the most part those monies were limited to the schooling of paupers. Theorists extolled the necessity and virtues of publicly supported systems of education and common schools, yet as the nineteenth century opened, education still remained largely a random, disorganized, and haphazard affair. The Founders, with a few notable exceptions such as those we have considered in this chapter, continued to follow colonial precedent in devoting public funds to education mainly at the two extremes: colleges and academies (both public and private) for the well-to-do, and pauper schooling for the embarrassing and troublesome poor.

One must also take into account the strong force of tradition in determining the fate of proposals for public schools in the early days of the American republic. In colonial America as in Europe, education had historically been considered an individual or private matter, a concern of family or church, or in tightly knit communities, perhaps a local affair. Whatever its source and form, schooling was, at least for the *parents* of the children, essentially a voluntary affair. It was also an affair involving others of like class, religion, ethnicity, or gender. The notion of truly common schools, open to the rich and poor, girls and boys, and eventually embracing children of all races and conditions, was still an idea that could be grasped only by a few, if any. The American Revolution had changed people's minds on many things, but the adoption of genuine equality of opportunity in education cannot be counted among the changes.

The Outsiders: Women

A few theorists discussed plans for female education, but most of the proposals of the post-Revolutionary era were, in keeping with the social arrangements of the time, limited to the education of the male population. Thomas Jefferson responded to a correspondent in 1818 that female education had "never been a subject of systematic contemplation with me." He nonetheless advised his fellow Virginian on a plan of reading that he had followed with his own daughters. In addition to books carefully selected (with but little fiction, most of which he termed "a mass of trash" and "poison [that] infects the mind"), Jefferson advocated the study of French, dancing, drawing, music (the latter to be attempted only if the girl "has an ear"), and the domestic arts.[48]

Benjamin Rush was among the Revolutionary theorists who gave the matter of female education more thought. He agreed with Jefferson that it was important that women be capable of educating their daughters and "even their sons, should their fathers be lost, or incapable, or inattentive." In an address presented to the board (of which he was a member) of the Young Ladies' Academy in Philadelphia in 1787, he detailed the studies he thought proper for American women. Rush discussed the advantages of a proper command of English grammar, handwriting, arithmetic and bookkeeping, history, biography, travel books, astronomy, and natural philosophy (the latter two recommendations calculated to prevent superstition by "explaining the causes or obviating the effects of natural evil"). Music, dancing, poetry, and moral essays should accompany the study of Christianity as essential ingredients in the shaping of the properly instructed American woman.

Rush parted company with Jefferson regarding the value of French and drawing in the education of women. Rush contended that in Britain, where company and pleasure are the principal occupations of women and daily discourse is maintained with Frenchmen and others who speak that language, its acquisition may be quite necessary. In the United States, however, "where nursery and the kitchen" occupy women's time and there is little occasion to use the language, its study would be a waste of time. To end the matter, Rush stated: "It certainly comports more with female delicacy, as well as with the natural politeness of the French nation, to make it necessary for Frenchmen to learn to speak our language in order to converse with our ladies than for our ladies to learn their language in order to converse with them!" Drawing he dismissed with the observation that the duties of the American woman were so numerous and difficult that little time would be available for this "elegant accomplishment."[49]

Rush certainly recognized the prejudice of the time that made some men object to the education of women. To this objection he gave two responses: First, opposition to female education "springs from the same spirit which opposes the general diffusion of knowledge among the citizens of our republics." Second, and surely in a much less charitable vein, Rush contended that "If men believe that ignorance is favorable to the government of the female sex, they are certainly deceived, for a weak and ignorant woman will always be governed with the greatest difficulty." Women as well as children needed education so that they could be controlled.[50]

There were a few courageous women who, in the midst of Revolutionary fervor, raised their pens in advocacy of a wider sphere of influence for members of their sex in the new society. Abigail Adams urged her husband, John, to "remember the ladies" in the new code of laws, and to give married women protection from tyrannical husbands. She lamented the terrible deficiencies in female education at all levels and challenged her husband by saying, "If we mean to have Heroes, Statesmen and Philosophers, we should have learned women." The awareness of Abigail Adams, Judith Sargent Murray, Mercy Warren, and a few other women who questioned traditional gender relations and educational conventions was rooted in the same Enlightenment faith that motivated their husbands and other patriots, and bespeaks a feminist perspective long before there was a feminist ideology.[51]

The Outcasts: Native and African Americans

The American Revolution was premised on the natural equality of all men. When writing those lines, Jefferson made no distinction among men on the basis of race or color. Yet, in the world in which he lived, however much it was changing for the better for white Americans, a blanket of racism and an institutionalized system of slavery marred the noble dream at the outset.

Jefferson, of course, was not unaware of the contradictions between his proclamations and his complicity in the unholy system. As a young man, heir to plantation slaves, he declared the system morally wrong and an outrage against humanity, yet by circumstance and choice born of economic necessity, he held on to his property. At the onset of his public career he made several efforts to end the system of slavery. As a young lawyer, he accepted a case without fee in which he argued against the law that extended slavery to the descendants of those already in bondage. He pleaded in vain that "we are all born free." As Dumas Malone observed, "such an assertion carried no weight with a practical-minded court in a slave-owning society."[52]

When Jefferson drafted a constitution for Virginia and in the original draft of the Declaration of Independence, he again strongly condemned slavery, but in the first instance his document was bypassed in favor of a committee version, and in the case of the Declaration of Independence, the paragraph condemning the slave trade was deleted. He managed to get the Virginia legislature to pass a measure in 1778 that ended the importation of slaves from abroad, but that measure did little to undermine the institution. As the author of the Ordinance of 1784, by which Virginia was to cede its western lands to the federal government, Jefferson proposed that slavery be prohibited south as well as north of the Ohio River, but he came up one vote shy of the number necessary to endorse his proposal. However, in the better-known Land Ordinance of 1787, slavery was prohibited in the more limited region northwest of the Ohio.

At other times in his life, Jefferson condemned slavery and his own involvement in the system. Nowhere is his hostility to slavery more apparent than in the pages of his *Notes on the State of Virginia*. This book, written in 1781 for a small audience of French savants and not initially intended for publication, carries an indictment by Jefferson against himself and his countrymen as caustic and strident as any made by latter-day abolitionists. He asserted that the system of slavery had produced an "unhappy influence on the manners of our people" and had given rise to "unremitting despotism on the one part, and degrading submissions on the other." He was saddened by the knowledge that the children of slave owners, in imitating the behavior of their parents, gave rein to their worst passions. Children who were thus "nursed, educated, and daily exercised in tyranny," he said, "cannot but be stamped by it with odious peculiarities." Jefferson then painfully and poignantly laid bare the damning contradiction between the ownership of slaves and his and the nation's commitment to liberty and equality. He wrote:

> Can the liberties of a nation be thought secure when we have removed their only firm basis, a conviction in the minds of the people that these liberties are the gift of God? That they are not to be violated but with his wrath? Indeed I tremble for my country when I reflect that God is just: that his justice cannot sleep forever.[53]

Jefferson considered a revolution of the slaves against their masters as a very real possibility, and warned that in such a struggle, "the Almighty has no attribute which can take side with us." He hoped that some way could be found to end slavery without bloodshed, and found some encouragement in the observation that sentiment against slavery had been rising since the outbreak of the American Revolution. Jefferson indulged the belief that, "under the auspices of heaven," the way was being prepared for total emancipation.[54]

It was in connection with his desire to bring an end to slavery that Jefferson gave consideration to the systematic education of African Americans. In 1778 he prepared for the Virginia legislature a plan for the gradual emancipation of slaves. He proposed that all children of slaves born after a certain date be offered training at public expense in farming, the arts, or the sciences, according to their abilities. Upon arriving at adulthood, these descendants of slaves were to be provided with arms, tools, household implements, and domestic animals and then colonized in Africa as "a free and independent people" in alliance with and initially under the protection of the United States. To replace the expatriated slaves, Jefferson recommended the importation of white indentured servants from Europe.[55]

Jefferson's plan for education followed by emancipation represented in his mind the only feasible long-term solution to slavery and the tensions between the races that were a consequence of the "infamous practice." Whatever may have been his fundamental feelings about the mental and moral equality of white Americans, African Americans, and Native Americans—and these views remain subject to debate[56]—Jefferson faced what he perceived to be the realities of the situation and concluded:

> Deep seated prejudices entertained by the whites; ten thousand recollections, by the blacks, of the injuries they have sustained; new provocations; the real distinction which nature had made and many other circumstances will divide us into parties, and produce convulsions, which will probably never end but in the extermination of one or the other race.[57]

Although a few years later Jefferson contemplated freeing his slaves, providing them with 50 acres of land, and letting them remain as sharecroppers along with imported German farmers, he soon let go of this idea and reverted to his earlier, more resigned outlook. His pessimism was as out of character as was his ownership of slaves. As one scholar has noted, Jefferson's failure to find a solution to slavery was more than a personal tragedy: "it was the most conspicuous failure of American democracy, it was the most conspicuous failure of the American Enlightenment."[58]

Jefferson was less ambivalent about the equality of Native Americans with whites. He considered Native Americans equal in intelligence, physical strength, and moral sense to Homo sapiens Europaeus—in essence, they were white people who wore moccasins and breech-clouts. Consequently, he addressed Native Americans in a manner he would never have assumed toward African Americans: "Your blood will mix with ours and will spread with ours over this great land" until the two had become "one people" and "one nation." Jefferson was proud of the fact that both of his daughters had married descendants of Pocahontas and that, in consequence, royal Indian blood flowed in the veins of his grandchildren. By way of interesting contrast, he never boasted of the fact that through the Randolph side of his family he was descended from the British aristocracy.[59]

Jefferson preferred that the federal government rather than religious denominations or private societies "civilize" the Native Americans. As a good Deist, he feared the influence of Christian missionaries among the Native Americans and compared them to tribal medicine men—enemies of progress bent upon keeping the Native Americans in ignorance. Rather than missionaries, Jefferson wanted individuals with the spirit and respect of anthropologists to take the lead in dealings with the Native Americans. As governor of Virginia in 1779, he changed the "Indian School" at the College of William and Mary, which had been established to civilize and Christianize the original Americans, into an institution for studying Native American cultures.

As president, Jefferson could and did take strong measures to remove Native Americans from lands needed for the westward expansion of American society, but he endeavored to convince Native Americans to sell their land for a just price to the government and take up farming with their white neighbors. He held high hopes for the Cherokees, Chickasaws, Creeks, and the Choctaws, who showed a special aptitude as farmers and ranchers. When the Creeks asked to become citizens of the United States, Jefferson endorsed their application as the first step toward the fulfillment of his ideal of amalgamating the two peoples into a single society. He was especially encouraged by the Cherokees, who gave every sign of becoming orderly, industrious, and "virtuous" citizens: They created a written language, established a newspaper, and instituted a representative form of government.[60]

Conclusion

The educational legacy of the Enlightenment, the American Revolution, and the launching of the American experiment in republican government is thus a mixed one. Grand theories of educational systems were proposed, but the actual work of establishing schools of various sorts was undertaken largely at the local level by small groups of individuals. Rather than substantial government subsidies, schools received only erratic support from occasional governmental offerings of land or surplus income; tuition fees; church offerings; individual benefactions; and, especially in New England, local town support. Still, in spite of the random spread of schools and the rather elaborate plans that received attention from enlightened segments of the society, little concerted action was taken on the educational front. Women, Native Americans, and African Americans received only passing notice and, being excluded from citizenship, were essentially outside the scheme of things. While there was a great outpouring of testimonials in favor of extending education to the masses, most states limited their support to institutions of higher education.

In spite of the fears of those who saw the imminent collapse of the American society if government-initiated schooling were not immediately instigated, the country survived its founding years. The United States began the nineteenth century with a patchwork array of educational institutions that, through common books if not common schools, were instilling ideas of Americanism. In one sense, the faith of Jefferson, if not his specific proposals, remained alive. That faith was expressed most clearly in a letter written in 1816:

Enlighten the people generally and tyranny and oppressions of body and mind will vanish like evil spirits at the dawn of day. Although I do not, with some enthusiasts, believe that the human condition will ever advance to such a state of perfection as that there shall no longer be pain or vice in the world, yet I believe it susceptible of much improvement, and most of all in matters of government and religion; and that the diffusion of knowledge among the people is to be the instrument by which it is to be effected.[61]

It would remain for later generations responding to the demands of a rapidly changing society to try once again to create a "system" for the more general diffusion of knowledge.

Further Reading

Bailyn, Bernard. *To Begin the World Anew: The Genius and Ambiguities of the American Founders.* New York: Alfred A. Knopf, 2003. How the framers' provincialism allowed them to spring free of European modes of thought to create something genuinely new, as told by a prize-winning historian.

Crawford, Alan Pell. *Twilight at Monticello: The Final Years of Thomas Jefferson.* New York: Random House, 2008. The story of Jefferson's post-retirement years, 1809–1826, with emphasis on the personal, political, and financial decline that he faced in the closing years of his life.

Cremin, Lawrence. *American Education: The National Experience, 1783–1876.* New York: Harper & Row, 1980. Describes the shaping of the institutions, agencies, and social arrangements that fostered educational growth from the Revolution into the nineteenth century, chronicled in elaborate detail.

Ellis, Joseph J. *American Creation: Triumphs and Tragedies at the Founding of the Republic.* New York: Alfred A. Knopf, 2007. An examination of issues, alliances, and conflicts among the icons of America's founding: Washington, Adams, Jefferson, Madison, and Hamilton.

Ferling, John E. *Setting the World Ablaze: Washington, Adams, Jefferson, and the American Revolution.* New York: Oxford University Press, 2002. A demystification of these three Founding Fathers, transforming them from icons into remarkable, fascinating, and flawed men who were passionate in their struggles to form a new republican nation.

Graff, Harvey J. *The Labyrinths of Literacy: Reflections on Literacy Past and Present*, rev. ed. Pittsburgh: University of Pittsburgh Press, 1995. Essays on the relation of literacy to society and the problem-solving, knowledge-creating, and communication side benefits of the ability to read and write.

Gundersen, Joan R. *To Be Useful to the World: Women in Revolutionary America, 1740–1790.* Chapel Hill: University of North Carolina Press, rev. ed., 2006. An interpretation of the Revolutionary period from the perspective of three women who lived in different circumstances.

Holton, Woody. *Forced Founders: Indians, Debtors, Slaves and the Making of the American Revolution in Virginia.* Chapel Hill: University of North Carolina Press, 1999. An argument that Virginia elites such as Jefferson and Washington joined with leaders from other colonies in declaring independence from Britain partly in response to grassroots rebellions to their own rule.

Ketcham, Ralph. *Framed for Posterity: The Enduring Philosophy of the Constitution.* Lawrence, KS: University Press of Kansas, 1993. An exploration of the debates over the framing of the Constitution with an argument that "original intent" is best discerned by studying the political climate that nourished the Constitution and the Bill of Rights and, more particularly, by understanding the broader meanings, intentions, and purposes of the Framers.

Longaker, Mark Garrett. *Rhetoric and the Republic: Politics, Civic Discourse, and Education in Early America.* Tuskaloosa: University of Alabama Press, 2007. A rhetorical analysis of "Republicanism" and the articulation of education and shifting hegemonies in early America.

Maier, Pauline. *American Scripture: Making the Declaration of Independence.* New York: Vintage Books, 1998. A meticulous and pathbreaking analysis of the popular origins of the document that has defined American nationhood.

Meacham, Jon. *American Gospel: God, the Founding Fathers and the Making of a Nation.* New York: Random House, 2006. A penetrating examination of the role of religion in the United States from the Puritans to Martin Luther King.

Pangle, Lorraine Smith and Thomas L. Pangle. *The Learning of Liberty: The Educational Ideas of the American Founders.* Lawrence, KS: University Press of Kansas, 1993. An analysis of the emergence of the American ideal of a public education that puts civic education at the core, traced in the writings of Franklin, Jefferson, Washington, and other Founders.

Wagoner, Jennings L., Jr. *Jefferson and Education.* Chapel Hill: University of North Carolina Press (Monticello Monograph Series), 2004. Chronicles Jefferson's interest in education and his accomplishments and failures as an advocate of public education in the Revolutionary and early National period of American history.

Wood, Gordon S. *Revolutionary Characters: What Made the Founders Different.* New York: Penguin Press, 2006. An examination of the character of the self-made men who shaped the character of the United States at its founding.

Notes

1. Henry Steele Commager, *Jefferson, Nationalism, and the Enlightenment.* New York: G. Braziller, 1975, p. 3.
2. Although there is considerable debate among historians over the conserving as opposed to the liberating effects of literacy, as well as over definitions and measures of "literacy" itself, it is suggestive that a leading scholar of literacy has maintained that literacy was nearly universal in New England by the eve of the American Revolution. See Kenneth Lockridge, *Literacy in Colonial New England: An Enquiry into the Social Context of Literacy in the Early Modern West.* New York: W. W. Norton, 1974. For a provocative analysis of the state of literacy studies, see Harvey J. Graff, *The Labyrinths of Literacy: Reflections on Literacy Past and Present.* London, New York and Philadelphia: Falmer Press, 1987, especially chap. 6.
3. Crane Brinton, *Ideas and Men: The Story of Western Thought,* 2d ed. Englewood Cliffs, NJ: Prentice-Hall, 1963, p. 289. (Isaac Newton's *Mathematical Principles of Natural Philosophy* was first published in 1687; John Locke's *An Essay on Human Understanding* appeared in 1690.)
4. Clarence J. Karier, *The Individual, Society, and Education: A History of American Educational Ideas,* 2d ed. Urbana: University of Illinois Press, 1986, p. 21.
5. Brinton, *Men and Ideas,* pp. 289–290.
6. See John Locke, *Essay Concerning Human Understanding,* ed. with intro. by A. D. Woozley. Cleveland, OH: World Publishing, [1690], 1964. See also Kenneth D. Benne, "The Gentleman: Locke," in Paul Nash, Andreas M. Kazamias, and Henry J. Perkinson (eds.), *The Educated Man: Studies in the History of Educational Thought.* New York: John Wiley, 1965, pp. 190–223.
7. Jean Jacques Rousseau, *Émile,* trans, by Barbara Foxley. London: J. M. Dent & Sons, [1762], 1911; Rousseau, *The Social Contract,* trans. and intro. by G. D. H. Cole. London [1762], 1913. See also Stanley E. Ballinger, "The Natural Man: Rousseau," in Nash et al. (eds.), *The Educated Man,* pp. 224–246.
8. Brinton, *Men and Ideas,* pp. 300ff.
9. Voltaire as quoted in Peter Gay, *The Enlightenment: An Interpretation,* vol. 1: *The Rise of Modern Paganism.* New York: Alfred A. Knopf, 1968, p. 122.
10. Thomas Paine as quoted by Karier, p. 23. Thomas Jefferson, rejecting charges that he was "anti-Christian," confided to his friend Benjamin Rush that while he was opposed to the "corruptions" of Christianity, he was certainly not opposed "to the genuine precepts of Jesus himself." "I am a Christian," said Jefferson, "in the only sense in which he [Jesus] wished any one to be; sincerely attached to his doctrines, in preference to all others; ascribing to himself every human excellence; and believing he never claimed any other." Thomas Jefferson to Dr. Benjamin Rush, April 21, 1803, in Adrienne Koch and William Peden (eds.), *The Life and Selected Writings of Thomas Jefferson.* New York: Modern Library, 1972, p. 567, emphasis in original.

11. The leaders of the American Revolution were convinced that there existed a "conspiracy" against freedom and that history revealed all too clearly that republics, the most fragile and delicate of political structures, were ever prone to degenerating into anarchy and tyranny. See Bernard Bailyn, *The Ideological Origins of the American Revolution.* Cambridge, MA: Harvard University Press, 1967, esp. chap. IV.
12. Thomas Jefferson, "A Declaration by the Representatives of the United States of America, in General Congress Assembled," in Koch and Peden (eds.), p. 22.
13. See Paul S. Boyer, Clifford E. Clark, Jr., Joseph F. Kett, Thomas L. Purvis, Harvard Sitkoff, and Nancy Woloch, *The Enduring Vision: A History of the American People.* Lexington, MA: D. C. Heath, 1990, pp. 167–168, 181.
14. Thomas Jefferson to Colonel Charles Yancey, January 6, 1816, in Paul L. Ford (ed.), *The Writings of Thomas Jefferson.* New York: G. P. Putnam's Sons, 1892–1899, vol. 10, pp. 1–4; Thomas Jefferson to George Washington, January 4, 1786, in Julian P. Boyd (ed.), *The Papers of Thomas Jefferson.* Princeton, NJ: Princeton University Press, vol. 1, pp. 150–152.
15. See Jennings L. Wagoner, Jr., *Jefferson and Education* (Monticello Monograph Series). Chapel Hill: University of North Carolina Press, 2004.
16. Thomas Jefferson to John Adams, October 28, 1813, in Ford (ed.), vol. 9, pp. 424–430. For a detailed analysis of the history and composition of the "Report of the Committee of Revisors," see Boyd (ed.), vol. 2, pp. 395–665. See also Jefferson's *Autobiography*, in Ford (ed.), vol. 1, pp. 58–69, and Jefferson's commentary in his *Notes on the State of Virginia*, William Peden (ed.), University of North Carolina Press, Chapel Hill [1787], 1954, pp. 135–149.
17. Thomas Jefferson, "An Act for Establishing Religious Freedom [1779]," in Koch and Peden (eds.), pp. 311–313. Some years later Jefferson expressed agreement with a Baptist association in Connecticut in their belief that "religion is a matter which lies solely between man and his God." It was in this letter that Jefferson insisted that there should be "a wall of separation between Church and State." See Thomas Jefferson to the Danbury Baptist Association, January 1, 1802, ibid., pp. 332–333.
18. Thomas Jefferson to George Wythe, August 13, 1786, in Ford (ed.), vol. 4, pp. 266–270; Thomas Jefferson to John Adams, October 28, 1813, in ibid., vol. 9, pp. 234–301.
19. Thomas Jefferson, "Bill for the More General Diffusion of Knowledge [1779]," in Roy J. Honeywell (ed.), *The Educational Work of Thomas Jefferson.* New York: Russell & Russell, 1964, pp. 199–205; or Ford (ed.), vol. 2, pp. 220–237; Jefferson, *Notes*, in Peden (ed.), p. 146. Although Jefferson did not believe that the state had a responsibility for educating girls beyond the elementary level, he approved of additional education for women and made special arrangements for his daughters. Even so, Jefferson adhered to the prejudices of his day regarding the restriction of women to the domestic sphere. See his letter to Nathaniel Burwell, Esq., March 14, 1818, in Koch and Peden (eds.), pp. 687–689. See also Jon Kukla, *Mr. Jefferson's Women.* New York: Alfred A. Knopf, 2007.
20. Thomas Jefferson to John Adams, October 28, 1813, in Ford (ed.), vol. 9, pp. 424–430; Thomas Jefferson to James Madison, December 20, 1787, in Koch and Peden (eds.), pp. 436–441. See also Richard Matthews, *The Radical Politics of Thomas Jefferson.* Lawrence, KS: University Press of Kansas, 1984; Garrett Ward Sheldon, *The Political Philosophy of Thomas Jefferson.* Baltimore: Johns Hopkins University Press, 1991; Jennings L. Wagoner, Jr., "Jefferson, Justice, and the Enlightened Society," in Deborah A. Verstegen and James G. Ward (eds.), *Spheres of Justice in Education.* New York: HarperCollins, 1991.
21. See Wagoner, *Jefferson and Education*, esp. 53–70 and Robert M. S. McDonald, *Thomas Jefferson's Military Academy: Founding West Point.* Charlottesville: University of Virginia Press, 2004.
22. Thomas Jefferson to Edward Carrington, January 16, 1787, in Koch and Peden (eds.), pp. 411–412.
23. An examination of "aristocratic" student life at the University of Virginia during the early decades of the institution's existence is provided in Jennings L. Wagoner, Jr., "Honor and Dishonor at Mr. Jefferson's University: The Antebellum Years," *History of Education Quarterly*, vol. 26, 1986, pp. 155–179. As a condition pressed upon Virginia in its bid to rejoin the Union after the Civil War, the state legislature passed a law providing for public education for all children in 1869—ninety years after Jefferson first proposed the idea.
24. See David Tyack, "Forming the National Character: Paradox in the Educational Thought of the Revolutionary Generation," *Harvard Educational Review*, vol. 36, 1966, pp. 29–41.
25. Benjamin Rush to Richard Price, May 25, 1786, in L. H. Butterfield (ed.), *Letters of Benjamin Rush*, vol. 1. Princeton, NJ: Princeton University Press, 1951, pp. 388–389.

26. Benjamin Rush, "A Plan for the Establishment of Public Schools and the Diffusion of Knowledge in Pennsylvania; to Which Are Added, Thoughts upon the Mode of Education, Proper in a Republic" [1786], in Frederick Rudolph (ed.), *Essays on Education in the Early Republic*. Cambridge, MA: Harvard University Press, 1965, pp. 3–23, at p. 9; Thomas Jefferson to John Banister, Jr., October 15, 1785, in Boyd (ed.), vol 8, pp. 636–637; Edgar W. Knight (ed.), *A Documentary History of Education in the South before 1860*, vol. 2. Chapel Hill: University of North Carolina Press, 1930, pp. 4, 17, 21–22.
27. Rush's basic plan called for grants of land and public taxes to be used in support of free elementary schools in every township or district of size; academies located in each county; and four colleges: "One in Philadelphia; one at Carlisle, a third, for the benefit of our German fellow citizens, at Manheim; and a fourth, some years hence, at Pittsburgh." The commonwealth's university would be located in the capital city.
28. Ibid., pp. 9–10.
29. Tyack, "Forming National Character," pp. 17–18.
30. Ibid., pp. 9–10.
31. Rush, pp. 10–11.
32. Ibid., pp. 12–13. See also Hyman Kuritz, "Benjamin Rush: His Theory of Republican Education," *History of Education Quarterly*, vol. 7, 1967, pp. 432–541. Noah Webster's comment can be found in his "On the Education of Youth in America" [1790], in Rudolph (ed.), p. 51.
33. Rush, p. 14. See also Jonathan Messerli, "The Columbian Complex: The Impulse to National Consolidation," *History of Education Quarterly*, vol. 7, 1967, pp. 417–431. On the land ordinances, see Peter S. Onuf, *Statehood and Union: A History of the Northwest Ordinance*, Indiana University Press, Bloomington, 1987.
34. The most useful discussion of the recurring idea of a national university is David Madsen, *The National University, Enduring Dream of the U.S.A.*, Detroit: Wayne State University Press, 1966. For Rush's specific proposal, see Benjamin Rush, "To Friends of the Federal Government: A Plan for a Federal University," in Richard Hofstadter and Wilson Smith (eds.), *American Higher Education: A Documentary History*, vol. 2. Chicago: University of Chicago Press, 1961, pp. 152–157.
35. Rush Welter, *Popular Education and Democratic Thought in America*. New York: Columbia University Press, 1962, pp. 25–26.
36. A provocative study of Webster's advocacy of "quiet and meek Christianity" and his fear of disorder is provided by Richard M. Rollins, *The Long Journey of Noah Webster*. Philadelphia: University of Pennsylvania Press, 1980. For a rhetorical analysis of "Republicanism" and the articulation of education and shifting hegemonies in early America, see Mark Garrett Longaker, *Rhetoric and the Republic: Politics, Civic Discourse, and Education in Early America*. Tuskaloosa: University of Alabama Press, 2007.
37. Webster, "On the Education of Youth in America," in Rudolph (ed.), pp. 43–77.
38. Messerli, p. 420.
39. Noah Webster, *Dissertations on the English Language with Notes Historical and Critical*, I. Boston: Thomas & Co., 1789, as quoted in Robert L. Church and Michael W. Sedlak, *Education in the United States: An Interpretative History*. New York: Free Press, 1976, p. 18; Messerli, pp. 420–421.
40. Richard M. Rollins, "The Wordmonger," *Pennsylvania Gazette*, May 1980, pp. 24–30; Joel Spring, *The American School 1642–1985*. New York: Longman, 1986, p. 37.
41. Church and Sedlak, pp. 19–20.
42. Lawrence A. Cremin, *American Education: The National Experience, 1783–1876*. New York: Harper & Row, 1980, pp. 391–394.
43. Rudolph has included both essays in his *Essays on Education in the Early Republic*. See also Allen O. Hansen, *Liberalism and American Education in the Eighteenth Century*. New York: Macmillan, 1926.
44. Samuel Harrison Smith, "Remarks on Education," in Rudolph (ed.), p. 214.
45. Samuel Knox, "An Essay on the Best System of Liberal Education, Adapted on the Genius of the Government of the United States," in Rudolph, (ed.), *Essays on Education*, p. 332.
46. Welter, pp. 23–41.
47. Merle Curti, *The Social Ideas of American Educators*. Totawa, NJ: Littlefield, Adams, [1935], 1974, p. 41.
48. Thomas Jefferson to Nathaniel Burwell, Esq., March 14, 1818, in Koch and Peden (eds.), pp. 687–689.
49. Benjamin Rush, "Thoughts on Female Education, Accommodated to the Present State of

Society, Manners, and Government in the United States of America," [1787], in Rudolph, (ed.). pp. 28–40, at p. 35.

50. Ibid., p. 39.

51. Barbara Miller Solomon, *In the Company of Educated Women: A History of Women and Higher Education in America*. New Haven: Yale University Press, 1985, pp. 8–9.

52. Dumas Malone, *Jefferson the Virginian*. Boston: Little, Brown, 1948, pp. 121–122. See also Thomas Jefferson, "Argument in the Case of Howell vs. Netherland," in Ford (ed.), vol. I, pp. 373–381.

53. Thomas Jefferson, *Notes on the State of Virginia* [1787], William Peden (ed.). Chapel Hill: University of North Carolina Press, 1955, pp. 162–163. In light of DNA evidence that has added support (but not definitive proof) to assertions that Jefferson may have fathered at least one child by Sally Hemings, a Monticello slave, Jefferson's agony over slavery perhaps becomes all the more understandable. See Annette Gordon-Reed, *Thomas Jefferson and Sally Hemings: An American Controversy*, Charlottesville: University Press of Virginia, 1997; and Jan Lewis and Peter Onuf (eds.), *Sally Hemings and Thomas Jefferson: History, Memory, and Civic Culture*. Charlottesville: University Press of Virginia, 1999.

54. Jefferson, *Notes*, p. 163.

55. Ibid., pp. 137–139. See also John Chester Miller, *The Wolf by the Ears: Thomas Jefferson and Slavery*. Charlottesville: University Press of Virginia, 1991.

56. In addition to Miller, cited above, see Garry Wills, *Inventing America: Jefferson's Declaration of Independence*. New York: Vintage, 1978.

57. Jefferson, *Notes*, pp. 137–138.

58. Commager, p. 55.

59. Miller, p. 65; Bernard W. Sheehan, *Seeds of Extinction: Jeffersonian Philanthropy and the American Indian*. New York: W. W. Norton, 1973, p. 175.

60. Miller, p. 72.

61. Thomas Jefferson to DuPont de Nemours, April 24, 1816, in Ford (ed.), vol. 10, pp. 22–25.

4
The Common Man and the Common School
1820–1860

Overview

The two uses of the word common in the title of this chapter have distinctly different connotations. The term *common man* refers to individuals identified with occupational groups in American society that, prior to the 1820s, had lacked a strong voice in the political realm. Farmers, artisans and merchants were among these new claimants for power and recognition. The term *common school* refers to a type of schooling that would educate all in common, using the same curriculum. Before discussing the common school and its most famous promoter, Horace Mann of Massachusetts, a brief look at the political rise of the common man is in order.[1]

The Jacksonian Era

"The mobs of great cities," wrote Thomas Jefferson in 1787, "add just so much to the support of pure government, as sores do to the strength of the human body." Jefferson's America, a land of noble farmers tending their own small freeholds and removed from the corruptions of industrialization, was in the process of disappearing even before the end of Jefferson's administration. Jefferson himself had to admit over a quarter century later that ". . . experience has taught me that manufactures are now as necessary to our independence as to our comfort." However preferable it might have been to send American raw materials to Europe for manufacture, it slowly became more profitable to bring industry to the materials.[2]

The farm still remained the statistical center of American life, but business enterprise grew rapidly as the nineteenth century unfolded. With the growth of manufacturing came the growth of cities. In 1820 less than a twentieth of the nation lived in communities of 8,000 or over. Two decades later more than a twelfth lived in cities of that size and more than a ninth lived in towns of 2,000 or more. The number of people engaged in manufacturing increased by 127 percent between 1820 and 1840, while agricultural labor increased by only 79 percent. Private businesses increased and chartered corporations emerged on the scene. The beginnings of the organized labor movement began in 1827 when skilled craftsmen in Philadelphia united into the Mechanic's Union of

Trade Associations. Following on the heels of craft associations, industrial unionism began with the organization of the New England Association of Farmers, Mechanics, and Other Workingmen in Providence, Rhode Island in 1831. A market revolution took hold as cash crop agriculture and capitalist manufacturing replaced an artisan and agrarian based economy. Banking and insurance enterprises flourished as the capitalist economy expanded.[3]

In the background of this market revolution was a visible increase in urban poverty. Long hours and low pay marked the lives of those who scrambled for jobs in the nation's cities. Vice and dissipation became ever more visible as workers and the unemployed sought escape from the tensions of urban life. Particularly in North eastern cities, immigrants and their children presented special problems. Fears about the failure of immigrants to assimilate and the crime and disorder that often erupted in their neighborhoods created anxiety among "nativists." As one self-styled patriot and public school advocate would later put the matter, choices had to be made. "To govern men," wrote Orville Taylor in 1848, "there must be either Soldiers or Schoolmasters, Books or Bayonets, Camps and Campaigns, or Schools and Churches—*the cartridge or the ballot box.*"[4]

In rural areas as well as in urbanizing America, the "little man" or "common man" was seemingly being swept aside in the emerging capitalist order and disorder that accompanied it. It was into this scene that General Andrew Jackson emerged as the avowed political champion of the common man. It was his campaign, election, re-election, and the subsequent election of his anointed successor, Martin Van Buren, that gave the era of the 1820s and 1830s the *common man* label.

Many factors contributed to Jackson's image as the spokesman for the ordinary person. He was, after all, a war hero, a general who had defeated the British in the War of 1812 at the Battle of New Orleans, and had succeeded in battles against Native Americans in the South. As president, Jackson's insistence on pushing south-eastern Indians across the Mississippi and onto western reservations cemented his image among white settlers of the South and the West who were competing with the Native Americans for land. Jackson's policies toward aboriginal Americans often included slaughters that were brutal and unnecessary. To many Americans of the 1830s however, removing the Indians by any means necessary seemed to justify excessive force.

Another factor supporting Jackson's image of commonness was that he was born in the state of Tennessee that was then considered both southern and western in character. Jackson's predecessors in the presidency had all been from Virginia or Massachusetts, two states with long histories and stable social structures that included landed elites. Tennessee could boast neither of these attributes, so Jackson's origins spoke to Americans from his own and other less established southern and western states on the fringes of American economic development. These frontier states faced different problems than the more settled regions of the nation, and Jackson appealed to those who knew

Figure 4.1 President Andrew Jackson.

Source: Library of Congress, Prints and Photographs Division, LC-USZ62-5099.

the differences as well as those in every state who felt the condescension of the Virginia and Massachusetts social, economic, and political aristocracies.

Jackson understood these circumstances and used them astutely in his political campaigns. In the 1824 presidential election, Jackson won the popular vote but did not achieve a majority of the electoral vote. This threw the election into the House of Representatives, which elected John Quincy Adams of Massachusetts. In the campaign of 1828, Jackson claimed that in 1824 he had been denied his rightful victory by establishment politicians who ignored the voters and chose one of their own. In the election of 1828, Jackson achieved a substantial majority in both the popular and electoral balloting. He came into office as the champion of the ordinary citizen, as a leader who would change the nation's power structure from one managed on a top-down basis by political elites to one that honored and respected its common citizens.

Other events associated with Jackson's presidency reinforced his image as the champion of the common people. At his inauguration in 1829, he opened the White House to his supporters who celebrated so enthusiastically that they caused substantial damage to the property. Jackson's opponents claimed that the "rabble," their word for those whom Jackson championed, had overrun the White House. As President, Jackson relied on his "kitchen cabinet," a group of informal advisers who shared his background, rather than the official cabinet composed of more established political figures such as those he had fought to gain the presidency. Jackson is also remembered as the initiator of the *spoils system*, under which appointments to various offices were made more on the basis of political support than on a merit system of qualification. Jackson thus appeared to assume that every man was qualified for office, a posture calculated to endear him to those ordinary people who voted for him.

One of Jackson's major economic undertakings as President also fueled his image of commonness. Jackson spent a considerable amount of time and effort during his terms of office in forcing the breakup of the Bank of the United States. This Philadelphia-based bank, the official national bank, was at that time a vehicle by which the economically powerful maintained their position by regulating economic activity through policies such as controlling interest rates. Jackson and his followers saw such regulation as positive for rich and powerful creditors, those who lent money, and negative for debtors, those who borrowed.

In his war against the bank Jackson gained the approval of ordinary citizens who felt neglected by their government. In fact, Jackson's economic philosophy of *laissez-faire* ("let things be") was directed at getting government out of the economic lives of its citizens. As long as government was powerful, Jackson and his followers reasoned that it would act on behalf of the rich and influential. Only by removing government from economic activity would ordinary folk, the common people, be able to compete for economic and other benefits.

Historians of the Jacksonian era have generally concluded that this image of Jackson as champion of the common people is overdrawn. Jackson himself was much better educated than he was reputed to be; his appointments to office were as qualified by standard educational criteria as those of his predecessors; his political supporters were not all from common or ordinary backgrounds and his fight against the national bank resulted in the establishment of state banks, which were almost as restrictive economically to ordinary citizens as the national bank had been. However, these facts do not change the perception of those who lived in Jackson's time and responded positively to his causes. Neither do these historical revelations change the perspective of Jackson's political opponents, many of whom opposed him as a dangerous person with untried ideas who was committed to changing the social and economic status quo.[5]

Jackson's political influence outlasted his two terms as president. After his re-election in 1832, he was succeeded in 1836 by Martin Van Buren of New York, an almost handpicked successor who pledged to continue Jacksonian policies and ideals. Thus the period from 1824 (when he was denied the

Figure 4.2 This 1833 caricature of Andrew Jackson depicts him as a heavy-handed monarch whose use of the veto, destruction of the national bank, and refusal to consult with Congress and his official cabinet in favor of his unofficial "Kitchen Cabinet" were seen as measures destroying the Constitution.

Source: HarpWeek

presidency by Congress) to 1840 became known as the "Age of Jackson," years in which the national political consciousness was influenced heavily by appeals to the wisdom of the common man—the farmer, the frontiersman, the artisan—all of whom counted themselves as ordinary Americans.

Jackson's political influence was so substantial that his political opponents had to re-form themselves in order to compete with the Jacksonians. They formed a new political party, the Whigs, which not only opposed Jackson but also simultaneously attempted to reach his frontier supporters. The Whigs were descended politically from the Federalists, who had vied with the Jeffersonian Republicans for national leadership since the nation's birth. Among the most notable Whigs were John Adams and Alexander Hamilton. Hamilton was secretary of the treasury in Washington's administration and was the force behind the establishment of the Bank of the United States. The bank's existence institutionalized the Federalist belief that the central government should be strong and, further, that it should function in the interest of the established economic order. Given the growing strength of the Jacksonians and their suspicion of centralized government and of the established groups in society, the Whigs could no longer operate as a group devoted primarily to preserving the existing order. Consequently, they recast their ideas and their image in a way that sought to recapture some of the voters who had defected to Jackson and his party, the Democratic Republicans (later simply the Democrats).

The Whigs did not abandon the Federalist commitment to an active central government. They simply tried to make that government work for more of the people than just the political and economic elites. One idea with which the Whigs are often identified is that of "internal improvements." To the Whigs, this meant government support for railroads, turnpikes, and canals that would develop remote areas of the country. Whig devotion to internal improvements combined Federalist affinity for government action with the Jacksonian objective of benefiting previously forgotten groups in society.[6]

Among the most significant of the internal improvements advocated by the Whigs was the common school. This institution was to be developed and managed through increased governmental activity at the state rather than the federal level. Its advocates offered the benefits of education to all citizens of a state, not just the elite population.

Given the preceding discussion, one should not be surprised to find that many of the most famous advocates of the common school were affiliated with the Whig party. Thus, in a real sense, one can say that the common school was a political response to the popularity of Andrew Jackson and his identification with the common people. Before elaborating on the relations between the Whigs and the common school, however, it is best to step back and contrast this new institution with other educational efforts, both prior to and during its time.

The Common School

Common schooling was more the ideological slogan of a reform crusade than it was a description of a particular type of formal educational institution. In defining the common school as an institution, one can begin by noting its early association with New England states such as Massachusetts and Connecticut. (More is said about this association in the next section.) Another early characteristic was its involvement with younger children, mainly those in the primary school years, although common school advocates also argued that a public high school should be the capstone of a system of local, common elementary schools. Furthermore, the common school was free; that is, no tuition was charged for attendance, and poorer citizens did not have to sign a pauper's oath in order for their children to attend. Common schooling was also "universal," that is, open to all children regardless of station or status. This "universal" standard did not necessarily include either black children or white children with "strange" religious beliefs, such as Irish Catholics, however.

Common schools were also supported by taxes, mostly by local property taxes. Relying for operating expenses on local taxation, common schools retained a closeness to and dependence on their immediate communities, a characteristic of the district schools that had existed previously. Finally, in some tension with the sense of localism implied by the property tax, the common school was more centralized than its predecessors had been. Whereas district schools had been organized on a geographic or neighborhood basis, the common school organization normally involved more than one district or neighborhood, and included a town, city, or township Board of Education. Centralization also meant that some educational initiatives, if not directives, came down to the local schools from the state level.

The common school did not produce large increases in enrollment. Historical studies of schooling in New England have shown conclusively that increased school attendance preceded the common school crusade waged in the 1830s and 1840s. What the common school crusade was designed to accomplish, however, was a more efficient form of school governance and management, one that would permit the schools to assimilate the great numbers of students they were currently enrolling and the increasing numbers that would come in succeeding years.[7]

Common school reform was more political and organizational than pedagogical or curricular. That is, life within the common school resembled that in other types of schools more than it differed from them. Recitation was the norm in the classroom, although the great common school reformer, Horace Mann, was not in favor of this practice. Teachers faced relatively large classes, most of which were not organized according to pupil age or ability. Reading was a staple of the curriculum, with readers such as those compiled by William Holmes McGuffey embedding moral lessons within the school exercises. In fact, moral lessons were the most important aspect of teaching in the antebellum common school, whatever the subject matter.

The McGuffey Readers

No book or series of books rivaled the *McGuffey Readers* in popularity throughout the nineteenth century and into the twentieth. It has been estimated that at least 120 million copies were sold from the beginning of the series in 1836 through 1960. Approximately 1.3 million have been published since then. Sales are continuing in the twenty-first century as some parents who choose to home school their children, as well as teachers in private (particularly religious) schools and even some in public schools (for use as supplements to the state-approved texts), find these readers to be pedagogically and morally in tune with their values.

William Holmes McGuffey was born in 1800, the son of strongly religious Scottish Presbyterians. His parents adhered to a strict Calvinist theology and stressed the importance of education. Young McGuffey began teaching in a one room school with 48 students in Ohio when he was just 14 years old. A precocious youngster who memorized entire books of the Bible, he had a strong desire to teach and spread Protestant Christianity. As author of the series that bore his name, McGuffey was able to do both by including Bible stories as well as moral lessons, poems, essays, and speeches in each of the six "graded" levels of his book series. Beginning with basic lessons in the *Eclectic First Reader* and progressing to more advanced content in the upper levels of the series, McGuffey not only introduced students to moralistic and Christian stories, but gave them an acquaintance with the writings of John Milton, William Shakespeare, Alfred Lord Tennyson, Sir Walter Scott, Lord Byron, and other luminaries of the literary world. For many, perhaps most, of the students who learned to read by advancing through the McGuffey series, the excerpts provided in these books were probably the only exposure they had to polite literature.

Figure 4.3 Portrait of William Holmes McGuffey by unknown artist.

Credit: Betty Hollow, *Ohio University, 1804–2004.* Ohio University Press, Athens, Ohio.

McGuffey, who between teaching jobs eventually graduated in 1826 from Washington College (now Washington & Jefferson College), undertook the writing of his series while serving as Professor of Languages at Miami University in Oxford, Ohio. He had already begun to make a reputation as a lecturer on religious and moral subjects when his longtime friend, Harriet Beecher Stowe, recommended him to a small Cincinnati publishing firm that was casting about for someone to author reading textbooks. McGuffey took the assignment and completed the first four books in the series within two years of signing the contract. He received $1,000 for his work.[8]

McGuffey was on the faculty and served as President of three colleges before becoming Professor of Moral Philosophy at the University of Virginia. He died in 1873 and was buried in the University of Virginia cemetery, but his impact on shaping the character of the nation reached into the far West and into and beyond the following century.

Politics and Common School Reform

The notable early advocates of common schooling were found not among the teaching force, but in the ranks of state education officials, most of whom were members of the Whig party or men who advocated Whiggish ideas. Horace Mann of Massachusetts was the most famous advocate of the common school. He labored on its behalf as secretary of the Massachusetts Board of Education from 1837 to 1848. Prior to that period, he had served in the Massachusetts state legislature as a member of the Whig political party. In 1840, after Mann had served three years as secretary, a bill was introduced into the Massachusetts legislature to abolish the State Board of Education. The legislation was defeated. An analysis of the vote on that bill shows that party affiliation was by far the strongest influence on a legislator's vote, with Whig legislators over-whelmingly favoring continuation of the board and Democrats supporting its abolition.[9]

Other famous Whig advocates of the common school included Henry Barnard in Connecticut, Calvin Stowe in Ohio, and Calvin Wiley in North Carolina. Most of the early common school crusades were carried on in the Northeast, with fewer in the Midwest, and even fewer in the South. Social and economic variations among the regions explain, to a great degree, the differences in the pace of school reform activity.

Social and Economic Conditions in Massachusetts

In the early nineteenth century, Massachusetts was undergoing a substantial amount of social and economic change as a result of heavy migration from rural to urban areas. Fueling this demographic shift was an economic transition from agriculture and merchant capitalism to an increasing dependence on industrial production in textiles, shoemaking and other enterprises in which goods could be mass produced. With the rise of these new industries, a new form of labor arose. Artisans such as shoemakers and tailors, who had produced finished goods while working from their home or a nearby shop, were gradually being replaced by centralized factories whose operatives specialized in a particular part of a manufacturing process. This industrialization of factory work, together with the population shift to towns and cities, meant a substantial physical and psychological dislocation among Massachusetts' workers. The incidence of strikes in response to factory conditions increased substantially in these years, reflecting both the economic grievances of the workers and the psychic damage that ensued as they lost control of their work to impersonal industrial processes. Dislocation was experienced by women as well as men. As young rural women began moving into towns to find work in the new textile mills, they began living more anonymous lives in boarding houses far away from their families.

In addition to the dislocations that accompanied urbanization and industrialization, Massachusetts also experienced a heavy immigration of Irish Catholics during this period. In the eyes of Protestant Whigs, this influx of European peasants with a strange culture signified that Massachusetts was in danger of falling apart. Horace Mann, the most famous Whig advocate of common schooling in Massachusetts, believed that the school was the institution best suited to solve Massachusetts' major problems: the threat of class warfare, the dislocations that accompanied the population shift from rural to urban areas, and the need to assimilate culturally diverse immigrants into mainstream American life.[10]

Mann was by far the most famous of all of the nation's common school reformers. Since his actions and the reactions they stimulated have been subjected to much scrutiny in the historical literature, a close look at him and his educational work in Massachusetts is in order.

Horace Mann

It is dangerous to let one man stand for an institution, even if he was its most famous advocate. However, studying an institution through its most notable proponent can allow one to see concretely and vividly how that institution touched people's lives. Furthermore, the complexity of Horace Mann's personal makeup and the dazzling variety of arguments he used in favor of the common school work against any tendency to be simplistic in an analysis of his ideas. Also, since he was in touch with common school advocates in many states and since the common school was designed, at least in the minds of its advocates, to fulfill similar purposes in all those states, Horace Mann and his school reform activities can be seen in a very real sense to represent the essence of the common school movement.

Horace Mann was the third son and fourth of five children of a relatively prosperous Massachusetts farmer. His upbringing was conventional for that time and place. He was raised in an environment that valued family and church and imbued its youth with those moral and religious ideas associated with Puritanism. Yet the Mann family members, particularly Horace, were not completely comfortable with this harsh and confining belief system. In his later years, Mann adopted the Unitarian version of Protestantism that advocated more tolerant and less confining beliefs than those of the Puritanism of his youth.[11]

Mann attended a district school in the village of Franklin, Massachusetts. His school reflected closely the ideas and values of the Franklin area farmers who sent their children to school to learn to read and write. Mann felt estranged from the reigning theological orthodoxy in Franklin, particularly its severe representation by the minister of his own church. When he needed tutoring as a prelude to attending college, he chose a Baptist minister from a neighboring town whose beliefs were less restrictive than those of his own minister. Mann attended Brown University in Providence, Rhode Island, some thirty miles from Franklin. At Brown, he encountered a fixed curriculum of classical studies and worked hard to become first in his class. After graduation and brief stints working with a lawyer in Massachusetts and as a tutor at Brown, he attended a school for the training of lawyers that was run by a judge in Litchfield, Connecticut.[12]

Upon finishing his legal studies, Mann moved to Dedham, Massachusetts, a town that was larger than Franklin and closer to Boston, the state capital. After a brief apprenticeship with a local lawyer in Dedham, he established his own law practice. He quickly succeeded in his law work and also proved adept at politics. He was elected to the lower house of the state legislature as a member of the Republican Party (antecedent of the Whigs), which opposed both the Jacksonians and the Federalists. In the legislature, he worked for economic development through policies supporting railroads. He also pushed for social reforms such as temperance, the creation of institutions for the insane and alternatives to debtors' prison. During this period he married, but his young wife died within two years.

Devastated by his wife's death and still harboring psychological scars from his Puritan childhood, Mann left the legislature and concentrated on his law practice. He continued to succeed in the law and eventually moved his practice to Boston. There he decided to re-enter politics, this time as a Whig candidate for the state Senate. He won this election and later was named the presiding officer of the Senate. Still devoted to reform causes, Mann grew tired of the rough and tumble of partisan politics in the legislature. He was also concerned by the violence he saw in Boston and by the social and economic divisions that separated the various segments of Boston society. These concerns, combined with his continuing religious search, prodded him to accept the position of secretary of the newly created Massachusetts Board of Education. There he could devote himself to reforming the common schools of his state. This activity allowed him to build on his previous economic and social reform efforts, to escape the evils of partisan politics, and to speak to his own personal religious crisis by fervently taking up a quasi-religious cause, common schooling. Mann's twelve years of work as secretary of the

Figure 4.4 Horace Mann, "Father of the Common School".
Credit: Reprinted with permission from The Granger Collection, New York.

Massachusetts Board of Education earned for him the title "Father of the Common School."

Mann and His Crusade

When Horace Mann accepted the position as secretary of the Massachusetts Board of Education, he already had well-developed views about the social problems of his day but had only a little knowledge about educational problems and issues. Of course, he learned a great deal about education during his years as secretary, and yet, in many ways, Mann's fundamental accomplishments were as much social, economic, and political as they were educational. He encouraged the citizens of Massachusetts to support and to patronize the common schools and to embrace a variety of educational innovations. One way to assess the significance of his social and economic accomplishments is to see how Mann approached various groups to enlist them in the cause of salvation by school reform.

Mann's Nonsectarian Moral Views

Scholars have described the world view, or ideology, of Mann and other common school advocates as Protestant Republicanism. This ideology was based on the Protestant values that had pervaded Massachusetts since its founding in the seventeenth century. The school day in these "common" schools typically began with the Lord's Prayer and readings from the King James version of the Bible, usually read without comment. To most Protestants, this approach seemed right, good, and proper. Those who could not abide by this "nondemoninational open-mindedness" were seen as less Christian and certainly less American than those who supported common schools with a Christian [Protestant] bias. Even so, mainstream Protestantism was acquiring distinctively "modern" traits that distanced it from early Puritanism. Like the earlier Puritans, the common school advocates were moralists, but their brand of morality was often more secular than sectarian. In their eyes, the essential institution for nonsectarian moral improvement was the common school. These Protestant Republicans were cosmopolitans who believed in state intervention, or at least state influence, in local affairs. They also supported the assimilation of groups with different moral creeds or values into the Protestant Republican mainstream. It is important to note, however, that the nonsectarian Protestantism that Mann advocated for the common schools, the teaching of broad Christian principles free from narrow sectarian interpretations, was quite close in spirit to the teachings of the Unitarian sect that he had embraced when he cast aside the doctrinaire Puritanism in which he had been raised.[13]

Advocates of this broad view of morality ran into difficulty whenever they faced objections from members of religious sects that believed deeply in their particular views and wanted schools to reinforce their beliefs and practices. Mann never solved this problem completely, but he also never allowed it to present an insurmountable obstacle to his school reform crusade. One reason that religion did not become too controversial in Massachusetts was the tradition of local control that state-oriented common school reformers wanted to circumvent but never managed to overcome. Localism allowed for sectarianism to operate without being formally acknowledged. Schools in a locale with a dominant sect tended to reflect the tenets of that sect without having to proclaim themselves officially as sectarian. Members of other sects tended to make adjustments and concessions as necessary.

The lack of organization among the large Catholic minority in Massachusetts during Mann's time kept that group, which was most uncomfortable with Mann's nonsectarian Protestantism, from effectively voicing its opposition. The relative lack of religious controversy in Massachusetts allowed Mann to finesse, rather than solve, the religion issue by fixing responsibility for a school's religious orientation in the neighborhood or district where it was located.

Mann's Appeal to the Wealthy

In addition to difficulties in the area of religion, Horace Mann had to confront opposition to the common schools from powerful white Protestants in Massachusetts who opposed the lack of fit between the common school and their own personal interests. It is instructive to see how Mann tried to overcome the objections of these wealthy Massachusetts citizens who were then, and whose descendants still are, more likely to send their children to private than to common schools.

When Mann talked to powerful businessmen and industrialists, he was dealing with a group that he knew well from his law practice. He addressed this group quite directly in the fifth of the twelve annual reports that he wrote while serving as secretary of the Board of Education. In this 1842 report, he described how he had spent a good portion of his time during the year gathering information from employers about the relative merits of educated versus uneducated workers. In the report itself, Mann provided a long excerpt from a Lowell industrialist, a Mr. H. Bartlett, who had responded to a letter Mann had sent to employers asking them to comment on the productivity of educated versus uneducated workers.

Bartlett was emphatic in his preference for the educated worker. He argued that the educated worker was safe and malleable, whereas the uneducated worker was dangerous and recalcitrant. Employers, therefore, could count on substantially fewer labor problems if they hired workers who had a common school education. Sounding a theme that was at the heart of Mann's support of the common schools and his fear of a world without them, Bartlett linked the superiority of educated workers to their moral values. He argued that educated workers were less likely to be drinkers or to damage machinery, and more likely to attend church and to provide a stable life for themselves and their families. Bartlett concluded his letter with the following appeal to employers to support the common school as a means of protecting their businesses:

> [T]hose who possess the greatest share of the stock of worldly goods are deeply interested in this subject as one of mere insurance, that the most effectual way of making insurance on their property would be to contribute from it enough to sustain an efficient system of common school education, thereby educating the whole mass of mind and constituting it a police more effective than peace officers or prisons.

Bartlett went on to conclude that support for the common school would maintain the status quo in the relations between the rich and poor:

> The great majority always have been and probably always will be comparatively poor, while a few will possess the greatest share of this world's goods. And it is a wise provision of Providence which connects so intimately, and as I think indissolubly, the greatest good of the many with the highest interest of the few.[14]

Although the words are Bartlett's, there is little doubt that the sentiments are ones Mann wanted stated in the report. He stressed that if the wealthy did not support common schooling, they would be threatened and possibly overrun by an ignorant rabble. Schooled workers were not ignorant rabble, but rather, men and women infused with respect for property, for the work ethic, and for the wisdom of the property owners. This respect and docility were equated with morality, implying that those workers who acted in opposition to owners of capital and property were immoral. Strikes and other crimes could be avoided if common schools flourished.

The conservatism of this appeal is evident, and the "Fifth Report" documents the profoundly conservative impulses behind Mann's common school reform movement. Appeals to the propertied to support schooling as a form of insurance for their property are not limited to nineteenth-century Massachusetts. They have occurred continuously from that time to the present day.

Mann's Views of Property and Taxation

When addressing the wealthy, appealing to their self-interest was not the only strategy that Mann employed. One of his most eloquent arguments in support of the common school was included in his "Tenth Annual Report" of 1846. In this report, he addressed those who owned large parcels of property and who therefore paid the largest amount of the property taxes to fund the common schools. This time, however, he did not try to convince the wealthy that investing in education was good business. Rather, he spoke in anger about a situation that bothered him greatly and that has continued to bother public school people to the present day—the reluctance of the wealthy to pay property and other taxes that support public schools.

In his "Tenth Annual Report," Mann addressed directly the objections that taxpayers often gave in opposing payment of taxes for schools. One objection came from citizens who owned property but had no children and therefore felt no obligation to support an institution they would not use. Similar opposition came from people who already had raised children and now refused to pay taxes for the education of children of others. In addition, there were the citizens who sent their children to private schools and were thereby reluctant to pay taxes for an institution they chose not to support. For Mann, the answer to all of these objections was the same. The overarching reason to support the common school was that it was an institution that existed not for the benefit of any individual, but for the benefit of all, and that therefore demanded support from all. Furthermore, the amount of support was not to be determined by the willingness of the citizens to pay, but rather by the needs of the schoolchildren.

In making his argument, Mann relied on a theory of property that bears explication. It was unusual then, just as it is in our own time. It also contradicts those who see Mann simply as an economic conservative. Mann's theory was that property in society was more than private property. When viewed socially rather than egocentrically, property was as much a gift as it was something people created through their own labor. According to Mann:

> In the majority of cases, all that we call *property*, all that makes up the valuation or inventory of a nation's capital, was prepared at the creation, and was laid up of old in the capacious store-houses of nature. For every unit that a man earns by his own toil or skill, he receives hundreds and thousands, without cost and recompense, from the All-bountiful Giver. A proud mortal, standing in the midst of his luxuriant wheat-fields or cotton plantations, may arrogantly call them his own; yet what barren wastes would they be, did not heaven send down upon them its dews and its rains, its warmth and its light; and sustain for them the grateful vicissitude of the seasons.

For Mann, this meant that property was not something to be hoarded privately; it was created "for the benefit and subsistence of the whole race . . ., collectively."[15]

In Mann's view, property owners were at best stewards of nature's treasures, and their property could be best described as being "leased" rather than owned. The obligations of the lessees were those of stewardship. They needed to husband and improve their property for the next generation, and they needed to provide a portion of their property for the good of their contemporaries—the good that came from the education of all children. Mann could not have been more specific in expressing his views of the limits of private property when it came to supporting public education: "no one man . . . has any such title to, or ownership in these ingredients and substantials of wealth, that his right is invaded when a portion of them is taken for the benefit of posterity." That, of course, is exactly what the tax on property for schools was about. It took a portion of property for the benefit of posterity by educating all children.[16]

Mann argued that since Massachusetts had passed laws against infanticide, the state should also enforce laws to support common schooling. The principle that a child should not be robbed of life was related to the principle that a child should not be robbed of the right to an education and the enjoyment of life. Mann ended this report with a powerful statement of the "foundation on which the Common School system of Massachusetts reposes":

> The successive generations of men, taken collectively, constitute one great Commonwealth.
>
> The property of this Commonwealth is pledged for the education of all its youth, up to such a point as will save them from poverty and vice, and prepare them for the adequate performance of their social and civil duties.
>
> The successive holders of this property are trustees, bound to the faithful execution of their trust by the most sacred obligations; because

embezzlement and pillage from children and descendants are as criminal as the same offenses when perpetrated against contemporaries.[17]

Mann here advanced a theory of property that recognized the rights of all the citizens of Massachusetts, not just those of property owners. His position was, in fact, a mild form of socialism based on the biblical concept of stewardship. While it legitimated the notion of private property, it also legitimated society's claim to a portion of all property. This was a radical statement for its day, or for any day. Mann impressed on his readers the collective or social purpose of the common school. That institution, Mann and other reformers insisted, exists for the benefit of all society, not just for those who presently attended. In this report, Mann emerged as a reformer who was willing to embrace unconventional views to impress on the wealthy that it was their obligation to pay taxes to support the common schools.

Mann's Appeal to the Working Class

Mann did not ignore the issue of how individuals benefit from attending the common school. In fact, he repeatedly emphasized this point in trying to get poor or working people to support the common school movement. At that time, many members of the Massachusetts lower classes were inclined to keep their children at home to work rather than to send them to school. In his twelfth and final report, Mann stressed what the common school meant to those who worked for a living. He argued that it alone was the institution that would prevent class divisions in America from hardening as they had in Europe. The reason for this, he believed, was that the common school prevented the tendency toward "the domination of capital and the servility of labor." For Mann this was so because "education creates or develops new treasures—treasures not before possessed or dreamed of by any one." Mann based his argument for school attendance on a social value that it produced. He stated his point by using a metaphor for which he is often remembered: "Education, then, beyond all other devices of human origin, is the great equalizer of the conditions of men—the balance wheel of the social machinery."[18]

Mann's Common School Reform in an International Context

A full evaluation of Mann's ideas and of the American common school must take into account the comparable experience in Europe. Carl Kaestle has pointed out that the arguments of common school reformers such as Mann resembled those of liberal school reformers in early nineteenth-century England. Conservative opposition was also much the same on both sides of the Atlantic. However, the English conservatives tended to be much more vocal than their American counterparts, stating that schooling would make the working classes turbulent rather than submissive by teaching them to question the justice of their place in the social order. While Kaestle is careful not to make too much of this difference, he does see it as the single greatest difference between

English and American educational ideology. By presenting public education as a stabilizing rather than a destabilizing process, American common school advocates met substantially less opposition than did their English counterparts. Opposition arguments in America, while sometimes coming from conservatives opposed to the centralizing aspects of common schooling, more often came from citizens opposed to particular institutions such as the public high school.[19]

The differences in the educational reform movements in England and America were in part due to the unpredictable responses of the intended beneficiaries of those plans. Reformers could never guarantee any amount of social mobility as a result of their efforts, nor could they guarantee that recipients would feel better about themselves or about the educational process. Furthermore, there was no guarantee that the ideas contained in a school curriculum would be received as they were conveyed. These points resurfaced in later discussions of the public school's encounter with late-nineteenth- and twentieth-century working people.

Whatever political label one attaches to Mann and the common school, it is clear that he had a social vision that sought to use the school to overcome the economic divisions in Massachusetts. He also had ideas about educational issues and methods that were often as controversial as his theory of property and taxation.

Opposition to Mann and the Common School Idea

Mann's educational ideas and pedagogical reforms were often opposed by Massachusetts' leading educators and by working teachers. Many of his pedagogical ideas resulted from trips to Europe, where he studied schooling in Prussia and other countries. In Prussia, he admired the accomplishments of a centralized school system, which he sought to emulate in Massachusetts. While in Europe, he also learned of the pedagogical theories of Johann Heinrich Pestalozzi. This Swiss educator advocated a theory of education that started with the interests of the child rather than the demands of the subject matter. According to Pestalozzi, one must start with children as they are, and then lead them to where one wants them to be.[20]

The pedagogical method of Pestalozzi was popularly known as *object teaching*. In this theory, the teacher starts instruction with a concrete object in order to gain the child's attention. The object, which is related to the child's world, can then be used as a means of bringing the child to the world of the educator. Mann's advocacy of Pestalozzian devices has prompted at least one historian to label Mann an advocate of "soft-line" pedagogy, in contrast to the "hard-line" recitation approach advocated by most teachers of his day. These colorful labels distort the complexity of the views of both educational camps, but they also convey essential differences in pedagogy.[21]

At the core of these differences was disagreement over the basic purpose of education. For Horace Mann and other common school reformers, moral education was the heart of the curriculum. Only moral improvement could heal the divisions caused by the social and economic changes Massachusetts was then undergoing. Mann's opponents, seeing the situation from the point of view of their own locality rather than from that of the state at large, did not share his fear of social crisis. Even if some of them did sense emerging social problems, they rejected the idea that these problems might be ameliorated by school reform.

The differing views of the reformers and their opponents can be highlighted by the pedagogical dispute that arose between Horace Mann and the Boston grammar schoolmasters. These men, principals of the grammar or upper elementary schools of Boston, also supervised the primary schools that fed their grammar schools. They were powerful and influential educators in Massachusetts' largest city. They vigorously disputed Mann's praise of the Pestalozzian pedagogy that he had described in his "Seventh Annual Report." In that report, Mann praised the harmonious relationship that existed between the Pestalozzian teachers and their charges. He advocated a similar approach in Massachusetts' schools, one that valued children and their interests. Mann's views were perceived as a threat by the Boston masters, who preferred the doctrine of "emulation" based on the correctness of the teacher and the imposition of those correct views on the child.[22]

The dispute between Mann and the masters centered on two concrete issues, both of which are still evident in contemporary educational debates. One was corporal punishment, a nearly universal practice that Mann sought to abolish. For him, the practice of corporal punishment was worse than useless; it was actually counterproductive. The masters, however, believed that the "rod" was a necessary and valuable tool for the maintenance of order and decorum in their classrooms and, therefore, for the pursuit of learning. The second issue in dispute had to do with reading instruction. Mann advocated the whole-word method of teaching reading, while the masters defended phonics, the traditional approach of learning letters and then putting them together to make words. In each case, Mann's position was more child centered than teacher centered. The masters criticized Mann as an inexperienced dreamer with no practical experience. In their view, any teacher who had to confront the daily realities of a classroom knew that Pestalozzian ideas were unrealistic and, more important, dangerous to the cause of effective education.[23]

Much of Mann's pedagogy was based on his embrace of the "science" of phrenology that captured the attention of many reformers in Europe and the United States in the nineteenth century. Phrenology was a theory that assumed that the mind is composed of thirty-seven faculties (for example, aggressiveness, benevolence, spirituality) that govern an individual's attitudes and actions. Phrenologists claimed that they could measure the contours of the skull, which held the keys to revealing an individual's predisposition to act in certain ways. Behavioristic in outlook, phrenologists also maintained that human character could be modified by the cultivation and exercise of desirable faculties. Such views, which held out promise for the improvement of the human condition through scientific observation and educational effort, fit quite comfortably into Horace Mann's reform philosophy.[24]

Readers of this book will have their own ideas on phrenology, corporal punishment, the teaching of reading, and the primacy of the child's interests versus those of the teacher. The important thing to remember is that Mann's ideas were not those of the grammar schoolmasters, the high-status teachers of his day. Rather, his views represented an approach to education that was compatible with an important change that was then beginning in the teaching ranks: the increasing presence of women teachers.

The Feminization of Teaching

Several factors account for the increasing number of women teachers in the common schools. First, employing women as classroom teachers was less costly, since they were paid substantially less than men. In addition, the number of women available for teaching was increasing rapidly as young Massachusetts girls moved from the farm to the city in search of economic betterment. Teaching was regarded as respectable employment for a woman because it was consistent with the dominant view of women as innately nurturing. In fact, the image of women teachers, particularly as teachers of young children, not only allowed the common schools of Massachusetts to employ teachers for less money but also furthered the image of the school as a nurturing institution like the home.[25]

Of course, Mann's "soft-line" Pestalozzian pedagogy also furthered the cause of women's entry into teaching. He worked hard with the leaders of Massachusetts' new normal schools to train their women students in a new pedagogy and to facilitate their entry on a large scale into Massachusetts' common schools.[26]

An additional reason for the acceptability of the feminization of teaching by more traditional elements in the state was that women teachers worked in educational arrangements managed by men. Men continued to dominate the upper ranks of the grammar schools and the few high schools, and men held the superintendencies and other administrative positions that increased as common school systems expanded.

In addition to being both affordable and compatible with traditional male–female hierarchical relationships, the feminization of teaching was also seen as a means of improving the teaching force. Many of the women who moved into the teaching ranks were trained to teach at the new normal schools, where the curriculum featured theories of learning, child development, and pedagogy, as well as common school subject matter. The old teaching methods of the masters required no pedagogical training since they were based on the assumption that subject-matter knowledge was the prime requisite of teachers and that knowledge was to be passed on to students through drill and repetition. Knowledge about the students themselves, or how to get them involved in learning, was considered unnecessary. In fact, pedagogical training was viewed as a dangerous substitute for subject-matter knowledge.

Mann's involvement with the state-run normal schools represented another unique aspect of his common school crusade, its attempt to prescribe pedagogy statewide. Although normal school training was seen by reformers as improving the teaching force, critics objected that by advocating Pestalozzian teaching methods, a more uniform curriculum and other reforms, common school supporters were intruding into the affairs of the local schools, most of which favored approaches similar to those practiced by the Boston masters.

The involvement of the state in educational affairs was a major theme of the common school era. In addition to state involvement in teacher training, Horace Mann pursued other centralizing measures. The creation of high schools as the capstone of common school systems was one such measure. These schools cut across the boundaries of district or neighborhood schools and, consequently, required the establishment of broader-based, more centralized governing boards. These boards had to deal with issues such as where to place the high school and whether those who had no direct involvement with it should pay taxes for its support. High schools also called for efforts by state educational officials other than the secretary of the Board of Education and thus represented the creation of an educational bureaucracy at the state as well as at the local level.

This discussion of Mann's pedagogical ideas and the new institutional arrangements they fostered has stressed the novelty of the changes. It is also true, however, that common schools were presented as improvements on older arrangements, not as radically new innovations. From this perspective, the common school reforms advocated by Horace Mann can be viewed as moderate improvements. Another way to illustrate the moderation of Mann's changes is to compare them with more radical educational reforms advocated by other individuals and groups of the time.

William Maclure and the Workingmen's Party

Mann's ideas seem quite moderate when compared to those of other Pestalozzian educators such as William Maclure. Maclure was a Scotsman who had emigrated to the United States after making a fortune in Europe. While amassing his fortune, he became devoted to various schemes for the reform of industrial society. He learned the Pestalozzian approach to educational reform from the Swiss master himself. Upon retiring from business, Maclure went to Philadelphia where he worked quietly as a schoolmaster. The radicalism inherent in his ideas did not become evident until he migrated to New Harmony, Indiana, in the 1820s, to become the schoolmaster at the utopian community founded by Robert Owen.

Like Maclure, Owen had made a fortune in industry and had tried to reform industrial life by making his factory at New Lanark, Scotland, into an ideal community where the evils perpetrated on workers by industrialism would be counteracted by a communal living arrangement. When Owen retired from industry, he came to America and purchased land in Indiana for his New Harmony community. This would be the laboratory in which he planned to implement and improve his ideas for economic, social, and educational reform.[27]

While Maclure shared Mann's Pestalozzian approach to pedagogical issues, he and Owen had far more radical social views than Mann. Maclure divided society into two classes, *producers* and *consumers*. The first group included all those who worked for a living, while the second included those who lived off the production of others. Maclure believed that schools should improve conditions for working people, the producers, by fostering the values of production and waging war on the values of consumers. In his eyes, the most notorious consumers were preachers, who did no productive work but siphoned off the productive efforts of others into the activities of organized religion. Although Mann was a Unitarian who wanted the common school to be nonsectarian, in no sense was he the implacable opponent of religion that Maclure was. Radical opposition to organized religion was not a position that would be countenanced in a religious society such as Massachusetts.

Pedagogically, Maclure and Owen preferred an environment that was more controlled than that of the common day school advocated by Mann. Maclure's school was a boarding school, where the students were kept safely away from the employers and politicians who dominated noncommunal arrangements. In such a controlled environment as a boarding school, it was possible to protect students from the dehumanizing effects of a profit-driven industrial order and from the influence of the family. Even though Mann might have secretly wished to have a controlled educational environment like the boarding school, he was too realistic to advocate that kind of institution. Further, he was not so set against the priorities of Massachusetts industrial society and the values of its families as to advocate the radical changes implemented by Maclure and Owen. Although Mann sought to improve society through the common school, he did not seek to remake it.

The Workingmen's Party

The Workingmen's Party, the nation's first labor-oriented political party, was formed in Philadelphia in 1828 and in New York in 1829 by reformers who championed the interests of craftsmen and skilled workers. Among the issues that energized the party were demands for universal male suffrage, a ten-hour workday, an end to the practice of putting debtors in prison, an end to competition from prison contract labor, and tax-supported free public education. The common school advocated by the Workingmen's Parties of New York, Pennsylvania, and other northeastern States in the late 1820s and 1830s resembled Maclure's educational plans more than Mann's. Like Maclure, the Workingmen's Party wanted the common school to speak directly to the interests of workingmen. These interests required educational arrangements quite different from those of Mann's common school. Political studies, eschewed by Mann for the common school as divisive, were regarded as necessary in order for workers to understand how they were being oppressed by employers and politicians. Schools would have to be boarding institutions if they were to eliminate completely the environmental differences that kept the working people and their children separated from the rest of society. In addition, the children would have to wear uniforms so that invidious social distinctions could not creep into their interactions with each other. Although the Workingmen's Parties' plans for a common school were never institutionalized, their plans, along with Maclure's, paved the way for less radical educational reformers such as Horace Mann to institutionalize a more moderate reform, the common school.[28]

Mann's political, social, and educational ideas, along with those of radicals such as Maclure and conservatives such as the Boston grammar schoolmasters, are summarized in the following extract, taken from the work of Charles Burgess and Merle Borrowman:

> It borders on the ironic that Mann, commonly remembered as a liberal, can as easily be seen as one who labored to establish an essentially socialistic education, public education, in the interests of enlightened conservatism.[29]

Any reader who can interpret how each of the labels in this extract (liberal, socialist, and conservative) can be correctly applied to Mann and the common school movement must have a nuanced understanding of that complex phenomenon. Yet the reality of the common school is only partly captured by the realm of ideas and ideology. To round out the picture, a brief look at how the common school functioned in relation to different social classes is informative.

The Sociology of Common School Reform

Examining the ideas of Mann and other, more radical, advocates of school reform is not the only means of studying the common school. In recent decades, historians have attempted to analyze the actions of the participants, as well as their ideas. This section begins with a brief look at one such behavioral analysis and the controversy it sparked.

Social Class and the Common School

In 1968, Michael Katz published *The Irony of Early School Reform*, a critical account of the educational reform movement in Massachusetts during and immediately after the common school era. With this work, Katz inaugurated a new movement in historical interpretation known as radical revisionism. The major point of Katz's book was that the common school was not the result of enlightened liberal reform as proffered by Horace Mann and his colleagues. Rather, the common school was an institution of social control through which the wealthy in Massachusetts society deliberately sought to control the lower classes while appearing to give them opportunity for social advancement. Control was achieved through schools that were deliberately structured to reinforce qualities essential to factory work: respect for authority, synchronization, monotony, specialization, and punctuality.[30]

Another of Katz's books provided the primary source material used in our discussion of Mann's "Fifth Annual Report," which Katz believes is a clear statement of Mann's fundamentally conservative designs for the common school. Katz does not discuss the "Tenth Annual Report" and its seemingly socialist theory of property in any of his many works.[31]

Putting aside Mann's highly publicized ideas, Katz concentrated instead on how the common citizens of Massachusetts actually reacted to Mann's educational reforms. In Katz's work, there is a lengthy discussion of a vote to abolish a high school in Beverly, Massachusetts, in 1861. According to Katz, this vote shows clearly that the working class of Beverly saw through the "smoke screen" created by the common school promoters. By a curious circumstance, the occupations of all those who voted on the high school issue were recorded along with their votes. Katz uses this record to support his contention that a clear anti-working-class bias existed among Massachusetts educational reformers. He points out in two tables that the opponents of the high school were mostly members of the lower classes, such as farm laborers, shoemakers, and fishermen, while the supporters were members of higher-status occupations such as master mariners, "gentlemen," professionals, and businessmen.[32]

For Katz, this is clear evidence of the class-based nature of common schooling, a characteristic that it still possesses in his eyes. What was trumpeted in Massachusetts in the mid-nineteenth century and throughout the nation in subsequent years as a "democratic" common school was in reality an institution through which the wealthy imposed their will on the poor and working people. According to Katz, Beverly's citizens saw through this smoke screen and voted down the high school.[33]

This is a powerful hypothesis that is examined repeatedly in our remaining chapters. However, it is not an argument without critics. Katz's critics have exposed some problems in his interpretation of the Beverly vote. They have shown how he miscalculated the totals in his own table, with the result that his data do not entirely support his conclusions. Critics have argued that Katz misinterpreted the actions of some of Beverly's voters, particularly the shoemakers, to fit his argument. The shoemakers were then on strike, and their vote against the high school may have had as much to do with their work situation as with the issue of the school itself. Katz's adversaries have also claimed that he ignored the historical context of the Beverly vote by failing to mention the town's subsequent vote to reestablish the high school. They concluded that he overemphasized class issues and understated the significance of other matters related to the vote, such as general economic conditions and geographic distance of voters from the high school. In short, Katz's critics claim that he oversimplified and distorted an enormously complex relationship between school and social class in order to support his critical view of the common school and its advocates.[34]

It would be presumptuous to try to resolve the dispute between Katz and his critics here. For purposes of this discussion, the central issue was not about who voted for or against the high school in Beverly and why. Rather, the issue was about the real, ongoing relationship between the common schools of Massachusetts and those they claimed to be helping: the poor, the working classes, and (later) minorities. While Katz saw the public school as an institution imposed by the establishment on the lower classes, his critics tended to see X the common school, and public schools in the twentieth century, as imperfect institutions that nevertheless attempted to overcome, or mitigate, social divisions in American society and to help the members of the lower orders of that society to better themselves.

Race and the Common School

Massachusetts' common schools faced a substantial difficulty in dealing with the state's racial minorities. One year after Horace Mann left his position on the Massachusetts State Board of Education, a black citizen sued the Boston schools because his daughter was required to journey past several white schools to attend an all-black public school. This suit was initially unsuccessful, for the state court ruled that racially separate schools were permissible as long as they were equal. A few years later, however, Massachusetts passed a law mandating integrated classes in the common schools. Although this law offered a formal solution to the issue of education for racial minorities, it did not completely prevent Massachusetts schools from allowing the same kind of racial segregation that occurred in almost every state.[35]

Thus, in the arena of race, the common schools of Horace Mann's era left unresolved an issue that would fester and resurface periodically. Only when black parents or political activists took it on themselves to fight racial segregation in public education would the issue of segregation be addressed fully. Even then, black actions would often lead only to a partial victory that meant a new fight for fairness a few years later. Some of those subsequent struggles are discussed in later chapters.

Religion and the Common School

Class and race were not the only controversial issues that common school advocates had to face. Although Mann found ways to soften potential religious opposition to the nonsectarian Protestantism of Massachusetts' common schools, his counterparts in other states were not always so fortunate. In New York City, for example, a highly organized Irish Catholic minority mounted a campaign of religious opposition to the policies of the nondenominational Protestant social welfare group that managed the city's public schools. Catholics in New York City refused to have their children educated by Protestant teachers using a Protestant Bible, and campaigned unsuccessfully in the state legislature for public money to establish Catholic schools. Eventually, a political compromise was reached that replaced the public schools managed by the Protestant beneficent society with a neighborhood or district system. This allowed the schools in Catholic neighborhoods to have a Catholic flavor and those in non-Catholic neighborhoods to have the nondenominational Protestant moral emphasis favored by Horace Mann in Massachusetts.[36]

This "solution" to the religious question in New York did not really satisfy many Catholics, however, since it did not recognize their right to educate their children with financial support in conformity with their beliefs. Consequently, New York Catholics proceeded to establish, at great cost, a system of parochial or parish schools. These parochial elementary schools were intended to protect the faith of, and provide rudimentary education to, the children of poor Catholic immigrants. As the common school became increasingly accepted as an "American" institution, Catholic schools were increasingly regarded as "foreign" institutions. Catholics themselves were often thought of as "foreigners" and hostile to things "American." In reaction, Catholic communities in many large northern and midwestern cities soon emulated the actions taken in New York. Later in the nineteenth century, America's Catholic hierarchy *ordered* its faithful to build and patronize Catholic schools because of the Protestant bias of the public schools, a development we will consider more fully in Chapter 7.[37]

It is somewhat ironic that in the late twentieth century, a growing number of fundamentalist Protestant sects are just as dissatisfied with the religious arrangements in public schools as were nineteenth-century Catholics. The fundamentalists object to the "Godless" character of public school textbooks and curricula, the court-mandated prohibitions on prayer, Bible reading, and other Protestant observances. Thus, like Catholics before have done, they are establishing Christian schools in reaction to the "failures" of the public schools to respect their position.[38]

Gender and the Common School

The content of women's education and the treatment of women in schools, a highly controversial issue in the late twentieth century, was not highly contested in the common school period. There are several reasons for this lack of controversy.

First, girls were admitted to the common school without prejudice. They sat alongside boys and pursued the same curriculum without apparent incident. This easy embrace of coeducation was due to the concentration of younger children in the common school. This allowed Mann and others to view the common schools as an extension of the family context, where young boys and girls were both socialized mainly by their mothers. As suggested earlier, this view of the common school as a "nurturing" institution allowed women to become an increasingly important presence in its teaching force. Women were viewed as more nurturing and men as more disciplining, according to nineteenth-century stereotypes. Thus men continued to dominate teaching in high schools, where disciplined scholarship was the goal, while women began to dominate common school classrooms, where a nurturing environment was sought. However, the predominance of men in supervisory and administrative roles ensured that women's influence would not become too pronounced, even where they were in the majority.[39]

Women's Seminaries

In contrast to the coeducational situation in the common schools, separate institutions for the education of older girls developed almost simultaneously with the common schools. In the seminaries headed by famous reformers such as Catharine Beecher, Mary Lyon, and Emma Willard, the curriculum ostensibly concentrated on equipping women for motherhood and domestic management responsibilities. This conservative focus helped mask the novelty of formal women's education behind familiar and accepted feminine roles.[40]

The net result was an equal education for women in the common schools, an expansion of educational opportunity for them in the women's seminaries, and expansion of employment opportunities in the teaching force as a result of the normal schools. Furthermore, this all occurred without ostensibly altering the patriarchal structure of nineteenth-century society and women's subservient status within that structure. One example of how a simultaneously traditional and autonomous education was secured can be seen by considering the life and work of Catharine Beecher.

Catharine Beecher and Her Schools

Daughter of a Presbyterian minister, Catharine Beecher grew up on Long Island and in Litchfield, Connecticut, in circumstances similar to those of Horace Mann. She was likely acquainted with Mann as a young child, and it is certain that she knew him socially when she was a young adult. Educated in her home by parents and private tutors, Beecher became engaged to a Yale College professor soon after she turned twenty-one. Upon the tragic death of her fiancé in a sea accident, she took upon herself his role as tutor to his younger siblings.[41]

From there, Beecher's educational activities progressed quickly. She moved to Hartford, Connecticut, where she soon opened the Hartford Female Seminary, and later moved with her family to Cincinnati, Ohio, where she opened the Western Female Institute. Both of these schools featured a fairly traditional academic curriculum, stressing the classics and scientific studies as providing the proper background for preparation in the domestic arts. Emphasizing academic traditionalism rather than a frivolous social agenda made her schools innovative in the education of young women. Beecher also made sure that all her schools held firm to a focus on moral rectitude and improvement as the cornerstone of domestic education.

In addition to running her schools, Beecher also engaged in a lively social and intellectual life. She set up her own household, with help from her sisters, as an independent base from which she pursued other interests. Soon after the death of her fiancé, she became convinced that her contribution to society would be made outside marriage, as an educator and publicist of educational and social ideas. She wrote much about education, women as teachers, and women's role in society. She became one of the leading advocates of the idea of "domesticity" that dominated advanced women's circles at that time.

Beecher's *Treatise on Domestic Economy* was first published in 1841. A year later, she published a refined version with a prominent national firm and saw it undergo multiple printings over the next decade. In the pages of the *Treatise* lay an argument for the home and the household as the proper sphere of women's influence in American life. Beecher covered every aspect of home life in that work, from building a house to setting a table.

The domestic roles emphasized by Beecher provided a new look at women's

Figure 4.5 Catharine Beecher.

Credit: Courtesy of the Harriet Beecher Stowe Center, Hartford, Connecticut http://en.wikipedia. org/wiki/Image:Beecherc.jpg

social and economic functions. While she revered the traditional roles of wife and mother, she also expanded the limits of those roles. Beecher saw that as husbands were increasingly lured away from the home to rough-and-tumble jobs in commerce and industry, women had begun assuming greater responsibility for home management and the early education of children. Without disturbing the existing gender hierarchy, Beecher made a place for women that linked them to the economic and political currents of the day. For Beecher, the home was an essential part of a national system of cultural maintenance and improvement. Women concentrated on moral, educational, and management roles in the home, while men pursued economic and political goals outside the home. Separate spheres for men and women did not challenge male superiority, but did secure for women an important and relatively independent place in society.[42]

The seeds of the twentieth-century feminist movements were sown in the soil of nineteenth-century women's educational institutions such as Catharine Beecher's seminaries. Further, those seeds were nurtured in the common school classrooms, where women taught their students as effectively, or perhaps even more effectively, than did men.

Conclusion

In spite of obvious disagreements and conflicts, Americans in the Northeast rallied around the concept of "the common school" for several decades before the Civil War. Democrats and Whigs, workingmen and capitalists, and country folk and urban dwellers joined forces in sufficient numbers to create what many considered to be indispensable institution of American democracy. Leaders of the movement, exemplified by Horace Mann of Massachusetts, generated enthusiasm for the idea of the common school by appealing to a variety of motives, not all of which were consistent or compatible. Essentially a movement that reflected the values of republicanism, Protestantism, and capitalism, the common school revival held out the promise that the educational frontier was as open and promising as the land itself.

The common school movement unleashed a set of ideas and a series of trends that are still in motion. Schools should be free, not based on fees. They should be open to all, not just a few. They should foster morality and ethics but avoid sectarian entanglements. Teachers should be prepared for their calling and temperamentally suited to deal with children from different walks of life. Schools should foster the public good as well as prepare individuals for success in life. The degree to which these and other objectives could be met through a system of schools more uniform in support, control, access, and ideology was problematic at best in the nineteenth century. As the later chapters of this book explain, the outcomes of the push for commonality in education remain problematic.

In the next chapter, however, we argue that the dominance of the common school idea was not uniform in the United States. In that chapter, we discuss the educational traditions and institutions of the American South, a region whose leaders were in general reluctant to adopt the common school idea when it was proposed by free school advocates. Only North Carolina, under the leadership of Calvin Wiley, the "Horace Mann" of that state, made significant headway in developing common schools before the outbreak of the Civil War. Even so, there was scattered sentiment in favor of tax supported schools throughout the region—and strong forces arrayed in opposition.

Our examination of educational developments and resistance in the southern United States leads us to recommend that scholars give similar attention to the Midwest, another region that was reluctant to adopt the common school nostrums of Mann and his fellow New Englanders. In fact, our discussion of the South is undertaken to show that regionalism is an important focus in American educational history. A more comprehensive treatment of that history should pay attention to regional accounts in addition to those of the northern and southern states. As regional studies accumulate, they will surely call into question the complete dominance of any single institutional pattern in the national experience.[43]

Further Reading

Brenzel, Barbara. *Daughters of the State: A Social Portrait of the First Reform School for Girls in North America.* Cambridge, MA: Harvard University Press, 1983. A comprehensive account of the establishment and operation of a girls' reform school in the common school era, which casts comparative light on common schooling for boys and girls.

Garvey, T. Gregory. *Creating the Culture of Reform in Antebellum America.* Athens: University of Georgia Press, 2006. Discusses social conditions, leaders, and strategies employed in the reform movements of pre-Civil War America.

Glenn, Charles. *The Myth of the Common School.* Amherst, MA: University of Massachusetts Press, 1988. A critical account of the establishment and operation of the common school, comparing it unfavorably to educational provisions in Holland in the same era.

Kaestle, Carl F. *Pillars of the Republic: Common Schools and American Society, 1760–1860.* New York: Hill & Wang, 1983. The "standard" account of the development of the common school in Republican New England, with discussion of events in other regions.

Kaestle, Carl F., and Maris Vinovskis. *Education and Social Change in Nineteenth Century Massachusetts.* New York: Cambridge University Press, 1980. A study of the social and political circumstances preceding and concurring with the rise of the common school in Massachusetts.

Katz, Michael B. *The Irony of Early School Reform: Educational Innovation in Mid-Nineteenth Century Massachusetts.* Cambridge, MA: Harvard University Press, 1968. A stinging revisionist account of the class and racial bias evident in the founding of the common school in Massachusetts and its development elsewhere.

Lannie, Vincent P. *Public Money and Parochial Education: Bishop Hughes, Governor Seward and the New York School Controversy.* Case Western Reserve University Press, 1968. A comprehensive political history of the battle of New York's Catholic hierarchy to protect its faithful from the Protestant religion it believed was taught in the public schools.

Messerli, Jonathan. *Horace Mann: A Biography.* New York: Cleveland, OH: Alfred A. Knopf, 1971. A thorough and sensitive account of the life and the work of the father of the common school in the state of Massachusetts.

Reese, William J. *America's Public Schools: From the Common School to "No Child Left Behind."* Baltimore: Johns Hopkins University Press, 2005. A thoughtful analysis of the pathways and detours faced by American schools from the nineteenth into the twenty-first century, gracefully written by one of the premier educational historians of the day.

Sklar, Kathryn. *Catharine Beecher: A Study in Domesticity.* New Haven: Yale University Press, 1973. The life and beliefs of one of the early pioneers in women's education, who worked in New England and in the Midwest to see that girls were properly educated.

Sullivan, Dolores P. *William Holmes McGuffey: Schoolmaster to the Nation.* Teaneck, NJ: Fairleigh Dickinson University Press, 1994. A biography of the editor of the early readers used in many common schools in the nineteenth century, and a description of the goals to which those readers were devoted.

Vinovskis, Maris. *The Origins of Public High Schools: A Reexamination of the Beverly High School Controversy.* Madison: University of Wisconsin Press, 1985. An evaluation of a critique of the common school that was based in part on quantitative historical evidence, by a quantitative historian who finds both the evidence and the argument using it to be inadequate.

Notes

1. The use of *man* here reflects the terminology of Andrew Jackson's time, a period almost a century before women gained the vote. As we will observe in this chapter, however, women were not invisible in school reform activities.

2. Thomas Jefferson, *Notes on the State of Virginia*, William Peden, ed. Chapel Hill: University of North Carolina, [1787], 1955, p. 165; Thomas Jefferson to Benjamin Austin, January 9, 1816, in Paul L. Ford, *The Works of Thomas Jefferson*, X. New York: G. P. Putnam's Sons, 1905. Most of our discussion here tracks with what one might call the "classic" interpretation of Andrew Jackson and his era by Arthur M. Schlesinger, Jr., in *The Age of Jackson*. Boston: Little, Brown, 1945. See also John William Ward, *Andrew Jackson: Symbol for an Age*. New York: Oxford University Press, 1955 and H. W. Brands, *Andrew Jackson, His Life and Times*. New York: Doubleday, 2006.

3. Schlesinger, *Age of Jackson*, pp. 8–18; Pessen, *Uncommon Jacksonians*. Albany: State University of New York Press, 1968, pp. 3–8.

4. As quoted by William J. Reese, *America's Public Schools: From the Common School to "No Child Left Behind."* Baltimore: Johns Hopkins University Press, 2005, p. 36.

5. For elaboration of these points, see Pessen, *Uncommon Jacksonians* and Frank Cobun, "The Educational Level of the Jacksonians," *History of Education Quarterly*, vol. 7, 1967, pp. 515–520.

6. See Michael F. Holt, *The Rise and Fall of the American Whig Party: Jacksonian Politics and the Onset of the Civil War*. Oxford: Oxford University Press, 1999.

7. Carl F. Kaestle and Maris Vinovskis, *Education and Social Change in Nineteenth Century Massachusetts*. New York: Cambridge University Press, 1980.

8. The 5th and 6th *Readers* were compiled by his brother, Alexander, in the 1840s. Down through the years the series underwent successive revisions. As the nation became more diverse in the decades following the Civil War, some of the more obvious derogatory references to non-Protestant religions and non-European immigrants were eliminated.

9. Kaestle and Vinovskis, *Education and Social Change*.

10. As other states began to experience similar problems they also began to turn to common schooling. Thus, the timing and regional pattern of common school development, starting in the Northeast and spreading to the Midwest and then to the South, followed the development of industrialization and its attending problems.

11. This description of Mann's early life is based on Jonathan Messerli, *Horace Mann: A Biography*. New York: Alfred A. Knopf, 1971.

12. On the district school and its relation to the common school, see Robert L. Church, *Education in the United States: An Interpretive History*. New York: Free Press, 1976, chap. 1.

13. See Carl F. Kaestle, *Pillars of the Republic: Common Schools amd American Society, 1780–1860*. New York: Wang, 1983, and David Tyack and Elisabeth Hansot, *Managers of Virtue: Public School Leadership in America, 1820–1980*. New York: Basic Books, 1982, part I.

14. Horace Mann, "Fifth Annual Report," 1842, as quoted in Michael B. Katz (ed.), *School Reform: Past and Present*. Boston: Little, Brown, 1972, pp. 146–147.

15. Horace Mann, "Tenth Annual Report (1846)," in Lawrence A. Cremin (ed.), *The Republic and the School: Horace Mann on the Education of Free Men*. New York: Teachers College Press, 1957, pp. 64–65.

16. Ibid., p. 66.

17. Ibid., pp. 77–78.

18. Horace Mann, "Twelfth Annual Report (1848)," in Cremin (ed.), ibid., pp. 86, 88, 87.

19. Carl F. Kaestle, "Between the Scylla of Brutal Ignorance and the Charybdis of a Literary Education: Elite Attitudes toward Mass Schooling in Early Industrial England and America,"

in Lawrence Stone (ed.), *Schooling and Society: Studies in the History of Education*. Baltimore and London: Johns Hopkins University Press, 1976, pp. 177–191. We discuss a case of opposition to the high school in Beverly, Massachusetts later in this chapter.

20. On Pestalozzi, see Gerald Lee Gutek, *Pestalozzi and Education*. New York: Random House, 1968. An earlier portrayal of the man, his theories, and his work is Roger de Guimps, *Pestalozzi: His Life and Works*. London: Kessinger Publishing, LLC, [1904], 2007.

21. Michael Katz, *The Irony of Early School Reform*. Cambridge: Harvard University Press, 1968, part II.

22. Horace Mann, "Seventh Annual Report (1843)," in Cremin (ed.), pp. 54–56.

23. Katz, *Irony*, part II.

24. On phrenology in the United States and England, see John D. Davie, *Phrenology: Fad and Science*. New Haven: Yale University Press, 1955; Roger Cooter, *The Cultural Meaning of Popular Science: Phrenology and the Organization of Consent in Nineteenth Century Britain*. Cambridge: Cambridge University Press, 1984; and Steven Tomlinson, *Head Masters: Phrenology, Secular Education, and Nineteenth Century Social Thought*. Tuscaloosa: University of Alabama Press, 2005.

25. On this rationale for employing women teachers, see David Tyack and Elisabeth Hansot, *Learning Together: A History of Coeducation in American Public Schools*. New Haven: Yale University Press and the Russell Sage Foundation, 1990, chaps. 3 and 4. Later in this chapter the liberating aspects of the ideology of domesticity are discussed.

26. The term "normal" school was derived from the French *école normale*, a teacher training school established to serve as a norm, or model. The first public normal school in the United States was established in Lexington, Massachusetts, in 1839.

27. On Maclure and Owen, see Charles Burgess and Merle L. Borrowman, *What Doctrines to Embrace: Studies in the History of American Education*. Glenview, IL: Scott, Foresman, 1969.

28. On the educational plans of the Workingmen's Parties, see Joel Spring, *The American School, 1642–1996*, 4th ed. New York: McGraw-Hill, 1996, pp. 93–97, and Phillip R. V. Curoe, *Educational Attitudes and Policies of Organized Labor*. New York: Arno Press, [1926], 1969, pp. 8–21.

29. Burgess and Borrowman, *What Doctrines to Embrace*, p. 35.

30. See note 19.

31. Michael B. Katz, *School Reform: Past and Present*. Boston: Little, Brown and Company, 1971.

32. Katz, *Irony*, p. 273.

33. Katz would like his readers to have a similar understanding about the class bias of contemporary public education.

34. For criticisms of Katz, see Diane Ravitch, *The Revisionists Revised: A Critique of the Radical Attack on the Schools*. New York: Basic Books, 1978. See also Walter Feinberg, Harvey Kantor, Michael Katz, and Paul Violas, *Revisionists Respond to Ravitch*. Washington, D.C., 1980; Maris Vinovskis, *The Origins of Public High Schools: A Reexamination of the Beverly High School Controversy*. Madison: University of Wisconsin Press, 1985. Vinovskis and Katz have discussed their differences further in "Forum: The Origins of Public High Schools," *History of Education Quarterly*, vol. 27, 1987, pp. 241–258.

35. *Roberts v. City of Boston*, 59 Mass. 198, 200 (1849). This ruling preceded by about five decades the "separate but equal" principle enunciated in the *Plessy v. Ferguson* decision of 1896.

36. Vincent P. Lannie, *Public Money and Parochial Education: Bishop Hughes, Governor Seward, and the New York School Controversy*. Cleveland, OH: Case Western Reserve University Press, 1968.

37. Thomas C. Hunt, "Catholic Schools: Yesterday, Today, and Tomorrow," *Journal of Research on Christian Education*, Fall 2005, vol. 14, p. 163.

38. See William J. Reese, "Soldiers for Christ in the Army of God: The Christian School Movement in America," *Educational Theory*, vol. 35, 1985, pp. 175–194. See also Barbara Finkelstein, *Governing the Young: Teacher Behavior in Popular Primary Schools in 19th-Century United States*. London: Falmer Press, 1989.

39. Tyack and Hansot, *Learning Together*.

40. On Lyon, Willard, and other educators of women in this and later periods, see Barbara Miller Solomon, *In the Company of Educated Women: A History of Women and Higher Education*. New Haven: Yale University Press, 1985; John Mack Faragher and Florence Howe, *Women and Higher Education In American History*. New York: W. W. Norton, 1988.

41. This description of Beecher and her educational activities is based on Kathryn Kish Sklar, *Catharine Beecher: A Study in Domesticity*. New Haven: Yale University Press, 1973.

42. For a descriptive analysis of Southern female institutions and their leaders in the Antebellum Period, see Elizabeth P. Harper, "Socially Conservative, Academically Progressive: Higher Education for Southern Ladies. 1830–1900." Ph.D. diss., University of Virginia, 2005.

43. Carl F. Kaestle, *Pillars of the Republic*. In his last chapter, Kaestle maintains that the Midwest, like the South, was reluctant to embrace the largely New England gospel of the common school.

5
Class, Caste, and Education
in the South
1800–1900

Overview: Traditional Patterns of Education in the Antebellum South

The struggle over common schooling was not limited to New England and northern states. In the pre-Civil War South, however, those who opposed common school reform often managed to use their political power and their social and economic influence to thwart the designs of those who wanted to move forward with the Jeffersonian crusade against ignorance by creating statewide systems of publicly supported schools. It is ironic that a modified form of Jefferson's vision of a statewide system of common schools took root in the Northeast and the Midwest long before it was accepted in his own region. The reasons for this irony are complex and form the substance of our discussion in this chapter.

The tendency of southerners to rely primarily on voluntary parental, community, and church initiatives in educating their children persisted throughout most of the region down to the Civil War and with some, long after that. A spirit of individualism and independent localism, the dispersed population pattern, and traditional class and caste divisions worked against the establishment of statewide common school systems. Some children learned the four R's of reading, "riting," rithmetic, and religion from parents, ministers, or others, either in home settings or in neighborhood schools of varying descriptions and quality. Other children, especially those born into slavery or poverty, learned little or nothing from books and much from the hard lessons of life. Throughout most of the region during the antebellum period, there was no uniformity of textbooks, fees, teacher qualifications, length of school terms, "accreditation," or any of the other aspects of bureaucratization and systemization that were beginning to appear in northern and western states. There were some exceptions, but in general an attitude of laissez-faire prevailed.

Private academies became the dominant formal institutions for children of middle- and upper-class families during the post-Revolutionary decades. The attributes and quality of academies differed from community to community, influenced as they were by variations in the character, intelligence, and seriousness of purpose of schoolmasters, trustees, and patrons. A precise and uniformly applicable definition of "academy," especially in the nineteenth-century South, is almost impossible to provide. The only criterion that seems to apply across the board is that academies were usually (but not always) chartered by state legislatures or by circuit or county courts as private institutions intended to provide instruction beyond rudimentary literacy and computational skills.

Academies were established by religious groups, philanthropic and fraternal organizations such as the Freemasons, citizens who organized themselves (as trustees) into private corporations, wealthy donors, and enterprising teachers. The better ones served as college preparatory schools in the manner of the Latin grammar schools (and later high schools) in New England. Some even evolved into colleges or universities, such as Monongalia Academy, which became West Virginia University, and Liberty Hall Academy, which became Washington and Lee University. Many schools formerly known as "parson's schools," "old field schools," or "classical schools" gradually took on the "academy" label, and some in the antebellum period began to distinguish themselves by emphasizing "military training" or "manual labor" as a special feature of their offerings and identity.

Academies tended to offer a wider range of courses, especially in scientific subjects and business skills, than did either the more purely classical schools or private tutors sometimes favored by pre-ministerial students and some among the economic elite. Although most academies were limited to male students, some coeducational institutions existed from the time of the Revolution. Still other academies emerged during and after the Revolutionary era with the prefix "female" or "young ladies' " added to their titles. With the founding of Georgia Female College in 1836, the doors of higher education opened for southern women.[1]

Because of their impermanence, it is difficult to judge either the number or the influence of southern academies. One student of education in Georgia reported that more than 580 academies were chartered in that state between 1783 and 1860. This number, however, does not appear to take into account the institutions that failed to survive, that moved or merged to form new institutions, or that in some cases evolved into colleges. In compiling statistics for Virginia, Dale Robinson reported that at least 25 academies existed in that state before 1800. By 1835 the number was in excess of 380, including more than 20 female institutions. The 1860 census listed 398 academies in operation in Virginia. Only New York, North Carolina, and Pennsylvania could boast of more. Throughout the entire South in 1860, there were reported to be 2,445 academies in operation; in the western states, 1,396; in the Midwest, 1,688, and in all of New England, 872.[2]

Some defenders of the "Old South" have cited these or similar statistics in a strained attempt to argue that, while the South did little for the education of the masses, it was strongly committed to education for its political and social leaders. Clement Eaton, for example, noting that southern states were the first to establish state universities, pointed out that the 1860 census revealed that Virginia had 23 colleges with an enrollment of 2,824 students, while Georgia enrolled 3,302 students in thirty-two colleges. By way of contrast, he noted, New York had only 17 colleges with an enrollment of 2,970 students, and Massachusetts but eight institutions with 1,733 students. Drawing from statistics offered in the *Southern Literary Messenger* in 1857, Eaton calculated that there was one college man to every 666 white inhabitants in Virginia as compared with one to every 944 white inhabitants in Massachusetts at that time. Combined with figures indicating that Virginia annually spent $50,000 more than Massachusetts on colleges, Eaton insisted that Virginia and other southern states "realized the need of trained leaders."[3]

Eaton's numerical arguments conveniently overlook the ratio distortion caused by massive immigration into the northeastern states during the decades preceding the Civil War. His figures also downplay the huge gap that existed between the opportunities available to the few and the many in the South. Yet these numbers, whatever their accuracy, do underscore an argument long used in the aristocratic South against extending educational opportunity to the masses, whether white or black. William Harper, a pro-slavery lawyer from South Carolina, addressed the issue squarely in the 1850s:

> The Creator did not intend that every individual human being should be highly cultivated. . . . it is better that a part should be fully and highly cultivated and the rest utterly ignorant. To constitute a society, a variety of offices must be discharged, from those requiring but the lowest degree of intellectual power to those requiring the very highest, and it should seem that endowments ought to be apportioned according to the exigencies of the situation.

As Carl Kaestle noted, Harper and others who subscribed to this view gave voice to the fundamental aristocratic assumption that children would inherit the status and role of the parents. Lest there be any doubt about the prevalence of this assumption among the elite of southern society, *DeBow's Review* announced in 1856 that while southern states should provide some education for all whites, "beyond that it must educate the wealthy in order to maintain their position as members of the white, privileged class of our society."[4]

The Struggle for Common Schools in the Antebellum Years

Compared to northeastern and western states, the South was slow in embracing systems of common schooling. Strong caste, class, and sectional divisions, scattered population patterns, economic crises, and a widespread acceptance of the laissez-faire attitude explain in part the region's slowness in this regard. However, too hasty an acceptance of these explanations may hide more reality than it reveals. As noted in the previous chapter, public school advocates in all sections of the country experienced opposition to their plans for systems of common schools. Everywhere there were advocates of local or denominational control and individual initiative who resisted governmental intrusion into affairs that were deemed the rightful concern of the family, church, or local community. In these ways Americans living in the agrarian South were not unlike their neighbors in many parts of the North and the West.

Generalizations regarding the acceptance and rejection of the common school ideology must be tempered by sensitivity to exceptions, even as one seeks to understand regional patterns and distinctions. Those who lived in the rural sections of the Northeast, the Midwest, and the West often had more in common with the lifestyles and attitudes held by southern farmers and backwoodsmen than they did with those facing the industrialization and urbanization changes of the Northeast. Thus, rather than seeing the South as a monolithic entity standing in opposition to the spread of publicly supported common schools, one must reckon with the fact that pleas for common schools were loudly and frequently voiced throughout the southern states at the same time that advances were being realized in some northern and midwestern states.[5]

Public Schooling with a Southern Accent

Publicly assisted education, at the lower as well as higher levels of learning, had long been an accepted fact of life in many parts of the South. Most southern states in the decades before the Civil War had created "literary funds" whose monies could be expended on the education of indigent children. Some benevolent societies also reimbursed schoolmasters for the tuition of pauper students. In other communities, separate charity schools were sometimes established. In Alexandria and Petersburg, Virginia, for example, town grants and philanthropic donations supported charity schools conducted on the Lancasterian "monitorial" plan during the early nineteenth century. Likewise, Norfolk, Virginia, supported free evening schools for poor children from the 1830s to the 1850s. Charleston, South Carolina, supported five free schools for poor white children at about the same time, while Georgia officials approved expenditures from that state's pauper fund to support free schools for the poor as well as to pay the tuition of those who attended subscription or old field schools.

Public subsidies for charity education at one extreme and outlays, however meager, for higher education at the other did little to assist those in the middle who wanted more education for their children but whose limited means and fierce pride foreclosed the few options available. As a result, the accustomed way of financing and structuring education increasingly came into question. From the stump, pulpit, newspapers, and legislative halls, word spread of "common school" reforms underway in northern and western states and of innovative practices emanating from Prussia, Switzerland, France, and other European countries.

In Virginia, comprehensive school plans along the model introduced by Thomas Jefferson continued to be rejected by successive legislatures, but not because of an apathetic populace or a lack of visionary leaders. Virginia's Governor David Campbell urged the legislature in 1839 to establish a comprehensive public school system, describing the undertaking as the state's "first, great and imperative duty." When the census of 1840 revealed that one out of every thirteen white citizens in Virginia was illiterate, others joined with Campbell in clamoring for an extension of public education. Educational conventions publicizing the need for public schools and rallying support for the necessary expenditures were held in various localities in the 1840s and 1850s. Following one enthusiastic convention, the Richmond *Whig* editorialized: "That legislature would achieve immortal honor which would boldly mortgage the revenue of the state for 50 years to come, if nothing else would do it, for the education of the children of the commonwealth." Sadly for most Virginians, the legislature did not share that view.

Although Virginia did not enact a comprehensive school law until after the Civil War, there was enough interest in publicly supported education that by 1855 systems of common schools had become operative in ten counties and four cities. However, opposition to additional taxation, indifference on the part of some, and elite domination of the political machinery blocked the efforts of common school advocates in most parts of the commonwealth. As William A. Maddox observed in his study of *The Free School Idea in Virginia before the Civil War*, "perhaps in no other state were the friends of education so energetic and persistent." However, Maddox was forced to conclude that, unfortunately, "in no state was more to be overcome."[6]

Other southern states also had advocates of reform—and strong opponents with which to do battle. Georgia's constitution of 1777 had called for state-supported schools in every county. The chartering of the University of Georgia in 1785 was intended not only as an act to advance the higher education of a select group of citizens, but as a mechanism by which to oversee the development of the state's educational system. However, subsequent Georgia legislatures did little more than provide small amounts of aid to pauper schools and academies in the following decades. A common school law was passed in 1837, only to be repealed in 1840 in the midst of a depression that followed the Panic of 1837. Subsequent legislation (1843) allowed counties to levy taxes in support of pauper schooling, and in 1858 Georgia lawmakers enacted a "permissive" common school law that increased state aid and allowed counties to tax themselves for either pauper or common schools. These measures amounted to little, however, and even that little was washed away in the flood tide of the Civil War.

Of all the states that eventually formed the Confederacy, only North Carolina made impressive strides toward a statewide system of common schools before the outbreak of hostilities between the North and the South. The chartering of the University of North Carolina only four years after the University of Georgia had been granted its charter suggested that the Tar Heel state, like Georgia, intended to take education seriously. However, although public officials in both states were profuse with oratory proclaiming the virtues of the diffusion of knowledge, progress on the educational front was minimal for decades.

In a series of far-sighted bills introduced into the North Carolina legislature between 1815 and 1818, State Senator Archibald D. Murphey championed internal improvements and public education as part of a larger package of reform measures. Murphey proposed the creation of a state fund for public instruction and a state board to administer a system of public schools. The state board would be given power to create school districts, fix teacher salaries, prescribe the curriculum, and set up graded schools and examinations to determine promotion through the various grade levels. Murphey's bold plan also called for a state school for the "deaf and dumb" and generous state support for a broad course of studies at the university. He recommended that primary schools and academies be supported in part by state funds and in part by local taxes. The state would bear the full cost of the education of poor children in the primary schools for three years, and, as in Jefferson's 1779 plan, Murphey proposed that a select number of deserving students should be given free education at the secondary and university levels.

The North Carolina legislature rejected every one of Murphey's proposals, although it did authorize the establishment of a Literary Fund in 1825. University of North Carolina President Joseph Caldwell fought to keep the public education issue alive with the publication in 1832 of a series of newspaper essays entitled "Letters on Public Education." The efforts of Murphey, Caldwell, and others bore fruit with the eventual passage of the state's first common school law in 1839. In that year a bill cleared the legislature that allowed for the distribution of monies from the Literary Fund in support of "common and convenient schools."

By the terms of the 1839 common school law, every county was allowed to vote on whether its citizens wanted to create school districts, choose a county superintendent, and levy taxes for the support of common schools. In counties in which the majority opted for the provisions of this law, each district therein had to raise $20 and provide a schoolhouse in order to qualify for $40 in state aid. With this $60 minimum, a teacher might be employed for two or three months a year. Of the 68 counties then in existence in the state, all but seven initially voted in favor of the law; the seven holdouts soon followed suit. On 20 January 1840, the first public school in North Carolina was opened in Rockingham County. By 1846, every county had one or more public schools; by 1850, 2,657 common schools were in operation, with an enrollment of 100,600. Perhaps the most significant feature of the North Carolina school law was the complete absence of the charity idea. The schools were free and without tuition to all white children on equal terms.[7]

It is important not to overstate the results of North Carolina's initial venture into public schooling. For a decade or more, the new school system was a disappointment. Prejudice, inefficiency, poor supervision, and the failure of some counties to levy and collect taxes—or even to spend all their income from the state Literary Fund for schools—plagued the system. Not until 1852 and the creation of the office of State Superintendent of Common Schools did the system really begin to acquire a semblance of order and uniformity. Calvin H. Wiley, a young lawyer and novelist who was a Whig leader in the legislature, assumed the position of State Superintendent in 1853 and was so successful in organizing and developing the system that the Democratic legislature kept him in office until 1865.

In many respects, Wiley's work in North Carolina paralleled that of Horace Mann's in Massachusetts. Wiley enforced the state school laws, insisted on reports from the school districts, procured better books and equipment, and improved the supply and quality of teachers by establishing county training institutes and a system of examinations and certification administered by supervisory boards in each of the counties. By speaking to audiences all across the state and through his editorship of the *North Carolina Journal of Education*, as well as through his annual reports, Wiley publicized the gains being made in his state. In his Seventh Report, issued in 1860, for example, Wiley noted that nearly 70 percent of all (white) school-age children were enrolled in school, more than 90 percent of the teachers were licensed, schools averaged about 50 pupils and operated for four months per year, and the salaries of teachers in North Carolina were on par with those being paid in northern states. In light of the impressive gains made under Wiley's supervision, it is easy to agree with the state's historians who concluded that "The North Carolina system was the best in the South in 1860—better actually than it ever was later until after 1900, and better in comparison with the systems of other states than it has ever been since 1860."[8]

Although North Carolina took the lead among southern states in terms of establishing a statewide system of tax-supported schools, on the eve of the Civil War other states such as Alabama, Louisiana, Kentucky, and Tennessee were progressing in that direction. However, even with these exceptions in mind and before the disastrous effects of the Civil War brought financial ruin to the region, southerners typically displayed strong resistance to taxation for educational purposes. The South's intense spirit of localism, limited urbanization, East–West sectional rivalries, agrarian economic system, and rigid class and caste system all worked against efforts to spread education broadly among the masses, white as well as black. Moreover, the more homogeneous white southern population did not encounter the strains of ethnic and religious diversity or wrestle with the strife that was accompanying the industrialization and urbanization of the Northeast. The power of "social control" arguments being put forth in support of public school systems north of the Mason-Dixon line thus had less appeal in the states to the south.

In the pro-slavery South, concerns about social control actually worked against the development of public education. Perhaps more than any other factor, the existence and defense of slavery forestalled the acceptance in the

South of the republican ideals that helped stimulate educational advances in other parts of the United States. Although plantation masters who owned vast acreage and numbers of slaves held disproportionate political power, they had reason to fear dissenters in their midst—independent-minded farmers, a small but increasingly assertive urban merchant class, and religious groups that held the practice of slavery in contempt. Behind them stood the greatest threat of all, the presence of millions of Africans and their descendants, whose continued bondage depended on their being kept in ignorance of the very ideals on which the nation had been founded. The planter elites and their allies had much to lose and little to gain from the extension of public education.

Education Behind the Veil: Slaves, Free Blacks, and the Other South

By the eve of the American Revolution, blacks had been a presence in the country for more than 150 years. By that time the majority of blacks were native-born Americans who had no firsthand knowledge of Africa. Although the large-scale importation of slaves did not end until the opening decade of the nineteenth century, for successive generations of American-born blacks, as for new generations of American-born whites, tales of distant lands and customs across the sea had become second- and third-hand accounts, stories told by elders who had learned from their elders about life in another time and place. As historian Ira Berlin put it, "Slowly, almost imperceptibly, transplanted Africans became a new people. They spoke English, worked with English tools, and ate food prepared in the English manner. On the eve of the Revolution, many blacks had done so for two or three generations, and sometimes more."[9]

As with the contact between Euro-Americans and Native Americans, the acculturation process was by no means a one-way affair. Indeed, multiple African heritages fused together and influenced as well as blended into elements of Euro-American culture under the pressures of new world conditions. Moreover, during the time of mounting tensions with the British, some African Americans who had listened in on discussions about natural rights and liberty were prepared to fight for those ideals once the American Revolution began.

The promise of freedom, however, was initially extended to the enslaved descendants of Africans not by the American revolutionaries but by the British, who promised liberty to those who took up arms against the rebellious colonists. Thousands of African Americans responded to the British offer. In later years, some who served the British cause or escaped slavery under the protection of British troops migrated to Africa, the West Indies, Florida, or Canada. Others remained in or returned to the United States, passing into the ranks of the growing free black population. As the war progressed, colonial militias also began accepting blacks, and at war's end, many who had sided with the patriot cause passed from bondage to freedom as well, albeit to a freedom circumscribed by caste distinctions.[10]

The egalitarian spirit unleashed by the American Revolution, reinforced by a sense of evangelical brotherhood stemming from the religious revivals of the late eighteenth and early nineteenth centuries, spurred opponents of slavery to work against the "peculiar institution." Although opposition to emancipation existed in many parts of the North as well as in the South, by 1805 every northern state had enacted legislation providing for the eventual ending of slavery. Slave owners in New York and New Jersey received compensation for giving up their human property. Slaveholders in some northern states yielded to abolitionist legislation with grave reluctance. Fear, prejudice, and economic concerns fed resistance to the emancipation of slaves even in New England, where in 1790 blacks accounted for less than 2 percent of the population. Viewed in this light, the rigid defiance of abolitionist proposals in South Carolina, a state with a 44 percent black population, becomes more understandable.[11]

Education and the "Hidden Passages to Freedom"

In spite of all the legal and social obstacles in their paths, some African Americans, slave and free, found routes to education during the antebellum era that opened up limited opportunities for them both during and after slavery. In some instances, these educational openings were intentionally created by well-meaning whites; in others, whites unwittingly lowered or removed barriers that had been erected to keep blacks in ignorance. Still other ways to knowledge were quietly and discretely charted by African Americans themselves. These overt and covert approaches to education and training operated simultaneously with the "underground railroad" to create a "hidden passage" to freedom. Equipped with valuable skills and attitudes, some educated blacks managed to survive as free people in a society they had helped build but not design. Sketching the contours of the hidden passage is essential if one is to understand fully the educational history of a people who have been forced to follow a circuitous route in pursuit of the American promise of equality.[12]

Abolitionists and African Schools

Abolitionists in northern and southern states provided valuable help in creating educational avenues for African Americans during the long period before universal emancipation. As noted in Chapter 2, some religious groups were engaged in the education of both slaves and free blacks as well as Native Americans in the pre-Revolutionary period. As early as 1763, for example, the Anglican sponsors of the Society for the Propagation of the Gospel in Foreign Parts were promoting educational institutions for both Native and African Americans. Groups of Presbyterians, Baptists, Methodists, and other denominations also became engaged in educational activity among black Americans, both before and after the Revolutionary War. Indeed, in spite of laws and public opinion to the contrary, some religious groups in the South as well as throughout the North continued to work for black enlightenment and manumission until (and beyond) the outbreak of the Civil War.

Probably no group equaled the Quakers in their zeal to promote the education and freedom of African Americans. When financially able, Quakers purchased slaves and then released them as free people. So disturbing did this practice become to the pro-slavery forces in North Carolina that the state supreme court ruled in 1827 that Quakers could no longer buy and release slaves. "When Quakers hold slaves," reasoned the state's high court, "nothing but the name is wanting to render it at once a complete emancipation." It is perhaps worth noting that Quakers, working under the auspices of the North Carolina Manumission Society, had been largely responsible for securing the freedom of more than 2,000 slaves in the two years preceding the court's ruling. However, neither law nor social convention dampened Quaker enthusiasm for doing whatever could be done to improve life for African Americans. Both Carter G. Woodson and John Hope Franklin credit the Quakers with accomplishing more than any other sect in the task of educating blacks in antebellum North Carolina.[13]

The momentary respite in racial antagonism that followed the American Revolution encouraged some free blacks in cooperation with sympathetic whites to establish integrated academies. In 1802, for example, Quakers in Baltimore reported several "mixed schools" in operation, while in Alexandria, Virginia, a few teachers accepted both white and black students into their schools. Experiments in racial harmony such as these did not last, however, and "mixed schools" soon disappeared in many parts of the North as well as throughout the South. After 1820, most northern states either excluded blacks from schools altogether or created separate institutions for them. In 1787, Boston blacks petitioned the legislature to establish special facilities for their race, since they were receiving "no benefit from the free schools." The same complaint was repeated forty years later when John Russwurm, editor of *Freedom's Journal*, the nation's first black newspaper, editorialized:

> While the benevolence of the age has founded and endowed seminaries of Learning for all other classes and nations, we have to lament, that as yet, no door is open to receive the degraded children of Africa. Alone they have stood—alone they remain stationary; while charity extends the hands to all others.[14]

Although integrated schools tended to be short-lived and separate facilities were often only slightly more permanent, special academies for "the children of Blacks and people of Color" were established by some individuals such as Robert Pleasants, a Virginia Quaker abolitionist. Around 1781, Pleasants established a school on his own land, outside Richmond, with the hope that the institution would form the minds of blacks "on the principles of virtue and religion, and in common and useful literature . . . as the most likely means to render so numerous a people fit for freedom and to become useful citizens." In Charleston, South Carolina, the Minor Society established a school for orphans and the children of other free blacks in 1810. The *École des Orphelins Indigents*, established in New Orleans in 1840, received generous support from wealthy free blacks. Some free black parents hired private teachers for their children, and a few even sent their children abroad for education.[15]

One of the most striking—and exceptional—efforts to teach free blacks and whites during the antebellum period involves the work of John Chavis of North Carolina. From 1808 until he retired in the 1830s, Chavis, a well-educated African American, conducted a school in Raleigh in which he taught whites during the day and free blacks in the evenings. Chavis was held in esteem by many well-placed whites and had few equals in intelligence. His effectiveness as a schoolmaster won him the admiration and praise of many, including the editor of the Raleigh newspaper, who wrote in 1830:

> On Friday last, we attended an examination of the free children of color, attached to the school of *John Chavis*, also colored, but a regularly educated Presbyterian Minister, and we have seldom received more gratification from an exhibition of a similar character. To witness a well regulated school, composed of this class of persons—to see them setting an example both in behavior and scholarship, which their *white* superiors might take pride in imitating, was a cheering spectacle to the philanthropist. The exercises throughout, evinced a degree of attention and assiduous care on the part of the instructor, highly creditable, and of attainment on the part of his scholars almost incredible.[16]

The efforts of individuals like Pleasants and Chavis and of groups such as the Quakers and various abolitionist societies were notable but severely limited in impact. Emancipationists had difficulty establishing and maintaining African American schools. Apathy was often as great an obstacle as open resistance. After five full years of operation, for example, an African American school begun by the Delaware Abolition Society still met but once a week. "If abolitionists had difficulty generating enthusiasm for educating newly liberated blacks," observed Berlin, "small wonder that most whites remained unconcerned." Those who *were* concerned often stood in *opposition* to the development of white-sponsored African American schools. As those schools failed, freedmen in some communities organized and conducted their own schools. In the antebellum South, however, schools run by blacks often operated clandestinely—the school of John Chavis standing as a special exception to the general rule.[17]

Sensing that literacy and schools contained the seeds of insurrection, southern states began to clamp down on educational activities for blacks, especially in the wake of the slave uprising led by Nat Turner in 1831. Southern legislatures adopted "black codes" or laws that made teaching slaves to read and write a criminal offense. These laws meant that slaves freed after the 1830s were even less likely to have acquired literacy skills than had their predecessors.

Despite these restrictive laws, blacks in bondage as well as freedom continued to learn to read and write. John Hope Franklin noted that, while laws prohibiting the teaching of slaves to read and write after 1831 severely limited the practice in North Carolina, the teaching of *free* blacks and even slaves often continued in spite of public opposition. Franklin cited an 1854 article in the *New Bern Atlantic* in which the writer complained that it was a "notorious fact" that day schools were being maintained for the enlightenment of the people of color in that North Carolina coastal community.

Although there was no state law against the private teaching of free blacks, public opinion refused to countenance the activity. Nevertheless, the practice continued, even in schools. The census of 1850 reported 100,591 whites and 217 free blacks enrolled in North Carolina schools. Free blacks were attending schools in twenty-five counties. As Franklin noted, while the number of free blacks reported to be in school in 1850 was relatively small, there were undoubtedly many others who were receiving their training privately—indeed, secretly. His suspicions would seem to be supported by the fact that, although there are no records of any schools for blacks in Gates County, North Carolina, more than half the free black males in that county in 1850 reportedly could read and write. Moreover, of the 12,048 free black adults in the state, the 1850 census listed 5,191 (43 percent) as literate.[18]

Education for Colonization

The growth of the free black population in the United States, the rising tide of abolitionist sentiment, and the increasing threat of slave revolt heightened the fears of those who could not envision blacks and whites living together as coequal citizens. As mentioned earlier, these anxieties had prompted Thomas Jefferson to recommend the elimination of slavery through a process of education that would culminate in the emigration of blacks to Africa, an idea that James Monroe, Henry Clay, and other leaders came to endorse. Humanitarian and religious impulses motivated some who were interested in preparing Christian missionaries for service in Africa. Some free blacks saw the idea as a passage from marginal if not actual slavery to freedom and independence in a country of their own. Thus, a variety of motives led to the formation in 1816 of the Society for the Colonizing of the Free Blackman of the United States, more commonly known as the American Colonization Society. Under the auspices of this society, several religious denominations undertook the task of establishing schools in this country for the education of free blacks who were willing to emigrate to Africa.

In 1822, the Colonization Society established Liberia as the possible new home for free blacks from the United States. Another agency, the African Education Society of the United States, was formed in 1829 in an effort to stimulate the founding of schools that would "afford persons of colour destined to Africa such an education in Letters, Agriculture and the Mechanic Arts, as may qualify them for usefulness and influence in Africa." One free black who took advantage of the education-for-colonization scheme stated clearly his reasons for wanting to become one of the first black missionaries sent to Liberia by the Baptist Missionary Convention:

I am an African, and in this country, however meritorious my conduct and respectable my character, I cannot receive due to either. I wish to go to a country where I shall be estimated by my merits, not by my complexion; and I feel bound to labor for my suffering race.[19]

While this missionary's feelings were shared by some blacks, others, black and white, saw serious flaws in the movement. The entire colonization scheme came under attack by radical abolitionists led by William Lloyd Garrison. Garrison argued that the colonization movement did nothing to attack the crucial problem of slavery or to improve the conditions of free blacks who wanted to remain in the United States. Many free blacks also denounced the movement and stated that they would not abandon their brethren in slavery. Some whites opposed the program because they feared free blacks might gain an education and then decide to stay rather than to emigrate, creating further tensions between the races. Moreover, the transplantation schemes proved to be economically unviable.

The arguments for and against the colonization scheme were as varied and contradictory as were the coalitions that formed on both sides of the issue. Whatever the intentions and concerns of supporters and detractors of the movement, the conclusion must be drawn that, for the most part, the attempts to provide education for blacks who would emigrate to Africa amounted to little. Only around 1,400 free blacks migrated to Liberia from the United States during the decade 1820–1830, years when the colonization movement was at its peak. During the whole of the antebellum period, less than 15,000 free blacks emigrated from the country as part of the various colonization schemes.[20]

The Sunday School Movement and African American Education

Sunday schools first began to appear on the American scene in significant numbers in the 1790s. Based on similar institutions founded in Britain during the previous decade, Sunday schools came into being to provide rudimentary instruction to poor working children on their only free day of the week. Although some of those who founded Sunday schools were genuinely concerned about the religious instruction of children from working families, others were concerned with the roughness displayed by unsupervised children in urban areas who obviously had little or no respect for "the Lord's day." The fact that working children were slipping through the educational cracks by not attending weekday common schools made them, in the eyes of some reformers, a "social problem" in need of correction. Thus, Sunday schools appeared early in the American republic as institutions designed to offer literary and moral instruction to working-class children.[21]

In northern and southern communities alike, Sunday schools fulfilled a variety of functions. Some employed paid teachers to impart basic literacy to working children; others were staffed by volunteers who taught reading, writing, and religion to poor or black children; still others concentrated primarily on catechism classes for church members' children. In some localities, Sunday school supporters obtained public funds to advance their work. In 1824, for example, school commissioners in Richmond, Virginia, appropriated thirty cents for each Sunday school pupil, and the following year added a supplement for books and supplies.

Sunday schools became important sources for basic literacy in the early nineteenth century, especially among individuals or groups excluded from public or tax-supported schools. Black adults as well as children responded eagerly to opportunities offered by Sunday school teachers in northern and southern communities. Charleston, Nashville, and St. Louis were among larger cities in which Sunday schools included blacks, although usually in separate classes and at different hours from whites.

After the 1831 Turner Rebellion however, the passage of laws prohibiting the teaching of slaves and uneasiness on the part of whites severely limited African Americans' access to Sunday schools. For example, when white parents in Baltimore objected to the presence of blacks (even though in separate classes) at the Asbury (Methodist) Sunday Schools, the classes for the black students ended. Similarly, the white-sponsored Sunday schools in Washington, D.C., turned black children out following the Turner revolt. However, in Washington, D.C., Baltimore, and elsewhere, some of the slack was taken up by blacks who opened their own schools after whites withdrew their support. Although most of the black students were free persons, some slaves were allowed to attend Sunday schools in some sections of the South.

In spite of prohibitive legislation and negative public opinion, some white southerners continued to conduct Sunday schools until the Civil War. A white woman who established a Sunday school on her Louisiana plantation in the 1840s wrote that her school "was always well attended" by slave children, even though she was well aware that conducting Sunday schools at the time was "not a very popular thing to do." A southern correspondent for the Presbyterian New York *Observer* reported that his unnamed city contained eight Sunday schools for blacks, each of which had slave members. "*In all of these schools,*" he contended, "*the scholars are taught to read.*" The first Sunday school for blacks in Lexington, Virginia, was launched in the 1840s by a Presbyterian minister, William Henry Ruffner, who later became Virginia's first superintendent of public instruction.[22]

For at least some African Americans, then, Sunday schools opened up yet another passage to literacy and thus eventually to freedom. Generalizing to the entire antebellum population, Boylan advanced the assertion that, "as an agency of cultural transmission, the Sunday school almost rivaled in importance the nineteenth-century public school."[23]

Education within the Plantation Economy

In theory, slavery existed as a rational system in which master–slave relations were structured along purely functional lines: the profitable purchase,

production, and utilization of slave labor. In practice, however, the inter-
dependence that bound slaves to masters and masters to slaves gave rise to
educational necessities and opportunities that served both masters and slaves.
The goal of every plantation owner was to make his plantation as nearly self-
sufficient as possible. This goal could be approached only if slaves—the human
machinery of production—were trained to be efficient and loyal workers.
Thus, the slave regime itself required and encouraged the teaching and learning
of work skills and habits that were essential supports of the slave-based plantation economy. In addition to work or production-related skills, however, social,
cultural, and religious attitudes and values also came to be transmitted across
the caste and class lines on which the slave system was based.

Occupational Skills

On many of the larger plantations, some male slaves became quite proficient as
carpenters, blacksmiths, masons, machinists, cooks, and farmers. Slave women
also worked as farmers and cooks, and some acquired special skills in sewing,
weaving, and midwifery. Selected boys and girls learned these skills on the plantation as they were put to work with their parents, other slaves who had been
taught and mastered these skills, or white artisans. In some cases, masters paid
to have promising and trusted slaves apprenticed to master craftsmen for training in specific occupations. The renowned landscape architect, Frederick
L. Olmsted, reported encountering a slave whose master had paid $500 to have
him trained as a machinist. Olmsted noted that this slave was entrusted with
keys to all the storage buildings on the plantation, that he weighed and measured all the rations issued, and that he had made and supervised all the
machinery on the place, including the steam engine. To cite another instance,
Thomas Jefferson, as concerned about the preparation of his food as he was
about every detail in the construction of his mountaintop home, had one of his
slaves, James Hemings, accompany him to France where the young man was
instructed in the finer points of preparing French cuisine. James Hemings was
eventually freed by Jefferson, but only after he had passed on his skill to another
slave—his brother, Peter.[24]

Although the example of Jefferson's French-trained chef and the machinist
who caught the attention of Olmsted may be among the more notable examples
of slaves being trained through the apprenticeship system, these were not isolated happenings. Although field hands received little "training" beyond the
basic rudiments of farming, some among the 400,000 or so slaves who lived in
towns by 1850 had become quite skilled. For example, the Charleston industrial
census of 1848 listed more slave carpenters and coopers than free blacks or
whites in those trades. In addition, slaves were employed as tailors, shoemakers,
cabinetmakers, painters, plasterers, seamstresses, barbers, hairdressers, and
bankers, and in other occupations. In Charleston, free blacks were employed in
all but eight of the fifty census occupations listed, and slaves were engaged in all
but thirteen. Skilled slaves not only increased the income of masters who hired

them out or used them in their own businesses, but also, at sale, brought considerably more than field hands of similar age with lesser skills.[25]

Literacy Skills

Laws dating back into colonial times in many southern as well as northern states required that masters arrange for instruction in literacy as well as teach job-related skills. These laws, which applied to black as well as white apprentices, survived into the antebellum period. While such laws were not strictly enforced, some blacks, free and slave, were indentured to master craftsmen who took their obligations seriously. Even after the passage of laws restricting literacy instruction, free black apprentices in some sections of the South were, as late as 1850, bound by indentures stipulating that they were to be instructed in reading and writing as well as in specific occupational skills.[26]

Moreover, some blacks still bound by the chains of slavery became literate in spite of laws to the contrary. The estimate by W.E.B. DuBois that about 5 percent of the slave population had learned to read by 1860 is entirely plausible and may even be too low. Certainly, slaves residing in towns and cities had more opportunities to gain literacy skills than did slaves on the large plantations of the "Black Belt," yet literate slaves appeared everywhere. Slaveholders, ex-slaves, and travelers all agreed that many plantations had one or more literate slaves and that any given locality had some. A leading historian of southern slavery observed that even the most restricted and isolated plantation slaves normally had contact with someone who could transmit information about the wider world, thus making possible the rapid spread of political news among the slaves.[27]

How did these slaves gain literacy skills? In some cases, those who held them in bondage either became their teachers or else made provisions for reading and writing instruction. The occupations of some slaves made at least a degree of literacy necessary. Thomas Webber cites an example of a slave who was taught to read and write by his master, who was a doctor, so that he could take the addresses of visiting patients. In some cases the motive was religious, as is evidenced by an ex-slave who stated that after his baptism, his master "removed all objections to my learning how to read, and said he wanted all the boys to learn how to read the Bible." A mistress who found herself torn between the dictates of law and of conscience lamented: "This teaching of Negroes is a sore problem to me! It ought to be done and I ought to do it. . . . My difficulties I am convinced beset many a well-intentioned mistress who, like me does nothing because she cannot do what she feels she *ought*." House slaves tended to receive more attention because of their greater intimacy with whites. However, since slave children were rarely segregated according to the status of their parents, some masters, more mistresses, and even more white children defied the law, which was unenforceable on the plantations anyway, and instructed slaves for whom they had a special fondness.[28]

White children were especially active in teaching their black playmates who wanted to learn. "Playing school" became a favorite game of some. Among the white children who played "teacher" with their black "pupils" were Sarah and Angelina Grimke, daughters of the Honorable John Fouchereau Grimke, judge of the Supreme Court of South Carolina. The Grimke sisters took great delight in teaching their playmates late at night, fully aware that what they were doing was officially against the law. Sarah described their secretive activity: "The light was put out, the keyhole secured, and flat on our stomachs before the fire, with spelling books in our hands, we defied the laws of South Carolina." In Virginia, Letitia Burwell and her sister did not need to take such precautions, for their father rewarded them when they taught arithmetic to a slave boy he was training to be a mechanic.[29]

While the doors to literacy were opened for slaves by some friendly whites, the slaves themselves carried on the process. Sometimes a literate slave taught others with the permission of his master or mistress, but more often such teaching was done on the sly. An old black preacher in Georgia moaned on his dying bed that he had caused the death of many slaves by teaching them to read and write. Will Capers, ex-slave from St. Helena Island, told a northern missionary in 1862 that he had conducted "a secret night school for men" while still enslaved. Frederick Douglass, who as a young slave had surreptitiously learned to read, later conducted a clandestine Sunday school in order "to exercise my gifts and to impart to my brother-slaves the little knowledge I possessed." Douglass soon had twenty to thirty young men meeting with him on Sunday afternoons. Their eagerness to learn (and their stealth) impressed Douglass, who recalled: "It was surprising with what ease they provided themselves with spelling books."[30]

Cultural Transmission

Accompanying and transcending literacy and occupational skills was the process of cultural transmission that resulted from the human interactions of masters and slaves. At one level, the cruelty and degradation experienced by slaves inevitably aroused deep animosity against those who held them in bondage. On another level, however, some slaves and masters found themselves entwined in various degrees of personal intimacy that led to cultural diffusion, acculturation, and, on occasion, miscegenation.

Free blacks and house slaves, especially mulattoes, tended over time to absorb some of the values and prejudices of the "quality folks" with whom they identified. They learned to look down upon ill-mannered field hands and "poor white trash" and to form strong opinions regarding appropriate behavior and refined tastes. In manners, values, styles of dress, patterns of speech, and in other ways, some blacks were assimilated as deeply into the mores of the dominant culture as their complexion, circumstance, and public opinion would allow. Thus, even before the slave system and plantation economy were forcibly ended, class divisions among African Americans were forming along lines similar to those that divided American whites. This process of assimilation—and for some, attendant racial shame—also forms part of the educational legacy of slave life as it existed within the confines of the antebellum plantation economy.[31]

Reconstruction and the New Social Order

The Union Army and Freedmen's Education

The visions of freedom that had for so long inspired the spiritual laments ascending from the slave quarters began to acquire a semblance of reality after the bombardment of Fort Sumter in April 1861. Initially, Union officers were unclear as to what should be done with the sometimes jubilant and often confused men, women, and children who made their way into their military encampments. At the outset of the war, the official position of President Abraham Lincoln and the Congress was predicated on preserving the Union. As late as the day following the First Battle of Bull Run, Congress passed resolutions disclaiming any intention of freeing the slaves or interfering with "the rights or established institutions" of the states in rebellion. When General John C. Fremont took it upon himself to declare all of Missouri under martial law and asserted that the slaves of any person who resisted federal authority would be considered "free men," he was reprimanded by Lincoln and forced to recall the order.

General Benjamin F. Butler took a more circumspect course at his command post at Fortress Monroe, Virginia. When three runaway slaves reached his lines six weeks after the outbreak of hostilities, he declared them "contraband of war" and refused to release them to a Confederate officer who came for them under a flag of truce. Word of Butler's policy of protection quickly spread to other slaves in the vicinity, and within three days the General had $60,000 worth of human contraband on his hands. In September 1861, Mary Peake, an educated Christian woman born of a black mother and a white father, opened at Fortress Monroe one of the first schools for freedmen that were to spring up under the protection of Union guns during and after the Civil War.[32]

The Sea Island Schools

The question of what to do with the growing numbers of slaves who sought the protection of federal troops took on momentous proportions as the war progressed. On November 7, 1861, seven months after the fall of Fort Sumter, U.S. Navy gunboats cleared the way for Union troops to take possession of the Sea Islands off the coast of South Carolina. As the fleet sailed into Port Royal Sound and opened fire on the defending batteries, the white population fled the islands and headed inland. When Union troops entered Beaufort, the only town of consequence in the area, they found a solitary white man who, too drunk to move, had been left behind. Also abandoned along with large plantation homes and fields speckled with cotton were some 10,000 slaves. General William T. Sherman described the deserted slaves as being in a state of "abject ignorance and mental stolidity." He proposed that sustenance be provided the bewildered slaves until such a time as they could support themselves. Along with representatives of the American Missionary Association (AMA), Sherman also made appeals for teachers who would venture to the islands to offer instruction in "the rudiments of civilization and Christianity."[33]

In the spring of 1862, a band of fifty-three missionaries, young men and women mainly from Boston and New York, docked at Beaufort and confronted for the first time on slave territory the African Americans for whose freedom they had so long agitated and had now come to secure. In what became a "rehearsal for Reconstruction," the first extensive schools for former slaves were established on the Sea Islands and the assault on illiteracy began in earnest. By the end of 1862 there were more than 1,700 children attending school on St. Helena, Ladies, and Port Royal Islands alone, and perhaps 500 more on Hilton Head and Parris Islands. Abandoned lands were confiscated and tenuous titles awarded to freedmen. Participation in political rallies and local politics presented the promise of a new world opening before those who had been propertyless and voiceless only months before. Following Lincoln's Emancipation Proclamation, which went into effect on January 1, 1863, black soldiers were recruited into the 1st and 2nd South Carolina Volunteers. These units, composed of former slaves, were on hand for the assault of Fort Wagner in July 1863 that was spearheaded by the free black soldiers of the Massachusetts 54th Regiment. Colonel Robert Gould Shaw, who commanded the 54th and fell as a martyred hero in that battle, has been immortalized in a St. Gaudens' monument placed under the elms of the Boston Common and in the motion picture *Glory*.[34] By the time the Confederate battle flags were finally furled at Appomattox, a number of practices that were to shape Reconstruction policies had already been tested in the Sea Island communities.

The Army as Educator

In other parts of the South, soldiers, missionaries, and literate blacks also were at work during the war years to prepare the way for genuine emancipation grounded in literacy and civic education. As the Union army brought sections of the divided South under military control, commanding officers became involved in recruiting teachers, establishing school districts, outlining curricula, obtaining textbooks, and turning confiscated homes into schools for freedmen. Former slaves were given religious and secular instruction in schools that were supervised by military authorities and staffed by some southern and growing numbers of northern teachers. Within the army itself, chaplains and line officers joined with teachers supported by benevolent associations in efforts to educate black soldiers. The officers and men of the 62nd and 65th U.S. Colored Troops were so impressed with the instruction they received in training camp at Benton Barracks, Missouri, that they contributed $6,380 to establish the school that became Lincoln University (Missouri).

While not all ex-slaves were as inspired and eager as those who gave from their meager military salaries to establish a school, most gave evidence of a "great desire" to learn. The observation of Colonel Thomas W. Higginson, commanding officer of the 33rd U.S. Colored Troops, that his men's "love of the spelling book is perfectly inexhaustible," was by no means atypical, as John Blassingame and others have amply documented.[35]

The advance of northern armies thus did more than preserve the Union and free the South from the curse of slavery. The soldiers who rescued "contraband" ex-slaves also gave many their first lessons as free men and women. With both bullets and books, the military opened the way for a second invasion of liberators who came with the promise of freeing the human spirit and mind. Well before the battles had ended, legions of "Yankee schoolmarms" began to descend upon the South, armed with the word of God, Webster's blue-backed spellers, and the zeal of latter-day Puritans.

Yankee Schoolmarms and the "New Puritanism"

Drawn mostly from New England states, the missionary teachers who came south under the auspices of the American Missionary Association and other benevolent agencies had enlisted in what many considered to be a holy crusade. Like their ancestors of the seventeenth century, many of the "new Puritans" saw themselves as called forth on a special mission for God. Their aim was to impress upon the white South the errors of its ways and at the same time deliver the black masses from the ignorance and ignominy that had been their lot under the slave system. This work was to be achieved by implanting in southern minds and hearts, black and white, the essentials of the Puritan way of life.

As James McPherson has emphasized, the concept of a "new Puritanism" embraced far more than mere inspirational rhetoric, although rhetorical flourishes abounded. The New England Freedman's Aid Society in 1865 urged the recruitment of enough teachers "to make a New England of the whole South." A Methodist abolitionist from Boston hailed the first wave of teachers departing for the South as the new "Pilgrim Fathers," sent on a nineteenth-century errand into the wilderness to create "a New South after the Puritan and perfect pattern." Students at Oberlin College, a major outpost of New England religious and social values in the Midwest, were recruited as missionary teachers whose objective, they were told, was to convert and Puritanize the South.

Themselves driven by an acute sense of individual and social guilt and an attendant need for repentance, the new Puritans came south prepared to engage in "moral warfare." They expected—and found—that their lives would be full of sacrifice and self-denial. At the end of one particularly trying day, Sophia Packard, a native of New Salem, Massachusetts, who had taken the lead in the founding of Spelman College, could find only enough strength to write in her diary: "tired tired tired tired tired tired." A Savannah teacher deplored the "indolence, degradation and vice" of the freedmen under her care, but with stern Puritan resolve she renewed her dedication to the task at hand. "It is no time . . . to sit down and cry," she noted in a letter to friends back home. "The voice we hear today, is Go! work—This people must be educated, and may we rejoice that God permits us to aid in such a work."[36]

The Freedmen's Bureau

As the advance of Union armies and northern missionaries made clear, schooling was only one of many problems facing southern blacks and whites as the war moved toward its final chapter in April 1865. A month before the Confederate surrender at Appomattox, Congress established the Bureau of Refugees, Freedmen, and Abandoned Lands, better known as the Freedmen's Bureau. General Oliver O. Howard, appointed by President Lincoln as the first commissioner of the bureau, began at once to map out a program aimed at securing "health, sustenance, and legal rights for refugees" and providing them with the "foundations for education."

Between 1865 and 1869, the Freedmen's Bureau issued 21 million rations, approximately 5 million of which were given to whites. The bureau established hospitals and expended over $2 million attempting to provide health care to freedmen. It supervised colonies of infirm, destitute, and vagrant blacks in several states, and distributed small parcels of abandoned land to some freedmen. In areas where the interests of southern blacks could not be entrusted to local courts, the bureau organized special courts and boards of arbitration. Despite some corruption, inefficiency, and white southern hostility to the bureau, its role in providing relief to the war-torn South, and especially to the black population, was considerable.

The most significant achievements of the Freedmen's Bureau were in the field of education. The bureau assumed responsibility for coordinating the relief programs and educational activities of scores of benevolent societies that established operations in the South. John W. Alvord, the general superintendent of schools for the Freedmen's Bureau, appointed a superintendent of schools for each southern state. These superintendents and their agents supervised a vast network of reading, writing, and industrial schools that operated by day, night, and on Sundays. By 1869 there were more than 9,500 teachers working in the freedmen's schools of the South. By 1870, when the educational activity of the bureau came to an end, 4,329 schools had been established with a combined enrollment of more than 247,000 pupils.[37]

The Freedmen's Bureau cooperated with philanthropic and religious organizations to develop a number of institutions of higher education. Among others, the bureau assisted the American Missionary Association in supporting Fisk University, Talladega College, Hampton Institute, and Straight University (now Dillard). The Freedmen's Aid Society of the Methodist Episcopal Church founded Bennett College, Clark University, Meharry Medical College, Morgan College, and Philander Smith College. The American Baptist Home Missionary Society gave support to Benedict, Bishop, and Morehouse colleges, Shaw University, Spelman Seminary, and Virginia Union University. Atlanta and

Figure 5.1 Freedmen's Union Industrial School, Richmond, Virginia.
Source: Library of Congress, Prints and Photographs Division, LC-USZ62-33264.

Leland Universities were operated by independent boards of northern missionary groups. Howard University, named for the Union general who headed the Freedmen's Bureau and who later became the institution's president, had its beginnings among a small group of Congregationalists in Washington, D.C. Howard began operations in 1867 as an institution whose doors were open to all, regardless of race or gender.

Black churches and organizations also set up colleges that figure prominently among the historically black institutions in the United States. The African Methodist Episcopal Church founded Allen University, Morris Brown College, and Wilberforce, among others. Livingstone College was created by the African Methodist Episcopal Zion Church, while the Colored Methodist Episcopal Church and state conventions of black Baptists founded still other schools and colleges.

African American Self-Help Efforts

The strong desire of ex-slaves to learn was underscored in Superintendent Alvord's first report on the Freedmen's Bureau schools, issued in January 1866. In detailing the educational activity taking place in the former slave states, Alvord gave special attention to numerous instances of "self-teaching" and "native schools" found to exist among the freed men and women. "Throughout the entire South," he noted, "an effort is being made by the colored people to educate themselves." As if echoing the observations of Colonel Higginson and other northern commentators, Alvord reported:

> In the absence of other teaching they are determined to be self-taught; and everywhere some elementary textbook, or the fragment of one, may be seen in the hands of negroes.

He described one such "native school" that had arisen in Goldsboro, North Carolina:

> Two colored young men, who but a little time before commenced to learn themselves, had gathered 150 pupils, all quite orderly and hard at study.

Alvord estimated that there were "at least 500 schools of this description . . . already in operation throughout the South."

Even more illustrative of the freedmen's desire to learn and to have their children educated is the fact that African Americans in some communities petitioned military officers to levy an added tax on them in order to have sufficient funds for schools. Alvord recounted:

> I saw one [petition] . . . at least 30 feet in length, representing 10,000 negroes. It was affecting to examine it and note the names and marks (x) of such a long list of parents, ignorant themselves, but begging that their children might be educated, promising that from beneath their present burdens, and out of their extreme poverty, they would pay for it.

Citing the observations of Alvord and others, James Anderson has convincingly argued that black efforts at self-education have too often been underestimated and unappreciated. He notes, for example, that in 1865, African American leaders in Georgia formed their own education association to raise funds and supervise their own schools. By the fall of 1866, Georgia blacks were financing in whole or in part 96 of the 123 evening schools then operative and owned 57 school buildings. A black newspaper in Savannah reported that sixteen schools in operation in that city were "under the control of an Educational Board of Colored Men, taught by colored teachers, and sustained by the freed people." This same newspaper expressed the hope that missionary teachers were not in the South "in any vain reliance on their superior gifts, either of intelligence or benevolence; or in any foolish self-confidence that they have a special call to this office, or special endowments to meet its demands."

African American pride and Puritan missionary zeal sometimes shared common ends but differed in means. Some northern teachers were "taken aback" to discover that some African Americans preferred to teach in and operate their own schools without the benefit of external aid, advice, or personnel.

In light of these tensions, one can appreciate more fully why some missionaries complained that the ex-slaves displayed a conspicuous lack of gratitude "for the charity which northern friends are so graciously bestowing."[38]

Certainly, on one point most ex-slaves and missionaries agreed—literacy and formal education were essential ingredients of true liberation. The *New Orleans Black Republican* editorialized at war's end: "Freedom and school books and newspapers go hand in hand. Let us secure the freedom we have received by the intelligence that can maintain it." In state after state, black politicians and leaders joined with white Republicans in southern constitutional conventions to ensure that public education clauses were worked into the new constitutions of the former Confederate states. Although marked by controversy and often subverted in practice, by 1870 every southern state had made specific constitutional provisions to establish and support a system of public schools.[39]

Figure 5.2 "Emancipation" illustration by Thomas Nast. Abraham Lincoln's Emancipation Proclamation was signed January 1, 1863 in the midst of the Civil War. Central to artist Thomas Nast's vision of the blessings freedom would bring was the integrity of family life and security of home ownership. The cruelties of the "peculiar institution" of slavery depicted in scenes on the left stand in marked contrast to the independence and happiness that would flow from wage labor and private initiative bolstered by the elevating influences of the church and public school.

Source: Library of Congress, Prints and Photographs Division, LC-USZ62-2573.

The Establishment of Public Education in the South

Radicalism, Racism, and the Politics of Reconstruction

A century after Thomas Jefferson first proposed a statewide system of public schools, the southern states, as part of the conditions for their readmission to the Union, grudgingly adopted new constitutions that contained provisions for schools maintained at public expense and available to all. However, the provisions for systems of public schooling were framed less by the ideals of Jeffersonian republicanism than by fear that "Radical Republicans," who for a time dictated the conditions of Reconstruction, would use their power to impose racially "mixed schools" on the defeated South.

The Thirteenth Amendment, adopted several months after the end of the Civil War, officially ended slavery for some four million African Americans, three and a half million of whom were then living in the states that had been in rebellion. In 1866 Congress passed the Fourteenth Amendment, which, following ratification two years later, provided for due process and extended full citizenship rights to former slaves. The Fifteenth Amendment, adopted in 1870, declared that no person could be denied the right to vote because of race, color, or previous condition of servitude.

These amendments to the Constitution, which had to be ratified by the southern states before they could rejoin the Union, were accompanied by heated debates over other Reconstruction policies. Some radical Republicans declared their intent to reduce the ex-Confederate states to the status of territories so that they could then be made over in the image of an idealized North, complete with "small farms, thrifty tillage, free schools … and equality of political rights." Rejecting milder approaches that had been put into place by Lincoln and his successor, Andrew Johnson, Congress in 1867 began passing a series of vindictive Reconstruction acts. These acts reimposed military rule, withheld voting and office-holding rights from former Confederates, and established conditions that led to Republican-controlled governments in the conquered Confederate states.

Among the most inflammatory issues of the Reconstruction era was school segregation. Although this issue had been contested in some northern and midwestern localities and states before the Civil War, emancipation and Reconstruction politics forced the question onto the national stage. Senator Charles Sumner of Massachusetts led a band of congressional radicals who wanted to force southern states to adopt policies forbidding segregation, even though there was little popular sentiment for the idea in northern states. In fact, many northern states had long practiced racial segregation in some form in their public schools.

While under radical Republican control in 1868, two southern states, Louisiana and South Carolina, installed new constitutions that specified that all schools be opened to all children without regard to race or color. Five other states that adopted new constitutions in 1868—Alabama, Arkansas, Florida,

Georgia, and North Carolina—crafted general provisions directed toward equality in education without guaranteeing mixed schools as such. The next year, Virginia, Mississippi, and Texas also managed to forge legislation that provided for schools for all citizens but that avoided language requiring integration.

Even though southern states gained readmission to the Union without having to guarantee mixed schools, the issue continued to resurface in Congress into the 1870s. Mixed-school clauses were often included in bills calling for federal aid to education or as sections in proposed civil rights legislation. Until his death in 1874, Senator Sumner regularly presented bills prohibiting racial segregation in public schools—and in restaurants, inns, theaters, common carriers, and the like. Just as regularly, opponents of the measure fought strenuously against the proposals.

Although the mixed-school clause was sometimes used as a stalking horse to test party loyalty and as a tactic to keep African American voters in the Republican ranks, the possibility that the radicals might carry the day struck terror in those who thought it would undo the gains that had been made in the common school movement, North and South. As a consequence, some of the most ardent supporters of public education on both sides of the Mason-Dixon line took the position that public education could survive in the southern states *only* if created and maintained as a dual or racially segregated system.[40]

The Peabody Fund and the Shaping of Southern Educational Policy

The trustees and agents of the Peabody Fund were among those who saw in education—segregated education—the most promising road to reunion. George Peabody, a native of Massachusetts, was the first of a number of northern philanthropists who acted on a desire to aid educational work in the South in the years following the Civil War. In 1867, two years before his death, he established a fund bearing his name with an initial endowment of $1 million. The income from this gift was to be used "for the promotion and encouragement of intellectual, moral or industrial education" of young southerners. He specified that the fund should benefit the entire population, "without other distinction than their needs and the opportunities of usefulness to them."

He personally selected the fifteen men who were to administer the fund. Among the trustees were public figures such as Robert C. Winthrop of Massachusetts and Hamilton Fish of New York, as well as General U.S. Grant and Admiral David C. Farragut. Including Farragut, who was a Tennessean, six southerners were appointed to the board. No one named to the Peabody board could be considered a political extremist; indeed, he thought them to be among the wisest and ablest men in the country.[41]

The trustees selected Dr. Barnas Sears, Horace Mann's successor as secretary of the Massachusetts Board of Education, who was then serving as president of Brown University, as the fund's general agent or chief administrator. Sears, who claimed to eschew politics altogether ("I neither vote, nor discuss political questions, even privately"), encouraged the trustees to adopt a cautious policy of assisting only schools that were already established and receiving local support. Helping good schools to become better, he advised, would enable them to become models for others—a more judicious course than spreading the Peabody Fund too thinly in an effort to establish new schools across the South.

The board adopted a policy that required localities to provide matching funds at a ratio of up to three or four dollars for every one dollar in Peabody support. The general policy of the board was to assist public schools, institutions that were "established, supported and superintended by the Southern people themselves." Along with elementary schools, normal schools were to receive particular attention, especially a small number that would serve as "models of instruction" for others. "Literary" and "professional schools" were excluded from assistance.

Although Peabody had instructed that no distinction other than need and usefulness should enter into the board's decisions, racial considerations did come into play as Sears helped shape the Peabody Education Fund policies. In 1869 Sears proposed that grants to black schools be scaled to one-third less than for white schools, because "[it] costs less to maintain schools for the colored children than the white." Sears opposed "mixed" schooling and wanted to keep the Peabody Fund out of the controversy over this question that was so explosive in the South during Reconstruction. With the board's approval, he made it policy to give aid only to communities that maintained *separate* facilities for black and white students. Convinced that whites would not attend or support integrated schools, Sears privately referred to mixed schools as a "curse."

Controversy over attempts to mandate racially integrated schools in South Carolina and Louisiana during the period of Radical Reconstruction prompted the board to depart from its policy of aiding only public schools. The Peabody Fund contributed $17,000 to nonpublic schools that had been established in Louisiana for white children who, resisting integration, were considered as no longer being served by the public schools. Sears published a letter in *DeBow's Review* of New Orleans, an arch-champion of the antebellum way of life, justifying the actions of the Peabody trustees. Sears stated:

> We ourselves raise no questions about mixed schools. We simply take the fact that the white children do not generally attend them, without passing any judgment on the propriety or impropriety of their course. We wish to promote universal education to aid whole communities, if possible. If that cannot be, on account of peculiar circumstances, we must give preference to those whose education is neglected. It is well known that we are helping the white children of Louisiana, as being the more destitute, from the fact of their unwillingness to attend mixed schools. We should give the preference to colored children, were they in like circumstances.[42]

Although Sears insisted that he wanted no part of political controversy, an 1874 civil rights bill introduced in Congress by Charles Sumner drew him directly into the fray. True to form, the Sumner bill contained a clause requiring integrated schools. Sears declared that he could not sit by passively while unthinking men pushed a measure that would undo all the good being accomplished by the Peabody Fund. Sears lobbied congressmen—but, "not Sumner and his trained Negroes"—arguing that if the school proviso were left intact it would lead to the destruction of public schools in the southern states and leave both blacks and poor whites destitute of education altogether. He conferred with Ulysses S. Grant and was satisfied to learn that the president shared his opinion. Sears took his case to the people as well, writing anonymously in the education column of the *Atlantic Monthly* that if the mixed-school proposal survived, public schools in the South would not. Southern whites, he warned, "will seize the opportunity to *abolish* the public schools and to return to their favorite plan of private schools."[43]

Sears' efforts proved effective. When the Civil Rights Bill became law in March 1875, the controversial mixed-school clause was noticeably absent. Obviously, Sears was not alone in his opposition to integrated schooling. Although for different reasons, some blacks as well as most whites of the time thought the idea unwise and untimely. However, the opposition led by Sears on behalf of the Peabody Fund proved significant in terms of helping cement the agenda of segregated schooling in the southern states for decades to come. Later philanthropic efforts, state legislation, and eventually the Supreme Court of the United States, in the *Plessy v. Ferguson*[44] decision of 1896, extended the "separate but equal" educational policy far into the twentieth century.

White Philanthropy and African American Education

George Peabody and Barnas Sears only begin the list of countless men and women of both races who believed that, through education, racial harmony and progress could become a reality in the South and in the nation. Peabody's philanthropy encouraged other wealthy individuals of like mind to offer assistance to the racially divided South. In 1882, John F. Slater of Norwich, Connecticut, also established a fund of a million dollars, "the income of which was to be used to assist in the education of the Negro people of the South." As had Peabody, Slater selected his own board of trustees. He designated Rutherford B. Hayes as the board's president. Atticus G. Haygood, a Methodist minister and president of Emory College, became the Slater Fund's general agent. Among other men of distinction named to the board was J. L. M. Curry, a native Alabamian who had earned a law degree at Harvard and had represented his home state with distinction in the U.S. Congress until the division of the Union in 1861. During the Civil War, Curry served as a Confederate congressman and military officer. At war's end, he took the oath of allegiance to the United States and, intent on living "in the present and for the future," urged his defeated countrymen to learn from the "dead past" and take up the cause of universal education.

Following the death of Barnas Sears, Curry became general agent of the Peabody Fund in 1881, and in 1890 he succeeded Haygood as the educational director of the Slater Fund. The activities of the two foundations thus became tightly linked. The Slater Fund trustees focused their attention primarily on teacher training and industrial education for southern blacks.

In 1905, Anna T. Jeanes, a Philadelphia Quaker, began donating funds to assist in the improvement of rural schools for southern blacks. Two years later she established an endowment fund of $1 million to advance this work. Caroline Phelps Stokes in 1911 gave a like sum to aid the education of blacks in Africa as well as the United States. In 1912, Julius Rosenwald commemorated his fiftieth birthday by donating $25,000 to Booker T. Washington to support "offshoots of Tuskegee." These "offshoots" were to be normal schools that adopted the Hampton-Tuskegee model of industrial education as their basic curriculum for teacher training, a development that will be explored more fully in the following pages.

Rosenwald's philanthropy and the scope of his foundation's activity expanded in subsequent years as the foundation encouraged southern blacks to raise matching funds to provide "sweat equity" for the building of schools in rural areas. Rosenwald agents spread through the countryside, urging poor sharecroppers to give whatever they could for the education of their children. M.H. Griffin, a black Rosenwald agent in Alabama, recalled the efforts of a group of poverty-stricken tenant farmers in Greene County to raise funds for a consolidated school in their remote region. As one member of the gathering spoke with tears in his eyes of the generations of children in the vicinity who had grown to adulthood without any semblance of formal education, one old man, who had seen slavery days, slowly drew from his pocket an old greasy sack that contained all of his life's savings. The ex-slave emptied the contents on the table and said, "I want to see the children of my grandchildren have a chance, so I am giving my all."[45]

The largesse of northern philanthropists, the charitable gifts of churches and other organizations, and the sacrificial giving of labor and money by southern blacks themselves made inroads in the journey toward educational equality. But the road was far from straight. Barricades and detours marked the journey from the beginning. At times it must have surely seemed that, as the old saw has it, "you can't get there from here!"

Public Schooling as a Battleground: Virginia as a Case Study

To understand more fully the social and political realities that influenced those who bequeathed money or served as trustees of various philanthropic funds, a closer examination of politics at the state level is instructive. The situation faced by Virginia's first superintendent of public instruction and architect of that state's public school law, William Henry Ruffner, provides a specific example of the political crossfire in which nonradical advocates of public schooling and equality of opportunity were caught.

Ruffner was a Virginia native and Presbyterian minister who had openly opposed slavery and strongly supported equality in public education. As super-intendent, he faced intense opposition from unreconstructed Virginians who disliked the idea of public education in general and in particular railed against public schooling for the newly enfranchised black citizens who composed nearly one-half the population of the state. In their attempts to destroy the infant public schools, reactionary critics often twisted racial and religious opin-ions into knotty arguments that severely hampered the efforts of public school advocates. Periodic rumblings from Washington that threatened passage of civil rights legislation mandating mixed schools served only to heighten the resolve of anti-public school forces intent on dismantling the fledgling system.

Among the most hostile critics who attacked Ruffner and his pro-public school allies were clergymen who contended that public schools by definition were atheistic and immoral. In one rhetorical onslaught, a Baptist minister writing under the pen name "Civis" declared that the political principles on which the public school concept was based are "foreign to free institutions and fatal to liberty." Civis contended that "the education of children is not the business of government, but the sacred and imperative duty of parents." Expressly rejecting the idea of equal treatment of black and white children, this minister asserted that "the line of demarcation between the races is not acci-dental or the result of outward surroundings; it has been fixed by the finger of God." He contended further: "The law of nature, which is always the law of God, is inequality, not equality; diversity, not uniformity."[46]

Robert Lewis Dabney, a Presbyterian minister and former seminary classmate of Ruffner's, blasted the public school system as a "quixotic project . . . the cunning cheat of Yankee statecraft." Dabney condemned the "unrighteousness" of a system that "wrung by a grinding taxation from an oppressed people" enormous sums for use in the "pretended education of freed slaves." Asserting that many white citizens were keeping their children at home to labor in the fields in order to pay taxes to support public schools "for brats of the black paupers" who "loaf and steal," Dabney maintained that freedmen's low character, ignorance, lax morals, dependent nature, and lack of ambition could not be cured by education. He regarded as "utterly deceptive, farcical and dishonest" the argument that African Americans deserved and required educa-tion in order to become responsible citizens. He asserted that educated blacks would develop "foolish and impossible" ambitions and would become dis-interested in their "true calling, manual labor." The real aim of those who advocated public education for blacks, he charged, was the "amalgamation" of the races.

Such emotionally charged attacks were countered by Ruffner and his public school allies with the standard moral, civic, and economic arguments used since the days of Horace Mann to support the public school movement.

Although realizing that his reactionary opponents would remain intransigent, Ruffner hoped that the more moderate citizens of the state could be relieved of their anxieties. It is not surprising, then, that when faced with the threat of federal civil rights legislation containing forced integration clauses, Ruffner sided with Barnas Sears and other moderate reformers in a determined effort to kill the bills.

Writing in *Scribner's Monthly* in 1874, Ruffner, like Sears, endeavored to inform sympathetic northerners that forced integration would undo all the progress that had been made in the South. He asserted that in both ancient and modern history, power had destroyed slavery, but had not been able to legislate changes in racial attitudes or diminish the moral, intellectual, and cultural gaps that separated the two races. Only "the disintegrating work of time" could eliminate these attitudes and differences, he stated. Acknowledging the reality of racism in the North as well as the South, Ruffner observed that "the social repugnance between the races has not been obliterated anywhere." As if to zero in on the heart of the matter, Ruffner reminded his readers that integrated schools in Boston at the time were "barely tolerated" and were "avoided" by large segments of the white population.

In spite of the difficulties he and his society faced, Superintendent Ruffner remained optimistic about future relations between the races and hinted at the possibility of integration in coming generations. "Our children will be sufficiently progressive," he declared. "The prejudices which disturb us now will run their natural course." But conditioned as he was by place and time, Ruffner championed universal education with a caution: Attempts to mix the races in the schools at that time, he said, were "vain and foolish . . . base and malicious." Like Sears, with whom he collaborated, Ruffner was convinced that legislated mixed schooling would last "just as long as would be required to go through the forms of law needed to destroy it." To Ruffner, and to the majority of whites in both the North and the South, the choice was simple: segregated public schools or no public schools.

From Reconstruction Toward Reconciliation

Just as Reconstruction had begun before the war was over, so it began to end long before the final withdrawal of occupation troops from southern soil took place in 1877. In a sense, Reconstruction was a second, nonmilitary phase of the Civil War. All during that period die-hard whites had continued to fight, overtly and covertly, legally and illegally, to reinstitute "white supremacy" and limit advances blacks were struggling to make. The Yankee teachers who had invaded the South under the auspices of missionary societies or the federal government frequently found themselves no more welcome than had been the soldiers who preceded them. Missionary teachers and "carpetbaggers," the latter a term of scorn applied to northerners who came South after the war for political or financial gain, were shunned and harassed by some southern whites and taunted in newspaper editorials. Along with freedmen, they were tormented and sometimes violently attacked by furtive secret societies such as "Rifle Clubs" in South Carolina, the White League of Louisiana, or the Knights of the Ku Klux Klan, which originated in Tennessee in 1866 and spread quickly throughout the South and beyond. From the perspective of the newly emancipated and enfranchised African Americans and their allies, it seemed as if the war had been won but the peace was being lost—with less bloodshed, to be sure, but with no less bitterness.

The withdrawal of Union forces began in 1868 following Grant's election to the presidency. As the northern military presence decreased in the South, Republican idealism began to wane in the North. Most northerners, while hostile toward slavery, had never been racial egalitarians, and the popularity of the "radical" cause faded as "regular" Republicans began to make peace with southern Democrats who were eager to regain power in the South. In 1871 Congress repealed the act that had disqualified most ex-Confederates from voting or holding office. The following year a general amnesty restored the franchise to all but about 600 ex-Confederate officials. In one southern state after another, the "Redeemers"—southern Democrats—regained power and began to dismantle Reconstruction policies. Tensions between old-line agrarians or "Bourbons" and a new generation of aspiring businessmen who envisioned an industrialized "New South" sometimes caused dissension within the ranks of the southern Democrats, but they could put differences aside in pursuit of a common goal: ousting the Republicans from office and restoring "home rule."

For "home rule" to be attained, African American suffrage had to be restricted, an objective that was largely realized by policies of intimidation and legal disfranchisement. Some blacks, keenly aware of the deteriorating conditions surrounding their tenuous freedom, joined in an "exodus" from the South. A group of Louisiana blacks, after determining in 1877 that "there was no way on earth that we could better our condition," decided to become homesteaders in Kansas. Thousands more from Mississippi, Texas, and Tennessee caught "Kansas fever" by the end of the decade and headed north and west, but the great majority of freedmen, having little or no money, had no choice but to stay behind and scramble for a living as sharecroppers on lands they had earlier worked as slaves.

Toward Compromise and Accommodation

If politics is defined as the "art of compromise," then the politics that defined the place of black people in American society in the post-Reconstruction years must be acclaimed "high art." The political arena was filled with compromise. In an official sense, the "Compromise of 1877" marked the end of Reconstruction and of the campaign to grant full political and social equality to American blacks. The Compromise of 1877 occurred when southern Democrats, in order to break a gridlock caused by fraud in the election of 1876, acquiesced in the elevation of the Republican Rutherford B. Hayes to the presidency. In return, Republican party negotiators promised that Hayes would disengage the remaining federal troops in South Carolina and Louisiana and would grant other concessions to the South. Both sides also agreed that black citizens would be treated fairly. As if anticipating the real meaning of that compromise, Frederick Douglass had declared at the 1876 Republican convention just months before the deal was struck:

> When you turned us loose, you turned us loose to the sky, the storm, to the whirlwind, and worst of all . . . to the wrath of our infuriated masters. The question now is, do you mean to make good to us the promise in your Constitution?

The Compromise of 1877 made clear that, for the black men, women, and children of that and many subsequent generations, the answer was "No."[47]

Booker T. Washington and the "Atlanta Compromise"

Yet another compromise must be considered when explaining the retreat from Reconstruction that marked the end of the nineteenth and the opening decades of the twentieth century. Booker T. Washington's "Atlanta Compromise," as it has been called, also figures prominently in the politics of racism and segregated schooling in the United States.

Washington, born into slavery in Virginia in 1856, emerged as the nation's foremost black leader in the post-Reconstruction era. In his 1901 autobiography, *Up from Slavery*, Washington recounted his struggle to escape poverty, obtain an education, and achieve dignity and respectability as a black man in a nation tightly controlled by whites. Ambitious and hard working, Washington was sixteen when he enrolled in Hampton Institute in 1872. Hampton had been founded by General Samuel Chapman Armstrong, whose missionary parents in Hawaii had taught him to cling to the principles of the Puritan ethic. Armstrong's belief that labor was a "spiritual force" that "not only increased wage-earning capacity but prompted fidelity, accuracy, honesty, persistence, and intelligence" was not lost on the young mulatto student. Washington absorbed Armstrong's teachings, which emphasized patience, respect for lawful authority, the doctrine of self-help, and the wisdom of gaining and applying the skills and attitudes that would enable one to acquire land, own a home, and provide for one's family.

Washington left Hampton convinced that in order for black Americans to achieve success, they must develop a sense of racial pride, become responsible citizens, and engage in useful service. In 1881 Washington went to Alabama to organize a secondary and normal school that became Tuskegee University. There he made the work ethic and pragmatic outlook that had been instilled in him the cornerstone of the new institution's educational philosophy. At a time when education was considered by many to consist of acquiring an acquaintance, no matter how slight, with the classical languages and *belles lettres*, Washington emphasized the dignity of labor and the value of skilled trades.

Admirers praised Tuskegee for teaching blacks marketable skills that would enable them to become self-sufficient. Along with Hampton, Tuskegee became the model of black "higher" education most favored by philanthropists such as Peabody, Slater, and Rosenwald and the stewards of their funds. By the turn of the century, new financial backers such as Andrew Carnegie, the John D. Rockefellers, Sr. and Jr., and the trustees of the General Education Board (founded in 1901) also praised the practical approach to education championed by Washington and funneled support to Hampton, Tuskegee, and their "offshoots."

Many blacks also revered Washington, who was seen to have great acceptance among influential whites, including Presidents Theodore Roosevelt and William Taft. Over time Washington became a master at courting the favor of powerful white people and accommodated himself, at least outwardly, to the segregated system that had taken root in the South and in other parts of the nation. Instead of lashing out openly at racial discrimination, Washington chose to work behind the scenes to improve conditions for African Americans.

Figure 5.3 Booker T. Washington, 1903, c. Cheynes Studio, Hampton, VA.

Credit: Library of Congress, Prints and Photographs Division, LC-USZ62-49568.

In his public persona, he emphasized the necessity for decency and fair play and encouraged his black brothers and sisters to "cast down your bucket where you are" and create a better life through hard work and education. Behind the scenes, however, Washington quietly financed some of the earliest court cases against segregation and in other ways worked to decrease the injustices being done to his race. With scheming that rivaled that of any political boss, Washington developed a network of associates into the "Tuskegee machine" and maintained his power through patronage and shrewdness. As Louis Harlan has pointed out in his excellent biography of Washington, the man was much more complex and enigmatic than he appeared to be when highlighted in the public sphere.[48]

The event that catapulted Booker T. Washington into national prominence (and controversy) and that earned him the label as the great accommodationist occurred in 1895. Addressing a biracial audience at the Cotton States Exposition in Atlanta, Washington insisted that the great majority of his race had little or no interest in social equality, but rather sought goodwill and the opportunity to improve themselves and be of greater service to society. Washington won great applause from the whites who agreed with his pronouncement that, "in all things that are purely social we can be as separate as the fingers, yet one as the hand in all things of mutual progress."[49]

Booker T. Washington's perceived willingness to postpone civil and political rights in favor of economic opportunity earned him the wrath of some blacks at the same time that others rallied to his cause. One strident critic was William Monroe Trotter, the editor of the *Boston Guardian*, a black newspaper. Trotter editorialized in 1902 that Washington's acceptance of black disfranchisement was "a fatal blow ... to the Negro's political rights and liberty." Ida Wells-Barnett, a crusading editor whose Memphis newspaper office was destroyed by a mob in 1892, was another black spokesperson who criticized Washington's virtual silence on the subject of lynching at the time when the practice was near an all-time high in the southern states.[50]

W.E.B. DuBois and the "Talented Tenth"

No critic offered a more searching and potent challenge to Washington than did William Edward Burghardt DuBois. Born in Massachusetts of a line of free ancestry, DuBois was educated at Fisk, Harvard (where in 1895 he became the first black there to be awarded a Ph.D. degree), and the University of Berlin. Booker T. Washington offered him a position in mathematics at Tuskegee, but DuBois turned it down, having already accepted an offer to teach classics at Wilberforce. After two years at Wilberforce and a year-and-a-half stint at the University of Pennsylvania, DuBois was invited to Atlanta University in 1896. There, for the next thirteen years, he and his graduate students in sociology undertook an in-depth study of "the Negro problem" in the South.

As DuBois probed and exposed the wretched conditions and injustices that defined black peonage in the South, he became increasingly critical of

Figure 5.4 W. E. B. DuBois photo by J. E. Purdy, 1904.
Credit: Library of Congress, Prints and Photographs Division, LC-USZ62-28485.

Washington's equivocations on political rights, his submissive concessions to southern caste discriminations, and his narrowly materialistic conception of black education. The rupture between the two black educators became public with the publication in 1903 of DuBois's *The Souls of Black Folk.* In a chapter titled "Of Mr. Booker T. Washington and Others," DuBois took direct aim at Washington's public posture of submission and silence on civil and political rights. DuBois termed Washington's "Atlanta Compromise" a complete surrender of the demand for equality and a ploy to win the esteem of whites that had resulted in his becoming the "most distinguished Southerner since Jefferson Davis, and the one with the largest personal following."

DuBois found Washington's advocacy of industrial education particularly distasteful and harmful. He accused Washington of preaching a "gospel of Work and Money" to such an extent that the higher aims of life were almost completely overshadowed. In an essay entitled "The Talented Tenth," DuBois wrote:

If we make money the object of man-training, we shall develop money-makers but not necessarily men; if we make technical skill the object of education, we may possess artisans but not, in nature, men. Men we shall have only as we make manhood the object of the work of the schools—intelligence, broad sympathy, knowledge of the world that was and is, and of the relation of men to it—this is the curriculum of that Higher Education which must underlie true life.

For DuBois, the classics, humanities, and social and physical sciences held the knowledge of most worth. The "talented tenth" of the race, the leadership cadre, should be educated, not trained.[51]

Despite DuBois' emphasis on the "higher education of selected youths" and Washington's concern for industrial education for the masses, in actuality both men were seeking leadership of and influence over "the talented tenth" or the black intelligentsia. Whereas Washington wanted to persuade prospective teachers, editors, ministers, and businessmen to guide the race's social development along the self-help and accommodationist lines he favored, DuBois advocated leadership by a more assertive and articulate class of college-educated men and women like himself. Washington looked to Tuskegee, Hampton, and other industrially oriented normal schools for leaders; DuBois found in Atlanta, Fisk, and Howard the better models for emulation.

DuBois' more aggressive stance led him to confer with other black leaders who favored vigorous resistance rather than accommodation to racism. A series of strategy-planning meetings at Niagara Falls beginning in 1905 led to the formation in 1909 of the National Association for the Advancement of Colored People (NAACP). In time, this group and other civil rights organizations pried open the doors that had denied equal access and treatment to one-third of the South's population.

Conclusion: Dreams and Promises Deferred

In his penetrating study of *The Education of Blacks in the South, 1860–1935*, James Anderson sets forth a troubling thesis. Noting that the history of American education abounds in themes tying democratic citizenship to popular education, he suggests that in the United States, two types of "citizenship education" have existed side by side. According to Anderson:

Both schooling for democratic citizenship and schooling for second-class citizenship have been basic traditions in American education. These opposing traditions were not, as some would explain, the difference between the mainstream of American education and some aberrations or isolated alternatives. Rather, both were fundamental American conceptions of society and progress, occupied the same time and space, were fostered by the same governments, and usually were embraced by the same leaders.[52]

Our excursion into the history of education in the nineteenth-century South bears out Anderson's disturbing but entirely accurate observation. For more than half the century, African Americans were not included among the citizenry and only a small number gained access to the printed word. Following the Civil War and Reconstruction, the dreams of the old and the visions of the young stimulated many ex-slaves to seek education through whatever avenues existed. With the spread of missionary and Freedmen's Bureau schools and the establishment in the 1870s of public schools across the South, the dreams of education for liberty gave promise of becoming reality.

The Fourteenth Amendment to the U.S. Constitution held forth the promise of due process and equal rights under the law for all. New state constitutions contained clauses providing for publicly supported schools for all citizens. Even with the development of the "dual" system of "separate but equal" schools, African American citizens had reason to hope that their children and their children's children might gain the knowledge that Jefferson had stated kept people and societies free.

The dreams began to fade, however, as Reconstruction policies gave way to acts of reconciliation, redemption, and racism. The system of separate schooling perpetuated inequality. Northern philanthropists and southern reformers engineered educational policies that enabled black children to make only marginal advances. Southern legislatures and tax-resisting politicians followed rather than directed public opinion and often did little better in support of public schools for white children.

As the twentieth century dawned, many sections of the South remained impoverished in spirit and mind as well as economically. A southern "educational revival" ushered in the new century, but the tasks before the reformers of that generation loomed large. On every measure—per-pupil expenditure, length of school terms, teacher preparation and salaries, conditions of schools, attendance, and graduation rates—the gap separating the opportunities and performance of black and white children of the South was marked—and the gaps separating southern schools from those in many other parts of the nation were pronounced as well, as the statistics in Tables 5.1, 5.2, and 5.3 reveal.

An expatriate of the South, Walter Hines Page, created something of a stir in the closing decade of the nineteenth century when he gave a speech on "The Forgotten Man." What many failed to see for years to come was that the South's forgotten men and women, white and black, had been the region's forgotten children. A full century after emancipation, Martin Luther King, Jr. spoke to the lingering promise by declaring still, "I have a dream. . . ."[53]

Table 5.1 Southern School Statistics, 1900–1930

| | Illiteracy (Ten Years of Age and Older) | | | | | | | |
| | 1900 | | 1910 | | 1920 | | 1930 | |
	Native White (%)	Black (%)	Native White (%)	Black (%)	Native White (%)	Black (%)	Native White (%)	Black (%)
United States	5.7	44.5	3.7	30.4	2.5	22.9	1.5	16.3
Alabama	15.2	57.4	10.1	40.1	6.4	31.3	4.8	26.2
Arkansas	11.8	43.0	7.1	26.4	4.6	21.8	3.5	16.1
Florida	9.0	38.4	5.2	25.5	3.1	21.5	1.9	18.8
Georgia	12.2	52.4	8.0	36.5	5.5	29.1	3.3	19.9
Kentucky	13.9	40.1	10.7	27.6	7.3	21.0	5.7	15.4
Louisiana	20.4	61.1	15.0	48.4	11.4	38.5	7.3	23.3
Mississippi	8.1	49.1	5.3	35.6	3.6	29.3	2.7	23.2
N. Carolina	19.6	47.6	12.3	31.9	8.2	24.5	5.6	20.6
Oklahoma	8.1	37.0	3.5	17.7	2.4	12.4	1.7	9.3
S. Carolina	13.9	52.8	10.5	38.7	6.6	29.3	5.1	26.9
Tennessee	14.5	41.6	9.9	27.3	7.4	22.4	5.4	14.9
Texas	5.1	38.2	3.3	24.6	2.2	17.8	1.4	13.4
Virginia	11.4	44.6	8.2	30.0	6.1	23.5	4.8	19.2

Sources: *Abstract of the Twelfth Census of the United States, 1900 and 1910*. Washington, D.C. Government Printing Office, 1912, p. 245; *Abstract of the Fourteenth Census of the United States, 1920*. Washington, D.C.: Government Printing Office, 1923, pp. 432, 434; *Statistical Abstracts of the United States, 1933*. Washington, D.C.: Government Printing Office, 1933, p. 43.

Table 5.2 Annual Expenditures per Pupil in Southern States, 1912–1913 and 1928–1929

| | 1912–1913 | | 1928–29 | |
	White	Black	White	Black
Alabama	$8.50	$1.49	$37.50	$7.16
Arkansas	7.89	2.62	26.91	17.06
Florida	14.75	3.10	78.25	10.57
Georgia	9.18	1.42	31.52	6.98
Kentucky	8.63	6.45	25.27	25.77
Louisiana	16.60	1.59	40.64	7.84
Mississippi	8.20	1.53	31.33	5.94
N. Carolina	6.69	2.50	44.48	14.30
Oklahoma	16.29	12.20	40.48	20.83
S. Carolina	9.65	1.09	52.89	5.20
Tennessee	8.32	3.94	46.52	31.54
Texas	10.89	7.50	46.71	39.66
Virginia	10.92	3.42	47.46	13.30
Average	$10.50	$3.76	$42.30	$15.86

Sources: Monroe N. Work, *The Negro Year Book, 1914–15* and *1931–32*. Tuskegee, AL: Tuskegee Institute, 1915 and 1933, p. 223.

Table 5.3 Average Annual Salaries of White and Black Teachers in Southern States, Average Expenditure for Salaries per Pupil Enrolled, and Length of School Term, 1928–1929

| | Average Expenditure | | | | | |
| | Annual Salary | | for Salaries per Pupil | | Length of Term | |
	White	Black	White	Black	White	Black
Alabama	$832	$354	$25.26	$7.35	159	129
Arkansas	723	449	20.02	8.86	150	132
Florida	1,054	424	35.20	9.80	163	128
Georgia	768	260	22.45	5.65	158	137
Kentucky	875	829	24.66	25.44	160	146
Louisiana	1,159	496	38.40	8.68	174	112
Mississippi	908	350	29.80	6.70	141	130
N. Carolina	870	480	26.79	11.10	151	137
Oklahoma	1,071	858	30.06	23.98	162	153
S. Carolina	1,047	316	35.70	5.89	173	114
Tennessee	855	525	25.70	13.01	116	156
Texas	1,053	687	36.38	14.61	152	147
Virginia	902	502	29.17	12.68	174	157
Average	*$932*	*$502*	*$29.19*	*$11.83*	*146*	*127*

Sources: Monroe N. Work, *The Negro Year Book, 1931–32*. Tuskegee, AL: Tuskegee Institute, 1932, p. 1932, p. 206; Edward Byron Reuter, *The American Race Problem*. New York: Thomas Y. Crowell, [1927], 1938, pp. 276–277.

Further Reading

Anderson, James D. *The Education of Blacks in the South, 1860–1935*. Chapel Hill: University of North Carolina Press, 1988. A critical examination of the struggles, successes, and setbacks in the development of educational opportunity for African Americans from Reconstruction to the Great Depression.

Ayers, Edward L. *The Promise of the New South: Life after Reconstruction*. New York: Oxford University Press, 1993. A comprehensive exploration of the cultural and political complexities facing the post-Reconstruction South, including attention to the major social institutions and significant literary and cultural activity in the South during this period.

Butchart, Ronald E. *Northern Schools, Southern Blacks, and Reconstruction: Freedmen's Education, 1862–1875*. Westwood, CT: Greenwood Press, 1980. A carefully researched revisionist interpretation of the work of the secular and religious aid societies and the Freedmen's Bureau in educating free blacks.

Click, Patricia C. *Time of Full Trial: The Roanoke Island Freedmen's Colony, 1862–1867*. Chapel Hill: University of North Carolina Press, 2001. An insightful and fascinating study of a slave refugee colony set up by Union military officers and evangelical missionaries who hoped to establish a model for a new social order in the postwar South.

Cobb, James C. *Away Down South: A History of Southern Identity*. New York: Oxford University Press, 2005. Discusses six features that have shaped the region: agrarianism, class relations, race relations, gender and family traditions, and religious and political traditions.

Donald, David H., Jean Baker and Michael F. Holt. *Civil War and Reconstruction*. New York: W. W. Norton, 2001. Three respected historians lay out the twisted story of sectionalism, Civil War, and Reconstruction.

Foner, Eric. *Reconstruction: America's Unfinished Revolution, 1863–1877*. New York: HarperCollins, 1988. A classic work on one of the most complex periods in American history.

Genovese, Eugene D. *Roll, Jordan, Roll: The World the Slaves Made*. New York: Vintage Books, 1972.

A thoroughly researched and sensitive investigation of the differing world views of slave-holders and slaves in the antebellum South.

Harlan, Louis R. *Booker T. Washington: The Making of a Black Leader, 1865–1902*, and *Booker T. Washington: The Wizard of Tuskegee, 1901–1915*. New York: Oxford University Press, 1972 and 1986. A two-volume biography by the highly respected editor of the Booker T. Washington Papers that reveals the complexities, contradictions, and contributions of this masterful politician.

Holt, Michael F. *The Rise and Fall of the American Whig Party: Jacksonian Politics and the Onset of the Civil War*. New York: Oxford University Press, 1999. A masterly researched and well-written history of the Whig Party's 22 year history—the only comprehensive history ever written on this party.

Lewis, David L. *W.E.B. Du Bois: Biography of a Race*, and *W.E.B. Du Bois: The Fight for Equality and the American Century, 1919–1963*. New York: Henry Holt, 1993 and 2000. A probing and comprehensive two-volume examination by a Pulitzer Prize-winning historian of the life and times of the brilliant and often alienated black intellectual, whose life spanned the tumultuous decades from Reconstruction to the civil rights movement.

McMillen, Sally Gregory. *To Raise Up the South: Sunday Schools in Black and White Churches, 1865–1915*. Baton Rouge, LA: Louisiana State University Press, 2002. An argument that, although dedicated to teaching the same fundamental Christian principles and biblical truths, black and white evangelical Sunday schools differed in their approaches to matters of racial equality.

Webber, Thomas L. *Deep Like the Rivers: Education in the Slave Quarter Community, 1831–1865*. New York: W.W. Norton, 1981. A study showing that proscriptions against schooling for southern blacks did not prevent active learning on the part of African Americans held in bondage in slave communities.

Notes

1. It is important to be alert to points of contrast as well as similarity in the curricular offerings and aims of women's academies, seminaries, and colleges as compared with institutions of similar titles that were restricted to men. On the academy movement, see Theodore Sizer, *The Age of Academies*. New York: Teachers College, Columbia University, 1964. An informative study of female higher education in the South is Christie Anne Farnham, *The Education of the Southern Belle: Higher Education and Student Socialization in the Antebellum South*. New York: New York University Press, 1994.
2. Edgar W. Knight (ed.), *A Documentary History of Education in the South before 1860*. Chapel Hill: University of North Carolina Press, 1953, vol. 4, p. 1; Dale Greenwood Robinson, *The Academies of Virginia, 1776–1861*. Richmond, VA: Dietz Press, 1977, pp. 55–56 passim. These figures need to be balanced by noting that by 1860, there were 321 public high schools in the United States; 167 of these were in Massachusetts, New York, and Ohio.
3. Clement Eaton, *The Freedom-of-Thought Struggle in the Old South*. New York: Harper Torchbooks, [1940], 1964, p. 216.
4. William Harper, "Memoir on Slavery," in J. D. B. DeBow (ed.), *Industrial Resources of the Southern and Western States*. New Orleans: Office of DeBow's Review, 1852–1853, p. 279; and *DeBow's Review*, vol. 20, February 1856, p. 149 as quoted in Carl Kaestle, *Pillars of the Republic: Common Schools and American Society, 1780–1860*. New York: Hill & Wang, 1983, pp. 206–207.
5. See Kaestle, *Pillars*, esp. chap. 8.
6. William A. Maddox, *The Free School Idea in Virginia before the Civil War*. New York: Teachers College, Columbia University, 1918, as quoted in Virginius Dabney, *Virginia: The New Dominion*. Garden City, NY: Doubleday, 1971, pp. 247–250.
7. Hugh Talmage Lefler and Albert Ray Newsome, *North Carolina: The History of a Southern State*. Chapel Hill: University of North Carolina Press, 1954, pp. 313–319, 349–352; Kaestle, p. 202 passim.
8. Lefler and Newsome, *North Carolina*, p. 363.
9. Ira Berlin, *Slaves without Masters: The Free Negro in the Antebellum South*. New York: Vintage Books, 1974, p. 10. Although federal legislation in 1807 outlawed the African slave trade, the practice continued and in some areas even increased. Stephen A. Douglas asserted that more slaves were brought into the United States in 1859 than in any year when the trade had been legal. See John Hope Franklin, *From Slavery to Freedom: A History of Negro Americans*, 3d ed., New York: Vintage Books, [1947], 1969, pp. 182–184.

10. See Benjamin Quarles, *The Negro in the American Revolution*. Chapel Hill: University of North Carolina Press, 1961; and Donald L. Robinson, *Slavery in the Structure of American Politics, 1765–1820*. New York: Harcourt Brace Jovanovich, 1971.

11. Slavery was abolished by the constitutions of Vermont (1777), Ohio (1802), Illinois (1818), and Indiana (1816); by a judicial decision in Massachusetts (1783); by constitutional interpretation in New Hampshire; and by gradual abolition acts in Pennsylvania (1780), Rhode Island (1784), Connecticut (1784 and 1797), New York (1799 and 1817), and New Jersey (1804). See Leon F. Litwack, *North of Slavery: The Negro in the Free States, 1790–1860*. Chicago: University of Chicago Press, 1961, p. 3. See also Arthur Zilversmit, *The First Emancipation: Abolition of Slavery in the North*. Chicago: University of Chicago Press, 1961. Cf. Berlin, *Slaves without Masters*, pp. 20–23.

12. For the general concept of a "hidden passage" we are indebted to Henry Allen Bullock, *A History of Negro Education in the South: From 1619 to the Present*. Cambridge, MA: Harvard University Press, 1967. We depart from his line of analysis in a number of respects, however.

13. *Trustees of the Quaker Society of Contentnea v. Dickenson*, 12 N.C. 120, as cited in John Hope Franklin, *The Free Negro in North Carolina, 1790–1860*. New York: Norton, [1943], 1971, pp. 24–26, 166–167; Carter G. Woodson, *The Education of the Negro Prior to 1861*. New York: G. P. Putnam's Sons, 1915, p. 46.

14. As quoted in Litwack, *North of Slavery*, p. 114. John Brown Russwurm, who with Samuel E. Cornish founded *Freedom's Journal* in 1827, graduated from Bowdoin College, Maine, in 1826, making him the first African American to graduate from college. By 1860, only 28 African Americans had graduated from recognized American colleges, although a larger number had matriculated. On the struggle for equal schooling in pre-Civil War Boston, see Carleton Mabee, "A Negro Boycott to Integrate Boston Schools," *New England Quarterly*, vol. 41, 1968, pp. 341–361.

15. Berlin, p. 75, *Slaves Without Masters*; Franklin, *From Slavery to Freedom*, p. 230.

16. *Raleigh Register*, April 19, 1830, emphasis in original, as quoted in Franklin, *The Free Negro in North Carolina*, p. 172. On Chavis, who attended Washington Academy in Lexington, Virginia, and Princeton University, see E. W. Knight, "Notes on John Chavis," *North Carolina Historical Review*, vol. 7, 1930, pp. 328–329.

17. Berlin, *Slaves Without Masters*, pp. 74–75.

18. Franklin, *The Free Negro in North Carolina*, pp. 168–169; Franklin, *From Slavery to Freedom*, p. 202.

19. A thoughtful discussion of this movement is provided by Vincent P. Franklin, "Education for Colonization: Attempts to Educate Free Blacks in the United States for Emigration to Africa, 1823–1833," *Journal of Negro Education*, vol. 43, Winter 1974, pp. 91–103. See also John Hope Franklin, *From Slavery to Freedom*, pp. 237–241.

20. Among those who did leave the United States was John Brown Russwurm (see note 14). After editing the *Freedom's Journal* for a short time, Russwurm went to Liberia and started the *Liberia Herald*. He later became governor of the settlement at Cape Palmas, Liberia. See Archibald Alexander, *History of the Colonization of the West Coast of Africa*. Philadelphia: W. W. Marden, 1846, pp. 283–284, 431–433, as cited in V. P. Franklin, "Education for Colonization," p. 100, n. 40.

21. The best account of the Sunday school movement is Anne M. Boylan, *Sunday School: The Formation of an American Institution, 1790–1880*. New Haven and London: Yale University Press, 1988. Our discussion draws heavily on this excellent study.

22. Among the Lexington citizens who felt led to teach black children to read and gain an understanding of the fundamentals of religion in this Sunday school was a Presbyterian deacon, Thomas Jackson. Jackson, of course, is better known for the daring exploits that earned him the nickname "Stonewall" when some years later he served as a Confederate general. See Charles William Dabney, *Universal Education in the South*. Chapel Hill: University of North Carolina Press, 1936, vol. 1, p. 145.

23. Boylan, *Sunday School*, p. 33.

24. Frederick L. Olmsted, *A Journey in the Seaboard States, 1853–1854*. New York: G. P. Putnam's Sons, 1904, pp. 54–55; Jack McLaughlin, *Jefferson and Monticello: Biography of a Builder*. New York: Henry Holt, 1988, pp. 212–213. James Hemings' life as a free man proved to be short and tragic. After several years of travel and living in Paris, Hemings returned to Monticello and worked as a paid cook for six weeks. He then left Monticello and several weeks later committed suicide at the age of thirty-six. See McLaughlin, *Jefferson and Monticello*, pp. 222–228.

25. Franklin, *From Slavery to Freedom*, p. 196; Bullock, pp. 6–7.
26. See Franklin, *The Free Negro in North Carolina*, p. 165; and Franklin, *From Slavery to Freedom*, pp. 202–203.
27. W.E.B. DuBois, *Black Reconstruction: An Essay toward a History of the Part which Black Folk Played in the Attempt to Reconstruct Democracy in America, 1860–1880*. New York: Russell and Russell, 1935, p. 638; Eugene D. Genovese, *Roll, Jordan, Roll: The World the Slaves Made*. New York: Vintage Books, 1972, p. 563.
28. Thomas L. Webber, *Deep Like the Rivers: Education in the Slave Quarter Community, 1831–1865*. New York: W. W. Norton, 1978, p. 132; Genovese, *Roll, Jordan, Roll*, pp. 563–564.
29. For these and other examples, see Bullock, pp. 9–11, and the several works cited above.
30. Webber, pp. 132–133; Genovese, p. 564; Frederick Douglass, *Life and Times of Frederick Douglass, Written by Himself*. Hartford, CT: Park Publishing, 1881, p. 151; William S. McFeely, *Frederick Douglass*. New York: Simon & Schuster, 1991, p. 50.
31. A thoughtful examination of antebellum race and gender relations is provided by Elizabeth Fox-Genovese, *Within the Plantation Household: Black and White Women of the Old South*, Chapel Hill: University of North Carolina Press, 1988. Among free blacks in Virginia a pseudo-aristocracy formed as some with pride signed their names to documents with notations such as "f.c.p." or "f.n.w." (free colored person or free Negro woman). It was the proud boast of many black families after the war that they had not been "shot free," i.e., emancipated as a result of the war. See Ervin L. Jordan, Jr., *Black Confederates and Afro-Yankees in Civil War Virginia*. Charlottesville: University Press of Virginia, 1995, p. 202.
32. In the same month, September 1861, Mary Chase opened Columbia Street School in Alexandria, Virginia. Of the two, Chase's is considered to be the first wartime school for the state's ex-slaves. See Jordan, *Black Confederates*, p. 102.
33. See Willie Lee Rose, *Rehearsal for Reconstruction: The Port Royal Experiment*. Indianapolis, IN: Bobbs-Merrill, 1964, pp. 13–14 passim. This excellent account of early attempts to provide education for the freedmen of the Sea Islands of South Carolina provides the basis for our discussion of this sequence of events. Cf. Bullock, p. 26.
34. See Rose, pp. xviii, 230, 243–271.
35. John W. Blassingame, "The Union Army as an Educational Institution for Negroes, 1862–1865," *Journal of Negro Education*, vol. 34, Spring, 1965, pp. 152–159. See also Thomas W. Higginson, *Army Life in a Black Regiment*. New York: Crowell-Collier, [1870], 1962, p. 48.
36. The concept of nineteenth-century neo-Puritanism is more fully developed in James M. McPherson, "The New Puritanism: Values and Goals of Freedman's Education in America," in Lawrence Stone (ed.), *The University in Society*, vol. 2. Princeton, NJ: Princeton University Press, 1974, pp. 611–639. On freedmen's education—and examples of black resistance to the imposition inherent in some missionary activity—see Ronald E. Butchart, *Northern Schools, Southern Blacks, and Reconstruction: Freedmen's Education, 1862–1875*. Westport, CT: Greenwood Press, 1980; Jacqueline Jones, *Soldiers of Light and Love: Northern Teachers and Georgia Blacks, 1865–1873*. Chapel Hill: University of North Carolina Press, 1980; Robert C. Morris, *Reading, 'Riting, and Reconstruction: The Education of Freedmen in the South, 1861–1870*. Chicago: University of Chicago Press, [1976], 1981.
37. Franklin, *From Slavery to Freedom*, p. 308.
38. Quotations from John W. Alvord's *Inspector's Report of Schools and Finances, 1866*, and commentary on the self-reliance activities of ex-slaves are drawn from James D. Anderson, *The Education of Blacks in the South, 1860–1935*. Chapel Hill: University of North Carolina Press, 1988, pp. 4–16.
39. *New Orleans Black Republican*, as cited in Anderson, p. 18. Other examples of black press advocacy of uplift through education are provided in Martin E. Dann (ed.), *The Black Press, 1827–1890: The Quest for National Identity*. New York: Capricorn Books, 1971, pp. 293ff.
40. See Alfred H. Kelly, "The Congressional Controversy over School Segregation, 1867–1875," *The American Historical Review*, vol. 44, 1959, pp. 537–563.
41. A listing of the original board and subsequent appointees is provided in Dabney, *Universal Education in the South*, vol. 1, pp. 105–106. See also Earle H. West, "The Peabody Education Fund and Negro Education, 1867–1880," *History of Education Quarterly*, vol. 6, 1966, pp. 3–21; and William P. Vaughn, "Partners in Segregation: Barnas Sears and the Peabody Fund," *Civil War History*, vol. 10, 1964, pp. 260–274.
42. Barnas Sears, *DeBow's Review*, vol. 50, 1869, pp. 198–199, as quoted in Vaughn, p. 269.
43. [Barnas Sears], "Mixed Schools at the South," *Atlantic Monthly*, vol. 34, 1874, pp. 381–382; Vaughn, pp. 272–274.
44. 163 U.S. 537 (1896).

45. Dabney, vol. 2, pp. 432–483, discusses these and other foundation efforts. A more critical appraisal is presented in Anderson, *The Education of Blacks in the South*, from which the Griffin anecdote is taken, p. 165.

46. Citations to the "Civis" articles and other quotations to follow may be found in Thomas C. Hunt and Jennings L. Wagoner, Jr., "Race, Religion, and Redemption: William Henry Ruffner and the Moral Foundations of Education in Virginia," *American Presbyterians: Journal of Presbyterian History*, vol. 66, 1988, pp. 1–9.

47. Frederick Douglass, *Narrative*; Franklin, *From Slavery to Freedom*, pp. 238–239; Paul S. Boyer, Clifford E. Clark, Jr., Joseph F. Kett, Thomas L. Purvis, Harvard Sitkoff, and Nancy Woloch, *The Enduring Vision: A History of the American People*. Lexington, MA: D. C. Heath, 1990, p. 561.

48. The most authoritative account of Washington is the two-volume work by Louis R. Harlan, *Booker T. Washington: The Making of a Black Leader, 1856–1901*, vol. 1. New York: Oxford University Press, 1972 and *Booker T. Washington: The Wizard of Tuskegee, 1901–1915*, vol. 2. New York: Oxford University Press, 1983.

49. Washington's speech, which was widely reprinted and praised, is quoted in full in his *Up from Slavery*, pp. 218–225. On northern liberal endorsement of Washington's philosophy, see Jennings L. Wagoner, Jr., "The American Compromise: Charles W. Eliot, Black Education, and the New South," in Ronald Goodenow and Arthur White (eds.), *Education and the Rise of the New South*. Boston: G. K. Hall, 1981, pp. 26–46; and David W. Southern, *The Malignant Heritage: Yankee Progressives and the Negro Question, 1901–1914*. Chicago: Loyola University Press, 1968.

50. Boyer et al., *The Enduring Vision*, p. 770; C. Vann Woodward, *Origins of the New South, 1877–1913*. Baton Rouge, LA: Louisiana State University Press, [1951], 1974, p. 351.

51. W. E. B. DuBois, *The Souls of Black Folk: Essays and Sketches*. Chicago: A. G. McClurg, 1903; W. E. B. DuBois, *The Autobiography of W. E. B. DuBois*. New York: International Publishers, 1968; David L. Lewis, *W.E.B. DuBois: Biography of a Race, 1868–1919*. New York: Henry Holt, 1993; Franklin, *From Slavery to Freedom*, pp. 393–394.

52. Anderson, *The Education of Blacks in the South*, p. 1.

53. On the plight of the rural poor whites in the South, see Wayne Flint, *Poor but Proud: Alabama's Poor Whites*. Tuscaloosa, AL: University of Alabama Press, 1989. Dabney, *Universal Education in the South*, vol. 2, provides a useful discussion of the progressive reforms of the early twentieth century, as do Woodward, *Origins of the New South, 1877–1913* and Louis R. Harlan, *Separate and Unequal: Public School Campaigns and Racism in the Southern Seaboard States, 1901–1915*. Chapel Hill: University of North Carolina Press, 1958. For an excellent study of the situation in a single southern state, see William A. Link, *A Hard Country and a Lonely Place: Schooling, Society, and Reform in Rural Virginia, 1870–1920*. Chapel Hill: University of North Carolina Press, 1986.

6

Beginning a Modern School System
1865–1890

Overview

Many historians refer to the late nineteenth and early twentieth centuries as the period of modernization in our nation's development. Key ingredients in the modernization process included the nationalizing trend that was taking place in American society following the Civil War, the development of a majoritarian political sensibility, and the increasing urbanization that took place during these years. Economic changes also characterized this period, as vast new fortunes accrued to those few individuals who built and profited from the new industrial order. Finally, a new wave of immigration began late in this period, one that continued through the first two decades of the twentieth century. While consideration of this new immigration takes place in the next chapter, a brief look at these other modernizing trends occurs here.[1]

Centralized National Government

The Civil War and its immediate aftermath constituted an era in which the United States became a nation in a far different sense than it was before the conflict. In addition to preserving the nation, the Reconstruction process following the war found the national government dictating to the southern states the terms under which they would rejoin the nation. This movement toward a stronger role for the federal government was also enhanced by four other developments, all of which were in some way related to the war effort:

- federal control of the currency as established in the Legal Tender Act;
- extension of federal citizenship to all Americans;
- enactment of a military draft system; and
- direct federal taxation.

The cumulative effect of all of these changes was to make the United States a much more centralized nation than it had ever been before. Taken together, these changes amounted to a fundamental alteration of the federal government. It was becoming a much more significant factor in the lives of most Americans.[2]

Majoritarian Consciousness

If the creation of a more powerful national government was one aspect of modernization, another was an emerging "majoritarian" consciousness in the minds of American citizens that rationalized this nationalizing trend. One prominent instance of this political majoritarianism was the Reconstruction process imposed on the southern states. Eventually, this majoritarian domination was imposed on various ethnic and religious groups. For example, before the Utah territory could become a state, it had to renounce both its formal recognition of Mormonism as the state's primary religion and the traditional Mormon practice of polygamy. Majoritarianism was also a factor in the willingness of several states to pass compulsory school attendance laws in these years.[3]

Economic Changes

Two alterations in the living conditions and economy of late-nineteenth-century America also deserve discussion. The first of these was urbanization. From 1860 to the turn of the twentieth century, the proportion of city dwellers in the United States doubled. By the end of the nineteenth century, the nation's urban population was approaching 50 percent. Much of this urbanization was accomplished through domestic migration from farm to city. Mechanization in agriculture forced more and more farm families to seek their fortunes in the nation's burgeoning cities. This relocation process put great stress on traditional family structures, which, in turn, had a direct impact on the nation's school legislation.

Economically, this period can be described as one of "high" industrialization. Basically, it was a continuation of the industrialization process begun earlier in the century, primarily in the Northeast. However, "high" industrialization differed from early American industrialization in several ways. Factory size and complexity increased significantly in this period, while the number of independent artisans declined precipitously. Also, large-scale industry began invading rural areas, as mines sprang up to extract the natural resources needed for the new industrial processes. This change from an agrarian to an industrial workplace also seemed to call for a greater number of formally educated, literate workers. Thus, schools began to struggle with new, work-related curricula that had been largely absent in earlier times.[4]

Another aspect of high industrial development in the late nineteenth century was the emergence of visible extremes of wealth and poverty. A long post-war depression in the 1870s brought the realities of poverty closer to Americans, particularly urban Americans. The simultaneous rise of great industrial fortunes meant that Americans were now confronted with the development of a new wealthy class. Their ostentatious lifestyles, the ruthlessness of their business methods, and the enormous fortunes they accumulated caused many to believe that the nation was in an era of unprecedented excess.

Historical descriptions of the period as a "gilded age" marked by the activities of "robber barons" testify to the negative connotations that accompanied these economic changes.[5]

All of these developments directly influenced the nation's schools. Because both educators and politicians began to view the schools as instruments of social policy that could be used to solve the nation's problems, school affairs began to take center stage. As school planning became more comprehensive and detailed, individual schools began to be linked more tightly into centrally administered school districts and state "systems." The net result was the beginning of a codified, organized, and hierarchical collection of educational institutions.

The National Government and the Schools

One of the major new forces contributing to the development of an expanded educational system in the post-Civil War era was the national government. Both Congress and the executive branch took part in this development. Congressional support for national educational efforts was boosted by the loss of southern members during the war, most of whom were Jacksonian-style Democrats bitterly opposed to the central government. Most Republicans believed, like their Whig ancestors, in the positive effects of intelligent government activity. Acting on this belief, they proceeded to put into place a variety of national initiatives.

Morrill Acts of 1862 and 1890

Two major post-Civil War congressional initatives directly involved education. A few years before the Civil War, a land-grant act had been proposed by which Congress would make the proceeds from the sale or rental of federal lands available for the support of technical and industrial higher education. Although that initial land-grant bill was vetoed by Democratic President James Buchanan who questioned the constitutionality of the measure, the departure of southern congressmen at the outbreak of the Civil War and the election of Abraham Lincoln as President opened the way for passage of similar legislation in 1862. Authored by Justin Morrill, a congressman from the rural state of Vermont, the "Land-Grant Act" provided financial support for every state that sponsored at least one college "where the leading object shall be, without excluding other scientific and classical studies and including military tactics, to teach such branches of learning as are related to agriculture and the mechanic arts." Under the provisions of the Act, each state was to be allotted public lands within its borders or land script for lands elsewhere equal to 30,000 acres for each senator and representative in Congress. Each state was to sell or lease its lands to establish an endowment for the perpetual support of these land-grant institutions. States varied in the amount of income provided by their stewardship of the public lands. For example, whereas Rhode Island garnered only $0.41 per acre from its allotment, New York's script for heavily timbered land in Wisconsin yielded $6.43 per acre. Although the agricultural part of the Morrill Act appeared to be its most significant feature at the time of its passage, the support of mechanical and industrial education proved increasingly important in the latter part of the nineteenth century as the need for more trained engineers arose. Land-grant institutions in time expanded by absorbing formerly independent schools in professional fields such as medicine and law and initiated new programs in fields such as business. As a result, these multipurpose universities grew in size and influence in the late nineteenth and throughout the twentieth century.[6]

In 1890 a second Morrill Act passed by Congress extended the reach of the federal government into educational affairs even more. This Act not only provided additional funding for the colleges and universities that had been established according to the provisions of the 1862 Act, but set forth a new requirement for Agricultural and Mechanical (A&M) land-grant institutions seeking increased federal support: every state seeking Morrill Act funding had to either provide equal access to the existing A&M colleges or establish separate institutions for the "people of color" in their state. This requirement led to the formation of seventeen historically black colleges, some of which had been previously established and later transitioned into A&M colleges and others that were newly created to conform to the new federal mandate.

Other federal acts aided land grant colleges and the populations they served in additional ways. The Hatch Act of 1887 funded agricultural *experiment* stations at the A&M institutions. Scientists in these laboratories and on state farms engaged in research on farming techniques, animal diseases, foodstuffs, seed quality and the like in order to improve agricultural production across the country. The Smith-Lever Act approved by Congress in 1914 initiated federal (and state) funding that enabled land grant colleges and universities to establish agricultural *extension* stations. Extension services brought the colleges to the people as extension agents traveled through each state spreading information that proved to be useful to farmers, ranchers, and their families.

One of the most notable examples of this concept in practice occurred in the state of Wisconsin. There, under the progressive leadership of the University of Wisconsin's president, Charles Van Hise, and with the backing of the state's governor, Robert M. LaFollette, extension work was seen as a way to "send a state to college." As other state universities followed suit in investigating and disseminating practical knowledge, applied research became an established and important component of university research and service commitments.

Both Morrill Acts and subsequent A&M legislation provided opportunities for those who desired technical and vocational training, on or off campus, in agriculture, home economics, engineering, or other scientific fields. It is important to note, however, that just as the Reconstruction Congress had mandated that southern state governments submit new constitutions with explicit provisions regarding public education for *all* citizens (see Chapter 5), the second Morrill Act further revealed a shift in federal–state educational relations. The approach to education now being taken by Congress in the educational Reconstruction of the southern states, and in advancing agricultural, mechanical, and industrial higher education in all the states, was one that began to replace voluntarism with direct prescription.

This is not to say that Congress dictated integration of educational facilities in the South. However, it did not allow the southern states to put segregation in education or in any other realm into their constitutions. When Texas tried to mandate that its public schools would be racially segregated, Congress invalidated the constitution and sent it back for revision.[7]

Federal Indian Policy before the Civil War

The move toward majoritarian consensus and an expanding federal influence in matters of educational policy over the course of the nineteenth century is clearly seen in terms of governmental relations with the Native American population. To comprehend the shifting role of the federal government with respect to the education of Native Americans, one must view developments in the post-Civil War period against the backdrop of earlier events.

The relationship between Native Americans and new arrivals to the Atlantic (and Pacific) shores had been marked by cultural conflict from the very beginnings of settlement, as was emphasized in Chapter 1. As the United States government came into being and expansion into the South and West increased, conflict between the federal government and the Indian nations over land— and culture—increased as well. Whereas at the time of the Revolution the vast majority of the American people resided within a few hundred miles of the Atlantic Ocean, by 1840 one-third of the non-Native population lived between the Appalachians and the Mississippi River. The continued movement of settlers into Indian territory provoked hostilities on both sides of the cultural divide and brought the power of the federal government directly into the conflict.

From the Revolutionary War to the 1820s, the federal government had followed a policy of enacting treaties with Indians that enabled the government to buy Indian lands and provide support to missionaries who established schools to "civilize" and assimilate Indians to the dominant culture. In 1819 Congress passed the Civilization Fund Act that authorized the U.S. government to aid missionary educators in their quest to Christianize and civilize Native Americans—an action that then, unlike what would be the case today, was not countered with expressions of fear over excessive entanglement between church and state. The southern Cherokees, Creeks, Choctaws, Chickasaws, and Seminoles—referred to by non-Indians as the "Five Civilized Tribes"—had experienced over a century of contact with white missionaries and traders by the opening decades of the nineteenth century. Intermarriage with whites had created in all these tribes an influential minority of mixed-bloods who tended to heed the call of missionaries to embrace Christianity, agriculture, and the learning of the white people. A small number of Indians even adopted the practice of slavery along with agriculture.

Although some Native Americans seemed eager to embrace "civilization," the majority of full-blood Indians tended to resist encroachment into their ancestral lands and the denigration of their culture and were contemptuous of those who bartered away tribal land. When the Creek mixed-blood chief William McIntosh sold all Creek lands in Georgia and two-thirds of the Creek lands in Alabama to the government in 1825, he was executed by his people. In spite of resistance however, by the late 1820s, Creeks in Georgia and Alabama began bending to the steady encroachment of white settlement and started moving west.

The traditional policy of negotiating treaties piecemeal with the Indians began to be rejected by the time Andrew Jackson became president. Jackson, whose earlier exploits against the Native Americans had contributed to his popularity, had little respect for the "savages" and could see no justification in continuing to enact treaties with Indian tribes based on their status as independent nations. When Jackson became president in 1829, he initiated a coercive removal policy. In 1830 he secured the passage of the Indian Removal Act, thereby gaining congressional approval to use force, if necessary, to remove Indians from their lands. In 1836 the Georgia militia and federal troops engaged Creeks still clinging to their lands in that state. When the fighting ended, the state of Georgia laid claim to 25 million acres of Creek land; 15,000 Creek Indians, many in chains and handcuffs, were in turn forced west of the Mississippi.

The other civilized tribes faced a similar fate. The Cherokees, the most assimilated of all the southern tribes, attempted to challenge the Indian Removal Act by appealing to the U.S. Supreme Court. Although Chief Justice John Marshall initially ruled in *Cherokee Nation v. Georgia*[8] that the Cherokees were neither a state nor a foreign nation and hence lacked standing to bring suit, he asserted the following year in *Worcester v. Georgia* that they were a "domestic dependent nation" entitled to federal protection. President Andrew Jackson's purported response to the Chief Justice's legal opinion was both curt and chilling: "John Marshall has made his decision; now let him enforce it." Of course, neither the Court nor the Cherokees could do so in the face of a hostile chief executive and an unsympathetic public. Between 1835 and 1838, bands of Cherokees were herded west of the Mississippi along the "Trail of Tears." At least 2,000 died along the way and, as epidemics ravaged the weakened survivors, perhaps that many more died in the wake of removal.

Several years earlier, the visiting Frenchman Alexis de Tocqueville had witnessed Choctaws making their way across the Mississippi. He was struck by the sad caravan that included sick and wounded men and women, babies, and "old men on the point of death." The author of the classic study of equality, *Democracy in America*, recorded: "I saw them embark to cross the great river, and the sight will never fade from my memory. Neither sob nor complaint rose from that silent assembly. Their afflictions were of long standing, and they felt them to be irremediable."[9]

Tribes in the old Northwest Territory fared no better. By treaty and by force, the U.S. government pushed Indians from the path of land-hungry white settlers. Relocation beyond the Mississippi by no means settled the matter. In the West, Mexican as well as Indian lands were overrun as westward expansion and annexation added more and more territory to the United States. To the expansionists, the death or displacement of tens of thousands of nonwhites who stood in the way of "Manifest Destiny" seemed a small price to pay.[10]

The Federal Government and Indian Education

Federal policy regarding the treatment and education of Native Americans gradually entered a new phase in the post-Civil war period. Even while the "bluecoats" of the U.S. Army were still pursuing aggressive campaigns against

Figure 6.1 Print of Westward Movement. In this widely reproduced rendering of the advance of civilization, a diaphanous vision of America soars through the air with the "Star of Empire" on her forehead. Moving across the Mississippi with eastern commercial centers flourishing in the background, America faces westward with a schoolbook in one hand and telegraph wire in the other—symbols, along with the Pony Express, railroads, and the westward movement of rugged pioneers and homesteaders, of the forces that would bind the country and its diverse peoples together. Retreating into the receding darkness in the face of advancing Christian civilization are the wild animals and "savages" that must yield to the forces of enlightenment.

Source: Library of Congress, Prints and Photographs Division, LC-USZ62-737.

western tribes, a reformist temperament began to give rise to pleas for more just and humane policies toward the Indians. The publication in 1881 of Helen Hunt Jackson's *A Century of Dishonor: A Sketch of the United States Government's Dealings with Some of the Indian Tribes* moved readers to shame as they read of the decade after decade government deceit and bloody campaigns against Indians that had indelibly stained the nation's honor. Increasingly those concerned with Indian affairs began to argue that Indians needed to be saved from the white man *and* from themselves. As long as they remained "uncivilized" (ran the logic), they would continue to be at the mercy of unscrupulous whites and remain unprogressive as a people. Reservation living and tribal schools were seen by a growing number of reformers as obstacles to progress rather than as remedies for the "Indian problem."

With genuine concern about the plight of the American Indians, some well-intentioned humanitarians concluded that renewed effort should be made to assimilate Indians into mainstream society. This could best be done, they maintained, by tackling the Indian problem on two fronts: land reform and education reform. The object of both strategies was to wean Indians from their culture. In terms of land reform, advocates of change argued that by breaking up the reservations and dealing with Indians on an individual rather than a "tribal" basis, Indians would be encouraged to think of themselves as individuals, not members of a distinctive minority or subgroup. Educational reform was to involve renewed efforts to bring Indians under the influence of Christian civilization. In effect, the new reformers advocated eliminating the "Indian problem" by eliminating the Indians as a culturally distinct entity.

In 1887 Massachusetts Senator Henry L. Dawes sponsored the key measure that was designed to turn Indians into citizens who understood the "American Way" of doing things. The General Allotment Act (more commonly referred to as the Dawes Act) provided for the breakup of reservations and the distribution of land to the head of each Indian family who accepted the law's provisions. The remaining lands, often the choicest sections, were to be sold to speculators and settlers. The income obtained from the land sales would be used for the tribe's "education and civilization" and to purchase farm implements for the Indians. An important provision of the Act declared that Indians were henceforth to be citizens of the United States with all attendant rights and responsibilities. Senator Dawes and other "friends of the Indian" sincerely believed that citizenship and full assimilation into the mainstream of society not only offered the best protection for the Indians but was really the only way they could survive and have any chance of getting ahead.

In addition to—and typically in competition with—education offered within the tribe, "reservation day schools" had emerged by the time of the Civil War as "civilizing" agencies. Forty-eight reservation schools located on the outskirts of Indian villages had been established by the 1860s. By the end of the century, more than one hundred day schools were in operation throughout the Indian reservations of the American West. Most attention in these primary schools was given to language instruction, moral training, and basic concepts of industrial training. Although the missionary teachers who staffed the reservation day schools hoped the children would themselves become instruments of assimilation as they returned to their camps in the evening, the proximity of the school to the tribal community was eventually judged to be a major defect in the system. One Indian agent summarized the situation tersely: "It must be manifest to all practical minds that to place these wild children under a teacher's care but four or five hours a day, and permit them to spend the other nineteen in the filth and degradation of the village, makes the attempt to educate and civilize them a mere farce." Parental distrust and opposition as well as youthful resistance to the regimentation of schooling contributed to high rates of absenteeism. By the late 1870s the inadequacies of reservation day schools as civilizing agencies were becoming pronounced. Secretary of the Interior Carl Schurz complained to Congress in 1879 that the day schools "do not withdraw the children sufficiently from the influences, habits, and traditions of [Indian] home life." To the agents of civilization, a better alternative was clearly needed.[11]

Some reformers put their faith in "reservation boarding schools" as a desirable alternative to reservation day schools. Boarding schools were usually under the direct supervision of government Indian agents, with daily supervision of the schools in the hands of a superintendent and one or more teachers. With school terms lasting eight to nine months a year, the boarding school could exert a stronger influence over its charges. David Adams quoted the superintendent of the Indian Schools who, in 1885, summarized the attractiveness of the reservation boarding school as follows:

These schools strip from the unwashed person of the Indian boy the unwashed blanket, and, after instructing him in what to him are the mysteries of personal cleanliness, clothe him with the clean garments of civilized men and teach him how to wear them. They give him information concerning a bed and teach him how to use it; teach him how to sit on a chair, how to use a knife and fork, how to eat at a table, and what to eat. While he is learning these things, he is also learning to read and write, and, at the same time, is being taught how to work, how to earn a living.[12]

Although the reservation boarding school was more of a "total" institution than the day school, critics contended that Indian children still remained too close to the degrading influence of tribal life. Parental visits or the sight of smoke on the morning horizon or the faint sounds of ceremonial chants at night easily triggered emotions and longings to return to the life of the tribe. Some observers noted that, even though some students appeared to be transformed while in school, they often "relapsed" when they came back under the influence of the family and tribe during vacation time.

"Off-reservation boarding schools" emerged as still another, and to many, the preferred model for transforming Indians from "savagery to civilization."

The off-reservation boarding school idea stemmed from the experiences of an Army officer, Richard Henry Pratt. In 1877 Pratt had been placed in charge of a group of Indian prisoners of war that had been removed from the West to St. Augustine, Florida. Pratt began a school for the prisoners, an experiment that attracted the attention and support of Harriet Beecher Stowe and other philanthropically inclined reformers. Pratt then arranged for seventeen Indian males to enroll at Hampton Normal and Industrial Institute that had opened ten years earlier under the direction of Samuel Chapman Armstrong. Both General Armstrong and Lieutenant Pratt had commanded black troops during the Civil War, and both shared the belief that the oppression and degradation experienced by former slaves and Indians could be overcome through cultural uplift combined with moral and manual training. An 1878 Congressional appropriation to support Indian children in "special schools" made it possible for additional Indians, girls as well as boys, to join the original contingent at Hampton and come under the influence of the industrial education model that Booker T. Washington had come to embrace so enthusiastically.[13] A year later, 1879, Pratt obtained permission to conduct what became the first off-reservation school at a decommissioned army base in Carlisle, Pennsylvania.

Lieutenant Pratt founded the Carlisle Indian School in part out of restlessness in being second in command to General Armstrong and in part out of fear that Indians at Hampton might suffer from their association with blacks—not because black students would be a degrading influence but rather because white prejudice against blacks would inevitably spill over toward Indians. Again with Congressional backing, Pratt took charge of some unused military barracks at Carlisle, recruited teachers and students, and by 1 November, 1879 declared Carlisle Indian School officially open. For the next 25 years, Pratt directed Carlisle's affairs and remained the foremost authority on the Indian educational scene.

Pratt's ambition at Carlisle was to replace the popular western slogan that "the only good Indian is a dead one" with the principle "Kill the Indian in him and save the man." According to Pratt, the basis for the Indian's inferiority was cultural, not racial; the difference between a savage and a civilized man depended entirely upon environment. "There is no resistless clog placed upon us by birth," he contended. "We are not born with language, nor are we born with ideas of either civilization or savagery." The white child was potentially a savage, just as the Indian child was potentially civilized. To Pratt the formula was quite simple: for Indians to become civilized, they must be immersed in civilization.[14]

Carlisle proved to be the prototype for the off-reservation boarding school approach to Indian schooling. Between the founding of Carlisle in 1879 and 1905, twenty-five off-reservation boarding schools were founded. At these schools, and to the degree possible at on-reservation schools and day schools, the civilizing process required a twofold assault on Indian children's identity.

First of all, the school needed to strip away all outward signs of savage life—that is to say, the children's identification with tribal life. Second, the children were to be instructed in the ideas, values, and behaviors of the dominant civilization. For boys and girls the stripping away process typically began with the cutting of their hair. Standard school uniforms replaced tribal clothing. Names were changed in a variety of ways, but the basic purpose was to give Indian youth a new identity. Even the physical environment demanded a fundamental change in the accustomed ways of relating to space. The boarding school, new recruits quickly learned, was a world of lines, corners, and squares. Desks, beds, and tables were all carefully arranged in straight rows. All this represented a worldview very different, for example, from the Sioux touchstones of cultural reality—the sky, the sun, the moon, the tepee, the lodge, and the sacred hoop—all circular phenomena. At boarding schools, even the land was reshaped to reflect the order and conformity of a "tamed" society. The wildness and disorder of weeds, cactus, and meandering paths gave way to the symmetry and order of manicured lawns, pruned trees, contoured gardens, and parade fields. The lessons being taught far transcended the words in books.

It is important to note that Indian students were anything but passive recipients of the curriculum of civilization. Resistance was demonstrated in many ways—by running away, open defiance, passive disobedience, torching buildings, and various strategies of negotiating the system. Still, the civilizing process that marked Indian educational policy in the closing years of the nineteenth and early decades of the twentieth century certainly had a profound psychological and cultural impact on those who attended schools run by government agencies. Like it or not, David Adams has noted, returning students often became agents of cultural change, and over time "white education" constituted one of the major acculturative forces shaping Indian society. At the same time, the experience of tribal mixing at boarding schools resulted in an enlarged sense of identity as "Indians." At institutions such as Carlisle, students learned that "the Great Father" made no allowances for tribal distinctions; Indians were simply Indians. "Ironically," Adams concluded, "the very institution designed to extinguish Indian identity altogether may have in fact contributed to its very persistence in the form of twentieth-century pan-Indian consciousness."[15]

A marked contrast to the approach of the off-reservation boarding school was provided in the small number of schools maintained by a few of the southeastern Indian tribes in the second half of the nineteenth century. The Chickasaw tribe sought to establish and succeeded in running its own schools in this period. Prior to removal from their land in Mississippi and Alabama, the Chickasaw had cooperated with a few missionaries who established various schools for Chickasaw children. After removal and the end of the Civil War, the tribe began to support several neighborhood schools on the lands of the Chickasaw nation in the Oklahoma territory as well as academies for boys and for girls.

One of the most noted of these academies was the Bloomfield Academy for Chickasaw girls. Successor to a similar institution that had been established by missionaries before the Civil War, a school was begun at Bloomfield in 1867. In 1876, the tribe formally established a female seminary at the Bloomfield Academy that reflected the desire of the Chickasaw nation for self-control of its affairs. The curriculum at this institution featured the academic study of subjects such as reading, geography, history, algebra, and U.S. history and literature. Additionally, the school emphasized the fine arts, including music, art, and physical culture. Notably absent were the homemaking and other domestic studies that had prevaded the missionary education of Chickasaw girls before removal. Also notably diminished, though not eliminated completely, was the role of formal religion in the curriculum. The graduates of Bloomfield took their place as teachers in the other schools of the Chickasaw nation, where they tried to implement the same educational approach they had experienced at Bloomfield.[16]

In the last decade of the nineteenth century, the federal government moved in a number of ways to end the tribal schools of the Chickasaw. This was accomplished formally with the passage of an act in 1898 that established a federal superintendent for the Indian territory. While the Chickasaw resisted takeover of their schools for a few more years, the overwhelming power of the federal government and impending statehood for Oklahoma resulted in the transformation of Chickasaw schools into federal schools for native Americans. While these schools often kept the names of their predecessor institutions, they quickly readopted the nonacademic fields of domestic and industrial studies and opened schools such as Bloomfield to other tribes than the Chickasaw. Of course, this intermingling of the tribes may also have inadvertently contributed to the creation of the "pan-Indian consciousness" that persisted in subsequent periods.[17]

The Federal Education Agency

National education activity in the post-Civil War era went beyond policies designed to bring recalcitrant southern states and Indian tribes into line with dominant educational sentiments. The move toward increasing conformity was furthered by the creation of a federal education agency. Initially, this agency took the form of a cabinet-level Department of Education. This high-profile role for education did not last long, however. American politicians and citizens, as well as the leaders of the agency itself, were not yet ready for direct federal intervention in the day-to-day affairs of education. The new agency quickly lost its departmental status and was reorganized into a "bureau" of education whose main function was to gather educational data. Even though the new federal education agency was not particularly powerful, it did become a permanent part of the American educational scene. Moreover, those who gather and publish information about any institution are never completely powerless in that particular arena. The very existence of the federal Bureau of

Education, therefore, established and legitimized a federal administrative role in education that previously had been absent.[18]

Congress and the executive branch thus sent mixed signals concerning the federal role in education during this period. Congress supported state efforts with its land-grant legislation but then dictated state educational policy for the southern states seeking readmission to the Union. Having dictated educational policy, however, the federal government never attempted to supervise its implementation after the southern states were readmitted to the Union. Similarly, having established an activist role with its new federal educational agency, the federal government then adopted a passive role for that agency, rendering it little more than a compiler and disseminator of information.

Nevertheless, it seems clear that both the legislature and the executive branch carved out a distinct federal role in education during this period. It has remained for later generations, including our own, to continue the debate over the nature and extent of the federal government's role in education. This debate resurfaces in several later chapters. For now it is sufficient to note that federal influence in education was significantly enhanced in the post-Civil War years, just as it was enhanced in many other areas of American life.

Compulsion in American Education

Turning from the national to the state level, the postwar era produced a significant trend in the educational activities of state legislatures: the passage of compulsory school attendance laws. By 1890, twenty-seven states had passed such laws, and by 1918 all forty-eight states then in the Union had enacted such legislation. The first states to enact these laws were mostly in the North, the upper Midwest, and California, where there was an increasing trend toward large-scale manufacturing. As noted previously, this industrialization process was accompanied by a mass migration from farms to the cities where the factories were located. These migrants and the immigrants that came to the United States in the late nineteenth and early twentieth centuries were often forced to live in squalid city slums. Many observers saw in these conditions a threat of family breakdown resulting in hordes of uncontrolled children running free in the city streets. This atmosphere of fear, together with concern for young children being forced to work in factories, accounts in part for the wave of compulsory attendance laws that swept the country by the end of the nineteenth century.[19]

Much of the political support for the compulsory attendance laws came from citizens who were neither migrants nor immigrants, but feared those who were. Many supporters of compulsion belonged to the Protestant middle and upper classes and valued close family ties. These groups were fearful of urban children roaming the streets without the benefit of family supervision.

Opposition to compulsory school attendance is not as easy to characterize. Some Americans objected vigorously to the principle of government compulsion in any area. Others, particularly the urban poor and many farmers, acted on their need for the proceeds from their children's work to help their families survive and prosper.

Early Attendance Laws

The first compulsory attendance law was passed in 1852 in Massachusetts, the birthplace of the common school. That law, which required twelve weeks of schooling, at least six of which had to be continuous, was ineffective from its inception. Little if any attempt was made to enforce its provisions, and it was ignored by the state's education officials for at least two decades.[20]

A similar situation occurred in New York State in the 1870s. In 1874, the New York legislature passed a compulsory attendance law that required students between the ages of eight and fourteen to attend school for fourteen weeks a year, at least eight of which were to be consecutive. In spite of this legislation, ten years after passage of the law, a smaller percentage of the school-age population attended school than had been the case before passage. This situation was due to several factors. For one thing, legislators appeared to be more interested in the appearance of attendance than in its enforcement. Also, enforcement was left up to local school officials, who received no compensation for this additional task. Finally, truant children and their parents, when confronted with the issue, could simply lie about the child's age.[21]

Much of the impetus for passage of the compulsory school laws came from concern over child labor. The New York law, for example, required that a child between the ages of eight and fourteen had to provide a school attendance certificate to qualify for employment. Violations of this provision, however, were the responsibility of overworked school officials trying to cope with over-crowded schools. Assigning enforcement to them was a sure sign that the law-makers were not really serious about enforcing the statute they had created. When the legislature did respond to criticism from reformers disturbed at the failure of the law, they confronted the child labor issue head on, passing the first of a series of Factory Acts in 1886. This initial Act sought to prevent children under the age of thirteen from working in factories and to limit the work hours of children between the ages of thirteen and sixteen. However, enforcement of this and subsequent Acts proved to be no more effective than enforcement of the school attendance laws. The number of inspectors funded to enforce the law was minuscule in relation to the size of the problem, and the courts proved to be more sympathetic to employers than to those who sought to regulate them.[22]

The ineffectiveness of compulsory attendance laws before 1890 has caused one historian to label this period a symbolic phase in the history of compulsory school attendance. The significance was in what the laws symbolized—that is, the political acceptance by several states of the principle of compulsion. These laws established the responsibility of the state to intervene in situations where families were unable or unwilling to care for their children. The majoritarian mood that was sweeping the nation was partly responsible for their passage, as well as for the attempt to institutionalize compulsion in other aspects of American life.[23]

Public support for pre-1890 compulsory attendance laws can be gauged from school attendance trends. National figures reveal that between 1860 and 1890 the school enrollment rate of five to nineteen-year-olds increased from 49 percent to 64 percent, while the percentage of illiterates in the same period declined from 20 to 13 percent. In other words, in a time of rapidly increasing school attendance, these laws illustrated the public's growing commitment to schooling and its concern about the children of poor families who were not attending school. The lax enforcement of these laws, especially in the cities, can be attributed largely to the overwhelming number of students who were trying to enroll.[24]

Urban School Systems

Whereas it was the state legislatures that passed compulsory school laws in the last half of the nineteenth century, it was in the cities that educators began to confront the increasing enrollments that accompanied the laws. One way to characterize this encounter is to show how educators began to develop an educational bureaucracy to handle the problems related to growing enrollment. As used here, the term "bureaucracy" does not refer to an elaborate system of specialization and expertise. Rather, it connotes a series of rudimentary organizational attempts to accommodate larger numbers of students without proportionally increasing school budgets and staff.

The "One Best System"

David Tyack has characterized the development of urban schooling in the late nineteenth and early twentieth centuries as the creation of a "one best system" that would serve in every situation. Of interest here is Tyack's description of how the earliest attempts to create a system of urban education distinguished urban schools from their common school predecessors. First, urban schools were organized on a new principle, age grading. Previously, all schooling was conducted either in a one-room setting where students of all ages studied at their own level, or in multiroom settings with each room having a large, heterogeneous group of students. In the new urban schools, however, students were grouped into classes according to age, so that the city schools began to resemble egg crates. They contained several classrooms that were similar in size but differentiated according to the age and presumed ability of the students.[25]

Along with the egg-crate school came uniform courses of study, specifying just what subjects were to be taught in each grade, the order in which material in each one would be covered, and the activities that were to be used by teachers to cover the material. Basic mathematics, spelling, and grammar were staples in the courses of study. They represented areas that could be sequenced, could be handled through a closely planned set of student activities, and, most important, could be tested frequently and consistently.

Examinations were essential to the new urban school courses, providing immediate evidence of student achievement or failure. These examinations could be either written or oral, although the written exam eventually came to dominate. The value of written examinations was that they provided a clear and consistent record of what was taking place in classrooms. Uniformity was imposed at each grade level through the examination system. In most systems, the superintendent was intimately involved in both curriculum and test development. Superintendents sometimes claimed to know what was happening hourly in each classroom on any day of the term.

This highly structured and competitive atmosphere eventually gave birth to the sort of predictable bureaucratic behavior that characterizes all large impersonal organizations. Punctuality, regularity, obedience, and silence were expected and rewarded. Needless to say, their opposite qualities were punished. Given the numbers of students in their classrooms, teachers became committed to managing classrooms with a set of factory-like rules. The attention to every aspect of student conduct, the sequencing of classroom materials and activities, and the frequent measurement of student learning all contributed to the development of hierarchical, efficiency-oriented urban schools.

In many cities, a high school emerged as a capstone institution fed by the newly graded lower schools. Clearly intended for only a small portion of the students, its existence signified that the budding bureaucracy of urban education had a fitting end point, a culminating institution toward which the lower studies could all be aimed, at least in terms of aspiration. Further, the city high school, which was governed by a single citywide school board, could function as an educational unifier, offsetting the rivalry between elementary schools that were governed by neighborhood boards.

The Superintendent

The bureaucratic school system that was emerging in the nation's cities in the late nineteenth century needed a single person at the top of its structure. That individual, the superintendent, was conceived as the head of the system, the one responsible for all that was taking place in the ranks below. The early superintendent's responsibility, however, was largely instructional. It was the superintendent who presided over the development of the curriculum and was responsible for examinations and the yearly promotion or retention of students. Further, he was the one who made sure that the principals were doing an adequate job of supervising their teachers. In addition, he served in an almost clerical capacity to the boards of education that managed the schools. In this capacity, he would compile rudimentary data regarding the conduct of the schools, write reports to the board, make arrangements for the day-to-day repairs of school buildings, and buy supplies for the schools. In a very real sense, then, the superintendent was the instructional leader of the teachers and principals in the schools but still clearly subordinate to lay authorities.[26]

This left much to be desired from the point of view of those who valued a truly powerful school executive. While the superintendent was responsible for instructional supervision, curriculum development, and day-to-day maintenance he had little to do with the policy and management decisions that set the tone for the system. Teacher hiring, firing, salaries, and promotions were the responsibility of lay boards, as were negotiations regarding school buildings and supplies. Further, the superintendent had few, if any, support staff to help him with his supervisory work. Thus, depending on the size of a school system, a conscientious superintendent could spend his entire year visiting classrooms and have little time left for anything else.

The role of the late-nineteenth-century superintendent was in a transitional stage, moving from the paternalistic, clergylike leadership embodied earlier in the century toward the broader managerialism that would evolve in the next century. Because of his limited responsibilities and lack of formal training for the position, the superintendent was often less of a leader than he seemed. Given the system of divided responsibility between the board and the superintendent, the desire of many board members to keep the superintendent in his assigned place, and the often large number of schools and students in the nation's cities, the internal administration of the enterprise often seemed chaotic.

Educational leaders used their journals and associations to criticize the unclear lines of authority. The National Education Association (NEA), founded in 1857 by actual and aspiring school leaders, for the rest of the nineteenth century became a vehicle devoted largely to improving school administration. The NEA also served as a platform from which to criticize the extreme regimentation and trivialization of curricula in the nation's urban school machines. Too often, the schools seemed like educational factories or resembled prisons or asylums rather than institutions devoted to the growth and development of students. Unfortunately, the NEA lacked any means to ensure that its views would be heard in the school systems themselves.[27]

Given this situation, it is not surprising that the individuals who aspired to urban superintendencies left much to be desired. Charles Francis Adams, descendant of two presidents and chair of the school committee in Quincy, Massachusetts in the late 1860s, was dubious about the quality of applicants for the superintendency there. He described the pool of candidates as "lawyers without briefs, ministers without pulpits, schoolmasters gone to seed," and concluded that every species of educated man without a job thought himself uniquely qualified to lead the Quincy schools. It would take another generation for anything to be done about the issue Adams raised. In the meantime, however, the burgeoning urban school systems continued to grow, if not prosper.[28]

Gender in the One Best System

Despite increasing bureaucratization there was at least one aspect of late-nineteenth-century urban schooling that threatened traditional authority relations. The issue of whether or not to mix genders in urban schools had been a matter for much debate throughout the nineteenth century. While small student numbers guaranteed that the sexes would be mixed in rural schools, the large numbers of students in city schools presented the possibility of separate classes or schools for girls and boys.

In some older eastern cities with long-standing public education traditions, single-sex schools were numerous, if not the norm. Even there, however, the principles of "common" schooling argued against separation of the sexes. In other cities, whose schools developed as part of the common school movement, coeducation tended to be the norm. There, boys and girls were taught the same curriculum in the same classes.

Given this mixture of precedent, the issue of coeducation continued to be debated throughout the latter half of the nineteenth century. However, by the last decade of the century, coeducation emerged as the dominant form of public education in the nation's cities. More conservative areas such as the South joined the older eastern cities in leaning toward separate schools for boys and girls, particularly in the high schools. Generally speaking, however, coeducation won out.[29]

While advocates of single-sex schooling feared the consequences of exposing girls to the coarseness of male students, defenders of coeducation argued that the presence of girls actually improved the behavior of boys. To its advocates, coeducation meant healthier psychological and sexual development of both boys and girls, as well as improved school discipline. Better discipline would, they believed, lead to more effective instruction in the schools. By merging the different tastes and abilities of boys and girls, a better-balanced learning process would result, one that would avoid the excesses that each sex brought to the schoolroom.

What was often not mentioned in these debates was the fact that coeducation was advanced by the developing dominance of women as classroom teachers in this period. While tradition-minded fathers and mothers might fear for the fate of their daughters in classes taught by men, the same fear did not operate for the parents of boys, or girls, in classrooms taught by women. Thus, the feminization of the nation's teaching force helped to cement coeducation as a firm, if not completely dominant, presence in the nation's urban schools.

The fear of some that coeducation might undermine the male-dominated society never materialized for two reasons. First, traditional gender roles were reinforced rather than challenged within the coeducational classrooms. Girls were not taught to behave like boys, but rather to conduct themselves as proper young ladies. Boys, in turn, were reinforced for exhibiting masculine qualities, both inside and outside school. Thus, the potentially dangerous setting of a coeducational school turned into an effective prop for conventional, hierarchical gender relations. Much of the impetus for this came from the conservative, middle-class background of the young women who were entering the teaching force at this time.

The second way in which coeducational schooling reinforced a gender hierarchy was in staffing. The supervisory ranks were largely male and the teaching ranks were overwhelmingly female. Superintendents were invariably men, and principalships were also male dominated. The classroom teachers, or "assistants" as they were called, were almost always women. In the cities, their training was intentionally kept at a low level. Teacher preparation classes were usually organized in the city high schools, where girls could learn the rudiments of teaching in a male-dominated setting that resembled the family structure of the era. Thus, an important gender hierarchy was reinforced in the day-to-day conduct of coeducational schools.[30]

Education and Society

Another result of the emerging bureaucracies of late-nineteenth-century urban schooling was the socialization of the students into the authoritarian order they would encounter in the workplace. Devotion to organization, regularity, punctuality, and discipline meant that the schools in a very real way prepared their students to work in the new factories that were developing in the nation's cities. The same routinization that the young would face on the job was present in the schools they attended.

Another goal of this regimented school culture was to homogenize the school population. The stability of urban society in this period was threatened from several directions. Class divisions, corruption, ethnic conflict, crime, and violence were all part of the social fabric encountered by American city dwellers. The school, with its emphasis on order and conformity, offered an antidote to these divisive social currents. Schoolmen knew of these threats to urban life, often highlighted the problems to the point of unreality, and trumpeted their institutions as the only long-range solution to the situation.

However, schooling was not concerned entirely with social conformity and stability. While the primary ideal of the school authorities might be moral, political, and economic order, the content of school curriculum contained readings and other intellectual exercises that reflected the individualism of the Western intellectual tradition. Students who read the classics of their heritage could take from those works lessons of social and economic mobility as well as of stability, of intellectual and moral independence as well as of conformity, and of political participation and agitation as well as of obedience to authority. Even at its most organized then, the educational system held within itself the seeds of opposition.

Yet those who used the educational system for economic mobility, political liberation, and moral questioning were clearly in the minority. The "one best system" did much more to reinforce social barriers than it did to break them down. Its success in this regard was proudly noted by its leaders, most of whom came from the more conservative ranks of America's social structure. They were confident that the primary mission of schools should be the maintenance of order in a rapidly changing society. They were equally confident that this order was necessary to the maintenance of the social fabric.

Specialization in the Educational System

Despite the development of a budding educational bureaucracy in the late-nineteenth-century cities, the common curriculum adopted earlier in the century did not disappear. The appearance of specialized curricula aimed at different groups of students did not occur until after 1890. Prior to this time, superintendents lacked the advanced training needed to lead the development of differentiated curricula. Not until the twentieth century did specialized training programs for school administrators give them the background necessary for this type of school leadership.

Although the common school curriculum remained intact during most of the late nineteenth century, new types of specialized schools began to develop above and below the common schools. These specialized institutions were complementary to the common schools.

The Kindergarten

While the common school had always permitted a variety of beginning ages for children, the arrival of age grading in urban public schools meant that more and more children began to attend school at the same age, usually around six years old. This uniform starting age, along with innovations in early education borrowed from Europe, combined to spark the development of the kindergarten, a new educational institution that existed initially outside the public school. From its beginnings the kindergarten, like most other educational innovations in the United States, was very much an urban phenomenon.

The kindergarten, whose literal translation from the German means "children's garden," owed much to the German philosopher, Friedrich Froebel. His approach to early education emphasized leading young children out of their "self" orientation toward valuing social relationships with other children. Froebel's garden metaphor emphasized cultivating young children toward maturity much as a gardener cultivates plants. For Froebel, a confirmed philosophical idealist, a divine spirit was present in all humans and the job of the kindergarten was to unify children by cultivating that spirit. The way to promote this development was through an elaborate set of structured play activities that gradually induced a social order in the child's environment.[31]

American kindergartens resembled Froebel's ideal in their emphasis on warmth, naturalness, and play as well as in their vision of the classroom as a natural extension of the home. One of America's early kindergarten advocates was Elizabeth Palmer Peabody, a sister-in-law of Horace Mann. She shared with her brother-in-law a devotion to education as an affective, moral enterprise as well as a cognitive one, and she dismissed concern with discipline as unwarranted. Given these values, it is not difficult to see how the initial kindergartens of Massachusetts served primarily as educational springboards for well-to-do children whose home environments resembled those of the school.[32]

Within a few decades, however, the kindergarten acquired a different orientation, one aimed primarily at children from the lower classes of the nation's cities. In this context, the classroom was often set at odds with the home environment of the children. Exemplary here were the charity kindergartens established in the teeming North End neighborhood of Boston by Pauline Shaw, an associate of Elizabeth Palmer Peabody. Shaw's kindergartens were associated with, though distinct from, the public schools in the neighborhood. Unlike in kindergartens in the more affluent areas, Shaw and her teachers had to visit the families of the North End and persuade them to enroll their children.

Urban kindergarten advocates enthused over stories like "A Lily's Mission," which depicted ragged, dirty children carrying home a beautiful flower to their tenement apartment. Their mother, not in the habit of keeping house, was so impressed at the beauty of the flower that she quickly cleaned herself and the house. Her husband, returning from a bout of drunkenness, was so impressed with his changed home environment that he vowed not to drink again. The kindergarten was thus enlisted as a crucial element in the battle to reform urban lower-class families.[33]

St. Louis, Missouri, provided another setting where the kindergarten was seen as a tool of urban reform. The roots of the kindergarten in that city were found in the city's German immigrant population, which established Froebelian private play schools there in the 1850s. In St. Louis, a young woman from a prominent family, Susan Blow, saw the possibilities of extending these instructions into the public schools. Blow was educated in private schools and by tutors as well as through foreign travel. Her family and church activities helped her to develop a concept of social responsibility somewhat like that which motivated Pauline Shaw in Boston. While she had learned Froebelian ideas in Europe, Blow found her vocation as a teacher through a stint as a substitute teacher in the St. Louis public schools in 1871–1872.[34]

After experimenting with Froebelian techniques as a substitute teacher, Blow went to New York to study kindergarten ideas in more depth. She returned to St. Louis a year later and, with the approval of the superintendent, established the first public school kindergarten in the nation. Blow's intended beneficiary was the slum child. She used the Froebelian approach of emphasizing games and other play activities as her main pedagogical tool. The goal of the activities was to instill desirable skills and proper social sentiments in the children. Although part of the public schools, these kindergartens would not have existed without the financial support and participation of Susan Blow and other young women volunteers from the better St. Louis families. Their mission was to enrich the environment of the city's poor children, thereby saving them from the dire consequences of their impoverished existence.

In the 1880s, after rebutting an attack on the kindergarten as a foreign institution, the St. Louis advocates sought to enlarge the target audience to include wealthy families. They argued in this case that the education of wealthy young children was too important to be left in the hands of servants. Wealthy parents were often too busy with their business and philanthropic responsibilities to attend to their children's needs. Thus, it was argued, the kindergarten was needed to save both poor and affluent children from misdirection and underdevelopment.

This rationale was successful enough to establish kindergartens in most of the wealthy neighborhoods in St. Louis, alongside those in the poor neighborhoods. In a sense, then, the institution had come full circle. Beginning as a private enclave for the affluent in Massachusetts, it soon evolved into an institution devoted to the betterment of poor urban children and, eventually, broadened into an agency for the socialization of the very young, whatever their backgrounds.

The University

Just as the kindergarten was emerging to meet the needs of children too young for graded public schools, another institution, the university, began emerging for older students. This new institution eventually surpassed the college as the most influential part of the higher-education system.

As we have already discussed, colleges had existed in some form in the United States since the seventeenth century. In their first two centuries, colleges had developed mainly in New England, the Northeast, and Virginia. In the nineteenth century, they spread rapidly through the South and the Midwest. By the middle of the nineteenth century, despite numerous differences in financial sponsorship and student population, colleges had come to resemble each other greatly, particularly in their curricula. With only a few exceptions, they all featured a commitment to the classics as the heart of their curriculum, although a few paid some homage to the sciences as a field of study.[35]

Although Yale University boldly bestowed the first Ph.D. degrees in the United States in 1861, the beginning of the university movement is often attributed to the founding of Cornell University in New York in 1868. Cornell, funded by a private endowment established by Ezra Cornell, augmented by state support, and the state's recipient of land-grant funds, set out to become an institution in which, in the words of its founder, "any person can find instruction in any study." One year later, Harvard College began its journey toward becoming a university when Charles W. Eliot assumed the presidency and gradually introduced the elective system and upgraded professional studies.

In 1876, Johns Hopkins University was founded as the first university devoted primarily to graduate study. A new "investigative temper" began to take hold at Hopkins and in the leading universities of the day. Based on the model established by German universities, the growth of the research university promoted basic changes in the nature of American higher education. One fundamental change was a new emphasis on the increasing specialization of knowledge within the university. A second and related new emphasis was a commitment to research as a route to discovering new—and socially useful—knowledge. A third development was the liberation of intellect for its own sake. No longer did professors at leading research universities need to spend their time hearing recitations or worrying about chapel attendance or monitoring student conduct. These *in loco parentis* ("in place of the parent") concerns at the undergraduate level began to dissipate and become the province of deans and student affairs specialists that emerged as part of the transformation taking place in higher education. University professors were encouraged to pursue their research specializations in laboratories, archives, and libraries and to bring the most recent scholarly knowledge to light in lectures and seminars, themselves new modes of advanced inquiry and teaching. Standards were set for the Ph.D. that emphasized substantial "original" research that would result in a publishable dissertation, the merits of which would be judged by a committee of academic experts in the field. These standards were codified with the formation in 1900 of the Association of American Universities, initially a collection of fourteen universities that were considered by themselves and others as the *elite* institutions of higher learning. Beginning with the founding of the American Economic Assocation in 1885, professional societies formed to advance specialization, focus on standards within the disciplines, and promote academic freedom. The American Association of University Professors (AAUP), founded in 1915 by Arthur O. Lovejoy and John Dewey, came into being as a direct result of perceived abuses of academic freedom and in order to advance the practice of shared governance.[36]

In spite of the tremendous impact of these new and expanded universities and their related associations, smaller and older liberal arts colleges by no means disappeared. The American devotion to undergraduate study that lent stability to the colleges and universities proved resistant to total surrender. Undergraduate programs not only provided a pool of students for advanced study, they became a symbol of social and economic status in America's high industrial society. So fixed was the association of undergraduate liberal studies with the public (and academic) concept of higher education in the United States that even Daniel C. Gilman, Johns Hopkins' founding president, had to yield to pressure from the local press to add an undergraduate division to its graduate oriented programs of study.[37]

Another factor that somewhat restrained the widespread adoption of the Hopkins' model was that the German ideal of "pure" rather than applied research was not in tune with the research ideal taking root at most other American universities. In the United States—a rapidly developing nation with shifting frontiers, restless people, abundant resources, and a vast array of social problems—the climate was much better suited to applied research than to pure, disinterested inquiry. In short, university research in the late nineteenth century had to attach itself to the principle of social utility in order to survive.

The American university was thus a hybrid institution. Its graduate and professional schools focused on applied research within a utilitarian framework, while its undergraduate program retained many of the liberal arts values of the colleges it was seeking to supersede. Although the specialization that character-ized graduate and professional schools invaded the undergraduate curriculum, it never completely displaced prescribed studies. Also, while the principle of election did gradually meet acceptance in most universities, the radical elec-tivism favored by Charles W. Eliot was too much for most college faculty and administrators to tolerate. A compromise eventually emerged as the undergraduate curriculum was broken into an initial set of core studies in which prescription still reigned, accompanied by a "major" field of study. This compromise position honored both student preference and intellectual specialization, but without sacrificing liberal education completely.[38]

Although the hybrid American university developed apart from the pub-lic schools in the late nineteenth century, the issues that it faced—intellectual specialization and social utilitarianism—also faced public school educators. Intellectual specialization proved to be a particular problem for the American high school.

The High School

As mentioned earlier, nineteenth-century high schools varied according to the needs of the communities in which they developed. Whatever similarity they shared derived mainly from the mostly middle-class population they served. The lower classes had little enthusiasm for an institution they had no intention of patronizing.[39]

Boston, which had from colonial times provided for public writing schools as well as English and Latin grammar schools, also led the way with the intro-duction of the first formally organized public high school in the United States. In 1818 Boston's city fathers established public primary schools, thus making entry into grammar schools possible even for children of those who previously had been excluded because of lack of access to the few public or more numer-ous private reading and writing schools in the city. Three years later, in 1821, an alternative to the grammar schools was opened: the English Classical School of Boston. Designed primarily as an institution for boys between the ages of twelve and fifteen who would become merchants and craftsmen, the three-year curriculum emphasized English composition and mathematics, along with courses in social studies and science. It was not intended to prepare boys for college and, in spite of the term "classical" in its original name, did not offer foreign languages of any sort. The name of the institution changed to English High School three years after its opening.

The first public high school was not a coeducational institution, but in 1826 Bostonians established a high school for girls. Ironically, the very popularity of the Boston High School for Girls led to its demise. So many girls applied for admission that after two years the city refused to vote the funds needed for its maintenance and the institution was closed. Josiah Quincy, then mayor of Boston and later president of Harvard, thought little of the venture into public education for young women and feared the undertaking would bankrupt the city. He declared the school a failure, an opinion obviously not shared by girls who sought more educational opportunity. Boston's female population had to wait until 1852 for another chance at publicly supported "higher" learning. In that year the Boston Girls' High and Normal School opened as a teacher training institution.[40]

Girls in neighboring Worcester and Lowell enjoyed earlier success than their Boston counterparts. A high school for girls was established in Worcester in 1824, and the mill town of Lowell in 1831 established the first coeducational high school. Lowell's high school resembled some academies of the period by offering both an English and a classical course. As high schools spread, many adopted a similar dual curriculum.

In the pre-Civil War period, high schools appeared most frequently in areas experiencing industrial growth and rapid social change. In addition to Boston and several other Massachusetts towns, New York City and Portland, Maine, also established high schools during the 1820s. Over a dozen more appeared in the 1830s and by the 1840s, cities as far afield as Providence, Detroit, Cleveland, Cincinnati, and even New Orleans were supporting high schools. By the close of the Civil War there were over 160 high schools in New England, slightly more than 100 of which were in Massachusetts. An 1827 law in Massachusetts that was reminiscent of the Old Deluder Satan Act of the 1640s provided the model if not the stimulus for the spread of high schools in the area. The 1827 law, enacted largely through the efforts of James G. Carter, required the establishment of a tax-supported high school in all communities of 500 or more families. The law further mandated that Latin and Greek be offered in the schools when the towns or districts had a population of at least 4,000. Other New England and Midwestern states soon followed suit.

Laws requiring the payment of taxes in support of high schools and the growing bureaucracies associated with increased systemization did not go unchallenged. A citizen in Kalamazoo, Michigan, questioned the city's law requiring taxes in support of a high school in 1872. The case reached the state supreme court in 1874. In rendering the opinion of the court in the "Kalamazoo Decision" (30 Mich. 69), Chief Justice Thomas M. Cooley reasoned that legislators in establishing a system of public or common schools did not set any limit to the number of years that were to be embraced by the system. Having already established common schools and a state university, Cooley argued, the legislature clearly intended to create a complete system of schools. The high school, he determined, was a necessary stage in completing the path from elementary schools to the university. The Kalamazoo Decision was subsequently cited in several states when laws establishing tax-supported high schools came under fire.

Central High School of Philadelphia

Philadelphia's first high school emerged during the common school era in 1838. It was a prestigious school for boys only, whose head was called president and whose faculty were known as professors. Initially it offered three courses of study: a two-year course that continued the education of the lower schools, a standard academic course that prepared youth for entry into the city's commercial enterprises, and a classical course for those who intended to go to college. Rather quickly, however, the two-year and the classical options were dropped, and Central offered the standard curriculum to all its students.[41]

This commitment to commonality was balanced against an equally strong commitment to the "market" needs of the middle-class boys who attended the school. The boys' parents wanted them prepared for the city's burgeoning white-collar occupations. Central did not offer a specialized commercial course of study. Its task was to create a prestigious, undifferentiated curriculum that would also qualify its students for the city's commercial occupations.

Central's standard curriculum differed substantially, although not completely, from the two courses of study, classical and English, found in many other high schools of the nineteenth century. Central focused on the study of English language and literature as well as on scientific subjects for all its students. Latin was maintained, but only in an obviously subservient role to the other subjects. Thus, Central's common curriculum was modern in the sense that its language and science focus was indirectly related to the commercial world. Central assured that its graduates would be distinctive by instituting a rigorous set of admission and exit criteria. This ensured that its diploma would be a valued and scarce commodity. Philadelphia's middle class coveted the diploma both as a status symbol and as a way of accessing the city's emerging commercial world.

The principle of equal access to Central was maintained through its entrance examination and other objective admission criteria. This homage to the political principles of commonality was contradicted by the makeup of the student body however, more than two-thirds of whom were from middle-class backgrounds. Thus, the needs of the middle class dominated the school's commitment to equal access for all classes.

Central High's relationship to the city's other schools took different forms in the nineteenth century. Initially, it was completely autonomous; it had no governance relationship to the primary and grammar schools that fed it. Even so, it exerted considerable influence over the lower schools, whose ambitious headmasters tilted their curricula toward its entrance examination. The various lay boards that were responsible for Philadelphia's schools exerted little influence at Central, even the board specifically responsible for high schools.

The faculty at Central enjoyed substantial power, income, and prestige under the leadership of the president. They met regularly to conduct the business of the school. This collegial form of governance was challenged in 1858 when a new president tried to untie the long-standing relationship between discipline and grades. Unable to win faculty support for the change, the president, with the approval of the high school board, simply imposed it on the school. Central's faculty revolted at this usurpation of power but lost the battle when three professors were dismissed for insubordination. Four years later, however, the faculty gained revenge, as the president was dismissed along with three of his close supporters. Although the faculty were unable to restore the link between grades and discipline, they did reestablish the principle of collegial governance.[42]

Faculty influence continued at Central High until the 1880s. In that decade, the city's first superintendent of schools was appointed. He moved to install hierarchical administration throughout the system, a plan that clearly threatened the autonomy of Central High School. When opposition from Central High arose, the superintendent responded by opening a second high school to compete with it. A few years later, in 1888, a new president was hired whose job was to bring the Central High faculty into conformity with the new order. He did this simply by refusing to call faculty meetings for any meaningful purpose. Thus, the collegial tradition of governance at Central was permanently ended.

The bureaucratic taming of the Central High faculty was part of a total revamping of secondary education, including the curriculum, that took place in Philadelphia during the next several years. The substance of that change is a subject for the next chapter. As it developed through most of the nineteenth century, Central High illustrates the growing pains endured by an urban high school as it moved to meet the occupational needs of its citizens. In the case of Central, this move was made with a curriculum only indirectly related to the occupational futures of its students. The late-century fate of Central's faculty also illustrates the consequences for teachers of the growth of centralized bureaucracy in America's modernizing urban school systems.

Girls and the High School

Contrary to the situation at Central High School, boys did not dominate enrollment in nineteenth-century high schools. In 1872, the first year that national records were kept, girls composed 53 percent of the high school population, and by 1900 girls accounted for 59 percent. In cities, this disparity was even greater. In 1888, for example, girls composed 75 percent of the high school population in the nation's largest urban areas.[43]

The main reason for this disparity was the fact that high-school-age girls had much less access to the workplace than did boys. This situation reflected both a lack of available jobs and a fear on the part of middle-class Americans for the well-being of their daughters in the world of commerce and industry. In addition, girls seemed to welcome the intellectual challenge that came with advanced study in the high school. They seemed less concerned with monetary rewards than with the intellectual stimulation that resulted from their studies, an attitude that seemed to be shared by their parents.

There was one exception to the lack of vocational training offered to girls in the nineteenth-century high schools. That exception was the normal (teacher training) courses offered as part of high school studies in many of the nation's cities. Teachers trained in the cities' normal classes could expect to find early employment in the cities' graded classrooms. The benefit from the system's point of view was the availability of an inexpensive group of teachers who had come up through the hierarchically ordered city schools and who accepted their authority structure. Also, school teaching was not the type of job preparation that would challenge middle-class notions of propriety and social order. It fit the nineteenth-century ideal of women as natural caregivers.

With the exception of normal classes in some high schools, the curriculum of nineteenth-century high schools was only indirectly linked to the world of work. However, the potential for increasing such links was present in the minds of many high school reformers, some of whom began advocating a more work-oriented curriculum late in the century. A prelude to the vocational educational movement (which is examined in the next chapter) can be found in the manual education movement, beginning in the 1870s.

Manual Training

In 1876, Philadelphians celebrated the centennial birthday of the United States by sponsoring an exposition. There, fifty-eight foreign countries as well as many states and industries exhibited their technological innovations. This exposition not only marked the arrival of the United States as a world industrial power; it introduced the American people to the new world of technological development.

The Russian exhibit, for example, included a collection of tools used to train students at the Moscow Technical Institute. These tools proved to be a more efficient way to introduce students to industrial skills than the construction shops in which learners had traditionally been taught. Several prominent Americans, including the president of the Massachusetts Institute of Technology, John D. Runkle, were so impressed with these new instructional tools that they began their own program of industrial shops in schools. Runkle added to the new idea by starting the School of Mechanic Arts for students who wanted a career in industrial work itself rather than in engineering. He was so enthusiastic about the prospects for the new approach to industrial education that he advocated its inclusion in the general high school curriculum, not just in industrially oriented programs.[44]

Calvin Woodward and the Manual Training School

Another American engineering educator, Calvin Woodward, was even more zealous in his advocacy of what came to be known as manual training. He saw the need for manual training for his engineering students at Washington University in St. Louis when he found that they were unable to construct the simple wood models needed to illustrate a difficult mechanical problem. He put aside the mechanical problem and set himself to the task of teaching his students to use the woodworking tools they needed to make the models. Woodward was astonished to learn that the Russians had already developed an industrial shop program to teach these skills.

He was so enthusiastic about the new methods that in 1879 he opened the

Manual Training School at Washington University. The first of its kind, Woodward's school provided a three-year secondary program that divided the curriculum equally between mental and manual labor. In addition to academic subjects such as mathematics, science, language, history, and literature, he offered industrially related subjects such as mechanical drawing and instruction in carpentry, woodworking, and a variety of metalworking skills. The goal of Woodward's school was not job preparation, however. It was preparation for life in an industrial society. Therefore, he believed manual training was desirable for all students.[45]

Other educators quickly adapted the principles of manual training to the education of girls. Classes in sewing and home economics emerged to serve the end that the wood and metal shop classes were serving for boys. Again, the classes were not seen as vocational preparation but as preparation for the realities of life in an industrial world.

The manual training movement, although built around the instructional tools pioneered by the Russians, also tapped a long-standing American tradition regarding the education of the poor. Beginning with the early-nineteenth-century reformatories, social reformers had repeatedly prescribed manual labor training as the vehicle for the social and moral reformation of wayward youth. This emphasis on manual education for moral regeneration increased as the rapidly developing cities of the late nineteenth century produced more and more wayward youth in need of reformation.

Support for manual training also came from the ranks of working-class youth seeking careers in the new industrial society. Since a variety of technical schools and classes already existed when the manual training movement began, in many cases it was difficult to distinguish between the two approaches. Technical training schools were supposed to teach the actual knowledge and skills needed for industrial work, whereas manual training schools were introduced to teach the manual principles and practices underlying that work. In reality, the boundaries between the two programs were often blurred.

Despite the effort of reformers such as Calvin Woodward, most educators were opposed to manual training. They saw it as an unwarranted intrusion into the academic focus of their schools. Some combined this criticism with the rather acute observation that the relatively simple mechanical skills and understandings gained in a wood or metal shop bore little relationship to the skills and understandings needed in the new industries.

Manual training was never able to compete successfully with academic studies. However, it set the stage for another movement, vocational education, which would soon force a much more direct link between school and work. That link is explored in the next chapter.

Educational Leadership

This discussion of how modern, bureaucratic school systems emerged in late-nineteenth-century America concludes with a look at two of the leading educators of that period. Although both served terms as school super-intendents, their strikingly different approaches to that office show that bureaucracy was in its infancy, not in the advanced state it would soon reach. In that later era of bureaucratic development, it would be hard to tell one superintendent from another.

William Torrey Harris

Born in rural Connecticut in 1835, Harris migrated to the Midwest with his father and brother in search of the economic opportunities then emerging through land development. As was often the case with ambitious educated men, Harris took time out from his commercial pursuits to begin teaching and, eventually, took a position in the St. Louis public schools. In a sense, he never looked back. He rose quickly to the superintendency of the St. Louis schools, a position he held from 1868 to 1880. Later he served as U.S. Commissioner of Education. In many ways, Harris was a transitional figure, spanning the period from the end of the common school era to the beginning of the next great reform period that began in the 1890s.[46]

Harris combined his career in educational administration with a scholarly interest in the field of philosophy. This combination of interests showed that educated people of many kinds qualified as school superintendents in the post-Civil War era. Harris, however, was one of the last nationally visible practicing school leaders who yoked his educational efforts to a larger intellectual system.

Harris's orientation in philosophy was idealism, and his philosophical touchstone was Friedrich Hegel. Although he embraced the new industrial society and tried to link the school's program to it, his traditional backward-looking philosophy was less fitted to science, technology, and industry than was the new pragmatic approach being embraced by the leading turn-of-the-century American philosophers. Harris's views quickly became obsolete, bypassed in the search for an intellectual paradigm better suited to a fast-changing world.

Nevertheless, as both a school superintendent and a philosopher, Harris was an enthusiastic advocate of the new urban industrial society. He embraced an evolutionary philosophy that encouraged support of modernization. According to Harris, the modernization process was an agent of the divine spirit behind human progress.

Despite his advocacy of industrial and urban progress, Harris proved to be a conservative educational leader. Conscious of the accomplishments of the preceding generation of schoolmen, he sought to regiment the common schools that Horace Mann had pioneered. Lacking Mann's reformist zeal, he tried to organize the schools and classrooms of St. Louis along the lines of industry; that is, he concentrated on producing a uniform product. This meant an emphasis on order, punctuality, morals, and discipline in the schools. Good students would make good industrial employees, and good industrial employees would help make a model industrial society. Harris's belief in the school as a means of instilling social order underlay his support for Susan Blow's pioneering of public kindergartens in the working- and lower-class neighborhoods of St. Louis.[47]

The limits of Harris's educational commitments were clearly illustrated in his conflict with Calvin Woodward over manual training. Woodward believed firmly that an expanded curriculum was needed to reach all students and to link them intellectually to the new social order. Harris, however, vigorously resisted the intrusion of manual training into the public schools. For Harris, the moral and intellectual training required by the new order was contained in the existing public school curriculum. There was no need to replace study in the traditional subjects with exotic material that was unrelated to the student's higher mental functioning.

While Harris eventually lost the battle with Woodward, he did not yield while he led the St. Louis schools. The forces of the educational status quo found an intelligent, loquacious leader in William Torrey Harris. His eloquence and obstinacy played no small part in holding back the movements for educational change that were clamoring for attention in the late nineteenth century.

Francis W. Parker

Born in New Hampshire in 1837, Francis Parker began teaching in country schools at an early age. He broke off his school career to serve in the Union army during the Civil War and, because of this service, acquired the title of "Colonel," a label he used for the rest of his life. After resuming his teaching career, he gradually became disenchanted with conventional approaches to teaching and, while teaching in the schools of Dayton, Ohio, began reading widely in educational theory. Upon receiving a small family inheritance, he traveled to Europe, as Horace Mann had done some years earlier, to see firsthand the educational reforms taking place there. While in Europe, he became immersed in the theories of Pestalozzi and also learned of the pioneering ideas of Friedrich Froebel concerning the education of young children.[48]

Shortly after returning to the United States, Parker applied for and was granted the superintendency of the Quincy, Massachusetts, public schools. He achieved this position by convincing members of the school board of both his own personal magnetism and his commitment to the new European educational reforms. In his tenure as superintendent in Quincy, he showed what a school superintendent whose powers were limited to curriculum and school inspection could accomplish. Shortly after taking office, Parker began revamping Quincy's elementary curriculum. He discarded the existing emphasis on drill, recitation, and memorization and installed in its place a new system of pedagogy built around children's natural curiosity about the world around them. For example, he advocated learning to read with children's own words and simple sentences rather than memorizing the alphabet, learning arithmetic through the study of objects and their properties rather than memorizing rules, and studying geography through field trips to the surrounding countryside.

Parker advanced his reforms and endeared himself to his teachers by making his annual school visits much more than the routine events they had previously been. During these visits he would consult with teachers regarding their difficulties with the new curriculum. He was not afraid to take over classes himself to help teachers see how the innovations might be carried out successfully.

By most accounts, his efforts in Quincy were enormously successful. In fact, his success was so widely publicized that his innovations acquired a label, the "new departure" in the Quincy schools. Visitors came from around the nation to see what had been done under his leadership, and an outside evaluation showed the Quincy schools to be achievement leaders in several subjects. These accomplishments, moreover, were produced with innovative programs that did not make rote memorization and testing the arbiters of instruction.

After a few years, Parker left Quincy for a district superintendency in Boston where he attempted to introduce his innovations into a much larger and more complicated organization. This time he failed to convince teachers and parents of the value of his approach and thus failed to get a toehold for the new departure in this large city system. One historian has analyzed Parker's Quincy success and Boston failure as the result of conflict between Parker's charisma and the bureaucratic realities of a large city school system. In the smaller town of Quincy, where he was in charge of all the schools, Parker's forceful personality permeated the entire system and he was able to persuade most, if not all, participants of the value of his approach. In Boston, however, as the head of only one district, he was in charge of only one part of a huge system. That larger system proved impervious to his personality. Furthermore, the district in Boston over which Parker had control was substantially larger than the entire Quincy system. Also, the political diversity in a large urban area such as Boston produced forces opposed to the "new departure" that were more organized and resistant to his innovations, whatever their merits, than they had been in Quincy.[49]

After his failure to renovate the Boston schools, Parker landed the position of principal of the Cook County Normal School in the city of Chicago. Here again he was in charge of an institution that he could transform through the strength of his powerful personality. Once again he brought his school into contact with what was now becoming known as the "new education." Parker quickly drew attention to the practice school that was attached to his normal school. This practice school, which also served as the public school for the neighborhood in which the normal school was located, offered a place where he could build on his earlier ideas and turn them into a fully developed approach to educational reform. His organization of the practice school was built on the twin models of home and community and on the principle of democracy. His informal approach to teaching and learning pervaded the entire school.

Textbooks were replaced by student-developed materials, and the academic curriculum was reorganized with the subjects integrated with each other. For example, reading, spelling, writing, and grammar became "communications," and the students' own experiences (conversations and writing) became the "stuff" of the curriculum. Art was added to the curriculum in a way that stressed student expression through various media. Science was taught through nature study that also began with the students' own experiences. Other subjects such as music and physical education were also employed as vehicles for students' self-expression. In short, Parker embedded formal academic study in the children's own physical, social, and personal environment. In his own view, the child was valued intrinsically and was encouraged to express that value in many ways: "The spontaneous tendencies of the child are the records of inborn divinities."[50]

Parker's personal enthusiasm was as infectious at the Cook County Normal School as it had been in Quincy. He thus made the practice school into a nationally known laboratory in the new education. When John Dewey became a faculty member at the University of Chicago in 1894, hired with the mission of building the study of philosophy, psychology, and education, he quickly enrolled his children as students in Parker's school.

Conclusion

William T. Harris and Francis W. Parker represented contrasting approaches to education and educational leadership in late-nineteenth-century America. Neither of these men had specific occupational training for the position of superintendent. Harris rose to the position through the teaching ranks of the St. Louis schools. His intellectual qualifications were considerable, but they were not formally acknowledged through the receipt of advanced degrees, either in education or in philosophy. Parker attained his superintendency through the force of his personality. He communicated his commitments to school change in ways that won him a national audience, again without the benefit of formal training for his leadership positions.

Both men acknowledged the pioneering leadership of Horace Mann and attempted to emulate Mann. The drastic differences in the direction they took are a testimony to the diversity of Mann's ideas and commitments. Harris sought to consolidate and connect traditional curriculum and instruction to the new social order, while Parker wanted to discard traditional pedagogy in favor of new methodology that would enliven the school and enrich the society.

One way of crystallizing the difference between these two men is to note that Harris looked to the present to confirm, expand, and strengthen what had been done by the schools in the past. Parker, however, looked to the future. He was interested in opening up the schools and the lives of students through a drastically improved pedagogy that would help prepare them for the changes that they were sure to encounter.

Another way to estimate the value of each approach is to examine their influence on events that occurred after 1890. In terms of pedagogical developments and in social reform, Parker may have been the better prophet. His commitment to change was honored by many progressive educators and social reformers during the next quarter-century. In terms of system building and system maintenance, however, Harris's more hierarchical, bureaucratic approach to schooling survived and prospered in the next era, although the common school curriculum he cherished gradually disappeared.

Most of what is discussed in this chapter revolves around the notion of building a "system" of schooling that fit a modernizing society. The changes in school organization, such as age grading, uniform courses of study, testing, and the rise of the superintendency, are all examples of system building within the public schools. Likewise, adding kindergartens, manual training, and university education to the graded public elementary schools and the varied public high schools is evidence of increasing specialization and diversity.

Thus, the notion of a public educational system stretching from early childhood education to graduate study was present in rudimentary form in the late nineteenth century. It remained for the twentieth century to put these elements together into a coherent organization. That task would fall to the educational progressives who gave their name to the educational movement of the early twentieth century.

Further Reading

Edwards, Rebecca. *New Spirits: Americans in the Gilded Age: 1865–1905.* New York: Oxford University Press, 2006. Explores the rise of the American "wealthy class" and the excesses of the "Gilded Age."

Gomez, Laura. *Manifest Destinies: The Making of the Mexican American Race.* New York: New York University Press, [1995], 2000. The role of racial definitions and the place of Mexican Americans in the American social order from Colonial times to the present.

Katz, Michael B. *Class, Bureaucracy and Schools: The Illusion of Educational Change in America.* Westport, CT: Praeger Publishers, 1971. A revisionist account of the organizational changes taking place in schools that argues that the form of organization chosen, bureaucracy, led to undemocratic results.

Labaree, David. *The Making of an American High School: The Credentials Market of the Central High School, 1838–1939.* New Haven: Yale University Press, 1988. The history of the first high school in the city of Philadelphia, with emphasis on the social makeup of the student body and the social ramifications of the curriculum.

Lascarides, Celi. *History of Early Childhood Education.* London: Falmer Publishing Co., 2000. A descriptive study of childhood education from the days of Antiquity into the Modern Era.

Lazerson, Marvin. *Origins of the Urban School: Public Education in Massachusetts, 1870–1915.* Cambridge: Harvard University Press, 1971. The story of the educational changes that took place in a state that was rapidly industrializing, including the development of kindergartens.

Mattingly, Paul. *The Classless Profession: American Schoolmen in the Nineteenth Century.* New York: New York University Press, 1975. The details of the early professionalization of the men who worked in the schools, with special attention to the organizations they developed and patronized, including the early National Education Association.

Morris, Charles R. *The Tycoons: How Andrew Carnegie, John D. Rockefeller, Jay Gould, and J.P. Morgan Invented the American Supereconomy.* New York: Henry Holt, 2006. A penetrating re-examination of the means and motives of the "Robber Barons" who created the excessive wealth that marked the economic elite of the Gilded Age.

McAfee, Ward. *Religion, Race, and Reconstruction: The Public School in the Politics of the 1870s.* Albany: State University of New York Press, 1998. The role of religion in school politics, nationally and regionally, with the topic placed in the context of the larger politics of the period.

Reese, William J. *The Origins of the American High School.* New Haven: Yale University Press, 1995. A comprehensive treatment of the early development of the high school, detailing the variety that characterized the institution in its early years and the increasing uniformity that it underwent later in the nineteenth century.

Reyhner, Jon and Jeanne Eder. *American Indian Education: A History.* Norman, OK: University of Oklahoma Press, 2004. An interpretative history of American Indian educational pathways from the Colonial Period into the turn of the twenty-first century.

Rury, John L. *Education and Women's Work.* Albany: State University of New York Press, 1991. An exploration of the links between schooling and women's social and economic roles in the late nineteenth and early twentieth centuries.

Thelin, John R. *A History of American Higher Education.* Baltimore: Johns Hopkins University Press, 2004, pp. 135–138. A fresh perspective on American higher education and a successor to Rudolph's *The American College and University.*

Troen, Selwyn. *The Public and the Schools: Shaping the St. Louis System, 1838–1920.* Columbia, MO: University of Missouri Press, 1975. A thorough study of the St. Louis system, with a substantial treatment of its most famous early superintendent, William Torrey Harris.

Tyack, David B. *The One Best System: A History of Urban Education.* Cambridge: Harvard University Press, 1974. A classic treatment of urban education in the late nineteenth and early twentieth centuries, with emphasis on its organization, its personnel patterns, and its relation to city politics.

Warren, Donald R. *To Enforce Education: A History of the Founding Years of the United States Office of Education.* Detroit: Wayne State University Press, 1974. The beginnings and early history of the Office of Education and the significance of its activities in spite of its lack of status.

Notes

1. Modernization is the governing explanatory concept in this and the next two chapters.
2. David Montgomery, *Beyond Equality: Labor and the Radical Republicans, 1862–1872.* New York: Alfred A. Knopf, 1967.
3. Gustave O. Larson, *The "Americanization" of Utah for Statehood.* San Marino, CA: Huntington Library, 1971
4. This term is borrowed from an analysis of similar developments in European society and education. See Fritz Ringer, *Education and Society in Modern Europe.* Bloomington, IN: Indiana University Press, 1979.
5. See Sean D. Cashman, *America in the Gilded Age: From the Death of Lincoln to the Rise of Theodore Roosevelt.* New York: New York University Press, 1993 and Rebecca Edwards, *New Spirits: Americans in the Gilded Age, 1865–1905.* New York: Oxford University Press, 2006. On robber barons, see Peter d'A Jones (ed.), *The Robber Barons Revisited.* Boston: D. C. Heath, 1968; Charles R. Morris, *The Tycoons: How Andrew Carnegie, John D. Rockefeller, Jay Gould, and J. P. Morgan Invented the American Supereconomy.* New York: Henry Holt, 2006.
6. A good discussion of the Morrill Act and other nationalizing (modernizing) trends in the first Civil War Congress is found in Leonard P. Curry, *Blueprint for Modern America: Nonmilitary Legislation of the First Civil War Congress.* Nashville, TN: Vanderbilt University Press, 1968. On land-grant institutions, see, among others, Frederick Rudolph, *The American College and University.* Athens, GA: University of Georgia Press, [1960], 1990, pp. 252 passim; John R. Thelin, *A History of American Higher Education.* Baltimore: Johns Hopkins University Press, 2004, pp. 135–138. For convenient access to the Morrill Act, see http://higher-ed.org/resources/morrill1.htm.
7. For discussion of this point, see Wayne J. Urban, *Black Scholar: Horace Mann Bond, 1940–1972.* Athens, GA: University of Georgia Press, 1992, pp. 171–173.
8. *Cherokee Nation v. Georgia* 30 U.S. 1 (1831), *Worcester v Georgia* 31 U.S. 515 (1832).
9. Paul S. Boyer, et al., *The Enduring Vision: A History of the American People.* Lexington, MA: D. C. Heath, 1990, pp. 281–283; David Hurst Thomas et al., The Native Americans: An Illustrated History. Atlanta: Turner Publishing Co., 1993, pp. 293–298; Alexis de Tocqueville, *Democracy in America*, vol. 1, ed. Phillips Bradley. New York: Vintage Books, [1835], 1945.
10. See Andress Stephanson, *Manifest Destinies: The Making of the Mexican American Race.* New York: Hill & Wang, [1995], 2000.
11. David Wallace Adams, *American Indians and the Boarding School Experience: 1875–1928.* Lawrence, KS: University Press of Kansas, 1995, pp. 29–30. Much of the following discussion is based upon Adams's excellent study of the American Indian educational experience. See also Thomas G. Andrews, "Turning the Tables on Assimilation: Oglala Lakotas and the Pine Ridge Day Schools, 1889–1920s," in *The Western Historical Quarterly*, vol. 33, No. 4, Winter, 2002.

12. Adams, pp. 30–31.
13. On Washington and the Hampton model of education, see Chapter 5. Richard Henry Pratt's autobiography is *Battlefield and Classroom: Four Decades with the American Indian, 1876–1904*, ed. Robert M. Utley. New Haven, CT: Yale University Press, 1964.
14. Adams, p. 52.
15. Ibid., p. 336.
16. Amanda J. Cobb, *Listening to Our Grandmothers' Stories: The Bloomfield Academy for Chickasaw Females, 1852–1949*. Lincoln, NE: University of Nebraska Press, 2000.
17. Adams, p. 336. On the experiences of some Native Americans who ventured into higher education in the mid-nineteenth century and beyond, see Steven Crum, "The Choctaw Nation: Changing the Appearance of American Higher Education, 1830–1907," *History of Education Quarterly*, vol. 47, February 2007, pp. 49–68.
18. Donald R. Warren, *To Enforce Education: A History of the Founding Years of the United States Office of Education*. Detroit: Wayne State University Press, 1974.
19. On city conditions and modernization, see Gunther Barth, *City People: The Rise of Modern City Culture in Nineteenth Century America*. New York: Oxford University Press, 1980. For the link between city conditions and compulsory education, see Henry Perkinson, *The Imperfect Panacea: American Faith in Education, 1865–1965*. New York: Random House, 1968, chap. 3.
20. Michael S. Katz, *A History of Compulsory Education Laws*. Bloomington, IN: Phi Delta Kappa, 1976, p. 21.
21. On New York's compulsory school attendance law, see Jeremy Felt, *Hostages of Fortune: Child Labor Reform in New York State*. Syracuse, NY: Syracuse University Press, 1965, p. 7. On the situation ten years after the passage of this law, see Forrest Ensign, *Compulsory School Attendance and Child Labor*. New York: Arno Press, [1921], 1969, p. 121.
22. Felt, chap. 2.
23. Charles Burgess, "The Goddess, the School Book, and Compulsion," *Harvard Educational Review*, vol. 46, 1976, pp. 199–216.
24. John K. Folger and Charles B. Nam, *Education of the American Population*. Washington, D.C. U.S. Government Printing Office, 1967; Robert B. Everhart, "From Universalism to Usurpation: An Essay on the Antecedents to Compulsory School Attendance Legislation," *Review of Educational Research*, vol. 47, 1977, pp. 517–518.
25. David B. Tyack, *The One Best System: A History of American Urban Education*. Cambridge, MA: Harvard University Press, 1974.
26. The use of the pronoun "he" for the superintendent reflects the overwhelming dominance of men in the position in the late nineteenth century. See David Tyack and Elisabeth Hansot, *Managers of Virtue: Public School Leadership in America, 1820–1980*. New York: Basic Books, 1982, pp. 94–104.
27. Paul Mattingly, *The Classless Profession: American Schoolmen in the Nineteenth Century*. New York: New York University Press, 1975.
28. As quoted in Michael B. Katz, "The New Departure in Quincy, 1873–1881: The Nature of Nineteenth Century Educational Reform," *New England Quarterly*, vol. 40, March 1967, pp. 3–30.
29. David Tyack and Elisabeth Hansot, *Learning Together: A History of Coeducation in American Public Schools*. New Haven, CT: Yale University Press, 1990.
30. Ibid.
31. A devotee of Froebel, Baroness Bertha von Marenholtz-Bulow, published *Reminiscences of Friedrich Frobel* in 1894. The original was translated by Mary Peabody Mann, the sister of Horace Mann. This volume has been newly published with a foreword by Herbert Kohl. The new edition carries the title *How Kindergarten Came to America: Friedrich Froebel's Radical Vision of Early Childhood Education*. New York: New Press, 2007.
32. Marvin Lazerson, *Origins of the Urban School: Public Education in Massachusetts, 1870–1915*. Cambridge, MA: Harvard University Press, 1971.
33. Ibid., p. 55.
34. Selwyn Troen, *The Public and the Schools: Shaping the St. Louis System, 1838–1920*. Columbia, MO: University of Missouri Press, pp. 99–115.
35. Exceptions to this generalization would certainly include the U. S. Military Academy (1802), the University of Virginia (1819), Rensselaer Polytechnic Institute (1824), and the U.S. Naval Academy (1845).
36. Laurence R. Veysey, *The Emergence of the American University*. Chicago: University of Chicago Press, 1965, esp. chapter 3. See also Christopher J. Lucas, *American Higher*

Education: A History. New York: St. Martin's Press, 1994; Arthur M. Cohen, *The Shaping of American Higher Education*. San Francisco: Jossey-Bass Publishers, 1998; and Thelin, *A History of American Higher Education*, esp. chapters 3 and 4.

37. See Hugh Hawkins, *Pioneer*. Ithaca, NY: Cornell University Press, 1960.
38. See Hugh Hawkins, *Between Harvard and America: The Educational Leadership of Charles W. Eliot*. New York: Oxford University Press, 1972; Seymour Martin Lipset and David Riesman, *Education and Politics at Harvard*. Berkeley, CA: The Carnegie Foundation for the Advancement of Teaching, 1972.
39. Lower-class animosity to the high school was discussed briefly in Chapter 4. The class orientation of the high school in the nineteenth century is described in Robert L. Church and Michael W. Sedlak, *Education in the United States: An Interpretive History*. New York: Free Press, 1976, pp. 181–189. The most thorough account of the early high school is William J. Reese, *The Origins of the American High School*. New Haven, CT: Yale University Press, 1995.
40. On the development of coeducation in public schools, see David Tyack and Elizabeth Hansot, *Learning Together: A History of Coeducation in American Schools*. New Haven, CT: Yale University Press, 1994.
41. David F. Labaree, *The Making of an American High School: The Credentials Market of the Central High School, 1838–1939*. New Haven: Yale University Press, 1988.
42. Ibid. At the end of each term, a student's academic average was decreased by twice the number of demerits he had received during the term.
43. John L. Rury, *Education and Women's Work*. Albany, NY: State University of New York Press, 1991.
44. Lawrence A. Cremin, *The Transformation of the School: Progressivism in American Education, 1876–1957*. New York: Random House, 1961, pp. 23–34.
45. Ibid.
46. Ibid., pp. 14–20.
47. For more on Harris, see Troen, *The Public and the Schools*, pp. 159–166.
48. Cremin, *Transformation*, p. 129. This account of Parker and his career draws from Cremin, from Michael Katz's article, "The New Departure in Quincy," and from the biography of Parker by Jack Campbell, *Colonel Francis Parker, The Children's Crusader*. New York: Teachers College Press, 1967.
49. Katz, "The New Departure in Quincy."
50. Francis W. Parker, *Talks on Pedagogics*. Glacier, MT: Kessinger Publishing, LLC, [1894], 2003; Cremin, *Transformation*, pp. 134–135.

7

Organizing the Modern School System
Educational Reform in the Progressive Era, 1890–1915

Overview

The last decade of the nineteenth century and the first two decades of the twentieth century composed a period of great ferment in American life. The industrialization and urbanization that began in the nineteenth century continued to develop and to give rise to numerous economic, political, and social problems. In addition, Americans faced a massive new wave of immigrants from largely unfamiliar countries of southern and eastern Europe. Called by historians the progressive era, these years produced a myriad of reforms in response to the social problems.

Despite the variety of reform activities, there is a way to characterize most, if not all of them. The largest number of reform efforts were part of a movement to organize twentieth-century American society into an efficiently functioning unit that would be in harmony with the needs of a modern industrial society. This new society ideally would operate on principles of political nonpartisanship and scientific and professional expertise. Before we say more about the organizational focus of reform, however, some indication of the genesis and the variety of the era's multifaceted reform efforts may be helpful.

Economic Reform

The key economic development at the end of the nineteenth century was the growth of "trusts" in various areas of American business life. These trusts, later called monopolies, consisted of large corporations that gained complete or effective control over a particular business or industry. This control enabled them to set prices, regulate production to maintain these prices, and determine wages without regard to consumer demand or the needs of workers. Perhaps the most famous trust of the period was the Standard Oil Company, the enterprise that made John D. Rockefeller enormously wealthy and famous. As trusts became more and more prominent during the 1890s, their harmful effects became increasingly apparent and a movement to curb their economic power took form.

The year 1893 marked a major turning point in the economic life of the nation. That year saw the beginning of an economic depression almost unprecedented in American history, one so severe that it caused citizens to contemplate steps to redress the imbalance in economic power that they associated with the trusts. If any particular event can be said to have initiated the progressive reform movement, it was this depression and the chain reaction it provoked.

It is not unfair to characterize the national politics of the 1890s and the early twentieth century as an attempt to deal with the problems of the trusts. The most famous politician of this period, Theodore Roosevelt, carefully cultivated his image as a "trust buster" in his successful campaign for the presidency. Roosevelt was really not a trust buster, but rather a regulator of trusts. He believed that the way to deal with big business was to empower the government to regulate it. This was one of the major ideas behind Roosevelt's "new nationalism" program. It was also the idea behind such earlier legislation as the Interstate Commerce Act of 1887 and the Sherman Antitrust Act of 1890, as well as the Hepburn Act of 1906.[1]

An alternative approach to regulating big business was offered by Woodrow Wilson, Roosevelt's opponent (along with William Howard Taft) in the election of 1912. Born and raised in the South, Wilson's view of the trusts hearkened back to the laissez-faire principles of Andrew Jackson. Campaigning under the programmatic label of a "new freedom," Wilson hoped to break up the economic trusts and revitalize the economy by supporting small-scale enterprise and competition rather than through government regulation. Although Roosevelt and Wilson differed in their prescriptions for economic recovery, they both realized that the monopoly power of the trusts, if left unchecked, would gradually alienate rank-and-file Americans.[2]

The rise of organized labor during these years was still another way in which the issue of economic privilege was confronted. Trade unions developed in several crafts as an attempt to check capital's attack on traditional craft privileges as well as its control over the larger economy. The American Federation of Labor (AFL) evolved as a loose federation of craft unions seeking to preserve the autonomy and work practices of self-employed artisans who were losing work to factories organized and managed according to scientific principles. Labor also sought to protect its members from the predatory trusts through the passage of legislation such as child labor laws, workmen's compensation, and unemployment insurance.[3]

Political Reform

American politics in these years was another arena in which reform activity was important. Politicians at all levels of government succumbed to the financial favors that the wealthy could bestow on them in return for a contract or a favorable decision regarding some regulatory or tax issue. Another problem, particularly visible in the nation's cities, was the corrupt reign of political machines, which were often kept in power by the votes of needy members of the lower classes. Thus reformers focused on two problems: an indigent underclass whose needs made them vulnerable, and a wealthy upper class whose power and greed made them insensitive to the public good.

The response to these concerns was a multifaceted array of progressive political reforms. For example, citizens in several states managed to install one or more of the following electoral reforms: the initiative, referendum, and recall. Political initiatives gave voters the power to develop and pass legislation, referendums subjected pending or existing legislation to voters' approval, and recall gave voters the power to remove corrupt officials. The operating principle in each case was the voters' right to correct the mistakes and overcome the malfeasance of the politicians they put into office. The citizen was viewed as morally superior to the politician and these changes were to institutionalize that superiority.[4]

Another reform of this era was the women's suffrage movement that gave the vote to that half of the population that had long been without it. Enlarging the electorate made political control by a small, self-seeking group more difficult, or so the argument went. Again, the clear implication was that the voting populace was superior to those it elected.[5]

Other political reform movements sought to deal with the many problems the nation's large cities were experiencing. As the need for city services such as lighting, transportation, and sewage developed, private companies moved in to meet these needs. This often resulted in subversion of the public interest to the cause of private profits. To give only one example, in the 1890s the city of Atlanta needed streetcars to transport its citizens from its newly emerging suburbs to the city center. Consequently, one of Atlanta's private streetcar companies ran a line to a new development in which the owner of the streetcar line also had a large financial interest. Once the lots in the new development were sold, the owner simply shut down his streetcar line. Quite naturally, citizens who had purchased lots on the basis of having easy access to downtown turned to the city's politicians for redress. Similar protests against the excesses of private capital throughout the nation led to the movement for municipal ownership of essential services.[6]

Public utilities provided another, more moderate, response to the excesses of private ownership. Many of the private utility companies used the city politicians they controlled to resist the movement toward public regulation. One way to combat this corruption was to replace elected politicians with professional administrators. For example, the city manager movement emerged to replace politically corrupt mayors with people trained in the administration of large governmental enterprises. Similarly, city commissioners appointed to run various city departments were touted as a replacement for corrupt city councilmen who oversaw city services. City commissioners, according to their advocates, brought professional expertise to the management of their departments, which politicians, chosen by the electoral process, lacked.[7]

Social Reform

Social life was another area that concerned reformers in the late nineteenth and early twentieth centuries. The problems of the new immigrants and other urban poor were seen as a major crisis. One effort to meet these problems was the development of the social settlement house in urban neighborhoods. The most famous of these was Hull House, situated in Chicago's near west side. Headed by Jane Addams, it served the new immigrants from southern and eastern Europe. Hull House was a nonsectarian institution that ministered to its immigrant clients in a myriad of areas—language training, vocational skills, family life, cultural exhibits, and citizenship lessons. All these endeavors were undertaken to help the immigrants adjust to their new surroundings and to improve their lives.[8]

In other American cities, social settlements like Hull House were established to achieve the same objectives that Jane Addams sought in Chicago. In addition, many cities used their public schools as a base for Americanization classes for adult immigrants. These classes sought to accomplish many of the same goals that underlay the activities of Hull House and the other social settlements. On the whole, however, Americanizers were less interested than Addams in finding ways to use the immigrants' own background as a bridge to life in the new world. To use an anthropologist's term, Americanization was an acculturation program in which immigrants were socialized into an American culture that was assumed to be superior to that of the "old country."

Reform in this era was not limited to economics, politics, and social welfare. From journalism to religion to science to education, reform was a major theme during this period. Any one of the reform movements described earlier could be illustrated in far more detail than has been given here. The preceding account simply makes the point that reform was a dominant theme of the progressive era. It was during this period that the term "progressive" began to be used consciously to indicate reformers' commitment to critiquing and redressing the multitude of problems they found in virtually every American institution.[9]

Defining Progressivism

Recent scholarship has exposed the diversity of the reforms that have been grouped under the "progressive" label. As noted previously, Theodore Roosevelt's regulatory bent and Woodrow Wilson's penchant for decentralization were both seen as progressive ways of dealing with the trusts. Thus, to call both Wilson and Roosevelt "progressive" with regard to the trusts is to make the term elastic enough to encompass diametrically opposed strategies. Similarly, empowering voters through political initiative, referendum, and recall clearly involved an extension of the franchise. In direct contrast to such voter empowerment was the professional empowerment of the new city managers and city commissioners, who sought to take decision making away from both voters and politicians. In social reform the Americanization movement's way of acculturating immigrants differed strongly in assumptions and approach from the programs of the settlement houses.

Such contradictions led scholars to seek a more refined view of progressive reform, one that took account of the movement in all of its complexity. A productive way to accomplish this was to break the reformers into subgroups. This analysis often resulted in the division of progressives into two groups, liberals and conservatives, who differed from each other in ideology and social goals. Liberal progressives sought social justice by casting off restrictions of one kind or another, while conservative progressives sought social order through rational management by trained experts.[10]

Using these categories to analyze the antitrust activity discussed earlier, Woodrow Wilson fits the label of a liberal progressive and Theodore Roosevelt is best described as a conservative progressive. Similarly, in the political arena, initiative, referendum, and recall exemplify liberal progressivism, and city managers and city commissioners represent conservative progressivism. In social reform, Americanization was a conservative progressive program, while liberal progressives founded culturally sensitive settlement houses.

Of the two types of progressives, the conservative progressives were by far the larger and more influential group of reformers. Their centrally administered regulatory programs proved to be much more powerful in reshaping American society than the changes advocated by the liberals. Both parts of this larger progressive movement shaped the schools of this era.

Progressive Education

Like the larger reform movement, educational reform in the late nineteenth and early twentieth centuries was made up of a dazzling variety of particulars, some of which conflicted with each other. Attempts to analyze those contradictory particulars have led to refinements in the notion of educational progressivism that parallel those just mentioned with regard to the larger progressive movement.

The standard historical treatment of progressive education by Cremin enumerated the following particulars:

- the extension of educational opportunity;
- a shift from an eight-four elementary-high school organization to a six-three-three system that included the junior high school;
- expansion and reorganization of the curriculum;
- addition of the extracurriculum;
- reorganization of classes according to student testing and school consolidation;
- pedagogical innovations;
- incorporating principles of developmental psychology into textbooks and other instructional materials;

- improving the design and quality of school buildings;
- improving the education of teachers; and
- changes in school administration.

In short, progressive education was seen as a movement that "was marked from the beginning by a pluralistic, frequently contradictory character." What was seen as uniting these diverse reforms was the widespread effort to expand the functions of the school and to oppose restricted definitions of schooling.[11]

A later historical analysis of progressive education by Katz produced a smaller list of particulars that provides a more manageable view of the movement. In this view, progressive educational reform revolved around:

- change in the political control of education;
- change in educational thought;
- innovations in school curriculum and other school practices;
- justifications of schooling in terms of professionalism; and
- the importing of scientific management into school administration.[12]

Another account by Tyack divided progressive educators into two major categories: administrative progressives and pedagogical progressives. Administrative progressivism sought changes in school organization and management that gave power to a new class of professionally trained school administrators. Their agenda included reorganizing schools under "scientific" principles and administering them through the expert leadership of a professionally trained school superintendent. The agenda of pedagogical progressivism involved moving toward more child-centered teaching and more democratic relations between teachers and administrators.[13]

In terms of Katz's five-category analysis mentioned previously, administrative progressivism was related directly to the changes in four of them: political control, school curriculum, professional justification of school change, and scientific school management. Change in educational thought is best represented by pedagogical progressivism, especially if the notion of democratization of the school is included. Pedagogical progressivism took place largely outside the ranks of school administrators.

The following treatment of progressive education focuses more on administrative than on pedagogical progressivism. Before describing these reforms, however, it is useful to look at the underlying forces behind progressive education.

Why Progressive Education?

The multiple changes in American social, political, and economic life that occurred in the late nineteenth and early twentieth centuries produced enormous enrollment increases in the public schools. A trend toward increased enrollments before this period, passage of compulsory attendance laws, massive immigration from Europe and elsewhere, and internal migration from farm to city all contributed to the huge increases in the size of the city school systems. For example, enrollments in Cleveland, Ohio went from 45,000 to 145,000 between 1900 and 1930, while in Detroit they climbed from 30,000 to more than 250,000. Such stupendous increases were echoed in city schools throughout the nation, creating an atmosphere of public concern. Administrative progressives capitalized on this climate in several ways, most notably through school centralization and curricular differentiation.[14]

Centralization of Schools

Centralization refers to an increase in authority for some impersonal, objective, and distant governing body and a corresponding decrease in authority for more local, representative governing agencies. Centralization also can refer to a shift in control of schooling to the next highest level of government, be it local, state, or national. In the progressive era, this often meant a shift of authority from individual or neighborhood schools to control by the next highest level, the local school district. Specifically, in the nation's largest cities, power moved from neighborhood or ward boards to citywide school boards.[15]

Centralization in city schools did not occur in a single step. Rather, it took place in fits and starts and proceeded in different ways in various cities. More than a power shift from a neighborhood to a citywide school board, it was usually accompanied by an increase in power for school administrators. Thus this account of centralization also considers the rise of professional school administrators and the reaction of teachers to this rise. Before considering that issue, however, the process of centralization deserves attention.

The Centralization Process

Centralization took place in gradual, uneven patterns, as city schools attempted to grapple with increasing enrollments and the social problems that accompanied them. Variations in the pace and particulars of centralization from city to city did not mean that the process itself differed significantly from place to place. Most often, centralization was imposed on schools by outsiders who were convinced that the schools were ineffective. In New York City, for example, it was Nicholas Murray Butler, a college administrator, who led the fight for centralization. In Chicago, it was William Rainey Harper, president of the University of Chicago.[16]

The centralizers wanted to break the hold of neighborhood interests in city school affairs. Most often, city school lines followed neighborhood geographic lines, which divided cities into "wards." Butler, Harper, and others sought to give citywide boards of education more power over issues such as teacher hiring and firing, building construction and maintenance, and textbook selection. These areas traditionally had been the purview of the ward board and its administrative agent, the ward trustee. According to the centralizers, and there was substantial evidence to back up their charges, the schools were rife with political corruption and unable to educate their students effectively.

This is not to say that the centralizers were completely correct in their charges, but that, under the artful leadership of men like Butler, there was enough evidence to convince citizens and political leaders to change the system. Giving more power to a central board meant a distinct change in the kind of person who would become a school policymaker. The newly empowered central boards were made up of men chosen (usually elected) on a citywide basis, not on the grounds of affinity to a particular neighborhood. This meant that candidates were usually prominent businessmen or professionals who had citywide visibility. Their antagonists, the neighborhood (or ward) board members, were most often small businessmen such as insurance men or tavern owners, who were in close day-to-day contact with the inhabitants of the neighborhood.

Centralization and School Governance

Giving more responsibility to a central board meant that the schools would now be guided by the same men who guarded the larger reputation of the city. Being prominent, they were expected to act in the best interest of the largest number of citizens, not in the particular interest of some small neighborhood group. For example, under centralization, teacher hiring was done on the basis of individual qualifications rather than on familial or political contacts. Similarly, decisions on sites and building contracts or on choice of textbook publishers and other suppliers of school materials were made on the basis of broad educational benefit rather than personal relationships. In short, centralized schools were run according to the same principles as any large corporation. The school board functioned like a corporate board of directors, its members setting overall policy and monitoring its implementation while refraining from interfering in day-to-day operations.

Centralization and Democracy

The success of centralization did not mean that there was no public opposition to this process. From the beginning, objections were raised. While centralization advocates argued that central board members would set policies that benefited all children, many parents, particularly those most removed (geographically and socioeconomically) from the central board members, had reason to be skeptical. One recurring theme of opponents of centralization had to do with religion. Ward, or neighborhood, boards were generally attuned to the religious beliefs and practices of their constituents, whereas centralized boards were less sensitive to such matters. This was a threat to citizens who thought religion and other neighborhood concerns worthy of protection. One critic of centralization in New York City strongly stated his reservations as follows:

> New York is a peculiar city. It is a cosmopolitan city. If you do away with the [ward] trustee system you do away with the people's schools. The

trustees are in touch with the schools, and none others are or can be but those who live in the locality of the schools. We have a peculiar population, made up of all nationalities. They are people whose children we want to get in the public schools. There is a fear on the part of these people that we are going to interfere with their religion. If we have ward trustees representing all classes, confidence will be restored.[17]

These sentiments did not carry the day, however. In New York, and in most other cities, centralization swept away the localized approach to urban education.

Years after most city schools were centralized, concern about the social distance between central boards and the cities' rank-and-file citizens still existed. In 1917, for example, Scott Nearing published a study of boards of education that showed that more than 60 percent of the individuals who held these positions were from the commercial and professional classes—businessmen, manufacturers, bankers, doctors, lawyers, and real estate men. He argued that these men could hardly be expected to represent fairly the interests of all the citizens and, in particular, the laboring masses of the cities. Twelve years later, George Counts found that 76 percent of city board members were professionals, proprietors, or managers. He added that such a skewing meant that the common interests of the city's citizens were likely to be ignored by these individuals.[18]

Both Counts and Nearing criticized school boards on the basis of social class bias, rather than the demise of neighborhood interests. Yet the overlap between social class and neighborhood was, and is, considerable. The fundamental issue that both critics raised was the probability that the public schools were becoming less and less schools of the public. For Nearing and Counts, the public schools were becoming alienated from the ordinary working citizens they were supposed to serve. As long as policies were being set by upper-class citizens, there was little reason to expect that this alienation would disappear.

Centralization and School Management

Changes in school governance brought about by centralization were accompanied by changes in the role and qualifications of school superintendents. The superintendent and his office were separated from teachers by the development of an elaborate educational hierarchy. Within this hierarchy there were distinct differences in power, prestige, and economic reward.

The office of school superintendent, as noted earlier, did not exist in the common school period. Even Horace Mann, the father of the common school, was the secretary of the Massachusetts State Board of Education and not a state superintendent. Nor were there any local superintendents in Massachusetts. Not until later in the nineteenth century did the superintendency develop as a response to increasing enrollments in urban schools. At first the city superintendent had a highly circumscribed role. His main jobs were to keep records and to examine students to make sure that they were learning what they were supposed to learn. The superintendent had little or no control over teacher selection and promotion, over provisions for choosing texts and other school materials, or over the fiscal and personnel management of the schools.

With the move to a citywide board, however, the school superintendency often changed substantially. Advocates of centralization did not envision the same type of hands-on role for city board members that had characterized the local boards. Instead, following newly developed corporate organizations the citywide board made policy and hired a school superintendent (manager) to implement it. The new city superintendents had a much expanded role that required specialized training. Thus, in the early twentieth century, the professional education of school administrators began to flourish in universities. Prior to this, superintendents had usually been men whose wide-ranging educational, occupational, and intellectual experiences qualified them to lead their schools. As the notion of educational leadership was transformed into educational management, however, job-oriented skills and training became the norm. In a word, the superintendency became professionalized.

Major universities began to develop schools of education devoted to training school superintendents and other school administrators as well as high school teachers. The professors in these new schools of education were intent on making education into an applied science that could be mastered by their students. Professors of school administration developed innovations such as "school surveys," studies of school enrollments and facilities that resulted in recommendations for school improvement. The professors who trained the new superintendents were often hired as consultants by their own graduates to make studies and recommend improvements. This situation, which might have occasioned critical comment, usually did not.

The development of professional school administrators in this period has been chronicled and criticized by one educational historian as propagating a "cult of efficiency." The term cult symbolizes the faddishness that characterized the practices of urban school superintendents who consciously borrowed the term efficiency from the business world to justify the alterations being made. Since efficiency was then a watchword in business, it met with approval from most central school board members. Mapping business practices onto the schools was a questionable tactic for educators, however, since the development of human beings is quite different from the development of material goods that can be impersonally gauged and manipulated. School superintendents were not inclined to question policies or practices based on business principles they themselves upheld, however.[19]

Teachers and Centralization

The centralization of city school boards and the rise to power of school superintendents was a direct threat to the established work patterns of urban school teachers. One of the ways in which teachers differed from administrators and board members was by gender. Most teachers were women, and elementary teachers were overwhelmingly female. Further, urban teachers were likely to come from social and religious backgrounds more similar to their students than to school officials.

The experienced teachers who led the opposition to centralization had far different social and occupational backgrounds from the school administrators. Most of the teachers had been hired under the rules of the ward system, which emphasized whom one knew. Consequently, whatever status they acquired came through long years of teaching in the schools.

Seniority

What had developed in urban schools prior to centralization and the rise of the superintendency was a system of promotion that recognized experience as the criterion of excellence. A teacher often started her career as a paid substitute assigned to one school and then took her first full-time job in the lowest grade of the school when an opening occurred. She then worked her way up through the grades until arriving at the level of the seventh grade, where she would also be the assistant principal. Finally, she could be "promoted" to the eighth grade class, where she would also hold the rank of "principal," meaning "principal" teacher. In a sense, this was a consistent, coherent system of promotion whereby the individual who reached the eighth grade class and "principal" teacher status had literally done the work of all those who served under her. Needless to say, the women who worked in this system were devoted to its maintenance and suspicious of those who saw in it a "hidebound" approach that stifled innovation.

Teacher Associations

Prior to centralization, city teachers often formed themselves into mutual-aid groups that provided sick or burial benefits to their members. It was a short step from these kinds of groups into more formal teacher associations that sought to institutionalize the principles of the seniority system through salary scales and other occupational benefits such as tenure laws. In one way, centralization, combined with professional school administration, can be seen as an improvement for teachers, since it led to a more regularized system of employment and personnel policies. But this was not the situation that usually resulted. Rather, new qualifications for entering teaching were often introduced and also were often imposed on experienced teachers to prevent their promotion. Further, regularized salaries involved cuts or freezes as often as they meant raises for teachers. These developments led teacher associations and teacher unions to form during this period, usually in opposition to the new boards and superintendents.[20]

As superintendents developed a central office with a staff and a corps of supervisors to help them manage their schools, this organizational elaboration distanced the school officers even further from their teachers. In this new order, school principals were now to be chosen not on the basis of seniority, but on the basis of their ability to earn a graduate degree in education or to pass a test. This was seen by women elementary teachers as a direct assault on their own, self-chosen occupational standards and career patterns. The women understood that, given the realities of university or college attendance, tying a principalship to graduate study meant more men and fewer women principals.

Teacher unions were largely unsuccessful in combating this and other aspects of the new order of administrative progressivism. The timidity of some women prevented their joining the unions. Also, the existence of many diverse teacher associations, based on gender, subject matter, or grade level, made it difficult for teachers to unite into a single organization powerful enough to combat the hierarchy headed by the school superintendent.

Occasionally, teachers did forge coalitions with parent and community groups against the policies of boards and superintendents. These instances were exceptional, however. Teachers were thus incorporated into the bottom ranks of a developing hierarchy that sought professional status.[21]

Centralization and professional school administration were meant to bring the schools into line with developments in business, industry, and other white-collar occupations. Although this was accomplished, it is not clear that the changes yielded dramatically more effective schools for clients (students and their parents) or for the teachers. This problem of organizational restructuring without social betterment also applied to another significant administrative progressive reform, the differentiation of the high school curriculum.

Curricular Differentiation in the American High School

The phenomenon of curricular differentiation reversed, rather than built on, what had been accomplished in the common schools. The common school curriculum was the same for all students. The curriculum that was installed in the common schools of Massachusetts, for example, emphasized the common moral elements that Horace Mann thought important for all citizens of that state. By the 1920s, however, a major portion of America's public schools had a curriculum that had become quite diversified and largely uncommon for all students. It is this process of change from a common elementary curriculum to a diversified post-elementary curriculum that is now discussed.

One reason for the change in curriculum was a distinct change in the purpose of education. As just noted, the common elementary curriculum was based on a notion of schooling that saw its fundamental purpose as moral. Politically, this translated into citizenship education for a polity of equals. A common curriculum, then, had the goal of equalizing students as moral and political actors. All deserved, and needed, to be developed into good citizens with proper American values.

Differentiation, however, reflected a new, largely economic, purpose for education. The differentiated curriculum was an attempt to accommodate the differentiated economic roles that students would play in their later lives. Politically, differentiation was justified by the notion that the system provided equal opportunity for all students to develop to the fullest of their abilities. This change in the guiding purpose of schooling from moral virtue to economic betterment was a fundamental shift that occurred in the progressive era of American education. It developed gradually and most prominently in the area of the high school curriculum.[22]

Committee of Ten

In 1893, a high school study committee of the National Education Association (NEA), known popularly as the Committee of Ten, published a report sparked by the rapid development of colleges and universities. Although high schools had existed long before the formation of the committee, they were not the only institutions offering post-elementary education. Private academies existed in New England and other parts of the country and offered a variety of studies to those who enrolled. Some students went to academies and other private preparatory schools, and still others had private tutors to prepare them for college examinations. While the high school competed with these other institutions in preparing students for college entry, it also educated a number of students, particularly girls, who had no intention of enrolling in college. Therefore, a movement emerged in the late nineteenth century to introduce more technical and commercial studies into the high schools in order to equip students, both boys and girls, to deal with the realities of modern life.[23]

Thus, the Committee of Ten confronted an extremely untidy world of secondary education in which college preparatory study was only one of its purposes, though probably the major one. The solution offered by the Committee satisfied none of the competing interest groups completely. They outlined four alternative curricula for the four-year high school, all of which were seen as equally appropriate and defensible, depending on the desires of the students. In this respect, it reflected the orientation of its chairman, Charles W. Eliot, who had pioneered Harvard College's elective system. Through the Committee's recommendation, Eliot was able to bring the elective principle into the high school. Students chose their course of study depending on their goals and interests. Once that initial choice was made, however, the curriculum was largely prescribed, making it clear that the Committee opposed complete election by fourteen to seventeen-year-olds.

The four courses of study outlined by the Committee were the Classical, the Latin-Scientific, the Modern Languages, and the English. The major variation in them was the number and nature of the foreign languages prescribed. In the Classical, three foreign languages were required, including the two classical languages of Latin and Greek. In the Latin-Scientific, two foreign languages, Latin and a modern language, were required. In the Modern, two modern languages were required; and in the English only one modern language was required. The studies that would replace the classical and/or modern languages were almost all in the sciences, mainly in nonphysical sciences such as botany, zoology, and anatomy.[24]

Two other tenets of the Committee deserve attention. First, they believed that no difference in the course of study should exist for college-bound and non-college-bound students. Any of the four choices would be appropriate for an individual from either group. To Committee members, what was good preparation for collegiate studies was also good preparation for students who would enter work or adult domestic roles immediately after high school. Second, they recommended that any of the four courses of study would be equally appropriate as preparation for college entrance. Thus, though offering three alternatives to the traditional, classical course of study, they did not differentiate in any intellectual, social, or vocational sense among the purposes of these curricula or the students who chose them. The selection was to be based entirely on student interests.

The recommendation for equivalence among the four courses of study, three of which were nonclassical, earned Eliot and the Committee the enmity of many educational traditionalists who believed that classical languages were the key to intellectual and cultural achievement. This group was further offended by the assumption that college-bound students did not need a curriculum that differed substantially from that of the non-college bound. Although classicists wished to differentiate the college bound from the non-college bound, the Committee held to a commonality among high school students. For Eliot, the purpose of secondary education was the same, or common, for all students; it was to discipline their minds in preparation for whatever activity was to follow.

The enmity of the classicists is not what is remembered about the Committee of Ten report, however. It quickly became known as a most conservative document because it refused to accommodate those who wanted to diversify the high school curriculum to include subjects considered practical and relevant in the commercial and industrial worlds. From their perspective, the Committee of Ten had turned its back on the world in which many if not most of the high school students would take their places.

Opposition to the Committee of Ten Report

Pressure to reverse the Committee of Ten's sanctioned support of academic studies characterized the next two decades of debate over the American high school. Advocates of reversal included many of the young men and women then attending high schools, their parents, businessmen, and other men of affairs in the larger society. They wanted to see the high schools offer commercial subjects and also work in manual training, as pioneered by Calvin Woodward at the Washington University Manual Training High School. For a time, separate commercial and manual training high schools were advocated as institutions that would not abandon traditional or liberal studies, but that would supplement them with either commercial or manual subjects. In some instances, these separate high schools were founded and existed as alternative routes to liberal education and even to college entry. In the city of Atlanta, Georgia, for example, the Technological High School was established that offered technical subjects together with foreign languages and the sciences. It was intended to prepare students for study at the Georgia School of Technology.[25]

But such mild advocacy of more practical studies gave way rather quickly to the arguments of those who wanted to revamp the high schools completely by offering commercial and technical subjects. This group believed that modern social conditions made the existence of college-oriented high schools, which for them were all schools that did not offer commercial or vocational studies, a luxury that could not be afforded. In their eyes, the new commercial and industrial world needed high schools that would train students not just to live in but to work in that world.

Vocational Education

The National Society for the Promotion of Industrial Education (NSPIE), founded in 1906, was an influential group in the movement for practical studies. Although it was founded by educators who adhered to a manual training philosophy, the NSPIE was supported from the beginning by business and industrial leaders who sought to link schooling to employment. The NSPIE quickly became involved in advocating industrial (or trade) schools, where students could learn the skills needed for industrial and manufacturing jobs. Although enrollment in these schools was elective, it was not long before advocates were arguing that students who lacked academic aptitude or orientation should be channeled into industrial programs.

Many members of the educational community felt squeamish about separating commercial or industrial education students into distinct programs. Such a policy would completely isolate the industrial students and make the possibility of their return to academic studies highly unlikely. This was a new development in public education that directly contradicted both the old common school orientation of moral equality in the elementary schools and the principle of curriculum equality in alternative high school studies favored by the Committee of Ten.

Many both inside and outside education were particularly disturbed by the idea of separate industrial or trade schools whose major function was training students for employment. Their fears of an education dominated by employers were heightened as some in the business community began advocating separate industrial high schools under a private board that would be responsive to employers' needs, not necessarily those of students.

The Cooley Plan

Separate boards for what were now becoming known as industrial schools were advocated in several locales, most notably in Chicago in the 1910s. Chicago's plan became known as the Cooley plan, named for Edwin G. Cooley, a former superintendent of the city's schools who was a major supporter of a separate vocational board to be controlled by employers. However, a coalition of educators and labor leaders opposed this plan on the grounds that it would allow the public schools to be overwhelmed by the interests of one group. Such an arrangement, opponents argued, would not be in the interests of the students, the laboring classes, or society at large.[26]

The Cooley plan was defeated; other attempts to establish private boards for vocational schools were largely unsuccessful, and the momentum toward separate commercial and vocational high schools was largely halted. Curricular differentiation, however, remained the dominant issue that faced the high schools for the next decade.

Differentiation and Democracy

From the beginning, the differentiation of the high school curriculum into academic, vocational, and commercial emphases stirred concern about issues of social equality. It did not take a particularly keen eye to notice that the different courses of study included students from distinctly different social backgrounds. The academic track appealed mainly to upper- and middle-class students, the commercial track was populated largely by middle-class girls, and the vocational track was reserved for lower-class boys, quite often from immigrant backgrounds.[27]

Although educators developed guidance programs and standardized tests to place students into the "proper" curricular track, this did not stop the controversy. Despite the concerns of those who questioned the separate curricular tracks as class biased, support for differentiated studies came from all classes. For example, many in the organized labor movement and from the working and lower classes saw vocational studies as a recognition of the dignity and honor of their own way of life.

The legacy of curricular differentiation was substantial in first-twentieth-century public schools. A vast array of tests and other measures are still used to determine which students belong in which track. All these measures are subject to the criticism that they are sorting students on the basis of their class or race as much as on their abilities or talents. The common school, which professed a simple equality orientation based on moral goals, is now a distant memory, largely because schools in the twenty first century shifted their focus to economic goals. The relevance of specific curricula to specific economic skills, however, is questionable. It remains as hard to document as the proposition that sorting can be done in a manner that is free of class, culture, race, or gender bias. Arguing for differentiation on the grounds that it facilitates equality of educational opportunity obscures the relationship between social and economic discrimination and what goes on in the schools.[28]

The relationship between schooling and social and economic status was, and is, exceptionally important. In the progressive era, the public schools were confronted with new groups of students who brought with them a variety of orientations and expectations for the future. To examine this encounter more fully, a consideration of the administrative progressives' view of an unfamiliar group of students, immigrant children, and the experience of these students in the schools follows.

Immigrants and Schools

Immigration itself was by no means a new phenomenon in the progressive era. The United States had been a nation of immigrants from the time of its settlement by Europeans in the seventeenth century. The thing that was new in the late nineteenth and early twentieth centuries was the increased number of immigrants and their exotic backgrounds. The massive flow of these new immigrants merely intensified the administrative progressives' drive for more centrally controlled, scientifically managed, and differentiated city schools. However, the cultural diversity of the immigrants meant that the public schools were now facing students whose backgrounds they did not know, whose languages they did not speak, and whose habits they often found strange and threatening.[29]

Over the course of the nineteenth century and well into the twentieth, New York's Ellis Island was the main gate of entry on the east coast. In the West, Angel Island in the San Francisco Bay served as the main portal for Asians and Pacific Islanders who sought entry into the United States. The "new" immigrants crowding into eastern cities came heavily from Austria, Hungary, Bulgaria, Greece, Rumania, and Turkey. In New York City, most of the new immigrants were Jews and Italians.

The Catholic Question

The troubled relationship between Catholics and the public schools became more acute and pressing in the post-Civil War years. While uneasy compromises were sometimes considered in an effort to remove some of the obstacles that prevented some Catholics from attending public schools, for the most part the Catholic hierarchy saw in their own parochial schools the only viable alternative to the public schools.

As discussed in Chapter 4, moves toward establishing Catholic parochial schools were made as soon as the common school movement got underway, but in the late nineteenth century, the call to the Catholic faithful to support their own parish schools intensified. Both before and after the Civil War pleas and strategies were made to obtain public support for Catholic schools, but proponents of common schools and so-called "100 percent Americans" blocked such attempts. Increasingly the common school became identified as the "American" school and Catholic parochial schools were termed "foreign" institutions. As immigration increased and parishes became more identifiable along ethnic lines (German, Italian, Polish, etc.), the "foreignness" and exclusivity of Catholics increasingly became a political as well as religious and educational concern.

Senator James G. Blaine, a former Speaker of the U.S. House of Representatives, brought the matter to a head in 1875 when he proposed an amendment to the Constitution that would settle the question of whether or not public funds could be used to assist parochial schools. His proposed amendment read as follows:

> No State shall make any law respecting an establishment of religion, or prohibiting the free exercise thereof; and no money raised by taxation in any State for the support of public schools, or derived from any public fund therefor, nor any public lands devoted thereto, shall ever be under the control of any religious sect; nor shall any money so raised or lands so devoted be divided between religious sects or denominations.

The Blaine Amendment passed the House by a vote of 180 to 7, but it failed to garner the necessary two-thirds majority in the Senate. Supporters of the measure had greater success when they crafted similar amendments at the state level. All but eleven states then in the Union passed laws that accomplished the end toward which Blaine and his supporters were working. The message to Catholics (or any other sect) was clear: public funds were to be used for public purposes only.

In the face of such resistance and out of concern for the protection of their faith, in 1884 Catholic bishops convened in Baltimore for their Third Plenary Council. The bishops directed every parish to establish a parochial school within two years. Catholic parents were instructed to send their children to these schools unless the Bishop of the Diocese determined that an exception could be made under some circumstances.

As Thomas Hunt, a leading authority on religious education, has pointed out, "at no point in the nineteenth century were over one half of the Catholic children in the country enrolled in Catholic schools." As the century ended, the motto of "Every child in a Catholic school" remained just that: a motto, not a reality.[30]

Administrative Progressives and Immigrants

The administrative progressives' attitude toward the new immigrant groups was generally negative. Recall that centralization sought to remove corrupt school management from city schools. For centralizers, much of the corruption found in urban neighborhoods and exploited by urban machine politicians resulted from the presence of immigrant communities that did not understand American culture.

A compelling example of negativism toward immigrants on the part of administrative progressives is found in the writings of Ellwood Cubberley. A former school superintendent who became dean of the School of Education at Stanford University, Cubberley was the author of several textbooks used in the education of teachers and administrators. In the pages of one of these books, after discussing the virtues of older, nineteenth-century immigrant groups from northern and western Europe, Cubberley had this to say about the more recent arrivals:

These southern and eastern Europeans were of a very different type from the North and West Europeans who preceded them. Largely illiterate, docile, lacking in initiative, and almost wholly without the Anglo-Saxon conceptions of righteousness, liberty, law, order, public decency, and government, their coming has served to dilute tremendously our national stock and to weaken and corrupt our political life. . . . [T]hey have created serious problems in housing and living, moral and sanitary conditions, and honest and decent government, while popular education everywhere has been made more difficult by their presence. . . . The new peoples, and especially those from the South and East of Europe have come so fast that we have been unable to absorb and assimilate them, and our national life, for the past quarter of a century, has been afflicted with a serious case of racial indigestion.[31]

Cubberley's sentiments were shared by many others who were active in

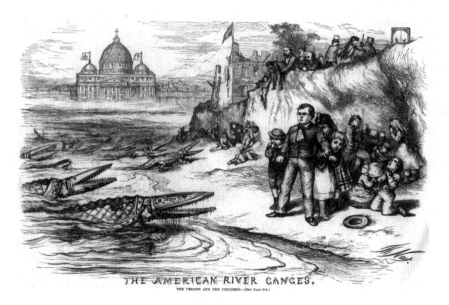

THE AMERICAN RIVER GANGES.
THE PRIESTS AND THE CHILDREN.—(See Page 915.)

Figure 7.1 "The American River Ganges" by Thomas Nast in *Harper's Weekly*, September 30, 1871. In an effort to win political support from New York's Irish Catholics, the Democratic political machine headquartered at Tammany Hall proposed providing public support to parochial schools. In opposition, Nast here warns of the result: Crocodilian bishops slithering out of the river, the public school in ruins, Tammany politicians dropping little children into the river, a public school teacher being led to the gallows, and the American flag hanging upside down, a universal signal of distress. The foreignness of Catholics is further illustrated by the Ganges River, the sacred river of Hinduism, another religion perceived to be primitive and fanatical and therefore un-American.

Credit: Provided courtesy HarpWeek, LLC.

the administrative progressive movement, both board members and super-intendents. The opposition to administrative progressivism included large groups of immigrants, usually Catholic, who expected and often received little consideration from the new school leaders. Yet it was precisely these new groups who needed to be reached if the public schools were to succeed in deal-ing with the problems of poverty and delinquency that were then rampant in many cities. The estrangement of the school leaders from the very groups that were most in need of school services was an irony that would be repeated later in the century. After the progressive-era immigrants made their way out of poverty, they were replaced by newer migrants and immigrants to the inner cities: African Americans, Hispanics, and Asians. These groups also would find themselves underserved by school systems focused on the needs of mainstream American culture.

Immigrants at School

The sentiments voiced by Cubberley illustrate the school–immigrant relation-ship from the point of view of the administrative progressive leadership of the progressive era. To get a more complete view of this relationship, however, it is also important to look at the school–immigrant encounter from the point of view of the immigrant children and their families.

In 1911, the Commission on Immigration was appointed to conduct a sur-vey of the lives of the recent immigrants. Evidence from that survey, as well as the results of studies regarding immigrant performance in several cities in the early twentieth century, shows rather convincingly that immigrant children with northern European backgrounds (English, Scottish, Welsh, German, and Scandinavian) did about as well in school as children of old-stock American whites. Children of eastern European Jews performed on a par with, or better than, other groups, but non-Jewish eastern and southern Europeans lagged significantly in school performance.[32]

Subsequent work has looked further into the causes of those differences. This work has noted both the similarities and differences between immigrants and non-immigrants in relation to schooling. For example, immigrant groups were as likely to be in school as non-immigrants and, at the elementary level, both groups made similar progress. Thus, the inference is that there was little difference in educational aspirations between the groups.[33]

Differences in achievement, however, clearly surfaced at the high school level. Much of that gap in school achievement can be explained by factors associated with social class such as wealth and occupational status. That is, immigrants experienced the same debilitating factors in regard to school performance as did non-immigrant students from similar socioeconomic back-grounds. Regardless of cultural background, students from families mired in poverty generally brought with them negative attitudes toward the school and, consequently, whether they were immigrant or non-immigrant, did poorly in school. The fact that more immigrant youngsters fared poorly in school, then, was in large part due to the fact that more of them were from the lower classes.

Yet this is far from the whole story. Scholars controlling for social class factors have shown that certain immigrant groups did better than others in school. Eastern European Jews were a classic example of immigrants who excelled in school, while Italians and Slavic groups generally did poorly. Further inquiry into the backgrounds of these various groups found that factors such as urban or rural origins and wealth or poverty in their native countries influenced immigrants' school success or failure. These factors surfaced in areas such as students' facility with words and abstractions, behavioral dispositions toward schooling, and responsiveness to school rewards—all of which related to school success or failure. These factors are culturally based and operate somewhat independently from socioeconomic characteristics.

Another finding that emerges from historical work on the school/immigrant encounter is that there were differences from city to city. Explanations of those differences await further study that compares the backgrounds of the immigrant populations in different cities against the arrangements of the educational enterprise in those cities.

Still another factor that is important in explaining differences in achievement is the relative participation and success of immigrant groups in public and nonpublic schools. Most southern and eastern European immigrants were Roman Catholics and were largely responsible for the increased enrollment in Catholic parochial schools through much of the twentieth century. Thus, the preference of a group for parochial over public schooling needs to be included in any complete explanation of the school–immigrant encounter as well as the possibility that this preference could vary from city to city.

Deeper insight into the school–immigrant relationship has come from a thorough study of the subject in the city of Providence, Rhode Island. In that city, Irish school achievement, which had lagged in the nineteenth century, paralleled that of "native" whites (Yankees) in the early twentieth century. The explanation offered for this is that as Irish gradually moved into positions of political, economic, and social power and came to occupy more teaching positions in the public schools, the school achievement of their children rose substantially. In addition, the school success of Jewish immigrants was qualified somewhat in this study by the finding that Jewish youngsters, although they did attend high school in high proportions, did not receive higher grades than other groups. Finally, although Italians were under-represented in high school, their occupational success was comparable to that of other groups, despite the educational differential.[34]

The Providence study indicates that the early-twentieth-century encounter between public schools and new immigrants is much more complex than many social commentators have thought. Unidimensional explanations of the immigrant experience—for example, that old-world customs and values or new-world occupational or social standing operated singularly or in combination as the most powerful determinants of the immigrant experience—do not hold up across group lines. Perlmann's study underscores the fact that ethnic groups are products of distinct histories. Moreover, within ethnic groups as within families, individuals chart different life courses. Efforts to ferret out a single consistently primary factor creating ethnic distinctiveness, or even a single generalization that will cover the relationships among several factors, seem doomed to failure.[35]

Americanization and the American Indian

As the only "non-immigrants" on the American continent, the experience of the Native American populations has always been a special case. During the progressive era, policies toward the acculturation of American Indians once again underwent change, although as in the case of different immigrant groups, inconsistencies in the application of policies and wide variations in responses among individual Indians and their tribal groups work against neat generalizations. It is clear, however, that the frontal assault on Native American languages, customs, and values that characterized the off-reservation boarding school experience began to soften somewhat during the progressive era.

An unmistakable signal that the nation's Indian policy needed revamping was given in the 1901 annual report by the Commissioner of Indian Affairs, William Jones. The Commissioner observed that over the previous thirty three years, the government had spent over $240 million in an attempt to move Native Americans from dependency to self-reliant citizenship. Public funding had provided food, clothing, plows, seed, wagons, and schools. The results of this investment, said the Commissioner, were extremely disappointing. The average Indian, he noted, "is little, if any, nearer the goal of independence than he was thirty years ago, and if the present policy is continued he will get little, if any, nearer in thirty years to come." However well-intentioned past policies may have been, he concluded, they were now seen to be wrongheaded; it was time to reassess.[36]

Special criticism was directed toward the boarding school policy. Francis Ellington Leupp, who succeeded Jones as commissioner in 1905, declared:

> It is a great mistake to start the little ones in the path of civilization by snapping all the ties of affection between them and their parents, and teaching them to despise the aged and nonprogressive members of their families. The sensible as well as the humane plan is to nourish their love of father and mother and home . . . and then to utilize this affection as a means of reaching, through them, the hearts of the elders.[37]

The shift from the goal of immediate assimilation toward one of gradualism was based on several assumptions that were emerging among educational elites during the progressive era. One was the conviction held by some that Indians, either because of inborn racial traits or sheer obstinacy, were simply incapable of rapid assimilation. Commissioner Leupp grounded his assertion that assimilationists had expected too much too soon in his conviction that "race characteristics" that had been transmitted across the centuries could not be changed in "a day, a year, or a good many years." Following the lead of scholars who were putting increasing stock in evolutionary theories of development, Leupp held that crossing the boundary between barbarism and civilization would take time, if indeed it could ever occur completely: "Ethnically he will always remain an Indian, with an Indian color, Indian traits of mind, Indian ancestral traditions and the like." Belief in the doctrine of inherited racial characteristics that were resistant to sudden change was similarly expressed by a speaker at the National Education Association meeting in 1909 who explained to an audience discussing the problem of Indian education that "the races of men feel, think, and act differently not only because of environment, but also because of hereditary impulses."[38]

Evolutionary and genetic explanations for the failure of past Indian assimilation policies were buttressed by a related criticism: boarding schools were inherently cruel and inhumane. The novelist Hamlin Garland charged that the practice of disrupting families and teaching the children to abhor the ways of their parents was "so monstrous and so unchristian that its failure was foretold to every teacher who understood the law of heredity." Popularized autobiographical essays by Indians themselves poignantly emphasized the alienation felt by many. A Yankton Sioux girl who had begged to go away to a missionary school and who later became a teacher herself nonetheless recalled the pain of separation: "Like a slender tree, I had been uprooted from my mother, nature and God. I was shorn of my branches, which had waved in sympathy and love for home and friends."[39]

The founder of the child study movement, G. Stanley Hall, helped popularize yet another notion that worked against the strenuous efforts of those who hoped to eradicate Indians through education. As an advocate of the "doctrine of culture epochs" or "recapitulation theory," Hall believed that each child, and each race, must progressively move through successive stages in the civilizing process. Hall held that there was a direct correspondence between the stages in an individual's physical and psychological development and the stages in the evolution of human society. In modern society and schools, he maintained, educators were in too great a rush to turn children into adults and in consequence placed too much emphasis on book learning and gave too little attention to the true nature and needs of childhood. Hall romanticized the slower pace of primitive societies where children engaged in play and physical activity and were allowed to develop naturally. He urged teachers of Indian children (indeed, of all children) to build on children's natural capacities and backgrounds rather than obliterate them. Similarly, John Dewey, who will be discussed in more detail later in this chapter, also emphasized the importance of children's development and building on natural ties with home life. Although Dewey never addressed the issue of Indian education directly, his proposition that education must begin with psychological insight into the child's capacities, interests and habits as well as his belief that the school should build upon activities with which the child is already familiar in the home certainly gave support to educators who were advocating reassessment of Indian educational policy.[40]

Another point of criticism of past Indian policy followed a different line of reasoning. Indian "uplift" policies, it was sometimes charged, encouraged attitudes of dependency rather than self-reliance and individual initiative. Government programs designed to feed, clothe, and house as well as educate Indian youth were thought by some to reward laziness and create an expectation that the government would and should provide for those who do not provide for themselves.

The campaign against off-reservation boarding schools thus drew from strains of thought that were at various points racist, pluralistic, humanistic, progressive, and socially conservative. Considered together and in the larger context of the long years of failure of assimilation efforts, they offered a compelling case for reassessing the ideological underpinnings of Indian education during the opening decades of the twentieth century.

Efforts to reform Indian education during this period were inconsistent in both theory and practice, but in that respect they reflected some of the same inconsistencies and definitional problems associated with "progressive education" in general. While more humane educational methods and approaches were often adopted as "means," the "ends" of greater efficiency and a greater degree of assimilation over time still remained paramount in the minds of those described above as "administrative progressives." At the same time, "pedagogical progressives," about whom more will be said below, also made their influence felt, not only in terms of modifying the curriculum and methods of teaching, but also in terms of advocating greater sympathy and respect for Indian cultural traditions and values. "Progressive educators" encouraged teachers to understand Indian children as products of a "different civilization" rather than a "lower civilization." Teachers began to incorporate Indian music and other arts and crafts into the curriculum. They attempted to improve students' facility with English by motivating them to retell tribal legends or describe aspects of home life in their writings.

In terms of government policy toward Indian education, emphasis began to shift away from off-reservation boarding schools back to on-reservation schools, day schools, and most significantly, public schools. The number of schools sponsored by the federal government declined as local public schools began to pick up more responsibility for educating Indian youth. Whereas in 1900 less than 1 percent of all Indian students were enrolled in public schools, by 1925 over half were in public schools—although there were still thousands of Indian children who were not enrolled in any type of school.

In 1928 a massive report authored by Lewis Meriam of the Institute for Government Research laid bare the distressing state of Indian life at that juncture in the nation's life. *The Problem of Indian Administration,* more commonly referred to as the Meriam Report, underscored the failed policies of the past. In its treatment of education, the Meriam Report was extremely critical of the boarding school system. Emphasizing the need for adoption of the "modern" view of connecting children's education to family and community, the report urged greater reliance on day and public schools and the pedagogy of progressive education. Still unsettled, however, was the question of the most desirable outcome of a more progressive approach to education. The report maintained that government policy must "give consideration to the desires of the individual Indians." Those wishing to enter the mainstream white society should be enabled to do so, while those wishing to remain Indian and live according to the old culture should likewise be aided toward that end. Implicit in the report was the assumption, however, that those who chose the latter path would have an increasingly difficult time facing the "advancing tide of white civilization."[41]

Character Education Outside the System

Concerns for the children of immigrants and Indians were not the only worries facing Victorian reformers in the closing years of the nineteenth and early years of the twentieth century. Middle-class Americans were becoming increasingly concerned about their *own* children, especially boys. As urban areas became ever more crowded with upwardly mobile families as well as families that seemed "stuck" at the bottom of the social order, fears were increasingly expressed regarding the pastimes of and character influences on urban youth.

Reformers who became referred to as "child savers" focused their attention on underclass delinquent children and brought into being a juvenile justice system to deal with the most wayward youth. But even children not labeled as delinquent—yet—caused concern. Families were under new forms of stress as fathers disappeared into large office buildings or factories for long periods each day and spent fewer hours at home. For an increasing number of young people, working side by side with their parents in fields or homes was becoming a story of the past, not a reality of the present. While schools underwent reforms in the progressive era to provide order and discipline for youth, it was seen that they could not carry the whole burden. Increasingly voices were raised lamenting not only the problems and conditions facing children of the urban working class and immigrant poor, but of "decent" boys and girls from middle-class homes who were experiencing the bodily changes and emotional turmoil of adolescence as well.

The theory of adolescence put forth by psychologist G. Stanley Hall highlighted the "storm and stress" experienced by young people as they entered their teen years. Based on his recapitulation or culture epochs theory (see previous section), Hall believed that activities normal for healthly adolescent development were being ignored or thwarted by parents, teachers, and others who pushed children to "grow up" and "act their age." According to Hall, acting their age was exactly what they *should* be doing, but modern society was denying opportunities and outlets for adventure, strenuous activities, and the free use of heroic imagination that romanticized the "manly" life exemplified by knights of old, explorers, frontiersmen, and, somewhat ironically, by American Indians. Thus, while educational reformers were trying to make the schools more inclusive and more responsible for the welfare of children, and the "child savers" were focusing their attention on children of the urban poor and a juvenile justice system, other concerned adults looked outside the legal and educational system for alternative or supporting paths to foster sound physical, spiritual, social, and moral development.[42]

Youth Organizations: The YMCA and Boy Scouts

Among the oldest of voluntary youth associations formed to combat the ills of urban life and negative influences among youth was the Young Men's Christian Association (YMCA). Founded in England in the 1840s, the purpose of the "Y" was to use prayer, Bible study, and streetside preaching as ways to combat the growing evils of industrial life. The movement spread to the United States and other countries in the pre-Civil War period. In 1851 Montreal and Boston became the first two YMCA affiliates to be established in North America.

The Civil War reduced the number of YMCAs and membership as young men were called to battle, but among the YMCAs that were still operating in the northern states during the war, attention was turned to aiding soldiers and prisoners of war. After the war the YMCA movement expanded and resumed its evangelical focus on soul saving. The movement gradually moved beyond its initial focus on boys and began to provide services to families regardless of social class, religious belief, race, or nationality. In 1853 the first YMCA founded expressly for African Americans was chartered in Washington, D.C.

It was the Boy Scouts of America (BSA), however, that came to exemplify organizations that came on the scene to provide alternative pathways through adolescence and into adulthood. Along with the YMCA, precursors to the Boy Scouts included such organizations as the Boys Brigades, Woodcraft Indians, and the Sons of Daniel Boone. The Woodcraft Indians was perhaps the most influential forerunner of the American Boy Scouts program. (There were also European versions of these and similar organizations.) Founded in 1902 by the artist and naturalist Ernest Thomas Seton, the Woodcraft Indians was organized to exalt what G. Stanley Hall had termed the "savage" stage of human development. Camping, swimming, nature study, Indian names, games, and awards were the focal points of these units. Himself something of a noncomformist, Seton made little effort to to inculcate conventional morality, piety, and patriotism in his boys.[43]

The Boy Scout program was the invention of a British general, Robert S. S. Baden-Powell (1857–1941). A veteran of various wars for the Empire, Baden-Powell took a special interest while in the army in reconnaissance work. Following a distinguished military career, and after a short stint working with the Boys Brigade, Baden-Powell conceived of an adventure-oriented and character-building program that blended some aspects of earlier boy-oriented organizations with new elements of his own devising. He wrote what became a widely popular book on scouting lore, *Scouting for Boys*, in 1908. The Scout motto, "Be Prepared" and the oath in which a boy promised "To do [my] duty to God and the King [British version], to help other people at all times, and to obey the Scout law" set forth the basic aims of the scouting program. The Scout oath and law, with minor refinements over time, affirmed characteristics of the good Scout and good citizen, e.g. trustworthiness, loyalty, helpfulness, cheerfulness, and obedience.

From its American founding in 1910, the Boy Scouts came to epitomize traits and activities that promised to build character in boys from twelve to eighteen years of age. Its chartering documents proclaimed that the BSA aimed "to promote, through organization and cooperation with other agencies, the ability of boys to do things for themselves and others, to train them in

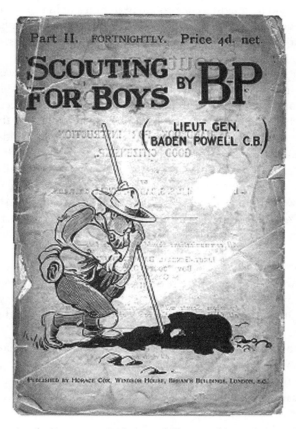

Figure 7.2 *Scouting for Boys* cover. Written and illustrated by Robert Baden-Powell, the second installment of *Scouting for Boys* included adventure stories as well as outdoor skills and lore. This 1908 copy of the original cover portrays a scout engaged in tracking.

Source: wikipedia.org/wiki/Image:Scouting_for_Boys-Part 2_cover.gif

Scoutcraft, and to teach them patriotism, courage, self-reliance, and kindred virtues. . . ."[44]

After Savannah native Juliette Gordon Low founded the Girl Scouts in 1912, an increasing number of middle-class Americans seemed to be placing their hopes and their children's values in the care and activities of new voluntary institutions not associated with schools or governmental agencies. There were, however, important differences in philosophy that kept the identities and activities of Boy Scouts and Girl Scouts separate. Girls were thought to be unhappy with their roles and status in society whereas boys, if given the chance, seemed to thrive in the rough and tumble of masculine life. Emphasis in the Boy Scout program was on competition, achievement, outdoor adventure, and individualism tempered by cooperation. Girls, it was assumed, needed to be taught to appreciate femininity and domestic achievement. If it was right and proper for boys to work on merit badges in pioneering, camping, signaling, and nature study, girls should be taught to be proficient in household tasks such as sewing, laundering, and cooking *inside* the house rather than on a campfire. The head of the Pittsburgh Girl Scout program urged that "the home-maker of tomorrow . . . must be made efficient in her task and happy in it."[45]

Girls were not totally shut out from outdoor pursuits, however. In 1902 Laura Mattoon opened Camp Kehonka on the shores of Lake Winnipesaukee near Wolfeboro, New Hampshire. Over the next several decades, private camps for girls began appearing throughout New England. For the most part, these camps were for the privileged daughters of upper-middle-class New Englanders. Democratization of camping for girls made inroads, however, as religious, fraternal, political, and ethnic groups began establishing camps for girls who had ties to these varied associations. The spread of the camping zeal among girls was boldly proclaimed when the Young Communist League and the Pioneer Youth of America founded camps for girls from families with communist or socialist sympathies.[46]

The Pedagogical Progressives

In terms of America's larger progressive movement, the pedagogical progressives were more aligned with the liberals than with the conservatives. Social justice was a goal of many of these pedagogical progressives, and they felt that school reform could be used to achieve that justice.

Two exemplars of pedagogical progressivism will be considered here. The first, John Dewey, was a brilliant philosopher and theorist who put his ideas into practice in a variety of educational and social settings. The second, Ella Flagg Young, was a practicing educator who brought progressive pedagogical ideas into her work in schools.

John Dewey

John Dewey was born in Burlington, Vermont, the son of a storekeeper in that small, New England college town. Dewey went to college at the University of

Vermont and graduated in 1879 with a degree in a classically oriented liberal arts curriculum. He then taught Latin, algebra, and science for two years at a high school in Pennsylvania. He returned to Vermont for a year and taught in an academy near Burlington while he studied philosophy with a tutor as a prelude to graduate study in that subject. In 1882, he enrolled in the philosophy department at the Johns Hopkins University in Baltimore, Maryland. He was quite successful in his graduate studies, earning both teaching assistant duties and a graduate fellowship.[47]

Upon completion of his doctorate, Dewey obtained a position teaching philosophy at the University of Michigan in Ann Arbor. He was hired there at the urging of one of his former teachers at Johns Hopkins who had gone to Michigan to build a program in philosophy. It also did not hurt Dewey's chances that the president of the University of Michigan was a former president of the University of Vermont and knew Dewey and his family.

During his tenure at Michigan, Dewey showed strong interest in the field of psychology. He saw a natural affinity between the empirical findings of the psychologists and the systematic thought of philosophers. He also exhibited a deep interest in social problems and was acknowledged as one of the two leading "liberals" on the faculty. In his final Michigan years, he used his previous high school and university teaching experience to develop an interest in the field of education. By combining his interests in philosophy, psychology, and social reform, Dewey became a uniquely practical philosopher, one who used scientifically organized experiments as a test of philosophical thinking and, in particular, of democratic social reform.

Dewey's use of scientific experiments to link his ideas to his social interests was leading him into the philosophy of "pragmatism." Dewey and other early pragmatists believed that ideas, like biological organisms, survived and evolved according to their ability to interpret and guide real-world events. Pragmatism was an ideal philosophy for a man who wanted to make a difference in the world, and John Dewey was such a man. He got the chance to begin making a large difference when he was called to the University of Chicago in 1894.

Dewey was appointed to the newly established and richly endowed University of Chicago as head of its department of philosophy, which also included the fields of psychology and pedagogy. This multifaceted department allowed him to combine all his developing interests under one academic umbrella and to have a major voice in all that would occur in each of the three fields.

Dewey at Chicago

As a condition of his coming to Chicago, Dewey made it clear that his department needed a laboratory school for educational experimentation. Enrollment in Dewey's school grew quickly as its fame spread throughout national academic and professional circles. Dewey's work received even more publicity when Francis Parker's teacher training school, recently detached from the control of the Cook County political apparatus, also became part of the university.

Parker's school functioned as a teacher training laboratory, while Dewey's school continued its mission as a testing ground for educational principles. When Parker died, the two schools were combined and then consolidated with the undergraduate program in education to form the School of Education with Dewey as the head. Graduate work in education continued to be done in the academic Department of Philosophy, which was also still led by Dewey.[48]

Parker's almost romantic belief in the potential of children became a subject for experimentation in Dewey's laboratory school and propelled the new education into a position of notoriety in the academic world. Dewey proceeded to lay out the intellectual foundations of his educational efforts in a series of books and articles, the two most famous being *The School and Society* (1899) and *The Child and the Curriculum* (1902). In both volumes, Dewey exhibited a characteristic thought pattern in which he described a problem involving two opposing forces and then demonstrated how a new formulation of the problem blended the two poles. For example, in *The School and Society*, Dewey took the vast differences between the culture of the school and that of the surrounding society and showed how the discrepancies could be overcome. For Dewey, the school itself was a social institution, a part of society, and needed to be consciously organized as such. In Dewey's formulation, learning was a natural by-product of concrete social activities. So, by organizing schools like other social institutions, Dewey believed learning would lose the abstract quality that permeated so much of the academic study that went on in schools.[49]

In curricular terms, this meant aligning school experiences with the real-life occupational and democratic experiences of the surrounding society. This real-life curriculum was formed cooperatively by students and their teacher. Together with a commitment to scientific methods and principles, this meant that the school functioned both as a learning laboratory and as a vehicle for the improvement of a democratic society. Pedagogically, this largely continued Parker's new education, in which primary grade children were encouraged to actively explore their surrounding environment. However, Dewey stressed two elements that Parker and other advocates of the new education did not.

First, Dewey did not assume that a child-oriented curriculum meant abandoning traditional subject matter. Rather, he saw his program as an occasion for reorganizing traditional subjects to fit the needs of both children and society. Although child centered, it still took the children from where they were to where the educators wanted them to be. Thus, for Dewey, teachers had to have knowledge of both children and subject matter in order to orchestrate the most productive blending of the two. Second, the activities that constituted Dewey's curriculum were intended to improve the classroom society and, thereby, to improve the larger society of which they were a part.

Democracy and Education

In his most elaborate educational statement, *Democracy and Education*, written in 1916, Dewey provided a systematic exposition of his educational philosophy.

While this volume was a philosophical treatise written more than a decade after Dewey left Chicago for a noneducational position at Columbia University, it built on the principles enunciated in his earlier volumes. Most important, *Democracy and Education* enunciated the principle of growth as the essence of educational activity. Education was growth, and growth took place through education. Any conception of education that saw it as an activity directed toward some "end" missed its essential developmental character. Growth needed no end to be effective: Growth was its own end.[50]

It was also in this volume that Dewey stated his view of democracy that guided his educational thought and, earlier, had guided his educational practice in the experimental school. Recall that Dewey's school was conceived of as a society in itself, or more specifically, as an embryonic democratic community. In *Democracy and Education*, Dewey made explicit the definition of democracy that underlay his educational philosophy. As the following passage makes clear, the ordinary political sense of democracy was only a small part of Dewey's own conceptualization:

> Upon the educational side, we note first that the realization of a form of social life in which interests are mutually interpenetrating, and where progress, or readjustment, is an important consideration, makes a democratic community more interested than other communities have cause to be in deliberate and systematic education. The devotion of democracy to education is a familiar fact. The superficial explanation is that a government resting upon popular suffrage cannot be successful unless those who elect and who obey their governors are educated. Since a democratic society repudiates the principle of external authority, it must find a substitute in voluntary disposition and interest: these can be created only by education. But there is a deeper explanation. A democracy is more than a form of government; it is primarily a mode of associated living, of conjoint, communicated experience.[51]

This statement attests to how important schools were to Dewey's vision of American society. They were the primary means for incubating the democratic way of life that he saw as our most important attribute. Thus, one can conclude that for Dewey the school was an essential, if not *the* essential, institution of social reform.

In spite of this emphasis on schools, Dewey was not just an educational reformer. To the contrary, he was active in a variety of social and political reform activities and organizations. He was an ally of Jane Addams and a frequent visitor and contributor to her activities at Hull House. He was also an inveterate writer on social and political issues in journals of political opinion such as *The New Republic*. He worked diligently through organizations such as the American Federation of Teachers (AFT) and the American Association of University Professors (AAUP) to see that educators were not prevented from influencing the policies that controlled their practice. In short, John Dewey was the archetype of the liberal progressive reformer whose commitment to reform permeated all phases of his life.

Dewey: Disciples, Critics, and Legacy

Dewey was remarkably influential on studies in the field of education, and somewhat less influential on practice in the schools. The popularity of his views made him a magnet for other educators to follow as well as a target for intellectual opponents on both the left and the right. We will try to give a brief indication of all three of these aspects of Dewey's impact in this chapter. He will come up again frequently in later chapters, a testimony to his reputation as the most significant thinker in American education in the twentieth century.

Dewey's disciples were numerous in professional educational circles. While some of his followers saw in his work mainly the impulse to liberate the interest of the child from the "dead hand" of subject matter, his opponents saw his work as an attempt to replace necessary subject matter with a pedagogy that privileged student interest erroneously over academic studies. Still others saw him as a powerful force for the unionization and professionalization of teaching through the invigoration of teacher organizations and other professional educational groups. In the next chapter, we will show the devotion to him of several educational practitioners and scholars in the 1920s and will suggest the limitations in that devotion. In the chapter after that, we will discuss those in the 1930s who saw Dewey and his disciples as a major threat to the intellectual integrity of American schools. Also in that chapter, we will show how some political radicals saw in him a powerful political voice for a collective response to the economic depression of that decade and a voice for educational improvement through a teaching force empowered by unionism. In later chapters, we will see how advocates of many positions not normally associated with him could invoke his name in support of practices and policies that seem remarkably anti-Deweyan. Dewey bears some of the responsibility for the diffuse influence he exercised on American education because of the complexity of his ideas and a rather frequent abstruseness in his writings that often obscured the major thrust of his ideas.

In the 1930s, Dewey took on both his pedagogical disciples and his pedagogical critics in an address to an educational honorary society that was subsequently published as *Experience and Education*. In this volume he used an intellectual strategy similar to the one he had employed in his pedagogical works of the turn of the twentieth century, *The School and Society* (1899) and *The Child and the Curriculum* (1902). In *Experience and Education* (1938), he showed the dichotomy between the child-centered educators' embrace of the child, unencumbered by subject matter, and traditional educators' endorsement of subject matter, to the point that education excluded any recognition of the interests of the child. For him, these two extreme camps, which he labeled progressive and traditional education, were equally off the mark. Only by combining the necessary content of academic subjects with the equally necessary influence of genuine interest in that subject matter by children could education yield a properly productive outcome. He adopted, thereby, a middle-of-the-road position that recognized the significance of both the child and school subject matter and, just as important, the role of the teacher. For Dewey, the teacher was the responsible adult in a school classroom, whose job was to link the interests of children to the subjects they were studying. He emphasized school activities such as gardening that began with the interest of children but then used that interest to develop activities and assignments that brought in the insights of disciplines such as, in the case of a school garden, mathematics, several of the sciences, history, and geography. These subjects were studied, not discretely or abstractly, but rather in terms of an interest that had attracted the attention of students.[52]

Despite his consistent advocacy of an approach that sought to mediate between the child and subject matter, he remained a beacon for many child-centered advocates who had far less commitment to subject matter than he did and a target for subject matter advocates who refused to understand that he himself was not opposed to rigorous studies. Dewey also became a controversial figure in scholarship on the social and political aspects of education, again because of some ambiguity in his thought and the interpretation of that thought as it played out in the classroom and the larger society.

For example, some historians looked at his educational formulations, particularly his emphasis on classroom community and cooperation, and saw them as having some profoundly antidemocratic implications. In spite of his reputation as a liberal reformer, these historians saw a strong conservative side to both his views and those of other liberal progressives. According to this interpretation, his emphasis on cooperative activity seems to leave little room for student autonomy, that is, for individuals who, for one reason or another, are not comfortable with the group living that he saw as the essence of democratic society. Similarly, his devotion to scientific inquiry seems to ignore literary and/or artistic ways of knowing. Also, in his advocacy of practical educational reforms such as vocational education, he seems to have paid insufficient attention to the socially and politically conservative ways in which this curriculum was used in the schools. To use a suggestive term, there is a "darker side" to Dewey's version of progressive education, one that involved an approach to education that appears to be insensitive to dissent and to difference.[53]

Dewey's activities in the Polish community of Philadelphia during World War I provide an illustration of progressivism's darker side. He brought a graduate seminar from Columbia University, where he was then teaching, into Philadelphia's Polish community to study the Poles and their adjustment to American life. One of the documents produced by that seminar, a report on the Poles in America, was submitted to the War Department in 1918. A brief account of the contents of that document indicates what bothers his critics. It seems that one of the subjects of inquiry in his seminar was the preference of many American Poles to enlist in the fight against Germany as members of a Polish army in exile then being formed in England. This army was dedicated to restoration of a monarchy in Poland if the Germans were defeated. He was chagrined at these choices and further bothered by the general tendency of Polish Americans toward an unthinking political conservatism. The entire situation was exacerbated for him by the tendency toward blind obedience on the part of Polish Americans to the clergy of the Roman Catholic Church to which they belonged in overwhelming numbers. In the report, Dewey contrasted the attitudes of these conservative Polish Catholics with a small group of Polish Jews who were much more liberal politically, who were willing to fight in the American army, and who supported the establishment of a socialist democracy in postwar Poland.[54]

Dewey's opposition to the ideas of the Poles was not the only wartime controversy in which he was engaged. Prior to American entry into the war, he had advocated pacifism as the policy to be followed by Americans. Once the nation entered the war, however, he switched from pacifism to vigorous pursuit of the war, arguing that, once involved, it was best to win and thereby ensure that the consequences of war would be positive both for American society and for the world at large. One of his allies in pre-war pacifism, Randolph Bourne, was also one of his associates at the progressive magazine, *The New Republic*. When Dewey abandoned pacifism after American entry to the war, Bourne published a series of angry essays arguing that Dewey's pragmatic allegiance to the world as it existed prevented him from maintaining the pacifist principles that the two had shared prior to America's entry.[55]

Of course, like most political controversies, it is not clear that Dewey was guilty of the charges brought by his critics. In the case of the Polish study, an entire issue of the *History of Education Quarterly* defended his actions against the charges of his critics. Similarly, his abandonment of pacifism, criticized so scathingly by Bourne, was defended by many of his contemporaries and by subsequent scholars who have carefully analyzed the circumstances.[56]

A recent scholarly account of Dewey's life takes a middle position on the issue. The conclusion of this work is that he treated Bourne shabbily, and it adds that Dewey's actions in this case conflicted with his intellectual principles. This is a different view from stating that his principles were fatally flawed, or that he was largely blameless in the Bourne affair and the Polish study. It is also a view with which the authors of this text are in substantial agreement.[57]

Ella Flagg Young

Ella Flagg Young's pedagogical progressivism was aligned with Dewey's views, but she operated in a quite different environment from that of the philosopher. She spent almost her entire adult life in the public schools of Chicago, which at first glance seems an unlikely place from which to either study or advocate pedagogical reform. The fast-paced atmosphere of school and classroom life leaves little time to think imaginatively about how things can be different.

Given her career, Ella Flagg Young should have been an administrative progressive, one who changed school governance and management to enhance her own occupational prestige. She did hardly any of that, however, perhaps because she was a woman who was attuned to concerns other than personal or occupational advancement. Or perhaps it is because the men who led the movement for administrative progressivism were little inclined to make room in their ranks for a female colleague. Whatever the reasons, Ella Flagg Young's career reveals just how different her priorities were from those of the administrative progressives of her day. Even if they had invited her into their fold, it is unlikely that she would have joined them.

Early Life and Career

Born in 1845 in Buffalo, New York, Ella Flagg moved with her family to Chicago in 1858. Prevented from entering high school because she had not completed a year of preliminary study in Chicago, she eventually enrolled in the normal department of a city high school and pursued a teaching certificate that was clearly differentiated from the diploma granted to regular high school students. In 1862, she began her career in the Chicago schools by teaching in an elementary school. She rose rather quickly through the ranks and eventually became principal of the "practice school" portion of one of the city's high schools that had been set aside for normal school students.[58]

She continued to win promotions, moving to the principalship first of a full elementary school and then of a larger school. In 1887, she was made an assistant (or district) superintendent with responsibilities for the curriculum of the elementary schools and the quality of the teachers in her district. In her work as an administrator, her supervisory responsibilities gradually expanded from the traditional elementary school curriculum to the newer subjects such as manual training and its counterpart for girls, domestic studies. In 1898, shortly after Chicago centralized its school governance and hired a new, authoritarian superintendent, Young resigned her position to become a full-time graduate student at the University of Chicago. Her progress was facilitated there by President William Rainey Harper and John Dewey, both of whom sought closer ties between the university and the city's public schools. She received her undergraduate degree on the basis of examinations and soon was admitted to candidacy for the doctoral degree.

After receiving her doctorate, Young was appointed a professor of education. She became a popular teacher and a colleague of Dewey's who helped develop his famous Laboratory School. Because of her close ties with Dewey, she became caught up in a clash between him and his colleagues in the School of Education at Chicago. In 1904, Dewey resigned under some pressure from the president and took a position at Columbia University. Shortly thereafter, Young resigned for unclear reasons. Although she had worked closely with him, her own career was not bound to his. She evidently was tired of bickering and faculty politics. She soon left for Europe, where she traveled and studied education, particularly the German school system.

Principal of Chicago Normal School

After her return from Europe, Young was rehired by the Chicago school system, this time as principal of the city normal school. Her graduate studies, her European experience, and her long years in the schools made her an ideal candidate for this position. She had a unique ability to combine theory with practice and also had a long record of positive contacts with the teachers of Chicago.

Young's doctoral dissertation, "Isolation in the Schools," gave her the chance to refine her educational views. In it she decried the lack of relationship between the various subjects that comprised the curriculum in the schools and also between the various elements (teachers, principals, superintendents) that composed the school bureaucracy. Her views of the dignity and importance of teachers made her the friend of classroom teachers and, potentially, the enemy of administrative progressives, who sought to mechanize the teachers' role in the new top-down form of school management. She brought these beliefs to bear on the curriculum and staff of the normal school, where she served until 1909, at which time she was chosen as superintendent of the Chicago schools.

Superintendent Young

Selecting a superintendent in Chicago in 1909 was a task fraught with problems. The schools were plagued by long-standing disputes among board members and were enmeshed in the city politics that often featured clashes between the mayor and the council. They were also reeling from fights with the growing Chicago Teachers Federation (CTF), an association of elementary teachers that had its roots in a pension protection group formed in the 1890s. Young's popularity with teachers and the teachers' federation, as well as her relative distance from the grubby city politics surrounding the schools, probably enhanced her candidacy. After her selection, she enjoyed a successful first year which culminated in being chosen as the first woman president of the NEA. In that capacity, she helped extricate the NEA from the clutches of an old guard that was trying to prevent the modernization of the association.[59]

Young served in the superintendency until the end of 1915. Her early years were quite successful, but in 1913 she attempted to resign because of political changes in the board. Her situation had been complicated by a dispute she engaged in with the Chicago Teachers' Federation over alternative methods of funding teachers pensions. Her resignation was not accepted by the board of education, which succumbed to political pressure on Young's behalf from the mayor's office. Still, Young's relations with the board were damaged and her last two years in office were marred by several acrimonious exchanges with board members. Finally, in 1915, faced with a new mayor and an increasingly fractious board, she again resigned from the superintendency, and this time her resignation was accepted.

Young's Progressivism

Ella Flagg Young's views were in direct opposition to those of the administrative progressives. The most important commitment she had was to foster collegial teacher–administrator relations. While she was a school principal, she had founded a club for her teachers where they could come for discussions of school affairs. This club soon became a movement, and Ella Flagg Young clubs flourished in most elementary schools of the city. Later, as an assistant superintendent, she founded a teachers' council in her district, a body that was to advise her in her administration of the schools. She had a long, cordial relationship with the Chicago Teachers Federation, the association founded to link the elementary teachers throughout the city with each other. Although the relationship with the CTF cracked a bit in the later years of her superintendency, the crack was superficial. Teachers remained committed backers of Young to the end of her superintendency.

Young's pedagogical views included support for object teaching, manual training, and other new subjects. A conscientious student of John Dewey and a collaborator with him in a variety of pedagogical experiments, she was clearly aligned with his real-life curriculum and inquiry-based teaching methods. It is her views about sharing authority with teachers, however, that most distinguish her from the administrative progressives and their budding authoritarian bureaucracies.

Conclusion

Both John Dewey and Ella Flagg Young failed to achieve victories in the battles they fought. Public education emerged from the progressive era more influenced by the organizational reforms of centralization and curricular differentiation than by the pedagogical alterations sought by Dewey or the empowerment of teachers sought by Young. To put it more succinctly, the pedagogical progressives lost out to the administrative progressives. Although pedagogical progressives made significant headway in experimental and laboratory schools and had a substantial influence over many teacher training institutions, they had little success in dislodging the traditional teacher-dominated, subject-centered curriculum that characterized most public and many private school classrooms.

These classrooms and the teachers who worked in them were now part of a streamlined, bureaucratic school system. Administrators were firmly in control of their teachers and deferential to their boards. A modernized educational apparatus had been firmly installed in the nation's urban schools.

Further Reading

Adams, David. *Education for Extinction: American Indians and the Boarding School Experience, 1875–1928.* Lawrence, KS: University Press of Kansas, 1995. A careful, comprehensive account of the ill treatment of American Indians in the off-reservation boarding schools sponsored by the federal government.

Blount, Jackie M. *Destined to Rule the Schools: Women and the Superintendency, 1973–1995.* Albany, NY: State University of New York Press, 1998. An explication of how and why women fared moderately well in the superintendency at times in the twentieth century although they have been excluded from that office during most of that century.

Kliebard, Herbert M. *The Struggle for the American Curriculum, 1893–1958.* Boston: Routledge & Kegan Paul, 1986. Examines what actually went on in schools, thus refuting both traditional and revisionist interpretations.

Macleod, David I. *Building Character in the American Boy: The Boy Scouts, YMCA, and Their Forerunners, 1870–1920.* Madison: University of Wisconsin Press, 1983. Macleod presents the history of boys' organizations to indicate their role in building character and in providing outlets for youthful interests in nature, camping, and personal achievement.

Miller, Susan A. *Growing Girls: The Natural Origins of Girls' Organizations in America.* New Brunswick, NJ: Rutgers University Press, 2007. Miller reveals the ideals and the realities of girls discovering camplife, naturecraft, and home life via volunteer organizations.

Murphy, Marjorie. *Blackboard Unions: The AFT & the NEA, 1900–1980.* Ithaca, NY: Cornell University Press, 1990. The story of the birth and development of the American Federation of Teachers, the countermovements in the National Education Association undertaken in response to the AFT, and some notable local and state organizations affiliated with the national groups.

Perlmann, Joel. *Ethnic Differences: Schooling and Social Structure among the Irish, Italians, Jews, and Blacks in an American City, 1880–1935.* New York: Cambridge University Press, 1988. A detailed analysis of the factors underlying the uneven success rates of different ethnic groups in the schools of Providence, Rhode Island.

Peterson, Paul E. *The Politics of School Reform, 1870–1940.* Chicago: University of Chicago Press, 1985. Peterson examined archival data in Atlanta, Chicago, and San Francisco to challenge standard revisionist accounts of the forces and ideologies that shaped urban public schools.

Reese, William J. *Power and the Promise of School Reform: Grass-Roots Movements during the Progressive Era.* Boston: Routledge & Kegan Paul, 1986. An argument that various lay groups, parents, club women, trade unionists, and so on were ardent advocates of democratic school reform in the early twentieth century.

Rousmaniere, Kate. *Citizen Teacher: The Life and Leadership of Margaret Haley.* Albany, NY: State University of New York, 2005. Focuses on Haley's political vision, role as a public school activist, and her life as a charismatic leader.

Ryan, Alan. *John Dewey and the High Tide of American Democracy.* New York: W. W. Norton & Company, 1995. A recapitulation of the politics and the social commitments animating Dewey's thought as well as the liberalism he and others espoused that captivated a large segment of the American intelligentsia through much of the twentieth century.

Smuts, Alice Boardman, et al. *Science in the Service of Children, 1893–1935.* New Haven: Yale University Press, 2006. Beginning with G. Stanley Hall and the Child Study Movement, the author presents the growth of science in education and social reform.

Townley, Alvin. *Legacy of Honor: The Values and Influence of America's Eagle Scouts.* New York: St. Martin's Press, 2007. A brief history of the Boy Scouts with special focus on modern-day leaders who attained the rank of Eagle Scout.

Urban, Wayne J. *Why Teachers Organized.* Detroit: Wayne State University Press, 1982. An account of the rise of teacher unionism at the local and national levels in the first two decades of the twentieth century.

Notes

1. Theodore Roosevelt, *The New Nationalism,* intro. by William E. Leuchtenburg. Englewood Cliffs, NJ: Prentice-Hall, [1913], 1961. The Sherman Antitrust Act enabled the government to regulate trusts in order to stimulate an open market economy. The Hepburn Act empowered the federal government, through the Interstate Commerce Commission, to regulate railroad fares if they were shown to be unreasonable.

2. Arthur S. Link, *Woodrow Wilson: A Brief Biography*. Cleveland, OH: World Publishing, 1961; H. W. Brands, *Woodrow Wilson, 1913–1923*. New York: Henry Holt & Co., 2003.
3. Daniel Nelson, *Managers and Workers: Origins of the New Factory System in the United States, 1880–1920*. Madison, WI: University of Wisconsin Press, 1975; Daniel Nelson, *Unemployment Insurance: The American Experience, 1915–1935*. Madison, WI: University of Wisconsin Press, 1969. On child labor laws, see the discussion in Chapter 6.
4. On the initiative and similar reforms, see Lloyd Sponholtz, "The Initiative and Referendum: Direct Democracy in Perspective, 1898–1920," *American Studies*, vol. 14, 1973, pp. 43–64.
5. Aileen Kraditor, *The Ideas of the Woman Suffrage Movement, 1890–1920*. New York: Columbia University Press, 1965.
6. Sarah Simms Edge, *Joel Hurt and the Development of Atlanta*. Atlanta: Atlanta Historical Society, 1957.
7. On the city commission and city managers, see Bradley R. Rice, *Progressive Cities: The Commission Government Movement in America, 1901–1920*. Austin: University of Texas Press, 1977.
8. On Jane Addams and Hull House, see Allen F. Davis, *American Heroine: The Life and Legend of Jane Addams*. New York: Oxford University Press, 1973; and Davis, *Spearheads for Reform: The Social Settlements and the Progressive Movement, 1890–1914*. New York: Oxford University Press, 1967; Dennis Fradin, *Jane Addams: Champion of Democracy*. New York: Clarion, 2006.
9. On the use of the term "progressive," see Daniel T. Rogers, "In Search of Progressivism," *Reviews in American History*, vol. 10, 1982, p. 127, n. 1.
10. Robert L. Church and Michael W. Sedlak, *Education in the United States: An Interpretive History*. New York: Free Press, 1976, pp. 251–259.
11. Lawrence A. Cremin, *The Transformation of the School: Progressivism in American Education, 1876–1957*. New York: Random House, 1961, pp. 226–228; x. Although this is a diverse and impressive list, it nevertheless ignores some relevant educational developments such as the rise of teacher unions. Several of Cremin's particulars, including the junior high, the extra-curriculum, and the project method, occurred in the post-World War I period. They will be dealt with in the next chapter.
12. Michael B. Katz, *Class, Bureaucracy, and Schools: The Illusion of Educational Change in America*. New York: Praeger, 1975, p. 114.
13. David B. Tyack, *The One Best System: A History of American Urban Education*. Cambridge, MA: Harvard University Press, 1974.
14. Jeffrey Mirel, "Progressive School Reform in Comparative Perspective," in David N. Plank and Rick Ginsberg (eds.), *Southern Cities, Southern Schools: Public Education in the Urban South*. New York: Greenwood Press, 1990; Mirel, *The Rise and Fall of an Urban School System: Detroit, 1907–81*. Ann Arbor, MI: University of Michigan Press, 1993.
15. Although the examples cited in this discussion will come from city settings, it should be remembered that a similar phenomenon, known usually as school consolidation, took place in rural areas, mostly in the years after 1920.
16. On centralization in New York, Chicago, and two other cities, see Tyack, *One Best System*.
17. *School* [Magazine], vol. 27, February 1896.
18. Scott Nearing, "Who's Who in Our Boards of Education," *School and Society*, vol. 5, January 20, 1917, pp. 89–90. George S. Counts, *The Social Composition of Boards of Education*. New York: Arno Press, [1929], 1969.
19. Raymond E. Callahan, *Education and the Cult of Efficiency*. Chicago: University of Chicago Press, 1962.
20. Wayne J. Urban, *Why Teachers Organized*. Detroit: Wayne State University Press, 1982.
21. Ibid., pp. 28–32. For an analysis of teacher association cooperation with parents in this period, see Marjorie Murphy, *Blackboard Unions: The AFT & the NEA, 1900–1980*. Ithaca, NY: Cornell University Press, 1990.
22. For a political analysis of school reform, see Paul E. Peterson, *The Politics of School Reform, 1870–1940*. Chicago: University of Chicago Press, 1985.
23. The standard source on the high school in this period, which contains a long account of the deliberations and report of the Committee of Ten, is Edward R. Krug, *The Shaping of the American High School, 1890–1920*. New York: Harper & Row, 1964. See also Herbert M. Kliebard, *The Struggle for the American Curriculum, 1893–1958*. Boston: Routledge & Kegan Paul, 1986.
24. Krug, pp. 61–62.
25. On Woodward and manual training, see Chapter 6. Wayne J. Urban, "Educational Reform in

a New South City: Atlanta, 1870–1925," in Ronald R. Goodenow and Arthur O. White (eds.), *Education and the Rise of the New South*. Boston: G. K. Hall, 1981.

26. On the Cooley plan and the opposition to it, see Julia Wrigley, *Class Politics and Public Schools: Chicago, 1900–1950*. New Brunswick, NJ: Rutgers University Press, 1982.

27. The best recent treatment on vocational education in this era is Harvey Kantor, *Learning to Earn: School, Work, and Vocational Reform in California, 1880–1930*. Madison: University of Wisconsin Press, 1988.

28. Ivar Berg, *Education and Jobs: The Great Training Robbery*. New York: Praeger, 1970. For a penetrating analysis of the negative legacy of curricular differentiation, see David L. Angus and Jeffrey E. Mirel, *The Failed Promise of the American High School, 1890–1995*. New York: Teachers College, Columbia University, 1999.

29. See Diane Ravitch, *The Great School Wars: A History of the New York City Schools*. New York: Basic Books, 1974, pp. 173 passim.

30. Thomas C. Hunt, "Catholic Schools: Yesterday, Today, and Tomorrow," in *Journal of Research on Christian Education*, vol. 14, Fall 2005, p. 164.

31. Ellwood P. Cubberley, *Public Education in the United States*. Boston: Houghton Mifflin, 1919, p. 338.

32. David K. Cohen, "Immigrants and the Schools," *Review of Educational Research*, vol. 40, 1970, pp. 13–27.

33. Michael R. Olneck and Marvin Lazerson, "The School Achievement of Immigrant Children, 1900–1930," *History of Education Quarterly*, vol. 14, 1974, pp. 453–482.

34. Joel Perlmann, *Ethnic Differences: Schooling and Social Structure among the Irish, Italians, Jews, & Blacks in an American City, 1880–1935*. New York: Cambridge University Press, 1988. The term "native" whites refers to those who were the children of earlier, northern immigrants and Western European whites.

35. Perlmann, p. 219; see also Reed Ueda, *Avenues to Adulthood: The Origins of the High School and Social Mobility in an American Suburb*. New York: Cambridge University Press, 1987.

36. Quoted in David Wallace Adams, *Education for Extinction: American Indians and the Boarding School Experience, 1876–1928*. Lawrence, KS: University Press of Kansas, 1995, p. 307.

37. Ibid., p. 308.

38. Ibid., pp. 309–310. For a penetrating critique of the rise of scientific theories of racial differences in intelligence, see Stephen Jay Gould, *The Mismeasure of Man*, rev. ed., Norton, New York, 1996; and Steven Selden, *Inheriting Shame: The Story of Eugenics and Racism in America*. New York: Teachers College, Columbia University, 1999.

39. Adams, pp. 311–313.

40. Adams, pp. 310–315. See Hall's autobiography: G. Stanley Hall, *Life and Confessions of a Psychologist*. New York: D. Appleton, 1924; Charles E. Strickland and Charles Burgess, eds., *Health, Growth and G. Stanley Hall on Natural Education*. New York: Teachers College Press, 1965; and Dorothy Ross, *G. Stanley Hall: The Psychologist as Prophet*. Chicago: University of Chicago Press, 1972.

41. Adams, pp. 328–333; Institute for Government Research, *The Problem of Indian Administration*. Baltimore: Johns Hopkins University Press, 1928; Margaret Szasz, *Education and the American Indian: The Road to Self-Determination, 1928–1973*. Albuquerque, NM: University of New Mexico Press, 1974, pp. 16–24.

42. Anthony M. Platt, *The Child Savers: The Invention of Delinquency*. Chicago: University of Chicago, 2nd ed., 1977; Judith Sealander, *The Failed Century of the Child: Governing America's Young in the Twentieth Century*. Cambridge: University of Cambridge Press, 2003.

43. David I. Macleod, *Building Character in the American Boy: The Boy Scouts, YMCA, and Their Forerunners, 1870–1920*. Madison, WI: University of Wisconsin Press, 1983, pp. 130–132.

44. As quoted in Alvin Townley, *Legacy of Honor: The Values and Influence of America's Eagle Scouts*. New York: St. Martin's Press, 2007, p. 7.

45. As quoted in ibid., p. 51.

46. See Susan A. Miller, *Growing Girls: The Natural Origins of Girls' Organizations in America*. New Brunswick, NJ: Rutgers University Press, 2007, p. 4 ff.

47. George Dykhuizen, *The Life and Mind of John Dewey*. Carbondale, IL: Southern Illinois University Press, 1973.

48. For a complete account of Dewey and his experimental school at Chicago, see Katherine Camp Mayhew and Anna Edwards, *The Dewey School*. New York: Appleton-Century, 1936. See also Laurel N. Tanner, *Dewey's Laboratory School*. New York: Teachers College Press, 1997. On Dewey's educational thought and practice at Chicago, see Arthur Wirth, *John*

Dewey as Educator: His Design for Work in Education, 1894–1904. New York: John Wiley, 1965.

49. John Dewey, *The School and Society.* Chicago: University of Chicago Press, [1899], 1915.
50. John Dewey, *Democracy and Education.* New York: Macmillan, 1916.
51. Dewey, *Democracy and Education*, p. 87.
52. John Dewey, *Experience and Education.* New York: Collier Books, [1938] 1963.
53. Clarence Karier, "Liberalism and the Quest for Orderly Change," *History of Education Quarterly*, vol. 12, 1972, pp. 57–80.
54. Ibid.
55. Bourne's essays and Dewey's reply can be found in *The New Republic* issues of July through September of 1917.
56. *History of Education Quarterly*, vol. 15, Spring 1975.
57. Robert Westbrook, *John Dewey and American Democracy.* Ithaca, NY: Cornell University Press, 1991.
58. Joan K. Smith, *Ella Flagg Young: Portrait of a Leader.* Ames, IA: Educational Studies Press, 1979.
59. On the Chicago Teachers' Federation and the NEA in this period, see Urban, *Why Teachers Organized.*

8
Completing the Modern School System
American Education, 1915–1929

Overview

World War I caused considerable confusion and conflict in the United States, both before the nation's entry into the conflict in 1917 and after the war's end in 1918. When the assassination of a minor European noble in 1914 plunged that continent's nations into conflict, American reaction was initially mild. Even as the hostilities began spreading across Europe, Americans still preferred to see them as a quarrel involving far-off groups with little connection to U.S. domestic welfare. Despite proclamations of neutrality, America's Anglo-Saxon heritage tilted the nation substantially toward the Allies, the group in which Great Britain was a major force, and against the opposing group, the Central Powers, which was dominated by Germany. Nevertheless, in the 1916 presidential election, both parties pledged to keep the nation out of the foreign war.

After that election, however, America began openly to favor the British and their allies. German U-boat atrocities such as the sinking of the trans-Atlantic cruise ship, the *Lusitania*, increased American allegiance to the Allies. When U-boat activities intensified and Germany essentially declared naval war on any ships off the coast of Great Britain, the United States reacted by joining the conflict on the side of the Allies.

Fortunately, by the time American troops entered combat, the European countries were largely exhausted from the war effort. Thus, American participation lasted for little more than one year. This meant minimum American casualties, at least when compared to those of the other combatants, but maximum American celebration in the Allied victory.

The United States also played an important role in the peace process following the war. President Woodrow Wilson carried his optimistic progressivism into the foreign policy arena, strongly advocating creation of the League of Nations to monitor world affairs and prevent conditions that might lead to another great war. However, many powerful congressmen saw the league as a dangerous vehicle through which America would be drawn into the quarrels of distant nations. After a long, exhausting battle, Wilson eventually lost out to his opponents, and American participation in the League was rejected by the Senate.

Domestic Effects of the War

Preparation for war and its actual conduct caused substantial changes in American society. Among these was increased involvement in the economy by the federal government. The war effort necessitated greater cooperation between business and government, with organized labor also participating as a minor partner. During this period, government economic policy shifted in the direction of stimulating business rather than regulating it. The federal government acted to ensure profits for business, which in turn pledged to help conduct the war effort as vigorously as possible. Government did manage to persuade business to grant a number of improvements for workers, such as an eight-hour day and collective bargaining rights for industrial workers. The net result of these policies was a substantial increase in union membership during the war.

Wartime conditions also motivated the government to initiate a deliberate push for unity among America's rather disparate populations. A national information agency was created and began cranking out large doses of propaganda in support of the war effort. Congress passed laws intended to curb sedition and sabotage. Eventually, opposition to the war was made a crime and resulted in jailing some noted labor leaders and socialists. Unlike their European brethren, American socialists did not let their nation's entry into the war silence their opposition to it. Eugene Debs, a pacifist, socialist, and labor leader, was jailed for his opposition to the war, although he never condoned the actions of Germany or its allies.

After American entry into the war, popular passions against war opponents rose and the government watched passively as mobs took various actions against dissidents. Immigrants, whose loyalty had often been an issue, now became the targets of loyalist citizens' groups of various kinds. Americans of German birth or heritage were particularly subject to reprisals, and Irish Americans, because of their homeland's long-standing antipathy to the British, were another target.

Postwar Conditions

In the aftermath of the war, the searching out and punishment of various dissident groups increased. Communist Russia, which had been allied with Britain and America during the war, became a target for Americans concerned about dangerous foreign ideas. When Russian leaders declared the birth of an international communist movement in 1919, American anticommunism intensified to a fever pitch.

Communism was suspected as the major force in various labor strikes of the postwar era. When Boston's policemen went on strike in 1919, many believed that the same sinister force that had infected Russia was now invading the most hallowed institutions of the United States. Other strikes were punctuated by violence, particularly in the West, where the radical Industrial Workers of the

World were often involved. A rash of bombings also occurred, one of which damaged the home of A. Mitchell Palmer, the attorney general of the United States. Palmer responded by orchestrating a series of raids on suspected subversives across the country that resulted in the arrest of more than 5,000 people. State and local governments and citizens' groups responded as vigorously and violently as had the attorney general. The climate of crisis created by this "red scare" eventually subsided, but the residual fear of foreigners and un-American doctrines and beliefs lasted through most of the 1920s.

Racial unrest also marked the postwar years. African Americans who fought in the war returned to a society that continued to discriminate against them in myriad ways. They responded with some militance and a sprinkling of violence. The reaction was swift. Lynchings in the South increased substantially, and whites in northern cities, which had received large numbers of black migrants during the war, responded in ways not unlike their southern cousins.

Labor and racial unrest following the war was caused, in part, by an unstable economy that featured dramatic inflation followed by a sharp downturn. Economic unease invaded the middle classes and provoked a suspicion of those who were worse off, especially striking workers and increasingly militant blacks. Ironically, those in the business community who had benefited from the war and were profiting from the less regulated economy were spared both criticism and blame.

Exhausted and fearful, Americans approached the election of 1920 desperately in need of reassurance about themselves and their country. Republican presidential candidate Warren G. Harding capitalized on the situation and reassured the nation of a "return to normalcy" if he were elected. Harding's election in 1920 ended the eight-year presidency of Woodrow Wilson, a progressive Democrat. The Republicans controlled the White House for the next twelve years, effectively ending the reformist thrust of the progressives. Harding and his successor, Calvin Coolidge, who as governor of Massachusetts had cracked down on Boston's police strikers in 1919, embarked on a new direction in American political life. They cut back on government regulation in many quarters while supporting the development of business through corporate tax reductions and the formation of business associations. Fears of collusion or monopoly were conspicuously absent from the concerns of government during these years.

The result was a period of high tide for big business and a prosperity that intermittently reached down and touched individuals in the middle and lower-middle classes. Mass production of consumer goods, such as the automobile, meant expansion of supporting industries such as steel, glass, and oil. An increase in suburban housing and road building also came with the automobile age. Technological advances facilitated the rapid and profitable extraction of oil, coal, and other natural resources from the earth. In short, the economy was soon booming, and more Americans were participating in the boom.

The labor movement, however, did not benefit from the changing economic conditions. American business embarked on an anti-union crusade in the early 1920s, advocating the "open shop" as opposed to the "un-American" union shop. The "American plan" of industrial relations sought to replace independent unions with a variety of company benefit plans that would make unions unnecessary. In some cases, employers developed their own "company unions" to compete with the independent labor organizations that sought to represent their workers.

Government during this period was a firm ally of employers, acting in a variety of ways to make sure that strikes would be unsuccessful. The courts, the Justice Department, and various other federal administrative agencies put obstacles in the way of striking workers and their leaders.

Labor was unprepared to deal with the changed economy. The American Federation of Labor (AFL) was a coalition of craft unions that looked backward to the pre-factory days when skilled craftsmen dominated production. In an economy that was increasingly keyed to mass industries, the AFL looked askance at the unskilled laborers who formed the bulk of industrial employees. AFL leaders feared communism among rank-and-file workers as much as, or more than, government or employers. Thus, while industrial workers enjoyed minimal participation in the boom of the 1920s, the labor movement went backward, losing almost a million members during the decade.

Society and Culture in the 1920s

Warren Harding's 1920 promise of a "return to normalcy" bore fruit in several aspects of American life. The advent of the automobile and other mass consumer goods brought the advertising industry into prominence in American life. The new products were invested with images of glamor and prestige, and the public responded with substantial increases in the number of goods purchased.

Developments in the communications industries allowed advertisers to reach the American public as never before. Newspapers became less localized as they joined various national chains, and magazines also began to reach untapped national audiences. Radio came upon the scene in 1920, and by the end of the decade, national networks were reaching more than 10 million families. National media networks encouraged a culture of fads that ranged from goldfish swallowing to ballroom dancing. The new media also popularized professional sports to an unprecedented degree.

Changes in the family also occurred in the 1920s. Industry and technology produced a variety of home appliances that combined to lessen the household burden of American women. This resulted in more women entering the workforce, particularly in traditional women's occupations such as teaching, nursing, and social work, and in enterprises that catered to women such as fashion and cosmetics. Traditional middle-class women used their new-found free time to play new roles in their husbands' and children's lives. Birth control emerged as another national movement, freeing women in still another way from traditional obligations. This liberation of women, most evident in the "flappers" who smoked, drank, and partied, resulted from the social and cultural changes affecting women and women's roles.

The social and cultural developments sparked by advertising and mass communications simultaneously expanded America's cultural horizons and limited perceptions of diversity in society. This, in turn, brought a variety of negative reactions from some segments of the population. Intellectuals and writers grew increasingly disenchanted with the materialism of American culture and produced a variety of works criticizing the society. Many writers eventually left the country for Europe, members of a "lost generation" in search of traditional intellect and high culture. Old-line progressive intellectuals also weighed in with their own negative evaluations of modern culture and society. And southern writers became increasingly disenchanted with industrial America, producing their own defense of agrarianism in the 1928 volume, *I'll Take My Stand*.[1]

It was not just intellectuals who were disenchanted with America in the 1920s. Defenders of the older, more sedate culture of previous generations fought for prohibition laws that made the manufacture and sale of alcohol illegal for more than a decade. Even though it resulted in a rise in organized crime, prohibition was a symbol of Anglo-Saxon dismay at social and cultural license.

This same Anglo-Saxon discontent was also directed at the new wave of immigrants that had flowed into America at the turn of the century. It produced immigration restriction laws in 1921 and again in 1924. The earlier legislation limited the number of immigrants from each country to a small percentage of its current American population. The latter law tied the number of immigrants from each country to a percentage of their number in 1890, before most southern and eastern Europeans had arrived in this country. This, of course, drastically reduced the flow of these groups.

The fear and intolerance that had fed America's "red scare" was also behind the growth spurt enjoyed by the Ku Klux Klan in the 1920s. Traditional southern, antiblack sentiment spread northward as blacks migrated to northern cities in the postwar era. Klan membership also grew as a result of adding Catholics and Jews to its roster of un-American groups that needed to be purged in the interests of national health. In the state of Oregon, the Klan helped pass a law that mandated attendance in public schools only, a direct slap at the Catholics in the state. The Supreme Court invalidated the law in the famous *Pierce* decision, but the court could not diminish the Klan's influence in Oregon, or elsewhere.[2]

Adding to the turbulence of the era, a wave of Protestant fundamentalism swept rural America, registering shock and dismay at the intrusions of science into the world of faith. The trial of John T. Scopes, a substitute science teacher in Dayton, Tennessee, for teaching evolution instead of creationism was the most noted result of the fundamentalist revival.

Thus, in the midst of economic growth, technological development, and social progress, angry voices of critique and reaction were being raised. Although these voices were forceful, they were unable to detour the nation's business-led drive toward material progress. The role of schools both during the war and in the postwar economic boom constitutes the focus of the rest of this chapter.

Schools During and After the War

As might be expected, America's war effort had substantial effects on its schools. Whereas the German language had been taught together with English in many cities with sizable German populations, the coming of World War I put an end to the study of the German language in most public and private schools. Similarly, school administrators and teachers with obviously German names became suspect, and school curricula were often examined for pro-German tendencies.

The schools themselves became quite active in support of the war. Groups such as the Student Army Training Corps brought military training to college campuses, and spin-offs began appearing in high schools. As the nation's schools mobilized to support the war effort, loyalty oaths were often imposed on staffs. Dissidents, such as three high school teachers in New York City who had the temerity to question American participation in the war, were hounded by patriotic groups, often to the point that they lost their positions.[3]

Intelligence Testing

One wartime development that directly influenced school policy in the postwar years was intelligence testing. Although mental testing had been present in the progressive era, its founder, the Frenchman Alfred Binet, was concerned primarily with testing individuals. During World War I, however, the army accepted the offer of the American Psychological Association to develop group intelligence tests. Initially, the tests were used to identify candidates for officers' training school, but they were later used for other tasks such as the screening of recruits who would have difficulty with the mental demands of military service.[4]

The success of the Army "Alpha" and "Beta" tests led their supporters to look for other applications in the postwar years. One of the most obvious markets was America's rapidly growing public school system, which was experiencing a measurement movement in educational research. School systems soon began developing elaborate bureaus of educational research whose major function was to purchase and administer the standardized tests that were believed to measure the educational potential and achievement of students.

Testing quickly grew popular in the public schools, but it provoked a sharp critical reaction. *The New Republic*, a journal of progressive liberal opinion, carried a series of articles by the noted journalist, Walter Lippman, that carefully scrutinized intelligence tests. Lippman acknowledged the utility of intelligence tests for the purpose of analyzing individuals but raised serious question about using them to classify people into groups. His criticisms were elaborated upon by John Dewey, who warned of the threat to democracy from the indiscriminate labeling of people on the basis of intelligence test scores.[5]

The most elaborate criticism of the tests came from an educational traditionalist, William C. Bagley. A Columbia Teachers College professor who was not part of its famous progressive group, Bagley wrote a volume titled *Determinism in Education* in which he attacked the intelligence test as unduly restrictive of educational opportunity. For Bagley, the tests were appropriate for diagnosing the readiness level of individual children but were inappropriate when used to restrict the educational services offered to any child.[6]

Black scholars and intellectuals also weighed in with criticisms of intelligence tests. Responding to racist use of test results to label blacks and recent immigrants as genetically inferior, black scholars demonstrably linked test results to cultural and environmental factors. Some blacks also noted the ironic aspect of some test scores. Horace Mann Bond, for example, showed that the scores of many white southerners were lower than those of black northerners. Despite these criticisms, a romance began in the postwar years between intelligence testers and American educators intent on restricting the educational opportunity of "unqualified" students, almost always members of racial or ethnic minorities or the working classes.[7]

Thus, the testing critics were unable to halt the reliance on tests by school administrators. The tests were an integral part of the change process called "modernization" that was sweeping America's schools. At the forefront of this modernization movement was the centerpiece of the new school system, the comprehensive high school.

The Fully Modernized School System

Chapters 6 and 7 describe how America's common schools gradually evolved into large, hierarchical school systems in the second half of the nineteenth century and the first decade and a half of the twentieth century. This evolution into a completely modernized school system culminated with a move to create a comprehensive high school.

The Cardinal Principles and the Comprehensive High School

As noted in the last chapter, the thrust toward separate commercial and vocational high schools was curbed, though not stopped completely, with the defeat of the Cooley plan in the city of Chicago. After that defeat the battle for vocational and commercial education shifted from separate high schools to a new institution, the comprehensive high school, which would accommodate multiple curricula (academic, commercial, and vocational) within the same school building. Comprehensive high schools allowed educators to maintain allegiance to the principle of common schooling while simultaneously permitting the separation that was thought necessary for learning commercial and vocational skills. However, the common aspect of the comprehensive high school was clearly overshadowed by the new commitment to curricular differentiation.

The comprehensive high school was championed in a report from the NEA in 1918. This report, the *Cardinal Principles of Secondary Education*, was developed under the leadership of Clarence Kingsley, a teacher in a New York City manual training high school. The principal objectives of a high school education, according to the *Cardinal Principles*, were health, command of fundamental processes, worthy home membership, vocation, citizenship, worthy use of leisure, and ethical character.[8]

The philosophy that underlay the cardinal principles was what Edward Krug has called "social efficiency." This philosophy saw the high school's role as preparing its students for their adult lives. Such preparation involved identifying the strengths and weaknesses of students and then fitting the students into appropriate social and vocational roles. For social efficiency educators, the multitrack comprehensive high school was an appropriate arena in which to implement their social engineering principles. Thus, social efficiency was the rationale that administrative progressives used to revamp and broaden the high school curriculum, just as they used business efficiency and the corporate model to justify their changes in school governance and administration.

Extracurricular Programs

Social efficiency educators aimed at more than curriculum revision. They also sought to provide students, parents, and community members with a variety of extracurricular activities aimed at increasing both the survival skills and the social cohesion of America's increasingly diverse population. Once again, the central setting for this expansion was the comprehensive high school.

The social efficiency reformers were sensitive to the social class separation that accompanied a differentiated curriculum, and they sought to compensate for this threat to social cohesion through a variety of extracurricular activities such as athletics, newspapers, and school clubs of various kinds. All these activities provided places for students from the various curricular tracks to interact with each other under the supervision of school personnel. Cooperation with a variety of other students in the pursuit of a common interest was the goal of these activities. Teaching students the importance of cooperation also served the needs of industrial society, which increasingly sought to link diverse workers together in cooperative enterprises.[9]

Student government was another vehicle through which cooperation was encouraged. In addition, it served as a way to develop democratic habits, skills, and responsibilities in a carefully controlled environment. Students could be kept from the political excesses that sometimes characterized real-life democracy.

Still another extracurricular activity that developed social unity and cooperation among high school students was the assembly. Programs of various kinds—concerts, talks, exhibits, drama, music, and patriotic exercises—were developed for school assemblies. Together with newly created "homerooms," they provided antidotes to the differentiated curricula of the comprehensive high school.

School playgrounds were initially developed in elementary and high schools to serve the needs of youngsters for physical activity during the school day. Supervision of school personnel ensured that students would engage in a wholesome range of activities free from the negative physical and social effects of unsupervised play. Playground programming was rather quickly extended to after-school hours and to school vacation periods and, in some instances, to adults in the school communities.

To summarize, the new comprehensive high school, with its differentiated curricula and its many extracurricular activities, represented a horizontal extension of school programs and influences. In effect, administrative progressives were turning their schools into efficient but inequitable arbiters of American economic and social opportunity. That the opportunity they dispensed was too often based on racial, social class, or other nonacademic criteria was not obvious to those who ran the modern school system. This, of course, was due largely to their own class and ethnic backgrounds, which were predominantly Anglo-Saxon, rural or small town, and middle class.

The American Educational Ladder

The creation of the comprehensive high school in the early part of the twentieth century completed the development of an educational ladder that served pupils from their early childhood years through graduate and professional school. All children entered school at the lowest rung of the ladder, but only a few climbed all the way to the top. At each successive rung on the ladder, some students left school and entered the world of work. While most students entered high school, substantial numbers left school for work during the high school years, and even more entered the work world after completion of high school. Even though college enrollments were relatively small and graduate school enrollments even smaller, the numbers of students emerging from those rungs of the ladder were sufficient to fill the ranks of the growing professions, including the academic profession. The emergence of each of these rungs on the educational ladder was discussed in Chapter 6, but a quick review might be helpful:

The Kindergarten

Begun in a variety of settings for a variety of purposes in the late nineteenth century, the kindergarten became a well-established bridge between family life and elementary school. In most large cities, public kindergartens were a fixture. In southern cities, small towns, rural areas, and other places where there were no public kindergartens, private institutions filled the gap for parents who aspired to the "best" for their children.

The Elementary School

The graded elementary school was also a fixture in all but the most rural settings. A lock-step progression through the grades was now the norm for most children, and those students who did not follow the progression were deemed a problem. The problem of out-of-step children was addressed in a volume by the director of the Russell Sage Foundation, *Laggards in our Schools*. The principal explanations for these laggards were twofold: deficiencies in the children's backgrounds and a lack of testing to assess exactly how students were performing. The proposed solution was to expand the testing program in education at all levels of the ladder. This "solution" was ineffective in that there is evidence that the elementary schools lowered their standards in the 1920s in order to make sure that most students passed each grade level.[10]

The High School

Following the graded elementary school came the new, comprehensive high school, which directed its students either into higher education or into the workplace. In addition, it aimed to serve as an agency of social cohesion for both its students and the surrounding adult community.

The College

Next came the network of private and public colleges that flourished as utilitarian training grounds for the middle and upper-middle classes. Undergraduate students were exceptionally important to American colleges and universities because they helped maintain a close relationship between these institutions and the rest of society.

The Graduate and Professional School

In the largest universities, graduate and professional schools were busy translating the latest scientific advances into technology that would support America's new industries. In addition, the graduate schools were supplying administrators for the upper ranks of the public school systems and professors for the undergraduate colleges.

Summary

On all levels of the educational ladder, the needs of the other levels were considered. Relationships between elementary and secondary schools were formal, while links between elementary schools and kindergartens, particularly if the kindergartens were private, were less formal. Although relationships between high schools and colleges were not highly formalized, no high school could long ignore the wants and needs of higher education without endangering the acceptability of its students. Thus the various rungs of the educational ladder provided a relatively smooth progression from one level to the next, a progression that was guided by an increasingly developed testing system.

New Rungs on the Educational Ladder

Two new rungs were added to the educational ladder in the post-World War I period. Their names, the junior high school and the junior college, indicate their primary relationship to the high school and the college.

The Junior High School

The junior high school began in the largest cities in the early twentieth century and became a fixture in most of the nation's school systems during the 1920s. It was established for two reasons. First, its services were targeted to the special developmental needs of early adolescence. Second, it helped to prepare students for the new curricular requirements they would encounter in the comprehensive high school. Although the first purpose was most often voiced by proponents, it was the second purpose that guaranteed the junior high its proper place on the educational ladder.

The curriculum of the junior high school introduced students to the subjects and teaching approaches most of them would face in the comprehensive high school. Although vocational studies were not usually offered, prevocational subjects such as manual training acquainted students with what was to follow. In addition, the junior high began to differentiate students in terms of their backgrounds and presumed futures. This, of course, facilitated their later placement in one of the tracks of the comprehensive high school. Finally, the junior high began to sort boys and girls into certain curriculum areas, such as home economics, that corresponded to their later adult lives.[11]

As its name implies, the junior high was closer in structure and purpose to the differentiated high school than it was to the common elementary school. It moved the high school's commitment to sorting and tracking students downward into two of the previous elementary grades. As with all levels of the educational ladder, this sorting reflected social class differences despite the fact that it was accomplished through the development of supposedly objective tests. These tests, produced by trained experts, were interpreted for students and parents by the burgeoning ranks of vocational guidance counselors who were fixtures in the new institution.

The Junior/Community College

The second new rung on the postwar educational ladder was the junior college. The junior college was inaugurated at the University of Chicago during the presidency of William Rainey Harper. With John D. Rockefeller's money, Harper was transforming a small Baptist College into a powerful university. Harper was concerned about what he perceived as the declining standards and misdirection of "general education," that is, the first two "preparatory" years of college before students should narrow their focus and became more serious as they pursued their "major" field of study. Harper wanted to push the general education phase of education downward into the secondary level of education and elevate the upper two years into "senior college" or university status. His concern was more about protecting the upper levels of education from the distractions and lack of seriousness of the first two years of college than it was to open access to a broader population of college goers. In fact, Harper foresaw the day when small colleges would disappear "in fact if not in name" and would become high schools or else absorbed into large universities.[12]

In the junior college at Chicago, subjects that extended traditional high school studies were at the center of the curriculum, while new elective courses introduced students to the higher studies that they would encounter after the junior college if they continued on with their academic pursuits. Early junior college advocates believed that the Chicago innovation could be used as an entering wedge in an effort to upgrade the high school by adding to it two additional grades of college-preparatory study.

During the 1920s, however, the junior college developed in a quite different direction. It did not become the capstone of the high school nor the junior part of the university. It became instead an institution separated from specific colleges and universities rather than a part of them. The separate junior colleges, in addition to their curriculum of two years of preparatory studies, began serving a variety of remedial functions for underprepared students. For some students, they functioned as a way station where the less mature could grow socially and emotionally while trying to improve their study habits. For others, the junior college was a retreat where those who had previously had difficulty with collegiate studies could regroup themselves for a second try. For some then, obtaining an Associate in Arts degree represented the end of the line academically; for others, it signaled a new beginning.[13]

Later in the twentieth century, the junior college evolved into a public community college, where a variety of vocational and life-related studies accompanied the traditional college-preparatory curriculum. In many states, proximity to students' homes and low tuition made community colleges the only form of postsecondary education available to low-income families. By the end of the twentieth century, community colleges could lay claim to the largest share of the college-going population, a solid indication of how important this rung on the educational ladder had become.

Administrators, Teachers, and Teacher Unions

As seen in Chapter 7, administrative progressives built complex hierarchies to administer elementary and secondary education in the nation's large urban school systems. This, of course, increased the distance between teachers and the top administrators of the school system who controlled the conditions of their work. In order to defend their occupational traditions and their salaries, teachers began to organize themselves into teacher associations. In a sense, teachers were defending themselves against the bureaucratic regimentation of the recently reorganized urban schools.

Generally, early teacher associations were local bodies that did not affiliate with labor organizations or with the NEA. The various labor groups, which were composed of skilled craftsmen, seemed alien to most women teachers. One exception to this generalization was the Chicago Teachers Federation (CTF), which was affiliated with the central labor federation in the city of Chicago. As for the NEA, it was a men's club run by an old guard that looked to the past and ignored women teachers. While it did appoint a committee on teachers' salaries in 1905, that group received little support for its activities and recommendations. The appointment of a second committee on salaries in 1912 was testimony to the ineffectiveness of the first effort. The election of Ella Flagg Young to the NEA presidency in 1910 marked the beginning of the end of the old-guard management of the NEA. It would be another decade, however, before the association attempted a formal reorganization to reflect the new realities within the educational profession.[14]

The American Federation of Teachers

In April 1916, as America was on the verge of entering World War I, a group of local teacher associations in and around Chicago, which included the CTF, joined together to form the American Federation of Teachers (AFT). The AFT quickly gained a charter from the American Federation of Labor, and a few other large-city local groups joined, including the high school teachers' union in New York City. With the addition of the New Yorkers, the AFT gained a journal, the *American Teacher*, and some valuable national visibility.

Using its journal and embarking on a national organizing campaign, the AFT experienced substantial growth during its first five years of existence. Wartime conditions were good for labor, both politically and economically. The national government needed labor's participation in the war effort and, consequently, was in no position to contest labor's organizing efforts. As a result, the AFT was able to expand to approximately one hundred locals by 1920.

Beginning in that year, however, the AFT began to suffer serious membership losses, due mostly to the changed economic and political conditions. The "red scare" years proved to be a bad time for all of organized labor, including teachers' unions. In addition, the AFT did not help itself when its job-oriented Chicago leadership was replaced by ideologically minded New Yorkers who spoke the language of socialism. The New Yorkers were not as adept at organizing as their predecessors. Also, their strange ideas and diverse backgrounds —many of them were Jewish—distanced the AFT from less cosmopolitan teachers in other areas of the country. The net result was that AFT membership, which had grown steadily until 1920, declined just as steadily throughout the 1920s.[15]

The National Education Association

The other national organization seeking the allegiance of teachers in this period, the NEA, had just the opposite experience. In 1917, just as America was entering World War I, the NEA moved its headquarters from the Midwest to Washington, D.C., and hired its first full-time executive secretary. This signaled a changing of the guard in the NEA's very top circles. The old guard was replaced by a group of professional educators, many of whom came from the administrative ranks of state normal schools. In a sense, the new NEA leadership was the equivalent of the administrative progressives who were revamping big-city schools.[16]

Casting aside its past history as a sort of national debating society on educational issues, the goal of the new NEA leadership was to become a powerful national lobby for education. This, of course, required the national visibility that came with a Washington, D.C., headquarters. The NEA believed that national prominence would come if it pushed successfully for the establishment of a department of education at the federal level. Making education a department would give the Secretary of Education full cabinet status and make that individual one of the leaders in the federal government.

The NEA found a way to pursue its own agenda in tandem with the war effort. It created a Commission on the National Emergency which instituted and publicized war work in the public schools. The commission also made sure to pursue the NEA goals of federal aid to education and a federal department of education. It added professional staff to pursue this program and to entice teachers into becoming members. Its relationship with the AFT at this time was basically cooperative, with both organizations pursuing establishment of a federal department of education. In fact, the AFT sometimes met at NEA conventions to refine its own agenda and attempt to enhance cooperation between the two groups. Thus, the NEA did not offer itself initially as an alternative to the teachers' union.

The postwar change in political climate provided both a barrier for AFT organizing activities and an opportunity for the NEA. As the "red scare" developed, the NEA's cooperation with the American Legion in a program to improve civic education in the schools, along with the clear dominance of the NEA by school administrators, insulated it from the anti-union sentiment that was hampering the more labor-oriented and ideological AFT.

Slow to take advantage of its new situation, the NEA gradually moved in the direction of teacher interests. In search of increased membership, the NEA tried to change its national convention from a town-meeting format, in which all members who attended had a vote, to a representative assembly, in which voting delegates to the national convention would be chosen by constituent local and state associations. Advocates of the change believed that it would facilitate the modernization of the association and allow it to accommodate a much larger membership and remain efficient.

Vocal teachers, however, felt differently. Under the old organizational format any member who attended an NEA convention could vote, so teachers from the convention city repeatedly turned out in mass and voted to block the proposed organizational change. Teacher activists believed that they would have less of a voice in the new delegate-controlled convention than they had under the old town-meeting format. The NEA finally steered the change through in 1920 when the association met in the state of Utah, where less independent teachers failed to organize opposition to the change.

The NEA moved quickly to conciliate teachers after the change in governance was finally approved. It hired a professionally active teachers' association leader from Denver to become a staff member at NEA headquarters. Her duties included pursuit of federal aid to education and the organization of teacher-oriented NEA groups in local school districts. In 1924, the NEA established a Department of Elementary Education as a part of its larger organizational structure. The department served both as a forum for teachers' concerns and as a career ladder within the NEA for ambitious teachers.

The overall effectiveness of the NEA's policies was mixed. Despite its avid pursuit of federal aid and a federal department of education, neither of these goals was achieved. On another front, however, the NEA managed to eclipse the AFT as an organization representing teachers. An indication of the NEA's success in this regard comes from its membership figures. In 1917, at the beginning of its organizational alteration, the NEA had 8,000 members. By 1920 it had 50,000, and by 1930 its membership exceeded 200,000.[17]

Internally, the NEA's teacher membership, which was largely female, was firmly controlled by the male administrators who held the top NEA offices and thereby managed the agenda and the actions of the national meeting. Thus, women teachers in the 1920s faced the same patriarchy in their own occupational association that they faced in their school systems.

Teacher Participation

As part of its 1920s program to conciliate and incorporate teachers within its modernized organizational format, the NEA advocated a movement for "teacher participation" in school affairs. This movement eventually gained the support of many school administrators who acknowledged that educational decisions were too important to exclude the practical wisdom of classroom teachers.

The vehicle chosen to institutionalize teacher participation in school districts was the Teachers' Council. Created by Ella Flagg Young while she was Chicago superintendent, the councils had languished under Young's successors. They were revived in the 1920s, however, and became the bodies through which teachers could provide advice to school administrators. Although their organization and agenda varied from one school district to another, their purposes were substantially similar. Councils were usually found at every level of school administration and gave advice to principals, district superintendents, and superintendents.

There were distinct limits to the amount and kind of teacher participation enjoyed by Teachers' Councils, however. The groups met only on the call of the school administrator they were supposed to advise and considered only those matters that administrators put before them. Finally, their recommendations were simply that—recommendations—that administrators could do with as they wished.

Thus, the teacher participation movement provided a facade of teacher involvement in school governance that seldom achieved substantial results. When councils threatened to behave in independent ways, as they tried to do in the city of Chicago in 1928, the superintendent simply abolished them. He refused to hear teacher objections to what they considered his arbitrary administrative style and his wrongheaded educational innovations.[18]

In fact, the councils strongly resembled the company unions that many employers formed in the 1920s as an alternative to independent unions. True autonomy and legitimate representation of teacher interests were problematic just as they were within the administrator-dominated NEA. Still, the NEA's creation of the Department of Elementary Education and district administrators' institutionalization of a teachers' voice through councils were effective enough to incorporate teachers into national and local educational bureaucracies.

Teacher recognition, though clearly limited, was enhanced by administrators' efforts to increase teachers' salaries throughout the 1920s. The NEA publicized the actual salaries earned by teachers throughout the nation, and this publicity was used by superintendents in poorer-paid districts to gain parity for their teachers. Other NEA activities such as the publication of a journal were also geared to gaining teacher allegiance. These efforts, combined with the decline of the AFT in the 1920s, resulted in the formation of the NEA into an organization that represented some of the interests of classroom teachers, though none which conflicted with those of school administrators.

Progressive Education after the War

One of the clear outcomes of American participation in World War I was a halt in the development of America's progressive reform movement. The war decisively shifted attention away from the domestic causes favored by reformers to matters connected to the prosecution of the war. In short, the war effort and the rise in patriotism that accompanied it left little room for those who questioned American political and social priorities.

The postwar "red scare" intensified the public devotion to America and Americanism and made the task of would-be reformers even more difficult. The progressives did not simply disappear, however; in fact, the Progressive political party unsuccessfully ran a candidate for president in the election of 1924. Progressive politicians continued to be visible in the Congress and in some state governments during the 1920s. These politicians had to contend with the relatively good times of the 1920s, however, and they proved to be no match for their opponents, who preached the gospel of less government and celebrated the accomplishments of big business.

The decline of social and political progressivism spilled over into the world of education. Although this did not mean the end of all pedagogical reforms, it did mean a retreat from those educational ideas, policies, and practices that were intertwined with the larger progressive reform movement. The educational progressivism that survived into the 1920s was the conservative brand of administrative progressivism that built the modern school system. Pedagogical progressivism, at least the versions such as Dewey's or Young's that shared much of their agenda with liberal progressivism, receded in influence.

Although pedagogical progressivism did not disappear completely, the versions that developed during the 1920s did not seek to link school experience with social and political life, as Dewey had sought to do. Dewey's own focus on educational affairs declined when he left Chicago and moved to Columbia's philosophy department, which did not house either psychology or pedagogy. As Dewey's contact with the schools and educational issues lessened, the leadership of progressive forces in education fell to his colleagues in education at Columbia's Teachers College.

Teachers College and Progressivism

Founded late in the nineteenth century as a free-standing school, Teachers College became a part of Columbia University near the turn of the century. Under the leadership of George Strayer and other apostles of administrative progressivism, it soon evolved into the leading graduate school of education in the nation. Although Teachers College could point to Dewey's presence in Columbia's philosophy department as one indication of its reform leadership, its links with the public schools came mostly from Strayer and his colleagues in the training program for school administrators.

In the 1920s, however, it did develop some of its own leaders in the area of pedagogical reform. Foremost among these was William Heard Kilpatrick, a Georgian who came to it after a brief career in the schools and colleges of his home state.

Project Method

Kilpatrick was best known as the developer of the project method of teaching. He first developed this innovation in an essay written as the war was ending and then elaborated on it in a book published in 1925. In these works Kilpatrick developed a child-centered pedagogical theory built on school activities that were both meaningful for children and relevant to the society in which they lived. Kilpatrick's method lacked two things that Dewey's reforms had featured. First, attempts to link school activities to social improvement in the outside world, and second, recognition of the importance of learning traditional subject matter.[19]

Kilpatrick's project method followed a four-step procedure: proposing, planning, executing, and judging. These processes were quickly standardized by others into a formula that, in hands less talented than Kilpatrick's, became an oversimplified recipe for pedagogical reform. Eventually the recipe became an end in itself rather than a pedagogical tool for enhancing student learning. In short, child-centeredness had become a goal rather than a starting point.

Other Progressive Educators

Other educational reformers in the 1920s who claimed to be working in the pedagogical progressive tradition encouraged child-centered activity that was explicitly devoid of social content as well as ignorant of traditional subject matter. One of these educators was Caroline Pratt, who developed a play-oriented curriculum at a private school she founded in the Greenwich Village section of New York City. Although Pratt sought a working-class clientele, she found that her approach was much more attractive to artists and intellectuals. These groups were alienated from the business values that dominated in this era and wanted their children to be liberated from conventional educational boundaries.

Another child-centered progressive was Margaret Naumberg, whose version of progressive education relied on Freudian psychology for its intellectual foundations. Naumberg ran an experimental school in New York's affluent Upper West Side. Working from Freudian notions such as sublimation, transference, identification, and fixation, Naumberg saw Dewey's emphasis on group activity as stifling the development of individual potential. She believed that engaging in creative activities in various artistic fields was the best way for children to realize the kind of self-development that was necessary in the postwar world.[20]

The pedagogies of Pratt and Naumberg were based on "the notion that each individual has uniquely creative potentialities and that a school in which children are encouraged to develop these potentialities is the best guarantee of a larger society truly devoted to human worth and excellence." Their schools, and a few others based on this ideal, were confined largely to a clientele derived from the upper class. If and when this approach was used in non-elite schools, it usually meant a ritualized education that ignored anything other than its pedagogical formulas. The net result of these movements was an abandonment of any meaningful link between pedagogical progressivism and the social and political world that surrounded the schools in the 1920s. Pedagogical reformers in that decade thus narrowed their vision to a school-centered universe.[21]

The Progressive Education Association

The Progressive Education Association (PEA) was founded in 1919 and quickly emerged as the major institutional voice for child-centered pedagogy. The

PEA became increasingly important as an organizational umbrella for various child-centered and project-oriented innovations throughout the 1920s. It started a journal, *Progressive Education*, which publicized various pedagogical experiments that were taking place in America and abroad.[22]

Although the specific ideas of the PEA are difficult to characterize, one thing is clear: The organization never provided a platform for ideas or policies that combined pedagogical change with social criticism. Instead, the PEA concentrated on the advocacy of child-centeredness, creativity, and freedom. Its leaders were most often associated with private schools, as were most of the pedagogical methods it promoted.

One thing the PEA did accomplish was to link these private school leaders with university developers of project-oriented curricula, particularly those curricula featured in college and university laboratory schools. Consequently, lab schools became the educational greenhouses in which pedagogical experiments took place. However, these lab schools were just as isolated as the private progressive schools from the social world and from the problems that were becoming increasingly prominent in the public schools in the 1920s.

The pedagogical emphasis that took hold in the public schools was a scientism that dovetailed nicely with the administrative progressivism that had become increasingly dominant in public school administration. The educational scientists of the 1920s stressed the development of tests and measurements that enhanced the expanding bureaucratic apparatus and contributed to further differentiation of the curriculum. In no way did this scientific approach pay attention to the surrounding social and political environment that inevitably influenced what went on in schools. Thus, the scientists, like the pedagogical progressives, concentrated solely on the school's internal affairs.

When John Dewey accepted the honorary presidency of the PEA in 1928, he made a speech in which he was critical of both pedagogical scientists and educational reformers for abandoning the social role of the school. For a brief time, it appeared that Dewey's words might bear some fruit within the PEA. Within a year of his speech, the group's stated principles added a concern for social development. After another year, however, that change was abandoned.

Progressive Education and African Americans

There is one final development that needs to be discussed before closing this account of progressive education in the 1920s, namely the relationship of progressivism to racial minorities, particularly to the nation's black population. To cover this topic fully, background events dating back to the 1890s need to be considered. These events illustrate that, despite their social and political interests, even liberal progressive reformers like Dewey were basically silent on the issue of race. This silence was even more emphatic in the progressive pedagogical reformers of the 1920s, who ignored all issues except educational innovation.

The South

One explanation for this silence is that the African American population was concentrated largely in the South before World War I and, consequently, was not directly visible to northern reformers like Dewey. The southern version of progressive social and political reform was much less liberal than progressivism in the rest of the nation and, more important, was utterly uninterested in rectifying the plight of southern black citizens. In fact, C. Vann Woodward's standard history of the South in the late nineteenth and early twentieth centuries titles its chapter on southern reform "Progressivism—For Whites Only." In this chapter, the author reports that the agenda of southern political progressives was more antiblack than the program of southern conservatives. The reason for this was the progressives' use of racism as a vehicle to win white citizens' allegiance away from the conservatives and toward the reforms that they championed. Southern progressives believed that supporting blacks was a recipe for failure. In fact, it was southern progressive governors and legislatures who often carried out the task of disfranchising black voters. Likewise, they vigorously supported the Jim Crow system of racial segregation that was sanctioned by the Supreme Court in the 1896 *Plessy v. Ferguson* decision.[23]

The negative social and educational consequences of this situation are well known to scholars. They have pointed out that the schools for southern blacks that survived into the twentieth century were rigorously segregated and woefully underfunded. Often, money that belonged to black schools was diverted by school boards to white schools. Blacks were forced to get by with the leftovers.[24]

These discriminatory actions were fought vigorously, though not always successfully, by southern black citizens. For example, in 1880, black citizens in Augusta, Georgia, under the leadership of the famous educator Richard Wright, managed to get Ware High School established as the public high school for blacks. Almost immediately, however, the white-dominated school board initiated a series of ongoing attempts to close the high school. In 1897, after the *Plessy* decision and after the issue of black disfranchisement became a significant factor in white political platforms, Ware High School was finally closed. Blacks took the issue to the Supreme Court but were rebuffed by that body in the *Cumming et al. v. Board of Education of Richmond County* case. Ignoring the racism behind the decision to close Ware, the court said that it could see no discrimination. Further, it added that education was a matter for states to manage, not the federal courts. Despite the board's contention that the closing of Ware was "temporary," and reversible when black enrollment and the system's finances improved, Ware remained closed for almost forty years.[25]

In Atlanta in the post-Civil War era, black citizens showed amazing resourcefulness as they sought to establish a high school for their children. Unlike Augusta, Atlanta's blacks had never enjoyed the benefits of a public high school. Their disfranchisement, however, was not complete. Although barred from primary elections, which in the one-party Democratic South was politic-ally devastating, they did retain the vote in general and special elections. Since school funding was usually determined through special elections, Atlanta's black citizens used this as their vehicle for pursuing a public high school.

In the years following World War I, blacks mobilized in special elections to defeat school funding measures desired by the board and by white parents. In order to gain the black votes needed for passage of the funding, the board of education agreed to establish a black public high school. The name of that school, Booker T. Washington, was significant. The board wanted and suc-ceeded in installing a mainly industrial curriculum at Washington, despite pressure from black citizens for a broader, more diversified course of studies. The Augusta and Atlanta examples show how public secondary education for blacks in the progressive-era South was almost completely absent and, in the 1920s, present in only a few cities in a severely limited version.

Blacks were not completely deprived of high school studies, however. Many of the private black colleges established after Reconstruction had preparatory departments where black youngsters could get the essentials of a secondary education. Even here, however, there was a constant battle to preserve aca-demic studies against the wishes of northern philanthropists who wanted to see Washington's industrial education installed in both the college and the preparatory curriculums.[26]

White-dominated school boards in the South did not prevent elementary schooling for black children. However, the public elementary schooling that was provided was meagerly financed and usually took place in facilities that were substandard by any definition. Thus, schooling for blacks in the progressive-era South was a largely dismal exercise at every level. The bright light in the situation, if there was one, was provided by the burning desire of many black parents, teachers, and children to get as much education as they could. Throughout the South, poor black parents supplemented the meager public resources available to them, and black teachers labored heroically under dismal conditions.

The North

World War I proved to be a watershed for African Americans. During and after that war, the "great migration" of the nation's black population began. Large numbers of blacks moved from the rural, agricultural areas of the South to southern cities and, in even larger numbers, to northern industrial cities such as New York, Chicago, Detroit, and Philadelphia. As blacks moved into north-ern cities, they were generally able to find work, although not in the skilled and high-wage jobs that they sought.

Although migrating blacks encountered somewhat improved educational conditions in their new urban homes, this improvement still left them far short of equality with white students. In Philadelphia, for example, the northern city with the largest black population at the turn of the twentieth century, schooling for black children was not as severely segregated as it was in the South. Some black children in Philadelphia went to school with white children, although they were often segregated into racially distinct classes as a result of ability grouping or intelligence testing.[27]

Conditions for black students in Philadelphia and other northern cities deteriorated during the 1920s, as growing black populations were crowded into ghetto areas that could not be escaped. These large concentrations of blacks enabled northern school boards to use a neighborhood school concept to segregate black children almost as effectively as laws segregated them in the South. School officials were generous in allowing whites to transfer out of their attendance area to escape going to school with blacks but very reluctant to grant black youngsters the same privilege. One historian has provided a detailed description of this development in the city of Chicago in the 1920s and 1930s in a book aptly titled *Down from Equality*.[28]

Events similar to those in Chicago were occurring in many other northern cities. The net result was that black education in most northern cities deteriorated to the point that it was often only slightly better than the situation that existed in the South. Also, as in the South, blacks had to fight attempts to confine their children to industrial education programs that offered virtually no academic study. Placement in these industrial programs was often justified by resorting to standardized intelligence tests, administered and interpreted by white guidance counselors who never questioned the appropriateness of the tests or the confines that they placed on black children.[29]

As segregation increased in the North, some black citizens fought it while others maneuvered politically, like their southern brethren, to obtain better facilities and equipment. Black teachers in both the North and the South had a particular reason to fight for all-black schools. Since in all southern and most northern schools blacks were not allowed to teach in racially mixed classes or in white classes, supporting segregated schools was a way to keep their jobs. This is not to say that black teachers were selfishly motivated, however. Many of them labored heroically under enormous handicaps to provide their students with the best education they could offer. In the poisoned atmosphere of twentieth-century American education, however, they could teach only if the schools remained segregated.

Finally, certain segments of the black community looked on segregated education as an opportunity to build up their communities. All-black schools could and often did become a focus for development of community pride and mutual benefit among black citizens. In many cases, black schools also functioned as social service institutions as well as educational ones. Conversely, blacks often resorted to other agencies, such as churches and fraternal organizations, to provide educational programs that could not be undertaken in their woefully underfunded and poorly constructed and maintained public schools.

The Modern School at High Tide

African Americans were well aware of the deficiencies in the education provided for their children in the 1920s. These deficiencies, which remained largely unaddressed for the new quarter-century, cast a shadow over the accomplishment of America's schools. Even with that shadow, however, one is still left with a 1920s legacy of a modernized public school system that could enumerate many accomplishments. Those accomplishments were most visible in the nation's largest cities.

Detroit, Michigan

In his recent history of the public schools in Detroit, Michigan, Jeffrey Mirel titled his chapter on the 1920s, "One of the Finest School Systems in the World." In that chapter, Mirel argues that there was a fundamental consensus among various political and economic interest groups in the city that allowed the schools to develop and prosper throughout the decade. Mirel does not deny that there were debates over particular proposals, as there almost always are in public school systems, but he argues that the consensus that underlay educational politics in this decade prevented those debates from developing divisions among the citizenry that hampered the progress of the public schools.[30]

In Detroit, as in most places in this decade, the schools succeeded in large part because they had strong leadership. In Detroit, one superintendent, Frank Cody, served in that office from 1919 to 1942. Cody did not fit the profile of the typical administrative progressive. He had only a master's degree, and it was from a state normal school rather than from one of the prestigious graduate schools of education. Yet he proved capable of developing in his schools the full range of administrative progressive policies and, furthermore, of heading off opposition to the school program that plagued many other systems.

In addition to having an effective leader, consensus on school issues in Detroit came from the support given the schools by the city's major interest groups. Organized labor, particularly important in Detroit, was a confirmed supporter of public education and a vocal advocate for school improvements. Although labor influence declined nationally in the 1920s, it declined to a lesser extent in Detroit. Labor's support of public education allowed it to ally with powerful business and lay groups and, thus, to maintain a positive image in the minds of the city's citizens.

An early test of labor's commitment to the public schools came in 1920, when a small group of male high school teachers and another of female high school teachers formed local affiliates of the AFT. Negative response came swiftly from the local press, members of the school board, and the administrator-dominated teachers' association. The superintendent informed the union teachers that if they remained union members, they would not receive a contract for the next school year. This threat was enough to cause both groups to give up their union charters. Instead, many of the teachers formed an unaffiliated teachers' council, a group to which the superintendent voiced no objection. The labor movement in the city, evidently understanding its limitations, chose not to contest the breaking of the teachers' unions. Instead, labor maintained its historical commitment to the principles of public education throughout the decade.

Another large interest group that upheld Detroit's consensus on public education during the 1920s was business. Through business associations such as the Board of Commerce, Detroit's business leadership made its commitment to public schools clearly and consistently evident throughout the decade.

Women activists were another vocal interest group concerned with school affairs. While they were most often allied with the business leadership that was made up largely of their spouses or other male relatives, they joined forces with labor and official school leaders in pursuit of public school improvement.

Oftentimes, the coalition in Detroit illustrated how different groups can advocate an educational policy for their own interest. Child labor laws presented an obvious example of this phenomenon. Labor wanted children kept in school, since their presence in the workforce threatened wage levels; women wanted children to be children and not to have the responsibilities or to be exposed to the vices of adulthood; and business thought the schools would provide workers who were better trained and socialized than those who had not been schooled.

In addition to pursuing education-related policies such as child labor provisions, the Detroit coalition obtained tangible improvements for their schools. Early in the decade, for example, teachers' salaries were increased substantially, at the suggestion of the school superintendent and without vocal objection from business groups. Similarly, the school board, after formal consideration of the issue, approved the continued employment of married women teachers. This was a move that might have caused controversy in other places that had narrow and moralistic views about teacher qualifications. These salary and hiring provisions ensured that Detroit would have a steady supply of qualified teachers throughout the decade.

The school budget was another area in which the Detroit coalition was successful. Inflation-adjusted per-pupil expenditure increased about 50 percent during the 1920s, despite a dramatic increase in the school population. To construct the new buildings needed for the expanding enrollment, both tax increases and the sale of municipal bonds were approved by the city's political leaders. While some political opposition to building expenditures did surface, it was not from the leaders of any of the organized interests in the city, and it did not succeed in turning public opinion against the schools.

In the area of elementary curriculum, Detroit school leaders successfully introduced a reorganization plan that had provoked substantial controversy in other cities. The Gary plan was named for the Indiana city in which it had first been implemented. The plan, which platooned two groups of students from each grade in the elementary school, was implemented in Detroit's schools with little opposition. In this plan, half the students were engaged in normal classroom instruction for half of the day and in various activity programs such as recess, crafts, and performance groups for the other half.

The Gary plan, supported by both administrative progressives and pedagogical reformers, had provoked substantial opposition from organized labor and tradition-oriented citizens in New York City. In Detroit, however, the superintendent carefully studied the New York situation and engaged in an effective public relations campaign prior to implementation. Labor in Detroit, used to supporting the public schools, was convinced that platoon school activities such as manual labor shops taught the dignity of work. Thus, labor did not succumb to the arguments of working-class leaders in New York or Gary that the platoon system represented an assault on working-class children that turned their schools into factories.

Along with the platoon school, the Detroit schools adopted other administrative progressive innovations such as intelligence testing and curricular tracking in the high school. Here again, class-oriented opposition to a multiple-track comprehensive high school program (vocational, commercial, general, and academic) was deflected by successfully associating tracking with democracy. The nonacademic tracks were perceived as democratic, since they made the school responsive to the interests of a far wider range of students. Offering only an academic curriculum in the high school meant that only a few students would attend. Offering four different tracks appealed to many more students and honored the work of their parents. This combination of financial support, a well-paid teaching force, and a curriculum that featured most of the favored innovations of administrative progressives guaranteed that Detroit's schools would become one of the leading systems in the nation.

While much of this and the two previous chapters have been critical of the administrative progressive program, the acceptance of that program by the Detroit coalition testifies to its appeal and to the success of the school leaders in selling the program. Whether the citizens' belief that their modernized public schools would broaden economic and social opportunity was true is open to question. What seems certain, however, is the very real commitment that both citizens and teachers had to the program.

Conclusion

The success of the Detroit schools during the 1920s was not duplicated everywhere in the nation. Few rural schools enjoyed the broadened curriculum and innovative organizational arrangements that occurred in Detroit, nor could they afford the improved teacher salaries and administrative specialists that characterized modern schooling. Less prominent cities, many of which were in the South, also lagged substantially behind Detroit and other northern cities. Nevertheless, nationwide improvements were made in school facilities, in teacher salaries, and in curricular diversification during the 1920s. These improvements resulted in a cadre of confident educational leaders presiding over growing and largely successful school systems. In retrospect, the 1920s may have been the time of the greatest accomplishment of American public education. That accomplishment would be sorely tested by the economic crisis of the next decade.[31]

Further Reading

Angus, David L., and Jeffrey Mirel. *The Failed Promise of the American High School, 1890–1995.* New York: Teachers College Press, 1999. An argument for the early promise of a democratic American high school that offered a rigorous curriculum to all classes and then compromised that commitment by offering different curricula for students from different social classes.

Banner, Lois W. *Women in Modern America* (4th ed.). New York: Wadsworth Publishing Co., 2004. Investigates the ways in which notions of gender difference have changed over time and examines the broad themes that have shaped women's experiences from 1890 to the present.

Franklin, Vincent P. *The Education of Black Philadelphia: The Social and Educational History of a Minority Community, 1900–1950.* Philadelphia: University of Pennsylvania Press, 1979. The relative powerlessness of the black community in obtaining quality education for its youngsters in the period up to 1920 is contrasted with the activism of an empowered black community in the 1930s and after.

Hayes, William. *The Progressive Education Movement: Is it Still a Factor in Today's Schools?* New York: Rowan & Littlefield, 2006. Chronicles the development and spread of progressive education from its beginnings through the last decade of the twentieth century with a final chapter that peers into the future.

Homel, Michael. *Down from Equality: Black Chicagoans and the Public Schools, 1920–1941.* Urbana, IL: University of Illinois Press, 1984. The relatively successful participation of Chicago blacks in the public schools in the 1920s is contrasted with a very different situation in the 1930s.

Krug, Edward A. *The Shaping of the American High School, 1920–1941.* Madison: University of Wisconsin Press, 1972. The second volume of the standard history of the American high school, with special attention paid to the writers on the high school in these years and the audience for their writings.

Leloudis, James. *Schooling the New South: Pedagogy, Self, and Society in North Carolina, 1880–1920.* Chapel Hill: University of North Carolina Press, 1996. A study that shows how, in much of the South, the rural nature of schooling gave way to a more structured, more bureaucratic, and in some ways more effective and in other ways a profoundly ineffective alternative.

Link, William A. *A Hard Country and a Lonely Place: Schooling, Society, and Reform in Rural Virginia.* Chapel Hill: University of North Carolina Press, 1986. An account of the staying power of the localism and suspicion of state authority that characterized Virginia's rural areas in this period and the less-than-successful schooling that the rural localists defended.

Miller, Nathan. *The New World Coming: The 1920s and the Making of Modern America.* New York: Scribners, 2003. This book examines themes that ran through the 20s by presenting key figures and the social, political, and economic events that defined the era.

Mirel, Jeffrey. *The Rise and Fall of an Urban School System: Detroit, 1907–1981.* Ann Arbor: University of Michigan Press, 1993. A chronicle of the great success of the Detroit public schools in the 1920s and the factors that led to the diminution of that success in later decades.

Null, J. Wesley. *A Disciplined Progressive Educator: The Life and Career of William Chandler Bagley.* New York: Peter Lang, 2003. A close look at an educator who was seen as an opponent of progressivism but yet had much in common with his progressive colleagues.

Null, J. Wesley. *Peerless Educator: The Life and Work of Isaac Leon Kandell.* New York: Peter Lang, 2007. A biography of a "democratic traditionalist" at Teachers College, Columbia University, who opposed his colleagues' progressive education ideas.

Semel, Susan and Alan Sadovnik. *Schools of Tomorrow, Schools of Today: What Happened to Progressive Education?* New York: Peter Lang, 1998. Documents some of the child-centered progressive schools founded in the first half of the nineteenth century and their subsequent histories.

Wallace, James M. *Liberal Journalism and American Education.* New Brunswick, NJ: Rutgers University Press, 1991. An account of the educational views of The New Republic and The

Nation, two leading liberal journals of opinion, from the post–World War I era to the onset of World War II.

Zilversmit, Arthur. *Changing Schools: Progressive Education Theory and Practice, 1930–1960.* Chicago: University of Chicago Press, 1993. Through a focus on actual classroom practices in several school systems in the Chicago area, the author examines the degree to which Dewey's ideas had an influence on American education at the local as well as national levels.

Notes

1. Malcolm Cowley, *Exile's Return: A Literary Odyssey of the 1920s.* New York: Viking Press, 1951. Twelve Southerners, *I'll Take My Stand: The South and the Agrarian Tradition.* New York: Harper, 1930.
2. *Pierce v. Society of Sisters of the Holy Name*, 268 U.S. 510 (1925).
3. Philip Taft, *United They Teach: The Story of the United Federation of Teachers.* Los Angeles: Nash Publishing, 1974, pp. 19–21.
4. Joel Spring, "Psychologists and the War: The Meaning of Intelligence in the Army Alpha and Beta Tests," *History of Education Quarterly*, vol. 12, 1972, pp. 3–15; Stephen J. Gould, *The Mismeasure of Man*, New York: Norton, 1996; Steven Selden, *Inheriting Shame: The Story of Eugenics and Racism in America.* New York: Teachers College, Columbia University, 1999.
5. On *The New Republic* in these years, see James M. Wallace, *Liberal Journalism and American Education, 1914–1941.* New Brunswick, NJ: Rutgers University Press, 1991.
6. William C. Bagley, *Determinism in Education.* Baltimore: Warwick & York, 1925.
7. Wayne J. Urban, "The Black Scholar and Intelligence Testing: The Case of Horace Mann Bond," *Journal of the History of the Behavioral Sciences*, vol. 25, 1989, pp. 323–334.
8. National Education Association, Commission on the Reorganization of Secondary Education, *Cardinal Principles of Secondary Education.* Washington, D.C.: Government Printing Office, 1918; Edward R. Krug, *The Shaping of the American High School 1890–1920.* New York: Harper & Row, 1964, pp. 295–296.
9. Krug, pp. 391–393, 443–444.
10. Leonard Ayres, *Laggards in Our Schools.* New York: Charities Publication Committee, 1909; Joseph L. Tropea, "Bureaucratic Order and Special Children: Urban Schools, 1890s–1940s," *History of Education Quarterly*, vol. 27, 1987, pp. 42–43.
11. Edward R. Krug, *The Shaping of the American High School, 1920–1941*, University of Wisconsin Press, Madison, 1972.
12. William Rainey Harper, *The Prospects of the Small College.* Chicago: University of Chicago Press, 1900; Frederick Rudolph, *The American College and University: A History.* Athens, GA: University of Georgia Press, [1962], 1990, p. 443.
13. See Steven Brint and Jerome Karabel, *The Diverted Dream: Community Colleges and the Promise of Educational Opportunity in America.* New York: Oxford University Press, 1989; Jennings L. Wagoner, Jr., "The Search for Mission and Integrity: A Retrospective View," in Donald E. Puyear and George B. Vaughan, eds., *Maintaining Institutional Integrity.* San Francisco: Jossey-Bass, 1985, pp. 1–15.
14. Wayne J. Urban, *Why Teachers Organized.* Detroit: Wayne State University Press, 1982, chap. 2.
15. Ibid., chap. 6.
16. Ibid., chap. 5.
17. Membership figures are in Edgar Wesley, *NEA: The First Hundred Years.* New York: Harper & Brothers, 1957, p. 397.
18. George S. Counts, *School and Society in Chicago.* New York: Harcourt, Brace, 1928.
19. William Heard Kilpatrick, "The Project Method," *Teachers College Record*, vol. 19, 1918, p. 330; and Kilpatrick, *Foundations of Method: Informal Talks on Teaching.* New York: Macmillan, 1925.
20. Both Pratt and Naumberg are profiled in Lawrence A. Cremin, *The Transformation of the School: Progressivism in American Education, 1876–1957.* New York: Random House, 1961.
21. Ibid., p. 202.
22. Patricia Albjerg Graham, *Progressive Education: From Arcady to Academe.* New York: Teachers College Press, New York, 1967.
23. C. Vann Woodward, *Origins of the New South, 1887–1913.* Baton Rouge: Louisiana State University Press, 1951, chap. XIV.
24. Louis Harlan, *Separate and Unequal: Public School Campaigns and Racism in the Southern Seaboard States, 1901–1915.* Chapel Hill: University of North Carolina Press, 1958; and

Horace Mann Bond, *The Education of the Negro in the American Social Order*. Englewood Cliffs, NJ: Prentice-Hall, 1934.

25. Edward J. Cashin, *The Quest: A History of Public Education in the Richmond County Schools*. Columbia, SC: R. L. Bryan, 1985, pp. 35–39.
26. James D. Anderson, *The Education of Blacks in the South 1860–1935*. Chapel Hill: University of North Carolina Press, 1988.
27. Vincent Franklin, *The Education of Black Philadelphia: The Social and Educational History of a Minority Community*. Philadelphia: University of Pennsylvania Press, 1979.
28. Michael Homel, *Down from Equality: Black Chicagoans and the Public Schools, 1920–1941*. Urbana, IL: University of Illinois Press, 1984.
29. Michael Homel, "Two Worlds of Race? Urban Blacks and the Public Schools, North and South," in David Plank and Rick Ginsberg (eds.), *Southern Cities, Southern Schools: Public Education in the Urban South*. New York: Greenwood Press, 1990, pp. 237–261.
30. Jeffrey Mirel, *The Rise and Fall of an Urban School System, Detroit, 1907–1981*. Ann Arbor: University of Michigan Press, 1993.
31. In Atlanta, Georgia, for example, the 1920s is seen as a golden era for public schools that had experienced wrenching political conflict in the 1910s and would suffer a dramatic downturn in the Depression.

9

The Effects of Depression and War on American Education
1930–1946

Overview

The period of the Great Depression and its immediate aftermath, the World War II years, present a special challenge to those who would make sense of its educational developments. In discussing these years, the enormous economic cataclysm that engulfed all of American society, including its schools, is examined first. Next, the massive social dislocations that accompanied the depression, including some substantial changes in the schools, are considered. In spite of these changes, schools during and immediately after the Great Depression resembled their predecessor institutions of the 1920s as much as they differed from them. The deterioration in economic support for the schools that took place during the depression, however, threatened their ability to prosper in the following decades.

School Continuity during the Depression

As the end of the last chapter suggests, American public schools and those who worked in them were remarkably inward-looking during the 1920s. The widespread appearance of prosperity, although an illusion for many, inhibited school people and others from examining the relationships between their institutions and the larger society. Also, as in most other segments of American society, school people hardly noticed the stock market crash of October 1929, since its effects did not immediately reach the schools and those who worked in them. Thus, although historians date the Great Depression to late 1929, financial support for public schools in all but a few cases remained remarkably stable until well into the 1930s.

Political and ideological circumstances, especially at the national level, also delayed any quick responses to the Depression by school boards and school administrators. For example, Herbert Hoover, elected to the presidency in 1928, would stay in office for almost three years following the stock market crash. A businessman and engineering expert, Hoover symbolized the commitment to business efficiency that characterized so many school administrators of that era. Thus, it was unlikely that schoolmen would easily discard their belief in efficiency, even as the Depression deepened and public opinion turned against business. Instead, like the President, school leaders believed that the economic prosperity of the 1920s would soon reappear. Thus, they continued to support the ideology of educational efficiency that had dominated their vision since early in the twentieth century.[1]

The schools' slow reaction to the Depression is also explained by the fact that teachers found their working conditions stable, at least into the early 1930s. The same could be said of most students. Unless their families were victims of the early crisis in banking, most students' school and home lives continued relatively untouched during the first few years of the Depression.

The Depression and the Lower Classes

For students at the lower end of the economic spectrum, the Depression was hard to differentiate from the circumstances they had encountered in the midst of the "prosperous" 1920s. For example, southern and eastern European immigrants and many other members of the working class had shared little, if at all, in the economic benefits of "prosperity." Farmers composed another group that failed to share significantly in the economic rewards of those years. Also, there were regional variations in the picture of economic success, with the largely rural South remaining well behind other regions of the nation. Finally, black southerners in the early twentieth century continued to lag behind white southerners economically as well as to suffer the debilitating effects of political disfranchisement. Although blacks who took part in the great migration from the South to the North fared somewhat better, they also suffered from a variety of discriminations that relegated them to the lower orders of the social structure.

The economic suffering of these groups during the 1920s was also accompanied by a substantial degree of educational deprivation. In a 1922 study of secondary schooling, George Counts found marked disparities in the access of various urban classes to high school. The lower one's social class, the less likely it was that one would attend high school. Similarly, rural Americans had been second-class citizens, both economically and in their access to schooling, long before the Great Depression. Black Americans suffered, both economically and educationally, even more than their white working-class or farm counterparts. High schools were strikingly absent for southern blacks in the 1920s. For example, in 1929, 286 southern counties with substantial black populations failed to provide them with high schools. Though high schools were available to blacks elsewhere in the South (and the North), racial discrimination and economic handicaps continued to hamper attendance rates. Thus, for many Americans, the Great Depression only intensified their previous suffering, while for others it provided a bitter introduction to economic deprivation.[2]

The Personal Experience of the Depression

It is hard to recreate the despair that pervaded the lives of many Americans in the 1930s. Statistics provide a startling, but relatively impersonal, look at the situation. Gross national product declined by almost one-half in the early 1930s, sinking from $103 billion to $56 billion. A similar decline occurred in personal income, and an even larger decline took place in corporate profits and stock prices. The number of bank failures increased astronomically, and the impact of these failures was felt in turn by the affluent leaders of the banking industry, bank employees, and bank depositors.[3]

Statistics alone, however, cannot begin to communicate the levels of shock, pain, and disbelief that scarred the adults and young people who lived in and through the Great Depression. Their trauma was never forgotten, and those of us who have followed must struggle to understand the scars that this calamity left on them.[4]

Oral histories have provided some of the most vivid memories of the depression years. Of these, one compilation stands out—Studs Terkel's volume, *Hard Times*. In its pages, one finds a series of riveting and disturbing accounts of life in the 1930s. Terkel's interviewees relate the personal circumstances and stories of those who were unemployed, those who stood in bread and soup lines, and those who became hobos and rode the rails in search of a job and a meal. These individuals experienced the utter destitution that characterized those years for so many.[5]

Utter destitution, however, was not the only experience of those years. Prosperous and middle-class families also suffered, as the following excerpt from Terkel illustrates:

> I remember all of a sudden we had to move. My father lost his job and we moved into a double-garage. . . . We had a coal stove, and we each had to take turns, the three of us kids, to warm our legs. It was awfully cold when you opened those garage doors. We could sleep with rugs and blankets over the top of us. Dress under the sheets.
>
> In the morning, we'd get out and get some snow and put it on the stove and melt it and wash around our faces. Never the neck or anything. Put on our two pairs of socks on each hand and two pairs of socks on our feet, and long underwear and lace it up with Goodwill shoes. Off we'd walk . . . miles to school.
>
> My father had owned three or four homes. His father left them to him. He lost these one by one. . . .
>
> He always could get something to feed us kids. . . . And he had a part time job in a Chinese restaurant. We lived on those fried noodles. I can't stand 'em today. . . .
>
> 'Cause he got a job in Akron, delivering carry-out food, we moved there. That was a dandy place: dirt, smoke, my mother scrubbing all the time. We lived right on the railroad tracks. . . . When the trains slowed down, he used to jump on and have us kids pick up the coal.[6]

This was the experience of one middle-class family as it confronted the Great

Depression. Far greater humiliations and deprivations were endured by the millions who lived a lower-class existence.

The Dust Bowl

The Great Depression was only one source of unemployment, dislocation, and spreading poverty in the 1930s. Wind storms that blew massive waves of dust across farm lands and into towns and cities were not new to farmers, but the devastation wrought in the 1930s by periods of prolonged drought and followed by dust storms that swept across the Plains states added greatly to the misery of farmers, merchants, and the agricultural suppliers and industries on which each segment of the rural economy depended.

Fourteen dust storms had been recorded in the Plains states in 1932 and thirty-eight more in 1933. By 1934 it was estimated that 100 million acres of topsoil had been carried away by the wind. There had been a series of dust

Figure 9.1 A man at the "Junk Market" on Houston St. in New York City trying to sell some possessions during the Depression. Photograph by Samuel H. Gottscho, March 10, 1933.

Source: Library of Congress, Prints and Photographs Division, LC-G623-19737-H.

storms in the Spring of 1935, but on April 14, 1935,—"Black Sunday"—the worst dust storm of all ripped through the southwestern plains. Tons of topsoil were blown off barren fields and carried in storm clouds for hundreds of miles. Technically, the driest region of the Plains—southeastern Colorado, southwest Kansas and the panhandles of Oklahoma and Texas—became known as the "Dust Bowl" and many dust storms did start there. However, the entire southwestern region, and eventually the entire country, was affected.

Some indication of the fear that gripped those caught up in the face of that catastrophe was captured by an observer who stated: "The impact is like a shovelful of fine sand flung against the face. People caught in their own yards grope for the doorstep. Cars come to a standstill, for no light in the world can penetrate that swirling murk. . . . We live with the dust, eat it, sleep with it, watch it strip us of possessions and the hope of possessions. . . ." Farmers told of trucks being blown down the road and chickens going to roost at midday because the sky was so dark, while their wives fought a hopeless battle with dust filtering in through every crack in their homes.[7]

John Steinbeck in his powerful 1939 novel, *The Grapes of Wrath*, captured the plight and flight of more than 500,000 people who left their homesteads and traveled west in hopes of getting a new lease on life:

> And then the dispossessed were drawn west—from Kansas, Oklahoma, Texas, New Mexico; from Nevada and Arkansas families, tribes, dusted out, tractored out. Car-loads, caravans, homeless and hungry; twenty thousand and fifty thousand and a hundred thousand and two hundred thousand. They streamed over the mountains, hungry and restless— restless as ants, scurrying to find work to do—to lift, to push, to pull, to pick, to cut—anything, any burden to bear, for food. The kids are hungry. . . .[8]

Depression, drought, dust, and then invasions of grasshoppers that ravaged whatever plants might peek above the thin soil—these were the forces driving homeless migrants westward. In their path and already at work in California fields were new tractors owned by large landowners that were pushing tenants off the land even there. Hard-scrabble camps—"Hoovervilles" they were called—sprang up on the outskirts of towns all along Route 66, the main road traveled to reach the Golden State. The "Okies" were not welcomed along the way or into the green fields of California. They were for the most part old stock Americans, not foreigners, Americans who hoped to find a better home but instead found only hatred. Going to school was not even an option for many children of depression and dust. The 1930s stood in dark contrast to the glitter and glamor that *some* thought was their due in the 1920s.[9]

The Great Depression and School Finance

As mentioned earlier, the consequences of the Great Depression were slow to be felt in the public schools, particularly in the urban public schools. For example,

Figure 9.2 A 32-year-old mother of seven living in a tent during the Dust Bowl migration. Photograph by Dorothea Lange.

Credit: Library of Congress, Prints & Photographs Division, FSA/OWI Collection, LC-DIG-fsa-8b29516.

city school systems actually had slightly larger budgets in the 1931–32 school year than they had in 1930–31. By 1932–33, however, the situation was becoming critical, with several large cities on the verge of bankruptcy. In the Depression's initial stages, city school systems responded with a variety of cost-cutting strategies such as increasing class size and closing small schools. Business "efficiency," a watchword in schools since the early twentieth century, was now emphasized even more. Detailed budgeting was seen as a way to stretch the dollars spent on public education. Inevitably, teachers' salaries, which comprised approximately 75 percent of most school budgets, became a target of budget cutters, and teacher layoffs and salary cuts became commonplace.

Additionally, many urban school districts launched campaigns to cut the "fads and frills" from school programs. This usually began with the elimination of nonregular schools and programs such as night schools, summer schools, kindergartens, and playgrounds, and then spread to non-academic subjects such as music, art, physical education, and industrial education, as well as to programs for the physically and mentally handicapped.

The Chicago Example

Perhaps the most notorious example of depression-era cutbacks in urban public schools occurred in the city of Chicago. The Chicago situation was dangerous even before the onslaught of the Great Depression, with school and other tax revenues being gutted in the 1920s by poor collection procedures and skimming on the part of corrupt politicians. The arrival of the Great Depression exacerbated the situation and led to a full-blown crisis. In April 1931, the school board claimed that it no longer had the funds to pay its teachers and, in the next two years, Chicago teachers were paid for only four of their nine months of work. To make matters worse, their payment was not by check but, instead, by a warrant that was redeemable for less than its face value. All this took place in the midst of a taxpayers' "strike" led by real estate interests but supported by many of the city's small property owners. Action by the city's mayor resulted in a symbolic victory for the teachers and the schools when he discharged from the city payroll a lawyer whose firm had represented the taxpayers' association. The mayor also intervened to prevent teachers from being arrested for not paying taxes on their vehicles, and arranged in March 1932 to have them paid the wages they had earned in December 1931.[10]

In 1933, the board of education announced that it would reduce expenses as its contribution to solving the schools' financial problems. This reduction resulted in the following actions: abolishing all junior high schools, closing the city's junior college, cutting the number of kindergartens by one-half, reducing the number of physical education teachers, abolishing all coaching positions, reducing the numbers of music teachers and supervisors, making elementary principals responsible for two schools, eliminating manual arts and household arts from the elementary schools, suspending all textbook purchases, closing all school swimming pools, and abolishing the position of dean in the high schools.

The response to these massive cuts was a protest rally attended by 25,000 Chicagoans. However, the rally failed to get the attention of the board members and, subsequently, many citizens sought court injunctions to stop the cuts. These injunctions, however, were not granted and the cuts were implemented. The result was that 300 kindergarten teachers, 455 junior high teachers, and more than 600 elementary teachers lost their jobs in September 1933. The remaining teachers found their class sizes and course loads increased substantially.

Although the mayor was unable to help the teachers who had been laid off, he was successful in obtaining a loan from the federal government to pay the remaining teachers a portion of the salaries they were owed. The situation then stabilized, though at a level of service far beneath what had been offered previously. Further stability came later in the decade as the state government moved to increase its contribution to school funding and, thus, decrease school dependence on local property taxes. This was particularly important since property values, both in Chicago and in the rest of Illinois, had decreased by over a third from 1927–35.

The Chicago situation resulted in an upsurge of union sentiment on the part of the teachers. While Chicago's teachers had participated enthusiastically in organizing teachers' unions in the early twentieth century, their various local unions had fallen victim to the anti-unionism that characterized America during the business-dominated 1920s. Teacher unionism will be discussed in more detail later in this chapter. For now, it is sufficient to note that the Chicago school crisis resulted in a revitalized teacher union movement during the depression years.

In some respects, the Chicago situation was atypical. Its financial crisis was as much the result of political corruption as of economic depression. Further, the fact that the city's schools depended on the local property tax for 90 percent of their revenue created a situation that was almost unique to Chicago. Because of this almost total reliance on the local tax levy, the city's schools could not take advantage of being located in one of the wealthiest states in the union.

The Detroit Example

A less contentious, and more representative, situation existed in Detroit schools during the Depression. In contrast to the situation in Chicago, Detroit's schools and teachers underwent a much less tumultuous upheaval. Few if any teachers lost their jobs; they were usually paid on time; their salaries were not cut severely; and the school program remained relatively untouched. In Detroit, the mayor supported the schools in their battle for loans from the business community, and school board members resisted attempts to lay off teachers, cut salaries, and abolish programs. Finally, Detroit's superintendent was much more interested than his Chicago counterpart in maintaining educational quality and was more politically adept at maintaining existing levels of services. Although there were some salary cuts for teachers, they came only during the depths of the depression. Despite an attempt to eliminate art, music, physical education, manual training, and home economics from the curriculum, a movement that had been successful in Chicago, the school board refused to accede and thereby preserved the existing curriculum. The board's reluctance to cut back was due in no small part to a large and active coalition of civic groups who defended these modern subjects.[11]

Jeffrey Mirel attributes a large part of Detroit's success in weathering the Depression to the actions of wealthy board members whose loyalty to the public schools outweighed their own immediate economic interests. Mirel points out that most board members came from the same economic background as those wealthy businessmen who sought to cut property taxes and thereby severely reduce public school programs and teacher salaries. However, instead of responding to their immediate economic interest, board members acted out of a long-term loyalty to public education. For Mirel, the wealthy board members in Detroit acted much more responsibly than the political hacks on the board in Chicago. Even this relatively positive action in Detroit had long-term negative consequences, however. Mirel concludes that the Depression put the business interests firmly on the side of the cost cutters and thus helped end the business–labor alliance that had supported the schools so effectively since the progressive era.[12]

Rural Schools

While Chicago and Detroit offered alternative examples of urban districts' ability to weather depression conditions, the situation in rural districts was more uniformly negative. Even before the Depression, rural schools featured the lowest-paid teachers, the shortest school terms, the oldest and most inadequate facilities and equipment, and the highest rates of student absence. Depression-era conditions intensified these problems and thereby increased the gap between urban schools and their rural counterparts. Property taxes, the source of almost all rural school revenues, were particularly hard hit by an avalanche of farm failures and their accompanying financial devaluation.

In addition to this upsurge in rural economic distress, there was an increase in rural birth rates, particularly in the poorer southern states. This placed a heavier burden on rural schools already faced with decreasing revenues. In addition to making the usual cuts in personnel and salaries, many rural areas simply closed their schools during the height of the Depression. An urban district, even when facing cuts of up to one-third of total revenue, was in a far better position to absorb such a reduction than was a rural district that started with only a fraction of the revenue of its urban counterpart.

The situation for rural black students, particularly in the South, was even more dismal. White rural leaders in the South had disproportionately distributed school support since the passage of Jim Crow laws at the turn of the century. Now, faced with disastrous economic conditions, these white decision makers acted as they had in the past; that is, meager provisions for rural schools became even more imbalanced in favor of white schools.

Educational Radicalism and the Great Depression

The reaction of educators to the Great Depression depended in many ways on where they were located in the world of the schools. The most radical reaction came from professors of education in colleges and universities. These radical professors called on various teacher groups to lead the way in educational reform. The teachers, however, responded haltingly, if at all, to the call. Nevertheless, there was a substantial upsurge in teacher unionism as a result of the depression. The reaction of school administrators was less radical than that of either the professors or the teachers, though in some ways they had the greatest potential for thwarting the decline in school conditions.

The Teachers College Group

Educational radicalism emerged during the Great Depression largely through the efforts of a handful of politicized education professors who taught at Teachers College, Columbia University, in New York City. The faculty radicals included leaders from a variety of educational fields: Jesse Newlon in educational administration, William Heard Kilpatrick in philosophy of education, Harold Rugg in social studies education, and George Counts in educational sociology. A few of them had been associated with progressive education at Teachers College in the 1920s. In the 1930s they participated in a wide range of activities that included a discussion group, the sponsorship of a new journal, and the writing of books, pamphlets, and textbooks. All of these activities were devoted to alerting teachers, administrators, and interested citizens to the new depression-era conditions and to the responses that the professors felt were appropriate to these conditions. John Dewey participated occasionally in their discussions, since he now worked full time in the philosophy department at Columbia.

The Teachers College radicals devoted themselves to serious social analysis. Their special interest centered around the relations between school and society. Although their discussions began in the late 1920s, before the stock market crash, that event and the subsequent devastations wrought on both the schools and the larger society intensified their discussions and provoked a variety of actions on their part.

The Challenge of George Counts

George S. Counts, whose early work had been based largely on quantitative studies, became increasingly concerned with social class issues in the 1920s. We have already noted his study of secondary education in 1922. In 1927, he published a study of the social composition of school board members that highlighted their privileged economic backgrounds and the negative consequences of those backgrounds for democratically oriented public schooling. One year later, he exposed the conditions of economic dominance and political corruption that characterized Chicago's schools just before the Great Depression.[13]

Counts's social interests and radical sentiments were heightened by a series of trips to the Soviet Union in the late 1920s and early 1930s. Here he came face to face with a nation that was larger and just as diverse as the United States and that was ostensibly attempting to democratize its social, cultural, and economic life. Moreover, Soviet ideology assigned education a crucial role in the democratization process. Counts did not, then, or later, see the Soviet experience as a panacea for America's economic problems. He recognized, however, the importance of the social and economic changes being attempted by the Soviet government and the usefulness of studying this experience as a laboratory for similar changes in other societies.

Later in the 1930s, Counts participated in a variety of activist ventures, including the founding of perhaps the only authentically radical journal ever sponsored by American educators, the *Social Frontier*. In the pages of this journal, Counts and others debated the authenticity of the Soviet experiment with democracy and the utility of centralized planning and government intervention in American economic and social life.[14]

A comprehensive discussion of Counts and his Teachers College colleagues is beyond the scope of this text. However, a brief look at a famous pamphlet that he wrote in 1932, *Dare the School Build a New Social Order?*, merits special mention. In the pages of this work, Counts issued a series of challenges to American educators as a response to the economic and educational crisis of the Great Depression.[15]

The pamphlet is made up of three speeches given to various professional educational groups in 1932. The general theme of all three speeches was that the United States and the rest of the world were in danger because of the far-reaching consequences of economic depression. In Counts's own words:

> We can view a world order rushing toward collapse with no more concern than the outcome of a horse race; we can see injustice, crime and misery in their most terrible forms all about us and, if we are not directly affected, register the emotions of a scientist studying white rats in a laboratory. . . . In my opinion, this is a confession of a complete moral and spiritual bankruptcy.[16]

The most famous of the speeches that composed *Dare the School* was "Dare Progressive Education Be Progressive?" presented at the 1932 meeting of the Progressive Education Association (PEA). This speech was so provocative to the PEA that the group suspended its remaining agenda in order to devote itself exclusively to a discussion of Counts's challenge. Basically, Counts told the progressive educators that they had withdrawn from the social arena and concentrated instead on a child-centered approach to education that was socially innocuous at best and, at worst, positively harmful. To Counts, the child-centered progressives were naive in believing that their complete attention to the child bespoke no social position. Rather, Counts charged, by concentrating on the nature of the child they were endorsing existing social arrangements and thereby perpetuating the crisis of the Great Depression. Counts further challenged:

> If Progressive Education is to be genuinely progressive, it must emancipate itself from the influence of this class [referred to on a preceding page as "the liberal-minded upper middle class who sent their children to Progressive schools"], face squarely and courageously every social issue, come to grips with life and all of its stark reality, establish an organic relationship with the community, develop a realistic and comprehensive theory of welfare, fashion a compelling and challenging vision of human

destiny, and become less frightened than it is today at the bogies of *imposition* and *indoctrination*. In a word, Progressive Education cannot place its trust in a child-centered school.[17]

Counts's tendency to countenance indoctrination or imposition deeply offended many of the child-centered progressives. His point was that a theory of society, social welfare, and social progress was going to be part of any child's school experience. A child-centered school lacking any explicit theory of social direction would, by omission, inculcate in the children a theory of individualism and adherence to the status quo. This was particularly disturbing to Counts, as he saw individualism as the principal cause of the Great Depression.

In place of individualism, Counts sought to substitute a viewpoint that was much more conscious of group or societal needs. In his more radical moments, he and other social reconstructionists called for "collectivism," which could mean group ownership of the society's productive resources. In other moments, Counts sounded like a mainstream progressive of the early twentieth century: Government regulation was needed to ensure protection of the public interest in the economic and social realms. This, in turn, was related to another economic idea, that technological progress was eliminating the condition of scarcity which he viewed as the basic justification for capitalism and free enterprise. In an age of abundance, government's primary economic role was to make sure that extreme inequalities were abolished.

To many, especially to pro-business conservatives, Counts and other like-minded educators were anti-Americans, communists. In fact, Counts was depicted as a "red" in many leading American newspapers and periodicals. His actions later in the 1930s and 1940s, when he participated in a campaign to rid teacher unions and the state of New York's Labor (political) Party of communist influences, indicate that the charge of communism was ill founded. Counts, however, went as far as almost any American educator had ever gone to get those who worked in America's schools to understand and respond to the challenge of the Great Depression.

The Response of Teachers

Teachers were a particular audience that Counts sought to reach. In *Dare the School*, Counts assigned teachers a crucial role in achieving a necessary educational, social, and economic reform. First of all, teachers needed to pursue democratic ideals in their classrooms. As already noted, democracy, for Counts, meant much more than child centeredness. It meant a commitment to equitable social, political, and economic policies.

Next, to be effective outside their classrooms, teachers needed to be organized. Once organized into labor unions, teachers could serve as leaders for the rest of the organized labor movement in the campaign to democratize American society. Counts reasoned that teachers, by virtue of their relatively common social origins and their higher education, were perfectly placed to lead their brethren in the labor movement on the road to social and economic reform.

The American Federation of Teachers

In one sense at least, teachers heeded the call of Counts. They joined teachers' organizations such as the AFT in large numbers during the 1930s. This contrasted sharply with the declining membership that teachers' unions had endured in the 1920s. As already shown in the discussion of Chicago, teachers' unions found their ranks enlarged greatly as a result of economic fears brought on by the depression. This pattern was repeated in many of the nation's largest cities. The consequence was a revitalized AFT that sought to protect its members locally and to advance the cause of teachers throughout the nation.

Unfortunately for Counts, teacher unions proved to be greater protectors of their members' jobs and pay than designers or advocates of a new social order. It was not for lack of effort on the part of some, however, that teacher unions failed to produce economic radicals and social and political visionaries. In New York, Philadelphia, and a few other large cities, the teacher unions were influenced, and occasionally dominated, by teachers who were Communist Party members or who were closely aligned with the politics of the American Communist Party. In fact, late in the decade, Counts ran for and won the presidency of the AFT on an anticommunist platform that promised to rid the teachers' union of this alien ideology.

What both Counts and his communist rivals shared was their devotion to political ideas and ideals and their belief that these were of crucial importance to the teachers' union. What most teachers, even most teacher unionists, appeared to believe, however, was that their unions' primary role was to help them protect their jobs and to survive the economic ravages of the depression years.[18]

The depression-era world of classroom teachers will be discussed later in this chapter. For now, however, a look at the reaction of still another group of professional educators which claimed to represent teachers during this time of crisis, the National Education Association, should be examined.

The National Education Association

The NEA, although it represented teachers, did so in a particular way. It operated under the belief that education was a unified profession and that teachers' interests were best cared for by the leaders of the educational establishment. Thus, the NEA represented teachers through the school administrators who dominated both the association and the public schools. These administrators, as noted in Chapter 8, had reorganized the NEA to become a national organization that might improve school conditions and advance the educational profession. Since the NEA sponsored a series of studies in school finance in the 1920s that included an analysis of teachers' salaries, teachers could see the link between their own welfare and the activities of the NEA.

Another part of the NEA's school finance thrust was the study of various ways to support public schools. This involved consideration of the relative merits of various types of tax levies as ways to raise money for public schools. As the Great Depression unfolded and the issues of school finance became increasingly important to everyone, the NEA pointed to its school finance studies as examples of its value to teachers.

In 1933, when the depths of the depression were being keenly felt by all Americans, the NEA established the Joint Commission on the Emergency in Education (JCEE). This body was charged with investigating the conditions and consequences of the economic crisis and making recommendations for its solution. In addition to expanding upon the NEA's earlier work in the area of school taxation, the commission was active in advising teachers and administrators nationwide on how they might stave off the consequences of economic doom in their locality or state.[19]

The commission advocated two major ways to solve the financial problems of local schools. One was the pursuit of federal aid for education, an objective it had been seeking for the past decade and a half. However, it advocated general federal aid to all school districts. In addition to being enormously expensive, this type of aid failed to target those places where the problems were the most acute. Further, general federal aid raised the specter of federal control of education, which was widely feared by diverse religious, political, and cultural groups. These groups pointed to the absence of education from the federal Constitution, along with the long-standing traditions of local control in school affairs, as reasons for their opposition. This opposition, combined with the enormous cost of general federal aid and some clumsy lobbying, prevented the NEA from achieving this objective.

In the area of tax reform, however, the focus of its second solution for the schools' problems, the NEA achieved partial success. Data generated through NEA studies allowed school districts to compare their methods of school finance with other districts of similar size and wealth. Highlighting the vast disparities in the taxation methods and results of local districts made it increasingly evident that state taxation was needed to counterbalance the educational inequities produced by dependence on local property taxes. As already shown, the state taxation equity thrust was relevant to cities like Chicago, where the existing state effort was remarkably small.

Equity achieved through state-level taxation was even more important for rural districts. In most, if not all, of these areas, the property tax burden was borne almost completely by farmers, since there were few businesses and industries to share it. In many rural areas, the property tax had been unable to produce a decent level of schooling even before the depression. Following the economic downturn, the situation worsened considerably, and many rural areas were forced either to close their schools or to cut the school term drastically. In response, the NEA advocated state taxation both on equity grounds and as a survival measure. Many poor, rural states followed the NEA lead and turned to state effort as the only way to salvage public schooling during, and after, the depression.

By the mid-1930s the worst of the depression had passed and the NEA prepared to disband its JCEE. As the JCEE ended, however, the NEA took steps to prevent the crisis from reemerging. It established the Educational Policies Commission (EPC), which was to make sure that the schools would be prepared for the negative consequences of future economic crises. The EPC lasted for the next three decades as a sort of "think tank" for educational problems. It represented the NEA's most enduring legacy from the Great Depression.

Child-Centered Progressivism in Theory and Practice

As discussed earlier, George Counts electrified the Progressive Education Association (PEA) with his 1932 address to that group. Although Counts's attack on child-centered education galvanized the 1932 meeting, it did not dislodge the child-centered wing from its dominance of the PEA. This group continued to advocate educational experimentalism and the liberation of students from the grasp of traditional curriculum as the solution to educational problems.

The Eight Year Study

The most notable effort of the child-centered progressives during the 1930s was the Eight Year Study. Conceived initially as a response to problems of college admission, the Eight Year Study became a landmark in the movement to revise the secondary school curriculum to meet the needs of a changing society. In order to evaluate the effects of curriculum experimentation by progressive educators, it was necessary to waive traditional college entrance requirements. Several noted colleges and universities agreed to do this for students who came from selected experimental high schools. These high schools, some public, some private, and some university laboratory schools, were allowed to make whatever curricular changes they deemed to be in the best interests of their students. Their effectiveness was judged in terms of how well their graduates did in college in comparison to the graduates of conventional high schools. The results showed no measurable difference in college success between graduates of experimental high schools and traditional high schools. Progressive educators interpreted these results as an endorsement of experimentation. Their student-centered programs seemed to provide the same chance of university success as traditional programs while simultaneously providing the active student learning that progressives had long advocated.[20]

Another curricular outcome that can be traced to the Eight Year Study was the development of the "core curriculum." The term was initially advanced to describe a course of study in one of the experimental schools that devoted half of its time to "functional" objectives such as health, citizenship, vocation, and leisure. While the breadth of this curriculum was not widely adopted, the term "core curriculum" endured. Eventually, it came to denote any attempt to combine studies in two or more academic subjects, usually English and social studies, with the pursuit of functional objectives. Such core curricula flourished throughout the 1930s, surviving in modified fashion into later decades.

Essentialist Opposition

The Eight Year Study, its core curriculum, and the larger cause of educational experimentalism did not survive without significant opposition from both educators and the lay public. In the pages of the *Social Frontier*, the radicals and child-centered progressives continued to debate the validity of educational experimentalism. Then, in the late 1930s, another group emerged to champion the cause of educational continuity against any kind of progressivism, be it child centered, social reconstructionist, or any other version of experimental education.

This new opposition group took their name, "essentialists," from the title of a manifesto they issued at the annual meeting of the American Association of School Administrators in 1938. The manifesto charged that American education had become "appallingly weak and ineffective," especially when compared to the levels of achievement in other countries. Essentialists contended that mass education and progressive, child-centered theories had spawned declining standards and the discrediting of rigorous academic standards.[21]

The essentialists took their lead from William C. Bagley of Columbia Teachers College. Bagley was a Teachers College colleague of some of the most famous social reconstructionist and experimentalist progressives. In the face of a rising tide of child-centered reforms, Bagley had been sounding a warning about the dangers of progressivism for a number of years. However, his views were clearly a minority position among the leading educational theorists and spokespersons of the Great Depression years.

The essentialists' critique of progressivism was built around a series of oppositions, such as that between freedom and discipline, the individual and society, and play and work. In the essentialist view, progressives wrongly stressed the first concept in each of these pairs. They either ignored, or undermined, discipline in classroom and community, the social goals of school study, and the value of work and workmanship. In opposition to the excesses of experimentalism and child-centered approaches, the essentialists called for a learning community based on a common core of ideas, understandings, and ideals. Their curriculum emphasized the essential subjects of reading, arithmetic, history, the sciences, and creative work in art. The essentialists criticized progressivism as academically weak and feeble in contrast to their own program, which was strong, virile, and positive.[22]

Public Reaction to the Educational Debates

The essentialists' manifesto received considerable press response. *Newsweek* magazine picked up on the assertion that progressives coddled their pupils and described essentialism as a return to traditional methods in classrooms that would correct the excesses of progressivism. Yet it would be an exaggeration to say that the essentialists, or essentialism, had any large impact on American educational thought or practice. While few schools were wholeheartedly committed to progressivism, neither were they committed in principle to essentialism. Rather, curriculum decisions were almost always the result of local conditions and the schools' interaction with local leadership.

Take the community of "Middletown," for example. *Middletown* is a pseudonym given to the midwestern town studied by sociologists Robert and Helen Lynd in the 1930s. In their study, the Lynds described a city caught in conflict between forces of cultural conservatism and pedagogical change. The result was a change of a "conservatively progressive" sort. New students with different social and/or ethnic backgrounds were offered new subjects such as business English or shop mathematics, geared specifically to their "needs" as determined by local school officials. In the case of Middletown's affluent students, the standard academic curriculum was kept intact.[23]

Curriculum change, however, was not the major alteration forced on Middletown's schools because of depression-era conditions. The most significant change was an enlargement in class size and a decrease in salaries for school employees, both undertaken to bring school costs under control.

Other examples of response, or the lack of response, to depression conditions were found in four Illinois communities in the 1930s. In these cases, wealth and tradition outweighed theory as the most important variables in accounting for school conditions during the Depression. In one wealthy suburb, Winnetka, the schools remained thoroughly progressive because of the long-standing commitment to innovation on the part of the superintendent and the board. In another wealthy suburb, however, there was no such tradition of innovation and support for the public schools. Here, the wealthy citizens who controlled the community sought a scaled-down basic curriculum for the public schools, while they sent their own children to private schools.[24]

In one less affluent, industrial community, the Depression meant increases in class size and drastic cutbacks in teacher pay, school offerings, and the length of the school year. These conditions meant that teachers retreated to the most traditional method, recitation, in order literally to "keep" school. In another ordinary community, while the negative economic consequences of the Depression were kept at bay, the system simply continued with its 1920s rote teaching method and traditional curriculum.[25]

The situations in the latter two communities were characteristic of those in most American school districts during the depression years. The drastic cutbacks that occurred in many communities were a clear antidote to any progressive changes advocated by educational leaders. In cases where cutbacks were not necessitated, inertia and reflexive devotion to traditional pedagogy prevented the adoption of curricular innovations. Other factors that contributed to keeping the status quo will be discussed later in the chapter, when the occupational lives of teachers are considered. For now, however, the next step is to look at the one arena where there was some genuine innovation in educational policy in response to the Depression, the federal government.

The Federal Government as Educator

As already noted, Herbert Hoover had been in office for less than a year when the stock market crashed in October 1929. This meant that he would stay in office for the first three years of the Great Depression. An economically conservative Republican, Hoover's response to the Depression was to try to re-create the prosperity of the 1920s through traditional free-market strategies. The very last resort for Hoover was governmental intervention in the economy. Federal government initiatives in the educational arena were particularly odious to Hoover because, like many Americans, he believed that education should be controlled by local communities. Interestingly, Franklin Delano Roosevelt, who defeated Hoover in the election of 1932, also relied, initially, on traditional responses to the Depression, responses that did not countenance government intrusion into educational, or many other, activities.

Roosevelt's initial policies did not work any better than Hoover's had. Consequently, FDR soon switched to a more experimental orientation toward economic and social policy. Education, however, remained on the back burner of the Roosevelt program. Given Roosevelt's reluctance to involve himself formally in the educational arena, it is not surprising that the NEA's long-held desire for general federal aid to education continued to be rebuffed. However, while direct federal assistance to education was turned away at the front door, some help managed to arrive from a different direction.

A major part of Roosevelt's New Deal strategy for combating the Depression involved agencies and programs created to employ the unemployed. Often these agencies also sponsored educational programs designed to supplement the established educational system. For example, the Civilian Conservation Corps (CCC) and the National Youth Administration (NYA) were two of the most famous New Deal work relief programs that had an educational component. The CCC, the first of these two agencies to be established, was begun in 1933 as a public works program that took unemployed young men, housed them in camp settings run according to quasi-military routines, and gave them jobs in preserving forests and other natural resources.

Education within the Civilian Conservation Corps

Educational activity in the CCC camps grew out of the need to engage recruits in their off-work hours. The military officers and technical advisors from the U.S. Forest Service, who were responsible for activities in the CCC camps, provided low-level educational activities that they believed were appropriate for the largely urban clientele of the camps. Basic drill in literacy skills characterized most of the CCC's educational efforts, accompanied by a strong emphasis on discipline, moral training, and the values of hard work and common courtesy. This occurred in spite of the efforts of the U.S. Office of

Education (USOE), the federal agency responsible for education, to upgrade the educational activities in the camps.[26]

Federal educational officials, and many public school leaders, believed that the CCC camps were too authoritarian, too interested in basic skills and values, and utterly uninterested in educational activities that were appropriate for a democratic society. These educators sought to include self-expression, cooperative activity, and vocational training and guidance as part of the educational program in the camps. Although they had some success in establishing buildings for education and expanding the use of films and other teaching materials, their influence was limited by the fundamental conservatism of the director of the CCC, a trade union official with old-fashioned ideas, especially in the areas of education and culture.

In one very real sense, however, education within the CCC was innovative. It brought a variety of work and training experiences to a clientele that was unable to get such training in a regular public high school. CCC courses ranged from remedial literacy courses to vocational training to various sorts of leisure pursuits. By the late 1930s, educational advisors from the USOE had become influential enough to help create better facilities as well as expanded enrollment in educational activities.

Despite this progress, the CCC's educational program never escaped the conservative influence of the military leaders who dominated the camps. Camp leaders actually feared educational efforts above and beyond their own disciplinary approach and sometimes banned books that were deemed "subversive." Often, when a conflict arose between the existing military approach and the more open, liberal approach of the educational advisors, President Roosevelt would intervene on the side of the director and the military. Roosevelt himself favored discipline and productivity in the camps rather than liberal courses that might encourage the corpsmen to ask questions or discuss issues.[27]

Education within the National Youth Administration

The National Youth Administration (NYA) was the other major New Deal agency set up to deal with unemployment and its educational implications. A non-residential program, it set out to address the program of youth unemployment without undertaking the considerable expense of putting the young into military camps. Also, in contrast to the CCC, the NYA took a much more imaginative approach to the economic, social, and educational problems experienced by its young clients. The NYA was headed by a social worker who was knowledgeable about his clientele and their needs. Also, lack of any military involvement in the NYA allowed the agency to be much more flexible and experimental in its programs.

NYA activities were organized in two ways. The first involved direct financial aid to current high school and college students. To receive this aid, the NYA paid the students for doing various kinds of jobs, usually at their school sites. NYA high school enrollees worked as teacher aides, as landscapers on school grounds, and in cafeterias, workshops, and school health programs. College-level enrollees worked as research assistants, library aides, or in community service activities. Both of these programs were small in terms of the total amount of money expended, but they often made the difference between an enrollee continuing in school or dropping out.

The second set of NYA activities involved the development of work and training programs for youth who were already out of school. These NYA workers served in parks' departments, YMCAs, settlement houses, hospitals, pre-schools, and in community building projects. In addition to providing work experience, the NYA developed training activities for youths that often related directly to the work they were doing. For example, young people who worked at maintaining or repairing automobiles would then study auto mechanics later in the day, or youngsters who worked on a construction project might study blueprint reading as part of their training activities. This type of educational activity meant that the NYA offered a real alternative to public school education. The link between education and work in the NYA programs appealed to some reform-minded social activists and a few vocationally minded educators.

The reaction of most educators to the NYA, however, was suspicious and hostile, just as it was to the CCC. Educators feared the NYA because it provided an attractive alternative to the regular school program for many young people. Its linking of education and work was much more real than the experience in vocational subjects offered in the public schools. These were still used as a weapon against the remoteness of traditional curricula or as a dumping ground for lower-class students. In short, most educators lacked the sense of social mission that characterized much NYA activity.

The NYA knew that it was dealing with the lower social classes and attempted to match its programs to their needs. Over nine out of ten NYA workers came from families on relief. This was in marked contrast to the approach of public school people, who wanted general federal aid for all school activities and refused to single out any one social segment or educational program as particularly in need.[28]

Another contrast between the NYA and both the CCC and public school advocates was the acknowledgment by the NYA of the special needs of African Americans. The NYA was particularly interested in enrolling blacks, and it institutionalized this interest by setting up the Division of Negro Affairs headed by the noted black woman educator, Mary McLeod Bethune. Estimates are that the NYA reached over a quarter of a million black youths through its various programs. Neither the CCC nor most public schools devoted special attention to black youngsters during the depression, even though blacks endured special hardships because of their concentration in the rural South and in the slums of southern and northern cities. Their hardships were aggravated, of course, because of the direct racial discrimination practiced against them by southern (as well as northern) whites.[29]

The antipathy of public school educators for the CCC and the NYA was part of the larger rift between the schoolmen and the Roosevelt administration. This rift, described briefly at the beginning of this chapter, was to last throughout Roosevelt's four terms. Politically, most of the educational leadership at all levels was made up of white Anglo-Saxon Protestant males who had traditionally been allied with conservative Republican political groups. Roosevelt's constituency was composed largely of poorer opposition groups: Catholics, labor, rural southerners, and various ethnic minorities, including African Americans. Roosevelt's opposition to general federal aid to education, while partly reflecting his own opinions, also reflected the views of his large Roman Catholic, working-class constituency, a group that feared that the NEA wanted the aid only for public schools. Catholics would favor federal aid only if it would also be available to Catholic schools, a position that they knew the NEA bitterly opposed.

Conflict between Roosevelt and the educational establishment persisted throughout the late 1930s and into the 1940s, culminating in 1941 when the NEA's Educational Policies Commission prepared a report on the CCC and the NYA. The educators recommended that both of these programs be disbanded and, further, that their functions be transferred to the public schools. In the view of the educational leaders, if sufficient support were given to the public schools, there would not be any out-of-work youth for which the CCC or the NYA had to be concerned.

One final point needs to be made about the relations between federal programs such as the CCC and NYA and the various kinds of educational reforms that characterized the 1930s. The innovative aspects of the federal programs were seldom, if ever, located in their pedagogy. Even their curricular innovations, such as linking work and training experiences, were not of the same order as the wholesale pedagogical and curricular changes favored by the child-centered and experimentalist progressives or the radical social alterations favored by the social reconstructionists. Thus, it was not just the educational establishment that looked askance at the educational activities of the federal government. Even committed educational reformers, who might have been expected to be less opposed to changes sponsored from outside the school system, turned out to be neutral at best. Generally they opposed the efforts of the CCC and the NYA on the grounds that they did not go far enough.

State Educational Reform

The Great Depression also triggered major educational changes in many states. Louisiana, for example, was led in the early depression years by Governor Huey Long, who believed firmly in the extension of educational opportunity. Long's educational program involved free textbooks for the schoolchildren of Louisiana, an upgrading of the state's public higher education system, particularly at Louisiana State University at Baton Rouge, and improvements in teacher training and instruction in both white and black schools. Most significantly, Long revised the method of financing schools, which had been based on local property taxes. As a result of that method, a two-tiered system of schools had evolved, one based on more expensive urban property and the other on less valuable rural land. Long centralized tax collection at the state level and installed a school equalization fund that allowed the poorer rural counties to improve their schools using state revenues. This, plus the favorable publicity emerging from his free textbook law, resulted in substantial growth in rural school enrollments between 1929 and 1935 and a sharp decrease in the state's high illiteracy rate.[30]

Long did not initiate his educational changes without substantial opposition. Part of Long's problem was due to his tendency to run roughshod over political opposition and to treat the state university, particularly its athletic teams, as an extension of his own person. He was also impatient with educators who questioned the validity of his programs or the purity of his motives in implementing them. Like Roosevelt, Long saw educational change more as a natural extension of general reform efforts than as a drastic attempt to alter educational programs or to spur social and economic change. The net result was that Long went forward with his educational programs with or without widespread endorsement from the state's established political and educational leaders.

Long's assassination in 1935 left a huge vacuum in the educational reform arena just as it did in other state governmental activities. His influence had permeated both state government and public education, despite the fact that he had left the statehouse for the U.S. Senate in 1932. While his political successors claimed to be following his reform agenda, those politicians proved to be more successful at maintaining themselves in office than in advancing policies of genuine reform, whether pedagogical, social, or economic.

Thus, attempts at educational reform during the depression, whether at the national or state level, failed to alter America's schools in any meaningful way. A full explanation of the lack of change, whether from progressive reformers or from governmental efforts, requires a close look at the backgrounds of school teachers and the values and orientations they brought to their work.

Teachers and the Great Depression

It would be foolish to argue that teachers were the main obstacles to school reform during the depression. Given their lack of power and influence over school policy and governance, one cannot claim that they were in a position to initiate or to alter school reforms. They were, however, in a position to resist reforms that called on them to change their traditional roles—and, as we will show, there were many reasons for teachers to resist such attempts at change.

Teacher Conservatism

Interestingly, in 1932, the same year that George Counts was calling on teachers to help schools build a new social order, a less apocalyptic educational scholar published a book that clearly explained why teachers were unlikely revolutionaries. Willard Waller's analysis focused on the microcosmic world of the school and those who worked in it. While Counts had described schoolteachers as coming from an ordinary social background, Waller went beyond Counts's analysis without contradicting it fundamentally. Waller found teachers to be predominantly native born, from rural areas, and from lower-middle-class families. While he was not sure what these characteristics meant in terms of teachers' occupational behavior, he concluded that mediocrity was a viable characterization of their lives and work.[31]

Waller was devastating in his description of what the job of teaching, as it existed in American school rooms in 1932, did to teachers. He talked of a long list of unpleasant qualities engendered in teachers by their work experience. Among these characteristics were inflexibility, reserve, a lack of spontaneity, and an artificial sense of dignity developed to mask teachers' uneasy and frequent alternation between roles of dominance in the classroom and subordination elsewhere.

According to Waller, the constant call on teachers to grade pupils tended to harness them firmly to the existing system and hamper their ability to evaluate that system critically. The net result was the development of "an early and rigid conservatism" as well as a habit of impersonality on the part of teachers. These traits were intensified by the constant need of teachers to maintain order in classrooms populated by students whose objective, for a variety of reasons, was often to disrupt that order. The teachers' occupational role, then, was one in which they were seldom treated as autonomous, self-directed people by the larger society. This led to occupational dissatisfaction for many teachers, with the bulk of the younger ones looking for ways to escape rather than change the system.[32]

Teachers' relations with their administrative superiors were no more positive, according to Waller, than were their other circumstances. While teachers often exhibited an exaggerated sense of loyalty to school executives, this loyalty masked a "latent rebellion" that occasionally came to the surface but more often festered inside the teacher. In terms of their peer relationships, teachers more often felt a sense of rivalry than of collegiality. This rivalry was hidden under an intense desire on the part of teachers to "talk shop" with other teachers whenever they interacted. However, the purpose of the shop talk was seldom, if ever, mutual support or improvement. Rather, it confirmed each teacher in his or her individual sense of occupational worth.[33]

While Waller did not develop this line of analysis fully, a sociological account of schoolteachers in the 1970s arrived at a similar set of conclusions about teachers' relations to each other. This later study by sociologist Dan C. Lortie focused on the negative consequences of teachers' classroom isolation as opposed to a working situation characterized by regular adult relationships.[34]

Although one need not accept every particular of Waller's analysis of teachers and their occupational role, the net effect of his work was to cast significant doubt on teachers' willingness or ability to lead, or even to participate in, the social and occupational revolution that George Counts sought to establish. This picture of teacher conservatism could even be applied to teachers' unions, which Counts saw as the vehicles through which teachers' educational activism would eventually be translated into larger social activism.

Union Conservatism

As already suggested, teachers' unions made some progress in membership during the Great Depression, particularly when these years are contrasted to the declining membership era of the 1920s. Union programs during the Depression, however, seldom matched the occupational expectations and desires of most union members. For example, union leadership in New York, Chicago, and many other cities where membership was healthy came largely from the ranks of male high school teachers, even though the occupation was composed mainly of female elementary teachers. Moreover, salary gaps often existed between men and women, and between high school and elementary teachers. Union leaders, coming from the more privileged ranks in terms of salaries, were seldom disposed to confront these inequities.[35]

Also, as suggested earlier in this chapter, teacher unions in large cities often became a battleground between communists and other social reformers and anticommunist activists with strong allegiance to the American political system. Neither brand of activism, however, seemed to be closely geared to the world of teachers, at least as it was depicted by Willard Waller.

Women Teachers

One extended examination of the relationship between teacher unions and women teachers during the Depression has been undertaken by Richard Quantz. In this discussion, the lack of fit between female members and their organizations is a dominant theme. First of all, this case study of teachers in Hamilton, Ohio, points out that the superintendent and other hiring officials took pains to employ only compliant teachers whose backgrounds predisposed them to be suspicious of union membership or other forms of independent activity. Hiring officials looked for "safe" young women to keep school, daughters of proper families who exhibited the "competent conformity" they were expected to instill in their students.[36]

The almost totally female teaching force in Hamilton typically came from the propriety-oriented lower-middle or upper-lower classes. After a successful career as students, they went on to obtain higher education but then returned home to live with their parents while they taught. Such an existence left little room for individual or occupational independence. These aspects of the Hamilton situation were hardly unique to that city. Rather, they characterized the situation of many, if not most, American school districts during the depression era.

A set of occupational expectations also militated against union membership among Hamilton's women teachers. For example, the teachers worked in a hierarchical structure that gave them dominance in their classrooms while requiring subordination in their relations with male administrators. In addition, school organization resembled a family more than an impersonal work setting. This family-like organization encouraged maternal-type behavior on the part of its women teachers, both inside and outside their classrooms. Needless to say, the maternal image had little in common with a militant teacher unionism.

Related to the familial image was the cultural image of teaching as a woman's occupation, particularly a single woman's occupation. Such an image made propriety and docility as opposed to social or political activism expected teacher behavior. Finally, Hamilton's women teachers were expected to exhibit a kind of dual selfhood. They were granted a modicum of professional respect in their teaching role but, in turn, were expected to behave as moral paragons both on and off the job.

This set of cultural expectations underlay the prohibition of married women as teachers. It was not that teachers could not act as human beings, have a social life, date, dance, and so forth. They were just expected to do these things out of sight of the community, thereby heightening their public image as paragons of virtue. As a by-product of this carefully maintained public image, both teachers and the local community had a grossly distorted view of teachers and teaching.

These cultural expectations did not mean that teachers did not join any organizations. It meant, rather, that they joined organizations which might, for lack of a better term, be called "professional" rather than occupational or union groups. The professional organizations included classroom teachers' associations, subject-matter or grade-level organizations, or groups such as the American Association of University Women. All of these groups functioned more like a women's club than a labor organization.

Historians are currently examining more closely the types of organizations that women teachers joined and are finding that some did represent women teachers in an occupational sense. The kind of representation they exhibited, however, was a far cry from the teacher unionism that characterized the AFT both in the 1930s and in later decades. In most cases, the NEA could more easily encompass women teachers within its local affiliates. Even here, however, the concerns of the local women teachers were not likely to dovetail with those of the male administrators who dominated all levels of the NEA. In the end, the women went their own way, usually without confronting the men who held the formal leadership positions.[37]

Teacher Work as Tradition

There is still another factor that militated against occupational activism on the part of both women and men teachers. Larry Cuban has documented the ways in which teachers tenaciously clung to traditional methods and orientations in their classrooms. Moreover, they did so in spite of many pedagogical innovations being recommended by progressive educators. Without explaining in any detail why teachers failed to adopt progressive pedagogical innovations, Cuban shows convincingly that, by and large, they failed to do so in the depression decade. Pedagogy in the 1930s was much more like it had been in the 1920s than it was different. Further, the high school teachers who seemed more inclined to favor teacher unionism were more reluctant to undertake innovation in their classrooms than were elementary teachers. Thus unionism seems to have had little impact on teachers' classroom behavior. Teachers who favored tradition in their work lives found it difficult to advocate change in other aspects of their occupational lives.[38]

For all these reasons, then, teachers in the depression decade found it difficult to entertain the visions of change offered to them by educational theorists, by social activists, and by union leaders. Teachers' fundamental occupational commitments, like their pedagogy, remained fixed on traditional roles and expectations.

Education and World War II

It is not clear whether the country ever brought itself completely out of the Great Depression. While there were a few upturns in the early 1930s and again in the middle of that decade, there were also several significant downturns, at least one of which occurred in the late 1930s. Thus, despite the unprecedented efforts of Roosevelt's administrations to lift the nation out of the depression, the economy grew in fits and starts and never completely shook off the effects of the stock market collapse of 1929. It is now the general consensus among historians and economists that it was the arrival of World War II and the conversion to a full-employment war economy that convincingly ended the decade-long Great Depression. The remainder of this chapter is devoted to discussing those events of the World War II years that had long-range significance on the educational world.

Despite the financial upheaval and related cutbacks that characterized education during the depression years, schooling itself continued to follow the familiar patterns of the 1920s. Interestingly, in some respects the World War II years provided more change for education and educators than the depression years. Yet these changes, as so often is the case in the history of American education, were influenced by external events and forces more than by the premeditated designs of educators or educational policymakers.

Changes in High Schools

One example of change during the war years stemmed from high-school-age boys enlisting in the military. To help prepare these boys for military service, many high schools began offering vocational courses to teach them the skills they would need either in the military or in military related defense industries.

The schools were simply contributing to the nation's effort to fight a war with multiple enemies on several fronts.

Other changes in high school life brought on by the war included low drop-out rates and a moratorium on school spending. The phenomenon of youth unemployment, so prevalent in the 1930s, practically disappeared as the demands of war and wartime production asserted themselves. High schools no longer faced a threat from government agencies such as the NYA and the CCC, both of which disappeared as alternatives for high-school-age youth. Wartime conditions also meant that schools put a moratorium on replacements and improvements in their physical plants. These tasks, which would have required substantial public expenditures, were not undertaken in an economy that was given over primarily to war production.

Equality among Teachers

Changes were also felt in the ranks of teachers, both during and after the war. As men joined the armed services, new opportunities opened up for women in the wartime factories. Women thus gained employment at relatively high factory wages in a sector of the economy to which they had previously been denied access. This had at least two effects on the occupation of teaching. First, the exodus of women teachers into better-paid factory jobs, together with the exodus of men into the armed forces, created an acute shortage of qualified teachers. Thus, teacher quality was diluted because of the war.

Second, and more important for the long term, those women who remained in teaching were not ignorant of the changes that were taking place for their sisters in factories. Women's employment gains outside of schools became a symbol that drove many women teachers to political action. Specifically, women teachers began pursuing a single salary scale in many American school districts. While women teachers in most districts had already been granted equal pay for equal work, either by law or by administrative rule, it was women's rising occupational expectations brought on by the war that fueled the movement for a single salary scale. Such a scale called for all teachers, whether elementary or secondary, to be paid according to the same (single) salary scale. Advocates of the single salary scale were out to repair the inequality that allowed largely male high school teachers to be paid on a higher scale than that which existed for elementary teachers, most of whom were female.[39]

Interestingly, it was the NEA, rather than the unionized AFT, that helped women teachers pursue this campaign. As already mentioned, the union's reluctance to fight for a single salary scale stemmed from its dominance by high school teachers. They could hardly have been expected to campaign for a policy that operated in opposition to their own immediate economic interests. However, it was well into the 1950s before the single salary scale became prevalent throughout the nation. In retrospect, it was the change in women's wartime roles and in their attitudes as a result of those role changes that paved the way for the ultimate success of the single salary scale across the nation.

A change that was related to women teachers' pursuit of the single salary scale occurred among southern black teachers during the World War II years. Despite the 1896 *Plessy v. Ferguson* decision,[40] which legitimized the "separate but equal" doctrine, black teachers' salaries and working conditions were greatly inferior to those of their white counterparts. Black teachers were denied financial equity regardless of their training or occupational achievement.

Black activists, many of whom were involved in the National Association for the Advancement of Colored People (NAACP), sought to combat the legal fiction of separate but equal in many aspects of southern social life. In education, the matter of unequal teacher salaries led to legal challenges in several cities and states. However, it was not always easy for NAACP lawyers to find a black teacher willing to put his or her name to a lawsuit, since retribution from school authorities often followed. When plaintiffs could be found, however, the result was often a court ruling that prohibited the existence of separate salary scales by race and pointed in the direction of a single salary scale for both races.[41]

Despite legal victories, the salary equity that black teachers sought was still often denied them. In Atlanta, for example, the school board responded to the campaign for a single, color-blind salary scale by abolishing salary scales altogether and paying all teachers according to estimates of their individual value and performance. This action, which was taken with the consent of the white teachers' union, effectively prevented the implementation of an equitable single salary scale for another decade. The state of South Carolina found another way to circumvent the legal demand for a single salary scale. After a court decision against separate salary scales, the state moved to require a standardized test for all teachers and to pay salaries according to scores on the test. This was done with full knowledge that black teachers would score lower on the test for a variety of reasons having to do with background and prior training.[42]

The movement against racial separatism was intensified by the wartime experience of black members of the armed forces. Blacks who fought on the European front experienced life in white nations that did not discriminate racially, a sharp contrast to their experience on the homefront. A few years after the war, President Harry Truman issued an order desegregating the armed forces of the nation, an order that was greeted with joy and anticipation in black communities, in both the North and the South. Truman's order, along with the return of black soldiers and sailors, fueled the black crusade against inequality in the South. The obstinacy of southern local and state officials in the area of race relations now stood in stark contrast to this powerful action by the federal government.

That contrast was not lost on black veterans, black teachers, and many black citizens. It encouraged black teachers to continue their fight for a single salary scale and black citizens to demand an improvement in the substandard schooling that had been provided for their children. These campaigns culminated in a Supreme Court decision in 1954 that reversed the *Plessy* principle. *Brown v. Board of Education*, which is discussed in detail in the next chapter, had many of its roots in the changing black consciousness that resulted from the successful performance of black soldiers and sailors in World War II.

The GI Bill

Still another significant educational result of World War II was the passage of the Servicemen's Readjustment Act of 1944, commonly known as the GI Bill. In an effort to avoid the substantial unemployment that threatened to occur when almost four million servicemen would simultaneously seek to reenter the civilian workforce, Congress provided veterans substantial financial support to attend schools and colleges to increase their qualifications and job skills. The Bill provided for one year of education for ninety days of service plus an additional month for each month served on active duty, for a maximum of forty-eight months. The government provided for tuition, fees, books and supplies up to $500 a year. Single veterans received a subsistence allowance of $50 a month while married veterans received $75.[43]

No one really anticipated the huge numbers of veterans who made use of the GI Bill. This flood of returnees entering schools and colleges brought new meaning to the notion of equal educational opportunity. Females and African Americans, however, did not share all the benefits available to their male white counterparts. Whereas women made up about 40 percent of undergraduate enrollment in 1939–40, by 1950 women constituted only about 32 percent. Campuses became masculinized in yet another way as the fields of study deemed appropriate for men and women created a divide. Although a number of women had been enrolled in business administration, engineering, law, medicine and other professional programs during the war, the returning male veterans flocked to these fields and women were guided into education, home economics, nursing, secretarial, and other "women's" vocational areas.

African American veterans were eligible for GI benefits and black enrollment did increase in the years following the war. However, there was no requirement in the Bill that prohibited racial discrimination by colleges and universities. Thus, opportunities for black veterans in higher education were limited by the same prejudices that had condoned segregation in the armed forces. Returning black veterans could only partially integrate into a society that had a standing—and often perverted—policy of "separate but equal."[44]

However limited in these respects, overall the GI Bill had a tremendous impact on improving educational and economic opportunity in the United States. Higher education was increasingly seen as being essential to one's success in life. The Bill markedly changed notions of who could and should seek higher levels of education. It also made it possible for the World War II generation to far surpass the occupational and status levels of their parents.

Conclusion

Before we leave the World War II years, a brief recapitulation of their impact on education seems in order. Although efforts to bring about curriculum reform and in working conditions for teachers have been stressed, along with the growing demand for equal educational opportunity, in some ways American education emerged almost unchanged from the war years. The basic school curriculum remained largely unaltered by the war, as did the structure of school governance, the training of teachers, classroom teaching practices, and most other educational policies and practices. School budgets recovered somewhat from the negative times of the depression era as the wartime economic prosperity trickled down to the public sector. The GI Bill increased opportunity for some two million veterans and opened the doors to mass education. Even so, America's schools emerged from the war showing more continuity than change when compared to schools of the 1920s and 1930s.

Further Reading

Beineke, John A. *And There Were Giants in the Land: The Life of William Heard Kilpatrick*. New York: Peter Lang, 1998. A biography of Dewey's most famous disciple in the field of professional education, in which his roots in the South and his development as the most noted professor at Teachers College, Columbia University are highlighted.

Bennett, Michael J. *When Dreams Came True: The GI Bill and the Making of Modern America*. Washington, D.C.: Brasseys, [1996], 2000. Lays out the political maneuvering and outcomes behind the GI Bill.

Bowers, C. A. *The Progressive Educator and the Depression: The Radical Years*. New York: Random House, 1969. A rigorous account of the development of social reconstructionism in educational thought in the 1930s, and a critique of that movement for its illiberal tendencies.

Cooper, Michael L. *Dust to Eat: Drought and Depression in the 1930s*. Boston: Houghton Mifflin, 2004. A moving narrative about the devastation leveled on American society by the Depression and the "Dust Bowl," augmented by Dorothea Lange photographs.

Cuban, Larry. *How Teachers Taught: Constancy and Change in the American Classroom*. New York: Longman, 1984. A remarkable portrait of the forces militating against pedagogical change in American classrooms since the advent of progressive education, with descriptions of both the intermittent adoption of and consistent opposition to pedagogical innovation.

Gutek, Gerald. *The Educational Theory of George S. Counts*. Columbus, OH: Ohio State University Press, 1971. A sympathetic look at the thought of the leading educational radical of the Depression Era and its evolution into the World War II years and after.

Kliebard, Herbert. *Schooled to Work: Vocationalism and the American Curriculum, 1876–1946*. New York: Teachers College Press, 1999. A profile of the forces behind the rise of vocational education and the various twists and turns the subject took within the school curriculum in the twentieth century.

Kridel, Craig and Robert V. Bullough. *Stories of the Eight-Year Study: Reexamining Secondary Education in America*. Albany, NY: State University of New York, 2007. A revealing blend of intellectual history and profiles of reform leaders that opens new ways of understanding this important (and often overlooked) study.

Olson, Keith W. *The G.I. Bill, the Veterans, and the Colleges*. Lexington, KY: University Press of Kentucky, 1974. An overview of the political climate that gave rise to one of the landmarks in the evolution of increased educational opportunity for Americans in the twentieth century.

Rousmaniere, Kate. *City Teachers: Teaching and School Reform in Historical Perspective*. New York: Teachers College Press, 1997. A challenging look at the occupational lives of women teachers and the values and understandings that made them suspicious of reformers, teacher unionists, and others who were ostensibly fighting for their welfare.

Tushnet, Mark. *The NAACP's Legal Strategy against Segregated Education, 1935–1950*. Chapel Hill: University of North Carolina Press, 1987. An account of the NAACP's attempt to use the "separate but equal" doctrine as a vehicle to improve black education. Leaders in that movement are profiled and their successes and failures are noted.

Westbrook, Robert B. *John Dewey and American Democracy*. Ithaca, NY: Cornell University Press, 1991. A political account of Dewey's life and work, in which his alliances and his rivalries are plumbed to show him as a democratic thinker working in the midst of many undemocratic rivals.

Notes

1. Raymond E. Callahan, *Education and the Cult of Efficiency*. Chicago: University of Chicago Press, 1961.
2. George S. Counts, *The Selective Character of American Secondary Education*. Chicago: University of Chicago Supplementary Educational Monographs No. 19, 1922; Edward A. Krug, *The Shaping of the American High School, 1920–1941*. Madison: University of Wisconsin Press, 1972, p. 120, 126–127.
3. *Historical Statistics of the United States: Colonial Times to 1970*. Washington, D.C.: U.S. Government Printing Office, 1975, vol. I, pp. 135, 224–241.
4. One historian has dealt at length with the long-lasting consequences of the "invisible scar" left by the Great Depression. See Caroline Byrd, *The Invisible Scar: The Great Depression, and What It Did to American Life, from Then until Now*. New York: David McKay, New York, 1966.
5. Studs Terkel, *Hard Times*. New York: Pantheon, 1970.
6. Ibid., pp. 116–117.
7. See commentaries at http://www.livinghistoryfarm.org/farminginthe30s/water_02.html.
8. John Steinbeck, *The Grapes of Wrath*. New York: Penguin, [1939], 2002, p. 233.
9. "Okie" was a derisive term used to refer to people from Oklahoma and other southwestern, midwestern and sometimes southern states who migrated West during the depression era.
10. Lyman B. Burbank, "Chicago Public Schools and the Depression Years of 1928–1937," *Journal of the Illinois State Historical Society*, vol. 64, 1971, pp. 365–381.
11. For our account of Detroit, we rely on Jeffrey Mirel, "The Politics of Educational Retrenchment in Detroit," *History of Education Quarterly*, vol. 24, 1984, pp. 323–358 and Jeffrey Mirel, *The Rise and Fall of an Urban School System: Detroit, 1907–81*. Ann Arbor: University of Michigan, [1993], 1996.
12. Ibid., esp. chaps. 3 and 4.
13. See note 2, above; George S. Counts, *The Social Composition of Boards of Education: A Study in the Social Control of Education*. Chicago: University of Chicago Press, 1927; George S. Counts, *School and Society in Chicago*. New York: Harcourt, Brace, 1928.
14. This remarkable journal began publication in the mid-1930s and lasted until the early 1940s. For an account of Counts and the *Social Frontier* that is friendly but critical, see C. A. Bowers, *The Progressive Educator and the Depression: The Radical Years*. New York: Random House, 1969.
15. George S. Counts, *Dare the School Build a New Social Order?* Carbondale, IL: Southern Illinois University Press, [1932], 1978. Much of what we say about Counts is drawn from the preface of this edition, written by Wayne Urban. Also, see Ronald Goodenow and Wayne Urban, "George S. Counts: A Critical Appreciation," *Educational Forum*, January 1977, pp. 167–174.
16. Counts, *Dare the School*, p. v.
17. Ibid., p. 7.
18. Joseph W. Newman and Wayne J. Urban, "Communists in the American Federation of Teachers: A Too Often Told Story," *History of Education Review*, vol. 14, 1985, pp. 15–24.
19. Edgar Wesley, *NEA: The First Hundred Years*. New York: Harper & Brothers, 1957, pp. 301–302.
20. On the Eight Year Study, see Krug, *The Shaping*, pp. 255–267 and especially Craig Kridel, Robert Bullough, *Stories of the Eight-Year Study: Reexamining Secondary Education in America*. Albany, NY: State University of New York Press, 2007.
21. William C. Bagley, "An Essentialist's Platform for the Advancement of American Education," *Education Administration and Supervision*, vol. 24, 1938, pp. 241–256.
22. Ibid.; see Krug, *The Shaping*, p. 292 and Herbert M. Kliebard, *The Struggle for the American Curriculum, 1893–1958*. Boston: Routledge & Kegan Paul, 1986, pp. 228–233. Essentialism has experienced a resurgence since the 1990s when E. D. Hirsch, Jr., initiated the Core Knowledge movement. This development will be discussed in Chapter 12.

23. Robert S. Lynd and Helen M. Lynd, *Middletown in Transition: A Study in Cultural Conflict.* New York: Harcourt, Brace, 1937.
24. Arthur Zilversmit, "The Failure of Progressive Education, 1920–1940," in Lawrence Stone (ed.), *Schooling and Society: Studies in the History of Education.* Baltimore: Johns Hopkins University Press, 1976, pp. 252–263.
25. Ibid. See also Arthur Zilversmit, *Changing Schools: Progressive Education in Theory and Practice, 1930–1960.* Chicago: University of Chicago Press, Chicago, 1993.
26. Our treatment of the CCC, as well as the NYA, relies mainly on David Tyack, Robert Lowe, and Elisabeth Hansot, *Public Schools in Hard Times: The Great Depression and Recent Years.* Cambridge, MA: Harvard University Press, 1984, chap. 3.
27. Ibid., p. 122.
28. Ibid., pp. 125–126.
29. George P. Rawick, "The New Deal and Youth: The Civilian Conservation Corps, the National Youth Administration, and the American Youth Congress," Ph.D. dissertation, University of Wisconsin, Madison, 1957, chap. 10.
30. On Huey Long, see T. Harry Williams, *Huey Long: A Biography.* New York: Alfred A. Knopf, 1969, for a basically favorable view. A more critical account is in William Ivy Hair, *The Kingfish and His Realm: The Life and Times of Huey P. Long.* Baton Rouge: Louisiana State University Press, 1991.
31. Willard Waller, *The Sociology of Teaching.* New York: John Wiley, [1932] 1965.
32. Ibid., p. 396.
33. Ibid., p. 425.
34. Dan C. Lortie, *School Teacher: A Sociological Study.* Chicago: University of Chicago Press, 1975.
35. On this and other situations within the occupation and its organizations, see Wayne J. Urban, "Teacher Activism," in Donald R. Warren (ed.), *American Teachers: Histories of a Profession at Work.* New York: MacMillan, 1991.
36. Richard A. Quantz, "The Complex Vision of Female Teachers and the Failure of Unionization in the 1930s: An Oral History," *History of Education Quarterly*, vol. 25, 1985, pp. 439–458.
37. Kate Rousmaniere, "Women Teachers and the Space between Teacher Unions," unpublished paper, American Educational Research Association, San Francisco, April 1992.
38. Larry Cuban, *How Teachers Taught: Constancy and Change in American Classrooms.* New York: Longman, 1984.
39. Urban, "Teacher Activism."
40. *Plessy v. Ferguson* 163 U.S. 637 (1896).
41. For a good account of the campaign, see Mark Tushnet, *The NAACP's Legal Strategy against Segregated Education, 1925–1950.* Chapel Hill: University of North Carolina Press, 1987.
42. Joseph W. Newman, "A History of the Atlanta Public School Teachers' Association, Local 89 of the American Federation of Teachers, 1919–1956," Ph.D. dissertation, Georgia State University, 1978.
43. John Thelin converted these amounts into year 2000-equivalent dollars, indexed for inflation. In "today's" currency (2000), this would amount to $4,800 per year for tuition with a subsistence allowance of $489 per month for a single veteran and $734 per month for a married veteran. See John R. Thelin, *A History of American Higher Education.* Baltimore: Johns Hopkins University Press, 2004, p. 263. See also Edwin Kiester, Jr., "The G. I. Bill May Be the Best Deal Ever Made by Uncle Sam," *Smithsonian*, vol. 25, November 1994, pp. 128–139.
44. Thelin, p, 257.

10

Education during and after the Crucial Decade
1945–1960

Overview

Most Americans greeted the end of World War II with relief as well as expectations of material improvement. Yet the period from 1945 to the mid-1950s was full of uncertainty because of crises in both domestic and foreign affairs. These crises were so monumental that one historian, Eric Goldman, referred to these years as a "crucial decade." Goldman later extended his analysis to the year 1960, believing that events from 1955 to 1960 were largely a continuation of the previous decade. It is Goldman's conception of the period that frames our own analysis.[1]

Federal Economic Activity

As World War II was drawing to a close, many Americans looked forward to a period of relative peace in foreign affairs and increasing prosperity at home. Instead, the decade following the war was characterized by substantial economic, political, and social upheaval.

Domestic conflict arose over the role the federal government would play in the nation's future. The most important single issue was the degree to which the federal government involved itself in the American economy. The Roosevelt administrations, first in response to the Great Depression and then in reaction to wartime conditions, had charted a course of substantial federal involvement in the nation's economic affairs.

This federal economic activity resulted in policies and practices that helped lower- and working-class Americans, particularly those represented by organized labor, to move into the nation's economic mainstream. An important issue faced by the Truman administration after World War II was whether or not federal economic intervention, on behalf of both economic prosperity and the interests of organized labor and other workers, should continue.

Truman's Postwar Policies

Harry Truman, from more humble economic origins than Roosevelt, had been a small businessman prior to becoming a politician. To some, he seemed to be bent on reversing Roosevelt's economic policies. Early in his presidency,

Truman clashed openly and vigorously with labor, threatening to draft unionized railroad workers, who were on strike, into military service. Settlement of this situation prevented the nation from learning whether or not Truman would have carried out his threat.

Whatever ambivalence Truman had regarding organized labor, the attitude of the Republicans who controlled Congress in the late 1940s was clear. They were intent on unleashing private enterprise from the federal shackles they believed had imprisoned it since the 1930s, when protection had been granted to union workers because of the Depression, and then because of the war.

Issues surrounding the role of organized labor took center stage nationally with the enormous publicity given to the strike of the United Mine Workers (UMW) in December 1946. The leader of the UMW, John L. Lewis, had clashed with President Roosevelt during World War II, and he seemed unafraid of President Truman or the federal judge who slapped an injunction on the UMW when its members refused to work without a contract. Lewis eventually capitulated to the injunction, but his willingness to stand up to the government made him a hero among the coal miners he represented and among many other working-class citizens as well.

Matters reached a critical stage in 1947. In that year, Congress passed the Taft-Hartley Act, a complicated measure that included a provision for delaying a strike during a "cooling-off" period that permitted further labor–management negotiations. Truman vetoed the Act and thereby restored some of his labor support, but the Republicans, aided by several conservative Democrats, mainly from the South, were powerful enough in both houses of Congress to override his veto.

Truman used his opposition to Taft-Hartley as a weapon in the 1948 presidential election. In that year, the national electorate refused to heed the congressional conservatives' leadership, foiled the *Chicago Tribune* and the many pollsters who had predicted a victory for Republican Thomas Dewey of New York, and reelected Truman. In domestic affairs, Truman's postelection agenda was consistent with that of the partial term he had served after Roosevelt's death. He sought basically to hold the line on the New Deal reforms and to preserve, though clearly not to enhance, government activity on behalf of ordinary Americans. He maintained the price controls imposed during wartime, thus enabling poor and working-class Americans to cope with postwar inflation. After the 1948 election, Truman's price controls seemed vindicated since a deflationary trend lowered prices for the first time in a number of years.

Truman sought specifically to reach out to farmers, labor, immigrants, and African Americans with proposals such as increases in farm subsidies and the minimum wage. He appealed to many Americans by advocating improvements in social security benefits and a more progressive federal income tax. Congress proved to be effective more often than not, however, in preventing Truman's plans from reaching fruition. Yet his 1948 reelection meant that for at least four more years the conservative "correction" to two decades of Democratic leadership would be sidetracked.

The Influence of American Communism

If the elections of 1948 and 1952 had been decided solely on domestic issues, it seems likely that Truman and the Democrats would have continued in power. However, domestic affairs were overshadowed by the specter of an insurgent international communism that bedeviled politicians of both parties. Truman reacted dramatically to communism in the late 1940s, with measures such as the airlift into Berlin to break the communist blockade of that city. He also pursued the Korean conflict in an attempt to contain the spread of communism in Asia. Despite such actions, Truman and the Democrats were successfully stigmatized as being "soft on communism," a charge that contributed significantly to Adlai Stevenson's defeat in the 1952 presidential election.

Truman's most vigorous and vocal critic on the communist issue was a Republican senator from Wisconsin, Joseph McCarthy. Through a series of charges that communists abounded in various governmental agencies, McCarthy managed to implant the threat of communism firmly in the minds of most Americans. First, he charged that the Department of State was riddled with communists who conducted national foreign policy in the interests of an alien power. In addition, McCarthy and other like-minded superpatriots combed the movie industry and the colleges and universities for hints of communist activity. Many Republicans and Democrats alike were alienated by McCarthy's cavalier attitude and his utter disregard for supporting facts. It became apparent that he frequently resorted to non-existent or flimsy evidence to "prove" his charges of disloyalty. Yet non-McCarthyite Republicans had to acknowledge the senator's success in rallying the American people to his cause, and thereby winning support for Republican candidates and policies.

Dwight Eisenhower's victories in 1952 and 1956 meant a calming trend in American domestic affairs, due largely to his ability to communicate an aura of confidence to the American people. The presence of a famous military general in the White House, as well as the increasing shrillness and unreality of McCarthy's claims, helped bring his destructive crusade to an end. When McCarthy charged that the U.S. Army was packed with communists, the hearings conducted to air those charges revealed to the nation the fantasy world in which he often lived. The swift decline in his reputation was an early testimony to the effectiveness of television, which covered the Army/McCarthy hearings in depth.

Domestic Affairs, 1952–1960

Under Eisenhower's leadership, the nation settled into a period of relative calm and prosperity. The suburbanization of the nation began in these years with the development of the Levittown community on Long Island, just outside New York City. Although Eisenhower did not care to be perceived as an advocate of

Figure 10.1 "You read books, eh?"

Credit: 1949 Herblock Cartoon, copyright by The Herb Block Foundation.

federal economic activity, it was his support for federal housing loans and the federally financed Interstate Highway System that fueled suburban development. Television was only one of a number of mass consumer goods which were marketed extensively to the American people. Widely available in American homes, TV projected an idyllic image of suburban prosperity through shows such as *Ozzie and Harriet* and *Father Knows Best*. Television comedy also became a mass-marketed phenomenon as entertainers such as Milton Berle, Sid Caesar, and Lucille Ball attained enormous recognition.

The paternal image of a benign "Ike" calmed day-to-day anxieties that Americans had about the changes the country was undergoing. Eisenhower encouraged acceptance of his administrations by refusing to rescind the pact that his Democratic predecessors had reached with organized labor. Although he was no avowed friend of labor, neither was he a committed enemy. Labor managed to share in the prosperity of the 1950s and to attain a comfortable portion of the material goods that its members were producing.

In spite of this large-scale satisfaction with American society and with the goods the economy was producing, critical voices could still be heard. The "beat" movement in literature emerged during this decade, led by such writers as Jack Kerouac and Allen Ginsberg. Journalistic criticism of American business emerged in works such as those of Vance Packard concerning the advertising industry and William Whyte's *The Organization Man*. Academics also were critical of the consequences of abundance and materialism in various segments of American life. In 1950, C. Wright Mills published an exposé of the negative changes in middle-class life in *White Collar*, and later in the decade exposed the inequitable distribution of power and wealth in society with *The Power Elite*. A team of academics produced a profile of the emptiness in the lives of many Americans, when compared to the lives of a preceding generation, in a book revealingly titled *The Lonely Crowd*. Ralph Ellison searingly profiled the demeaning existence endured by African Americans in his novel, *Invisible Man*. Despite the efforts of these and other critics, American life and American schools proceeded largely unchanged.[2]

The Soviet Threat

Although the "threat" of domestic communism diminished substantially with the decline of McCarthyism, the fear of international communism and the Soviet Union did not suffer a comparable decline. When the Soviet Union launched *Sputnik*, the first space satellite, in 1957, Americans feared that their nation had lost its scientific and technological lead. The international aggressiveness of Nikita Khrushchev, whose penchant for publicity was in marked contrast to that of his predecessors, helped stir the fears of American citizens. Khrushchev's combative stance during his trips to America, as well as his actions during the visits of American leaders to the Soviet Union, intensified fears about America's place in the world. His well-publicized remark, "We will bury you," served as a signature threat for many fearful Americans.

In retrospect, Khrushchev proved to be the most liberal leader of his nation until the last decade of the twentieth century. His overt bellicosity, however, hid the moderate stance he adopted in world affairs. Furthermore, the American government knew, through its intelligence agencies, that the Soviet Union, despite its successful satellite launchings, lagged far behind the United States in weaponry, in other scientific accomplishments, and in its standard of living. Thus, the government knew that Soviet power was overrated and that our nation could withstand Soviet military and economic competition.

The government's unwillingness to publicize its own surreptitious intelligence activities prevented a formal acknowledgement of our superior capabilities. In addition, the military establishment used the Soviet "threat" to maintain itself against those who wanted to cut the defense budget. This also militated against publicly recognizing America's superiority in relation to the Soviet Union. However, *Sputnik's* launching did evoke a substantial response from the federal government in the educational arena. How that response tried, but largely failed, to reach into the public schools is discussed later in this chapter. What contributed most to the social conflict of the 1950s, however, lay not in the area of international relations, but in domestic race relations.[3]

Race

The impact of the 1954 and 1955 decisions in the *Brown v. Board of Education* segregation cases was to be far reaching. *Brown* proved to be a most unusual decision in that it involved an issue of educational policy that had effects that were felt both inside and outside of schools. It may have been one of the few occasions in our history when an educational policy was the catalyst for substantial changes in social relations and policies outside the schools. Inside the educational system, *Brown* was wrenching for all school districts, whether they attempted to implement or fight its mandates. Outside the schools, *Brown* helped spark a civil rights movement that galvanized many African Americans into organized political and social action on their own behalf.[4]

The conflict over *Brown* certainly belied the standard picture of the post-World War II years as a time of domestic tranquility. Before looking closely at *Brown*, however, two other educational conflicts, the continuing debate over academic priorities and the educational reaction to *Sputnik*, deserve attention.

The Life Adjustment Curriculum and its Critics

The curriculum debate between educational traditionalists and innovators that raged in the late 1940s and early 1950s had its analog in several earlier eras of American educational history. Earlier chapters discussed the dispute between the innovator Horace Mann and the conservative Boston grammar schoolmasters, the quarrels over intelligence testing and curriculum differentiation early in the twentieth century, the coalescing of various groups in pursuit of curriculum changes in the progressive era, the battle between child-centered and social-centered progressives in the 1930s, and the critique of educational progressives by the essentialists in that same decade.

As suggested in Chapter 8, progressive education in the 1920s lost its link to a larger social reform movement. American society in that decade was less amenable to reform than it had been before World War I. Sensing this loss or experiencing it themselves in their own lives and thought, educational reformers began to think about and to plan educational reform without reference to any larger social agenda. The spate of social reconstructionist ideas that surfaced in the 1930s came mostly from a group of "frontier" thinkers, who were confined largely to Columbia University Teachers College, the Ohio State University, and a few other institutions. Social reconstructionism, although causing a stir in the Progressive Education Association (PEA) in the early 1930s, failed to take hold within the PEA or any other group of administrators or teachers.

The Functional Curricula

That is not to say that educational change was completely absent within professional circles in the 1930s and 1940s. Rather, the kinds of changes that did emerge were devoid of any social or political reform intention. Curriculum reform produced such approaches as the core curriculum, which combined English and history or social studies into instruction that centered on occupational and personal needs. Other types of curriculum reform also stressed vocational subjects or courses under the label of "life skills." The umbrella term for these different approaches to curriculum change was "functional" curriculum, and it quickly became an antonym for the standard academic, or college preparatory, curriculum. Whatever brand of functional curricular reform was tried in a particular setting, its presence usually entailed replacing one or another traditional academic subject.[5]

The progressive education movement after World War II continued to employ a number of different child-centered curricula that paid little attention to life outside schools, except when needing outside support for a specific curricular change. John Dewey, for one, had already attacked this type of anti-academic tendency in child-centered progressivism in his 1938 book, *Experience and Education*. However, the child-centered progressives of that decade were not inclined to hear Dewey's plea to combine or reinterpret traditional subject matter in light of the child's needs. Rather, they continued to focus on the irrelevance of the traditional academic curriculum. Although the functional curriculum advocates of the 1930s and 1940s were not attuned to their child-centered colleagues, the two groups shared an antipathy to traditional subject matter.

A new emphasis in curriculum reform literature arose in the immediate post-World War II years. It grew out of a meeting of vocational educators in 1945, and its leader was a noted vocational educator, Charles Prosser. Prosser was worried about the great number of high school students who were not being adequately served by a high school curriculum composed of academic, college preparatory studies on one end and vocational studies on the other. He estimated that students in the unserved middle represented 60 percent of the total enrollment. What Prosser and his colleagues felt would most benefit these students was "the life adjustment they need and to which they are entitled as American citizens."[6]

The particulars of life adjustment curricula varied significantly from place to place. Whatever the variation, however, life adjustment studies everywhere were based on principles of functionality and were touted as necessary for life in a "democratic" society. Invocation of the word "democracy" allowed the life adjustment educators to distance themselves from traditional subjects by implying that those were somehow "undemocratic." The life adjustment curriculum, with its goal of serving the needs of students living in a democracy, judged subjects on the basis of their social usefulness. For example, business arithmetic or business English were preferred to the more traditional versions of these two subjects, since these business-oriented courses dealt with problems and issues that students would soon be facing in their adult lives.

The goal of life adjustment education was to improve individuals and society through training geared to future experience as a home member, a worker, and a citizen. The student who emerged from this curriculum would be well adjusted and prepared to live effectively in modern society.

It is not clear whether or not life adjustment education had much impact on the public school curriculum. Searches for significant implementation of life adjustment curricula have turned up several examples but little evidence of a trend. However, it did capture the attention of the U.S. Office of Education, the federal educational agency, and many professional educational leaders. In general, life adjustment seems to have been another version of the functional curriculum movement and can be viewed as another assault in the recurring war on the traditional academic curriculum.

The long-term decline of traditional academic subjects that seemed to culminate with the life adjustment movement of the late 1940s was startling. According to one high school curriculum expert, while 83.3 percent of high school students studied a foreign language in 1910, by 1955 that percentage had declined to 20.6. Similar declines were registered in all history courses except American history. With the change in mathematics and English from traditional to functional courses, the alteration of the total high school curriculum in these years was substantial and dramatic.[7]

Critics of Life Adjustment

A series of books emerged in the late 1940s and early 1950s that bitterly criticized the anti-intellectualism of life adjustment and other curriculum reforms. Critics included laymen such as Mortimer Smith and Albert Lynd, military leaders such as Admiral Hyman Rickover, and college professors such as Arthur Bestor. They argued that the schools needed to be rescued from progressive educators who, in their minds, had come to dominate education. In many ways, the 1950s critics continued the attack on progressivism begun in the 1930s by the essentialists and by university faculty and administrators such as Robert Maynard Hutchins, president of the University of Chicago.[8]

Arthur Bestor

Understandably, the 1950s critics did not agree with their predecessors in every particular. Yet a common thread of antiprogressivism and a defense of academic traditionalism prevailed. A close look at the ideas of one representative critic, Arthur Bestor, is illustrative. A history professor at the University of Illinois, Bestor was familiar with the inside workings of professional education and thus was quite knowledgeable about the enemy he and his reformist colleagues were fighting.

Figure 10.2 "I've always said that the only teacher I need is life itself."

Credit: Reprinted by permission of Kyle Kaser.

Bestor had published in the area of nineteenth-century utopian reforms and knew well the educational ideas of William Maclure, as discussed in Chapter 4. In 1952 he published a journal article containing a direct assault on life adjustment education. His major theme in the article was that life adjustment and other curriculum changes sponsored by progressive educators were fundamentally anti-intellectual attempts that harmed the proper functioning of the public school. Bestor was not, like some critics, snobbish or elitist about education. In fact, he charged that the life adjustment movement's attempt to distance the middle 60 percent of high school students from the academic curriculum was an unwarranted attack on their intellectual abilities. Bestor believed that many if not most of these students could benefit from academic studies, if taught engagingly by committed instructors.[9]

In his article, Bestor specifically criticized developments in his own state of Illinois, where a substantial curriculum revision project had been instituted in the high schools in response to the life adjustment movement. He sarcastically exposed the triviality of some of the curricular components of the Illinois program, such as spending leisure time enjoyably, developing an effective personality, acquiring social skills through parlor games, selecting a family dentist, and "developing and maintaining wholesome boy–girl relationships." To Bestor's way of thinking, these and similar objectives were not within the purview of the school; rather, they were to be met by other social institutions such as family, church, and community. Bestor urged the school to concentrate on what it knew how to do and what it had done in the past, that is, provide instruction in academic subjects.[10]

Bestor saw several negative consequences of life adjustment curricula. First, he thought that they shortchanged students by preventing them from contact with academic studies. In addition, he felt they shortchanged colleges and universities by forcing them to deal with generally unprepared entrants. Most important, he argued, they shortchanged society by saddling it with a youth cohort that was unversed in academic knowledge and skills and thus unprepared to meet the intellectual and civic challenges of the twentieth century.

Bestor's response to life adjustment and other curriculum reforms was, in his own words, "to reaffirm our belief in the value of intellectual training to all men, whatever their occupation, whatever their background, whatever their income or position in society." To do this would be to recover the traditional and vital purpose of intellectual accomplishment in the public schools, a purpose that had been abandoned by the professional educators in charge of those institutions.[11]

Bestor's Criticism of Teacher Education

A year after his initial article was published, Bestor published a book that expanded on his ideas without fundamentally changing them. The title of the book, *Educational Wastelands*, indicated Bestor's opinion about what had happened to both the public schools and the schools of education that trained their teachers and leaders. In the book, Bestor lashed out at the intellectual flabbiness that he thought characterized the faculty in schools of education.[12]

Teacher training, according to Bestor, needed an overhaul as badly as did the public school curriculum. Scholars within the academic disciplines needed to reclaim their influence over the training of secondary teachers. Only through such a reclamation could high school teachers and high school studies alike be saved from the anti-intellectualism of the educationists.

Bestor and his colleagues were successful in capturing the attention of a large and influential segment of the American public. Publicity for his critique was fueled, at least in part, by Cold War fears that were surfacing about college campuses. The critics' attack on schools of education as bastions of anti-intellectualism succeeded, particularly among traditional arts and sciences scholars and often among their students.

The Demise of Progressive Education

Another accomplishment that Bestor and other academic reformers could claim at least partial credit for was the demise of progressive education as a cohesive movement in American education. According to Lawrence Cremin, historian of progressive education, the end of the movement came in the mid-1950s with two specific developments. The first occurred in 1955, when the PEA disbanded because of waning enthusiasm for the cause and due to a grievous shortage of members. Two years later the journal of the PEA, *Progressive Education*, suspended publication. The demise of the PEA and its journal did not mean the rebirth of academic ideas and values in America's public schools, however. In fact, as Cremin argued, progressive education was in part a victim of its own success. Its concern for the child and its skepticism about "pure" academic studies had captured a significant segment of America's educators, particularly those in colleges and universities that trained teachers.[13]

Thus, despite these considerable successes, Bestor and his colleagues did not make significant inroads into the ranks of public school curriculum makers. That penetration would be attempted again in the next decade, after the United States received one of the most visible setbacks ever in the international arena.

Sputnik and the National Defense Education Act

The most significant educational consequence of *Sputnik*, even more important in the long run than the attention paid to academic studies, was the impetus it gave to federal financing of public education. The battle over the issue of federal aid to education in the United States had been going on since before the birth of the nation. During the era of the Articles of Confederation, before the Constitution was adopted in 1789, the national legislature passed the Northwest Ordinance of 1785, which set aside parcels of land to be sold, with the proceeds used to support schooling. "Land-grant" monies were also used to provide federal funds for agricultural and mechanical education in the two Morrill Acts, passed in 1862 and 1890. Between the two Morrill Acts, Congress had considered but did not pass other bills that would have provided more general federal aid to schooling in all of the states.

In the twentieth century, first in the 1910s and again in the 1930s and 1940s, Congress passed vocational education measures that provided federal funding for vocational programs. Thus, by the end of World War II, when the nation and Congress addressed the issues of the postwar world, concern for education was in the forefront. In addition to the successful passage of the GI Bill, discussed in the previous chapter, during the war years Congress had approved measures that provided federal funds for overpopulated schools located adjacent to military bases. Given these traditions, Congress's consideration of a variety of postwar proposals to increase the federal role in education was in keeping with a long-standing tradition. President Truman supported advocates of increased federal funding, and in 1947 convened the national Commission on Higher Education.

In considering the federal role in education, members of Congress were scattered along a continuum of positions. At one end stood those who opposed any federal funding or federal involvement for schools and colleges. Their argument was based on the constitutional premise that education, not being mentioned specifically in any article or amendment, must be a "derived" power and, thus, according to Article X, was the sole responsibility of the states. However, these constitutional purists had to contend with at least two "facts" that belied their position. First was the long history of federal involvement in education, as already outlined. Second, world and national conditions since the onset of the twentieth century (e.g., involvement in two world wars) had offered substantial evidence that the United States was a very different, more complex, nation than could have been envisioned by those who framed the Constitution.

At the other end of the spectrum were those who saw federal aid as the all-encompassing answer to the nation's educational problems. As discussed in earlier chapters, the National Education Association was foremost in supporting this point of view. The NEA began its pursuit of what it termed "general" federal aid for education in 1917 and continued, undaunted by repeated defeats, through the 1920s, 1930s, and 1940s. What the NEA and its congressional supporters meant by general aid was discretionary money available for whatever school improvements seemed necessary, particularly higher teacher salaries. The NEA had to wrestle with the public's very real tendency to agree with opponents of federal aid, conditioned both by long-standing fears of federal domination and by the prospect of keeping down their taxes.

Most members of Congress, as well as many Americans, stood somewhere between these two extremes. They refused to respond to an issue primarily in terms of a principled, ideological stand. Instead, they evaluated each proposal for federal aid to education in terms of the immediate interests it purported to serve. By precedent, for instance, agricultural, mechanical, and vocational concerns were some of the educational considerations worthy of federal support.

Educational Consequences of Sputnik

As discussed earlier in this chapter, the years immediately after World War II found the nation involved in the "Cold War" with communism. That war escalated rapidly at the beginning of the 1950s, as America engaged Asian communists in the Korean conflict. During this period, conservative politicians fueled the threat of creeping communism, making certain it was kept firmly in the minds of the American public. Although the election of Dwight Eisenhower in 1952 calmed the excesses of McCarthyism, the perception of communist threat continued to plague the nation for the rest of the decade.

When the Soviet Union launched *Sputnik*, the world's first space satellite, in October 1957, the fears of Cold War were once again ignited in America. In fact, the Soviets launched a second satellite before the United States could itself make a successful launch. The successful American launching did not take place until after the humiliation of an unsuccessful U.S. launch, witnessed by many Americans on their television screens.

The National Defense Education Act

The successful Soviet launchings, as contrasted with the slow and only partially successful U.S. efforts, led to some unexpected consequences in American educational circles. The first of these was the passage of the 1958 National Defense Education Act (NDEA). Congress and the Eisenhower administration had considered a number of approaches to federal aid to education prior to *Sputnik*, but the Soviet space success galvanized American politicians into action on the educational front. Several books and articles were published in the aftermath of *Sputnik*, all arguing in one way or another that the Soviets were leading in the "brain race." A telling example of the tone of these volumes comes from one of the titles, *What Ivan Knows That Johnny Doesn't*. In this volume a professor of English at a midwestern university claimed to show that there was a terrible educational deficiency in the reading, writing, and mathematical skills of American youngsters as compared to their Soviet counterparts. This argument echoed the concern for academic achievement voiced by Arthur Bestor and other academic critics of the educational establishment earlier in the decade. This time, however, critics dramatized the point with the rhetoric of the Cold War, given renewed energy in the minds of many Americans by the Soviet technological success.[14]

The provisions of the NDEA reflected some of the wishes of the Republican administration as well as some of the desires of the majority Democratic Congress. The two Democrats who led the push for the National Defense Education Act in Congress (NDEA), Lister Hill in the Senate and Carl Elliott in the House of Representatives, were both from Alabama. They represented the economically poorer states of the South and thus were receptive to aid for education from the federal government. Elliott, additionally, was intent on extending educational opportunity to students whose economic circumstances handicapped them in taking avantage of it. Alabama and other southern states were particularly unable to keep up with the demand for classrooms and teachers caused by the baby boom of the post-World War II years.

Many southern states passed minimum foundation plans for their schools in the 1940s or 1950s. These plans provided state funds for schools in the poorer, rural districts of the state, which would have languished under a locally oriented property tax provision. Thus, to a considerably greater extent than most nonsouthern states, the South had already centralized its funding at the state level.

Sputnik allowed the advocates of NDEA to tie federal aid to the national defense effort, thereby disarming much of the conservative opposition. The most effective argument for federal educational aid at the time was that the Soviets were dangerously close to a superiority in science and technology, and perhaps in other fields as well. Thus, federal aid was a way to help America close the gap.

Although opposition to federal aid was weakened by the national defense rationale, it was not completely vanquished. In addition to ideological opponents of federal aid, NDEA advocates in Congress also faced a lack of enthusiastic support from two committed friends of federal aid, the National Education Association and the Council of Chief State School Officers. Both groups objected to what they described as the NDEA's narrow focus on science and technology. Furthermore, they objected to its affinity for the college- and university-oriented National Science Foundation as opposed to the educator-oriented U.S. Office of Education. They argued for a more general and more generous distribution of federal aid than the NDEA would allow, with its focus on only science and mathematics, and a few other "defense-related" subjects.[15]

Interestingly, these groups were basically wrong, at least about Senator Hill and Representative Elliott. While both men invoked the importance of science and technology, they did this for strategic reasons, knowing that educational improvement was needed in all subjects.

The NDEA's tortuous path through Congress and the White House eventually resulted in a bill that included some small parts of many desired changes. As passed in 1958, the NDEA provided financial assistance to undergraduate college students in the form of loans and to graduate students in the form of fellowships. It also provided financial aid to states to improve instruction in science, mathematics, and foreign languages, another area deemed important in an age of international competition. It specified funding for technological, audiovisual, and media services. For the stated purpose of channeling intellectual talent into defense-related fields, NDEA also provided funds to improve guidance and counseling services. Finally, it added some funding to existing vocational legislation to improve the education of technicians.[16]

The varied provisions of the NDEA were unprecedented in many respects, but, in reality, the total amount of federal aid finally appropriated to education was not enormous. The long-lasting effect of the legislation, however, was in the precedent that had been set. Rather than continuing the trend of single-purpose legislation, the passage of this Act legitimized broad-based federal aid to education for the first time. The full scope of the federal effort was not felt until midway through the next decade, when President Lyndon Johnson piloted through Congress a more comprehensive and wider-ranging educational aid law.

The School Curriculum Reform Movement

An indirect outcome of the NDEA and related federal educational activities was the school curriculum reform movement that began in the late 1950s and continued into the 1960s. Shortly after passage of the NDEA, scientists and mathematicians, supported by the National Science Foundation, began to develop courses of study that would resuscitate the study of science and mathematics in the schools. Innovative new courses in physics, chemistry, mathematics, and biology were produced by groups of disciplinary scholars such as the Physical Sciences Study Committee (PSSC), the Biological Sciences Study Committee (BSSC), and the School Mathematics Study Group (SMSG).

Late in 1959, a meeting of reform-minded scientists and psychologists interested in instruction took place in Woods Hole, Massachusetts. A slim volume emerged from that meeting that influenced the direction of curriculum reform for the next decade. In *The Process of Education*, Harvard psychologist Jerome Bruner published an account of the learning process that served as a manifesto for academic curriculum reform. Bruner argued that what was missing in schools was a carefully structured approach to learning the academic disciplines. With some developmental differences taken into account, young people of any age could learn to think like scholars. According to Bruner, "We begin with the hypothesis that any subject can be taught effectively in some intellectually honest form to any child at any stage of development." Bruner thus provided the intellectual underpinning for curriculum created by academics but informed by the findings of instructional and developmental psychologists. The revamped science and mathematics courses of the late 1950s were soon followed by similar developments in history and in the social sciences.[17]

The outcome of these curriculum renovations scarcely resembled their creators' expectations, however. Although they were developed by academic scholars, the reorganized courses were implemented by instructional supervisors and teachers who were far less versed in the nuances of the disciplines. What seemed novel and innovative in conception and design was largely reduced to formula and ritual in the schools. One of the greatest failures of the academic reformers was their ignorance of the realities of day-to-day schooling activities. The implementation of their reform plans suffered because of their reluctance to include the insights of school people in designing the new courses.

Another problem with the curriculum reforms was the designers' failure to predict the degree of discomfort that the new approaches caused the populace at large. The anguish of parents coming to terms with the "new math" being studied by their youngsters was unanticipated. How could parents react positively to an approach that seemed alien to everything they knew about mathematics? The gap between "set theory" and basic computational skills such as addition, subtraction, multiplication, and division made too many parents uncomfortable with the new math. The ultimate failure of the subject-matter reformers to transform instruction in the academic subjects was foreordained, in a sense, by their inability to convert teachers and parents, along with students, to the new ways.

Thus, the net result of direct federal legislative and executive activity in American schooling in the 1950s was, at best, mixed. The wishes of Congress or federal executive agencies such as the National Science Foundation were always filtered through and diluted by the actions of state educational agencies, teachers, and parents. The federal judiciary, however, provided another source of federal involvement in the schools that, potentially at least, indicated a more far-reaching outcome. This, of course, had to do with the desegregation of America's schools.

Brown v. Board of Education

Harry Briggs of Summerton, South Carolina, was 34 years old in 1949. He was a Navy veteran of World War II who had lived his entire life (excepting his war service) in Clarendon County, where Summerton was located. Employed as a gas station attendant, he had bought a lot and built a small home near the black school in Summerton, the Scott's Branch School. Because his name was first alphabetically, Briggs became the lead plaintiff in a law suit brought by 20 of Clarendon County's black citizens against the school authorities of South Carolina School District 22. The chairman of that school district was Roderick W. Elliott, a white sawmill owner with a history of dealing decisively with blacks who challenged his actions. A year earlier, he had used a legal technicality to defeat an attempt by local blacks to get school buses for their children, a service the district's white children had enjoyed for years. Briggs and Elliott were the named adversaries in one of five school desegregation court cases from diverse locations that eventually reached the U.S. Supreme Court in the 1950s.[18]

Initially, the plaintiffs in the *Briggs* case were seeking, with the help of attorneys from the National Association for the Advancement of Colored People (NAACP), school facilities and services equal to those granted to whites in the district. They were asking the whites to make real their adherence to the "separate but equal" doctrine that had been legalized in the 1896 *Plessy v. Ferguson* case.[19]

In fact, since the late 1930s, progress had been made in desegregating graduate and professional studies in southern public colleges and universities. There had also been substantial progress during the 1940s in getting white authorities in various southern locales to move toward creating more equal facilities in the lower schools. One problem with the lower school cases, however, was that each had to be fought locally, proving time and again in each individual school district what seemed obvious to all but the legal system—that blacks had separate facilities that were far from equal. The legal victory of black plaintiffs in any district was not generalizable; each district had to be the subject of its own case and a new ruling. This frustration, combined with desegregation victories in the higher education cases, led to a new and far-reaching strategy on the part of the NAACP and its lead attorney, Thurgood Marshall. The NAACP vowed to attack segregation directly by arguing that the practice itself was unconstitutional. But to do this involved reversing the precedent of *Plessy*, an action the federal courts would not take without substantial evidence and argument.[20]

The other four cases that eventually got the Supreme Court's attention were from Kansas, Virginia, Delaware, and the District of Columbia. In a move designed to minimize negative political reaction in the South, the Court decided against the normal procedure of naming the consolidated cases for the plaintiff who was first alphabetically, Briggs of South Carolina. Instead, that status was transferred to Oliver Brown, the plaintiff in the case from the border state town of Topeka, Kansas. Thus, we remember the consolidated cases as *Brown v. Board of Education of Topeka.*[21]

While the *Briggs* and other *Brown* cases were ruled on by the Supreme Court in 1954, the justices had been dealing with issues raised in the *Briggs* case since December 1952. Delay, temporizing, and earnest search for a common ground composed the main reasons for the delay.[22]

Relying to some extent on evidence offered by black psychologist Kenneth B. Clark that segregation irreparably damaged black children as well as on the legal argument of the NAACP, the Supreme Court finally responded with a landmark decision in the *Brown* cases. Speaking for a unanimous Court, Chief Justice Earl Warren wrote a brief but eloquent decision. In a famous pair of sentences from that decision, Warren declared: "We conclude that in the field of public education the doctrine of 'separate but equal' has no place. Separate educational facilities are inherently unequal."[23]

The ruling in *Brown* was legally decisive. Henceforth racial segregation in public schools was against the law. But the ruling left several issues undecided, including how quickly and to what extent desegregation was to take place. Again, the Court delayed its decision, arguing within its ranks as to how compliance might be achieved. It asked the attorneys for both plaintiffs and defendants to prepare arguments regarding implementation. Many southern states responded with a litany of arguments about why desegregation would not work. Thurgood Marshall responded by asking the Court to set a date for the end of segregation. The federal government brief recommended that the defendant school boards in the cases submit plans for implementing the decision within ninety days of the ruling. Finally, in mid-1955, fourteen months after the first ruling, a second *Brown* decision was announced regarding the implementation of school desegregation.

The Court ruling tried to be responsive to all of the litigants' concerns. This ruling, acknowledging both the importance of compliance and the significance of the forces massed in resistance, stated that desegregation should proceed "with all deliberate speed." In addition, it held the federal district courts and the appeals courts responsible for determining the suitability of local school compliance. The actions of southerners, then, would be judged by the southerners who inhabited the federal benches in the southern states.[24]

This ruling reflected the realities of the situation. Although the Supreme Court was clear in the enunciation of legal principles, it took into account its own inability to guarantee enforcement of its rulings. Therefore, enforcement depended initially on the willingness of whites to comply and, later, on the pressure brought to bear from further judicial rulings and public opinion.

Reaction to the Brown Decision

The reaction to this ruling in the old Confederacy was swift. White Citizens Councils in many localities emerged to fight the *Brown* ruling, and state governors and legislatures vowed to resist as well. Southern congressmen were no help either, passing a manifesto in 1956 that called the *Brown* decisions unwarranted, unconstitutional, and an abuse of the judicial power. Compliance, if it was to come, would come largely without leadership from the politicians of the southern states.

Where it did take place, compliance came with much more deliberation than speed. In some border states, compliance began slowly, but progress was made. "Freedom of choice" plans, forcing no student to attend any school, dominated. However, in most southern states, any form of compliance was delayed for several years and, when eventually undertaken, amounted to a "token" effort at best. "Progress" occurred, for example, in Atlanta, Georgia, where the effort received national approbation. The Atlanta plan called for a small group of carefully screened black students to attend a previously all-white high school. Further desegregation, using only token numbers of students, was to take place at the rate of one grade per year, continuing for more than a decade until the first graders would finally participate. For a time, this halting and partial desegregation was hailed as a national model of desegregation that worked.

While southern politicians, whether local, state, or federal, could be counted on to be of a single mind in their opposition to *Brown* and the cause of school desegregation, the actions of the federal executive and legislative branches were harder to predict. In 1957, Congress passed a civil rights law that, although timid in intent and mild in approach, put that body on the side of racial equity.

Little Rock, Arkansas

In 1958, in Little Rock, Arkansas, the federal executive branch was put to the test on the question of *Brown*. Arkansas seemed an unlikely place for violent opposition to desegregation. Although it had been one of the eleven Confederate states, it had as much in common with the West as with the rest of the South, and it was far from the hotbed of reaction to *Brown* that the deep South had become. Furthermore, Arkansas's governor, Orval Faubus, had been mild in his initial reaction to the decisions.

Little Rock was characterized by a newer generation of civic leaders who were wedded more to notions of civic progress and image than to die-hard resistance to desegregation. Court-approved plans for the desegregation of Little Rock's Central High School proceeded smoothly, with the admission of nine carefully selected black students. One of Little Rock's newspapers was edited by Harry Ashmore, a liberal on racial matters who did not want racism to interfere with the prospects for economic development of his city and state. The citizens and politicians of Little Rock and Arkansas, however, proved to be less malleable. Governor Faubus retreated from his moderate stance as he came under pressure from other southern governors who were determined that their ranks not be broken. Faubus was one of Arkansas's poor whites, and his political antennae told him clearly that his re-election to a third term as governor was assured if he blocked the pending desegregation. Thus, when the day appointed for the desegregation of Central High School arrived, Faubus ordered the Arkansas National Guard into action to prevent the plan from being implemented.[25]

The events that took place at Central High were recorded by television cameras, and the nation recoiled at the violence etched on the faces of the defiant white parents who massed at the school. When the first of the nine black students approached the school building, the crowd became a mob intent on preventing her entrance by whatever means necessary. The enactment of this and subsequent scenes of racial hatred on television proved its ability to make as well as to record the news. Little Rock quickly became a focal point for regional reaction to and anxieties about *Brown*.

President Eisenhower became a key, if unwilling, actor in the drama at Little Rock. Although he was torn over the situation there, his personal inclinations lay more with the opponents of desegregation than with the black citizens' aspirations. In Little Rock, however, he faced a governor acting in direct opposition to a federal court order. Downplaying the issue of desegregation, Eisenhower finally reacted firmly, treating this opposition as an act of insurrection. The President sent in federal troops and nationalized the Arkansas National Guard, which moved decisively to implement the desegregation of Central High School.

When federal troops were withdrawn after a few weeks of apparent order, the National Guard was put in sole charge and the situation took another turn for the worse. White students opposed to desegregation at Central High began a year-long harassment of the black students. Whites who might have been inclined to be friendly, or at least not overtly hostile, were threatened with

Figure 10.3 People holding signs and American flags protesting admission of the "Little Rock Nine" to Central High School, August 20, 1959.

Credit: Library of Congress, Prints and Photographs Division, LC-U9-2908-15.

reprisals if they acted in other than a negative or indifferent manner toward the blacks. This hostility eventually caused the withdrawal of one of the original nine black students from Central High. The remaining eight students endured, rather than prospered, for the rest of the school year. A year later, when a spokesperson for the students suggested they might benefit from a visit to the White House, the president and his advisors signaled clearly that they had no desire to embrace openly those who had desegregated Little Rock's schools.[26]

Aftermath

Little Rock and Central High proved to be prophetic in several ways. The actions of Governor Faubus showed other southern politicians how they could turn opposition to court-ordered school desegregation into direct political benefit, regardless of other consequences. And although formal compliance in Little Rock was achieved, it did not alter the unrelenting opposition of whites to the desegregation process. Thus, both desegregation and the resistance to desegregation were given sustenance at Central High School.

Nationally, the televised hatred of reactionary whites in Little Rock made whites outside the South noticeably uncomfortable. They might not favor racial justice in their own backyards, but the vivid image of bigoted, hate-filled southerners led many of them to acknowledge the need for federal intervention in that benighted region. The hesitant, then decisive, but seldom principled actions of President Eisenhower showed clearly the consequences of mixed messages sent by a chief executive. The actions of his two immediate successors, John Kennedy and Lyndon Johnson, reinforced the significance of a national leader's stance. Eventually, they would both lead the nation in a more positive direction in its race relations.

A final irony to the *Brown* decision is worthy of mention. There is no doubt that *Brown* signaled a distinct revolution in American race relations. As a direct result, Jim Crow was destroyed not only in the South, but also in the rest of the nation. The irony revealed in Little Rock, however, was that while desegregation might be accomplished in token numbers in the schools, it would be far harder to accomplish meaningful change. Thus, despite the fact that *Brown* involved the schools, its consequences were felt more significantly outside the schools than within.

The next chapter will recount the determined but largely unsuccessful drive to achieve racial equity in American schools in the decades of the 1960s and 1970s. If, as argued in the last chapter of this book, the 1980s represented a retreat from racial equity in the schools, the experience immediately after the *Brown* decision can be clearly seen to have foreshadowed that retreat.

While conflicts in educational affairs occurred over issues of race, curriculum, and federal aid in the 1950s, there was one other issue internal to the public schools that remained tense from 1945 to 1960, and beyond. That issue was teacher pay and working conditions.

Teachers' Strikes and Teacher Organizations

A number of school conflicts emerged in the immediate post-World War II years from a relatively unexpected source, the teaching ranks. Postwar price increases for consumer goods aggravated the unfavorable economic conditions that teachers had been experiencing. In the later stages of the Depression, teachers had begun to complain openly about their relatively low salaries and their lack of retirement benefits. In a decade when Social Security legislation brought retirement to the forefront of society's consciousness, teachers saw little improvement for themselves.

During the war years teachers had been as patriotic as any Americans, and had put their economic grievances aside as the nation pursued the conflicts in Europe, Asia, and North Africa. Although all workers labored under wartime wage controls, those in the private sector often ameliorated their situation by working "overtime," an option not available to teachers. In the immediate aftermath of the war, especially after price controls were lifted in the summer of 1946, inflation became a serious problem for teachers, whose wages had been held at the low levels established early in the war years.

The situation was aggravated for veteran teachers by soldiers returning to the teaching ranks, sometimes at salaries well above those of the women who had continued to teach during the war. In addition, teachers were feeling the effect of their flat, relatively meager salaries being subjected to a rising federal income tax that was used to offset wartime debts. As the nation moved into postwar hiring conditions, teachers increasingly began to vent their frustrations by engaging in strikes or similar job actions.

Strikes in Small Towns

In the fall of 1946, the first full school year after the end of World War II, teachers' grievances reached a boiling point in several school districts in smaller towns and cities. In Norwalk, Connecticut, teachers vowed not to report for the opening of school in September because their board of education refused to fund a salary increase it had agreed to the preceding February. As Norwalk's teachers made good their threat, the school board relented and granted a substantial portion of the agreed-on increase in response to direct pressure from the state commissioner of education. That fall, Norwalk's experience was repeated in small cities in Pennsylvania, Iowa, Wisconsin, Ohio, and Tennessee.[27]

As long as such activity was concentrated in towns or small cities, publicity about the increasing number of teachers' strikes was controlled, and the nation could overlook the phenomenon. However, as teachers in larger cities such as New York and Chicago contemplated strikes, the situation became more and more difficult to ignore. Although, for various reasons, teachers' strikes did not occur in these cities, strikes in the twin cities of Minnesota, as well as in Buffalo, New York, and suburban Detroit, Michigan, garnered national attention.

The Twin Cities Strikes

Teachers in St. Paul and Minneapolis, Minnesota, like their colleagues in smaller towns and cities, were interested in improving their pay and working conditions. Because of a limit on school tax revenues approved decades earlier, in 1946 the St. Paul school board presented its teachers with the "choice" of a pay cut, a shortening of the school year, or the elimination of kindergartens. In response, St. Paul's teachers demanded at least a $50-per-month salary raise and implementation of a new salary scale containing even larger increases. Teachers vowed to strike if their demands were not met. Although city and state politicians tried to act as peacemakers, the board threatened teachers with severe reprisals if they failed to report to work. On the first Monday after the Thanksgiving holiday, St. Paul's teachers carried out their threatened strike, and two-thirds of the city's teachers did not show up at school. The strike lasted through the Christmas holidays. Late in December, however, city leaders found a way to increase educational expenditures enough to partially meet the teachers' demands, and the strike ended.

In Minneapolis, teachers initially fared better than their colleagues in St. Paul. The teachers' unions in Minneapolis had reached an agreement with their board in 1946 on a contract that provided for substantial salary increases for three successive years. In 1947, however, the board faced severe limitations in its ability to raise revenue, and found that it had to borrow funds to meet its obligations to the teachers. In December 1947, the board announced that it would no longer borrow to meet its commitments and that teachers would face salary reductions and/or reductions in the number of school days in the following spring and fall.

This announcement resulted in a strike by the Minneapolis teachers in February 1948, which lasted for almost a month. When the teachers received a court injunction forcing them back to work, they responded by suing the board. This pushed both parties in the direction of a settlement. Eventually, the board agreed to borrow again to fund a salary increase, though the pay raises were not of the levels prescribed in the original agreement. Thus, like teachers in their sister city, Minneapolis's teachers could claim at least a partial victory as a result of their strike. Publicity from these two big-city strikes gave teachers' strikes substantial visibility nationally. That visibility increased further with strikes in Buffalo, New York, and a near-strike in Detroit, Michigan. Both of these job actions provoked responses from state legislatures as well as from the local school authorities.

City Strikes and State Responses

Late in February 1947, 2,400 Buffalo teachers refused to go to work, constituting the greatest number of teachers ever to have gone on strike. Teachers in Buffalo, having seen the 1946–47 school budget cut by the mayor because of a prospective decline in city revenue, were seeking both a cost-of-living adjustment and a new salary scale. They received neither, but the strike that ensued eventually led to partial fulfillment of their requests. In this case, state politicians joined city leaders to provide substantial relief for the teachers.

New York's state legislative action on behalf of Buffalo's public schools and teachers was also geared to appeal to teachers throughout the state, since circumstances similar to those in Buffalo existed in many New York school districts. The legislature enacted a proposal for a new state salary scale that provided substantial raises for both beginning and experienced teachers. In addition, and in a move not approved by many teachers' unions, the legislature passed a law prohibiting teachers' strikes like the one that had taken place in Buffalo.

Teachers in Detroit, Michigan, were contemplating actions like those of their colleagues in other cities. In December 1946, the Detroit Federation of Teachers (DFT) undertook a "poster walk" (a picketing outside the board of education headquarters) to dramatize teachers' salary grievances. At almost the same time, St. Paul's teachers went on strike, and Detroit's teachers quickly contributed to the St. Paul strike fund.

As the Detroit situation progressed, the DFT grew closer and closer to a strike of its own. The union was seeking direct negotiations with the school board when news of the Buffalo teachers' strike reached Detroit. Dispatching its own representative for a firsthand look at the situation in Buffalo, the DFT succeeded in winning a round of negotiations from the school board. These negotiations proved unfruitful, however, and, again, a strike seemed imminent.

The threat of the Teamsters' Union to honor teacher picket lines indicated that Detroit's teachers might well shut down the schools if they struck. Compromise emerged when city politicians with ties to organized labor intervened and engineered a settlement that substantially increased teachers' salaries. That settlement, however, provoked a bitter reaction from the city's powerful business leadership.[28]

The negative reaction of Detroit's business leaders was heightened by the actions of the teachers in East Detroit, a suburban school district. There teachers refused to report for work in May 1947, as the Detroit dispute neared resolution. Seeking a pay increase, the teachers were stymied by the refusal of East Detroit's citizens to increase property taxes to finance the increase. Thus, East Detroit's teachers struck again later in May. A subsequent special tax election in early June, undertaken to respond to the teachers' demands, was unsuccessful. Another election in the fall of 1947 provided a partial gain for the teachers, assuring them one-fourth the raise in salary they had sought.

Detroit's near-strike and East Detroit's strike also provoked a reaction from the state legislature. Spurred on by business and other opposition to the strikers, the Michigan lawmakers passed a measure that resembled the New York state law prohibiting teachers' strikes. However, unlike the New York measure, and perhaps in response to labor's strength in the state's industrial areas, the Michigan legislation also prescribed a grievance process that the state's teachers could use as an alternative to striking.

NEA and AFT Reaction to Strikes

The NEA and the AFT were markedly ambivalent in their reaction to the numerous post-World War II teachers' strikes. The Norwalk, Connecticut, strike and the threat of strikes in other small towns usually involved an affiliate of the NEA, while most of the big-city strikes were conducted by AFT locals. In every case, the national group tried to respond as positively as possible to the particular situation without condoning the strike specifically. Both national groups were officially on record as being opposed to teachers' strikes, and the AFT actually had adopted a formal no-strike policy. Neither group abrogated its opposition to teachers' strikes during this period, yet they both refused to condemn the actions of their striking members.

The contradictions and the tensions in the policies and practices of the national teacher organizations with regard to their striking members were mitigated in the next several years as the number of teachers' strikes receded and the publicity surrounding strikes diminished. Also, the Korean War meant a return to price controls, which tamed the inflation that had fueled the teachers' strikes after World War II. The news media's focus on the Korean War brought a renewed emphasis on international events, which diverted attention from striking teachers.

Teachers' strikes never ceased completely during the 1950s, but their number and intensity lessened as the decade wore on. However, the issues teachers had raised in the postwar strikes came into increasing prominence in the latter half of the 1950s. In that period, the differences in the leadership styles of the two teacher organizations became clearer.

NEA and AFT in the Late 1950s

The NEA celebrated its 100th anniversary in 1957 with a largely self-congratulatory series of publications and events. At the time of its centennial, and despite its many accomplishments during its first hundred years, the NEA was in several respects poorly placed to respond to growing teacher agitation. Its mixed teacher/administrator membership, with administrators dominating the association, meant that the NEA was not structured to respond to rising teacher militancy. Furthermore, it was dominated by a staff distinguished both by its long tenure in office and by its experience in school administration. The NEA's extremely large size and complex organizational structure militated further against the development of any independent teacher voice.[29]

While it would not be correct to say that the NEA opposed labor actions by teachers, it espoused a fundamentally different approach to teachers' interests than did the AFT. One difference was that the NEA saw teacher and administrator interests as compatible, if not identical. Another difference was its reliance

Figure 10.4 "Be sure to give mine special attention."

Credit: 1955 Herblock Cartoon, copyright by The Herb Block Foundation.

on persuasion and lobbying, rather than more direct job actions, in pursuit of its goals.

The AFT, however, was comfortable with more straightforward and sometimes confrontational practices such as collective bargaining, in which a school board and a teachers' organization would participate as equals in negotiating the terms of teacher employment. This is not to say that the NEA did not negotiate and that the AFT did not lobby. Rather, each group had a preference, related to its internal organizational structure and leadership, that influenced how it pursued teacher goals.

The differences between the NEA and the AFT were probed in depth by one organizational analyst of the 1950s, Myron Lieberman. His major premise was that teacher organizations were an essential component of any realistic attempt to professionalize education. Furthermore, he argued, teachers' strikes were a fact of life rather than something to be avoided at all costs. He wrote about strikes within a context that accepted teacher organizations as integral to the solution of teachers' occupational difficulties, not the cause of their problems.[30]

Lieberman acknowledged that teachers' strikes were often of questionable legality and admitted that they had caused severe problems in the public's view of teachers and the schools. He did not conclude from these observations, however, that striking was an action that teachers should eschew in principle. Rather, he saw strikes in an instrumental fashion: The issue was whether or not they managed to improve the working conditions of teachers and advance their movement toward professionalization.

In comparing the two national teacher organizations, Lieberman was as detached emotionally as he was in analyzing strikes. Yet he wrote in a way that made clear his own preference for the avowedly union American Federation of Teachers rather than the more "professional" National Education Association. The reasons for Lieberman's preference involved the AFT's more consistently "pro-teacher" stance and program. The NEA was hampered as an advocacy group for teachers by its claim to represent school superintendents and other school administrators as well as teachers. The AFT's straightforward advocacy of teachers' occupational betterment, and its refusal to confound that betterment with the often counterconcerns of school administrators, set the two groups apart for Lieberman and others.

New York City Teachers and Unions

As the 1950s drew to a close, events within the AFT affiliates in New York City showed that Lieberman was a prophet as well as an analyst. The AFT then had several local affiliates that claimed members within New York City's public school teaching ranks. Some of these included only high school teachers, only junior high school teachers, or only vocational teachers, while others, claiming to be open to all teachers, found most of their members in the high school ranks. In addition, there were groups not affiliated with the AFT, whose membership was composed either of elementary or secondary teachers. Some of the secondary teacher organizations recruited only teachers of a particular subject, such as history or English teachers. Non-AFT groups were either affiliated with the NEA or independent.

At the onset of the 1960s, several AFT affiliates amalgamated into the United Federation of Teachers (UFT). The ultimate victory of this group in securing the allegiance of all New York City's teachers was accompanied by a series of militant teachers' strikes (discussed in the next chapter) that occurred during that decade. This move toward militancy within the AFT, which was gaining momentum in New York and a few other large cities in the late 1950s, was in direct contrast with the organizational stasis in the NEA.

Gender and Unions in New York

Another difference between the two organizations was not so obvious. Specifically, in the late 1950s, as the AFT and its affiliates in New York moved toward a stance of greater teacher militancy, they reflected their numerical domination by high school male teachers. The NEA, on the other hand, in response to its large number of elementary and female teachers, proceeded more cautiously.[31]

As noted in the previous chapter, the NEA's tilt toward the orientations of female elementary teachers involved factors other than an opposition to strikes. In the late 1940s, the NEA in New York, as it had in many other states, helped push through the state legislature a "single salary scale" that guaranteed elementary teachers the same salaries as high school teachers of comparable experience and educational background. This single salary scale reversed a long-standing trend in which predominantly male high school teachers were paid higher salaries than their elementary teacher colleagues. The New York law also addressed a grievance that female teachers had felt since the end of World War II, when returning male soldiers were hired at salaries well above those paid to women with more teaching experience.

One analysis of the teacher unionization process in New York in the 1950s highlighted this situation from a male perspective. In accounting for the formation and early success of New York's United Federation of Teachers, Stephen Cole stressed how the union institutionalized the militant preferences of its mostly male, junior high and high school teachers. Cole related their militance to the resentment that men felt when the state's new single salary scale cost them the status and income advantages they had previously held over female elementary teachers.[32]

Conclusion

The fifteen years after World War II were, indeed, a crucial decade and a half for America's schools. Teachers struggled to find their place in the postwar economy and to guarantee their place in the future. Teacher organizations took on an increasingly important role in determining teachers' occupational conditions. The curriculum lurched along in response to the competing forces of life adjustment education and the academic reaction to it. *Sputnik* provided the occasion both for a spurt in academically based curriculum reform and an increase in federal educational activity. Finally, the specter of *Brown* loomed over the entire era, dominating the scene in the final five years. The issue of racial justice raised by *Brown* has not gone away. As it was in the 1950s, 1960s, and 1970s, it is still a major educational concern.

Further Reading

Berube, Maurice. *Teacher Politics: The Influence of Unions.* Westport, CT: Greenwood Press, 1988. The story of how both national teacher unions, the National Education Association and the American Federation of Teachers, participated in national politics, educational and at-large, in the second half of the twentieth century.

Clowse, Barbara Barksdale. *Brainpower for the Cold War: The Sputnik Crisis and the National Defense Education Act of 1958.* Westport, CT: Greenwood Press, 1981. A full picture of the educational politics surrounding the passage of landmark federal aid to education legislation in a politically conservative era.

Cole, Stephen. *The Unionization of Teachers: A Case Study of the UFT.* New York: Praeger, 1969. The forces behind the first substantial unionization of American teachers in New York City in the late 1950s and the winning of the first collective bargaining contract.

Cuban, Larry. *Teachers and Machines: The Classroom Use of Technology since 1920.* New York: Teachers College Press, 1986. A study of the overselling of technological solutions for the problems of American schoolrooms and the resistance of school people to this movement.

Dow, Peter B. *Schoolhouse Politics: Lessons from the Sputnik Era.* Cambridge, MA: Harvard University Press, 1981. A chronicle of the failure of a social science subject matter reform program, Man A Course of Study (MACOS), to repeat the successful changes achieved in the natural sciences in the aftermath of *Sputnik.*

Fairclough, Adam. *Teaching Equality: Black Schools in the Age of Jim Crow.* Athens, GA: University of Georgia Press, 2001. The author, Professor of American History at the University of East Anglia, examines the work of black teachers as both "liberators" and "race traitors" during the era of white supremacy.

Kliebard, Herbert. *The Struggle for the American Curriculum,* 2d ed. New York: Routledge, 1995. An evaluation of the participants in the debates over the nature of the curriculum in American schools from the time of the initial controversy over progressivism to the 1950s.

Kluger, Richard. *Simple Justice: The Story of the Brown Decision.* New York: Alfred A. Knopf, 1976. A comprehensive, award-winning study of the events leading up to the *Brown* decision, the arguing and implementation of the decision in the courts, and its initial aftermath in schools.

Patterson, James T. *Brown v. Board of Education: A Civil Rights Milestone and Its Troubled Legacy.* New York: Oxford University Press, 2001. A searching account of the meaning of the *Brown* decision for American education and American life since its promulgation.

Ravitch, Diane. *The Troubled Crusade: American Education, 1945–1980.* New York: Basic Books, 1983. A compellingly written narrative of the course of educational development in the political and social turbulence of the post-World War II decades.

Rudolph, John L. *Scientists in the Classroom: A Century of Failed School Reforms.* New York: Simon and Schuster, 2000. Details the high school science subject matter course reforms of the early 1960s. Emphasizes the failure of the scientists to alter substantially what was going on in high school science classes.

San Miguel, Jr., Guadalupe. *"Let All of Them Take Heed": Mexican Americans and the Campaign for Educational Equality in Texas, 1910–1981.* Austin, TX: University of Texas Press, 1987. The evolution of different strategies in relation to schools and to the Mexican American community that were adopted by Mexican Americans in Texas in their quest for equality of educational opportunity.

Zimmerman, Jonathan. *Whose America? Culture Wars in the Public Schools.* Cambridge, MA: Harvard University Press, 2002. An insightful and well-told story of the conflicts, compromises, and renewed conflicts over the teaching of history and morality in twentieth-century America.

Notes

1. Eric F. Goldman, *The Crucial Decade: America, 1945–1955.* New York: Alfred A. Knopf, 1956, and Goldman, *The Crucial Decade and After: America, 1945–1960.* New York: Alfred A. Knopf, 1960.
2. Vance Packard, *The Hidden Persuaders.* New York: David McKay, 1957; William F. Whyte, *The Organization Man.* New York: Simon & Schuster, 1956; C. Wright Mills, *White Collar.* New York: Oxford University Press, 1951; and Mills, *The Power Elite.* New York: Oxford University Press, 1956; David Riesman with Revel Denney and Nathan Glazer, *The Lonely Crowd.* New Haven, CT: Yale University Press, 1950; Ralph Ellison, *Invisible Man.* New York: Random House, 1952.
3. This hesitancy of our government to acknowledge our superiority because of its unwillingness to admit to its intelligence activities is discussed in David Halberstam, *The Fifties.* New York: Villard Books, 1993, p. 8.
4. *Brown v. Board of Education of Topeka,* 347 U.S. 483 (1954) and 349 U.S. 294 (1955).
5. Diane Ravitch, *The Troubled Crusade: American Education, 1945–1980.* New York: Basic Books, 1983.
6. U.S. Office of Education, *Life Adjustment for Every Youth.* Washington, D.C.: U.S. Government Printing Office, n.d., p. 15.
7. Edward A. Krug, *The Secondary School Curriculum.* New York: Harper & Brothers, 1960. See

also David L. Angus and Jeffrey E. Mirel, *The Failed Promise of the American High School, 1890–1995.* New York: Teachers College, Columbia University, 1999.

8. On the essentialists, see Chapter 9. For Hutchins's ideas, see his book, *The Higher Learning in America.* New Haven, CT: Yale University Press, 1936.

9. Arthur E. Bestor, Jr., " 'Life Adjustment' Education: A Critique," *American Association of University Professors Bulletin,* vol. 38, 1952, pp. 413–441.

10. Ibid., p. 425.

11. Ibid., p. 440.

12. Arthur E. Bestor, Jr., *Educational Wastelands: The Retreat from Learning in Our Public Schools.* Urbana, IL: University of Illinois Press, 1953.

13. Lawrence A. Cremin, *The Transformation of the School: Progressivism in American Education, 1876–1957.* New York: Alfred A. Knopf, 1961, p. 270.

14. Arthur S. Trace, *What Ivan Knows That Johnny Doesn't.* New York: Random House, 1961.

15. Barbara Barksdale Clowse, *Brainpower for the Cold War: The Sputnik Crisis and National Defense Education Act of 1958.* Westport, CT: Greenwood Press, 1981, p. 72.

16. Ibid., p. 162–167.

17. Jerome S. Bruner, *The Process of Education: A Searching Discussion of School Education Opening New Paths to Teaching and Learning.* New York: Vintage Books, 1960.

18. *Briggs v. Elliott,* 98 F. Supp. 529 (1951).

19. *Plessy v. Ferguson,* 163 U.S. 537 (1896).

20. On the special role of black teachers in segregated schools before desegregation took hold, see Adam Fairclough, *Teaching Equality: Black Schools in the Age of Jim Crow.* Athens, GA: University of Georgia Press, 2001.

21. The full legal citation for the *Brown* cases is *Brown v. Board of Education of Topeka,* 347 U.S. 483 (1954) and 349 U.S. 294 (1955).

22. The source for most of what we say about the *Brown* decision is Richard Kluger, *Simple Justice.* New York: Alfred A. Knopf, 1976. Also relevant is a biography of NAACP attorney and later Supreme Court Justice Thurgood Marshall: Carl Rowan, *Dream Makers, Dream Breakers: The World of Justice Thurgood Marshall.* Boston: Little, Brown, 1993.

23. *Brown v. Board,* as cited in Kluger.

24. Kluger.

25. Halberstam, *The Fifties,* pp. 667–692.

26. Ibid.

27. For this action and most of the other postwar teacher strikes described herein, see Russell C. Oakes, "Public and Professional Reaction to Teachers' Strikes, 1918–1954," Ed.D, thesis, New York University, 1958.

28. This account of Detroit is based on Jeffrey Mirel's book on the Detroit schools in the twentieth century. The 1940s reversal of the situation from the 1920s, when business and labor cooperated in support of the public schools, is analyzed at some length by Mirel. He sees the origins of the dispute between business and labor as having arisen initially over school finance in the 1930s. See Jeffrey Mirel, *The Rise and Fall of an Urban School System: Detroit, 1907–1981.* Ann Arbor: University of Michigan Press, 1993, pp. 176–186, for the postwar salary conflict.

29. For elaboration of this argument, see Wayne J. Urban, "The Making of a Teachers' Union: The National Education Association, 1957–1973," *Historical Studies in Education,* vol. 5, 1993, pp. 33–53, esp. pp. 39–42.

30. Myron Lieberman, *Education as a Profession.* Englewood Cliffs, NJ: Prentice-Hall, 1956; and Liebermann, "Teachers Strikes: An Analysis of the Issues," *Harvard Educational Review,* vol. 26, 1956, pp. 39–70.

31. Of course, the NEA's hesitancy to embrace militant action also served the inclinations of its male administrators, who had dominated the organization, and its female teacher members, since its inception.

32. Stephen Cole, *The Unionization of Teachers: A Case Study of the UFT.* New York: Praeger, 1969.

11

The Pursuit of Equality
1960–1980

Overview

The two decades covered in this chapter constitute a period of marked contrast. To characterize the divergent events in each of them is no easy task. The 1960s were a time of great turmoil and political activism in the United States as well as in its schools. The 1970s, however, marked both a retreat from the conflict and activism of the 1960s and a period of reassessment and redirection for the nation. That redirection may have been more symbolic than substantive, but the symbols of redirection had a distinct effect on the nation.

The 1960s

The 1960 presidential election, in one sense, marked a clear turning point in American political life. John Fitzgerald Kennedy, who was elected to the presidency in 1960, was the first Roman Catholic chosen to hold the nation's highest office. Many Protestant leaders and churchgoers opposed Kennedy's candidacy on the principle that a Catholic would never be independent enough of the Pope and the Vatican bureaucracy to lead the nation. In addition to the controversy generated over the issue of religion, the 1960 election was also markedly partisan. The Republican candidate, Richard M. Nixon, was a master of the art of political conflict and innuendo. Kennedy's narrow victory in the 1960 election was attributed by many to his success in a televised debate between the two candidates shortly before the election. Kennedy put forth an image of vigor and an air of assurance during that debate that contrasted markedly with the uneasy, somewhat sinister image that Nixon conveyed. The emergence of television as a force in the 1960 election presaged the increasingly important role that it and other mass media played during the rest of the twentieth century.

Kennedy moved quickly after his election to reassure non-Catholics that he was a president for all Americans by distancing himself from the Roman Catholic hierarchy. He also stamped his presidency with a youthful activism that contrasted markedly with the grandfatherly aura of his predecessor, Dwight Eisenhower. The Kennedy family's youth, vigor, and glamor, and the positive tone of the Kennedy White House, caught the imagination of many Americans.

Despite the positive image surrounding the Kennedy presidency, the youthful leader was soon plunged into a series of national and international crises that tested the limits of his abilities and his vision for the nation. Two of the international conflicts involved Cuba, a country undergoing significant social and political change under its own young revolutionary leader, Fidel Castro. Castro's developing relationship with the Soviet Union led Kennedy into one of the greatest defeats and then into one of the greatest public relations successes of his young administration. The halting, and totally disastrous, invasion of Cuba at the Bay of Pigs by forces backed by the Central Intelligence Agency was quickly marked as a fiasco, a failure from a new administration carried away with its own activist image. Yet the subsequent confrontation with the Soviet Union and its leader Nikita Khrushchev over the presence of Soviet nuclear missiles in Cuba yielded Kennedy a positive result. After days of tense saber rattling on both sides, the Soviet leader backed away from armed confrontation with the American naval forces that blocked the arrival of the Soviet ships. Although some considered Kennedy's willingness to use nuclear weapons in this confrontation a foolhardy act, most Americans took heart from his forcing the Soviet leader to "blink" or back down from the consequences of this confrontation. The missile crisis, along with other Kennedy administration foreign policy activities, intensified the Cold War anticommunism that had characterized all post-World War II administrations.

President Kennedy's domestic program was overshadowed initially by these foreign policy crises. Before he could clarify for Americans his own intentions on domestic matters, on November 22, 1963, Kennedy was assassinated. The graphic televised pictures of the actual assassination, of the funeral that followed, and of the subsequent shooting of Lee Harvey Oswald, the man generally accepted to have been the sole assassin, marked television's unquestioned arrival as the dominant mass medium. The televising five years later of the events surrounding the assassinations of Robert Kennedy and of Martin Luther King, Jr., as well as the attention devoted to their funerals, allowed much of the nation to be involved in an intimate way in the tragedy and immediate consequences of all three of these assassinations.

John Kennedy's assassination brought Lyndon Johnson to the presidency. Johnson's long and successful tenure as a congressional leader enabled him to guide a multitude of domestic legislation through Congress. Many of his admirers compared his legislative record with that of Franklin Roosevelt's New Deal. Johnson pursued a "Great Society" image, which included his war on poverty as well as his pursuit of civil rights for African Americans and other minority groups.

Johnson's domestic agenda was short-circuited, however, by his entrapment in the Vietnam War, a conflict he had inherited from the Eisenhower and Kennedy administrations, but one that he quickly made his own. He presided over a rapid and steady escalation of the war, which in turn provoked an increasingly loud and sustained opposition centered, to a large extent, on American college and university campuses.

Youthful dissent over the Vietnam War was one ingredient in a youth culture movement that swept up many of the nation's young people, on and off the college campuses. A dissident youth culture developed and expressed itself through oppositional music, clothing, and the use of various types of drugs. The 1960s appeared to be a time of genuine fracturing in relations between America's young people and their elders.

The "invasion" of the British rock group, the Beatles, whose embrace of the drug culture was evidenced by such songs as "Lucy in the Sky with Diamonds," heralded a significant cultural shift. This type of music spotlighted the use of drugs at massive rock festivals such as the one that took place at Woodstock, New York, in 1969. Such events testified to the oppositional quality that characterized relations between the established parts of American society and great numbers of its young people.

The objection to the Vietnam War by young people and increasing numbers of adults who followed their lead became so widespread that by 1968 President Johnson chose not to run for reelection. The Democratic nomination went instead to his loyal vice president, Hubert Humphrey, following a bitter primary fight with Eugene McCarthy, a peace candidate, and Robert Kennedy, an outspoken supporter of minorities. A series of disturbing events surrounding the 1968 election suggested to many the possibility that American society was dissolving. These included police beatings of anti-administration demonstrators during the Democratic national convention in Chicago; the backlash against war opponents and against the liberal accomplishments of Johnson's Great Society from the American Independent Party and its presidential candidate, Governor George Wallace of Alabama; and Richard Nixon's overwhelming defeat of Humphrey in the presidential election. In fact, the phrase "coming apart" became the title of William O'Neill's historical account of the 1960s.[1]

As president, Nixon moved to counter opposition to the Vietnam War by trying to wind down the war without acknowledging defeat. Before the war was finally settled through American abandonment of the conflict, the United States underwent cataclysmic uprisings on many of the nation's college campuses. In May 1970, students were killed during antiwar demonstrations at Kent State University in Ohio and at Jackson State University in Mississippi. These shootings punctuated the end of a violent decade that also witnessed riots by poor blacks in Cleveland, Detroit, and Los Angeles, among other cities. Desperate for change, minority citizens had begun to react violently to the helplessness of their social and economic circumstances.

The urban riots as well as the student uprisings in the 1960s indicated both the success and the failure of social protest. The Civil Rights movement, pioneered in the late 1950s by young African Americans, flowered in the 1960s and led to tangible victories for blacks seeking entrance into mainstream institutions, including the public schools. Their success sparked other groups, including middle-class women and school teachers, to become active in pursuit of their own social, political, and economic advancement. The feminism of the

1960s, begun symbolically with the 1963 publication of Betty Friedan's book, *The Feminine Mystique*, eventually took a more radical direction as it discovered new leaders and new agendas.[2]

The 1970s

Political protest by various youth, minority, and feminist groups reached radical proportions by the late 1960s and triggered a reactionary movement on the part of many conservative Americans. As already mentioned, George Wallace represented the "white backlash" against the pursuit of African American equality and against the youthful war protesters. Skillfully building on these reactionary sentiments, Richard Nixon was able to lead the nation in a new, more conservative direction. By winding down the Vietnam War, he was able to neutralize one of the more volatile issues that had sparked the youth rebellion of the 1960s. Nixon also managed to harness the rising sentiment against "forced busing," which had been employed as a tool for school desegregation in compliance with the *Brown* decision. The seeming exhaustion of the young, particularly after the killings at Kent State and Jackson State, also contributed to the demise of liberal activism. Finally, Nixon was able to move the Supreme Court in a more conservative direction through the judges he appointed. All these events signaled a sharp swing toward conservatism in America's political climate.

In other ways, however, Nixon continued the social programs of the 1960s, although in a muted manner. Before he could consolidate his program, Nixon ran afoul of his long-standing tendency toward "dirty tricks" against his political opponents. In the Watergate affair, a team of burglars who were eventually linked to the White House was caught breaking into the political headquarters of the Democratic Party. The clumsy and unsuccessful attempt to "cover up" those links eventually resulted in the resignation of the nation's thirty-seventh president after the House of Representatives began impeachment proceedings. Once again, television brought the Watergate affair into America's homes through lengthy live coverage of the Senate Watergate Committee hearings. Senators such as Committee Chair Sam Ervin of North Carolina gained celebrity status from their conduct of the hearings.

Nixon's 1974 resignation, in disgrace, also tarnished the presidency of his successor, Vice President Gerald Ford. Most Americans were shocked when Ford pardoned Nixon of all charges stemming from the Watergate affair, an act that contributed to Ford's defeat by Jimmy Carter in 1976. Carter's presidency, however, proved as much a continuation of the two preceding Republican regimes as a rebuilding of the liberal agenda established in the 1960s by Presidents Kennedy and Johnson. The international energy crisis that plagued the world during Carter's term in office led to runaway U.S. inflation that greatly harmed his presidency. Carter's inadequacies as a politician and a leader, and his inability to free American hostages held by terrorists in Iran, also contributed to his failure to win re-election in 1980. (Carter turned out to be a much better ex-president than a chief executive. For his humanitarian work during the decades after his presidency, Carter received the Nobel Peace Prize in 2002.)

The 1970s constituted a period of rhetorical retreat from the excesses of the preceding decade, although there was never a blanket repudiation of the policies of the 1960s. The tumult of Watergate, the economic battering from the energy crisis and the inflation that accompanied it, and the political maladroitness of the Carter administration all led the nation further and further away from the euphoria, the social agenda, and the political activism of the 1960s.

The Civil Rights Movement and the Schools

The 1954 *Brown* decision helped motivate African Americans to launch a series of civil rights campaigns on their own behalf. The boycott of the segregated buses in Montgomery, Alabama, in 1955; the series of sit-ins by black college students begun in Greensboro, North Carolina, in 1960; the march on Washington, D.C., led by the Reverend Martin Luther King, Jr., in 1963; and the ongoing series of voter-registration campaigns were some of the more visible examples of political activism that first swept through the South and finally the entire nation. The impact of the Civil Rights movement in educational affairs came mainly through a series of legislative acts passed in response to pressure from blacks and other minority groups or from court decisions rendered in response to suits filed by various minorities.

The 1964 Civil Rights Act

The 1964 Civil Rights Act was originally proposed by the Kennedy administration in 1963, when prospects for passage of meaningful civil rights legislation were mixed at best. The Bill's enactment in 1964 was aided by Kennedy's assassination the previous year and by the widely publicized mistreatment of black civil rights demonstrators in Birmingham in the same year.

The Bill that was passed contained several titles mandating enforcement of the civil rights of black Americans in different areas. Title VI, the part affecting segregation in education, received minor attention when Congress debated the Bill. But that provision, which allowed federal education funds to be withheld from districts that segregated their schools, proved to be highly significant after the Johnson administration increased the flow of federal dollars to school districts. Initially, enforcement of Title VI was the responsibility of the secretary of the Department of Health, Education, and Welfare (HEW). Because of its size and its wide-ranging responsibilities, however, neither the agency nor its leader were prepared to implement such a widely publicized and highly controversial measure. As a result, in 1967 a subagency within the Office of Education of HEW was created to administer Title VI. That sub-unit was the Office for Civil Rights (OCR). It would play a major role in the adjudication of civil rights claims for many groups.[3]

The Coleman Report

One massive social science study, undertaken in response to a special mandate of the 1964 Civil Rights Act, provided substantial support for civil rights activism. James S. Coleman, a distinguished sociologist then at Johns Hopkins University in Baltimore, was chosen to conduct an inquiry into the lack of educational opportunities for the poor. Coleman led a research team that responded broadly to this mandate and produced a volume that brought into play underlying issues relating social class to minority and majority students' educational achievement.[4]

Coleman went beyond questions of differences in the resources available to minority and majority students in schools by attempting to link those differences to the achievement of various groups. In considering these differences, Coleman reached two rather startling conclusions. First, he noted that differences in school resources were only mildly related to differences in educational achievement. Second, he noted that achievement differences were strongly related to the educational backgrounds and aspirations of a student's peer group. Poorer students performed substantially better when put into classes with higher-achieving students from the more advantaged backgrounds. This finding provided ammunition for those seeking to move poor black children, and other poor children, out of inferior schools and into mainstream educational environments. Yet Coleman's analysis, like much social science research, was so complex that it raised more questions than it answered. Although the Coleman report offered no definitive answer to the problem it addressed, underachievement of poor students, its greatest contribution was to bring into mainstream social scientific inquiry the question of the links among economic class, race, and school achievement.

Civil Rights and the Mexican American

The success of the black Civil Rights movement in the late 1960s and 1970s was not lost on other heretofore oppressed or forgotten groups in American society. Mexican Americans constituted the largest and one of the poorest subgroups of Spanish speakers in the United States. Concentrated largely in the state of Texas, with lesser but significant concentrations in states like California, Mexican Americans had endured a long history of struggle to obtain the benefits that many other immigrant groups to the United States had almost begun to take for granted.[5]

Mexican Americans had begun agitation on their own behalf in the late 1920s with the formulation of the League of United Latin American Citizens (LULAC). In the beginning, LULAC developed a two-pronged agenda: a battle against discriminatory treatment of Mexican Americans by public school officials and the promotion of education as an essential improvement strategy within Mexican American communities. In the post-World War II years, LULAC began to confront and combat the segregation of Mexican American youngsters in public schools. With the *Brown* decision in 1954, these efforts were intensified, but LULAC began to lose ground to newer advocacy organizations, particularly the Mexican American Legal Defense Fund (MALDEF), which had been formed with advice from the NAACP and support from the Ford Foundation to pursue desegregation and other legal avenues of educational and social redress.

One of the problems with the LULAC approach became obvious in the post-*Brown* era, when the striving to have Mexican Americans declared "whites" backfired as legislators and school officials in the state of Texas hit on the strategy of using Mexican American children as the "whites" to be paired with African Americans to meet desegregation mandates. This policy left Anglo children untouched by the desegregation process. MALDEF and other Mexican advocacy groups abandoned this "other white" strategy in the late 1960s and eventually succeeded in having Mexican Americans declared as an identifiable ethnic group to which *Brown* and its successor decisions could be applied. The issue was settled finally in the 1973 *Keyes* desegregation case covering Denver, Colorado, in which the Supreme Court ruled that Mexican American children in that city had been illegally segregated, just as African Americans had been.[6]

The subsequent experience of Mexican Americans, in Texas as in other states, was that in spite of legal rulings, their children continued to face segregation and other discrimination in public schools. As the pace of desegregation slowed in the late 1970s, advocates of Mexican American children turned more attention to a parallel strategy that they had developed to achieve equal educational opportunity for their children: bilingual education.

Bilingual Education

The bilingual education movement began in the 1960s as a response to the comprehensive problems that Mexican Americans and other Spanish-speaking youngsters confronted in schools with an all-English curriculum. In districts where some desegregation had been achieved for Mexican Americans, the profound language and cultural difficulties of a completely English curriculum were often left untreated. Early recognition of the low educational achievement of many Spanish-speaking children related it to their lack of facility in the English language. Improved achievement, it was believed, would result from using these students' first language as a bridge to achievement in English. Bilingual education programs were developed in which some instruction was offered in Spanish and some in English.

Bilingual educational approaches were initially legitimized in 1968 when Congress passed a Bilingual Education Act. The Act did not mandate bilingual programs, however, thus leaving their existence dependent on the political leverage that could be mustered by supporters and opponents.

In 1974, the Supreme Court appeared to permit bilingual education in its ruling in the *Lau v. Nichols* case. This suit had been filed on behalf of Chinese American children in San Francisco who spoke little or no English. Their advocates argued that these children needed more than the usual instruction in English. They required special attention from school authorities that took into account their lack of facility in English.[7]

Spurred by this court ruling, several approaches to bilingual education were developed. Total immersion in English classes designed specifically for non-English speakers was one approach. A second approach involved enrolling non-English speakers in special English language classes until they acquired sufficient mastery of English to return to regular classrooms. The third method was bilingual education, which emphasized study and practice in both the child's native language and in English. Advocates of this last approach sometimes emphasized biculturalism as well as bilingualism. They wanted children to be taught in ways that preserved and enhanced their original culture and language while they were simultaneously being taught the English language and the mainstream culture that accompanied it.

Bilingualism was often supported by politicians and other leaders of Hispanic communities as a way to maintain their communities against the onslaught of cultural and linguistic assimilationists. It was opposed by many teachers, Anglo politicians, and some Hispanic intellectuals, who saw assimilation into mainstream culture as the natural outcome of the educational process.[8]

Civil Rights and the American Indian

D. H. Lawrence once remarked that while American Indians would never again control the continent, they would forever haunt it. In terms of the shifting policies pertaining to the status and education of the original Americans, it seems that government officials have constantly been uneasy and dissatisfied with—dare we say haunted by?—whatever policy has been in place at any particular time.[9] As we have noted in earlier chapters, government policies at the national, state, and local levels have rarely been consistent in conception or application. To further complicate a very complicated situation, different circumstances among tribal groups as well as divided opinions among individual Indians and tribes have made Indian and government relations continually problematic. And, as with any group in American society, the rights or agendas of tribes (or ethnic or cultural groups) and the rights and desires of individual Indians have sometimes worked at cross purposes.

From at least the time of the Dawes Act in the 1880s, the U.S. government worked to diminish tribal identity and authority by subdividing Indian lands and stressing assimilation of Indians as individuals. "Progressive" policies toward Indians that began early in the century appeared to gain momentum in the 1930s when Bureau of Indian Affairs (BIA) Commissioner John Collier convinced Congress to restore and promote tribal rights to self-determination. The Indian Reorganization Act of 1934 halted further allotments of Indian lands and established tribal governments and courts. Critics of government policy were quick to point out, however, that BIA officials drafted tribal constitutions for Indian tribes based on Anglo-American rather than Indian values and traditions.

By the early 1950s, yet another turn (or return) in policy was placed in motion—termination of all Indian-aid programs combined with efforts to promote relocation of Indians in cities. This destructive and ill-conceived policy involved the unilateral termination of the United States' relationship with tribes, with the ultimate goal of assimilating all Indian people into the dominant culture by breaking down Native American cultural and tribal bonds. By 1961, Congress had terminated its relationship with 109 bands and tribes.[10]

It is one of the ironies of the Civil Rights era that while blacks and Hispanics were engaging in protests and devising strategies to gain access to mainstream society, some Indian activists were redoubling efforts to resist termination and all other policies designed to force them to yield to the cultural mindset and political realities of the dominant society whether they wanted to or not. As one writer has noted, where other groups have suffered deliberate discrimination and oppression, American Indians have been "the only group whose oppression [has come] primarily from an effort to help them change into replicas of the white man." Although the political agenda of Indian activists was sometimes at odds with objectives of the Civil Rights movement, Indian leaders adopted some of the same tactics in order to direct attention to their concerns. In the fall of 1969, the abandoned federal prison on Alcatraz Island was "reclaimed" for a short time by about 300 Indians. Briefly, Alcatraz became the focal point of Indian protest and a symbol of the reassertion of tribal independence from government-dictated policies. In 1972 a group of Indian activists invaded the Bureau of Indian Affairs building in Washington, D.C., and the following year, Sioux Indians and others under the leadership of Russell Means and the American Indian Movement (AIM) occupied Wounded Knee, South Dakota, site of the last fateful Indian massacre by the U.S. Army in 1890. AIM held Wounded Knee and the nation's attention for seventy-two days in a dramatic declaration of independence.[11]

The obvious failure of the policy of termination and forced assimilation was not lost on the Nixon administration. In 1970 President Nixon announced a new era of self-determination for American Indians. Acquiescing to the reality that "Indian people will never surrender their desire to control their relationship both among themselves and with non-Indian governments, organizations and persons," Nixon proclaimed that "the time [had] come to break decisively with the past and to create the conditions for a new era in which the Indian future is determined by Indian acts and Indian decisions." In essence, self-determination gave official recognition to the tripartite nature of citizenship to which many Indians could lay claim. As members of a tribe as well as citizens of a state and the nation, they should be able to enjoy three separate sets of rights: federal, state, and tribal. The question of balancing these loyalties and identities continues to divide Native Americans and those who seek to better their condition through education.[12]

Passage of the Indian Self-Determination Act of 1974 granted tribes the right to manage federal-aid programs on the reservations and to have oversight of their own schools. Indians also began to have success in asserting long-ignored treaty rights. The Eskimos, Aleuts, and other native peoples of Alaska won 40 million acres of land and nearly $1 billion in settlement of old claims in 1971. On the mainland, the Sioux were awarded $107 million in 1980 for South Dakota lands illegally taken from them more than a century earlier, and the Penobscot Indians in Maine received $81 million based on a federal law of 1790. Along with these gains came an increased sense of Indian pride and tribal loyalty. Nearly 1.4 million persons identified themselves as American Indians in the 1980 census, in contrast to fewer than 800,000 in 1970. Obviously, over the course of a decade many thousands of people chose to identify themselves as Indians who had been reluctant to do so earlier.[13]

New directions in federal policy and the willingness of the white majority to recognize the validity of ancient treaties clearly marked an advance over past neglect and injustice. Exercise of tribal rights has enabled some tribes to benefit from casinos and fishing, mineral, and logging rights and other profit-making ventures, although in terms of traditional cultural mores, the "value" of some of these undertakings might be seriously questioned.

School retention rates suggest that educational policies may be becoming more attuned to the needs and cultural values of the native population. High school completion rates increased from 67 to 75 percent between 1980 and 1990. By 1990 about 9 percent of the Native American population (compared to 20 percent of the general population) had attained a bachelor's degree or higher and 3 percent (as compared to 7 percent) held graduate or professional degrees. However, these encouraging signs hardly offset the continuing realities of unemployment, alcoholism, disease, and poverty that persist both on reservations and among Indians in urban areas. As in the larger society, educational and social conditions among individuals and among tribes vary considerably.[14]

Women's Rights Activity

An activist women's political movement also flourished in the 1960s, emulating the black Civil Rights movement. The women's movement did not have much impact on the schools, however. Women, who made up the majority of the teaching force, had different social, cultural, or intellectual backgrounds from the feminists of that era. Thus, women teachers turned a largely deaf ear to the militant cries of the feminists, who in turn exhibited little sympathy for or understanding of the needs and desires of school teachers.

Despite the lack of rapproachment between feminists and women teachers, educational institutions were affected by the women's rights movement. For example, Title IX of the Higher Education Act, passed in 1972, provided for gender equity in colleges and universities. Title IX has been consistently used to close the enormous funding gap between men's and women's sports in colleges and universities. In more recent years, Title IX has been applied to the funding of public school sports as well. Further, the principle of gender equity, as enunciated in Title IX, has supported efforts at all levels to increase the number of women administrators in the schools. Despite these efforts, women remain under-represented in school principalships and in district and state administrative ranks.

Public Law 94–142

One of the most significant acts of educational legislation during the 1970s recognized the educational rights of Americans with disabilities. The Education for All Handicapped Children Act (PL 94–142), passed by Congress in 1975, was designed to assure that children with disabilities received the most appropriate free public education available. What Congress deemed most appropriate, however, proved to be much more extensive than had heretofore been provided in local school systems. The legislation provided for education for handicapped children in the least restrictive educational environment possible. This meant that more and more disabled students would be "mainstreamed," that is, placed in regular classrooms.

Another significant outcome of this law was that an Individualized Education Plan (IEP) was to be developed for each student enrolled in special education programs. This IEP would indicate present levels of performance for each eligible student, annual goals and instructional objectives, remedial services keyed to these goals, and class participation reports and evaluation procedures also keyed to the goals.[15]

For children enrolled in special education programs, and for their parents, PL 94–142 represented a substantial advance in the quantity and quality of educational programs available. To some state and local school officials, however, it represented an unwarranted intrusion into educational affairs by federal officials who prescribed expensive and personnel-intensive remedies without providing funds for their implementation. To some parents of non-special education students, as well as to some teachers, the attention given to disabled students detracted from the education offered to the main body of students. The reality of mainstreaming and other special education programs did not completely meet the expectations or the fears of either supporters or critics. Each group had such zealous advocates that satisfactory enforcement of the law became a difficult, if not impossible, endeavor.

School Desegregation

By far the most controversial educational outcomes of the Civil Rights movement were felt in the attempts to desegregate the public schools. Although school desegregation had been mandated by the 1954 *Brown* decision, implementing that decision proved far more difficult than most proponents ever imagined. Although some early progress was made in the border states, where public sentiment was mixed, the South experienced only "token" integration, with small numbers of carefully chosen black students attending white schools.

There were several reasons for this difficulty. First, the federal courts had no agency available to enforce their mandates. Second, the office of the president, particularly under the Eisenhower administration, failed to act decisively on behalf of the *Brown* mandate and third, Congress, through its seniority and committee system, was controlled by southern legislators pledged either to the ideology of "massive resistance" to *Brown* or to a studied inaction that amounted to the same thing.[16]

The implementation of the fiscal penalties imposed by the 1964 Civil Rights Act on school systems that refused to desegregate significantly increased the pressure for meaningful desegregation in southern schools. In addition, a 1968 Supreme Court decision, which declared voluntary or "freedom of choice" plans to be unconstitutional violations of the principles enunciated in *Brown*, further intensified the pressure for meaningful desegregation. And so the movement for substantial school desegregation reached a high tide in the late 1960s and early 1970s, at the same time that political reaction to desegregation also reached a fever pitch.[17]

Charlotte, North Carolina

Perhaps the most impressive victory for school desegregation was achieved in Charlotte, North Carolina. Desegregation in that city was helped by the fact that the city and county schools had already been consolidated into one system, thereby precluding the existence of an inner-city black school district surrounded by white suburban districts. Within the consolidated district, however, substantial desegregation could not be achieved without threatening the existence of neighborhood-based schools. Redrawing subdistrict lines and busing students were the available remedies to combat the racially exclusive character of Charlotte's neighborhood schools. The Supreme Court sanctioned these remedies in its 1971 ruling. The legitimacy this ruling gave to school busing came at the same time that strident opposition to "forced busing" was being expressed throughout the nation.[18]

Denver, Colorado

Shortly after creation of the Office of Civil Rights within the HEW and the Charlotte ruling, the eyes of the nation turned to the situation in school districts outside the old Confederacy. In a 1973 ruling in a Denver, Colorado, case, the Supreme Court found that school officials had pursued a variety of policies, including zoning, selection of school sites, and school staffing, that perpetuated racially segregated education. The principles of desegregation, heretofore applied mainly in southern states where segregation had been practiced by law, were now applied to districts that enforced it through a variety of extralegal procedures.[19]

Detroit, Michigan

The year after the Denver ruling, however, the decisions against segregation turned in a new, and different, direction. In 1974, in a case involving the schools of Detroit, Michigan, the Supreme Court refused to allow the largely black schools within the city of Detroit to be consolidated with the white suburban school districts that surrounded the Motor City. In this case, the Court ruled that, in order to be the target of a cross-district plan, the suburban districts must be shown to have acted illegally to deny Detroit's black plaintiffs their constitutional rights. This standard proved to be extremely difficult to meet, and thus the *Millikin* ruling meant that the tide of desegregation that involved transporting large numbers of students outside neighborhood schools was beginning to ebb.[20]

Three years after the initial *Millikin* decision, a second decision took desegregation in Detroit in a direction distinctly different from pupil assignment plans. The district court ruling in the second *Millikin* case imposed a series of specific educational measures, which eventually became labeled "compensatory" education, to remedy the segregation in the Detroit schools. The mandating of remedial reading programs, teacher training activities, and specific testing and counseling programs set a precedent that could be, and was, used in subsequent desegregation cases. After *Millikin* II, any district court could impose specific educational practices on a district that had denied children their constitutional rights to an education.[21]

Boston, Massachusetts

Perhaps the most notorious school segregation case during the 1970s was the one in Boston, Massachusetts. It is somewhat ironic that a bitter school desegregation suit was decided in Massachusetts, where the common school and its ideal of equal educational opportunity were born. Yet the opposition of vocal whites in Boston to schooling their children with black children reached a level of intensity thought to occur only in the deep South. The open opposition to the federal court by the city's school committee and its refusal to implement desegregation mandates also smacked of stereotypically southern resistance.[22]

Beginning with his 1974 ruling in the case, the federal district judge, Arthur Garrity, took on an extraordinarily visible role in Boston's school affairs for most of the next decade. A resident of a Boston suburb, Judge Garrity dealt with the recalcitrance of the Boston School Committee by creating a series of outside bodies and agencies that developed plans for operating several aspects of the Boston schools. In addition to implementing a mandatory transportation plan for some of the city's black and white students, Judge Garrity and his team of experts prescribed a wide variety of school policies and practices in school facilities, teacher assignments, and special programs such as bilingual education. In their own published account of Boston school desegregation,

Figure 11.1 "One nation . . . indivisible . . ."

Credit: 1977 Herblock Cartoon, copyright by The Herb Block Foundation.

some of the experts who assisted him pointed to the implementation of a number of magnet schools as one of their greatest successes.[23]

Magnet Schools

Magnet schools, developed around a specific theme or area of interest such as mathematics/science, performing arts, or traditional academics, were becoming increasingly popular in the 1970s as opposition to busing and other pupil assignment plans coalesced into a powerful national movement. Magnet schools offered a different means for achieving racially balanced enrollments in large cities, where white enrollment was swiftly diminishing with or without busing. In Atlanta, Georgia, for instance, where both a metropolitan district consolidation plan and mandatory pupil assignments had been withdrawn, magnet schools, along with a voluntary majority-to-minority (m-to-m) pupil assignment plan, became the sole avenues to school desegregation. Plaintiffs in Atlanta, eschewing pupil assignment measures, settled for a commitment to place meaningful numbers of black administrators and teachers within the existing schools, along with magnet schools and the voluntary m-to-m plan.[24]

In effect, school desegregation had come almost full circle by 1980. Whereas the Supreme Court had ruled in the mid-1960s that strictly voluntary pupil assignment plans were unsatisfactory, less than two decades later voluntary plans had again become acceptable. Voluntarism was now condoned if accompanied by compensatory remedies for students who had been discriminated against and positive incentives for biracial attendance, such as those presumed to exist in magnet schools. While reflecting the nation's ambivalence toward desegregation, such mixed-strategy plans did achieve a definitive political compromise between the rights of minorities and those of majorities.

Poverty and its Consequences

Along with race, the phenomenon of poverty was high on the national agenda in the first few years of the 1960s. Soon thereafter, its eradication became the overriding goal for many, and its amelioration became the goal of many more. A telling illustration of how poverty was discovered in this era is found in the work of a leading educational and public policy thinker, James Bryant Conant.

James Bryant Conant

A renowned chemist, former president of Harvard University, the official leader of educational reform in post-World War II West Germany, and the head of a Carnegie Corporation team investigating American education, Conant was sure to be heard when he spoke on topics of public interest. In 1959, he published *The American High School Today*, an analysis of secondary education in small- and medium-sized cities (population 10,000 to 60,000). In this study, Conant stressed the need for comprehensive high schools large enough to offer both the diversity of courses and the academic rigor needed to match graduates to the educational and work opportunities they would encounter.[25]

Much of Conant's study addressed national defense issues, such as improving science and mathematics education, that had been addressed by Congress in its 1958 National Defense Education Act. In this regard, Conant was especially concerned with the education of those gifted and talented secondary students who, for a variety of reasons, he found to be underachieving in existing high schools. Specific gifted and talented programs, ability grouping to ensure that students of high ability would be properly challenged, and extended work in academic subjects such as science, English, and foreign languages were a few of Conant's most important recommendations.

Two years after the publication of his initial high school study, Conant wrote a book that reflected different priorities and was more in line with the themes that characterized the rest of the 1960s. In *Slums and Suburbs*, Conant focused on the educational needs of the nation's metropolitan areas and the burgeoning suburban rings developing around them. Their significant and troubling problems differed substantially from those delineated in his earlier volume, addressed to small- and medium-sized city high schools. In both urban and suburban settings, Conant found that the main problems stemmed from the concentration of poor students in the inner cities and the more affluent students in the suburbs.[26]

A major problem in suburban high schools was created by anxious parents who wanted their children, regardless of ability, to qualify for admission to a prestigious college. Conant's advice to those parents was to rethink their view of their offspring's place in high-status colleges. Parents, he said, should accept the fact that those institutions were intended to attract students of high ability rather than high social standing. No longer should wealth and upper middle-class status guarantee a prestigious college education for children of average or below-average achievement, argued Conant.

For Conant, the greatest problem for the suburban high school lay in challenging the academically talented students who made up as much as one-half of the student body. For these students, his prescription was an enriched academic curriculum with substantial doses of English, mathematics, science, and foreign languages. An additional goal was emphasis on advanced placement classes. Conant went so far as to advocate rigorous college entrance examinations, developed outside the high school, to challenge suburban high schools and ensure that their academic offerings were sufficiently demanding. He briefly turned his attention to students of average and below-average ability, suggesting that small but substantial vocational curricula be created to meet their needs.

Conant's recommendations for inner-city high schools were similar: academic enrichment for the able and vocational curricula for the less talented. However, the proportion of the student body affected by these curricula was almost exactly the reverse of that recommended for the suburbs. Because of the concentration of poor, deprived families in the urban slums, large numbers of inner-city students would qualify for the vocational curricula, but only a small minority could benefit from enriched academic studies. In stark contrast to the unrealistically high expectations that suburban parents had for their schools and children, the residents of urban slum areas lived in a climate of overwhelming despair, haunted by the problem of early school dropouts. Even those who remained in high school did not face the relatively rosy economic future that awaited their suburban counterparts.

Conant's recommendation for large-city high schools was to develop a realistic and challenging vocational program that would attract and hold the interest of young people prone to drop out of school. This was particularly the case with male students, who represented the majority of those leaving high school before graduation. For example, Conant advocated starting an automobile shop program in these high schools, to be taught by an experienced automobile mechanic rather than a college-trained vocational or industrial arts teacher. The link between the school auto shop or other vocational programs and the surrounding labor market had to be explicit and recognizable to students and their families if there were to be any hope of attracting these at-risk students. For academically talented inner-city students Conant advocated the same program of enriched academic studies he proposed for suburban youth.

The difference in the proportion of academically talented and vocationally oriented students in the two settings, however, resulted in Conant's advocating very different priorities for the high school programs in urban and suburban settings. Academic improvement was his major focus for the suburbs, while vocational education was his most important priority in the cities. Conant's differing priorities merely intensified the discrimination endured by the nation's poor populations, which were increasingly being concentrated in the inner cities. Thus, although Conant's study of high schools consciously addressed the nation's growing poverty, his recommendations were tied to the 1950s and earlier, when concern for an educational elite, not social and educational equity, dominated the schools.

Michael Harrington and the Discovery of Poverty

Two years after the publication of *Slums and Suburbs*, a book that represented a very different approach to the problems of poverty appeared. In *The Other America*, Michael Harrington produced a ringing exposé of the dire poverty that was beginning to characterize more and more urban Americans. A member of the radical Catholic Worker movement that had begun in New York City in the decades before the 1960s, Harrington explained how the numbers of poor had increased in the 1950s with little or no notice. He wrote of the "invisible" poor, and he used graphic language, statistics, and wrenching individual stories to make the new poverty visible to mainstream American society. After showing the degree to which poverty had expanded and was concentrated now among the elderly, blacks, and other minority groups, Harrington concluded with the argument that the United States was now made up of two nations: one that was largely affluent and white and one that was largely nonwhite and mired in poverty.[27]

A prominent characteristic separating the new poor from their predecessors was the difference in their values and expectations. The new poor had developed a "culture of poverty," characterized by a lack of expectation for long-term betterment. Unlike earlier poor, who visualized improved economic and social status for their children if not for themselves, the poor Harrington wrote about were so trapped in their situations that they could see no way out. For this group, in contrast to their predecessors, education was not a way out of poverty but, rather, one more way in which they were made to feel inferior. To change this situation, the "culture of poverty" had to be attacked on a variety of economic, educational, and social fronts.

Harrington, a journalist and a talented writer, struck a sympathetic chord with the American public, awakening many to the momentous problems that were facing the nation. The warning his book carried clearly reached President Kennedy, but the president was assassinated before he could mount a response.

His successor, Lyndon Johnson, however, declared a "war on poverty" and implemented various antipoverty programs largely in response to Harrington's ringing exposé. In fact, the back cover copy in later editions of Harrington's book referred to its link with the War on Poverty.[28]

Education and the War on Poverty

Lyndon Johnson's War on Poverty had wide-ranging goals. The goal of his Economic Opportunity Act of 1964 was direct economic improvement for the poor. That Act created an agency, the Job Corps, to improve employment prospects for poor youngsters. It also created community action programs to help the poor mobilize themselves in the fight to improve their conditions. Another new agency, Volunteers in Service to America (VISTA), enlisted volunteers into various domestic programs to combat poverty. Ultimately, dissatisfaction with the community action programs led to the creation of Head Start, the most famous educational outcome of the 1964 Act.

Figure 11.2 "Kindly move over a little, gentlemen."

Credit: 1965 Herblock Cartoon, copyright by The Herb Block Foundation.

Head Start

Since many American cities and states were reluctant to accept funds to help their poor mobilize themselves, federal planners were left with surplus funds to apply to other programs. Using these surplus monies, the Head Start program was planned and developed as a way to prepare poor children for school. Planners feared a negative image for Head Start if it became part of the federal educational bureaucracy so, from the beginning, Head Start operated as an independent federal agency. From its inception, it was also more than just an educational program. It featured an unprecedented strategy, involving parents in a program that would help their children develop intellectually, socially, and physically.

Head Start proceeded with one eye on creating a favorable political climate for itself and the other on developing an effective program. It was this combination of priorities that accounted, in large part, for the longevity and success of the program. A large part of Head Start's permanence can be attributed to its direct appeal to the parents of poor children and to policymakers concerned both with children and their parents.[29]

Elementary and Secondary Education Act

Shortly after the Head Start program was initiated, Congress passed one of the most influential pieces of educational legislation in American history, the Elementary and Secondary Education Act (ESEA) of 1965. It was by far the most costly and comprehensive federal educational law that had ever been passed. A wide-ranging consensus on the gravity of the educational problems of the poor motivated ESEA's initial passage. Accordingly, disadvantaged poor children were targeted for most of the program's funds. Those who developed the legislation and guided it through Congress noted that these children were largely concentrated in the nation's largest cities and that they came predominantly from the ranks of African Americans and other minority groups.

From 75 to 85 percent of the funds appropriated through ESEA went to various Title I programs, all of which were geared specifically to the needs of educationally deprived children. Much of the work supported by the other five titles of ESEA involved direct or political support to fighting the educational consequences of poverty. ESEA-funded activities in local school systems included cultural and social enrichment programs, library innovations, parental involvement activities, nutrition programs, and social and medical services. Another title of ESEA supported innovations in teaching practice.[30]

Like Head Start, ESEA combined the pointed purpose of serving the poor with a wide political appeal. Although the poor were the clear target of ESEA programs, there were at least some poor children in almost every school district, guaranteeing a wide distribution of ESEA funds. Furthermore, school districts were encouraged to develop their own alternative programs for combating poverty.

Unlike Head Start, however, ESEA did not maintain its funding base. The developing Vietnam War began to monopolize the attention of both President Johnson and the Congress, thereby gradually diluting the supervision and funds available for the War on Poverty. In addition, the community action programs sparked by the Economic Opportunity Act created a political mobilization among the poor, particularly the urban poor. They became increasingly sensitive to the social-class bias implicit in terms such as the "culture of poverty" and "educationally disadvantaged" that characterized ESEA programs. The parent focus of the Head Start program, however, appealed to the urban poor and captured their political support, a key explanation for why it remains effective and popular today.

The Federal Government and Education

The passage of the ESEA in 1965 under President Johnson raised the expectations of the NEA that its long-sought goal of a federal partnership role in educational finance would be fulfilled. However, these developments also fueled the fears of opponents of a federal presence in educational affairs. Both opponents and proponents of federal educational involvement found arguments for their programs within the academic community.

Social Science and Educational Achievement

The nature and consequences of the links among ethnicity, wealth, social class, and educational achievement captured the attention of social scientists in the 1960s. As already discussed, the Coleman report found that educational achievement seemed most directly related to a student's peer group, a relationship that encouraged proponents of school desegregation.

Opponents of desegregation and other efforts to ameliorate the educational conditions of poor, minority children also found support in academic research findings, however. In 1969, Arthur Jensen, an educational psychologist at the University of California, Berkeley, published an explosive article that argued that the low educational achievement of African American children was due, to a large extent, to hereditary factors that were immune to amelioration. Needless to say, Jensen's article encouraged those who questioned the expenditure of funds for various compensatory educational programs, especially those for poor black children.[31]

The relationship of wealth to school success was explored in a 1972 study of schooling and family background conducted by a team led by a noted sociologist, Christopher Jencks. In this study, Jencks and his co-authors found that the educational achievement of students was best accounted for by their family background. This argument posed a dilemma for formal education. A logical conclusion was to lessen the emphasis on educational spending in favor of more straightforward public welfare measures that would speak to the financial inequalities in individual and family backgrounds. This tack was suggested to the Nixon administration by its domestic advisor, Daniel Patrick

Moynihan, a former Harvard University professor and a member of the Democratic Party.[32]

Moynihan, a New Yorker, had been a sub-cabinet official in the Kennedy and Johnson administrations. During that time, he was responsible for a report that identified the structure of the black family, particularly the absence of adult males within the family unit, as being primarily responsible for the social and economic plight of African Americans. The report proved to be quite controversial, provoking a storm of critical reaction that labeled both the author and the ideas as racist. Moynihan survived this controversy, however, and when, in the 1970s, he took a position in the Nixon administration, he again advised the president to substitute direct economic aid to poor people for the complicated entitlement programs that had emerged from Johnson's War on Poverty. Moynihan's suggestion, in addition to aiding the poor directly, also served the Republicans' preference for limited federal governmental activity, an ideal combination for the Nixon administration.[33]

Nixon's Educational Policies

The record of the Nixon administrations in education did not really reverse the trend toward more federal involvement and expenditure in education. Nixon's preference for federal support of educational research over direct financial involvement in school programs altered the direction of the federal effort somewhat without seriously diminishing it. As it turned out, the twin forces of a declining economy and a lack of political will did result in somewhat diminished spending for existing educational and economic entitlement programs in the Nixon years. Also, no new program of economic subsidies, such as that suggested by Moynihan, was attempted. After Nixon resigned due to the Watergate scandal, neither Gerald Ford, his immediate successor, nor Jimmy Carter, the southern Democrat who defeated Ford in 1976, proved capable of reviving President Johnson's devotion to economic or educational reform.[34]

The U.S. Department of Education

In the 1976 election, Jimmy Carter's victory put a Democrat in the White House for the first time since 1968. Carter's campaign for the presidency was helped enormously by support from the NEA, which for the first time in its history endorsed a presidential candidate. In addition, the NEA spent a sizable amount of money and contributed a number of workers to support Carter's campaign. Its organizational rival, the American Federation of Teachers (AFT), countered with support for Carter's rival for the Democratic nomination, Edward M. (Ted) Kennedy. Carter's success in gaining the nomination and his victory in the election secured for the NEA a position of increased power and influence in American educational circles.

In return for the NEA's support for his candidacy, Carter pledged to work for the establishment of a Cabinet-level Department of Education. Such an agency had been formed during the Reconstruction era, but it was quickly downgraded from cabinet status to that of a minor, data-gathering agency housed in the Department of Interior. Later, in a mid-twentieth-century reorganization of the federal government, educational responsibility was transferred to the large, multifaceted HEW. As Carter assumed the presidency in 1977, the NEA jubilantly waited for him to deliver on his promise of a federal department of education.[35]

Carter's eventual creation of the Department of Education represented the continuation of a trend toward increasing federal involvement in education that had been unfolding since early in the twentieth century. Yet, even in the moment of triumph for NEA supporters of the new department, there remained a substantial amount of doubt about the power and significance of the new body.

There were several reasons for that doubt. First, Carter seriously considered not honoring his commitment to create the federal department. Indeed, it took him well over two full years to fulfill his promise. His southern roots made him suspicious of federal intrusion in state affairs, and his oft-stated desire to bring Americans together, and thereby minimize the influence of interest groups (such as the NEA), kept alive the possibility that he would reverse himself on the issue. Finally, his clumsy relations with Congress threatened nearly all of his legislative agenda, including this new department.

In the end, however, a combination of honoring commitments to loyal supporters such as the NEA and his desire for efficiency in government prodded Carter into pushing the new department through Congress. It was not surprising that Congress acquiesced in establishing the new department, given its own legislative history in the 1950s and 1960s of increasing involvement in educational affairs.

Carter's initial choice of secretary of the new department dampened the enthusiasm of the NEA and other advocates of strong federal involvement in education. He selected as the first secretary of education Shirley Hufstedler, a rather obscure federal judge from the state of California. Hufstedler's lack of relationships with anyone in the professional educational community diluted educators' enthusiasm about the secretary and the new department. Thus, even in the ranks of its supporters, serious doubts about the significance and the power of the Department of Education remained.

Questions about the effectiveness of spending federal dollars on schools also did not disappear. Data on the effectiveness of ESEA, including its Title I antipoverty programs, were mixed at best. Some of this may have been due to the fact that federal monies to support poor children had to be channeled through state departments of education and then through local districts. Both of these groups had to respond to broad political constituencies not necessarily enamored with the plight of the poor. Head Start, the one federal educational program that was generally recognized as a success, was not even housed within the Department of Education. Thus, despite increased federal commitment to educational programs for the poor, there was little hard evidence that federal spending had produced substantial improvement in the educational accomplishments of poor children.

Pedagogical Currents

During the 1960s and 1970s, academic scholars, investigative journalists, and social critics all sought to change the curriculum and the instructional methods used in American classrooms. However, most long-lasting changes in school operations did not come from their ranks, but from federal laws and court decisions. Thus, efforts to change pedagogy in these years achieved, at best, a record of mixed success.

Curriculum Experiments

The major thrust for curriculum change in the early 1960s had its roots in the preceding decade. The National Defense Education Act (NDEA), passed in 1958, eventually yielded a variety of curriculum reforms, particularly in the sciences. As noted in Chapter 10, the BSSC, the PSSC, and the SMSG all developed course syllabi for high school studies in their respective fields. The various committees' motivation for reforms was based partially on their distrust of school teachers, the education faculty who had trained them, and the administrators who were responsible for their in-class performance. Consequently, the new curricula were developed largely in isolation from public school staffs and were then presented to them for implementation, with little or no consultation.

Romantic Critics

One group of educational critics that did attend to the budding educational equality movement was the "romantic critics" of the late 1960s. This group, some of whom were journalists, successfully used firsthand accounts of harsh, punitive schools and classrooms to strike a chord that resonated among many minority parents, intellectuals, and even among some educators.

Perhaps the most famous of these romantic critics was Jonathan Kozol. A Harvard-educated writer and journalist, he was for a time a substitute teacher in the inner-city schools of Boston. His account of life in those schools burst onto the national scene with the publication in 1967 of a book titled *Death at an Early Age*, which was clearly an indictment of public schools in Boston. The negative implication of Kozol's book was reinforced by its subtitle: *The Destruction of the Hearts and Minds of Negro Children in the Boston Public Schools.*[36]

Kozol's indictment of the treatment given to inner-city black children was scathing. He argued convincingly that these children were the victims of prejudiced, unfeeling teachers and an ignorant, rigid school bureaucracy. For Kozol, the result of this perilous situation was that the children in these schools were just not being taught. Rather, they were being warehoused by their teachers and the school authorities. Kozol's critique of the punitive pedagogy then practiced in Boston was echoed in other works of the time, one of which was Herbert Kohl's book on New York's schools. Kozol, Kohl, and other authors documented how innocent school children were the victims of teacher bias and gross educational malpractice. According to Kozol, the racial and social class differences between children and teachers was a significant cause of teachers' lack of affinity for their students.[37]

This line of argument served to link Kozol and his ideas to the educational equity movement then being waged on behalf of minority, mainly black, children. The argument about class differences was also used against Kozol, however. Although he linked himself emphatically to his African American students, he exhibited little understanding of and much personal disdain for the lower-middle-class backgrounds of the teachers who were working in the schools.

This failure to analyze fully the cross-cultural factors underlying the differences between urban school students and their teachers was not limited to Kozol. Few if any educational theorists of this period accounted for the very real cultural gap that existed between themselves, the urban minority students they championed, and the teachers of those students.

The limits of the romantic critics became clearer as their criticism flourished. So many of them came from private school and private college backgrounds that it became difficult to tell if their defense of urban minority children and their criticism of urban schools and teachers reflected genuine understanding of the situation or an elite bias against the lower-middle- and middle-class backgrounds of most teachers. The romantic critics often became involved in free schools, institutions that safely practiced radical pedagogy outside of the public schools. This reliance on non-public school settings exacerbated the situation to the point that one could believe the critics were waging class war on behalf of urban children but against the public school system that served them.[38]

Not all pedagogical criticism of the 1960s concentrated on urban children. Some critics decried the stodginess of the teaching that existed in both urban and suburban public schools. In 1970, journalist Charles Silberman published a stinging indictment of the pedagogy practiced in most public schools and in many private schools, colleges, and universities. Silberman characterized much of the existing pedagogy as "mindless," an indictment that saw the situation as one of neglect rather than of calculated prejudice against pupils. Silberman's remedy was a form of child-centered pedagogy then being practiced in British primary schools. Informal classrooms, freedom of movement for students and teachers, problem-centered learning, and other inquiry-based strategies formed the core of Silberman's recommendations. He also noted particular places where the informal methods were already being practiced.[39]

On close analysis, this pedagogy seemed to differ little from what many of the child-centered progressives had advocated in the United States three or four decades earlier. Like their progressive forebears, the romantic critics and child-centered educators of the 1960s and early 1970s left little in the way of a lasting legacy. Their movement flourished in the publishing industry but languished in the public schools. What the romantics did accomplish, however, was to keep the child-centered progressive legacy alive by refashioning its language and its social focus to suit the time.[40]

Problems of School Bureaucracy

While Jonathan Kozol and other romantic critics concentrated on the deadening pedagogy and unsympathetic personalities of many urban teachers, other critics focused on the numbing organizational arrangements that characterized urban education. Peter Schrag, for example, in *Village School Downtown*, profiled in scathing prose the entire structure of the Boston public schools, from the school board and the larger political leadership to the central bureaucracy and the teaching force that it oversaw. The Boston school hierarchy, according to Schrag, was dominated by white ethnics: Italians, Irish, and others who had little sympathy or empathy for the black students trapped in Boston's inner-city schools. This educational power structure may have been appropriate for the Boston of a century earlier, but it was hopelessly out of touch with the problems of the mid-twentieth century.[41]

In New York, the mantle of organizational critic fell to a political scientist, David Rogers. His work critiqued the massive and horribly rigid New York school bureaucracy, which was failing miserably to serve the increasing minority population of the city's schools. Rogers wrote that the New York public school system had failed to educate its minority populations at least since the time of the 1954 *Brown* decision. In New York as in many cities, that decision sparked a controversy between civil rights groups seeking meaningful desegregation on the one hand and white neighborhood groups seeking to protect their children's educational and social advantages on the other hand. The school organization's contribution to bridging the gap between these two groups turned out to be negligible. Rather than alleviating the situation, the clumsiness, mendacity, and bias of school officials exacerbated it.[42]

Like the romantic critics, the organizational critics tended to agree with minority students and parents who perceived their problems in terms of inherent cultural conflicts between themselves and the middle-class teachers and administrators who were responsible for running the schools. Although there was certainly some truth in this analysis, it also seems clear that any long-lasting solution to the problems of urban schools had to involve alliances between the groups.

Emerging Political Activism Within the Schools

Within the formal educational arena, the political activism of the 1960s eventually reached teachers and parents, although conflicting agendas between these two groups quickly surfaced. Eventually, the activist impulse even reached the students.

Teacher Unionism

Public school teachers were chafing under the burdens of a deteriorating economy and new patterns of student behavior, particularly at the high school level. These changes were most noticeable in the nation's large cities, and it was there that the teacher union movement found the most fertile soil for growth.

As noted in Chapter 10, teachers had been vocal about their grievances prior to the 1960s. However, the prosperity of the 1950s had muted this activism. As that decade came to a close, a series of developments began to take place in New York City that proved to be the beginnings of a new and more militant wave of teacher organizing and strike activity.

The United Federation of Teachers

New York City had a number of teacher organizations in the 1950s, some affiliated with the trade-union-oriented AFT, some with the antiunion but occupationally oriented NEA, and some with neither of those groups. In the late 1950s, a movement toward the consolidation of many of these groups began under the leadership of the AFT affiliate for high school men teachers. This consolidation of organizations into a combined AFT local resulted in the birth of the United Federation of Teachers (UFT). Albert Shanker quickly emerged as the dominant leader of both the UFT and the teacher union movement that swept the nation's largest cities in the 1960s.[43]

During that time the UFT engaged in a series of controversial but largely successful strikes and political campaigns. The results were a substantial raise in teachers' salaries and a collective bargaining agreement institutionalizing the increases and other improvements in teacher working conditions. The UFT also assured itself a position of political power in both city and state government. None of these gains was achieved without substantial opposition or cost, however. New York State moved to curb the occurrence of teachers' strikes by passing legislation that, while it encouraged collective bargaining agreements, made strikes illegal and threatened both fines and personal incarceration for those who led them. However, the union's vast political power successfully neutralized most of the attempts to punish strikers.

Teachers throughout New York State and in much of the rest of the nation were encouraged by the swift and dramatic victories of the UFT and began to join unions in large numbers. Large industrial cities in the Northeast and Midwest, as well as cities on the West Coast, quickly became sites of substantial union organizing among teachers. Strikes, or the threat of strikes, followed, and collective bargaining agreements accompanied by substantial salary increases ensued. The teacher union movement swept urban America during the 1960s, giving urban teachers new energy and positive expectations about their occupational lives.

NEA Response

The NEA, until this time largely a broad, poorly focused professional organization for teachers, repeatedly lost to the AFT in elections to choose a bargaining agent for the nation's largest urban school districts during the 1960s. Smarting under these defeats, the NEA began analyzing how it could respond more successfully to the AFT's challenge. Moving toward collective bargaining, but calling its own version "professional negotiations" in an attempt to avoid the stigma of unionism, the NEA enjoyed some initial successes in negotiating collective agreements in several small cities. Next, NEA state affiliates engaged in job actions such as the 1968 walkout in the state of Florida, which won them national publicity as teacher advocates. The NEA then moved to reorganize itself so that it could compete better with the AFT in collective bargaining elections throughout the nation. This reorganization resulted in a new constitution for the NEA in the early 1970s, which confirmed the association as a genuine teachers' union.

The new goals of the NEA were virtually indistinguishable from those of the AFT, and the two organizations now competed on a more equal footing. While the AFT continued to dominate in the largest cities, the NEA gradually succeeded in bargaining elections in suburbs and in smaller cities and, at the state level, sponsored state laws that permitted collective bargaining. These campaigns to organize teachers resulted in a largely unionized teaching force operating under collective bargaining agreements in most American cities and in many of the surrounding suburbs. The position of the nation's teachers was, in at least one sense, transformed during the 1960s and 1970s. By the end of this period, the clear majority of teachers belonged to unions and bargained collectively with their school boards over issues of wages, hours, and working conditions in the schools.[44]

Merger Attempts

Despite heated competition between the AFT and the NEA for the allegiance of teachers in elections to choose a collective bargaining agent, there were some attempts at cooperation between the two groups. In New York State, in fact, a merger between the AFT and NEA occurred in the 1970s. That merger proved to be unsuccessful, however, and the NEA eventually started its own new organization in the state to compete with the merged group. Dissatisfied NEA loyalists felt that the merger had been, in reality, a takeover of the New York NEA group by the New York City union and their ambitious leader, Albert Shanker. Despite the failure to achieve a meaningful merger, the prospect of unity appealed to many members of both groups. After all, fighting a rival teacher organization siphoned off time and money from both groups that might otherwise have been directed toward the pursuit of contract negotiations and other occupational improvements.[45]

Community Control and Teacher Unionism

Teacher unions, whether AFT or NEA, prospered throughout the 1960s and 1970s. However, one movement that originated in inner-city districts tested the limits of teacher unions' traditional devotion to liberal political causes. Community control—a catch phrase for a variety of attempts to give poor urban parents and citizens some meaningful role in the conduct of their children's schools—became an issue of great controversy in 1968.

In that year, New York City's black residents expressed their disenchantment with both the desegregation and compensatory education efforts being waged on their behalf. Their discontent was channeled into a movement to decentralize the schools of the city, initially through an experiment involving three neighborhoods in the city. Ocean Hill–Brownsville, one of the three demonstration districts, became a flashpoint of controversy when its newly established community board of education tried to transfer a number of teachers out of the district's schools. These teachers were seen by community activists as insensitive or even hostile to the interests of the community and its children. The attempted transfer of teachers put the community board immediately at odds with Albert Shanker's UFT, because the union's contract with the central board of education prohibited such transfers without just cause and due process.

Tempers flared on both sides of the issue, and the dispute over teacher transfer became embedded in an ethnic conflict between the largely African American neighborhood of Ocean Hill–Brownsville and the primarily Jewish teachers union. Extremists on each side made it increasingly difficult to reach a compromise, and a series of union strikes ensued to protect the rights of teachers against arbitrary transfer. The final outcome was a victory for the UFT, but one that estranged the union from the minority communities its members were increasingly being called on to serve.[46]

The conflict between teacher unions and community activists was repeated in other cities, such as Detroit, but the controversy did not flare out of control as it did in New York. However, the result in Detroit, although less inflammatory, was no more favorable for either the activists or the unionists. In fact, the dispute over community control has been seen by one historian of Detroit's schools as an important cause of the eventual breakdown of the consensus between teacher unionists, other liberal and labor leaders, and their allies in the minority neighborhoods.[47]

Student Activism and the Schools

Student activism in the 1960s and 1970s tended to be confined to college and university campuses. A dichotomy existed between college activists and elementary and high school students similar to that which characterized relations between feminists and women teachers. Some high school unrest related to the Vietnam War did occur in these years, however, and a famous case from a school district in Iowa reached the Supreme Court in 1969.

At stake in that case, *Tinker v. Des Moines*, was the right of students to wear black armbands as a sign of protest against the war. The local school board banned the armbands as disruptive to the operations of the school. The Court ruled, however, that wearing armbands was an appropriate exercise of the students' free speech rights. This ruling contradicted earlier rulings that had permitted educators to operate on the principle that students' rights to free speech while in school were severely limited, if not completely absent. *Tinker*, therefore, was a landmark decision in establishing students' right to free speech in school.[48]

The *Tinker* decision culminated a line of argument that had begun at least a decade earlier. In 1959, Edgar Z. Friedenberg, a sociologist and social critic, published the first in a series of books profiling the American adolescent. Friedenberg argued that modern social conditions were creating a crisis for the healthy development of adolescents and children. In his view, extended and largely harmful schooling reduced adolescents to the status of a minority group excluded from meaningful participation in social and political life. Friedenberg believed that both the school and the larger society were at war with adolescents' attempts to develop a meaningful response to modern life. The *Tinker* decision reinforced Friedenberg's analysis and ensured that at least some rights of young people were protected from school authorities bent on imposing a rigid conformity.[49]

In a series of decisions in the 1970s, the federal courts applied *Tinker* free speech rights to student publications. Early in the decade, the attempts of administrators to suppress unofficial, or underground, student publications were partially rebuffed. In addition, a case decided in the same year as *Tinker* upheld the rights of high school student journalists to publish articles and ads opposed to the Vietnam War. In other cases, the rights of student editors to publish materials on controversial topics such as sex education were also upheld. Although no decision completely enjoined school officials from overseeing student newspapers, the general trend during these two decades was to expand substantially the rights of both students and student newspapers.[50]

Teachers and Academic Freedom

At about the same time that the federal courts were expanding students' rights, they also heard a series of cases related to the issue of teachers' academic freedom in their classrooms. In the late 1960s, the Supreme Court protected a teacher's right to use in class a magazine article that contained a highly offensive word. In subsequent cases, however, the right of teachers to use controversial words or ideas in class was limited. Issues such as the educational relevance of the controversy or the controversial language, the purpose of the teacher in using the material, the quality of the material being used, and the age and maturity of the students all had to be considered.[51]

Generally speaking, the courts extended teachers' academic freedom in and out of their classrooms during this period. As is often the case, however, not all court decisions supported teachers' rights to the same degree. In more conservative areas such as the South or the Midwest, teachers' academic freedom continued to be severely restricted by state courts responsive to the wishes of citizens who objected to their children's exposure to what they considered controversial ideas.[52]

The trend toward court recognition of both students' and teachers' rights was clear in the 1960s and 1970s, but the consequences of the trend were not. Conservatives pointed to student and teacher rights as simply more evidence of a social permissiveness that was undermining the educational fabric of the nation. Others claimed that, despite legal principles, the freedom teachers and students had won did not affect pedagogy at all. Educational practice continued largely unchanged by the court decisions.

Conclusion

In the beginning of the 1980s, the educational climate, like the political climate, was one of wide disarray. As Ronald Reagan campaigned against Jimmy Carter and the Democrats as the party of failed solutions, his indictment could have easily been applied to the educational arena. Instead, Reagan preferred to campaign on the more emotional and vote-rich issues of tuition tax credits for private school parents, a return to prayer in the schools, and the establishment of school choice programs that included public funding for private schools. Reagan's victory presaged a substantial shift away from the focus on equalizing educational opportunity for the poor and minorities that had characterized the federal agenda for the preceding twenty years.

Further Reading

Deloria, Vine, Jr. *American Indian Policy in the Twentieth Century.* Norman: University of Oklahoma Press, 1985. A thorough survey of the larger policy of the federal government toward the American Indian within which the educational provisions for Native Americans can be considered.

Donato, Ruben. *The Other Struggle for Equal Schools: Mexican Americans during the Civil Rights Era.* Albany, NY: State University of New York Press, 1997. A look at the multifaceted campaign by Mexican Americans to try to assure equal educational opportunity for their children in public schools.

Franklin, Barry M. *From Backwardness to At Risk: Childhood Learning Difficulties and the Contradictions of School Reform.* Albany, NY: State University of New York Press, 1994. A consideration of the early attempts to accommodate special needs children in public schools that compares and contrasts those attempts to the policies and practices for special education of the Civil Rights era.

Graham, Hugh Davis. *The Uncertain Triumph: Federal Education Policy in the Kennedy and Johnson Years.* Chapel Hill: University of North Carolina Press, 1984. A searching analysis of the often-halting, half-hearted, and politically motivated steps that constituted a substantial intensification of federal educational efforts under these two presidents.

Jeffrey, Julie Roy. *Education for Children of the Poor: A Study of the Origins and Implementation of the Elementary and Secondary Education Act.* Columbus, OH: Ohio State University Press, 1991. A consideration of the social and political background within which the ESEA was proposed, debated, and adopted, as well as the subsequent maneuvering in federal, state, and local jurisdictions in relation to its implementation.

Kirp, David L. *Just Schools: The Idea of Racial Equality in American Education.* Chapel Hill: University of California Press, 1982. A profile of desegregation in five California school districts, which reveals the complexities and peculiarities of the process in a non-southern setting.

Kliebard, Herbert. *Changing Course: American Curriculum Reform in the 20th Century.* New York: Teachers College Press, 2002. A survey of the school curriculum and its evolution in a search for a rational consistency that is not found.

Orfield, Gary. *The Reconstruction of Southern Education: The Schools and the Civil Rights Act of 1964.* New York: Wiley Interscience, 1969. A look at the politics of the passage of the Civil Rights Act in Congress and the enormous intensification of desegregation activity in the South that its passage sparked.

San Miguel, Guadalupe, Jr. *Brown Not White: School Integration and the Chicano Movement in Houston.* College Station, TX: Texas A&M University Press, 2001. A sensitive account of how Mexican Americans in Houston moved from having their children declared "white," and integrated only with African American children in the public schools, to a declaration of minority status that empowered them in their fight for educational equity.

Wolters, Raymond. *The Burden of Brown: Thirty Years of School Desegregation.* Knoxville, TN: University of Tennessee Press, 1984. Case studies of the desegregation process in the districts of the original plaintiffs of the *Brown* case, leading to a conclusion that the desegregation process had unfortunate outcomes that call the effort itself into question.

Notes

1. William L. O'Neill, *Coming Apart: An Informal History of America in the 1960s.* New York: Quadrangle Books, 1971.
2. Betty Friedan, *The Feminine Mystique.* New York: W. W. Norton, 1963. We deal separately with teacher activism in a later section of this chapter.
3. Gary Orfield, *The Reconstruction of Southern Education: The Schools and the 1964 Civil Rights Act.* New York: Wiley Interscience, 1969.
4. James S. Coleman, Ernest Q. Campbell, Carol J. Hobson, James McPortland, Alexander M. Mood, Frederic D. Weinfeld, and Robert L. York, *Equality of Educational Opportunity.* Washington, D.C.: U.S. Government Printing Office, 1966.
5. This account relies in large part on Guadalupe San Miguel, Jr., *"Let All of Them Take Heed": Mexican Americans and the Campaign for Educational Equality in Texas, 1910–1981.* Austin, TX: University of Texas Press, 1987.
6. *Keyes v. School District Number One, Denver, Colorado,* 413 U.S. 189 (1973).
7. *Lau v. Nichols,* 414 U.S. 563 (1974).
8. This conflict, rooted in the legal and curricular battles of the 1970s, was echoed in later decades in the battles over issues such as "Afrocentric" curricula for black students.
9. Attributed to D. H. Lawrence by Vine Deloria, Jr., *God Is Red.* New York: Delta, 1973, p. 74.
10. This discussion of Indian rights is drawn from Sharon O'Brien, "Federal Indian Policies and the International Protection of Human Rights," and other essays in Vine Deloria, Jr., ed., *American Indian Policy in the Twentieth Century.* Norman, OK: University of Oklahoma Press, 1985, pp. 43–44 and passim.
11. See Vine Deloria, Jr., *Behind the Trail of Broken Treaties.* New York: Delta, 1974. The quotation is from Deloria, *God Is Red,* p. 50.
12. Message from the President of the United States Transmitting Recommendations for Indian Policy, H.R. Doc. No. 363, 91st Cong., 2d Sess. (1970).
13. Paul S. Boyer, et al., *The Enduring Vision: A History of the American People.* Lexington, MA: D. C. Heath and Co., 1990, pp. 1142–1143.
14. National Center for Education Statistics, *American Indians and Alaska Natives in Postsecondary Education,* U.S. Department of Education, Washington, DC, 1998. For a view of this problem across the Canadian border, see Peter Cheney, "How Money Has Cursed Alberta's Sampson Cree," *Globe and Mail,* April 24, 1999, p. A1, A12.
15. Diane Ravitch, *The Troubled Crusade: American Education, 1945–1980.* New York: Basic Books, 1983, pp. 308–309.
16. Numan Bartley, *The Rise of Massive Resistance: Race and Politics in the South during the 1950s.* Baton Rouge, LA: Louisiana State University Press, 1969. See also Matthew D. Lassiter and Andrew B. Lewis, eds., *The Moderates' Dilemma: Massive Resistance to School Desegregation in Virginia.* Charlottesville: University Press of Virginia, 1998.
17. *Green v. County School Board of New Kent County,* 391 U.S. 430 (1968).
18. *Swann v. Charlotte-Mecklenburg,* 402 U.S. 1 (1971).

19. *Keyes v. School District No. 1, Denver, Colorado*, 413 U.S. 189 (1973).
20. *Millikin v. Bradley*, 443 U.S. 267 (1974).
21. *Millikin v. Bradley*, 443 U.S. 267 (1977).
22. *Morgan v. Hennigan*, 379 F. Supp. 410 (D. Mass. 1974).
23. Robert A. Dentler and Marvin B. Scott, *Schools on Trial: An Inside Account of the Boston Desegregation Case*. Cambridge, MA: Abt Books, 1981.
24. Majority-to-minority plans allowed students who were enrolled in a school in which their race was in the majority to transfer to a school where their race would be in the minority. The practical outcome of these plans was that black students could transfer from predominantly black schools to majority white schools.
25. James B. Conant, *The American High School Today: A First Report to Interested Citizens*. New York: McGraw-Hill, 1959.
26. James B. Conant, *Slums and Suburbs: A Commentary on Schools in Metropolitan Areas*. New York: McGraw-Hill, 1961.
27. Michael Harrington, *The Other America: Poverty in the United States*. Baltimore: Penguin Books, [1963], 1966.
28. Ibid.
29. Edward Zigler and Susan Muenchow, *Head Start: The Inside Story of America's Most Successful Experiment*. New York: Basic Books, 1992.
30. Ravitch, *The Troubled Crusade*, p. 159, states that five-sixths of the funds went to Title I, while Joel Spring, *The Sorting Machine Revisited: National Educational Policy since 1945* New York: Longman, 1989, p. 148, states that 78 percent of funds went to Title I.
31. Arthur O. Jensen, "How Much Can We Boost IQ and Scholastic Achievement?," *Harvard Educational Review*, vol. 39, 1969, pp. 1–124.
32. Christopher Jencks, Marshall Smith, Henry Acland, Mary Jo Bane, David Cohen, Herbert Gintis, Barbara Heyns, and Stephan Michelson, *Inequality: A Reassessment of the Effect of Family and Schooling in America*. New York: Basic Books, 1972.
33. The Moynihan Report was produced while Moynihan was Assistant Secretary of Labor in the Johnson Administration. It was published, along with a full account of the controversial reaction it provoked, in Lee Rainwater and William L. Yancey, *The Moynihan Report and the Politics of Controversy*. Cambridge, MA: MIT Press, 1967.
34. Nixon's successor, Gerald Ford, did not have a meaningful impact on educational issues.
35. See our discussion in Chapter 6. Also, see Donald R. Warren, *To Enforce Education: The Founding and Early Years of the United States Office of Education*. Detroit: Wayne State University Press, 1974.
36. Jonathan Kozol, *Death at an Early Age: The Destruction of the Hearts and Minds of Negro Children in the Boston Public Schools*. Boston: Houghton Mifflin, 1967.
37. Herbert Kohl, *36 Children*. New York: New American Library, 1967.
38. Allen Graubard, *Free the Children: Radical Reform and the Free School Movement*. New York: Random House, 1972.
39. Charles E. Silberman, *Crisis in the Classroom: The Remaking of American Education*. New York: Random House, 1970.
40. Joseph Featherstone, then a writer for the *New Republic* and later a faculty member at the Harvard Graduate School of Education, noted the links between the British Infant School and earlier pedagogical reform sentiments.
41. Peter Schrag, *Village School Downtown: Boston Schools, Boston Politics*. Boston: Beacon Press, 1967.
42. David Rogers, *110 Livingston Street: Politics and Bureaucracy in the New York City Schools*. New York: Random House, 1968.
43. Philip Taft, *United They Teach: The Story of the United Federation of Teachers*. Los Angeles: Nash Publishing, 1974.
44. Allan M. West, *The National Education Association: The Power Base for Education*. New York: Free Press, 1980.
45. The issue of merger between NEA and AFT lay nearly dormant after the New York failure. In the 1990s, however, merger again became a distinct possibility at the national level and a reality in a few local settings such as Los Angeles and San Francisco.
46. The literature on community control, and particularly the Ocean Hill–Brownsville situation, is substantial. For example, see Marilyn Gittell and Alan G. Hevesi, *The Politics of Urban Education*. New York: Frederick A. Praeger, 1968; and the essays in Maurice R. Berube and Marilyn Gittell, eds., *Confrontation at Ocean Hill–Brownsville*. New York: Praeger, 1969. For a set of interviews with participants in the controversy, see Melvin Urofsky, *Why*

Teachers Strike: Teachers' Rights and Community Control. Garden City, NY: Doubleday, NY, 1970.

47. Jeffrey Mirel, *The Rise and Fall of an Urban School System: Detroit, 1907–1981.* Ann Arbor: University of Michigan Press, 1993.

48. *Tinker v. Des Moines Independent School District,* 393 U.S. 503, 506 (1969). An explanation of the particulars and significance of this case, as well as many others related to student and teacher rights is in Louis Fischer and David Schimmel, *The Rights of Students and Teachers.* New York: Harper & Row, 1982.

49. Edgar Z. Friedenberg, *The Vanishing Adolescent.* New York: Dell Publishing, 1962 [1959]. Also see Friedenberg, *Coming of Age in America: Growth and Acquiescence.* New York: Random House, 1965; and *The Dignity of Youth and Other Atavisms.* Boston: Beacon Press, 1965.

50. Fischer and Schimmel, pp. 42–75.

51. *Keefe v. Geanakos,* 418 F. 2d 359 (1st cir. 1969).

52. Fischer and Schimmel, pp. 94–111.

12
From Equality to Excellence
American Education, 1980–2008

Overview

While it is somewhat of an exaggeration to have characterized the 1960s and 1970s as devoted to the pursuit of equality in education, such a description seems quite defensible when this era is compared to subsequent decades. Beginning with Ronald Reagan's term in the White House and continuing through the terms of his successors, George Herbert Walker Bush, Bill Clinton, and George W. Bush, the emphasis on using the schools to pursue egalitarian goals and equity objectives was diminished severely. Reagan set the tone for his successors by successfully depicting the two decades before his accession to the presidency as a period of egalitarian excess accompanied by moral degeneration.

In education, the end of federal involvement in pursuing equity through school desegregation began with the Reagan presidency and continued under his successors. The Office of Civil Rights and the federal courts, both of which had been heavily involved in the active pursuit of desegregation in American school districts, turned their attention to policies and practices that protected the rights of individuals rather than those of racial minorities. Reagan and his Republican successors sought the appointment of conservative federal judges who were devoted to individual liberty and suspicious of group-conscious policies as a threat to that liberty. While Clinton sought to fashion a more "centrist" judiciary, he faced a Congress that often looked askance at, and proved effective in, blocking approval of his proposed appointees, particularly after the 1994 congressional elections. The second George Bush has proved intent on continuing the pursuit of the conservative federal judiciary that was the goal of his two Republican predecessors—his father and Ronald Reagan.

Reagan's election to the presidency in 1980 rallied economic, cultural, and religious conservatives to the agenda of the Great Communicator, as he became known. Reagan's antipathy to government regulation of the economy appealed to free market advocates, his devotion to family values appealed to the cultural and the religious right, and his intention to rebuild the military spoke to those who believed that the national defense effort had been grievously hampered by budget cutters in the Carter White House and in Congress. Reagan promised a revived, confident nation that would resume its role of world leadership, for

389

many a welcome contrast to what they considered the undue caution of the Carter years. Further, Reagan's devotion to deregulation and to tax cuts, both of which built on and greatly intensified trends begun by his predecessor, had great appeal for wealthy Americans and for corporate America, the most obvious beneficiaries of those policies. Reagan, however, managed to couch those policies in ways that appealed not just to the wealthy and powerful, but to all those working and middle-class Americans who believed that economic wealth and its attendant political power were within their individual reach and that national prosperity and international dominance were within the country's reach. This latter segment proved to be substantially larger than the group that benefited directly from Reagan's policies, large enough to win him a landslide reelection in 1984 and to elect his vice president, the first George Bush, to the presidency in 1988. In spite of Bush's obvious difference in background (New England versus the Midwest and California), education (private schools and Ivy League college versus public schools and midwestern college), and instinctive orientation (insider versus outsider) to his immediate predecessor, Bush's domestic policies basically followed directions set by Reagan.

The 1990s proved to be a more complex political decade than the 1980s. Bill Clinton's defeat of George Bush in 1992 and then his reelection in 1996 indicated at least some discontent with the conservative agenda of Reagan and his successor. Yet Clinton's first presidential victory gave way two years later to the Republican landslide of 1994 in which the Republicans took control of both houses of Congress and promised in the "Contract with America" a renewed commitment to conservative principles, both domestically and internationally. Clinton, an astute politician, learned from the congressional defeat of his medical insurance reform program that traditional Democratic, or governmentally activist, reform was unable to carry the day. After this defeat, he managed to co-opt some of the conservative agenda, with the successful achievement of long-sought conservative goals such as welfare reform, at the same time that he assumed the traditional conservative mantle of fiscal responsibility with his pursuit and eventual achievement of balanced budgets. While one is tempted to characterize Clinton as a liberal sheep in conservative wolf's clothing, it must also be said that his combination of fiscal restraint through balanced budgets and internationalism in trade and foreign policy, added to his political ability to connect with both ethnic and working-class minorities and the middle-class majority, effectively represented the goals of the centrist wing of his party. This is in contrast to the more traditional Democrats who supported a government more actively engaged in the pursuit of economic and social equality.

Despite his many political talents and accomplishments, Clinton also proved to be the kind of politician who thought himself able to ignore the moral standards most Americans expected of their leaders. His personal behavior proved controversial enough to arouse the venomous animosity of many in Congress and the concern and disapproval of many Americans.

This animosity, as much as anything, contributed to the ability of the second

George Bush to attain the presidency in the 2000 electoral contest against Clinton's vice president, Albert Gore. While a case can be made that Gore won the election in Florida as well as in the popular vote nationally, the narrowness of the margin allowed the election to be thrown into the courts, where, depending on one's political views, Gore was robbed or Bush was properly declared the winner. However, the heated controversy that accompanied the election and its aftermath all but disappeared with the September 11, 2001, assault on the World Trade Center and the Pentagon. Americans rallied to their president in a time of national emergency and responded positively to his declaration of a "war on terrorism" that turned attention to the nation's role in world affairs and away from domestic pursuits.

Even so, Bush managed to achieve a good bit domestically, especially in the initial brief period in which his party controlled both houses of Congress. Most notably, he gained congressional approval for a large tax cut that effectively neutralized any plans for substantive improvements in domestic areas such as education, health, or social welfare. Especially dangerous politically to Bush was the controversy over his support for the privatization of at least a part of the social security accounts of the nation's retirees and his diffidence on the crisis in the Medicare system. The essence of Bush's domestic agenda, along with his program of tax cuts, was his consistent proclamation of the "compassionate conservatism" that he had announced in the presidential campaign. His ability to speak Spanish and his penchant for appointing high-profile minority people such as Colin Powell and Condoleezza Rice to Cabinet-level positions meant that he had a chance to gain support from among some of those who might have been seen as the targets of his policies rather than the beneficiaries of his compassion.

Ronald Reagan's Educational Policies

While the above characterization of the various presidencies in the period since 1980 has emphasized some similarities and even more differences between the recent Republican and Democratic occupants of the White House, the similarities are substantially greater when the issue of education is considered. In many ways, there has been more continuity than discontinuity in federal educational policy since 1980, though there were some differences in the agendas of the various presidents. In large measure the tone for educational policy in the closing two decades of the twentieth century and the opening years of the twenty-first century was set by President Ronald Reagan.

The Reagan–Bush Agenda

Ronald Reagan came to the presidency intent on reversing the course that the nation had been following during the four-year presidency of his Democratic predecessor, Jimmy Carter. The Georgian had proved to be a rather clumsy politician in handling Congress, and he was further weakened politically both by his inability to control the inflation caused in large part by an Arab oil embargo and by his failure to free Americans taken hostage by Iranian fundamentalists.

Reagan promised to change things drastically and to stem the tide of failure that had seemed to swamp the nation under his predecessor. Reagan's landslide victory in the 1980 election indicated that most Americans were eager to join him in reviving a nation that had seemed to many to be plagued by defeatism. Reagan quickly moved to cut taxes, thereby in his view releasing American capital from the government that had fettered it and prevented economic development. At the same time, he drastically increased military spending, which, when combined with the tax cut, put a substantial strain on the federal budget. The tax cut and increased defense spending meant that there was little or nothing left for domestic expenditures. Reagan set out to reduce or eliminate a number of social support programs from the federal budget but met with only mixed success.

Reagan had made it clear even before his election that public education would not be in line for any significant increase in support from his administration; but this did not mean that he had no educational policy. Reagan had advocated three educational changes in the 1980 campaign. First, the abolition of the federal Department of Education (just created by Carter in 1979); second, tax credits for the tuition paid by parents of private school children; and third, returning prayer to a prominent place in public schools. As part of his overall domestic agenda of a less intrusive government, Reagan also sought to trim federal educational spending and, if possible, to abolish it altogether, along with the Department of Education. Each of these objectives was pursued by Reagan and by his successor, George Herbert Walker Bush.

The President and the Department of Education

Given Ronald Reagan's stated goal of abolishing the Department of Education, the fact that the Secretary of Education was the last Cabinet officer he selected in his first administration was not surprising. Yet the individual Reagan chose to be Secretary of Education, Terrell Bell, who was then serving as commissioner of higher education in the State of Utah, was a member of the nation's educational establishment who proved to be unwilling to carry out what appeared to be Reagan's conservative agenda. Under Richard Nixon, Bell had served as Commissioner of the U.S. Office of Education, the sub-Cabinet federal educational agency that was housed within the HEW. Furthermore, Bell had testified in favor of the proposed federal Department of Education when the Carter-backed bill establishing it was winding its way through Congress in the late 1970s.[1]

Bell's own description of his selection and his tenure as Secretary of Education stresses that Reagan was more flexible in his educational agenda than the president's campaign rhetoric indicated he would be. In Bell's first meeting with Reagan, prior to Bell's selection as Secretary of Education, the two agreed on the goal of downgrading the federal educational agency to sub-Cabinet status, but still letting it function as a separate agency. Bell was adamant on the latter point, as he did not wish to see educational concerns circumscribed or diluted within the agenda of a large, diverse department such as the old HEW.

Throughout his years as secretary, Bell confronted, usually successfully, the anti-public education bias of Reagan's most conservative advisors. He also waged a largely effective, behind-the-scenes campaign to maintain Cabinet status for his department. Though he often clashed with presidential counselor Edwin Meese and other ideological opponents of federal support for public education or any other involvement in educational affairs, Bell managed to forge a positive relationship with the president that kept the ideologues at bay. He realized quickly that there were enough Republican supporters of education in Congress to ensure the continuation of the Department of Education.

Despite his success in keeping it, Bell was less able to counteract most of the federal funding cuts for education that characterized Reagan's years in office. Bell fought, at best, a rear-guard action aimed at minimizing these budget cuts and preserving threatened federal programs such as aid for low-income college students. Under George H.W. Bush and his Secretaries of Education, the overt attack on the federal department and the public schools was minimized, though the stringent restraints on federal spending were not lifted. The net effect of the Reagan–Bush period was a substantial diminution of almost every aspect of federal financial support for education, and, if not an overt disdain, an obvious lack of support for public education. Financial aid for college students was especially hard hit in these years, with grants being severely slashed in favor of student loans. The Reagan and Bush administrations, reflecting the Republican devotion to private enterprise, advocated student loans, most of which were privately offered by banks and involved substantial repayment commitments that could last for several years, even decades.

The one area of federal financial support for education that did not suffer substantial cuts during the Reagan and Bush presidencies was the Head Start program. The explanation for Head Start's protected status involves at least three factors. First, Head Start was as easily seen as an antipoverty program for poor and minority children as an educational program. As such, it was touted as an important part of the Reagan–Bush "safety net" for the poor, their counter to those who argued that federal domestic policies favored the rich over the poor. Second, the Head Start program was not housed within the Department of Education and its administration did not involve state departments of education directly. Instead, Head Start programs were usually run within a local community development (or other) agency and were thus safely removed from the normal, bureaucratic educational administrative apparatus. Thus, support of Head Start did not imply approval of the existing educational establishment. Third, some empirical evidence showed that Head Start programs were at least moderately successful in preparing poor and minority children to succeed in school.[2]

Terrell Bell's rear-guard support for a meaningful federal role in education eventually became unacceptable to the Reagan White House. After almost four years as Secretary of Education, he resigned under some pressure from the administration. His successor, William Bennett, was in many ways Bell's opposite. Bennett immediately alienated the educational establishment with pointed and extreme criticism, the body of which appealed to the religious right and other conservatives. Unlike Bell, Bennett supported completely the administration's education agenda, including the abolition of the Department of Education. By the second Reagan term, however, it was clear that Congress was in no mood to abolish the recently established department, and Bennett turned his attention to issues of cultural and moral renewal.

After George Bush replaced Reagan in the White House, his choice for Secretary of Education was made to shore up his standing with minority political constituencies. Bush chose a rather obscure Texan of Latino background, Lauro Cavazos, to lead the federal educational agency. Neither Bush nor Cavazos was able to carve out a meaningful educational agenda distinct from the policies supported by Ronald Reagan.

Moral Education and School Prayer

William Bennett's tenure as Secretary of Education, as well as his subsequent career, turned on the issue of a decline in the cultural and the moral fabric of the nation, a platform that dovetailed nicely with Ronald Reagan's advocacy of prayer in the schools. Widely publicized instances of school violence, capitalized on by Bennett and other conservatives, fueled the image of an out-of-control student population and of a group of professional educators that was clueless as to how to address the causes, treatment, and prevention of the problem.

Bennett, along with the Republican-appointed chairperson of the National Endowment of the Humanities, Lynne Cheney, castigated college professors for what they perceived to be the academics' extreme secularism, a position that seemed to Bennett and Cheney to be overtly hostile to religion, ignorant, and morally offensive. Bennett called for a return to school prayer and to traditional, morally based, classroom discipline as the best vehicles for the moral betterment of the nation's youth. The enthusiasm with which Bennett espoused his ideas endeared the Secretary of Education, a practicing Catholic, to both the leaders and the rank-and-file of the Christian right. While Bennett seldom pushed the linkage between moral decay and public education itself, those who listened to him had no need to be so careful and could easily reconcile his views with a position that was implacably opposed to secular public education as inferior to religiously based private schooling.

Bennett's tenure as Secretary of Education was not as long as Terrell Bell's, but Bennett assumed a much higher public profile while in office. He became an avowed spokesman for the conservative critique of secular public education as amoral if not immoral. He quickly became a target for educators, both in the public schools and in colleges and universities, who tended to see him as a dangerous spokesman for the more extreme views of the religious right. Bennett's continued devotion to school prayer, as a force for moral regeneration, went generally unheeded as most public school teachers and officials adhered to the strictures of the Supreme Court. However, some states, such as Georgia, passed "moment-of-silence" laws that prescribed a time for reflection in the public schools every day. Both advocates and opponents interpreted such laws as substitutes, religiously meaningful substitutes, for prayer in the schools. Bennett's tenacity in pursuit of school prayer and moral regeneration earned him political points with many fundamentalist Christians and their leaders. While Bennett's advocacy of religion, more particularly Christianity, as the foundation of moral education did not enlist overt support from many public school educators, a movement for greater attention to moral education based on religiously free content did take place within the educational profession.[3]

After leaving the Department of Education, Bennett continued his devotion to moral education as based on the religious and cultural traditions of the West, and spoke out often as an authority on morality, personal and political. He was especially active as a critic of Bill Clinton's sexual misconduct during Clinton's term in the White House and provided support for those who sought to impeach him. Additionally, Bennett served as editor and author of books devoted to the crusade for moral betterment in the United States, particularly in the education of its young people. To many, and perhaps even to himself, Bennett seemed to function far more effectively as a critic of government, of government officials, and of government policies than as a member of government.[4]

Tuition Tax Credits and School Choice

The final aspect of the initial Reagan agenda, the pursuit of a tax credit for parents who paid private school tuition, yielded the same largely unremarkable immediate results that characterized the efforts to abolish the Department of Education and to establish prayer in the schools. Many in the administration, particularly those devoted to ideological conservatism, openly espoused private education and almost all private services as being superior to secular public education and other public services. This was the context within which appeals for tuition tax credits for private school parents were made, even though the appeals failed to carry the day in Congress.

Administration support for private schools was accompanied by repeated criticism of the public schools for failing to maintain academic standards and guarantees of personal safety for students and teachers. Beginning in Reagan's second term and continuing like a drum beat throughout the 1990s and into the new century, these attacks on public schools were accompanied by a push for programs that institutionalized "school choice."[5] The idea of school choice had been around for some time, although it had been most often described in earlier iterations in terms of school vouchers or a voucher plan. The basic ideas behind vouchers and school choice are quite similar. Both plans seek to allow students, or rather the parents of students, to apply their individual "share" of public school funds (usually a portion of the amount that a state grants to a school system for each student in attendance at a public school) to the cost of any school, private or public, that the parent/student chooses to attend. Practically speaking, this amounts to a redistribution of some of the tax monies assigned to public education to students in private schools.[6]

Advocates of school choice advance their case with both economic and educational justifications. Economically, the school choice plans institutionalize the essentials of a free market system in education. According to market economic theory, this policy allows supply and demand to determine the unsuccessful and the successful schools, just as supply and demand separate the unsuccessful from the successful business enterprises. Public education, seen as a monopoly undisciplined by the forces of supply and demand, allows poor schools to continue functioning, even if they fail to educate their students.

Figure 12.1 "Money is not the answer—except for private schools."

Credit: 1983 Herblock Cartoon, copyright by The Herb Block Foundation.

Supply and demand also would minimize the need for the large bureaucracies—local, state, and federal—that are necessitated by current educational arrangements.

The Reagan–Bush era movement for school choice had powerful academic supporters, including free market economists such as Milton Friedman and other famous social scientists. Noted social scientist and educational researcher James S. Coleman, for example, author of an influential report on equality of educational opportunity in the 1960s discussed in the previous chapter, published a study in the late 1980s responding directly to the critics of school choice. Many critics had charged that private schools produced superior educational achievement largely because they were able to lure the best students and keep out those such as the poor, the disabled, or immigrants with poor English language skills, all of whom could lower total school achievement. In his complicated study of high schools in the public and private sectors, Coleman claimed that private schools were convincingly superior to public schools in the production of academic achievement even when family wealth was taken into consideration. That is, Coleman argued that private high schools produced more academic achievement, even among poor students, than did public high schools. Whether or not this gain could be held in private schools with large concentrations of poor students was an issue not addressed in Coleman's work.[7]

The school choice movement received another powerful dose of academic support in 1990, when two political scientists, John Chubb and Terry Moe, published a book arguing that an educational choice program was the only viable alternative to a public school system that was numbed by a huge, unresponsive bureaucracy. Chubb and Moe argued that public schools were the prisoners of their system of hierarchical control. The existing system of placing public schools under the control of a local school board and an administrative bureaucracy that responded, directly or indirectly, to the political wishes of that board, and the board and the bureaucracy in turn being subjected to the supervision of a politically sensitive state educational bureaucracy, guaranteed that public education could not respond effectively, that is, nimbly and quickly, to the challenges it was facing. The publication of the Chubb and Moe report by a relatively liberal think tank, the Brookings Institution, indicated that the school choice movement had now reached more than just a conservative political constituency.[8]

Despite the evidence offered by Coleman and the powerful arguments of Chubb and Moe, the school choice movement made relatively little headway in the 1990s. On several occasions, states included school choice initiatives on their ballots and, in every case, voters rejected the policy. Many factors contributed to these defeats, perhaps including voters' instinctive recognition that school choice could function only as a release for individual students and parents dissatisfied with the public schools and not as a large-scale replacement for public schooling. Strong lobbying against the school choice measures by most members of the educational establishment, particularly by teacher organizations such as the NEA and the AFT, also contributed to their defeat.

In spite of these results, two cities, Cleveland and Milwaukee, managed to mount successful school choice programs in which children from failing public schools could enroll, with a substantial subsidy (though not the full amount granted to public schools for each attendee), in private schools, including religious schools. Additionally, the state of Florida instituted a program in which public school students from failing schools receive financial support from the state to enroll in other schools, public or private. Private funding has been provided to underwrite choice efforts in other parts of the country as well. The largest of these efforts, to date, is the Children's Educational Opportunity Fund that was established in 1999 to subsidize voucher programs in over 40 cities.

Evidence on the educational value of voucher experiments has been mixed, at best. John Witte's official evaluation of the Milwaukee choice program found no gains in performance for the children in the private choice schools, while Paul E. Peterson and his associates countered that there are data, in Milwaukee especially, that indicate superior performance on the part of the choice students. Princeton economist Cecilia Rouse's study of Milwaukee offered some support for Peterson's claims, though none of these early reports could be considered conclusive. The problem is so complex and the measures are so imprecise that observers often seem able to find support for antithetical positions on the issue of the effectiveness of voucher programs, positions that tend to support the presumptions that the observers held before analyzing the data.[9]

The Cleveland plan began in 1996 when the state undertook to provide tuition assistance for Cleveland grade school students who wanted to attend private schools, special city schools, or suburban public schools rather than what were deemed to be substandard Cleveland public schools. While the plan did not explicitly favor the private school option, the realities of Cleveland and its surrounding school districts made the plan one in which 96 percent of the students involved in the program attended religious (overwhelmingly Catholic) schools. The predominance of Catholic schools was due to at least two factors. Cleveland had a long history of Catholic parochial schools within the city and in nearby suburbs, schools that in the 1990s had places for transfer students because of the movement of younger Catholic families to the outer suburbs and the decline in the number of children among the aging Catholic families that remained in the city. Second, these Catholic schools, subsidized by the Church and the religious orders that taught in them, charged tuition that was substantially less than that required by independent private schools. This lower tuition meant that these Catholic schools were realistic options for those who got a tuition voucher from the state, a voucher that amounted to only a portion of the amount the state and the school district spent on each student in the public schools.

The school choice issue received renewed attention in the summer of 2002 when the Supreme Court announced a legal ruling that covered both the Cleveland and the Milwaukee plans. A legal objection had been lodged against both plans charging that they were inappropriately violating the establishment clause of the First Amendment to the Constitution; that is, that the plans, insofar as they supported Catholic schools, amounted to government sponsorship of religion. In a ruling specifically on the Cleveland voucher plan, *Zelman v. Simmons Harris*, the Court found, by the slimmest of margins (five to four), that the voucher program in Cleveland did not violate the First Amendment. The Court's ruling was based on the fact that each voucher went initially to the parents of students in failing schools, and only after their endorsement, to the religious schools. This distinction for many was a fatuous one, because the money eventually wound up in the coffers of the religious institutions; however, for the short-term future, at least, the ruling seems to open the door to the further development of voucher plans involving religious schools as one of their options.

Many in the public schools fear that significant increases in voucher activities threaten the very existence of public education, at least in urban areas. This seems rather alarmist since the existence of a substantial number of private religious schools in midwestern "Rust Belt" cities like Cleveland and Milwaukee is not characteristic of most large cities in other regions of the country. Also, most non-Catholic private schools, religious and nonreligious, charge substantially more in tuition than the per-pupil amount that was spent in Cleveland or Milwaukee, meaning that most new plans would require a voucher substantially larger than the amount spent in those two cities. Further, many, if not most, private schools distinguish themselves by being highly selective in choosing their student bodies and are not likely to line up to enroll low-achieving students from failing public schools. Just as important, choice plans must conform to state constitutional mandates that may be stricter on aid to religious schools than the federal constitution. Finally, the large reservoir of satisfaction with public schools that exists in many American suburbs, where the schools seem to be doing a reasonable if not a superior job, is a favorable omen when their future is considered. Thus, though the Supreme Court's endorsement of a voucher plan certainly has given new life to the voucher movement, the politics and demographics of American education seem to militate against the growth of that movement to the extent that it would threaten the hegemony of the public school.[10]

This does not mean, however, that conservatives will cease their war with public education. Recently in Georgia, for example, the Republican dominated legislature passed a law providing funds for parents of special education students to seek educational services for their children in private schools.

Home Schooling and the Christian Right

Home schooling is a policy that seems clearly aligned with the desires of those who advocate school choice. If parents can choose which schools their children can attend, home schoolers argue, then surely they should be able to choose to educate their children at home. The substantial increase in home schooling in the last decade or so, when the number of children schooled at home has increased exponentially, is testimony to the strength of this movement.

Prior to the 1980s, most people who chose to school their children at home did so mainly for academic reasons. Many were dissatisfied with the quality of education in both public and private schools and the authoritarianism that often characterized the schooling process in both sectors. The rigid bureaucracy in public schools and the elitism or snobbery that often came with private schooling were also sources of dissatisfaction. These home school parents were often members of academic families, cultural dissidents who sought to provide their children with an education substantially less constricted than that offered in existing schools, whether public or private.

In the 1980s and 1990s, however, a new wave of home schoolers came on the scene, many of whom were fundamentalist Christians appalled at the secularization they saw happening in the public schools and the amorality such secularization encouraged. Educating their children at home allowed them to reinforce the morality of family and church, and not let it be challenged by a school devoid of formal religious and moral influence. Displeasure with public schools on the part of religious believers was not a new phenomenon, as readers of the earlier chapters of this book will remember.[11]

The Reagan and Bush administrations of the 1980s and early 1990s, and the administration of the second George Bush at the dawn of the twenty-first century, sought, and garnered, substantial political support from the Christian right. While this support did not always make these administrations opponents of public schooling, it did make them conscious of the desires and needs of a substantial political constituency that tends to be more enthusiastic about private and home schooling than about the public school system. Further, a substantial commercial market has emerged consisting of those who provide services to home schoolers, such as curriculum materials, assessment vehicles, and social strategies and activities. The protection of the producers and consumers involved in this market is a priority for political conservatives implacably opposed to big government and its institutions. Home school "fairs" and "conferences" often feature the products and services offered by a variety of commercial (and often religious) vendors. The net result is a vibrant home school movement in the first decade of the twenty-first century, one that moves forward vigorously, knowing that it has substantial support in Congress and in the federal administration, as well as in the ranks of fundamentalist Christian groups that are its main sponsors.

In response to the religious right, many have suggested changes in public schooling such as the nondoctrinal teaching of religion and morals in the public schools in the form of comparative world religions or Bible-as-history courses. Many committed Christians have found this insufficient, however. They demand moral education taught in conformity with their own understanding of Christian religion and its moral absolutes. This, of course, has led to conflict with those who espouse different religious beliefs, as well as with committed secularists who demand that any moral education be divorced from all religious doctrine. One result of this situation has been the proselytizing of many of their fellow students by fundamentalist Christian students in public schools, an activity that has sparked its own round of legal actions both for and against the activity. Another result has been the decision by increasing numbers of committed Christians to pull their children out of the public schools in favor of home schooling.[12]

Results of Reagan–Bush Educational Policies

Returning to the larger question of the efficacy of the Reagan–Bush educational agenda, their formal educational efforts must be judged as a mixed success at best. Neither of these presidents was able to abolish the Department of Education, to establish school prayer, or to legalize tuition tax credits. They did succeed, however, in curtailing and sometimes reducing federal educational spending, in raising public concern over moral education and school violence, and in sustaining nationwide momentum for school choice plans. Rhetorically, they set an educational agenda in terms of moral education, educational choice, and home schooling that has come close to dominating educational discourse in the last two decades. When the second George Bush took office in 2000, advocates of those avowedly conservative educational priorities were reenergized by the presence of an ally in the White House.

The most important educational initiative of the Reagan–Bush years was not any policy advocated by the administration, but one that happened almost by accident. Nevertheless, that initiative, the "educational excellence" movement, proved to be substantively far more influential than any policy or practice advocated by the two chief executives of the 1980s. The beginnings of the excellence movement were sparked in 1983 by the publication of a small pamphlet titled *A Nation at Risk* by the Department of Education.

Educational Excellence

As already noted, when Terrell Bell became Ronald Reagan's first secretary of education, his major concern was to protect his department from those in the administration who wanted to see it abolished. Further, he wanted to map out a meaningful federal educational agenda in an administration that had no intention of spending any more money on public education and that sought to reduce educational expenditures wherever possible. Given these priorities, Bell searched for an agenda that he could pursue that would maintain high visibility for his department and educational concerns without much financial cost. Bell hit upon this agenda by pursuing a concern that he had long held over what he considered to be an alarming decline in educational standards and achievement. To explore the sources and circumstances of this decline, he had a commission appointed shortly after he took office in 1981. The

National Commission on Excellence in Education was headed by David Gardner, who had been president of the University of Utah when Bell was that state's commissioner of higher education. Other members of the excellence commission, all appointed by President Reagan with close consultation from Secretary Bell, included individuals representing a wide variety of educational constituencies. Parent groups, teachers, school board members, school and college administrators, and private school staff were all represented on the commission.

In April 1983, after two years of data gathering, public hearings, and deliberation on the causes and consequences of educational decline, the National Commission on Excellence in Education published a report of its activities and conclusions. That report, apocalyptically titled *A Nation at Risk*, sought to persuade the American public that there was a real crisis in American education, and that the solution to that educational crisis should become the major educational objective of the era.[13]

Secretary Bell, wise in the ways of Washington maneuvering, arranged to have the report launched officially at a White House press conference featuring the president. On that occasion, President Reagan briefly alluded to the report and then went on to focus his remarks on two of his pet themes, school prayer and tuition tax credits for parents of children in private schools. In spite of his speech, the presidential presence and Bell's astute understanding of how to publicize an issue produced a public reaction that was clearly positive. The media, looking for an issue with some weight that might excite public interest, began to address the concern for educational excellence and achievement raised by the commission, thereby focusing the public's attention on Bell's educational concern.

In a very real sense, the report was sensational. It was peppered with references to the United States as a competitor in the new world economy. The rivals the report referred to were not the Communist nations, those who had been the target of the post-*Sputnik* subject matter reform movement of the late 1950s and 1960s, but rather contemporary American political allies such as Japan, Korea, and Germany. These nations were referred to in the report as outstripping the United States economically and in the production of better cars, tools, and electronic equipment. The core of their economic superiority was alleged to be their educational superiority, the evidence of which was their higher scores on international measures of educational achievement in subjects such as reading, mathematics, and science. These areas, with the addition of computer science, were the most important subjects for the technological accomplishments that were seen as absolutely critical to the age. Though in the *Sputnik* era the military threat to the United States had been the lever used to incite the nation to action, the "Excellence Report" invoked the image of a nation threatened economically by its political allies who were also economic rivals. Bell and the report's authors took this tack in the hope that the alarm, if sounded and heeded, would provoke both attention to the report and support, including financial support, for its suggested solutions to the problem.

Despite its sensationalism, *A Nation at Risk* raised a concern that many political, educational, and business leaders considered to be of the utmost importance. These groups saw that behind the metaphor of an education-based global economic competition lay real phenomena alluded to in the report—declining test scores in reading, mathematics, and science; lessened academic requirements for high school graduation and college admission; and school curricula and textbooks that had been "dumbed down" for the benefit of students who were not as capable as their predecessors or their global competitors. Journalists, university academics, state and local politicians, and some K-12 educators responded positively to these and other aspects of the reports, as well as to the image of the economic threat posed to the United States by its global economic competitors.[14]

Educators and Educational Excellence

Prior to the 1983 report of the National Commission on Excellence in Education, there already existed a group within the ranks of the U.S. educational community that was developing a coalition devoted to the causes of school improvement in the interest of educational excellence. The leaders of this coalition, most notably Diane Ravitch, had begun in the mid-1970s to identify problems like those pointed to by the Excellence Commission. Ravitch and other educational excellence advocates decried what they perceived as permissive, child-centered pedagogical strategies that they traced back to the 1960s and the earlier "progressive education" movement. As an antidote to educational decline, these Excellence supporters advocated a return to basic academic subjects and to traditional disciplinary policies in the schools.[15]

Many other educators were, however, troubled by *A Nation at Risk*. They saw the report as another instance of public school bashing by an administration that seemed to exhibit contempt for all public enterprises, seeing them as inherently inferior to the private sector. Further, these educators knew that the schools were an easy target for state and local politicians looking for a scapegoat to blame for the economic decline plaguing much of the nation. These educators argued that the schools were more a victim of the larger social and economic environment in which they existed than they were the cause of that environment. Thus, these educators saw something disingenuous in the motives of political leaders and members of economic elites who placed blame for a national economic crisis on an overburdened school system that lacked broad support from politicians and the business community.[16]

This line of argument reached a zenith with the publication of a scathing account of the unfair attack on the public schools. This account, written by two leading educational researchers, was titled *The Manufactured Crisis*, indicating what the authors thought was taking place in the wake of *A Nation at Risk*. In their preface, David Berliner and Bruce J. Biddle expressed their "outrage" at the conduct of the federal government in regard to public education under the Reagan and Bush administrations. Their position was that the criticism of the public schools was basically composed of a number of overstatements and out-right lies by government officials. Specifically found wanting by Berliner and Biddle were the claims that elementary student achievement had fallen, that college students also exhibited a marked decline in academic performance, and that America's schools were inferior in student performance to those in other nations. They argued, using substantial amounts of data that were often the same as those used by critics, that our schools were doing an excellent job in a difficult situation. Given this, they saw the critics, especially the politicians and business leaders, as using the schools as a cover for the nation's economic and political failings. They charged that critics scapegoated teachers and adminis-trators, as they had often done in the past. Although the authors hardly men-tioned the criticism of the schools in the 1950s and 1960s provoked by the launching of the *Sputnik* satellite by the Soviet Union, it seems clear that this was one of the forerunners of what they saw as the school "bashing" of the 1980s.[17]

Still other educators tried to find a middle ground between the extremes of whole-hearted support and outright opposition to *A Nation at Risk* by critically evaluating its arguments and those of its opponents. Many in this middle group believed that the vaunted test-score decline decried in the Excellence Commission report was at best a half-truth. The decline itself had not lasted for two decades (the 1960s and 1970s), as many excellence advocates contended. Rather, it was concentrated in the 1970s and had begun to subside near the end of that decade, prior to Reagan's election in 1980. Furthermore, much of the test-score decline could be attributed to the fact that during the 1970s the school-age population that took tests had broadened to include a much larger portion of the high-school-aged student cohort than had taken the tests in previous years. In those years, high-achieving students had been greatly over-represented in the ranks of test takers. Now, their proportion in relation to all test takers had slipped substantially as more lower achievers took the tests. Finally, and perhaps most important, these middle-ground critics decried the one-sidedness of the report's emphasis on tests and test scores to the exclusion of other educational concerns, its devotion to the back-to-the-basics curric-ulum movement in place of the broader approach to subject matter favored by many educational experts, and its endorsement of a return to traditional, teacher-centered instruction, a method that in many ways had never been abandoned, particularly in the high schools.[18]

According to these critics, more testing, back-to-basics curriculum, and tra-ditional instruction and discipline were overly simplistic solutions for genuinely complicated educational problems. Standardized test-oriented instruction, for example, ignored many advanced areas of study such as logical reasoning and advanced writing that are related directly to any meaningful conception of educational excellence. For these critics, touting a return to authoritarian, teacher-centered classrooms ignored the complexity of modern classrooms in which teachers had to develop a learning community in the context of an increasingly culturally diverse group of students with substantially different learning styles, many of whom came to school with little of the preparation that students in earlier decades and from more favorable circumstances had acquired.

These critics did not deny the Excellence Commission's contention that a crisis existed in American education. However, the crisis the critics saw was related to demographic and economic shifts more than to any concrete pattern of educational decline. This crisis was also not related to the global economic competition that animated the analysis in *A Nation at Risk*, nor was it subject to the relatively simple, and simplistic, solutions offered by President Reagan and other political leaders. Administration critics maintained that the alterations and complex realities of late-twentieth-century life presented the real challenge to established curricular, instructional, and school organization patterns, whether or not there had been a meaningful decline in test scores dating back to the 1960s.

Cultural Literacy

Substantial evidence that the Excellence thrust of the president's commission had support in the academic community was provided by the success of the cultural literacy movement. The publication in 1987 of E. D. Hirsch, Jr.'s *Cultural Literacy: What Every American Needs to Know* was both a contribution to the growth of dissatisfaction with the content of public schooling in the United States and a prescription for what to do about the problem. Professor Hirsch of the University of Virginia contended that American education had taken a wrong turn early in the twentieth century when "progressive" child-centered ideas first began to make headway in educational thought and practice. He pointed to Jean Jacques Rousseau and John Dewey as the leading philosophers who popularized "progressive" notions about the natural development of children, and whose warnings against the attempts to impose on young children content that was inappropriate for their age had gone awry. Rousseau, wrote Hirsch, "thought that a child's intellectual and social skills would develop naturally without regard to the specific content of education." While this view had started with Rousseau in the distant past, it was widely diffused in the twentieth century through the writings of Dewey and his educationist disciples. Hirsch charged that this diffusion encouraged a "content-neutral conception of educational development that has long been triumphant in American schools of education and that has long dominated the 'developmental,' content-neutral curricula of our elementary schools."[19]

Hirsch's rendition of a familiar litany of "failures" and shortcomings in American education and his polemical indictment of "progressive education" were less novel and stimulating to many of his readers than was the list—5,000 terms that every literate American should know—contained in the appendix

Figure 12.2 "But I could always look up that stuff—if I could spell."

Credit: 1987 Herblock Cartoon, copyright by The Herb Block Foundation.

to *Cultural Literacy.*[20] Anxious middle-class parents worried about the eventual success of their children in gaining admission to the "right" college or university and about their attaining a satisfying professional career turned to "the list" to test their own and their children's grasp of those things that Hirsch and his colleagues had determined everyone should know. To provide direction regarding steps needed to stimulate reform, Hirsch published a series of graded books detailing the subject matter content every elementary school child should learn in each successive grade.[21]

Much more important in principle to Hirsch, however, was the main thrust of his argument, that is, that shared knowledge—cultural literacy—is "the oxygen of social intercourse." Without shared understandings and a common base of knowledge, he contended, there could be little hope of closing the gaps between the culturally literate and illiterate, the advantaged and the disadvantaged, the rich and the poor. He maintained that to close those gaps and to spread and to share the cultural capital that is the only available ticket to full citizenship, agreement on and implementation of a common body of "core knowledge" should constitute the most urgent agenda for educational reform. Hirsch explicitly framed the matter as follows:

> Literate culture is the most democratic culture in our land: it excludes nobody; it cuts across generations and social groups and classes; it is not usually one's first culture, but it should be everyone's second, existing as it does beyond the narrow spheres of family, neighborhood, and region.[22]

Not unexpectedly, Hirsch's call for universal cultural literacy and renewed attention to "mainstream knowledge" sparked controversy. Pundits were quick to point out that knowledge is constantly changing and that what is important in one cultural enclave or subgroup may not have the same currency in another—points with which Hirsch hardly disagreed and, in fact, which he emphasized. Hirsch's initial "provisional list" of cultural items was scrutinized for sins of omission and commission by spokespersons on the left and the right of the political and cultural spectrum, and especially by those prone to apply measures that point to ethnic, gender, and other social divisions. Professional educators took particular exception to his overgeneralizations and to his condemnation of educational research and practice that differed from his own position. Hirsch's subsequent publication in 1996 of *The Schools We Need and Why We Don't Have Them*, in which he presented a sharpened critique of progressive education and its pernicious consequences, hardly stemmed the tide of negative criticism from his opponents. At the same time, the adoption of core curriculum materials by hundreds of schools marked a steady increase in his influence as the decade grew to a close. As suggested above, the appeal of any prescriptive list of content to anxious middle-class parents meant that Hirsch would stay in the forefront of popular discussions of education, if not in the mainstream of academic discussion of educational issues. Parental anxiety was also intensified by the major educational accomplishment of the George H. W. Bush administration, the adoption of the *America 2000* program.[23]

George Bush and America 2000

When then Vice-President George Herbert Walker Bush campaigned for the presidency in 1988, he rode the wave of political popularity that still adhered to the Reagan presidency while simultaneously trying to fashion his own identity. One of the ways that he accomplished these dual objectives was by campaigning on the issue of educational improvement. None of Reagan's main educational proposals—school prayer, tuition tax credits for private school parents, and abolition of the Department of Education—had been enacted into law. This allowed Bush to distinguish himself from Ronald Reagan by couching his discussion of educational improvement in a less overtly ideological context, promising that if he were elected, he would become "an education president."

Despite the rhetoric of an education presidency, education was not a prominent issue in the 1988 presidential campaign. During his time in office, Bush's educational policies differed little from those of his predecessor and were not really the type of policies that an educationally active president might pursue. School prayer and tuition tax credits for private school parents remained prominent, at least rhetorically. However, given Reagan's inability to abolish the Department of Education and Bush's record as a federal insider and traditional political leader, the presidential war against the federal educational agency diminished substantially. In its place, Bush maintained, and even intensified, the Reagan advocacy of school choice, particularly choice plans that involved private schools, as the solution to the nation's educational problems.

Most of Bush's other school improvement ideas were rather safe, politically oriented proposals, that would enhance his popularity with the voters. In this regard, the president had much in common with the nation's governors. This commonality was reflected in the joint adoption by the president and the governors of an educational platform for the nation. At the "Presidential Summit on Education," held in late September 1989 at the University of Virginia, the president and the governors conferred for two days on educational problems. The outcome was the *America 2000* program that was subsequently pushed vigorously by the Bush administration. It consisted of a series of goals, published in pamphlet form, which the political leaders had agreed constituted a needed educational agenda for the nation.[24]

In his April 1991 remarks about his new educational program, published as a preface to the pamphlet outlining the goals, Bush sounded some familiar educational themes with equally familiar political overtones. He remarked that it was time to abandon the status quo in education in order to meet the challenges of the twenty-first century. Instead, he remarked, it was time to put America's genius into play to solve educational problems. He was quick to add, however, in traditional Reagan Republican fashion, that it would do no good simply to throw money at the nation's educational deficiencies. The body of *America 2000* more or less reiterated several earlier educational pronouncements that almost sounded clichéd: The schools were in need of a revolution, school people would have to be held accountable for their results, the schools were destined to become learning communities, and the students within them should prepare for "lifelong learning." The pamphlet also echoed themes of international economic competition taken from the pages of *A Nation at Risk.*

A potentially controversial idea was at the core of the program in the pamphlet, however: a statement of the need for national standards as the key aspect of educational improvement. This idea stood in stark contrast to conservative Republican (and much Democratic) ideology that the schools, which were locally controlled, should not be dictated to by any national initiative. Bush's solution to this problem was to make the standards voluntary, not mandatory. What Bush did not address was how a national standard that sought effective universal application through voluntary adoption differed in practice from a mandatory standard. A similar contradiction was involved in the Bush administration's advocacy of a national system of voluntary certification for teachers.[25]

As already noted, the *America 2000* program involved cooperation with the nation's governors, a group that had officially endorsed the proposals. However, this same bipartisan support prevented the *America 2000* program from emphasizing the more controversial aspects of the Republican educational agenda, such as school prayer, tuition tax credits, and school choice. The meat of the *America 2000* program was in the six stated educational goals it posited. These goals, all to be reached by the year 2000, were as follows.

1 All children in America will start school ready to learn.
2 The high school graduation rate will increase to at least 90 percent.
3 American students will leave grades 4, 8, and 12 having demonstrated competency in challenging subject matter including English, mathematics, science, history, and geography; and every school in America will ensure that all students learn to use their minds well, so that they may be prepared for responsible citizenship, further learning, and productive employment in our modern economy.
4 U.S. students will be first in the world in science and mathematics achievement.
5 Every adult American will be literate and will possess the knowledge and skills necessary to compete in a global economy and to exercise the rights and responsibilities of citizenship.
6 Every school in America will be free of drugs and violence and will offer a disciplined environment conducive to learning.

Several characteristics of these goals deserve comment. First, they represent a strong statement about some ideals to which American education was to be directed. However, the lack of specific proposals relating to implementation of the goals constituted an obvious shortcoming. Insofar as the goals spoke to problems of preschool and adult education, they involved constituencies and concerns traditionally left unaddressed by the nation's K-12 and college and university educators. Additionally, requiring substantial reliance on increased educational testing of many kinds, and report cards for individual schools and school districts that sought to guarantee successful test performance, indicated that, in the most basic sense, *America 2000* was every bit as much a political event as it was a plan for school improvement.

The political attractiveness of the program was certainly a reason that it was embraced by the nation's governors. One of them, Bill Clinton of Arkansas, had already won a reputation as one of the nation's most accomplished education governors. He helped convene the conference and was a leader in the movement to adopt *America 2000* in Arkansas and other states. After he defeated George Bush in the 1992 presidential election and after he criticized his opponent for not making good on his promise to become the "education president," Clinton proceeded to build on *America 2000* by developing his own program. In fact, however, the Clinton program, called *Goals 2000*, differed little from its predecessor in its statement of goals. It simply added two goals to Bush's six; first, it advocated parental involvement in education, and second, it established programs for improving the professional education of teachers.

The major differences between the educational agendas of Bush and Clinton were in areas such as school prayer and tuition tax credits, both of which were opposed by Clinton. In the area of school choice, Clinton advocated a program that limited choice for students in public schools to other public schools, in contrast to the Bush program that included private schools as legitimate alternatives. Clinton was also less penurious in federal educational expenditures, though his increases were seldom very large and were as often in response to political factors as they were to strictly educational concerns.

In short then, the educational improvement efforts sparked by Republicans in the 1980s continued largely unchanged in the 1990s, despite the change in administrations. As if to underscore this continuity, Clinton selected Richard Riley, the Democratic education reform governor of the state of South Carolina, as his first Secretary of Education. In that position, Riley succeeded Lamar Alexander, the Republican education reform governor of the state of Tennessee who served as the last Secretary of Education under Bush. Clinton himself, as already noted, had been the education governor of the state of Arkansas. All these men shared an affinity for stated educational goals, standardized testing as a measure of achievement, and accountability standards for schools and school districts that relied heavily on standardized measures. Similarly, all came to prominence as governors of relatively poor southern states that clustered near the bottom of most national rankings of educational performance. The relative improvement in performance in the southern states still often left them well behind their nonsouthern sisters. All this indicated a strong possibility that the prospects for reform of American education were in hands that were much more conversant with the political usefulness of educational issues than with substantive educational concerns.

Education in the Clinton Administration

One significant change in educational policy in the two administrations of Bill Clinton was the lowering in intensity of the public criticism of schools and school people. This diminution of school and teacher bashing was welcomed by educators and was seen as a possible harbinger of a much more favorable period in terms of tangible support for schools. This did not turn out to be the case, however, as the record in education over the Clinton terms showed that the fundamental orientation of the Reagan–Bush years—an emphasis on school reform led by politicians along with a lack of infusion of meaningful amounts of federal funds for education—continued.

Unlike Reagan, Clinton had not promised to abolish the Department of Education, but, like George Bush, he did not substantially increase the department's power, influence, or funding. The Republican victory in the 1994 congressional elections meant that, two years after his own election, Clinton faced a Congress in which the opposing party, and especially its conservative wing, controlled both houses. This put a firm brake on any changes in educational direction the Democratic president might have had in mind, if he indeed had such changes in mind. Clinton's posture as a "New Democrat," one who understood and acquiesced in the political realities of the conservative revival of the late twentieth century, also signaled that the recovery of an active role for the federal government in education, as in most areas of domestic affairs, was unlikely. After the 1994 election, Clinton affirmed the new political reality by announcing that the age of big government had come to an end. Thus, the Democratic president explicitly affirmed his intent to embrace, or at least to co-opt, the conservative agenda by pushing his own less contentious and controversial versions of policies the conservatives had sought to enact.

In education, this meant a Department of Education under Clinton that, despite its change in leadership and rhetoric, was not significantly strengthened through new funds or mandates. Rather, stand-pat or retreat policies were adopted, with rhetoric that made them sound like substantial improvements. For example, the consequences of cuts in direct grants to students were softened by increases in the availability of student loans, and these loans were as likely to come from private banks under government guarantees as directly from government funds. This allowed Clinton to pose as a friend to students without confronting the negative impact on the working classes and the poor that the change from grants to loans portended. Similarly, Clinton's advocacy of school choice, even though limited to choice within the public sector, nonetheless was a move in the direction desired by social conservatives. Clinton, who as a governor, had cooperated with George Bush in the adoption of the *America 2000* plan, simply added a few goals to the plan as his contribution.

The educational content of Clinton's 1999 State of the Union address, offered to Congress and the nation in the midst of his impeachment trial over a sexual encounter with a White House intern, illustrates the modesty of his agenda. Salting his address with phrases such as "No child should graduate from high school with a diploma he or she can't read," "All states and school districts must turn around their worst performing schools or shut them down," and "We must empower parents with information . . . on the quality of local schools," the president offered no analyses or explanations of how these situations had arisen, the ways in which they did or did not represent substantial changes from the past, or how they could be addressed in any meaningful way. One national political journal, not unfriendly to the Clinton presidency, commented on the inadequacy of these sentiments, urging the president to "use federal legislation to promote competition and choice within public education instead of using the federal pulpit for empty rhetoric." While the charge that the president's words were empty rang true, the journal's call for public school choice as the solution for educational problems hardly represented a serious challenge to the policies of the previous administrations. In fact, some cynics dubbed the public school choice programs favored by many Democrats as a school choice "lite" version of Republican plans. Thus, the language of educational policy issues in the 1990s remained much the same as it had been in the 1980s.[26]

Bill Clinton left the White House after the election of November 2000 without having had a substantial impact on American education. The problems, at least those problems that got the attention of politicians, were the same as when he took office in 1992. The concrete educational goals of the *America 2000* program, such as universal readiness for kindergarten or a 90 percent high school graduation rate, were almost as distant from being fulfilled in the year 2000 as they were when they had been adopted in 1989. Furthermore, the tension between these national goals and a locally managed public school system was left unaddressed. While school people, particularly public school people, might have felt slightly less under attack by the Clinton White House than by its predecessors, they could point to few tangible policies or programs of the Clinton administrations that helped them in their work.

Education and the Second George Bush

The controversy over the results of the 2000 election plagued the early months of George W. Bush's first term as president. This meant that he devoted substantial amounts of his energy that might have gone to policy formulation to legal and political efforts to confirm his election. Of course, as the heir of two conservative Republicans whose achievements had been interrupted but not substantially reversed by the Clinton years, Bush had had no new plans for substantive improvement efforts in domestic affairs, including education. The events of September 11, 2001, horrific in their impact and outcome, energized Bush as commander-in-chief and legitimized a turn to foreign policy, national defense, and war readiness as the proper purview of the nation's chief executive.

In education, Bush was able to build a somewhat positive image in spite of his essential disinterest in spending money on substantive change. Part of the favorable regard for the chief executive was the image cast by his wife, a former school teacher and school librarian who seemed to have a genuine personal affinity for children and a regard for teachers. Bush himself also proved to be adept at projecting positive personal views about children and their parents. Further, Bush had some facility in Spanish and he was not afraid to use Spanish on strategic political occasions to enhance his image as a "compassionate conservative" with a strong commitment to minority achievement in education and in other arenas. Moreover, his high-profile appointments of minority persons to positions of importance in his administration earned him support from liberal factions. Along with the already-mentioned appointments of Colin Powell and Condoleezza Rice, he chose an African American who had been superintendent of the Houston, Texas, schools, Roderick Paige, as his first Secretary of Education.

Bush also had a record as an education governor of the state of Texas. In cooperation with the state legislature, Bush imposed an accountability system on that state's schools, a system that used substantial standardized testing as a basis to indicate whether or not the state's schools had indeed improved. While the idea of standardized testing as the arbiter of any school or school system's accomplishments continued to generate controversy within professional educational circles, it clearly had carried the day in the political arenas in which national and state educational policies were made. Bush's accomplishments in Texas were thus seen as a beacon of reform, as were similar accomplishments being stimulated by Jim Hunt, a Democratic education reform governor in the state of North Carolina. Again, as in the Republican administrations of the 1980s and the Clinton administrations of the 1990s, the idea of positive educational reform on which the nation's efforts could be modeled originating in southern states with substandard educational records won the approval of the media and the American public.

No Child Left Behind Act

George Bush used the regular renewal of a federal educational law that dated back to Lyndon Johnson's administration, the Elementary and Secondary Education Act, to put his mark on national educational policy. The Bush version of ESEA was known as the "No Child Left Behind" (NCLB) Act and was passed by Congress in 2001 and signed into law by President Bush on January 8, 2002. This Act, in addition to continuing the previous patterns of federal educational provision and funding, institutionalized standardized testing as the

Figure 12.3 "Let's not get alarmed . . ."

Credit: Reprinted with permission of Jimmy Margulies.

vehicle by which public schools would be measured. Gone was the invocation of voluntary national standards that had been favored by Bush's father. In its place was a provision that mandated testing in all public schools (at least all of those that received federal funds of any kind) and that, further, imposed negative consequences on those schools that did not measure up. Parents of children in individual schools that did not achieve satisfactory scores in two consecutive years of testing were now entitled to substantive relief, either in the form of tutoring for students or through the option of enrolling in another, more successful, public school. The implementation of these provisions in the 2002–03 school year was fraught with confusion. Especially troublesome were notices of failure received in the summer or later that conveyed mixed messages about exactly what options would be available to children in which schools.

Of course, a smooth and timely administration of the program would not have obviated the difficulties that it ignored—namely, that failing schools were too often, if not always, predictable in terms of the socioeconomic backgrounds of the students rather than in relation to any specific educational concerns. Allowing individual students to enroll in higher-achieving schools, again most likely those with student bodies less burdened by poverty and its consequences, did nothing to alleviate the situation for the bulk of students who were left behind in the "failing" schools to fend for themselves. The morale of teachers and students in these failing schools, necessarily an issue of deep concern, was ignored completely. Moreover, the impact on the schooling process itself was and remains a concern in a system in which test results can have such dire consequences. "Teaching to the test" may not only have negative consequences for the curriculum and pedagogy, but in its most extreme form can motivate some teachers to use past (and, illegally, present) test items as the basis for their instruction.[27]

Yet, the Bush agenda seemed clearly dominant as the federal mandates were implemented in the states. To get a clearer indication of the extension, and the nature, of this dominance, as well as another view on educational reform since 1980, we turn now to a consideration of educational reform at the state and local district level.

State and Local School Reform

The rather constant drumbeat for school reform, a feature of the educational landscape since *A Nation at Risk* was published in 1983, sparked and/or intensified changes in educational policy and practice at the state level. These changes, in turn, had a substantial impact on the conduct of schooling in local school districts. Although many state and local educators and educational officials agreed with the stated belief of many political conservatives of the 1980s that stultifying federal control of education threatened the ability of local districts and of individual schools to adjust to their particular situations, the net effect of the state school reforms that followed publication and the arguments in *A Nation at Risk* imposed more regulations on local schools than federal educational officials had ever contemplated. There follows a close look at the sources and outcomes of this ironic situation.

The First Wave of State School Reform

State educational reform in the 1980s stemmed from several sources, not just the challenges and mandates of the federal government. Interstate groups devoted to educational affairs, such as the Council of Chief State School Officers and the Educational Compact of the States, had existed prior to Ronald Reagan's election and his National Commission on Excellence in Education. These interstate groups served as forums in which state educational leaders, political and professional, could discuss the substance and the politics of state educational reform. Similarly, regional accrediting agencies had been engaged in the business of evaluating individual schools since early in the twentieth century, and they used this evaluation process to prod school districts toward change. The educational excellence movement presented a spur to both of these groups, and the eventual result was an explosion of state school regulations and other reform efforts throughout the 1980s.

This activity can be characterized as having occurred in two waves, or movements. The first wave concentrated on reforms that promised quick response to excellence and other immediate results-oriented reformers. The concentration here was on policies that could be implemented rather easily and that could be easily measured. Examples included changes in teacher certification and/or reward regulations, changes in financial support plans and provisions for school districts, and the adoption of national or newly developed state testing programs. Ironically, in addition to providing measurable outcomes by which the efforts could be judged and compared within and among states, these changes further increased the trend toward national uniformity in educational policies and practices that conservatives had traditionally resisted.

A more obvious problem with this first wave of reforms, however, was their indirect relationship to the educational process that was taking place in the schools in any state. For example, basing rewards, whether tangible or intangible, on standardized test scores sometimes led to unwanted outcomes that reflected poorly on the process itself. In South Carolina, for instance, one teacher was found to have given her students actual questions from a state-mandated test that they were scheduled to take. The teacher was prosecuted for this obvious legal violation, but other teachers throughout the country were praised for drilling their students with questions taken from previous versions of state-mandated or nationally standardized tests. In other cases, tests that closely resembled those to be given were given to students to use as practice activities. Such practices, which substituted test-based activity for regular school instruction, narrowed the educational process severely, dangerously limiting the repertoire of teachers and oversimplifying the educational process.

Regardless of any substantive educational questions raised about the educational process under such reforms, governors proceeded with their school improvements, learning from each other and ignoring their critics. In fact, as we already have noted, the annual conferences of governors in the 1980s often had school reform at the top of their agendas and proved to be settings in which governors could trade reform ideas with each other, as well as adopt the national goals for education that stemmed from the Charlottesville summit on education in 1989. Governors often vied with each other to earn the reputation of being "education governors," and, again as already noted, several of these education governors moved up to hold high national office, either as President, as Bill Clinton and the second George Bush did, or as Secretary of Education, an office held by governors Lamar Alexander and Richard Riley. The motives behind the creation of the image of "education governor" likely were mixed. Perhaps chief among them was an interest in creating a record of having accomplished something in the school reform arena, preferably without raising costs substantially. An equally plausible motive was that the most educationally active governors also had a sincere, if somewhat educationally naive, interest in school improvement.

In retrospect, an important outcome of the first wave of 1980s school reform was a shift in regulatory power from the federal to the state level of government. This shift did not lessen the flow of regulations that plagued school districts and local schools, as promised by conservatives. Instead, state departments of education proved to be just as able as, or more able than, federal education officials in imposing arbitrarily fixed mandates on the conduct of local schooling. From the perspective of local educational leaders, parents, and teachers, the amount of regulation to which they were subject did not diminish in the 1980s (and the 1990s) and the educationally confining aspect of the regulatory activity may well have increased. Further, although the states were granted more discretion as to how federal educational support dollars could be spent during the Reagan–Bush years, the amount of federal money made available was severely limited.[28]

Site-Based Management: A Second Wave of Reform

Dissatisfaction with the confining nature of the first wave of school reforms in the early and mid-1980s led to a second wave of school reforms later in the decade, the goal of which was to unshackle schools from stifling regulatory and top-down administrative arrangements. An important, and a representative, example of this second wave was the push for school-based or site-based management of the educational enterprise. The essence of this movement was the decentralization, or devolution, of control over local school affairs to an individual school-based team that stressed parent, teacher, and sometimes student participation in decision making. Whatever combination of these actors any particular plan empowered, site-based management focused on the individual school as the unit for achieving school improvement. Site-based management received substantial support in professional educational circles, where it was seen as a vehicle for freeing the local school from bureaucratic incursions, whether from the federal or state government, or the local district lay board or administration. The aim was to free individual schools from the confines of local, state, and federal bureaucracy and to empower those who were constituent actors in the drama of American education to participate directly in its improvement.

The ultimate success of any site-based management governance plan was tied, ironically, to the willingness of the local school principal to facilitate and to cooperate in its implementation. That is, despite its distinctly bottom-up orientation, site-based management depended on the local school administrator for its success. In another ironic aspect of site-based management, those called to participate in the day-to-day management of a school often claimed not to have time to participate in that activity. Many teachers resented time taken away from instruction and instructional planning by management planning, and many parents found that jobs and other responsibilities left them little time to be available for wide-ranging consultations on issues of school management. Thus, among teachers and parents, skepticism about site-based management plans was often equal in intensity to their questions about increased, and stifling, state mandates that had begun to control classrooms during the 1980s. These and other difficulties made site-based management a bit of a flash-in-the-pan, a policy that seemed to burn itself out within a decade of its enactment.[29]

"Systemic" School Reform in the 1990s

The reality of state school reform, as implemented in the 1990s, showed that the first wave of concerns in the 1980s about measurable school achievement and improvement had much more long-lasting influence than the site-based management movement of the last years of that decade. In truth, it should not be surprising that the most significant educational alterations of the 1990s, or any other decade for that matter, would come from the state level. In fact, as alluded to in earlier chapters, our Constitution makes education a function of the states, not of the federal government. Traditionally, any emphasis on local institutions in education has come about through the states' devolving their educational responsibilities to local school districts, a devolution that has proved to be reversible, as we shall now discuss.

In 1990, Michael Cohen, an advisor to the National Governors Association, described an educational agenda that came to be adopted in many states as the decade progressed. Cohen contended that for meaningful improvement in education to occur at the state level, there would have to be a more meaningful assumption of control over education at that level. This assumption of state control was to be achieved through a process of "restructuring." Restructuring meant that states should engage in the business of demanding educational accomplishment from local school districts and individual schools. The main vehicle to be used in making this demand, and in responding positively to it, was to set measurable educational standards, national or state, especially in academic subjects, and to enforce those standards through a system of mandatory testing of students. This aspect of restructuring clearly dovetailed with the *America 2000* program.[30]

Other aspects of school restructuring, such as devolving more authority to individual schools, lengthening the school year to allow more time for academic instruction, and focusing the curriculum on those academic subjects in which achievement was lacking, echoed both the Excellence movement and the site-based management movement of the 1980s. Relatively new initiatives included providing incentives to schools and teachers identified as high performing and disincentives to low-performing schools and the teachers in them. These incentives and disincentives were frequently termed part of a school "accountability" system that provided an attractive label for politicians to use in selling the school restructuring process to voters. Images of slothful teachers, unprepared or uninterested in their tasks, were sometimes proffered as one of the main causes of low school achievement.

A closer look at restructuring can be taken by describing the twelve-year-long school reform movement in the state of Texas. Begun in the late 1980s when Democrat Ann Richards was governor, the school reforms in that state were sparked by concern over the state's dropout rate as well as its poor performance, especially by minority students, on national tests. The reforms accompanied a major renovation of the state's system of financing schools that followed a state court ruling identifying the existing system as inequitable. Additionally, preschool and kindergarten enrollments were expanded drastically, and kindergarten programs went increasingly from half-day to full-day sessions. At the heart of the school reforms was the creation of more precise curricula and standards to measure the ability of school children to master them. These standards were institutionalized in the statewide Texas Assessment of Academic Skills (TAAS) program. By the 1990s George W. Bush had replaced Ann Richards as governor and, though he instituted many changes in state government, he continued, and even intensified, the educational reforms that had begun under Richards.

The results of these changes, at least as measured by the TAAS, proved heartening to advocates of structural reform. Between 1992 and 1996 math scores for Texas fourth- and eighth-graders increased by 14 percent, almost twice as high as gains in other states. Also, reading gains were realized, though they were not as great as those in mathematics. Additionally, the gaps between white and Latino and between white and black children closed substantially, the black–white gap, for example, being reduced from 40 percent in 1994 to 21 percent in 1998. These gains were also evident in Texas scores on the National Achievement of Educational Progress test (NAEP), where the state's children ranked second and fourth among the forty-two participating states in 1998. George W. Bush cited the Texas program and its accomplishments in the 2000 presidential campaign and, after he entered the White House, used Texas as a model for his "No Child Left Behind" federal legislation. Thus, what began as a state-level testing and accounting system became institutionalized at the federal level.[31]

Developments in the state of Georgia, another state that underwent substantial school restructuring in the 1990s, can be compared and contrasted with those in Texas. Early in the 1990s, the Democratic governor of Georgia, Zell Miller, pioneered a series of educational improvements, including substantial increases in pre-kindergarten programs and educational technology spending at all levels of education (including higher education), as well as an impressive scholarship program at state colleges for both public and private high school students who were graduated with a B average. Miller was able to support his programs with an infusion of new money by persuading voters to approve a state lottery, the proceeds from which were to go only to his educational programs. Additionally, Miller garnered the backing of the state's teachers for his program by promising to raise the state's teacher salaries to the point that they were competitive nationally. Miller made good on this promise by instituting a 6 percent raise for teachers for four consecutive years in the mid- and late 1990s.

While Miller mentioned improved test scores as an objective of his program and the state did develop a state testing system that was tied to a curriculum reform program, he did not specifically tie scores to existing school practices. That link was made by Miller's successor, Roy Barnes. A Democrat like Miller, Barnes instituted a rigorous state testing and accountability program modeled on the programs in Texas and North Carolina. However, Barnes initiated a major move away from the Miller focus of enrolling teachers on the side of state reforms when he instituted a policy of removing tenure rights for beginning teachers shortly after he took office. The state's teacher organizations, particularly its NEA affiliate, were outraged by what they considered to be a betrayal of support, and Barnes seemed to revel in the opposition, positioning himself as a politician intent on taming a group of teachers that wanted to protect its own incompetents through maintenance of teacher tenure. Barnes, in spite of teacher opposition, continued his imposition of a statewide testing and accountability program that identified schools that were failing their children and, indirectly for the moment, seemed to threaten the careers of some teachers working in those schools. Barnes justified his program by arguing that it was very much in line with what George Bush was in the process of mandating for the nation's schools.[32]

While it is too early to get a good picture of exactly how effectively the Georgia program is working, it seems likely that substantive increases in the state's own standardized test scores, and perhaps in NAEP scores, will result. Also, the hope is that minority–majority gaps in Georgia will close as much as they did in Texas. On the other hand, the anger of teachers at Barnes's highhandedness has proved to be at least moderately long-lasting. Teacher activists in other states, whether or not they enjoy collective bargaining rights, can look to Georgia as a possible harbinger of what could develop nationally if school restructuring is pursued under the spur of the "No Child Left Behind" Act. While the attack on teacher tenure may prove to be an extreme, the identification of test scores by school, by class, and by individual students threatens negative consequences such as transfers, salary reductions, or other penalties for teachers who are held accountable for the low performance of their students.

The consequences of a curriculum narrowed in the interest of elevating scores on standardized tests are yet to be calculated. While restructuring advocates have argued that teachers should be free to adjust their teaching in ways they see fit to meet the defined test standards, the current implementation of restructuring in public schools suggests that the tests could become so dominant in classrooms that teachers will be forced to redesign their entire approach to teaching in order to meet the standards, leaving room to accomplish little else. Critics who raise this issue are often dismissed as fuzzy-minded, although they are usually closer to the ranks of working teachers than are the state politicians who have pioneered restructuring and the national administration that is intent on institutionalizing it.

Other critics of restructuring, whether by state or federal mandate, have noted that it is an assault on the prerogatives of local school districts, and the schools in them, to adopt a curriculum and instructional standards that do not fit their local circumstances. In some instances, those critics have pursued a positive agenda of making public schools more responsive to the needs of parents and students through the adoption of charter schools.

Charter Schools

Charter schools constitute a reform movement that in some ways is clearly in tension with, if not in opposition to, the school restructuring movement that has pervaded state and local schooling since the 1990s. Yet reformers in both camps have been less likely to pay attention to the tensions between the two movements and more likely to concentrate on how their particular version of school reform will achieve the elusive goal of genuine educational improvement and how even the other version of school reform, though perhaps in opposition to the favored version, is preferable to business as usual in education.

There has been no national charter school initiative to parallel the charter movements in several states, or the national movement toward restructuring in the "No Child Left Behind" Act of the Bush administration. The difference between charter school legislation and the administrative arrangements to institutionalize the legislation in various states has been substantial. Thus, it is difficult to characterize the charter school movement comprehensively. The attempt here will be simply to elucidate the nature of charter schooling through a discussion of its development in several state and local contexts.

By the end of the 1990s, 37 states had passed some version of charter school legislation. Some of these provisions have been referred to as relatively strong or weak charter laws, depending on the amount of release from centralized educational authority a given law provides. Under weak charter laws, state and local school boards retain substantial control over the schools that are chartered through the chartering process itself as well as in terms of other restrictions once a charter has been granted. Under a strong charter law, a school is chartered, receives funds from the state and possibly from a local school district, and is given wide freedom to develop as an enterprise, subject to only a periodic review of the charter and, perhaps, to legal or other standards that are imposed.[33]

Bruce Fuller, one of the leading students of charter schools, sees the charter school movement as unfolding in tandem, chronologically and ideologically, with the school choice or voucher movement. Seen in this sense, the charter school movement is a radically decentralist attempt to correct the evils that have been imposed on parents and children by public schools so wrapped up in bureaucratic controls—federal regulations, state laws and mandates, and school district regulations—that they are often unable to deal effectively with the education of children in contemporary society. Fuller is careful to note that despite this relatively coherent political analysis of the charter movement, the impetus for charter schools in the several states has been wide ranging. Some proponents have supported state laws allowing for charter schools based on concern for increased student achievement. Others have pursued school innovation as a good in itself, while still others see decentralization as the only effective road to true accountability and a good way to widen student and parent choice in education. Thus, despite Fuller's characterization of charters as radically decentralist, he is also aware that many charter proponents view the movement more in terms of the results it can produce than from any principled commitment to a political process that seeks to reinfuse the democratic control of the nineteenth-century village, or district school, into twentieth-century public education.[34]

In schools with strong charter laws, state money can flow to any group that has its application for a charter approved—including parent collectives, teacher–parent cooperatives, privately financed entities, for-profit corporations formed to run charter schools, and religious groups committed to school improvement. In weak charter states, on the other hand, the application for a charter has to be approved by a local school district that has substantial organizational incentive not to fund radical departures from its educational norm. In these states, oftentimes existing public schools can petition for a charter that might free them to adopt a different scheduling pattern, curricular orientation, or other relatively minor variation from what is imposed on the schools in the district by the district board and administration.

Fuller is committed to the cause of charter schools on principle, that is, he is an advocate of highly decentralized, localized institutions that can present alternative realities to the increasingly centralized public sphere of twenty-first-century America. Even so, he understands that charter schools will live or die on their ability to produce enhanced educational achievement for the poor and minority populations that are not being empowered under conventional educational arrangements. The political challenge facing charter schools is that in their commitment to radical decentralization, they cannot allow middle-class students and parents to use a charter to escape from the equity and empowerment commitments that its democratic advocates seek to guarantee.

While the jury is still out on the accomplishments of charter schools, particularly in terms of their ability to raise student achievement, the evidence that is beginning to come in is not such that charter advocates can take heart. For example, an extensive study of charter schools by the American Federation of Teachers, which, along with the NEA, envisioned charter schools as a possible way to unleash the power of teachers to change education, has found these schools to have been largely unsuccessful in raising student achievement scores over those of comparable students in regular public schools.[35] One problem is that in many states, achievement data are not reported for charter school students and such data are not required for renewal of charters. Additionally, the report notes that "In the 2000–2001 school year in Texas . . . approximately 40 percent of charter schools were on the state's low-performing list compared to about 2 percent of other public schools." Similar results were found in California and Massachusetts.[36] Moreover, charter schools have not excelled in meeting state fiscal accountability requirements relevant to their operations, have hired less experienced teachers and paid them less than regular public schools, and have proved to be no more innovative pedagogically than regular public schools.

More important, especially for the democratic advocates of charters, the performance of poorer students in charter schools has not eclipsed that of their peers in regular public schools. Additionally, the report notes that "It appears that charter schools, for the most part, isolate students by race and ethnicity, and enroll fewer students classified as English language learners and special needs than the comparable local school districts."[37] Of course, committed charter school advocates have condemned the report as the product of an organization that is implacably against genuine educational reforms like charter schools and have pointed to other studies that show that charter schools do indeed increase the achievement of their students. However, another study from the state of North Carolina, where significant numbers of charter schools exist, has raised the same concerns as those found in the AFT study.[38] While those whose primary commitment is to parental choice in education may ignore evidence that calls charter schools into question and proceed to support charters strictly on ideological grounds, many Americans are likely to agree with the AFT's skepticism about charter schools if they are found not to fulfill the major educational goals that sparked their establishment.

Other Educational Reforms

The word "reform," like "crisis," has been sorely overused in the last several decades of discussion of American education. A perusal of the titles of the various sections of this chapter should give the reader one piece of evidence of such overuse. We seem to have come to the point that anyone who advocates any change can get at least a positive initial hearing by calling the proposal a "reform." This begs the question of just exactly what is being called for by any particular proposal and what the outcome signifies in terms of educational accomplishment. We turn in this section to a discussion of two "reforms" that deserve the title of reform, if that concept bears any connotation of school improvement and, particularly, school improvement for those who have been deprived of effective education in the United States. After those two movements have been discussed, we return to a more generic educational reform, one that involves the training of America's teachers.

Fiscal Equalization Reforms

Although federal and state reform efforts of the 1980s generally represented a retreat from the equality movement of the 1960s and 1970s, in at least one area, events of the 1980s built on earlier precedents. In the school finance arena, efforts to close the enormous funding gap between rich and poor districts dated back to the late 1960s and 1970s. At issue was the fact that some students attended school in districts where property values were too low to generate adequate school funds, while in other districts, with high property values, students benefited from affluent school budgets. As might be expected, the better-funded districts usually enjoyed higher academic achievement.

The earliest efforts to pursue equity in school finance date to the 1960s in states such as Illinois and Virginia.[39] Although those efforts proved unsuccessful, a lawsuit filed in the early 1970s in the state of California (*Serrano v. Priest*) had a different outcome. In that case, tried in a state rather than a federal court, the plaintiff, who was from a property-poor district, argued that children in that district were denied their right to equal protection under the law as specified in both the state and federal constitutions. In this case the court ruled that the quality of a child's education must be based on the wealth of the state rather than that of the particular school district in which the child lives.[40]

The ruling in *Serrano* was seen initially as a precedent that would be applicable in many, if not all, states, but a clear limitation was soon placed on the *Serrano* ruling. In 1973, the U.S. Supreme Court ruled in the *San Antonio Independent School District v. Rodriguez* case that inequities between school districts in Texas did not violate federal constitutional provisions. This ruling meant that any future battles on behalf of children in poorer school districts would have to be fought in state courts using the particular educational provisions set forth in each state constitution.[41]

Despite the *Rodriguez* ruling, by 1992 plaintiffs had filed school financial equity suits in more than thirty states. Depending on the wording in a state's constitution and on the state court's willingness to interpret that wording, the outcomes of those suits have varied. More often than not, a system of finance in which poorer districts suffer in relation to their wealthier counterparts has been allowed to continue. The rationale for these findings has often been that, while disparities in funding exist, no child was denied a minimum level of funding and, concomitantly, a minimum standard of schooling.

Rulings in other states, however, have been in favor of the plaintiffs. These rulings have substantially altered state school finance formulas to rectify the most grievous imbalances in district funding. Even in states such as Georgia, where the state Supreme Court ruled against plaintiffs in a school equalization suit in 1981, the court acknowledged the legitimacy of the plaintiffs' complaint but looked to the legislature to redress the inequities. In 1985, the legislature and the governor answered the court by passing a school reform law that included a substantial movement toward equalization of expenditures across school districts.[42]

Some rulings in school equalization suits have moved far beyond the area of school finance in an effort to ensure educational equity. In West Virginia, Kentucky, and a few other states, the courts chose to rule broadly on inequity issues, and major reform efforts resulted. In West Virginia, for example, a trial court insisted that equitable proposals for staffing, school facilities, and curricula be developed. The resulting standards in all these areas were to be applied to all school districts. The reason for this decision and others like it, of course, was that a quality education involves much more than the amount of funding received by a school.[43]

It would be difficult to argue, however, that these funding reform suits set the tone for educational policy in the 1980s and 1990s. Most equalization efforts, when they have occurred at all, have narrowly addressed funding and stayed away from other aspects of educational policy and practice. Further, state legislatures in states such as Ohio have largely ignored state court directives to make school funding more equitable.

Many leading state equity suits to date have involved cases in which the tax base of rural districts was compared to that of suburban districts. These cases have largely ignored inequalities found in large city school systems. Here, equity suits have accomplished little. In New York, for example, the contention that city school systems are overburdened financially because of higher service costs than in suburban or rural districts, and are therefore entitled to financial relief from the state, was denied by the state Supreme Court.[44] This reluctance to address the special needs of poor urban students indicates that the United States is a long way from addressing some of the most persistent and troubling aspects of educational inequity of the late twentieth century.

The problems of urban schools, many of which stem from the funding problems faced by those school districts, have been highlighted most recently in *Savage Inequalities*, a book by Jonathan Kozol.[45] In this provocatively titled volume, Kozol chillingly depicted the many educational deprivations that affect the largely poor and minority student populations in the nation's largest cities.

However, Kozol did not refer to the issue of "overburden," a term that points to the high cost of educating the urban poor, as brought up in the New York

State school equity case. If he had, he would have been better able to answer those who point out that in some large cities, such as Atlanta, Georgia, the per-pupil expenditure substantially exceeds the state average, without yielding any corresponding increase in achievement.

Although the pursuit of funding equity became a permanent part of the educational scene in the 1980s, it failed to alter the educational debate over the adequacy of the nation's classrooms. That debate continues to be influenced by a federal government in no mood to spend money on public schools, by state governments that demand measurable, short-term improvement for every dollar spent, and by intellectuals and educators who see issues of standards and excellence as more important than issues of equality or equity. Whatever the federal or state influences on reform, however, substantially meaningful changes, if they are to be realized at all, are likely to happen at the individual school level.

School-Level Reforms

In contrast to federal accountability standards as well as to state mandates for systemic school reform that sometimes place actual restraints on the ability of teachers to react to the particular needs and interests of their students, there are still some cases in which pedagogical innovations that connect with student interests have occurred. Much of this innovation takes its inspiration from the ideas of John Dewey and his progressive disciples whose work has been considered in earlier chapters of this book. These cases of innovation, many of which occur in small private schools but others of which happen in public schools, are notable for their rarity, as well as for their success. Most of these innovations have taken place in smaller schools or schools within schools, a way to import the benefits of small size into large school settings.

One significant and fairly wide-ranging example of this kind of work is provided by Theodore Sizer. Founder of the Coalition of Essential Schools, a group of over 1,000 individual schools in 38 states, Sizer is a former education professor and dean of the Harvard Graduate School of Education, as well as a former school administrator. His prescriptions for members of the coalition are minimal, consisting mainly of a genuine commitment to serious innovation in the conduct of schooling. He has fleshed out his ideas in a series of books on American education, all of which feature a fictional high school English teacher named Horace Smith. In the second of these three works, *Horace's School*, Sizer indicates what he considers to be exemplary educational reform for the American high school. He subdivides a large high school into several self-contained units called "houses," and makes each teacher responsible for no more than eighty students, a welcome reduction from the loads of well over a hundred students that face many high school teachers today. The teachers work together in multidisciplinary faculty teams that plan and conduct the work of the school. All teachers are responsible for the core skills of oral and written expression, inquiry, and study techniques. Additionally, the teachers in the school have reached a consensus on what high school graduates should be able to do and have come up with serious assessments, such as designated student exhibitions, to use in measuring that ability. For Sizer, individual school autonomy and teacher autonomy in individual schools are the keys to meaningful school reform.[46]

Central Park East

A notable elementary school that has transformed itself in the last several years is Central Park East, a New York City public elementary school that was led in the process of change by an especially dynamic and knowledgeable principal, Deborah Meier. Central Park East was founded in 1974 on the premise that poor minority students in New York City could benefit from the same approach to education that has proved successful for affluent students in prestigious private schools. A major assumption of the educational program at Central Park East is that the schooling that students receive there should begin with things that are of interest to students. This approach is a far cry from the back-to-basics, standardized test-oriented, accountability-laden programs that became more and more prevalent in public education in the years since publication of *A Nation at Risk*.

Stunningly, at least to many, the basically child-centered approach to education undertaken at Central Park East yielded a level of measured educational achievement by students far above what was expected of them. For example, among students whom the researchers were able to reach, 94 percent of the graduates of the school in the first ten years of its existence had graduated from high school or had received a high school equivalency credential. This percentage compared favorably with almost any New York City elementary school and far outstripped that of other schools in neighborhoods with demographic characteristics similar to those of Central Park East. Just as important, Central Park East was a community school in which the parents of the students, the teachers, and the students themselves all cooperated in accomplishing academic, social, and political achievements. The school was a vehicle for personal and social growth, for community regeneration, and for neighborhood political involvement, thereby serving as a poignant example of the success of progressive education and of social and political reform that accompanied that regeneration.[47]

Central Park East principal Deborah Meier was the spearhead in the development of the school, yet she worked hard to empower parents, students, and teachers to participate in the joint effort to fulfill the goals they set for themselves. Meier, a democratic socialist as well as a progressive educator, has sought to emulate the successes of Central Park East in other cities, most recently in Boston, without seeking to impose the Central Park East model on other school communities. Rather, for Meier, the road to success is different in each school and it must be found jointly by all those involved in the individual school before it can be followed. As Meier has noted, "strong and idiosyncratic public schools, each different from the others, could offer to all young people what Central Park East offered [its] youngsters."[48]

For Meier, the contemporary educational crisis is not one of low achievement or a lack of standards, but rather a situation in which the idea of democratic schools has become lost. Indications of this loss are the incredibly low voter turnout in American elections, the clumsiness of schools that have become too large and too distant from their communities, and the alienation of parents and students from these schools.[49] Only through individual school reform, such as that at Central Park East, can democracy reassert its claim on public schools and, in turn, on the communities in which those schools exist; only thus can we combat the stultifying standardization that has resulted as politicians have forced schools to march to the drum of standardized tests and accountability.

Teacher Education Reforms

The pages of *A Nation at Risk* contained more than just complaints about student achievement in American elementary and secondary schools. The report was anything but complementary about the content of American teacher training programs, and it intensified anew a criticism of the education of American teachers that had been ongoing at least since the 1950s and 1960s. Specifically, the authors of *A Nation at Risk* argued that the "teacher-preparation curriculum is weighted heavily with courses in 'educational methods' at the expense of courses in subjects to be taught."[50] This line of criticism echoed the complaints of Arthur Bestor, Mortimer Smith, Admiral Hyman Rickover, and others who railed against the education of the nation's teachers in the 1950s and 1960s.[51] While those critics managed to provoke modest changes in some education programs and certification requirements during the Cold War era, politicians and the educational establishment appear to have been much more responsive to the more recent challenges to the teacher education status quo following upon the heels of *A Nation at Risk*.

Alternative Teacher Preparation Programs

In recent years, alternative teacher preparation programs have increased their presence significantly on American college and university campuses. On the one hand, the location of these programs in higher education institutions at the master's, or graduate, level indicates that something serious is afoot. On the other hand, the incessant drumbeat of criticism of existing undergraduate, and graduate, teacher education programs indicates that there is more to the alternative teacher preparation agenda than improvement of those graduates who are placed in positions in the nation's schools.

Before we try to assess the alternative programs, however, some description of their origins and their content is in order. It is somewhat difficult to characterize something as wide-ranging as the movement for alternative teacher preparation in American higher education, since each state may have a different wrinkle, or set of wrinkles, in its alternative programs and each institution that implements an alternative program may be able to adjust, either minimally or perhaps substantially, program requirements mandated by its state. Nevertheless, most of the newer alternative teacher training and certification programs involve preparation leading to a master's degree and tend to minimize professional education course requirements while increasing the amount of preparation in subject matter. Some new or alternative programs require a fifth year of study in programs leading to the attainment of B.A. and M.Ed. degrees simultaneously. Others add on a year or more of training beyond the baccalaureate and award Master of Arts in Teaching (MAT) or Master of Teaching (MT) degrees to graduates of these extended programs. Still others, however, provide quicker alternative routes into teaching for those who have bachelor's degrees in other fields than professional education. Many of the more streamlined routes to certification were developed to help relieve the shortage of qualified teachers in subject areas such as mathematics and the natural sciences. These alternative programs enable graduates with degrees in science, mathematics, or related fields such as engineering to engage in short-term studies in education and pedagogically related fields, along with intense internship programs under the guidance of "master" teachers and close supervision from university academic and pedagogy specialists.[52]

At their best, these "fast-track" programs do provide ways to attract and place people with appropriate subject matter backgrounds into teaching careers more quickly. Subject matter competence is an especially important factor in high school teaching, where disciplinary mastery is an obvious requisite. However, efforts to apply fast-track alternative routes to elementary and special education preparation programs are extremely problematic. Teachers who lack a solid understanding of child development and essential teaching skills may be able to "fill the spot," but they are likely to be poorly equipped to motivate students and to direct their learning in ways that will lead to successful student academic and emotional growth. Movements in certain states—such as Texas, which limits the number of education courses in *any* teacher preparation program, and New Jersey, where an alternatively trained teacher can bypass even the requirements of the alternative programs if he or she has a bachelor's degree in a field and is needed in a classroom—indicate that some alternative programs exist as much to bypass traditional routes into classrooms and to provide bodies for classrooms, whatever the qualifications of those bodies, as they do to provide competent professionals who can function effectively in classrooms. Reports that the mentoring and supervision of some teachers-in-training in alternative programs are nearly non-existent or lacking in intensity compared to what was deemed adequate by program developers are a further indication that not all is what it purports to be in the arena of alternative teacher preparation.[53]

Holmes Group Teacher Preparation

A movement that was sparked initially by departments and schools of education at the nation's largest research universities to move teacher preparation
almost exclusively to the master's level provided another model in the alternative teacher preparation movement. The argument of the institutions in the
Holmes Group was that professional teacher preparation was too important
and too advanced to be conducted at the undergraduate level, and instead
should take place at the post-Baccalaureate level, as do most other professional
preparation programs. Opposition to the Holmes approach came from research
universities skeptical about the rationale behind the program; from other
large public institutions concerned about losing the massive enrollments in
undergraduate teacher education programs; and from smaller undergraduate
institutions, private and public, that did not wish to go out of the business of
teacher training. This opposition worked against widespread adoption of
the Holmes agenda of elevating initial teacher preparation to an essentially
post-Baccalaureate activity.

The Holmes Group thus was unsuccessful in getting research universities to
buy in completely to the idea of graduate preparation and it eventually
developed into a larger group of research and non-research universities with a
related but substantially different agenda from that initially proposed. In its
second iteration, Holmes institutions placed heavy stress upon university–
school cooperation through devices such as professional development schools
as sites for much of teacher preparation and development activity. The Holmes
Group, now larger and more loosely characterized as a consortium, thereby
reoriented its agenda and, like many of the alternative programs, emphasized
internship experiences as the key element in the reform of teacher education
programs.[54]

NCATE and National Teacher Certification

Whatever approaches to teacher education are considered or adopted on the
campuses of colleges and universities, these institutions, particularly if they are
public institutions, are subject to the influence, if not the overt control, of governmental bodies as well as of the "voluntary" accrediting agencies to which
individual institutions belong. Every state has a licensing or accrediting agency
that approves the teacher education programs of institutions, public and private, in the state. These arrangements vary from state to state in their level of
specificity and usually reflect rather long-standing relationships between the
state accrediting agency and colleges and universities. Two relatively recent
movements, voluntary accreditation by a national accreditation agency and
national teacher certification through a body supported by the national government and other national forces, deserve our attention in that they bring a
relatively new sphere of influence into play.

The National Council for the Accreditation of Teacher Education (NCATE) has been in the business of accrediting teacher education programs for a number of years. With the recent push for accountability and standards in education, however, NCATE has managed to raise its profile as an accrediting agency and to make major changes in its accreditation standards. Rather than concentrate on inputs such as faculty quality, library holdings, and the abilities and academic records of teacher education students, NCATE is moving now to a more output-oriented model of accreditation in which it requires teacher education programs to show that their graduates know what to teach in classrooms and that they are capable of teaching that content. NCATE has aligned its standards with various subject matter standards being developed by disciplinary associations and has worked to bring standardized testing of teacher education students into line with those standards. While NCATE accredits less than a majority of teacher education programs, it has parlayed its new, output-oriented approach so as to become a major force in the teacher education world. Whether this approach will better serve the needs of teacher education students or of students in the public schools is debatable, but NCATE has proved itself to be politically astute in its responsiveness to the standardization and accountability movements that have characterized public education since the 1980s.

NBPTS and Standardization

Another movement toward a standardization of teaching and teacher education is the development of the National Board for Professional Teaching Standards (NBPTS). This organization, begun under the presidency of the first George Bush, has used foundation funding and the push for standardization from the White House in the last decade to position itself as a leader in the improvement of school teaching. Sidestepping the ambiguity of being an agency that has developed "voluntary" national standards for teachers, NBPTS has used the anxiety of states over the condition of their schools and the qualification of their teachers to develop an elaborate program of national certification of teachers. The process is lengthy and time consuming, featuring the development of teaching portfolios as well as other indications of superior work on the part of the teachers who choose to become candidates for national certification. Incentives for national certification vary from state to state, but they often involve salary supplements or other increases as well as supervisory roles for those teachers who become nationally certified. Both major national teacher unions became involved in the national certification movement. The AFT moved earlier and more forcefully in this direction than did the NEA, but both organizations see national certification as a way to enhance the remuneration of their members as well as to improve the teaching profession.

These national involvements in teacher education and certification have intensified the standardization of American public education that has taken place in the years since *A Nation at Risk*. Whether or not they have led to real improvement in the conduct of public education, improvement that is having a meaningful impact on the intellectual, social, and personal lives of the young people in those schools, is a question yet to be answered. Indeed, given the nature of social pathologies that plague our society and our children, the challenges that teachers face sometimes seem all but overwhelming. It is to a closer examination of some of the pressing realities that bear on our schools and our society that we now turn.

Educational Realities in Schools

There are a number of problem areas in contemporary education that may be little altered by reform plans such as those discussed above. The following discussion of some of the most pressing of these problems begins with one area that was mentioned in the *America 2000* pamphlet.

Drugs and Violence in Schools

There seems little doubt about the reality of violence in some of America's schools, although there is great disagreement about the extent of the problem. A goal of "safe, drug-free schools," however, as stated in the *America 2000* program,[55] recognized the problem but did little to resolve it meaningfully. Linking violence to drugs certainly identified one aspect of a serious problem that is thwarting the best attempts of America's teachers to instruct the youth of our nation. However, no proposal has yet been articulated to show how drugs or weapons can be kept out of the hands of children—and thus out of our schools.

In fact, schools are but one of the social settings within which drugs have sparked a crisis. This illustrates an important point: Pervasive social problems such as drugs and violence are not solely or even preponderantly a school problem. To look to the schools for a solution to the drug problem, therefore, is to try to solve a problem within a setting that is only tangentially related to its source or sources. This, of course, is naive educational and social policy.

Poverty

Student poverty, particularly within the nation's large cities, is another profound social problem that many have expected the schools to solve. Of course, no one has asked the schools to abolish poverty directly or alone, but schools have been asked to educate the children of the poor so that they can escape poverty. Once again, the schools have been compelled to address a multifaceted problem. Historically, the link between education and socioeconomic mobility has been indirect at best. There is little doubt that a relationship exists between economic success and educational success, but as in the riddle of the chicken and the egg, it is hard to know which is the cause of the other. To some researchers, it appears that the causal element in that relationship has been the economic variable, not education.[56] Furthermore, the economic trends in the early twenty-first century indicate that the problem is getting worse, not better. As the ranks of the poor grew substantially in the 1980s and 1990s, the economic gap between the rich and the poor also increased. This is a problem that stems from changes in our economy rather than from deficiencies in our educational system.[57]

There is little doubt that in myriad ways poverty makes education more difficult. Poor nutrition, atypical learning styles, and lack of a literate home environment are some of the many conditions that impede poor children's school performance. Yet schools and teachers are expected to attend to these realities without the benefit of a proven method of intervention. Some programs, such as Head Start, have shown consistent progress, but their lessons are too often ignored because of their cost and because of antitax, antigovernment interference sentiments. In spite of their substantial operating costs, preschool programs for poor, at-risk children appear to be a necessary—but hardly sufficient—ingredient in any serious effort to help these children negotiate the school system successfully.

Another reality facing schools that have large numbers of poor children is poor school attendance. This is often related to families' moving frequently from one housing situation to another and, thus, from one school to another. The children of migrant farmers are especially at risk in this regard, but the children of many urban dwellers are likewise subject to frequent moves—and even homelessness. It is clearly unrealistic to expect the schools to provide effective teaching for children who, by virtue of their changing residences and social conditions, are intermittent consumers of whatever education is offered.

Desegregation

The failure of school desegregation to fulfill the expectations of educational improvement and social harmony promised in the *Brown* decision constituted one of the great missed opportunities of the second half of the twentieth century. In a sense, this failure can once again be attributed to inflated expectations, that is, asking the schools to solve a racial problem that permeates the entire society. Nevertheless, enough experience with school desegregation has been gained to analyze the phenomenon in some detail.

The obstinacy of white opposition to school desegregation must be counted as a primary cause of its failure. As Jennifer Hochschild, Gary Orfield, and others have argued, desegregation has failed because, in a very real sense, it has not been tried.[58] White resistance—particularly in the subtle form practiced by wealthy whites who move to suburban communities or who pay for private schooling for their children—has been a constant and chronic obstacle to desegregation. In reality, the burden of busing and of other policies to implement desegregation has been borne most heavily by black children who have been involved in one-way busing schemes. Within the white population, it was the working-class whites who, left with blacks and other minorities in the nation's cities, were expected to desegregate the increasingly black schools.

It would be unfair, however, to say that desegregation has failed completely in every setting. In many southern school districts, usually in small- or medium-sized cities or in rural areas, desegregation has been relatively successful. The ingredients for success seemed to be first, a commitment to the process on the part of school and community leaders and second, a reasonable and steady ratio of black to white students in all the schools involved. Of course, even in the midst of these success stories, troubling phenomena such as resegregation within a desegregated school caused by tracking and other forms of curricular differentiation continue to occur.

In the large southern cities, such as New Orleans, Birmingham, and Atlanta, however, one finds a situation much like that in northern cities—wrenching urban poverty gripping a largely minority population concentrated overwhelmingly in the city schools. It is difficult to see how urban desegregation can be accomplished without combining the urban and suburban districts for attendance purposes. The Supreme Court, however, dominated by a "strict constructionist" ideology that dates back to the 1970s, has made clear in its decisions that combining districts across independent government lines is out of the question.[59]

The present trend in desegregation is toward "magnet" or theme schools that will entice rather than coerce students to attend. The lack of substantial studies of magnet schools, along with the historically fleeting tastes of the American public, warn that this solution to desegregation may, at best, be illusory, at least in terms of any large-scale movement. In truth, the failure of school desegregation remains a symptom of the larger failure of American society to deal fairly with its racial and ethnic minorities and the social divide that has resulted. As long as racism remains a pervasive social problem, it is not likely to be eradicated in the schools. At best, we might hope that effective schooling can gradually move the rising generation to greater levels of acceptance, mutual understanding, and a commitment to social justice.

Multiculturalism

The difficulties faced by schools in dealing with their African American students—and the problems these students and families have had with the schools, especially in the context of desegregation—have been repeated down through the years as language minority and "new immigrant" youngsters have entered American classrooms. Toward the closing decades of the twentieth century a movement to pursue "multicultural education" emerged as a solution to these problems. Multiculturalism means making a commitment to respect and teach about the many cultural backgrounds that children bring into the schools. It builds on predecessor movements such as making February "Black History Month" in school. A multicultural approach to black history brings the perspectives of African American culture into continuous contact with the school curriculum, rather than concentrating those perspectives in a one-month period. Programs such as the Portland, Oregon, "Baseline

Essays" offer materials for infusing African American traditions into all school subjects.[60]

Of course, a true multicultural approach to schooling and curriculum involves more than an African American perspective. Other minority groups, such as Asian Americans, Hispanic Americans, and Native Americans, seek their proper place in the social and cultural life of the school. A comprehensive multicultural approach also would include the perspectives of the disabled, of women, and of gay and bisexual people.

Multiculturalism has captured the attention of a vocal group of American scholars concentrated in the fields of educational studies, the social sciences, and the humanities. In terms of a prescription for the school curriculum, however, multiculturalism may turn out to be a better idea in theory than it has been in practice. The constituency for multiculturalism is clearly larger in colleges and universities than it is in the schools and other parts of American society. Thus, educators and intellectuals who seek to introduce one or another aspect of multiculturalism into the schools often find a school system or a larger community that is uncomprehending of the problem or indifferent to the proposed solution.

Furthermore, it cannot be said that multiculturalism has completely captured the nation's colleges and universities. Some scholars have raised serious questions about the tendency of multiculturalism to fracture and fragment a diverse American society that, in their view, is in need of unifying experiences, particularly in its classrooms.[61] Whatever the outcome of the current educational controversy over multiculturalism, a related issue is the actual success or failure of various minority groups, especially the newest immigrant groups making their presence felt in schools across the country toward the end of the twentieth century.

Immigrants and School Success

One way of looking at the recent immigrant–school encounter is to compare it with the similar encounter that occurred in the late nineteenth and early twentieth centuries. Some students of that era point to the relatively rapid assimilation of many immigrants by schools whose curricula were intended to induct students into mainstream culture as a model experience for the current groups to emulate. This assimilation, however, was neither completely painless nor evenly and eagerly embraced by all groups. Children were often put at odds with their parents and other members of the immigrant community who had less access to mainstream culture. Some schools ignored the language spoken by the immigrant children and their parents, preferring instead to immerse them in the English language that was spoken in mainstream culture.

As noted in Chapter 7, the school experience of late-nineteenth-century immigrants was far more complex than modern-day assimilationists like to admit. For example, the schools in the earlier period, like those of today, were not devoid of attempts to honor immigrant cultural experiences. The existence

Figure 12.4 "After smoking awareness . . ."

Credit: Reprinted with the permission of Paul Nowak.

of German language instruction in the rural Midwest and in urban communities such as St. Louis and Milwaukee, where sizable German-speaking communities had political muscle, calls into question the notion that immigrants of that era had no say in school affairs. Furthermore, many urban public schools had faculty and administrators who were either of the same background as their immigrant students or empathetic with the situations of both students and parents. In addition, many European immigrants sent their children to Catholic parochial schools in parishes with a dominant ethnic population that was represented in the teaching staff as well as in the parish community.

On balance, however, it seems clear that the public schools of the late nineteenth century were not uniformly successful in assimilating immigrant children. Historically, the educational success or failure of immigrant groups is best understood by considering the cultural characteristics and economic conditions that made different groups more or less receptive to the culture of the school and the larger society.

Several interesting studies of recent encounters between minority and immigrant groups and the public schools shed light on this complex issue.[62] Before considering those studies, however, several cautions need to be stated. First, it must be remembered that group studies cannot explain what happens to any particular individual within a group. Second, as already mentioned, the encounter between group and school is incredibly complex. It can vary from individual to individual within a group, from school to school, and from one city or state to another. Third, the immigrant–school encounter involves analyzing and matching both the culture of the group and the equally complex culture of the school. Finally, much of the understanding of any immigrant group's encounter with the school depends on factors outside the group's culture, particularly socioeconomic factors.

Neither cultural nor socioeconomic factors alone can be used to explain the "success" or "failure" of certain groups to assimilate in school and society. For example, certain Asian immigrant groups have done well in American schools, whatever their economic background. This success is clearly related to cultural factors in the students' backgrounds, although not necessarily to their willingness or desire to assimilate. Rather, successful Asian immigrant groups have cultures that value success in school without denigrating their own cultural backgrounds. In a sense, these groups seek to enter the mainstream on their own terms, not on the more assimilationist terms that the larger culture might prescribe. Their success and its sources are strikingly similar to those of certain Jewish children of prior generations. This success has caused Asians to be labeled by some assimilationists as "model minorities."

While the "model minority" appellation might apply in general to Asian Americans, the recent experience of Chinese immigrants in public schools seems to parallel more that of other recent immigrant groups from the Caribbean, Mexico, and Central America than that of previous Asian immigrants.[63] The Chinese immigrant experience in schools, like that of other immigrant groups, is dependent on factors such as the makeup of the schools in which the children are enrolled and the level of services provided in those schools, as well as on cultural and socioeconomic conditions in the neighborhoods where they live.

John Ogbu has offered still another interesting—and controversial—explanation of variations in the acculturation process among ethnic and cultural groups such as African Americans, Native Americans, and Mexican Americans. Ogbu argued that there is a great difference between the school experience of what he refers to as voluntary and involuntary minorities. Voluntary minorities are made up of immigrant groups who have come to this country willingly, much like the immigrants at the turn of the nineteenth century. These groups see the obstacles put in their way by the schools and the larger society as things to be overcome on the way to economic and social advancement. Conversely, involuntary groups such as African Americans, Native Americans, and many Mexican Americans were born into subordinate positions in this country and do not have a sense of positive expectation. They often exhibit oppositional traits conditioned over time by their unsuccessful encounters with majority institutions, including the schools. Unlike immigrants who see cultural differences as barriers to be overcome, involuntary minorities see cultural differences as markers of identity to be maintained.[64]

Ogbu's theory is controversial and not fully sustained by research on the topic. What it does provide, however, is one plausible explanation for the obvious difference in school success between African Americans and other involuntary minorities on the one hand and other "new immigrant" minority groups on the other hand.

Educational practices that follow from Ogbu's theory are not fully developed. His work does seem to support strongly the cultural reinforcement sought by advocates of Afrocentric curricula and pedagogy. However, a clear definition of relevant curriculum and pedagogy has not yet emerged. Furthermore, it has not yet been demonstrated convincingly that Afrocentric education is the answer. In fact, stating that one or another approach is "the answer" for the education of African Americans, Native Americans, Mexican Americans, or any other cultural group seems beyond the reach of educational research as it now is constituted. What does seem clear is that African American and other minority students need teachers and schools that regard them as genuinely educable pupils and that are willing to reach out to their families and communities for assistance in their education.

That political agendas sometimes trump what many educators might consider to be "best practice" when it comes to the education of minorities was conveyed dramatically in California in 1997 when the state's voters passed Proposition 227, the law that dismantled the existing bilingual programs in the state. Proposition 227 mandated that bilingual education should be replaced by English immersion programs for immigrant children. The law stipulated that immigrant students be "immersed" in English for one year prior to being placed in regular classes in which English is the language of instruction. While there is no solid research basis for this decision, and in fact there is evidence to suggest that students who speak a language other than English should be taught to master reading in that language before being taught to read in English, California voters voiced their concerns about illegal aliens and a growing Spanish-speaking population with a "reform" that was clearly more political than educational in intent.[65]

Conclusion

The dominance of political over educational concerns has been a relatively constant feature of most of the educational reform initiatives since 1980. While this is not a new phenomenon in American educational history, the political has seemed to take on an increasingly dominant role in contemporary educational policy discourse and decision making, with educational professionals proving largely inept at providing a counter-discourse that centers on teaching, learning, and meaningful social experiences in real, individual schools. The accountability and standards movements are prime examples of the trend, presenting a situation in which education is represented by test scores and other numbers that are interpreted like the scores of athletic events by the press and the public. State rankings, school system rankings, individual school rankings, and individual child scores are all bandied about, too often with little or no qualification or clarification, as the indicators of educational success or failure.

Like accountability and standards, some other educational reform initiatives of the recent two decades often have been characterized by a narrow single-mindedness of purpose. Whether reformers are conservative Christians, adamant secularists, free marketers advocating school choice, advocates of ethnic solidarity, or proponents of multicultural curricula, they have often exhibited an ideological certainty and singleness of purpose that have made compromise seem anathema. Too infrequently have leaders of these and other groups seen merit in a moderate or compromise solution achieved in a school setting where they might have to give a little in order to achieve a portion of their particular reform agenda.

If this type of advocacy becomes more prevalent in educational affairs, the prospect of a strong public school system in anything like its present form will be substantially diminished. For better or worse, as we have seen often in this book, the American public school system was built on compromise. At its strongest, the public school was forged by coalitions of individuals and groups who worked in farm communities, villages, towns, and large cities to hammer out the differences that separated them as adults in order to provide better opportunities and a more decent and just society for their children. The baser dimensions of this process of compromise came into play when power relations and insensitivity gave advantage to some at the expense of others and placed the school in roles that were in fundamental contradiction to its nobler ideals. Yet today, we have seen a situation in which the ideological purists of free enterprise have seen fit to question the very idea of public education, or at least to redefine it in ways that seem to distance it from its historical antecedents.

The complex history of the public schools described in earlier chapters shows that, from their inception, they have served a multiplicity of purposes and agendas. The most crucial issue facing public schools in the new millennium is whether the current system can—or even should—survive the pressures of disintegration that have come to the fore in recent years.

In our own discussions, we, the authors, find ourselves somewhat divided—but far from settled on this issue. From one perspective it seems imperative that the public school, if it is to survive, must find a way to continue to be responsive to multiple groups. It must continue to be an institution of compromise, one in which both the principle of serving the public at large and the principle of serving the particular needs of individuals and groups are respected.

From another perspective, however, it can be argued that continued compromise may in fact result in the final undermining of sound public education. The energy and allegiances that motivated nineteenth- and early-twentieth-century coalitions of reformers to build the public school system of the United States seems to be dissipating as schools collapse under the weight of state and federal mandates that represent an ever-expanding agenda of social obligations that the schools seem ill equipped to handle. Uncomfortable though the notion is, it almost seems as if the system must be destroyed in order for it to be saved—that is, it seems that the very idea of public education needs to be reconsidered and redefined.

As we have seen, almost from the very beginning there has been the nagging question of how common the common school could—or should—be. This question remains unanswered. The task of the American public, and especially of the parents, teachers, and school administrators who are most intimately and directly involved with the welfare and happiness of our children, is to frame an answer that will best serve all children as they make their way into adulthood and the demands of the twenty-first century.

Further Reading

Bloom, Allan. *The Closing of the American Mind.* New York: Simon and Schuster, 1987. A scathing indictment of contemporary intellectuals and the banality of their activities in pursuit of liberal goals and cultural permissiveness.

Chubb, Jon E., and Terry Moe. *Politics, Markets, and America's Schools.* Washington, D.C.: Brookings Institution, 1990. A powerful critique of the inappropriate but unavoidable politicization of local school boards and an argument for school choice as the solution for the problem.

Cuban, Larry. *Oversold and Underused: Computers in the Classroom.* Cambridge, MA: Harvard University Press, 2001. A study that highlights the failure of computers to deliver on their promise to revolutionize the American schoolroom, and puts that failure into the historical context of the overselling of technology.

Fuller, Bruce, ed. *Inside Charter Schools: The Paradox of Radical Decentralization.* Cambridge, MA: Harvard University Press, 2000. An anthology of accounts of charter schools in different settings, and a persistent advocacy of this reform.

Hacsi, Timothy A. *Children as Pawns: The Politics of Educational Reform.* Cambridge, MA: Harvard University Press, 2002. A thoughtful analysis of recent educational reforms, which points out that the education of children is a minor priority in most of these efforts.

Kozol, Jonathan. *Savage Inequalities.* New York: Crown Publishing, 1991. A compelling survey of the barren landscape of urban schools in the United States, which makes the case for fiscal equity as a necessary beginning in the reform process.

McGuinn, Patrick J. *No Child Left Behind and the Transformation of Federal Education Policy, 1965–2005.* Lawrence, KS: University Press of Kansas, 2006. McGuinn asserts there have been "two revolutions" in educational politics over the past 40 years: the Republican embrace of a federal role in educational policy and the acceptance by Democrats of national testing and accountability measures.

Phillips, Kevin. *American Theocracy: The Peril and Politics of Radical Religion, Oil, and Borrowed Money in the 21st Century.* New York: Viking, 2006. A penetrating political analysis of the impact of American greed, growing religious fervor and commitment to faith over reason, and increasing government debt on the declining future of American society.

Ravitch, Diane. *Left Back: A Century of Failed School Reforms.* New York: Simon and Schuster, 2000. A history of progressive education that sees the movement as intellectually bankrupt and directly responsible for the intellectual deficiencies of contemporary schools.

Sizer, Theodore. *Horace's Compromise.* Boston: Houghton Mifflin, 1992. A chronicle of the life of a fictional high school English teacher, the difficulties he encounters in doing his job, and the intellectual compromises he makes in order to do it.

Suarez-Orosco, Carola, and Marcelo M. Suarez-Orosco. *Children of Immigration.* Cambridge, MA: Harvard University Press, 2001. A thorough and historically sensitive account of immigrants and schooling and an argument about the ways that immigrant children can succeed in contemporary schoolrooms.

Urban, Wayne J. *Gender, Race, and the National Education Association: Professionalism and Its Limitations.* New York: Routledge/Falmer, 2000. An analysis of the contemporary crisis of teacher organizations, as they struggle to make their way in an inhospitable political climate, in relation to earlier political commitments that are now under consideration for remaking.

Notes

1. This discussion is based on Bell's own memoir of his years as Secretary of Education. See Terrell Bell, *The Thirteenth Man: A Reagan Cabinet Memoir*. New York: Free Press, 1988.
2. Edward Zigler, *Head Start: The Untold Story of America's Most Successful Educational Experiment*. New York: Basic Books, 1992.
3. See, for example, John L. Goodlad, Roger Soder, and Kenneth A. Sirotnik, eds., *The Moral Dimensions of Teaching*. San Francisco: Jossey-Bass, 1990.
4. See, for example, William Bennett, ed. and comp., *The Book of Virtue: A Treasury of Great Moral Stories*. New York: Simon & Shuster, 1993. Bennett's own moral standards were brought into question when, in the spring of 2003, it was revealed that he had long been a high stakes gambler. See Jonathan Alter and Joshua Green, "Bennett: Virtue Is as Virtue Does?," *Newsweek*, May 12, 2003, p. 6.
5. Interestingly, neither the term school choice nor anything related to it appeared anywhere in Bell's *Thirteenth Man*.
6. Some experiments with voucher plans were tried in the 1970s, but they proved unsuccessful. Voucher advocates always argued that the lack of success was due to improper implementation of the plans, rather than to any flaws in the idea of vouchers. On these early voucher efforts, see James A. Mecklenburger and Richard W. Hystrop, *Education Vouchers: From Theory to Alum Rock*. Homewood, IL: ETC Publications, 1972.
7. James S. Coleman and Thomas Hoffer, *Public and Private High Schools: The Impact of Communities*. New York: Basic Books, 1987.
8. John E. Chubb and Terry Moe, *Politics, Markets, and America's Schools*. Washington, D.C.: Brookings Institution, 1990.
9. John F. Witte, "The Milwaukee Voucher Experiment," *Educational Evaluation and Policy Analysis*, vol. 20, 1998, pp. 229–252; Jay P. Greene, Paul E. Peterson, and Jiangtao Du, "Effectiveness of School Choice: The Milwaukee Voucher Experiment," *Education and Urban Society*, vol. 313, 1999, pp. 190–213; and Cecilia-Elena Rouse, "Private School Vouchers and Student Achievement: An Evaluation of the Milwaukee Parental Choice Program, *Quarterly Journal of Economics*, vol. 113, 1998, pp. 553–602.
10. A Florida state judge ruled in 2002 that the Sunshine State's school choice plan is in violation of the state's constitutional mandate for separation of church and state. The plan allows parents whose children are in public schools deemed to be substandard a number of alternative placements for their children, including religious schools. It is the appearance of religious entanglement that caused the judge to declare the plan unconstitutional. See *Zelman v Simmons-Harris* 536 U.S. 639, 122 S. Ct. 2460 (2002).
11. Many thoughtful public school people agree with the concern for moral education voiced by these home school activists; unlike the activists, however, these people wish to invigorate moral education in the public schools. See note 3.
12. On the phenomenon of home schooling, see Jane Van Galen and Mary Anne Pitman, eds., *Home Schooling: Political, Historical, and Pedagogical Perspectives*. Norwood, NJ: Ablex, 1991. See also Isabel Lyman, "Why Homeschooling Continues to Grow," *Teachers College Record*, May 16, 2005 http://www.tcrecord.org ID Number: 11878.
13. National Commission on Excellence in Education, *A Nation at Risk: The Imperative for Educational Reform*. Washington, D.C.: U.S. Department of Education, 1983.
14. On the genesis of the report and the early reaction to it, see Bell, *The Thirteenth Man*, pp. 114–144.
15. Diane Ravitch, *The Schools We Deserve: Reflections on the Educational Crises of Our Times*. New York: Basic Books, 1985. Ravitch's book, a collection of essays, included some that dated back to the mid-1970s. Ravitch eventually took a position in the Department of Education in the Reagan administration.
16. Much of the opposition to the Reagan–Bell excellence agenda came from the National Education Association, the organization that had supported Jimmy Carter in 1976, had pushed hard for the creation of the U.S. Department of Education by Carter in 1979, and had supported Carter against Reagan in the 1980 election.
17. David C. Berliner and Bruce J. Biddle, *The Manufactured Crisis: Myths, Fraud, and the Attack on America's Public Schools*. Cambridge, MA: Perseus Books, 1995, pp. xi, 310 passim.
18. Lawrence C. Stedman and Carl F. Kaestle, "The Great Test Score Decline: A Closer Look," in Carl F. Kaestle, Helen Damon-Moore, Lawrence C. Stedman, Katherine Tinsley, and William

Vance Trollinger, Jr. (eds.), *Literacy in the United States: Readers and Reading since 1880.* New Haven, CT: Yale University Press, 1991, pp. 129–145. On the persistence of traditional methods in teaching, especially in high schools, see Larry Cuban, *How Teachers Taught: Constancy and Change in American Classrooms.* New York: Longman, 1984.

19. E. D. Hirsch, Jr., *Cultural Literacy: What Every American Needs to Know.* Boston: Houghton Mifflin Co., 1987, p. xv, passim.

20. Two of Hirsch's colleagues at the University of Virginia, historian Joseph Kett and physicist James Trifel, contributed to the compilation of the 5,000-item appendix listing of "What Literate Americans Know," and to publication the following year of *The Dictionary of Cultural Literacy.* Boston: Houghton Mifflin, 1988 (rev. ed. 1993).

21. For example, see Hirsch, *What Your Fifth Grader Needs to Know: Fundamentals of a Good Fifth Grade Education.* New York: Doubleday, 1993. Hirsch's Core Knowledge Foundation also provides lesson plans and college course outlines detailing "what elementary teachers need to know" in various subject matter areas. See also www.coreknowledge.org.

22. Hirsch, *Cultural Literacy*, pp. 19, 21.

23. E. D. Hirsch, Jr., *The Schools We Need and Why We Don't Have Them.* New York: Doubleday, 1996.

24. *America 2000: An Education Strategy Sourcebook.* Washington, D.C: U.S. Department of Education, 1991.

25. This system will be discussed in some detail later in this chapter under the topic of teacher education reform.

26. *The New Republic*, February 8, 1999, p. 11.

27. For examples of continuing criticism of NCLB, see Lowell C. Rose, "No Child Left Behind: The Mathematics of Guaranteed Failure," *Educational Horizons*, Winter, 2004; Jonathan Weisman and Amit R. Paley, "Dozens in GOP Turn Against Bush's Prized 'No Child' Act," *Washington Post*, March 15, 2007, p. A01; and Erik Gleiberman, "Teaching Even 100 Hours a Week Leaves Children Behind," *Phi Delta Kappan*, February, 2007, pp. 455–459.

28. Deborah Verstegen, "Educational Fiscal Policy in the Reagan Administration," *Educational Evaluation and Policy Analysis*, vol. 12, 1990, pp. 355–373.

29. The literature on site-based management is enormous. For example, see B. Malen and R. T. Ogawa, "Professional-Patron Influence on Site-Based Governance Councils," *Educational Evaluation and Policy Analysis*, vol. 10, 1988, pp. 9–23. For a discussion of how teachers saw this movement, as well as several other reform movements, see Sharon Conley, "Review of Research on Teacher Participation in School Decision Making," in Gerald Grant., ed., *Review of Research in Education*, vol. 17, 1991, pp. 225–266.

30. Michael Cohen, "Key Issues Confronting State Policy Makers," in Richard Elmore, ed., *Restructuring Schools: The Next Generation of Educational Reform,*. San Francisco: Jossey-Bass, 1990, pp. 251–288. Restructuring is also referred to in the literature as "systemic reform." On this topic, see Maris Vinovskis, *History and Educational Policy Making.* New Haven, CT: Yale University Press, 1999.

31. On black–white scores, see David Grissmer, Ann Flanagan, and Stephanie Williamson, "Why Did the Black–White Score Gap Narrow in the 1970s and 1980s?" in Christopher Jencks and Meredith Phillips, eds., *The Black–White Test-Score Gap.* Washington, D.C.: Brookings Institution, 1998, pp. 182–228. Also see Texas Association of School Boards, "Reasons you Should Stand Up and Cheer for Texas Public Schools," *Texas Lone Star*, 1998.

32. Barnes lost his bid for reelection as governor in November 2002, at least in part because of teachers' anger over his educational policies.

33. Bruce Fuller, ed., *Inside Charter Schools: The Paradox of Radical Decentralization.* Cambridge, MA: Harvard University Press, 2000, p. 32.

34. Fuller notes that David Tyack, when he read a draft of Fuller's edited book on charter schools, remarked that charters were reinventing the "one room schoolhouse" of the district school form of organization that had been replaced by the common school in the nineteenth century. Fuller, *Inside Charter Schools*, p. 28.

35. American Federation of Teachers website: www.aft.org/edissues/downloads/charter report02.pdf.

36. Ibid., p. 60.

37. Ibid., p. 19.

38. Julie Blair, "Critical Union Report about Charter Schools Raises Ire of Advocates," *Education Week*, August 7, 2002, p. 14.

39. Michael W. La Morte, "Courts Continue to Address the Wealth Disparity Issue," *Educational Evaluation and Policy Analysis*, vol. 11, 1989, pp. 3–15.

40. *Serrano v. Priest*, 5 Cal. 3d 584, 487 (1971).
41. *San Antonio Independent School District v. Rodriguez*, 411 U.S. 1 (1973).
42. *McDaniel v. Thomas*, 248 Ga. 632, 285 S.E. 2d 156 (1981).
43. The ruling in *Pauley v. Kelly*, 162 W. VA. 672, 255 S.E. 2d, 859 (1979), returned the case to a lower state court, which in turn required the drafting of the state of *West Virginia Master Plan for Public Education* (1983).
44. *Board of Education, Levittown Union Free School District v. Nyquist*, 94 Misc. 2d 466, 408 NYS. 2d 843 (1981), rev'd, 57 N.Y. 2d 27, 439 N.E. 2d 359, 453 N.Y.S. 2d 634 (1982), *appeal dismissed*, 459 U.S. 1139 (1983).
45. Jonathan Kozol, *Savage Inequalities: Children in America's Schools*. New York: Crown, 1991. For Kozol's earlier criticism of urban school pedagogy, see *Death at an Early Age*, as discussed in Chapter 11.
46. Theodore R. Sizer, *Horace's School: Redesigning the American High School*. Boston; Houghton Mifflin, 1992. Also see Theodore R. Sizer, *Horace's Compromise: The Dilemma of the American High School*. Boston: Houghton Mifflin, 1984; and Theodore R. Sizer, *Horace' s Hope: What Works for the American High School*. Boston: Houghton Mifflin, 1996.
47. David Bensman has conducted several studies of Central Park East. For the high school graduation rates discussed above, see David Bensman, *Central Park East and Its Graduates: "Learning by Heart."* New York: Teachers College Press, 2000, p. 10.
48. Ibid., p. ix. For a fuller look at Meier's ideas, see Deborah Meier, *In Schools We Trust: Creating Communities of Learning in an Era of Testing and Standardization*. Boston: Beacon Press, 2002.
49. Meier and others have contributed to a critique of standardized testing in public education, published as *Will Standards Save Public Education?* Boston: Beacon Press, 2000.
50. *A Nation at Risk*, p. 22.
51. See the discussion and citations of Bestor's work in Chapter 10. See also Mortimer Smith, *The Diminished Mind: A Study of Planned Mediocrity in Our Public Schools*. Chicago: Henry Regnery, 1954; and H. G. Rickover, *Education and Freedom*. New York: E. P. Dutton, 1959.
52. C. Emily Festritzer and David T. Chester, *Alternative Teacher Certification: A State-by-State Analysis 2000*. Washington, D.C.: National Center for Education Information, 2000.
53. Arthur E. Wise and Linda Darling-Hammond, "Alternative Certification Is an Oxymoron," *Education Week*, September 4, 1991.
54. The initial report of the Holmes Group, which advocated graduate preparation in research institutions, was published two years after *A Nation at Risk*; see Holmes Group, *Tomorrow's Teachers: A Report of the Holmes Group*. East Lansing, MI: Holmes Group, 1986. For the later development of an emphasis on professional development schools, see Holmes Group, *Tomorrow's Schools: Principles for the Design of Professional Development Schools*. East Lansing, MI: Holmes Group, 1990.
55. *America 2000: A Sourcebook*, p. 19.
56. Convincing evidence on the economic causes of low educational achievement can be found in Henry Acland, Mary Jo Bane, David Cohen, Herbert Gintis, Barbara Heyns, and Stephan Michelson, *Inequality: A Reassessment of the Effect of Family and Schooling in America*. New York: Basic Books, 1972.
57. See, for example, "Study Says Wealth Gap Is Growing," Richmond (VA) *Times-Dispatch*, July 24, 1990; or Robert Reno, "Economic Gap between Rich, Poor Widens, but No One Seems to Care," Charlottesville (VA) *Daily Progress*, October 10, 1999.
58. Jennifer Hochschild, *The New American Dilemma: Liberal Democracy and School Desegregation*. New Haven: Yale University Press, 1984; and Gary Orfield, *The Reconstruction of Southern Education: The Schools and the 1964 Civil Rights Act*. New York: Wiley-Interscience, 1969.
59. *Millikin v. Bradley*, as discussed in Chapter 11.
60. The Baseline Essays were compiled by a group of African American scholars as curriculum guides for the infusion of African perspectives into the various subjects taught in the schools. They are available from the Portland, Oregon, Public Schools. See www.pps.k12.or.us/depts-c/mc-me/essays.php.
61. Arthur M. Schlesinger, Jr., *The Disuniting of America: Reflections on a Multicultural Society*. New York: W. W. Norton, 1988.
62. This account relies in part on Michael Olneck, "Immigrants and Education," in James A. Banks, ed., *Handbook of Research on Multicultural Education*. New York: Macmillan, 1994.

63. Gary Orfield and John T. Yun, *Resegregation in American Schools*. Cambridge, MA: Harvard Civil Rights Project, 1999.
64. John A. Ogbu, "Variability in Minority School Performance: A Problem in Search of an Explanation," *Anthropology and Education Quarterly*, vol. 18, 1987, pp. 312–334.
65. Catherine Snow, "Bilingualism and Second Language Acquisition," in Jean B. Gleason and Nan B. Ratner (eds.), *Psycholinguistics*. Fort Worth, TX: Harcourt Brace, 1993, pp. 392–416.

Epilogue

We are finishing revisions for this edition of *American Education: A History* in the midst of the 2008 presidential campaign. While the issues of defense against terrorism, global warming, health care, and an economy teetering on the brink of recession are clearly dominant, the almost absolute absence of education as a major point of emphasis for the main contenders in both parties is notable. Unlike George W. Bush, and his two immediate predecessors, Bill Clinton and George Herbert Walker Bush, no candidate in 2008 has either declared her or himself to be interested in being an "education president" or in significantly reforming the nation's schools. In one sense this is a good thing. It means that at least for awhile, the schools may be out of the limelight of national attention. That limelight, as least in the last quarter century, has almost always yielded scathing criticism of the schools rather than positive commentary or productive intent or result. On the other hand, it also may mean that education will simply languish as a national concern, or, more ominously, be given serious attention only by those who have an ideological interest in voucher plans, home schooling, or other more or less veiled attacks on the public schools.

The contemporary fate of George Bush's singular educational accomplishment, the No Child Left Behind Act of 2001, is worthy of special mention here. Its initial passage by Congress was a bi-partisan effort with leading Democrats such as Edward Kennedy of Massachusetts playing a major role. Its implementation since then has resulted in an albatross of rigid standardized testing requirements being imposed on the schools with negative occupational consequences threatened for both the teachers and administrators associated with schools that are identified as "failing." While some of the rigidity has been moderated since the inception of NCLB, it still stands as a bureaucratic behemoth that threatens to remake schools into testing factories that, at best, address only a very limited portion of a complex educational and social reality.

Renewal of NCLB in 2008 is problematic. However, the dissatisfaction of educators with the implementation and outcomes of NCLB is clear. In spite of George Bush's wishes to the contrary, NCLB will almost certainly undergo substantial changes in the years ahead *even if* it survives in anything like its present form. In 2007 new members of Congress were largely skeptical of NCLB because of the ramifications of federal interference in what has traditionally been a state and local undertaking, federal directives void of sufficient funding, perceived insensitivity regarding differences among children, and in part because of generalized unhappiness with the increasing impotence of the Bush administration. While we cannot predict the future, modification of NCLB

445

resulting in the elimination of some of its most rigid aspects seems likely. As we near the 2014 deadline in NCLB at which time all students are to meet an arbitrary standard—no less arbitrary for being termed as being "at grade level"—we expect to see more modifications aimed at removing the sting of failure from students, teachers, and schools that underperform as measured by test scores.

Less certain, for us at least, is the future of the public school itself as a common and comprehensive institution serving the needs of all the people. In the final chapter of this book, we pointed to our own ambivalence about the public school and the mixed prospects for its future. It is not lack of appreciation for the ideal of the common school as the force animating public education that causes our uncertainty. Rather, our concern stems from the growing abandonment of the public school by those who once were its strongest supporters. There has been a veiled but not unexpected backlash from efforts at desegregation that has caused some parents, especially in urban and suburban areas, to pull their children out of the public system. Some of those same parents, and others, have lost faith in the public school system because of Supreme Court decisions that have declared in-school prayers, Bible reading, and observances that include religious music or symbols as being contrary to the Constitution. The lack of explicit moral teaching combined with the increasing secularization and permissiveness in our society as well as in our schools has alienated many. Still others lament the widely proclaimed decline in academic standards and the movement away from traditional approaches to education. These criticisms of the public schools have been reinforced by the almost uniformly negative attention that has been paid to public education by a national media that tends to highlight negative assessments of school quality. A great deal of publicity has been given to groups seeking the demise of the public school while at the same time trying to gain funding via vouchers, tax credits, and other avenues to support, at least in part, various kinds of alternative schools.

Unfortunately, groups set in opposition to public schools have more than their ideological interest to use as a motivating force in their campaign. Public schools have only occasionally fulfilled the common school ideal of an equal education for all children regardless of their background. Those occasions have had too much to do with local economic, social, and political circumstances to serve as ready examples for emulation. Until the public schools give serious attention to, and yield positive results for, demands for academic excellence along with demonstrable educational improvement for those whose social, economic, and/or ethnic status are in fact causing them to be left behind, they remain vulnerable. In short, public education, for all of its progress and achievements, so far remains unable to serve everyone's needs and wishes. Perhaps, to use the title of another history of education text, it has always been, at best, an "imperfect panacea."[1] It is, nonetheless, a goal, however impossible, that we think is worth pursuing.

It is not that progress has not been made. We certainly educate more of our population for longer periods of time than we have in the past. Yet, we also live in an era when educational requirements for economic success, political participation, and social fulfillment are significantly greater than they have been in the past. The Three R's are no longer enough, if they ever were. Now we need much greater numeracy than in the past just to function in our increasingly technological society. Oral and written communication skills are also in much greater demand in our contemporary world than they were in the past. This means that our progress has been made relative by rising expectations of the educational system, expectations that seem worthy of fulfillment at the same time that educators and policy makers seem largely bereft of ideas for getting that fulfillment within groups that have not traditionally done well in school.

One thing does seem clear, at least to us. The legacy of progressive education, defined broadly as educational methods and policies that seek to serve students where they are rather than where we might want them to be, is mixed at best. The liberating aspects of progressive education are a decided improvement over the buttoned-down and restrictive approach once dominant in American schools. However, the culture and domination of progressive educational theory and practice in departments, schools, and colleges of education provoke concern in terms of intellectual weaknesses in professional preparation programs as well as with results in many of our public schools. Even though we are part of the "educational establishment," however contrary may be some of our views, we are uneasy with the fact that progressive education has led to a negating of intellectual achievement as a legitimate goal of American education. Progressivism has been equated with relativism in all things; adjusting the curriculum to meet the interests and perceived abilities of the child has too often led to activities for the sake of activity. Faculties who train most of the nation's teachers have taken only part of Dewey's admonitions to heart. It was not his intent to degrade subject matter and intellectual achievement. Progressivism was a means to an end, not an end in itself.

We do agree with progressives who maintain that students must be met where they are when they enter our classes. Yet we do not believe that such a stance means the abandonment of subject matter for some mainly therapeutic or otherwise anti-intellectual approach to education. The stakes are too high intellectually in our time to allow schools to become either factories for manufacturing test results or play pens where children and youth fulfill their immediate needs as they themselves define them. Like John Dewey, we believe that student interests stand as the starting point for education, but only as a starting point. Those interests must be shaped through the minds and hands of good teachers to facilitate their productive interaction with academic subjects and to attain an outcome of meaningful intellectual accomplishment.

At the outset of the first and subsequent editions of this book, we invited you, the reader, to join with us in a conversation. Our approach to the conversation and the conclusions we draw are driven in large part by the history detailed in these pages. We do not for a moment think that our views are the only ones that follow from that history. Yet, in formulating our views and understandings, we have tried hard to acknowledge the complex reality that has been American education and the even more complex reality of the present. Attention to complexity is surely a necessary quality for any serious contemporary educational practitioner, policy maker, or interested citizen. We hope that our textbook addresses many of the most enduring complexities underlying our educational system and provides perspective for those who seek to understand and improve upon what history has wrought.

Note

1. Henry J. Perkinson, *The Imperfect Panacea: American Faith in Education, 1865–1965.* New York: New York University, 1968.

Index